GERMANS IN THE CIVIL WAR

CIVIL WAR AMERICA

Gary W. Gallagher, editor

GERMANS IN THE CIVIL WAR

The Letters They Wrote Home

Edited by
Walter D. Kamphoefner
and
Wolfgang Helbich

Translated by Susan Carter Vogel

The University of North Carolina Press
Chapel Hill

Originally published in German with the title
Deutsche im Amerikanischen Bürgerkrieg:
Briefe von Front und Farm, 1861–1865,
© 2002 Ferdinand Schöningh, Paderborn.

Set in Janson with Champion display
by Tseng Information Systems, Inc.

This book was published with the assistance of
the Fred W. Morrison Fund for Southern Studies
of the University of North Carolina Press.

Part of this book has been reprinted in revised form from Walter D.
Kamphoefner, "German-Americans and Civil War Politics: A Reconsideration
of the Ethnocultural Thesis," *Civil War History* 37:3 (1991): 226–40, with
permission of the Kent State University Press.

The paper in this book meets the guidelines for permanence
and durability of the Committee on Production Guidelines
for Book Longevity of the Council on Library Resources.

Library of Congress Cataloging-in-Publication Data
Deutsche im Amerikanischen Bürgerkrieg. English.
Germans in the Civil War : the letters they wrote home / edited by Walter D.
Kamphoefner and Wolfgang Helbich ; translated by Susan Carter Vogel.
p. cm. — (Civil War America)
"Originally published in German with the title *Deutsche im*
Amerikanischen Bürgerkrieg: Briefe von Front und Farm, 1861–1865, © 2002,
Ferdinand Schöningh, Paderborn"—T.p. verso.
Includes bibliographical references and index.
ISBN-13: 978-0-8078-3044-4 (cloth : alk. paper)
ISBN-10: 0-8078-3044-5 (cloth : alk. paper)
1. United States—History—Civil War, 1861–1865—Participation, German American.
2. United States—History—Civil War, 1861–1865—Participation, Immigrant. 3. United
States—History—Civil War, 1861–1865—Personal narratives. 4. United States—
History—Civil War, 1861–1865—Personal narratives, Confederate. 5. German
Americans—Correspondence. 6. Immigrants—United States—Correspondence.
7. Soldiers—United States—Correspondence. 8. Soldiers—Confederate States of
America—Correspondence. I. Helbich, Wolfgang Johannes, 1935–
II. Kamphoefner, Walter D. III. Title. IV. Series.
E540.G3D48 2006
973.7092'331—dc22   2006014016

10 09 08 07 06   5 4 3 2 1

CONTENTS

WESTERN THEATER

MAP, TABLE, AND ILLUSTRATIONS

PREFACE

This edition (like its German-language predecessor) presents an anthology of hitherto unpublished letters written by German immigrants from Civil War America, mostly to relatives and friends back in the Old Country. Selected from the holdings of the North America Letter Collection, or NABS,[1] in Gotha, Germany, it includes the writings of soldiers and civilians, men and women, North and South. This ethnic component of the Civil War has largely faded from public memory, and it has been seriously neglected by scholars as well. Nearly one-quarter of all Union troops were foreign-born, and Germans alone accounted for about one-tenth of the Union army, about 200,000 of some 2 million troops. Germans thus made up as large a contingent as African Americans, whom most historians rightly see as essential to the Union war effort. This is not to disparage the importance of either group at the expense of the other. In fact, each played a crucial role at a particular time—blacks in the late phases of the war, because they first had to fight for the right to fight; Germans at the war's outset, and especially in border states, where they were often among the most reliable and decisive Unionists.

Neither of these groups—the two elements who stood out most conspicuously in the Union ranks—was without controversy, and they pose other interesting parallels and contrasts. While blacks were compelled to fight in segregated units, many Germans preferred and chose to do so. At the war's outset, some thirty "German regiments" were raised, sometimes using German

1. NABS (Nordamerika-Briefsammlung), now part of the Forschungsbibliothek Gotha, will be a frequent reference in this volume. The collection was established at the History Department of Ruhr-Universität Bochum during the 1980s under the name Bochumer Auswandererbriefsammlung (Bochum Emigrant Letters Collection), abbreviated BABS. As such, it has been frequently cited in many publications, and it was also microfilmed in 1997 by the Library of Congress—including the full German text of the letters excerpted and translated here (except two by Herbst and Ruff [nos. 30 and 48], which were acquired after 1997). The move to Gotha in 2002 and an expansion of the collection's scope made the name change desirable to avoid confusion. So NABS contains all the material of BABS, plus some 2,400 recently acquired letters as of the end of 2005 and those expected to come in as a result of ongoing solicitation. Both editors are now involved in a German Research Foundation (DFG) project headed by Professor Ursula Lehmkuhl of the Free University of Berlin that aims to collect and make accessible immigrant letters written to the area of the former German Democratic Republic, which was inaccessible to the collection efforts of BABS.

as a spoken and even written language of command as late as 1863. In mixed regiments Germans were often concentrated in a company or two, and even at higher levels, the XI Corps was heavily German and popularly identified as such. But the majority of Germans in blue ended up serving in mixed units, whether by choice or necessity. Blacks had to be satisfied with fighting under white officers; Germans beleaguered the Lincoln administration with demands that positions of command, even generalships, be granted to their compatriots. Although both historians and the popular media have done important "catch-up" work within the last generation in documenting the role of black soldiers, the immigrant soldier—not to mention the interactions between the two groups—has largely escaped notice, if only because much of the evidence is hidden away in foreign-language sources.

This anthology is designed to help remedy this deficit. Yet even a brief perusal reveals that the editors have no intention of "celebrating" the German contribution to the Civil War or telling tales of immigrant heroism. Filiopietistic adulation is not our goal, nor is vindication. Rather, it is the intercultural refraction created as immigrants experienced and interpreted the war that fascinates us and led to the publication of these texts. Immigrants brought different values, images, and experiences to bear on the war, which provide a contrast to the perspectives shared by most American letter-writers. They could make different comparisons, often had different motives for volunteering and fighting, and almost always experienced a different set of social relationships in the military. Some adapted quite easily to the war situation, others less so, and some not at all. But in almost every case, regardless of their confessional or regional background or level of education, these immigrants described the American Civil War from a distinctly German standpoint.

Preceding the letters and providing overall context is an introductory section on the Civil War era and the role that German immigrants played in it; although partly synthesis, it also draws on our own research and on examples from the letters. The main corpus of this edition consists of selections from 343 letters written during the Civil War era by some 78 German immigrants in 57 different family groups. Thirty-five were written by men in uniform and 22 by civilians; counting persons who cowrote letters or added a few lines of their own, the number of civilians increases to 47, including 19 women. Each letter group contains a biographical introduction and often a sequel, with the amount of detail depending somewhat on the amount of information that could be unearthed, as well as on the length of the letters.

In terms of content, the selected letters offer the broadest imaginable spectrum both of the situations of writers and the topics and points of view their writings encompass. Some soldiers served in ethnic companies or regiments;

others were practically the only Germans in their respective units; one was even a surgeon in a black artillery regiment; a couple wore the gray rather than the blue. We see the Union and Confederate home fronts as experienced by both men and women, in some cases the wives or other family members of soldiers. The editors have resisted the popular tendency to see the Civil War as a purely military drama that ended in 1865. Where material from before or after the war is available, the introductions and sequels to letter groups cite passages illustrative of writers' initial political socialization in America or their attitudes toward postwar politics and Reconstruction. The letters present the full array of German American opinions on the war and the related issues of slavery and race. However, the edition does not simply juxtapose such contrasts and let them cancel each other out; rather, the personal characteristics and social milieu of the writers, as uncovered through background research and profiled in the letter introductions, help explain many of the writers' attitudes. Besides functioning as a primary source collection that future historians will mine for their own purposes, this edition can stand on its own as a combined narrative and interpretive work illustrating the ethnic role and providing an ethnic perspective on the Civil War.

The conventional wisdom of historians is challenged at a number of points by these letters. It becomes clear, for example, that immigrants' opinions on American issues were closely tied to their democratic aspirations for Germany and the rest of Europe. Ordinary immigrants speaking in their own words provide evidence that the republican and egalitarian ideology manifest in the 1848 Revolution extended farther down the social scale than previous scholars have realized. Particularly among recent arrivals, however, Union enlistment often had purely economic motives. There were some divergences in attitudes between Protestants and Catholics, but they were far from absolute. One striking contrast did come to light: the nearly unanimous and indiscriminate adulation of immigrants for German generals and the valor of German regiments—whereas American officers, soldiers, and newspapers usually held to diametrically opposite opinions, seeing only incompetent political generals and cowardly "flying Dutchmen" in battle. These letters thus cast doubt on the venerable and conciliatory claim, made by contemporaries as well as many historians, that the Civil War was the great "melting pot" that eradicated nativism and ethnic prejudice—on the part of both Germans and Anglo Americans—as natives and immigrants stood shoulder to shoulder and shed their blood together in a common cause.

Nonetheless, for present-day Know Nothings who equate the use of languages other than English with disloyalty to the United States, the examples of dedication or even the ultimate sacrifice to one's adopted country by persons who were largely ignorant of English may have a salutary effect. But above all, for the majority of specialists in American history who lack facility in the German language, this edition provides the raw materials for a more complete and accurate understanding of many aspects of the Civil War. With the record presented here, the successors to standard works such as Bell Wiley's *The Life of Billy Yank* or James McPherson's *What They Fought For* will have to take on a somewhat different accent—in both a literal and a figurative sense.[2]

2. Wiley (1952); McPherson (1994).

ACKNOWLEDGMENTS

The present volume would not have been possible without the thorough preparatory work on the Bochum collection of immigrant letters, which was greatly facilitated by five years of essential and generous support from the Volkswagen Foundation. This work, which began in 1979 and intensified after 1984, included transcribing and cataloging the letters, as well as biographical and archival research. It led to publication of our first letter edition, *Briefe aus Amerika* in 1988 (in English, *News from the Land of Freedom*, 1991), thanks to the dedicated support of many research assistants. In 1992 the editors began work on this second volume, but although most of the time-consuming work of transcription had already been completed, other academic obligations—and the need to conduct background research on fifty-seven diverse and widely dispersed immigrant families across the transatlantic divide—delayed completion of the manuscript for another decade.

The final publication as *Deutsche im Amerikanischen Bürgerkrieg* (2002) owes much to our competent and dedicated research assistants Bettina Struckmann, Anke Müller, and in particular Antje Kreipe, who accompanied it on the home stretch. Michael Musick's expertise and commitment were indispensable: as an archivist in the Military Division of the National Archives in Washington, he proved able to trace documents in even the most hopeless cases. Additional transatlantic planning, coordination, and research were made possible by generous travel grants from the DAAD (Deutscher Akademischer Austausch Dienst) in 1991 and 1994–95. Our special thanks go to the people without whom we could never have published these letters—their owners, who not only permitted publication but also provided important additional information. A list of their names is included at the end of the book.

With the English translation we have incurred an additional round of indebtedness, above all to the National Endowment for Humanities for a Collaborative Research Grant, which funded the translation, and to the Fritz Thyssen Stiftung, which provided additional matching funds under this grant. Finally, both editors want to thank the third member of our team, translator Susan Carter Vogel, coincidentally a great-great-granddaughter of Robert E. Lee. Her dedication to accuracy and excellence showed no regard for the time, effort, or financial reward involved—or for how the South came off looking in the letters. Although the translator is ultimately responsible for all matters of language, the editors take full responsibility for all matters of fact and content.

ABBREVIATIONS

AB	Adressbuch (German city directory)
Batn	Battalion
Baty	Battery
Br. LHA P	Brandenburgisches Landeshauptarchiv Potsdam
Cav	Cavalry
CD	City Directory
Co.	County
Comp	Company
CSA	Confederate States of America
DAB	*Dictionary of American Biography*, edited by Allen Johnson and Dumas Malone, 20 vols. (New York, N.Y., 1927–36).
Desc. Books	Descriptive Books
Div.	Division
e.d.	enumeration district
fl.	guilder* (approximately 41 cents)
GA	Gemeindearchiv (Town Archives)
GLA Ka	Generallandesarchiv Karlsruhe
HArt	Heavy Artillery
HPL	Hamburg Passenger Lists
Hs. StA Da	Hessisches Staatsarchiv Darmstadt
Ind. Baty	Independent Battery
Inf	Infantry
KB (ev., lu., rk.)	Kirchenbuch (Parish Register) (Evangelical, Lutheran, Roman Catholic)
LArt	Light Artillery
LHA	Landeshauptarchiv (Central State Archives)
ll.	lines
MC	Manuscript Census
MCA	Manuscript Census, Agriculture
MC MN	Manuscript Census, Minnesota State Census, 1885, Minnesota Historical Society
NABS	Nordamerika-Briefsammlung, Gotha
NatA	U.S. National Archives, Washington, D.C.

NOPL	New Orleans Passenger Lists
Ns. StA	Niedersächsisches Staatsarchiv
NYPL	New York Passenger Lists
OAR	*Official Army Register of the Volunteer Force of the United States Army for the Years: 1861, '62, '63, '64, '65*, edited by United States Adjutant General's Office, 9 vols. (Washington, D.C., 1865; Gaithersburg, Md., 1987).
OR	*The War of the Rebellion: A Compilation of the Official Records of the Union and Confederate Armies*, 128 vols. (Washington, D.C., 1880–1901).
Pct.	Precinct
Regt.	Regiment
Regt. Books	Regimental Books
RG	Record Group
StA	Staatsarchiv (State Archives)
StateA	State Archives
StdA	Stadtarchiv (City Archives)
Subd.	Subdivision (of city ward)
Twp.	Township
USC	U.S. Census, Population
USC A	U.S. Census, Agriculture
USC M	U.S. Census, Manufacturing
Vol.	Volunteers
W.	Ward
WHMC	Western Historical Manuscript Collection, Columbia, Missouri
#	sequential family number (in MC)

EDITORIAL APPROACH

Although it may seem unusual in the introduction to a new edition of letters to make repeated references to an older publication, this proves to be the
best way to delineate the character of the present volume. With the publication of *Briefe aus Amerika* and its complete English translation *News from the
Land of Freedom*, the editors (together with Ulrike Sommer) set wide-ranging
goals.[1] Above all, we attempted to present letters written by immigrants to
their relatives and friends back home as documents of the process of adaptation and integration and as individual, social historical sources, rich in meaning. To provide context and enhance their value as source material, we added
extensive biographical data on the letter-writers and explanatory footnotes to
the texts. At the same time, we made a case for letters, especially those written by uneducated immigrants, as documents of everyday life and as almost
uniquely authentic sources for the study of individual impressions, evalua-
tions, and feelings. Finally, given the parallels between migration then and
now, we wanted to contribute to the present-day debate on immigration and
assimilation.

In that first volume we tried to cover roughly a century of German immigration (from 1830 to 1930), and in the interest of illuminating social historical
development, we chose not to present a mere collection of still shots, such as
might be provided by individual letters. Instead, we only included individuals
from whom we had an entire *series* of letters. And concern for the authenticity
of the historical documents meant that these series were presented in their
entirety and only lightly abridged, primarily in the case of repetitions.

The present volume of letters from German immigrants during the Civil
War has a more restricted perspective and addresses a more limited range of
questions. The documents included here are almost exclusively letter *excerpts*,
no less authentic and reliable than those in the previous edition, but chosen
when they contained one or more of the following:

— immigrant perspectives on politics, war, and slavery
— descriptions of battles, hardships, and everyday life in the military

1. Helbich, Kamphoefner, and Sommer (1988); Kamphoefner, Helbich, and Sommer (1991).
For the sake of simplicity these are referred to as *News from the Land of Freedom*, or *News*.

— depictions of interethnic relations, especially between Germans and
  Americans
— references to the socioeconomic situation or political events in
  Germany
— comments on the reputation of Germans in American society
— information about German immigrants as part of the military
  (primarily the Union army)—German officers, regiments, and their
  culture.

The choice of letters and excerpts also reflects our interest in highlighting the
various ways in which German immigrants—the 1.3 million who were living
in the United States in 1860 and particularly the approximately 200,000 who
fought in the Union army—experienced this time of drastic upheaval in their
new homeland.[2]

It is impossible to say exactly how "representative" this sample might be
with regard to "life situations": writers' civilian occupations ranged from
farm owners, tenants, and farmhands, through businessmen and entrepre-
neurs, artisans and bartenders, down to the unemployed. There are letters
from common soldiers, noncommissioned officers, and higher officers, including surgeons; men who volunteered, were drafted, or deserted; some who
were wounded, taken prisoner, or ultimately lost their lives. But with the
broad range covered by our eighty or so letter-writers, it seems likely that a
large majority of German males living in the United States between 1861 and
1865 would fit into one or more of the categories presented here. The same
may not hold true, however, for women and children, since female letter-
writers are underrepresented here—not as the result of any editorial decision,
but because there are so few letters written by women during the Civil War
in the original collection.

A different kind of representativeness, however, can be established more
precisely. We have enough information, for example, about the correlations
between religious denomination and partisan affiliation, being a freethinker
and opposing slavery, different social classes and their racial attitudes, and so
forth to establish which of our letter-writers conform to statistical expectations and which ones (and they are not all that rare) do not fit into neat categories.

2. The figure refers to all immigrants born in Germany, including those who had naturalized. In 1860 a total of 4.1 million immigrants (of all nationalities) were registered, at a time when
the total U.S. population was 31.4 million. About one American in twenty-four was German-
born; with so few Germans living in the South, the proportion in the North was correspondingly
higher—one out of seventeen.

In this volume we have reversed our editorial policy when it comes to abridging the letters: in *News from the Land of Freedom*, the goal was to "keep everything that is not redundant"; here we have tried to "cut everything unrelated to the issues." But we have not adhered too slavishly to this policy. We did not want to reduce the texts to a mere string of quotations but to preserve the character and personality of these documents as actual letters, and so, for example, salutations and greetings are included. We have also kept our list of issues fairly open, retaining passages that shed interesting light on important aspects of the problematic nature of immigration in general. We cut more severely from longer series than from those consisting only of one or two letters, and we gave preference to eyewitness or participant accounts over writers who passed along hearsay or information they had merely gleaned from newspapers. Finally, in making our selections, along with our scholarly criteria we looked for passages that are also captivating in their own right — human-interest stories, tales of unusual events, as well as observations and criticisms that are relevant to the situation in the United States even today. In such cases, we cut rather sparingly.

Immigrant Letters

The North American collection of immigrant letters (NABS) contains 956 letters written by 258 German immigrants from the years 1860–65. In this volume we have included excerpts from 343 letters written by 78 individuals. During these years, nearly 4 million letters were written in the United States and sent by mail to Germany, most but certainly not all of them by German immigrants.[3] On top of this, there were tens of thousands of letters that travelers to Europe took along with them, and probably more than 500,000 letters sent by German Civil War soldiers to their relatives on the American side of the Atlantic.[4] In short, the collection contains only a miniscule fraction of the letters written at the time, perhaps 1 out of 4,000.

In the letters printed in *News*, next to inquiring and reporting about the family, the second most important topic was addressing the crucial question — always implicit if not stated explicitly — of whether other family members and friends back home should follow. In the letters written during the war, when the number of German immigrants to the United States initially dropped (the 1862 figure was down by half from the already low 1860 total),

3. See Kamphoefner, Helbich, and Sommer (1991), 27, n. 1.

4. In this volume, letter-writers Schmalzried, Brucker, Weinrich, Voigt, Simon, and Lehmann (nos. 7, 32, 44, 54, 55, and 57) belong to this category.

this question became somewhat less important. It did remain a major issue, however, since by 1864, immigration was back up and had surpassed the 1860 numbers (and by 1867 immigration had soared to more than twice the level of 1864). Reports about the family also moved down in the list of priorities — to second place—and the most important topic became the war: from its political and economic ramifications to details of battles and military life, the letter-writer's encounters with danger or the heroic deeds of his unit, hardships and sickness, injuries and death.

Peacetime letters seldom contained exaggerations about life in the United States or glossed over the difficulties connected with immigrating, since letter-writers ran the risk that new arrivals could be a financial burden or be disappointed and reproachful. Traffic back and forth across the Atlantic, too, was brisk, and many people returned to Germany and could report on conditions in the United States. The war letters, however, may have a less straightforward relationship to objective reality and truth. Perhaps the most striking case, though not included in this volume, is found in the letters of the Hecks, where Angela describes every step of her husband Nikolaus's remarkable Civil War career as he advances from private to colonel. The military files, however, tell another story: although the tailor served as a private in three different regiments, he never rose in rank.[5] The fact that the risk of being "found out" was lower during the war, combined with the exceptional circumstances the war itself created, meant that misinformation had a greater tendency to be passed along. And so we find fictitious or at least premature reports of being promoted, individuals or units whose significance and success are overstated, gross overexaggeration of enemy losses, and wild rumors of all kinds. Here, Alexander Dupré (no. 2) is in a class by himself.

The editors have tried to verify these claims. When statements turned out to be false or seriously off the mark, this is usually noted and corrected, often in a footnote, with reference to standard works for general information and to special sources, described below, in individual cases. Positive corroboration of claims is given only in exceptional cases: if a statement is not contradicted by the editors, it was judged to be correct or only slightly misleading—or proved impossible to verify.

As in *News*, we have tried to make the texts as accessible as possible, even to readers unfamiliar with the details of the Civil War or nineteenth-century

5. Kamphoefner, Helbich, and Sommer (1991), 367–82. Heck was mustered in for three years on October 1, 1861, and served in the 52 N.Y. Inf until he was discharged on grounds of illness in June 1863. On March 3, 1865, he received a $100 bounty when he reenlisted in the 45 N.Y. Inf for one year. His unit later became part of the 58 N.Y. Inf, and he was mustered out in October 1865. Muster Rolls, Pension File, NatA.

vocabulary. Clarifications, notes, and editorial comments are provided either in the letter texts (in square brackets) or in the footnotes. Terms that show up in more than one letter series (especially minor military or political figures and battles) are explained in a glossary and marked in the text with an asterisk (*).

Far more time and effort went into researching the biographies of the letter-writers, their lives both in Germany and in the United States, before the war and afterward. Information on each letter-writer is presented in the introduction to each series, as well as in footnotes and usually in a sequel to the letters. The amount of information varies considerably: in some cases we could only find enough to fill a few lines, and in others, due to space limitations, we have only included a fraction of the details we were able to discover.

We placed special emphasis, as we did in our previous edition, on finding out as much as possible about a letter-writer's regional and social background in Germany, his or her religious affiliation, family, education, occupational training, economic situation, and motives for emigrating. We also tried to trace what happened after the letter-writer arrived in the United States: where he or she first settled, any subsequent moves, job changes, and the like. In addition, we tried to find out what we could about the recipients of the letters. And in this particular volume, a new set of issues became important as well — the reasons why a letter-writer joined the military, what type of unit he served in, his military career, any injuries, decorations, or disciplinary measures, and what happened to him after the war. Such information is of interest not only for reasons such as satisfying natural curiosity or checking the credibility of a particular letter-writer, but also to aid in the assessment of the contents of the letters. Letter-writers, after all, are not journalists addressing the general public; instead, they are people who are often untrained in writing, engaged in a dialogue with their correspondents (who may, of course, have then passed the letters on or read them aloud to a group). The relationship between the writer and the recipient, their shared background and experience, is therefore significant, as is the personality of the letter-writer and his or her relationship to family and others.

In the German version of this volume, the editors decided it was advisable to include a brief account of the Civil War era, roughly the third quarter of the nineteenth century, to help the reader understand the economic, social, and political context of the letters without having to turn to additional sources. In the present edition, this introduction has been pared down, restricted mainly to material on the German presence and role in politics and the military in Civil War America (sections 2 and 5 of the German version). We assume that American readers will be familiar with the general outline of the Civil War

German Birthplaces of Letter-Writers

Königsberg

Danzig

Op

Wp

22

Pm

Stettin

Bromberg

R. Vistula

Po

R. Warte

Posen

R. Oder

Russian Empire

Bresslau

Si

14

8

Kingdoms

KB	Bavaria
to KB	Palatinate
KS	Saxony
KW	Württemberg

Duchies

DBr	Braunschweig
DMS	Mecklenburg-Strelitz

Grand Duchies

GB	Baden
GH	Hesse
GM	Mecklenburg
GO	Oldenburg

Free Cities

HB	Bremen
HH	Hamburg

Prussian provinces

Br	Brandenburg
Ha	Hanover
HNa	Hesse-Nassau
Op	East Prussia
Pm	Pomerania
Po	Posen
Rp	Rhine Province
Sa	Saxony
SHo	Schleswig-Holstein
Si	Silesia
We	Westphalia
Wp	West Prussia

Principalities

Th	Thuringia
Ho	Hohenzollern

Numbers correspond to the numbering of letter series in the table of contents and show places of origin of letter-writers

——— national boundaries

------- boundaries between German states/ Prussian provinces

——— rivers

Cartography: C. Vogel

and have access to reference works if they need them. The introductory material we have retained should be new to most American readers.

Sources of Background Information

The most important biographical sources on the German side, apart from information provided by the donors of the letter series and family traditions (either written or oral), are parish registers. Additional information about the economic and social situation in the various regions in Germany is provided by contemporary collections of statistics, along with state and county historical and geographical publications.

The emigration process itself was often documented in special emigration files and lists, another invaluable source of information. These files were kept by local officials, and they included entries for all the emigrants who had fulfilled the formal requirements. Potential emigrants had to make a public announcement in the newspaper of their intention to emigrate and prove that they would be leaving no unpaid debts or needy dependents behind, and males had to prove that they were not liable for military service. Fewer than half of the people who emigrated, however, were noted in the files—the rest tried to avoid the complicated bureaucratic procedure, did not meet the requirements, or wanted to keep their options open in case they wanted to return to Germany sometime in the future, something that was difficult once one had received an official "discharge" from German authorities.

Although there is no guarantee that their names, ages, and occupations were recorded or even spelled correctly, all of the persons who emigrated from Hamburg are to be found in the passenger lists that were kept by shipping agents there as of the mid-1850s. For the other important ports of emigration—Antwerp, Bremen, Le Havre, and Rotterdam—such lists were either not kept at all on the European side or have not survived.

Beginning in 1820, federal law in the United States required all ports of immigration to keep lists of all arriving passengers, and these lists are comprehensive and have survived largely intact. But it is often extremely time-consuming to find the records of a particular immigrant, unless the specific port and date of arrival are known and the individual's name is less common than, for example, Heinrich Müller or the like. Recently, however, computerized indexes have become available that have considerably eased the search process.

The most useful sources of information about where immigrants lived in the United States after their arrival are city directories and, above all, the U.S. Census. Except for the originals of the 1890 census, of which only a special enumeration of Union veterans escaped destruction by fire, and the post-1930 returns, still closed for confidentiality reasons, all of this information is available on microfilm and, increasingly, online as well. Name indexes for each state and decade are also available, making this information easily accessible.[6] Other useful sources are published U.S. Census returns for basic economic and demographic information at the county level[7] and county histories that were published widely throughout the United States, which provide descriptions of the communities and accounts of local events, as well as biographical sketches of prominent local citizens.

Information about persons (immigrants or otherwise) in the military can be found in a completely different set of records, all of which are located in the National Archives in Washington, D.C., and in some instances published on microfilm. In particular, the Muster Rolls are important sources because they offer an almost complete set of records for the entire time a person was in the Union army, including the date mustered in, name, rank, promotions or punishments, monthly presence or absence from the regiment, injury, illness, capture, and more. Similar records for Confederate soldiers have survived on a much spottier basis, usually in the respective state archives. Other principal sources are the Regimental Books, available for most, but not all, Union regiments. The most important types of these regimental documents are order books (containing all orders given and received), descriptive books (giving detailed descriptions of the men in the regiment, including information about place of birth, occupation, age, and so on), morning reports (day-to-day events), and "letters sent" books (copies of all letters sent).

Pension Files are a major source for the life of military men after the war (if they survived or left behind dependents): pension applications were accompanied by affidavits, often written by a third party, that included not only detailed descriptions of health problems incurred during the war but also information on applicants' lives after they were mustered out, including their marriage and children. And court-martial proceedings are an inexhaustible source for questions of military discipline, everyday life, ethnic conflicts, and

6. For more detailed information on sources see Kamphoefner, Helbich, and Sommer (1991), 36–42. Within the last five years, census indexes with advanced search capabilities for other characteristics besides names, and linked directly to digitized census images, have become available from HeritageQuest and Ancestry.com, but most of the research for this volume was completed before these methods became available. They were used to track down a few "stragglers," but we do not indicate where we drew on scanned images as opposed to census microfilm.

7. Published U.S. Census returns are cited according to the numbering system in *Bibliography and Reel Index* (1975).

many other issues; none of our letter-writers were court-martialed, but they often mention such cases and give the names of the accused.

These are the most important sources, in that they were consulted most often, but the National Archives, where the bulk of the records of the Civil War—the best-documented war in history—are located, contain vast amounts of other material on every imaginable aspect of the conflict, not all of which was or could be consulted.

Editorial Policy

One major goal of the original German edition was textual authenticity. No attempts were made to correct the orthography, punctuation, regional dialect, grammar, or idiosyncrasies of the original texts, even when unusual forms were difficult to understand. Occasional help was provided—usually in square brackets—but the texts were not modernized to make them easier to read. Had we done so, the information that can be gleaned from an authentic text—for example, use of a local dialect as opposed to High German, educational background, expressive ability, the influence of English or German American terms—all would have been lost. The goal was to produce a text so accurate that ideally—except for issues of penmanship—no scholar would ever need to consult the original letters.

The goal of the English translation, however, is necessarily rather different. Here, we have tried to maintain the impression of texts produced by letter-writers with different levels of education and amounts of training. Some writers never set a period and thus wrote one continuous sentence; others, by contrast, wrote formal and pedantically correct letters. We did not attempt to reproduce antiquated forms, the flavor of regional dialects, erratic punctuation, or grammatical errors. Spelling also reflects modern norms, but with one important exception: the original spelling of personal and place names has been retained. This adds a touch of "local color" to the texts without impeding comprehension, and gradual shifts over time—for example, from Ludwig to Louis—can provide some evidence for adaptation to life in America. The basic goal of the translation, however, has been to achieve, in clear, idiomatic, and contemporary English, the same level of colloquialism or formality and the same degree of lexical sophistication or simplicity as in the originals.

As mentioned above, many of the letters included here have been abridged, and these cuts are indicated according to the following policy: cuts of three lines or less of print are marked by conventional ellipses in square brackets. In the case of longer cuts, the square brackets contain the number of lines cut and a brief summary of the topics discussed or important information included in the omitted passage.[8] Square brackets are used exclusively to mark the editors' comments, including the summaries of cuts just described, reconstructions of letters or words that are illegible or have been destroyed, and modern equivalents of words no longer in use.[9]

With the exception of personal and place names (where we have consistently retained the original spelling without any further indication), any other words and phrases taken directly from the original German (or interspersed English) have been put in italics. Italics are thus used to indicate instances in which the letter-writer used an English word or provided explanations or translations of English terms (often giving their German equivalent, which is also italicized), or in very rare occasions when a German word proved untranslatable, often due to difficulties in transcription.[10] German weight, measure, and currency terms have been left in German but written out in standard orthography (and hence not italicized), even when abbreviated or represented by symbols in the original texts. German legal terms and administrative titles, many of which have no direct English equivalent and may be unfamiliar to the reader, have been translated into idiomatic English as consistently as possible. The translation of biblical passages cited in the letters is based on the Authorized King James Version. All dates have been changed to conform to U.S. norms (month, day, year).

Division of Labor

Both editors share responsibility for this entire volume, although the editing of each letter series, the various introductions, and the background research

---

8. Some of the terms used in these summaries are quite general. "Correspondence," for example, covers thanks for letters received, requests for letters, comments on the writer's own letters, postage, mail delivery, the time it takes for a letter to be delivered, and so forth.

9. Thus, "ne[xt]" usually means that only the first two letters were legible, but the editors are almost certain that this reading is correct, while "ne[xt?]" indicates that they were not. And "[----]" signals that four letters were so illegible that no reasonable interpretation was possible. Occasionally, but very rarely, something has been added in square brackets to aid comprehension.

10. A few further notes on the treatment of the texts: (1) German handwriting of the time used a different script than English, but some Germans also used a second, "Latin" script similar to English handwriting for English or other foreign words, often for proper names, and sometimes for emphasis. While we distinguished between the two scripts in the German edition, we do not do so here. (2) Words or phrases underlined in the letters are also underlined in the translation. (3) Separate paragraphs in the original letters are usually indicated by separate paragraphs in both the German and English editions; but to save space, short lines frequently found at the beginning or end of a letter are occasionally combined, separated by a slash (/). This means that a new line was begun in the original.

were divided, with only the preface, Editorial Approach, and material in the back matter drafted jointly. Walter Kamphoefner wrote the "German Immigrants and Politics in the Civil War Era" section of the introduction, and Wolfgang Helbich wrote the "German Immigrants in the Union Army" section. The selection of letters for the edition and the establishment of general editorial principles were also a matter of mutual agreement. Research in archives and primary sources on both sides of the Atlantic, however, was done cooperatively and not restricted to one's "own" series or native land. Otherwise, work on the introductions and texts was done independently.[11] Wolfgang Helbich was responsible for letters in the Eastern Theater grouping, and Walter Kamphoefner handled letters in the Western Theater grouping. Although letter selections were made jointly, the drafting of introductions, footnotes, and annotations to a given letter group, as well as the decisions on abridgments, were made by the individual editor. However, drafts of these introductions, annotations, and other material were read and critiqued by the other editor and in some instances discussed rather intensely. But the final decisions and responsibility rested with the editor of the respective section. The result is, or is intended to be, a volume with a common structure and framework, but upon close examination, the individual viewpoints, concerns, and accents of the two editors still show through to the discerning eye.

For the English version, Wolfgang Helbich added notes at the beginning of every introduction characterizing each letter-writer's original German handwriting, orthography, grammar, style, and overall linguistic competence. General translation policies were set by the editors together with the translator, Susan Vogel. The editors, with much input from Vogel, also decided on changes in the annotation from the original German version to suit the needs of an American readership. The translator worked closely with the two editors, often circulating multiple drafts. Each translation draft was given a reading by both of the editors, and the person with prime responsibility for the series did a line-for-line check against the German original. Problematic

---

11. Since there was no logical, a priori way to group letter-writers, our grouping by combat theater is somewhat arbitrary, in part reflecting our division of labor. Maritime and West Coast letters were assigned to Helbich to even out the editing load, and grouped with the Eastern Theater letters as a matter of convenience. Civilians were assigned to the two theaters by whether or not they resided in states bordering on the Atlantic. With soldiers, distinctions between the Eastern and Western Theaters were somewhat imprecise since several eastern units were transferred west; soldiers from Michigan and Wisconsin ended up in both theaters depending on where their units were assigned. Within the Eastern Theater, writers are arranged in roughly chronological order since many had no firm geographic base; within the Western Theater they are grouped geographically by state to keep writers from Union, border, and Confederate areas together.

passages were worked out in a final editorial round by all three team members. Walter Kamphoefner, the chief editor of the English version, assembled the final manuscript.

Literature and Sources on Immigrants in the Civil War

The ethnic component of the Civil War has been largely forgotten in the public image and seriously neglected by scholars as well. The popular and critically acclaimed PBS television documentary on the Civil War by Ken Burns gave virtually no mention in its eleven hours to ordinary immigrants, except for their role in the New York City draft riot of 1863. Academic accounts show somewhat greater awareness of the immigrant presence but still are badly handicapped by the dearth of material on foreign-born, and particularly foreign-language, soldiers. For example, Bell Wiley's classic account *The Life of Billy Yank* devotes scarcely two pages to Germans, and not much more to other immigrants. James I. Robertson Jr.'s *Soldiers Blue and Gray* is intended as an update of Wiley, but it hardly gets beyond the mere numbers of immigrants in the ranks. Neither of these works explores how the experiences of immigrant soldiers were similar or different from those of their native-born comrades.[12]

Though more than a half century old, Ella Lonn's *Foreigners in the Union Army and Navy* still remains the best in its field, despite a strong emphasis on elites and particularly Forty-eighters and a concomitant lack of perspective on the rank and file.[13] Another, more recent treatment of ethnic Yankees cites only a minimum of German-language material and is heavily dependent on the coverage of secondary sources. Moreover, the author rides his "melting pot" thesis rather heavily, and he overlooks ways in which the Civil War experience often reinforced ethnic rather than American identity—or sometimes did both by convincing immigrants that they understood the essence of America better than those who were citizens by accident of birth.[14]

As for work focused specifically on Germans, the era leading up to the Civil War, and especially its politics, has been much more thoroughly studied than the war itself.[15] Besides the pioneering works by Carl Wittke on two overlap-

12. Wiley (1952); Robertson (1988). Wiley (1943), the companion volume devoted to "Johnny Reb," includes even less on ethnic soldiers, but justifiably so given their small presence in the Confederate army.

13. Lonn (1951). Her predecessor volume, *Foreigners in the Confederacy* (1940), is still in print, attesting to its continuing value. Lonn (2002).

14. Burton (1988).

15. See especially Luebke (1971); and Levine (1992).

ping subjects, the Forty-eighters and the German-language press, there is a compilation of ethnic press reports from one of the "storm centers" that provides some military commentary along with the political, though mostly from the perspective of the ethnic elite.[16]

On the military side, Wilhelm Kaufmann's pioneering 1911 work was recently translated from the German; however, the footnotes and annotations of the English edition do virtually nothing to correct the author's ethnocentric hyperbole.[17] Two of the most prominent German generals, Carl Schurz and Franz Sigel, have been the subjects of modern biographies.[18] But the perspective of immigrant common soldiers, both their military role and especially their motivations for fighting, is still greatly in need of elucidation. One of the best editions of German letters is typical of what little has appeared in English: the writer was the son of political refugees in the "Latin Farmer" settlement of Belleville, Illinois; he was a well-educated officer and American-born to boot.[19] Material on German Confederates is similarly atypical: the best such letter collection, *Lone Star and Double Eagle*, deals with the family of a German count.[20] Letters of ordinary immigrants and common soldiers, or of their families and other civilians writing from the home front, are even more rare, although a couple of recent publications have improved the meager fare.[21] German Jews should be a part of this story; when Jewish companies were raised, they often served in German regiments.[22] Unfortunately, there are no Civil War letters from Jews in the material from which this anthology was selected, although letters by others occasionally provide glimpses of Gentile-Jewish relations. The published letters penned by one of

16. Wittke (1952), 221–43; Wittke (1957), 135–58; Rowan and Primm (1983).

17. Kaufmann (1911); Kaufmann (1999).

18. Trefousse (1982); Engle (1993).

19. Hess (1983). Domschcke (1987) presents a memoir written in German shortly after the war, but it, too, is from a well-educated officer, Forty-eighter, and professional journalist.

20. Goyne (1982). Similarly, Patrick (1999) presents the diary of a well-assimilated German merchant who was a Confederate captain. The diary published by Spurlin (1992) was revised after the war; its author was an ordinary soldier but still atypical in that he was one of the few Germans in his company or regiment who did not go over to the Union side after being taken prisoner in 1863; see v–vi, 14, 66–67.

21. Nevertheless, even the most recent publications offer little of the perspectives of ordinary soldiers. Reinhart (2004) presents translations of the diary of one Kentucky German Union soldier and the letters of another; one was an artist, the other a journalist and correspondent for a Louisville ethnic newspaper. Gould and Kennedy (2004) offer the "war memories" of a Wisconsin German infantry captain. Macha and Wolf (2001) do offer a bilingual edition of a common soldier's diary, but the introduction and annotations provide more linguistic than historical context.

22. See, for example, Brinkmann (2004), 57–59.

the highest-ranking Jewish Union officers would at first glance appear quite atypical of German Jews as a whole, since he wrote in English to his Quaker wife. However, his letters reflect not only his own personal sentiments but also those of his relatives and other members of the Jewish community in Chicago, so the gap in this literature is actually less serious than with other Germans.[23] Ironically, given their small numbers, there is nearly as much material from German Confederates as from Germans in the Union army.

For one celebrated Ohio Turner* regiment, a history originally written in German at the turn of the century is now available in English. But such accounts written long after the fact leave much to be desired for the important new investigations of soldiers' motivations and the psychology of combat.[24] As a leading historian in this field, James McPherson, convincingly argues, "there is no better way to recover what motivated [Civil War soldiers] from 1861 to 1865 than to read their letters and diaries written in the immediacy of experience."[25] However, he readily concedes that the foreign-born are seriously underrepresented in the sample of Civil War letter-writers and diarists he used for his masterful study of soldier motivation. Although Germans made up about 10 percent of the Union army (and immigrants generally almost one-quarter), only 9 percent of the soldiers in McPherson's sample were foreign-born, and of the few he cites, the majority were English-speaking Irish.[26] This is no reflection on McPherson; it simply illustrates the scarcity of available material from Germans in blue (not to mention German Confederates), particularly in the English language.[27] An important new study of Union combat psychology by Earl Hess includes even less of an ethnic perspective; the German Yankee whose letters this author had previously edited is one of the very few he cites.[28]

This edition thus offers an important complement to such work by McPherson and Hess and helps illuminate the motivations of a substantial component of the Union army. Moreover, these letters may offer greater in-

23. Byrne and Soman (1985).

24. Grebner (1987). There are three other histories of regiments that were all or part German; however, are all secondary accounts, not primary sources: Martin (1987); Pula (1976); and Bacarella (1996).

25. McPherson (1994), 68–69.

26. McPherson (1997a), ix.

27. An extensive bibliography of nearly 2,000 items from Civil War eyewitnesses lists fewer than a dozen by German immigrants, including poems, single letters, and several of the books cited above. See Cole (1988); Cole (2000). No attempt has been made here to reference German-language publications, but it is clear that they, too, are few in number. One such letter edition, Holtmann (1999), has just come out in English translation; Holtmann (2005).

28. Hess (1997b); Hess (1983).

sights into soldiers' motives than those of the native-born because most were written to people with whom the writer was no longer in face-to-face contact before enlistment. People writing back to Europe had a greater need to explain just what the war was about and what led this individual to participate—or not to, as the case may be. In fact, it is very rare to find letters from Anglo Americans in which "slackers" explain their motives for avoiding Civil War service. With about two-fifths of the letters herein penned by noncombatants, we are confronted with an array of factors and motivations that kept men out of the army, and we gain additional insight into immigrant civilian life during the war.

Not only men, but also some women writing from the home front, are represented in this volume. While women's voices and two-way correspondence between spouses are fairly common among published Civil War letters of Anglo Americans, they are a rarity among immigrants.[29] Two translated letter collections do offer some women's perspectives on the era, although both involve elite women, and neither is likely to show up in a Civil War literature search.[30] Thus, the nineteen women represented in this collection add greatly to our understanding of how ordinary German women viewed the Civil War and the extent to which they shared or contradicted their husbands' views on the subject.

This volume is unique on both sides of the Atlantic in that it presents a cross-section of letters written by ordinary German immigrants during the Civil War era. Other possible selection criteria, such as gender or whether the letter-writer actually served in the military, did not play a role. The letters and excerpts were chosen on the basis of the language (German), the geographical background of the letter-writers (territory of the German Empire as of 1871), and the fact that the letters were written during the Civil War years (from the 1860 election campaign to the end of 1865). There are a few exceptions to this rule—letters from the time before or after these years—but the reasons for their inclusion should be self-evident from the content.

29. A 796-item bibliography on women in the Civil War does not even include a subject entry for Germans (or immigrants), nor could any be located through the name index. McDevitt (2003).

30. Schroeder and Schulz-Geisberg (1988) presents sixty years of letters by Jetta Bruns, a mayor's daughter and doctor's wife who lost a son and stepson in the war; her husband was heavily involved in Missouri Republican politics. Cheeseman (2002) offers letters from a Texas German woman of the nobility whose husband saw Confederate service and whose daughter married a Union solder during Reconstruction.

GERMANS IN THE CIVIL WAR

INTRODUCTION

German Immigrants and Politics in the Civil War Era

The events of the year 1848 had major ramifications both for the United States in general and for its German American population in particular—consequences that would be especially felt from 1860 to 1865. For the American republic, 1848 saw the successful conclusion of the war with Mexico and ratification of the peace terms. Texas was secured in its generous boundaries reaching to the Rio Grande, and California and most of the intervening territory was annexed from Mexico. But the Mexican War itself had been a bone of contention between North and South, and the resulting territorial acquisitions once again brought the latent question of the expansion of slavery to the top of the national agenda.

In Germany the March revolutions of 1848 brought a springtime of hope for democratization, national unification, and greater international recognition. Prince Metternich, the symbol of reaction for a generation, fled Vienna, and Prussia saw the prospect of a constitutional monarchy. On May 18, 1848, an elected national assembly met at the Paulskirche in Frankfurt in an attempt to establish a new Germany based on liberty, democracy, and national unity. By the next year these hopes were dashed, and several thousand German revolutionaries found themselves in European exile, which was for most of them just a way station on the road to America. Although these "Forty-eighters" accounted for less than 1 percent of the Germans who immigrated to the United States in the 1850s, they had a significance far greater than their numbers, leavening the whole loaf, as it were, with their democratic and egalitarian ideals. Within a decade of their arrival, a number of Forty-eighters met on Civil War battlefields with veterans of the Mexican War: some as allies, some as adversaries.[1]

Waging war on Mexico proved to be an easier task than disposing of the spoils. Slavery had been prohibited by Mexican law in the newly annexed areas, and southerners were already threatening secession in the fall of 1849 if their "rights" to human property were not respected. Ultimately, a legislative solution was achieved in the Compromise of 1850, but it was a grudging settle-

1. Friedrich (1950), 3–9.

ment at best; one historian has called it an armistice.[2] If all the compromise accomplished was to delay the outbreak of the Civil War by eleven years, this delay helped assure a northern victory. Every year brought a greater population advantage for the North. In relative terms, the 1850s saw the heaviest rate of immigration the nation has ever experienced. The years from 1850 to 1860 inclusive brought an influx of over a million Germans and nearly as many Irish. There was a net increase between the two censuses of nearly 700,000 Germans, more than doubling their numbers. Moreover, the concentration of immigrants in the northern states, already high to begin with, intensified during the decade, and it was higher for Germans than for other major groups. While only about one-third of the Union's net population gain in the decade before the Civil War was attributable to immigration, its impact on military potential was even greater because of its demographic makeup: disproportionately young, male adults.[3] Negligible as the 70,000 Germans in the eleven Confederate states were, nearly 20,000 of them resided in New Orleans, which was in Union hands from May 1862 on.

Well educated and articulate, the Forty-eighters who arrived in the early 1850s provided an important stimulus to immigrant cultural life and political participation. They nearly doubled the size of the German-language press in just four years, founded numerous *Turnvereine** that were hotbeds of republican idealism, and flocked to the newly established Republican Party, viewing the crusade against slavery as a continuation of their revolutionary struggles in Germany. Historians are still debating, however, to what extent their ideals were shared by the rank and file.[4]

The bulk of the German newcomers had more in common with their Irish counterparts than with their Forty-eighter countrymen. They were first and foremost economic refugees, even if they were not quite as desperately poor as the average Irish immigrant and were blessed with more marketable skills. Still, the distinction between economic and political motives for emigration is not as clear in practice as it might appear in theory. The economic burdens of the German lower classes were related to their political impotence and their lack of a voice in village self-administration. They bore the brunt of compulsory military service since the more prosperous members of peasant society could avail themselves of the option of hiring substitutes. For the first time, in 1848, not just bourgeois liberals but occasionally also ordinary immigrants

---

2. Potter (1976), 90–120, uses the term as the title of a chapter.

3. In the years 1852, 1856, and 1860, over 28 percent of arriving German immigrants were males in the prime military age group of sixteen to thirty years old. Thanks to Ira Glazier for this information from the Center for Immigration Research at the Balch Institute in Philadelphia.

4. Wittke (1957), 262–63; Levine (1992); Nagler (1984).

commented on the European political situation in their letters home.[5] The greater symbolic egalitarianism in the United States, even though it may have amounted to little in substance, certainly did not go unnoticed by ordinary Germans.

The German immigrants of the 1850s arrived in the United States to find a political situation that was in flux; in fact, they themselves contributed to the instability. Although an occasional German liberal such as the early political refugee Karl Follen was closely allied with the abolitionist movement (and lost his position at Harvard because he was frightening away potential southern students), most Germans kept their distance.[6] The revivalist tone of the abolitionists was especially repellant to freethinking political refugees, even if they pursued many of the same goals relative to slavery. Germans, however, stressed the "rational" basis of their humanitarian antislavery program in contrast to the "fanaticism" of their religiously motivated Anglo American counterparts.

This distance from antislavery reformers had other grounds as well. Reforms usually came in a package that included the temperance movement or outright prohibitions on alcohol—laws forbidding what most Germans considered to be innocent pleasures of beer gardens and brass bands—and injected a militantly Protestant tenor into public institutions such as schools. For example, the same Lyman Beecher who fathered the author of *Uncle Tom's Cabin*, Harriet Beecher Stowe, and her militant Free Soiler brother Henry Ward Beecher had in 1834 delivered violently anti-Catholic sermons at three Boston churches that inspired a mob to burn the nearby Ursuline convent the next day. In 1846 the elder Beecher had attended the World Temperance Conference in London along with William Lloyd Garrison, the founder of militant abolitionism. Such associations repelled not only German Catholics but many freethinkers and Old Lutheran separatists as well.

Yankee reform impulses, which originally found their vehicle in the Whig Party, took on a more explicitly antiforeign tone in the so-called Know Nothing movement that sprung up out of the party's ashes in the mid-1850s. Since this movement operated as a secret society rather than as a conventionally organized political party, there was considerable overlap between it and the newly formed Republican Party. By 1860, the Republicans had outmaneuvered the nativists and established themselves as the majority party in the North. Nativists usually had nowhere else to go but to join the Republican fold, but they no longer set the tone. However, their subterranean presence,

5. Kamphoefner (1987), 61–67; Harris (1989), 8; Kamphoefner (1997), 92–93.
6. *DAB*, 3:491.

which was stronger in some states than others, gave pause to many religiously conservative Germans.

What applied to immigrants from Luxembourg also held true for many other German-speaking Catholics: "it was only natural that they turned to the Democrats, who were conservative in their principles, well-disposed towards immigrants, opposed to centralization, and supported by other fellow Catholics." They remained Democrats "not because they were friends of the slaveholders, no, but because they did not like the elements that had combined to form the new Republican Party. Instinctively, [. . .] they stood in opposition to the party of centralization and Puritanism."[7]

Whig and Republican zeal for individual, as well as national, improvement went so far that proponents were not always willing to leave things to chance or personal choice. Not just southern slaveholders, but also many of the impoverished, immigrants, Catholics, or tipplers (sometimes all wrapped up in one), felt threatened by Republican "do-gooders" with their tendency to want to improve others regardless of whether they felt they needed improving. Whigs and Republicans had taken the lead in humanitarian areas such as building orphanages and improving schools, but they had often given these new institutions an unmistakably Protestant tone, to the point of reading the Protestant Bible translation in schools and proclaiming the pope as the Antichrist.[8]

This "ethnocultural" interpretation of antebellum politics (in the terminology of recent historiography) offers an important corrective to an earlier generation of self-congratulatory German American scholarship and its claim that the unanimous support of the "freedom loving Germans" for Abraham Lincoln proved decisive to the outcome of the 1860 presidential election. Scholars who have examined voting behavior and electoral issues more carefully have concluded that the legacy of nativism in the Republican Party and the anticlerical tendencies of its most articulate German leaders often proved to be insurmountable obstacles with rank-and-file voters of Catholic or conservative Lutheran backgrounds. However, one must beware of religious determinism and not assume that voters followed religious leaders unquestioningly. Even though Germans across the North were less likely to vote Republican than were Anglo Americans, and may have cast a slight majority

7. Gonner (1985–86 [1889]), 1:229–30 (our translation); the translation in Gonner (1987), 199, tones down the original language somewhat.

8. McPherson (1982), 20–22, 82–84. Zophar Mills—characterized by letter-writer Emile Dupré (no. 2), Mills's son-in-law, as a nativist—served on a citywide New York committee resolved to oppose all candidates for any school office except for known Protestants who supported daily Bible reading in all public schools. *New York Times*, November 15, 1858, p. 1.

of their votes against Lincoln in 1860, they were still probably the social group that made the largest net shift away from the Democratic Party during the decade of the 1850s. Thus, earlier perceptions of their decisive role were not so far off base after all.[9]

One strong piece of evidence against religious determinism is the fact that Germans of the same local origins and religious affiliation ended up supporting different political parties depending on where they happened to settle, a fact that has become increasingly apparent through recent scholarship utilizing work in transatlantic tracing.[10] The Republicans made greater efforts than the Whigs ever had to meet immigrants, and particularly Germans, halfway. Lincoln had not only taken a firm stand against nativism, but in 1859 he also went so far as to secretly purchase an interest in a German-language newspaper in his hometown of Springfield, Illinois.[11] There was a prominent German presence at the 1860 Republican convention, including earlier immigrants as well as Forty-eighters, and a handful of Catholics as well as Protestants. The convention, with four Germans on the drafting committee, enacted a party program containing several "Dutch planks," in particular one opposing any tightening of naturalization laws such as nativists were demanding and had actually enacted in Massachusetts.[12]

A number of German-language orators, headed up by Forty-eighter Carl Schurz,* but also including prominent "Dreissiger," politically motivated emigrants of the 1830s such as Friedrich Muench and Gustave Koerner, were sent out on the campaign trail to bring the Republican message into ethnic communities. Still, as best as can be determined, the Democrats retained a majority of German voters in Wisconsin, Iowa, Indiana, and the cities of New York, Albany, Baltimore, and Philadelphia. Republicans won greater or lesser majorities among the Germans of Missouri, Illinois, Minnesota, and the cities of Brooklyn, Buffalo, and perhaps Pittsburgh. Michigan Germans presented a contrast between Republican Detroit and Democratic rural areas. Cincinnati Germans likewise produced a Republican majority that contrasted with their compatriots in Cleveland and rural Ohio. (Lincoln obtained barely 1 percent of his votes in the South; the only counties he carried in the slave states were St. Louis and Gasconade Counties in Missouri, both dominated by Germans.)[13]

9. Many of the most important articles on this subject are collected in Luebke (1971); see also Kleppner (1979), 73–74; Gienapp (1986); and Kamphoefner (1991).

10. Further details in Kamphoefner (1991).

11. Wittke (1957), 145.

12. Bergquist (1989).

13. In addition to the literature in Luebke (1971), see Gienapp (1986); Kamphoefner (1991);

Clausewitz's old dictum, "War is the continuation of politics by other means," is perhaps nowhere more literally true than with reference to the Civil War. While this applies particularly to the South, in the North the means and ends of the war also continued to be a political issue throughout the conflict. Northern Democrats were willing to fight for "the Constitution as it is and the Union as it was," but they were usually reluctant to go any further.[14] Republicans, however, came increasingly to see a restoration of the old Union without the elimination of the root cause of secession, slavery, as a task only half done and a source of recurring problems. Political affiliation had significant implications for both military recruitment and military appointments.

At the outbreak of war, both sides had more volunteers than they had the means to train or equip, but as the harsh realities of combat began to sink in, both were forced to resort to conscription. During the Civil War and ever since, charges have been raised that it was a "rich man's war and a poor man's fight." Certainly, there were legal provisions that would have made this possible. Both sides allowed the purchase of substitutes, which enabled the wealthy to escape military service if they chose (a practice Germans were familiar with back home). However, several case studies of northern service found little or no class difference in recruitment rates. Although the letter-writers herein include several ardent Republicans of bourgeois origins who purchased substitutes rather than serve, as well as some impoverished immigrants who enlisted mainly for economic reasons, this does not constitute an overall trend. Most studies have found that Irish immigrants, one of the poorest elements of northern society, were underrepresented in the Union ranks, thus underscoring the influence of non-economic factors. One of the most obvious of these factors is political affiliation: Democrats were decidedly cooler toward the war effort than Republicans. A case study of one Wisconsin county suggests that Republicans were twice as likely to enlist as Democrats.[15]

Although Germans generally complied, if sometimes reluctantly, with Union conscription laws, there were several cases of collective resistance, one serious enough to cause arrests. Not coincidentally, this took place in Wisconsin, where Germans predominantly stuck with the Democratic Party and where it was necessary to impose a draft already in 1862 to meet the state's troop obligations. As the drawing was about to get under way in Port Washington, the Ozaukee County seat, local Luxembourgian and German Catho-

---

Kawaguchi (1994); and Lorenz-Meyer (2000). For the cities of New York, Brooklyn, Albany, and Buffalo I have conducted my own regression analysis of German voting behavior.

14. McPherson (1982), 296–97.

15. Logue (1996), 14, 28; Rorabaugh (1986); Vinovskis (1990b), 16–17; Hackemer (1999). For a thorough assessment of the class issue, see McPherson (1988), 603–15.

lics revolted. It was little comfort to them that the state governor was fellow immigrant Edward Salomon (who had moved up from lieutenant governor); he was also a Prussian Lutheran Forty-eighter. A drunken mob of about 200 people seized and destroyed the draft lists and drove off the officials in charge, wrecking the houses of the head of the draft committee and four others who were associated with him. Eight companies of Federal troops were immediately sent to Port Washington where they remained for more than a month, allowing conscription to be carried out without further resistance. Eighty-one persons were arrested and held at military stockades, though eventually they were set free without prosecution. There were several other incidents of draft resistance in Wisconsin's German communities, including at least two that led to the sending of troops. Often, such resistance took on a more passive form: many of those subject to conscription fled, and those who were inducted often proved to be almost useless for the war effort. The mostly German 34th Wisconsin, consisting entirely of nine-month draftees, could be trusted only for garrison duty, never heard an enemy shot, and still saw almost 30 percent of its men desert during its short term of service.[16] But nowhere did German resistance approach the magnitude and virulence of the largely Irish 1863 draft riots in New York City, which left more than 100 dead in their wake.[17]

The differing political affiliations of Germans in various states clearly affected the degree to which they supported the Union military cause. A leading Civil War historian sees these differences purely as a matter of confession: German Protestants "enlisted in proportion to their percentage of the male population[. . . .] German Catholics did not."[18] Much more accurate would be to say that Republican immigrants enlisted more eagerly in the Union army than did Democrats; these categories overlapped with confession, but far from completely. In fact, the overall level of German representation in the Union forces was so high as to make it doubtful that a segment as large as the Catholics (at least one-third of the total) was made up of consistent slackers.

Information on the ethnicity of soldiers was compiled by B. A. Gould of the U.S. Sanitary Commission, who then set up "quotas" for each nationality group based on its share of the population. According to his figures, Germans were the group most overrepresented in the Union army (except for Canadians, many of whom were not permanent U.S. residents). Germans sur-

16. Gonner (1985–86 [1889]), 1:206–10; Current (1976), 310–19, 324–35, 353, 412.

17. A detailed study of the riots is offered by Bernstein (1990); see also McPherson (1988), 609–11. A contemporary account is the letter of July 28, 1863, in the Wesslau series (no. 3).

18. McPherson (1982), 358. Many Catholics, especially the better educated, tended to support the Union cause. Kamphoefner (1997).

passed their quota by almost 50 percent, British by 19 percent, and Irish by only 4 percent, while native white Americans were 8 percent under quota. It is unclear whether Gould took into account the disproportionate share of immigrants who were young males (the overrepresentation of the Irish suggests that he did not), but one local study that does so still shows Germans as the most willing recruits. According to the 1865 New York census, in Buffalo only 9 percent of the Irish aged nineteen to thirty-five had seen Union service, as opposed to 10 percent of the natives and 16 percent of the Germans in the same age group.[19]

When one compares levels of German recruitment from state to state, there are some immediate contrasts that reflect the group's local affinity for the Republican Party (see table). These calculations are not without their problems. As was the case with a number of letter-writers, some immigrants fought in units outside their state of residence. Big cities had an easier time filling their recruitment quotas because they could offer larger bonuses. In New York and Pennsylvania, where despite largely Democratic affiliations, Germans showed rather high recruitment quotas, newly arrived immigrants — some of whom, like letter-writer Wilhelm Albrecht (no. 9), probably came over specifically to enlist — certainly helped out. Recent arrivals such as letter-writers Gustav Keppler (no. 21) and Eduard Treutlein (no. 27) (neither of whom was enumerated in the 1860 census) obviously account for the good showing of the few Germans in New England, New Jersey, Delaware, and the District of Columbia.

These exceptions aside, however, Missouri Germans, the strongest Republican supporters, also had far and above the highest level of Union army participation. Though sixth in the size of its German population, Missouri was second only to New York in the number of German troops it furnished. The contrast is particularly stark with other border states such as Kentucky and Maryland, which did not have an appreciable German Republican movement. The poor showing of Iowa can be explained by both partisanship and the state's rural character. Michigan and Indiana, states with little Republican success among Germans, also rank well below Illinois and Minnesota, probably the only states besides Missouri with German Republican majorities. The contrast between Cincinnati and the rest of Ohio in German party affiliation gave that state a middling ranking in German recruitment.

The most puzzling feature of the table is the relatively good showing of Wisconsin, the only state to see German draft riots. Gould assumed that the 1 million recruits from the beginning of the war, for whom no nationality data

19. Kaufmann (1911), 118–31; Lonn (1951), 574–79; Yox (1985), 156.

Number of German-Born Union Soldiers
in Relation to German Immigrant Population by State

	Germans in Union Army	German-Born in 1860	Proportion of State German Population
New Hampshire	952	412	231.1%
Maine	244	384	63.6
Delaware	621	1,263	49.2
Vermont	86	219	39.3
Missouri	30,899	88,487	34.9
Connecticut, Rhode Island	2,919	9,340	31.3
Kansas	1,090	4,318	25.3
District of Columbia	746	3,254	22.9
New Jersey	7,337	33,772	21.7
Massachusetts	1,876	9,961	18.8
Minnesota	2,715	18,400	14.8
New York	36,680	256,252	14.3
Illinois	18,140	130,804	13.9
Wisconsin	15,709	123,879	12.7
Pennsylvania	17,208	138,244	12.5
Ohio	20,102	168,210	12.0
Indiana	7,190	66,705	10.8
Michigan	3,534	38,787	9.1
Iowa	2,850	38,555	7.4
Maryland	3,107	43,884	7.1
Kentucky	1,943	27,227	7.1

Source: Calculated from Wilhelm Kaufmann, *Die Deutschen im amerikanischen Bürgerkrieg* (Munich: Oldenbourg, 1911), 121–22.

was available, were distributed across nationalities the same way as later recruits. For Wisconsin, this was clearly not the case. Foreigners, of whom Germans were the largest element, made up half of Wisconsin's men of military age, but only 40 percent of its soldiers overall and only about one-third at the beginning of the war.[20]

The low level of Wisconsin recruitment becomes especially apparent in comparison with Missouri. Though Wisconsin Germans outnumbered those in Missouri by 40 percent, and made up twice as large a share of their state's population, they supplied barely half as many troops. The ancestor-worship-

20. Current (1976), 313–35, 353–54.

ping legend of German "Wide-Awakes" saving Missouri for the Union at the outbreak of the war is only a slight exaggeration. Together with a handful of Anglo political and military leaders, they prevented the Federal arsenal in St. Louis from falling into Confederate hands, despite the best efforts of a prosouthern state governor. Of the five, three-month regiments recruited at the outbreak of the war, four and a half were German. Besides these, among the first twenty Missouri regiments, the 12th and 17th were overwhelmingly German, the 15th was German and Swiss, and there were two German companies in other regiments. In Wisconsin, by contrast, the most German state of the Union, of the first twenty regiments only the 5th Militia and the 9th were overwhelmingly German, though the 18th and 20th were both more than half. There can be no doubt that political affiliation weighed heavily in such varying enthusiasm for the Union cause.[21]

The Civil War brought a military buildup of unprecedented proportion. The peacetime U.S. Army before the Civil War seems incredibly small by European standards, or even for Americans of the post-1945 era. Its official strength consisted of only 16,367 soldiers, including 1,108 officers of various ranks. This was not even one-twelfth the peacetime strength of the Prussian army. In such an enormous military buildup, there was no alternative to placing into command many men who lacked previous military experience or training. Given the political nature of the conflict and the fact that soldiers initially elected their own officers, it is not surprising that political, regional, and ethnic considerations weighed heavily in many appointments, even up to the level of general, which was the president's prerogative. Then and ever since, this has led to acrimonious charges of incompetence on the part of "political generals," charges that were not entirely groundless but certainly exaggerated. As several historians have pointed out, whatever drawbacks political appointments had from a military standpoint, from the viewpoint of national strategy they integrated important ethnic, regional, or political constituencies into the Union cause. Moreover, even the two generals most responsible for Union victory, Ulysses S. Grant and William T. Sherman, obtained their initial appointments at least partly because of political connections. Also in the case of Peter Joseph Osterhaus,* one of the most competent ethnic officers, Lincoln stated that his promotion to major general in 1864 was based "on what we thought was high merit, and somewhat on his nationality." Whatever the shortcomings of the hapless Alexander Schimmelfennig—chosen by Lincoln over several other German nominees primarily for his conspicuously ethnic name, and singled out by one historian for mak-

21. Blum (1948); Lonn (1951), 669–70.

ing a "real ass" of himself—he was not a rank amateur. Trained as a Prussian officer, he had fought on the liberal side in Schleswig-Holstein and Baden before emigrating. But he never lived down having spent most of the battle of Gettysburg in a pigsty.[22]

One biographer describes Carl Schurz as "a competent officer who had risen too high too fast." The second half of the characterization would apply equally to fellow Forty-eighter Franz Sigel,* a prime beneficiary of ethnic lobbying—though again not an amateur soldier. He had graduated at the top of his class at the military academy in Karlsruhe and spent four years in the Baden army before casting his lot with the 1848 revolution. Sigel was probably the Forty-eighter with the most military training and battlefield experience in Germany. This, along with his devotion to the revolutionary cause, won him a place in the hearts of German Americans and assured him a position of command at the outbreak of the Civil War. He spent the first year of the war in the Missouri-Arkansas campaign as a brigade and division commander, punctuated (as was his entire career) by quarrels with superiors and threatened and actual resignations. The political lobbying of German Americans as much as any military achievements led to Sigel's promotion to major general and transfer to the eastern theater.[23]

Sigel was a good administrator and a master of orderly retreat, but despite personal bravery in battle, he showed timidity of leadership and proved to be neither a competent and dependable subordinate nor someone capable of independent command. He was no match for Stonewall Jackson (though neither was any other Union general), but when he proved equally unsuccessful against Jubal Early, he was removed from command in July 1864. Lincoln's appointment of Sigel to brigadier and even major general made sense on military as well as political grounds. What is less understandable is the continued "uncritical enthusiasm" of German Americans for Sigel, especially given the superior record of other compatriots such as General Osterhaus.[24]

Another issue that subjected the president to a crossfire of criticism from both radicals and conservatives was Lincoln's decision to issue an emancipation proclamation and employ black troops in the Union army. Lincoln did a

22. Williams (1952), 10–13; McPherson (1990), 70–71; Work (2004); Basler (1953), 5:463–64; Hattaway (1997), 178; Zucker (1950), 336–37; Trefousse (1982), 138.

23. Trefousse (1982), 149; Engle (1993), 116–22, 145–48, 229–33, 267 n. 27; Lonn (1951), 175–80, 182–84. Examples of lobbying for Sigel in the German press are presented in Rowan and Primm (1983), 297–300, 308–9, 310–11, 313–14. See also letters by Dupré (no. 2), Rossi (no. 6), Albrecht (no. 9), Hermanns (no. 10), Knoebel (no. 17), W. Krause (no. 22), Dieden (no. 36), and Stähler (no. 51).

24. Engle (1993), 232.

masterful job of holding together a diverse and factionalized political coalition and of using the office of the president to educate the American public and prepare the way for black emancipation and military participation. He showed an exquisite sense of timing, resisting extreme pressure if he considered a measure to be premature, but moving decisively when he felt the time was right. He usually remained slightly ahead of public opinion, but not so far as to precipitate a backlash, and once he took a new step he almost never backed off. Nonetheless, both the slow process of emancipation and perceptions of ethnic discrimination in military appointments had alienated many German Americans from Lincoln. They formed an important component of the political forces that opposed the president from the left and attempted to nominate a more radical candidate in 1864.

Some of these tensions went back all the way to the beginning of the war, especially in Missouri, a slaveholding border state. There, conservative or pragmatic unionists had clashed with idealistic abolitionists over a number of issues. Missouri Germans were much dismayed when the president rescinded General John Frémont emancipation order in 1861 and removed him from command. Beginning in March 1864, a number of German-language newspapers endorsed Frémont for the presidency, and in May a convention in Cleveland nominated him as candidate. But what had started out in Missouri as a radical emancipationist party took the national stage as the Radical Democratic Party, making concessions to the Democrats with an opportunism that made Lincoln's pragmatism appear statesmanlike by comparison. Lincoln's differences with the radicals were more about timing than about ultimate goals; after the visit of a largely German delegation from Missouri in 1863, he remarked that such radicals were "devils [. . .] to deal with" but conceded that "their faces are set Zionwards." In September Frémont withdrew his fading candidacy, and many German radicals gritted their teeth and supported Lincoln, or at worst stayed home. But this may explain why the number of German votes for Lincoln—besieged from the right as well as the left—failed to increase between 1860 and 1864, and the percentage of support in German areas actually declined slightly. Milwaukee was one of only two big cities where Lincoln lost ground between elections. The only congressional race that Wisconsin Republicans lost in 1864 was the 4th District, which included the heavily German counties of Washington, Sheboygan, and Ozaukee—the last the scene of earlier draft riots.[25] Ethnic politics was a factor

25. Basler (1953), 5:463–64. The most thorough treatment of the German Frémont movement is Nagler (1984); an English summary can be found in Nagler (1989a). German Democrats have received less attention. Schick (1994) offers a fine analysis of the rhetoric of the German Democratic press in Illinois, but the author gives insufficient attention to its reception by the

that Lincoln had to contend with from his first presidential campaign until the end of the war.

There was also a small but significant ethnic presence in the South. Two prominent German names in southern leadership circles, immigrant Christopher Memminger as Confederate secretary of the treasury and immigrants' son John A. Quitman as governor of Mississippi and one of the leading "fire-eaters" until his early death in 1858, might lead one to believe that Germans in the South identified easily with the slaveholding aristocracy. But it is questionable to what degree either of these figures shared or identified with German culture.[26] In general, it seems that Germans of a bourgeois background, like these two, especially when they migrated alone and settled in areas without a substantial German presence, were among those most likely to adopt the "southern" way of life. One such example in the letters is "Herr Traun" of Alabama, an acquaintance of letter-writer Heinrich Stähler (no. 51).

A recent study of Germans in the Confederacy (focusing primarily on the cities of Charleston, Richmond, and New Orleans) estimates their overall level of military service as close to that in the Union: 16.1 percent of the German population in the South joined the military, as opposed to 16.6 percent in the North. At first glance this might suggest considerable Confederate sympathies. But given that a much higher proportion of southerners in general saw service (61 percent of military-age males versus 35 percent in the North), Germans in the South were evidently much less enthusiastic than their Anglo neighbors or their compatriots in the North.[27] The Confederate draft was im-

---

rank and file and provides no comparison with the English-language press. See also McPherson (1988), 714–16, 776; Dennett (1939), 108; Kleppner (1979), 83–84; Parish (1975), 546; Current (1976), 353.

26. Quitman's "mother" tongue was Dutch. His maternal grandfather had been governor of Curacao in the Dutch West Indies, where his father, a pastor born and trained in Germany, spent twelve years, met his wife, and adopted the custom of slaveholding before settling in Rheinbeck, New York, where John was born in 1798. Groomed for the ministry, John no doubt understood German, but he soon turned his back on the Lutheran confession and his father's ambitions, settling at age twenty-three in Mississippi. Although born in Germany, Memminger was probably less exposed to its culture than Quitman. He immigrated as an infant with his grandparents and widowed mother and, after her death, was placed at age four in a Charleston orphanage. Taken in at age eleven by a future governor of South Carolina, Memminger went on to a successful career in law and finance. He was so assimilated to an Anglo American world that letters from his German relatives had to be translated into English. May (1985), 2–5; letter of Robert May to Walter Kamphoefner, September 30, 1995, in author's possession; Capers (1893), 7–13, 19–20; Mehrländer (1998), 354.

27. Mehrländer (1998), 314; Vinovskis (1990b), 9. The military potential of foreigners in the South was increased by the higher ratio of males to females: 60 percent of the Germans in the South were male, but only 56 percent of those in the North were male. Of all Germans in

posed a year earlier than in the Union, it encompassed a broader age group, and it was revised to require service for the duration of the war. By allowing the purchase of substitutes, it held the same potential for class inequities as the Union draft, and more. The Confederacy in October 1862 passed the notorious "twenty Negro rule," which freed one white man as overseer for every twenty slaves, further lightening the obligations of the planter class. But studies of who actually did serve in the Confederate army paint a rather different picture. At least in Mississippi, the more slaves a family owned, the more likely its members were to fight for the Confederacy. Though the military burden was more equally shared across classes than is often realized, the economic burdens of inflation and taxation in kind fell disproportionately on the poorer members of southern society. The South grasped the expedient of a 10 percent tax in kind on all agricultural produce beyond subsistence, a measure that weighed especially heavily on yeoman farmers and even more on their wives back home (see the Lehmann letter series, no. 57).[28]

Some interesting contrasts can be observed between the Germans in the Confederacy's three largest cities. The German community of Charleston, the oldest, richest, most homogeneous, and most prone to slaveholding of the three, also gave the greatest support to the Confederacy. Richmond's Germans, many of whom had recently arrived and were concentrated in the artisan class, were strongly suspected of disloyalty.[29] New Orleans had the largest and most diverse German community in the Confederacy. Its leading German newspaper supported the Stephen Douglas (northern) Democratic ticket in 1860; a rival organ backed the moderate Constitutional Union ticket, and its editor opposed secession to the end as a member of the legislature. The ethnic community did manage to produce five companies of the 20th Louisiana Infantry to form the Confederacy's only German battalion, but it also proved fertile recruiting grounds for the Union army, whether from economic or ideological motives, once the city was in Union hands.[30]

---

the North, 40.7 percent were men of military age; in the South the figure stood at 46.9 percent; German men in the South were slightly older and thus less likely to serve, but the difference in average age amounted to a negligible 0.3 years. So other things being equal, Germans in the South, being more heavily male, should have had a higher ratio of soldiers to total German population than those in the North. These figures are based on calculations from the 1 percent 1860 IPUMS (Integrated Public Use Microdata Series) census sample; see Ruggles et al. (2004).

28. Parish (1975), 314–21; McPherson (1988), 437–40, 615–17.

29. Mehrländer (1998); see also Bright (1999), a thesis entitled "'Nothing to Fear from the Influence of Foreigners': The Patriotism [*sic*] of Richmond's German-Americans During the Civil War." Tellingly, the thesis that Bright seeks to overturn is the Germans' "reputation for universal disloyalty" to the Confederacy. Bright (1999), ii.

30. Clark (1980 [1937]); Deiler (1980 [1901]).

Outside of Texas and New Orleans, there were a mere 30,000 Germans in the South: a few urban clusters and a negligible rural diaspora. What cities there were in the South did have a relatively high foreign-born population, but Germans formed a lower percentage even of the white population in cities of the Confederacy than they did in the North. Five Confederate states had no German newspapers whatsoever; and New Orleans was the only southern city with competing German dailies beyond the duration of the 1860 presidential campaign. From June 1862 on, the *Richmond Anzeiger* remained the only German-language paper in the Confederacy east of the Mississippi.[31] Texas, which was home to more than 20,000 of the 70,000 Germans residing in the eleven Confederate states, presented a rather different situation. It was the only place in the South where Germans were concentrated enough in rural areas to form a critical mass and maintain an ethnic community life, so that they were a factor to be reckoned with in politics and war.[32]

Geographer Terry Jordan has pointed up important distinctions between Germans in eastern and western Texas as far as attitudes toward slavery and the Civil War are concerned. Eastern settlements were older, their immigrants more acculturated to American values, their local economies well suited for plantation agriculture and slavery. The Hill Country, west of Austin, by contrast, was more recently settled. With its semiarid ranching economy, it had very few slaveholders, Anglo or German. As a frontier region, it was exposed to the dangers of Indian attacks should federal military protection be withdrawn—a consideration that also promoted unionism among neighboring Anglos. But while Jordan has provided a needed corrective to Texas-German ancestor worship, exploding the myth that his forebears were overwhelmingly unionist and abolitionist, he goes too far in characterizing Texas Germans as "unremarkable" in their race attitudes, and he underestimates the degree to which Germans stood apart from their fellow Texans on the issues of the Civil War era.[33]

Moreover, the regional differences among Texas Germans should not be overestimated. Although geographic conditions in the Hill Country may have discouraged slavery, Jordan's own work shows that in three counties where 11 percent of the Anglo families owned slaves, not a single German did. According to Jordan, lack of capital was the main factor restricting slaveholdings among Germans in eastern Texas. Indeed, a recent study of Austin, Fayette, and Colorado Counties (the neighborhoods of letter-writers Hermann Nagel, Robert Voigt, and Georg Wilhelm Schwarting [nos. 53, 54, and 56])

31. Rousey (1992), 154–56, esp. n. 4; Arndt and Olson (1965); Mehrländer (1998), 496–97.
32. Further details in Kamphoefner (1999), on which the following sections are based.
33. Jordan (1989), 92.

has documented about sixty Germans who did own slaves between 1840 and 1865. Still, despite the strong presence of Germans in these eastern counties, they made up less than 5 percent of the local slave owners and possessed only 2 percent of the area's slaves. Moreover, at every level of wealth a higher proportion of Anglos than Germans owned slaves. For example, among persons worth from $3,000 to $6,000, over half of the Anglos but barely 2 percent of the Germans were slave owners. People of the servant-keeping class in Germany, especially those of noble origins, were especially prone to slaveholding. But even among the wealthy worth over $15,000, only half of the Germans owned slaves, in contrast to 92 percent of the American-born. Granted, slaveholding was a voluntary act among Germans unless they married into an Anglo family, whereas many native Texans became slave owners through inheritance. But contrasts of this magnitude could hardly have arisen without a conscious choice by many or most Germans against human property. One sees similar patterns in Missouri, the only other slave state with large numbers of Germans.[34]

The secession referendum of February 23, 1861, provides another measure of Texas German attitudes toward southern independence and institutions. German and Anglo unionists were not the natural allies one might suppose. Many of the latter had earlier expressed their nationalism in the form of nativism, especially in the Know Nothing movement of the mid-1850s. Thus, Germans were faced with a devil's choice between an alliance with southern fire-eaters or political opponents of the foreign-born.[35] Across Texas, secession won by a landslide, with less than a quarter of the voters opposing. In an appeal to ethnic voters, the declaration of secession had been printed not only in 10,000 English copies but also 2,000 each in Spanish and German. The German copies, however, largely fell on deaf ears. Two German frontier counties, Gillespie and Mason, led the state with a 96 percent margin against secession. Some largely Anglo counties also turned in majorities against secession.[36] But wherever precinct-level returns are available, they show the German communities of a county to be most hostile.

The older Texas German settlements farther east also show little evidence of enthusiasm for secession. The 64 percent support level in Colorado County masks an internal polarization. Three German precincts voted 86

34. Jordan (1966), 106–11, 180–85; Jordan (1989); Küffner (1994), 17–20, 46–68, 110–14, 123–26. Another recent study, Kelley (2000), examines the triangular relationship of Germans, blacks, and Anglos in Texas before and after the Civil War. On Missouri see Kamphoefner (1987), 116–17.

35. Buenger (1984), 26–33, 91–94.

36. Ibid., 67, 151, 174–75.

percent against secession, whereas five Anglo precincts cast all but six of their votes in favor; only the county seat with its mixed population fell near the average.[37] Some Anglos as well as Germans must have contributed to the 52 percent majority against secession in Fayette County (where precinct returns are unavailable), but a local paper with the telling name *State Rights Democrat* blamed the "sauer-kraut dirt-eaters" who were anything but fire-eaters. Only in Austin County did Germans perhaps give a slight majority vote for southern independence, still a rather lukewarm result compared with the 96 percent in favor in the Anglo precincts of the county.[38]

In heavily German Comal County, the one western county that voted almost three-quarters for secession, immigrants trusted the advice of the venerable Ferdinand Lindheimer and his *Neu Braunfelser Zeitung*: "When in Texas, do as the Texans do. Anything else is suicide and brings tragedy to all our Texas-Germans." Lindheimer's editorials said little about the merits of the secessionist case but instead stressed that his constituents would suffer less trouble if they were seen as supporting rather than opposing it.[39] In general, the factor of intimidation must be kept in mind when examining German behavior in the winter of disunion. Wherever they fell below a certain threshold, perhaps 15 percent of the voters, Germans hardly dared to stand against secession. The vaunted American freedom of speech and the press counted for little when the issue of slavery was involved. Southern postmasters routinely removed abolitionist literature from the mails, on the pretext that it threatened public safety by encouraging slave revolts (and that in a region where almost every state prohibited the teaching of literacy to slaves).[40] Nor was this censorship restricted to English-language publications: some German and even Czech periodicals containing antislavery opinions were harassed or suppressed. Urban Germans were more acculturated to southern society and more subject to intimidation; both factors worked against unionist voting. Although Galveston was perhaps one-third German and home to unionist editor Ferdinand Flake, with a low turnout it voted 96 percent in favor of secession. Mob violence had destroyed one of Flake's presses the month before, sending an unmistakable message to unionists.[41]

37. Weyand and Wade (1936), 244–45. Similar voting patterns are evident in Bastrop County precinct returns in Moore (1977), 77–78.

38. *La Grange (Tex.) State Rights Democrat*, March 7, 21, 1861; *Bellville (Tex.) Countryman*, February 27, 1861, March 17, 1861.

39. Buenger (1979a), 395–96; Metzenthin-Raunick (1953), 15–16; Auspurg-Hackert (1984), 150–51.

40. Fehrenbacher (1981), 57–59; Eaton (1964).

41. Buenger (1979b), 294–99; Buenger (1984), 12, 164.

New Braunfels was one of the few places in Texas where Confederate sympathizers were subject to intimidation. Editor Lindheimer's pragmatism was not universally appreciated. Even ninety years later, the centennial issue of his paper admitted, "Because of its strong southern tendencies during the war the *Neu Braunfelser Zeitung* attracted the bitter enmity of the loyally unionist part of the German population in West Texas and especially in Comal County, which made the further existence of the paper nearly impossible." So incensed were some New Braunfelsers that they threw the paper's type into the Guadalupe River, but Lindheimer fished it out of the clear water so that the paper did not miss an issue.[42]

Willingness to serve in the Union or Confederate military provides yet another measure of the attitudes of Texas Germans. Published muster rolls of the 1st and 2nd Texas Union Cavalry show these units included disproportionate numbers of Germans. Persons of German stock made up about 7 percent of the state's population but over 13 percent of its Union troops, despite the fact that they were recruited largely in the Brownsville area at the mouth of the Rio Grande, far from centers of German settlement.[43] At the outbreak of the Civil War, Texas Germans faced an unenviable choice: to go or to stay. Flight from the Confederacy was theoretically possible, but the experiences of those who tried it probably gave pause to many others. It took a strong dose of ideological conviction, especially if escape involved abandoning hard-earned property and leaving wife and children to an uncertain fate. Consequently, Texas Germans in the Union army were obviously outnumbered by German Confederates. There is strong evidence, however, that many of the latter served reluctantly.

According to Terry Jordan, "many or most" Texas Germans became "inaccurately" stereotyped as unionists because of a single incident, the 1862 skirmish on the Nueces River involving Hill Country refugees from the Confederacy, reported in the letters of Ernst Cramer and Ferdinand Simon (no. 55). But here, too, regional contrasts among Texas Germans can be exaggerated. Not only Gillespie or Kendall Counties in the Hill Country but also the eastern counties of Austin, Fayette, and Colorado were placed under martial law in January 1863 because of German draft resistance. A list of thirty-two draft resisters from Austin County included only four who were not German or Czech. A resistance meeting held at the end of 1862 attracted 400 to 600 Germans from five counties.[44]

---

42. Arndt and Olson (1965), 628; Metzenthin-Raunick (1953), 15–16.

43. Marten (1990), 26, 76–77.

44. Jordan (1989), 92; Elliott (1947), 472–74; Bailey (2001); *OR* 1:15, 887, 925–29. See also the references in the letters written by Robert Voigt (no. 54), February 11 and March 30, 1863.

Victoria and DeWitt Counties, near Corpus Christi, produced few votes against secession despite a substantial German population, which also contributed one and a half companies to the 6th Texas Infantry, CSA. But a closer examination reveals contrasts between immigrant and Anglo Texans in gray. When the regiment was captured at Arkansas Post in January 1863, 152 of its men, mostly Germans and Poles, took an oath of allegiance to the United States. Captain C. P. Nauheim resigned his commission because his German Company I had virtually disappeared. The rest of the regiment was exchanged and served to the bitter end in the Army of Tennessee.[45]

Whatever their position during the war, Texas Germans apparently took a distinctly unsouthern view of Reconstruction, making the boys in blue feel right at home. When one Anglo Yankee ended his occupation duty in December 1865, he noted in his diary, "Some of them shed tears almost. I never felt so bad at leaving any place as that[,] except home in 1861. Farewell Braunfels."[46] Less than six weeks after Texas officially surrendered, New Braunfels celebrated the Fourth of July in what sounded like a huge sigh of relief: the Stars and Stripes was unfurled from the highest hill, a marching band led a well-attended parade throughout the town, and a number of dances rounded out the evening and the next day. In Austin County farther east, New Ulm had displayed the Union flag already on May 20 and marked Independence Day 1865 with an equally rousing celebration.[47]

The Civil War experiences of Germans north and south exhibit both parallels and contrasts. The nativist antecedents of many northern Republicans and southern unionists posed obstacles to cooperation with Germans, but in neither case did they prove insurmountable. During the war, tensions with Anglo authorities occasionally surfaced in both sections, but they were much more serious in the South, particularly in Texas. Confederate conscription was instituted earlier and enforced more stringently than the Union draft; nevertheless, although comprehensive studies of Confederate recruitment are lacking, there is little doubt that the German presence in rebel ranks was even smaller than their meager presence in the southern population. In the Union army, by contrast, Germans were overrepresented relative to their share of military-aged males. Among the underlying factors at work were both aversion to slavery and devotion to the Union.[48]

---

45. Spurlin (1992), 12–14, 60, 93–96.

46. Mosman (1987), 399–401.

47. *Neu Braunfelser Zeitung*, July 14, 1865; letter to the editor from Austin County, July 28, 1865, in an unidentified clipping, Box 301-48, Folder 9, A. J. Hamilton Papers, Texas StateA, Austin.

48. See, for example, Buenger (1984), 83.

German Immigrants in the Union Army

The 1860 census listed 1,276,075 persons living in the United States who were born in Germany. Most of them were certainly more surprised by the outbreak of the Civil War than the Americans who had been following political developments longer and more closely. Our letter-writers generally regarded the war as a dreadful disaster: it was bad for business and, later on, a waste of countless lives. Some explained to their relatives how and why it had come about, some were emphatic supporters of the Union, some were opposed to the war altogether, and some ignored it almost completely, though virtually no one, not even those in the Confederate ranks, defended the rebel cause.

More than 200,000 Germans, however, almost 10 percent of the men who served and fought for the Union, became soldiers in the U.S. Army. Most of them volunteered—either out of conviction or in light of their own circumstances. Only about one in six was drafted.[49] Four out of five served in regiments in which they comprised a small ethnic minority of 5 to 15 percent, often together in one special "German company" due to language problems. Probably 15,000 men belonged to units that were one-third to one-half German (about thirty regiments), and more than 30,000 fought in the roughly thirty "German Regiments" made up almost exclusively of German-speaking soldiers and officers—at least at the beginning of the war. Later on, recruits were assigned more randomly, without much consideration of ethnic background or language.[50]

On August 30, 1863, Christian Härring (no. 23) wrote the following about German soldiers and officers: "so for the workers there was no other way to earn a living except to enlist. And others who didn't have to make their living as laborers found it a good opportunity to play the role of an officer, and so it went, nothing but a competition to raise one regiment after the next, just to make money."[51]

This may have been a one-sided view, but many aspects of the organizing of German regiments had little if anything to do with the lofty goals of preserving the Union or the abolition of slavery. In fact, in many ways it seems as if the German regiments were little more than an extension of traditional German associations and clubs, adapted to the war situation. This was most obvious in the "Turner* regiments," recruited almost exclusively from members of German *Turnvereine*. These regiments displayed many of the charac-

---

49. According to the official numbers, 36,740 were drafted. Kaufmann (1911), 118.
50. Ibid., 184–90; Lonn (1951), 666–72.
51. Härring (no. 23), August 30, 1863.

teristic features of German immigrant communities (minus the women and children). The official language of command and communication, spoken as well as written, was German, at least until mid-1862 when English became dominant. Troops were supplied with sauerkraut and sausages and received generous rations of beer. In the early months of the war, they wore uniforms based on German models and drilled according to German regulations. And they found other ways to maintain, demonstrate, and even flaunt their German identity.

From winter camp in February 1863, for example, letter-writer Wilhelm Francksen (no. 16) wrote about the tidy rows of houses with tasteful furnishings, just like in Germany. Wilhelm Albrecht (no. 9) from Mecklenburg described how his German regiment, serving in Virginia in the summer and fall of 1863, had established all the clubs and amenities dear to Germans. First they organized a glee club, then they set up a gymnastics field. They also had a reading room decorated with German and American flags and stocked with eight German American newspapers and magazines, as well as the *Leipzig Gartenlaube*, a popular illustrated family magazine, and several "English" papers.

Some German commanders made it abundantly clear that their troops were not normal American soldiers who happened to speak a foreign language. On February 9, 1862, General Louis Blenker issued Order No. 31 (in German, of course), according to which "the designation of the Division under my command is not '5th Division' [. . .] but 'Blenkers Division'; only this designation is to be used in all written records."[52] More than a year before the debacle at Chancellorsville* firmly established the reputation of German troops as cowards, the same general complained about "the venom of the press and of persons," though he asserted that they "could not prevent that all men of my *Division* have kept up their good spirit."[53] And on the same day, Colonel Henry Bohlen issued the following brigade order, No. 390: "The German fighter for the preservation of the Freedom and Union that Washington fought for and won will not stand back when tribute is to be paid to his memory."[54]

In a circular written in the fall of 1864 (in English), Lieutenant Colonel Adolphus Dobke of the 45th New York Infantry noted that two "*of our brother Officers*" had lost their lives in Confederate prisons: the officers of the 45th, to which they had belonged, were to wear bands of mourning for a month.[55]

---

52. General Order No. 31, February 9, 1862, 35/74 Pa. Inf Regt. Books, Order Books, NatA.
53. General Order No. 13, February 21, 1862, in ibid.
54. Order No. 390, February 9, 1862, in ibid.
55. 45 N.Y. Inf Regt. Books, Order Book, NatA.

In short, the German regiments placed great emphasis on their own separate identity—they were pursuing goals that were almost identical to those of the Americans, but they did so in different ways and with different means.[56]

Why were there separate German regiments? The most important practical reason was the fact that so many German recruits spoke so little English. But even when they could speak English, many preferred to serve with comrades of the same cultural background and to be commanded by officers they could trust because they were Germans. These language and cultural concerns are plausible enough. A number of our letter-writers, however, show how strong and even desperate they could be.

A Saxon who had arrived in the United States in 1861, for example, made the following complaint: "when you send a sick man out on picket duty just because the doctor can't understand him, then you have less freedom here than the lowest secessionist's *Nigger*."[57] Even a soldier who was so well integrated and such an enthusiastic supporter of the Union as Sergeant Albert Krause (no. 22) wrote home during the Advent season of 1864 that he was a stranger in a strange land with a foreign language, "so it is like music to my ears when I occasionally hear a few familiar, German, good, pithy words."[58]

On the subject of social contacts or friendships, one officer wrote that he only associated with Germans—by which he meant German officers. Similar reports from enlisted men arouse more sympathy. Alphons Richter (no. 8), for example, wrote, "Charles and I live a rather isolated life. My socializing is almost completely restricted to him." Gustav Keppler (no. 21) reported that after the departure of his two German-speaking friends he was all alone and had little contact with his comrades. And Wilhelm Albrecht (no. 9) went so far as to desert from his primarily English-speaking regiment (55th New York Infantry) to join a German artillery unit.[59] The language problems seem to have diminished during the course of the war, but cultural distance remained as large as ever: many letter-writers expressed feelings of isolation, either directly or indirectly. Even more significant is the fact that references to friendship, sympathy, or even an occasional shared activity with Americans are extremely rare.

Other reasons for raising separate German regiments were rather second-

56. The sense of distinctiveness in German regiments extended to the point of blatant discrimination against American officers who happened to serve in one of those regiments. Most of these men clamored to be transferred away from the "Dutch." Keller (2001), 52–54, 65.

57. Petasch (no. 37), December 11, 1861.

58. Krause (no. 22), December 1, 1864.

59. Uterhard (no. 18), May 27, 1863; Richter (no. 8), March 2, 1863; Keppler (no. 21), November 19, 1864; Wilhelm Albrecht (no. 9), May 1863.

ary. American observers at the beginning of the war had high hopes for European units with previous military experience and assumed that immigrants would more willingly volunteer if they were under the command of officers of their own nationality. The latter point was also particularly relevant for those Germans who had a vested interest in the participation of as many of their countrymen as possible. These included German American community leaders who sought to demonstrate their influence and prove their patriotism by having large numbers of Germans enlist; German American politicians who hoped to gain from impressive recruitment figures; others who believed the German sense of self-sacrifice and bravery would vanquish nativism; the German business community, which understood how much money and honor were involved in supplying goods to German regiments; and finally, serious or self-appointed military experts who saw the war as a chance to have a career, win glory, and become wealthy. And many politicians, officers, and recruits were no doubt motivated by genuine idealism as well.

Given the Germans' sense of being different, their strong roots in German immigrant communities, and their intense involvement in day-to-day politics and election campaigns—and here the campaign speeches of Generals Sigel and Schurz for the Republicans are only the tip of the iceberg—one might almost be tempted to see the German regiments not as American troops who happened to speak a different language and eat different food but rather as allies who were fighting under U.S. supreme command.

Had there been no German regiments, or had they been less conspicuous, the "German element" would have been less vulnerable to criticism. Being distinctly different, however, made the German regiments a collective target of contempt and ridicule even before Chancellorsville, and far more so after that battle. What is fascinating is that hardly any of the Germans themselves seem to have been aware of this criticism—on the contrary, almost all German Americans believed their troops were the bravest and their officers were the most superb. This was expressed most clearly by August Horstmann (no. 13), who wrote, "And indeed the enemy has tremendous respect for German soldiers, so that even the farmers come running from all directions to see the *flying dutchmen*, as they call our German *Division*." [60]

The letters contain no hint of the German reputation for cowardice. Instead, the letter-writers (including five civilians) emphasize that German officers were the better commanders, German soldiers fought more courageously, German camps were cleaner, and German soldiers were healthier and commanded great respect from the military. Carl Hermanns (no. 10) put it

60. Horstmann (no. 13), fragment of a letter written shortly before June 16, 1862.

this way: "The Germans are always the ones who are the most honest and fight the best, and the bravest fighter of all is the German General Major Sigel."[61]

These hymns of praise were also echoed in Germany. In the Black Forest, the almanac *Lahrer Hinkender Bote* contained the following entry in 1863: "The Germans have won such respect from their enemies that when the cry is heard 'The Germans are coming, Sigel is coming!' entire regiments turn and flee without firing a shot."[62]

On June 2, 1863, an "indignation meeting" organized by German American leaders was held in New York, in an attempt to restore the honor of the German troops. After the battle of Chancellorsville, they had become the target of a massive anti-German press campaign. In the *New York Times* there had been talk of "the panic-stricken Dutchmen," "the cowardly retreating rascals," and "the retreating and cowardly poltroons."[63] The meeting's speakers claimed that nativism alone was behind this horrendous slander. It is hard to imagine that a meeting like this would have changed the journalists' opinions, but all attempts at whitewashing became even more difficult when the American officers voiced the same opinion as the English-language press (the German press, naturally, supported the goals of the meeting). One captain from Boston who had taken part in the battle at Chancellorsville reported the next day: "And this is all, because the 11th Corps, Sigel's Dutchmen, broke and ran, all of them, at the first shot, as I always knew they would, losing 16 pieces[. . . .] It is horrible awful. Every man in Sigel's Corps ought to be hauled off the face of the Earth."[64] And in the fall of 1863, another New Englander wrote, "The Eleventh Corps has the comparatively easy duty [of protecting the railroad] by virtue of their being such excellent skedaddlers in time of battle. Our boys were cruel in their jokes on these fellows, and take every occasion to let them know that their peculiarities are appreciated."[65]

Anti-German sentiment, however, did not originate at Chancellorsville. It had existed from the beginning of the war, and it lasted through to the end: it seems reasonable to assume that American nativism played a major role. German troops may not have been particularly tough, let alone heroic, but they were not as hopelessly demoralized as was widely claimed.

The German letter-writers fought back, too, when it came to Yankee character and soldierly qualities. Half a dozen at the most complained about dis-

61. Hermanns (no. 10), April 12, 1862.

62. *Lahrer Hinkender Bote* (1863), 253.

63. *New York Times*, May 5, 1863. On this meeting see Lonn (1951), 594–95; and Nagler (1984), 119–20.

64. Scott (1991), 176.

65. Rosenblatt and Rosenblatt (1992 [1983]), 154.

crimination, but twice as many described the Americans in terms that are hardly flattering: uncultivated, hypocritical, money-grubbing swindlers— people who stop at nothing. Many of the letter-writers voiced approval of the basic ideals that America represented—freedom, the Union, the abolitionist movement—but there is not even one case in which "the Americans" or any individual Yankee (except Abraham Lincoln) are seen as people to admire or emulate.

It is indisputable that some German (and Irish and American) regiments fought well, and others did not, and that there were excellent, mediocre, and incompetent officers of all ethnic backgrounds. Collective stereotypes, there-fore, seem to have been operating on both sides. Disparagement of other ethnic groups and praise for one's own seem to have little to do with reality but rather with psychological needs and most of all with insecurity, intensi-fied by constant confrontation with the existence of cultural differences, in what was seen as a competitive situation.

The unpopular Germans insisted on believing they were the better soldiers and could thus win the respect of the Americans, and many Americans were eagerly waiting for a chance to prove that these incompetent foreigners were inferior to real Yankees. The mutual demand for recognition seems to have been so strong that both sides were blind to the irony of the situation. For-eigners and Americans may have occasionally been aware of the position of the other group, but this awareness did not diminish their prejudices or lead to an increase in mutual respect.

The most authoritative expert on the Civil War, James McPherson, who is frequently cited in this volume, has studied thousands of letters and calculated that 62 percent of the soldiers and no less than 79 percent of the officers wrote about their patriotic convictions or even ideological goals (such as freedom or democracy). In his extensive sample, however, only 8 percent were written by foreigners, although immigrants made up 24 percent of the Union army.[66] Our sample consists of letters written by thirty-six Germans who served in the Union army: nine of them either were or became officers during the war, five of them in German regiments. Seven of these officers expressed "patriotic feelings": the same percentage as the Americans.[67] This congruence among the officers, however, makes the vast difference between the percentages for

66. McPherson (1997a), 101–3. See also the preliminary findings in McPherson (1994), 35.

67. Only Peter Boffinger (no. 15) and Carl Uterhard (no. 18) (the latter a sojourner or re-turn migrant) were indifferent or critical. All of the letter-writers mentioned in notes 67–75 are included in this volume, with the exception of Heck, Klein, and Lenz, whose letters are in Kam-phoefner, Helbich, and Sommer (1991), 370–82, 383–405, and 130–48; and Zimmermann, in Hel-bich (1988), 97–100.

the enlisted men all the more remarkable—only 11 percent (3 of 27) of the German immigrants mentioned their patriotism, as opposed to 62 percent of McPherson's sample.[68] Even if allowances are made for the relative smallness of the German sample, error margins, definition problems, and difficulties of interpretation, a factor of five leaves no doubt that German enlisted men in the Union army were strikingly less "patriotic" than their American comrades. How can this discrepancy be explained?

One theme found frequently in the letters is a full-blown conspiracy theory: financiers, politicians, and high-ranking Union officers were drawing out the war by not fighting energetically enough and not taking advantage of northern superiority in order to continue making money on the war for as long as possible. Such convictions would probably preclude feelings of patriotism.

The simplest explanation, however, is that men who were born and raised in the United States, with American values and traditions, were more likely to be patriotic than foreigners who did not share this background and knew little about American history, institutions, or way of life. Most of them probably did not care at all about such things—as long as they could improve their own standard of living and be left alone by the authorities.

It may also be the case that the letter-writers did not think their relatives at home were particularly interested in American ideals, or they may have identified themselves more strongly with Germany. Alphons Richter (no. 8), for example, newly promoted to lieutenant in an American regiment (56th New York Infantry), wrote the following: "But, oh, with what sublime feelings would I go into battle, if I could draw my sword in defense of my own fatherland."[69] And finally, some letter-writers may have either actually experienced discrimination or merely imagined it, making them rather suspicious of American ideals.

But one other important reason can be found elsewhere. When one examines the reasons why immigrants signed up for military service, some noteworthy results emerge. Of the twenty-seven enlisted men in our sample, three volunteered out of patriotic conviction, two were drafted (one of them deserted after only four days), one enlisted in the face of impending conscrip-

68. Bullenhaar (no. 50); Krause (no. 22); Ludwig Kühner (no. 35). Bauer (no. 46), Gerstein (no. 34), Miller (no. 47), Penzler (no. 49), Ruff (no. 48), Schorse (no. 42), Treutlein (no. 27), and Zimmermann (Helbich [1988], 97–100) clearly or vaguely showed sympathy for the Union, though not "patriotic feelings." Alexander Dupré (no. 2), Francksen (no. 16), Hoffmann (no. 14), Petasch (no. 37), Schmalzried (no. 7), and Schwarting (no. 56) opposed the Union cause or essential aspects of it. Ten soldiers were indifferent or made no relevant remarks.

69. Richter (no. 8), October 11, 1862.

tion, and in ten cases, the reason is unknown.[70] Two probably had economic motives, and nine clearly stated they had enlisted because they were unable to find another job or because the pay was attractive.[71] Gustav Keppler's (no. 21) fate was probably quite typical for this group. In debt and looking for employment, he got a job working for a baker; but then the baker went bankrupt and did not pay him: "I went and enlisted only when I had no other choice." August Strohsahl (no. 26) had similar problems. Unable to find a job in San Francisco either on land or at sea, he concluded that "therefore there was nothing I could do but become a soldier."[72]

This means that at least one-third of these soldiers joined the army either as a last resort or as a way to make a decent living.[73] And, given the fact that military service was deeply hated in Germany—the main reason that two or possibly even three of our letter-writers had left Germany was to avoid the army—it is clear that a German immigrant must have been in dire straits indeed before taking such a step. It seems reasonable, therefore, to assume that people who had no alternative to manual labor and were unable to find any other kind of employment, who came from a different culture and knew little about the United States, would not tend to write professions of patriotism to their relatives back in Germany. Or to put it more bluntly: they did not know "what they were fighting for"—aside from the pay, their own survival, and perhaps vague hopes of recognition and advancement in American society.

A comparison with McPherson's findings is not possible with regard to our twenty-three male civilian letter-writers who were old enough for military service, since he deals only with men in the military. None of them reported being unemployed or in dire poverty. On the issues of the war and Union politics, only two were neutral or indifferent; and for a variety of reasons

70. Krause, Ludwig Kühner, Miller (volunteered); Lenz (Kamphoefner, Helbich, and Sommer [1991], 130–48) and Schwarting (drafted); Gerstein (volunteered to avoid conscription); Wilhelm Albrecht (no. 9), Bauer, Bullenhaar, Francksen, Krieger (no. 41), Karl Friedrich Kühner (no. 35), Penzler, Rossi (no. 6), Ruff, Schorse (no. 42) (unknown). Carl Anton Ruff's letter demonstrates how difficult the attribution of one motive can be. From his writing, one may legitimately conclude that he volunteered (1) to exact personal revenge, (2) to defend freedom, or (3) for economic reasons.

71. The two are Heck (Kamphoefner, Helbich, and Sommer [1991], 370–82) and Heinzelmann (no. 20). The nine are Böpple (no. 39), Alexander Dupré, Hoffmann, Keppler (no. 21), Petasch, Schmalzried, Strohsahl (no. 26), Treutlein, and Zimmermann.

72. Keppler (no. 21), July 28, 1864; Strohsahl (no. 26), November 4, 1864.

73. By adding the "probably economic" cases and some of the men in the "unknown" category one could easily arrive at one half. The fact that most of the "last resort" volunteers were quite recent arrivals in the United States indicates, however, that our sample should not be considered representative for all German-born soldiers.

and to different degrees, six were opposed or critical.[74] On the positive side, ten expressed or probably felt sympathy for the North, strong in some cases and barely perceptible in others, while another five even showed evidence of "patriotic feelings"—thus about two-thirds of our civilian sample expressed some measure of support for the Union cause.[75]

It is not surprising that the critics did everything they could to avoid the army (at least one, Emile Dupré [no. 2], paid for a substitute), but it is somewhat inconsistent when an avid (verbal) supporter of the war used a loophole in residence formalities to avoid conscription (as Victor Klausmeyer [no. 29] did) or fled to a different state for the same reason (Heinrich Müller [no. 31]). Much of the positive support from civilians seems to have been only lip service for the Union cause, in view of the fact that the other eight sympathizers and all five of the "patriots" apparently never seriously considered volunteering, and most did their best to avoid the draft.[76]

It is certainly true that the life situations of soldiers and civilians differed so greatly that any direct comparison is impossible. The fact remains, however, that professions of patriotism were obviously not directly related to being willing to risk one's own life, and this might add to the questions about the meaning and the weight of such declarations made by the military men. The reaction of the civilians to the war, however, is completely understandable. The average immigrant, who had started a new life to improve his lot, could hardly be expected to rush off to follow the flag, especially one that was not yet his own. He may have quickly developed political opinions, sympathies, or even convictions, but that was a far cry from deciding to put his own life at risk. Yet three of the soldiers and several of the officers in our sample took that step without any economic pressure, apparently and sometimes even expressly for patriotic reasons.[77]

74. Buschmann (no. 43), Jacob Odensaß (no. 4) (neutral); Bönsel (no. 40), Dünnebacke (no. 12), Härring (no. 23), Hermanns (no. 10), Monn (no. 33), Pack (no. 24) (opposed).

75. The ten are Otto Albrecht (no. 1), Emile Dupré (no. 2), Herbst (no. 30), Heubach (no. 19), Kessel (no. 52), Klausmeyer (no. 29), Leclerc (no. 25), Müller (no. 31), Julius Wesslau (no. 3), and Karl Wesslau (no. 3). The five are Augustin (no. 5), Barthel (no. 4), Dieden (no. 36), Klein (Kamphoefner, Helbich, and Sommer [1991], 383–405), and Nagel (no. 53).

76. It is true that half of them were over age thirty-five (though only one was over forty-one) and many had families, but with conscription affecting ages eighteen to forty-five, these men would still have been considered fit for military service.

77. It is interesting to have a look at the other side of the coin, at the attitudes held by German immigrants about political and social conditions in Germany. Walter Kamphoefner has done this in his article "'Auch unser Deutschland muß einmal frei werden'" (Our Germany must also become free one day), based on many of the letters printed here. Kamphoefner (1997).

It would be desirable though quite complicated to establish how "representative" our military letter-writers are in terms of their background, religion, occupation, education, and so forth. The data for our sample are easily accessible, but such an analysis is impossible since comparable information does not exist for the total number of Germans in the military. Still, the existence of a very significant gap in expressions of patriotism between McPherson's soldiers and those in the German sample — 62 percent versus 11 percent — does not seem to be open to question. What is certainly open to doubt is the representativeness of our sample, and not only in the terms just mentioned. Assuming that McPherson's results were generally based on a lengthy correspondence, our letter-writers — from some of whom we have only a page or two — had comparatively fewer chances to express their patriotism. And there seems to be a high correlation between recent arrival in the United States, poverty, and the probability of writing home. If one takes these considerations into account, the factor of five of the patriotism gap would most likely be lowered, though it is difficult to say by how much. A considerable gap would no doubt remain.

The repercussions of ethnic tension and conflict in the Union army are much better documented than cases of ethnic harmony. We have already described the letters as a source on the role of ethnicity. Other important documents include newspapers and military correspondence, reports, and orders. The most fascinating and, in my opinion, the most trustworthy sources are court-martial records. Their reliability is enhanced by the fact that both sides received a hearing, and further details of a case often emerged during cross-examination.

These records show that tension and bitter conflict could arise not only between ethnic groups but also within a particular group. In the German 74th Pennsylvania Infantry, for example, Captain Henry Krauseneck was accused of cowardice in the face of the enemy.[78] In his defense, he argued that "the Colonel [Adolph von Hartung] bears me a long time grudge, and the officers having witnessed against me had been placed under arrest during my command and [are] wreaking revenge[. . . .] The actual cause of charges is to keep me out of promotion, now having been my turn." Krauseneck was found guilty anyway and received a dishonorable discharge.[79]

Using a similar defense tactic, Colonel Robert J. Betge of the German 68th New York Infantry was acquitted. His charge contained no fewer than twelve

78. Knoebel's (no. 17) unit.
79. Krauseneck proceedings, February 1–3, 1864, RG 94, Box 588, No P-2935 VS 1864, NatA.

specifications of "conduct unbecoming an officer and gentleman," but according to Betge, the list consisted of nothing but "fabrications" by Lieutenants August Volkshausen and Louis Leibuscher.[80]

The files on this trial also provide insight into interethnic relations and even information about a business deal made by one of our letter-writers. Betge testified that the quartermaster of his regiment, a man named Simon, had left the regiment in early October 1861. Six weeks later, Betge found out that Simon had sold 400 pairs of shoes belonging to the U.S. Army to a German merchant in Washington.[81] He had Simon arrested. The deposition continued: "Simon had been of great assistance to me in raising the regiment—he was a German. The German name had already begun to suffer reproach upon those grounds, I was desirous if the Government could be made secure [i.e., repaid] to stop the prosecution, and thus avoid further Exposures and discredit to the German name."[82]

Ethnic slurs often played a role in court-martial cases, though usually together with more serious offences. One of the charges brought against Private Constantine McJulien in Company C of the 119th New York Infantry, for example, was "offering violence to his superior." Among other things, the accused had insulted one of his comrades, and he was then reprimanded by Second Lieutenant Kolomb. Thereupon McJulien "called said Lieutenant Kolomb a damed [sic] Dutchman" and picked up a rock. The officer struck him with his sheathed sword, drew it—and McJulien dropped the rock. He was sentenced to two months of hard labor without pay.[83]

The clerks who recorded such proceedings, almost always Anglo Americans, frequently amused themselves by writing down exactly what an accused German said in his broken English. More serious and significant than such teasing, however, is the fact that in the majority of the cases involving both Anglo Americans and Germans, witnesses testified—almost without exception—in favor of members of their own ethnic group. Aside from obvious ethnic tension or conflicts between Americans and immigrants, the court-martial proceedings also illustrate the classic conflict between West Point graduates and volunteer officers, especially if they were foreigners, as well as officers with a European military background.[84]

80. Betge Court-Martial, December 23, 1861–February 14, 1862, RG 153, CRR, 4WA-4-3, Case File KK 407, NatA.

81. The buyer was letter-writer Emile Dupré (no. 2), whose brother mentions Colonel Betge in his letter of August 1, 1861.

82. Betge Court-Martial; see note 80.

83. RG 153, Judge Advocate General, Court Martials, NN 131, NatA.

84. See, for example, Helbich (2004), 312–18.

As the conventional wisdom of generations of historians has it, fighting side by side in the Civil War eliminated nativist prejudice. In 1963 one of the leading experts on immigration, John Higham, argued, "The war completed the ruin of organized nativism, by absorbing xenophobes and immigrants fighting in a common cause. Now the foreigner had a new prestige; he was a comrade at arms. The clash that had alienated sections reconciled their component nationalities."[85]

Even contemporaries regarded this as a reliable fact. In March 1862 the *New York Times*, referring explicitly to German volunteers, wrote that "all nativism, all proscription of foreigners is forever broken up." In June 1863 an article about immigrants in the Union army claimed, "Their fighting, side by side with the descendants of those who laid the foundation of the Republic, will do more to Americanize them and their children than could be effected in a whole generation of peaceful living. The war will prove itself a wonderful school for instilling American ideas, sentiments, sympathies and convictions."[86] German immigrants, too, believed the war would have positive effects. In August 1861, for example, Peter Klein, a young miner from the Saar who was putting his professional skills to use as a gold digger in California, wrote, "For us Germans this war is very good, for since the Germans have shown themselves to be the keenest defenders of the constitution, and provide entire regiments of the best and bravest soldiers and officers, they're starting to fill the native Americans with respect. Now the Americans don't make fun of us anymore since they know that we are the mainstay of their country and their freedom."[87]

Did the Civil War really speed up the melting-pot process; was it a blast furnace that incinerated nativism, an inferno of blood and iron that cleansed the nation of ethnic tensions, a miracle weapon of Americanization? One should always be suspicious of such superlatives. Several points, however, can be conceded immediately. There was a dramatic decrease in politically organized nativism as it had been known in the 1850s, though there is little evidence that this was the result of fighting for a common cause. Tens of thousands of immigrant soldiers, especially those in predominantly American regiments, had improved their English by the end of their term of service, and immigrants in uniform certainly learned a considerable amount about American customs and attitudes. This acculturation, however, might have happened in civilian life as well, where it might have been even faster and af-

---

85. Higham (1981 [1963]), 13.
86. *New York Times*, March 16, 1862, June 4, 1863.
87. Kamphoefner, Helbich, and Sommer (1991), 402–3.

fected spheres of life beyond the military. But if one views the Civil War as part of the ongoing attempt, over several decades, to subject workers to industrial labor discipline, and if one even agrees that "the whole concept of assimilation/Americanization has been at heart merely a subterfuge for the initiation of new working classes, particularly immigrants, into the American system of class stratification based upon to the needs of 'corporate capitalism,'" then exposure to military discipline may well have accelerated such a process.[88]

On the other hand, it is evident that in the Union army general fraternization across ethnic lines simply did not happen. Although interethnic friction could not occur in ethnically homogeneous regiments, these soldiers suffered from collective discrimination and individual abuse when they came into frequent contact with American units posted nearby. And in the American and mixed regiments, in which more than 80 percent of the immigrant soldiers served, there were a host of cases of ethnic tension and friction, conflicts and incidents, well documented in the literature. There is hardly any trace of evidence to the contrary; there are precious few examples of well-meaning attempts to overcome cultural differences or promote tolerance and no indication of friendly conviviality with—let alone admiration for—soldiers or officers of different ethnic backgrounds.

But aside from incidents of ethnic tension, be it one group making fun of the "Dutchmen" or the other ridiculing the Yankees, patterns of behavior in the military were remarkably similar to what was found in civilian life. Ethnicity was relatively unimportant at work and in one's daily routine, and in the army the job routine consisted of drills, target practice, guard duty, marching, and parades. But in terms of social contacts—who one cooked and ate with, who became a friend, or who one went to visit (German officers were very successful at tracking down German families, even in enemy territory)—social groups of men with a similar ethnic background seemed to form automatically, even when these groups were restricted by class and educational barriers and only included two or three people. These small groups were usually very exclusive, and social contact with outsiders was extremely limited or even non-existent. It is of interest, too, that spontaneous and practical ethnic solidarity was found not only within the army, both on duty and off, but also in the care and treatment of wounded soldiers by civilians. Thus, it seems that prewar patterns continued during the war and after the war, and there is no plausible reason why it should have been different. A "job" in the military was one thing, but men shared their thoughts about the horrors of war and their

88. Catalfamo (1989), 11.

innermost feelings with other ethnic insiders. The war brought little or no change in this context, and it is hard to imagine how such change could have occurred.[89]

"Americanization," however, can also be understood somewhat differently. It could mean, for example, stronger identification with the United States, looser ties with the German American community, or a decrease in one's identification with Germany. Unfortunately, we have no way to examine these processes systematically. But the vast wave of German patriotism that swept through the entire German American community in 1871, when Germany won the Franco-Prussian War and the German Empire was founded, belies the notion that emotional ties to the homeland were significantly weakening. Certainly, a very large majority of German immigrants identified with the old homeland enough to share the joy and pride and to participate in the enhanced recognition of the "German name." There is also little evidence that veterans withdrew from German American activities after the war.

Albert Krause (no. 22) certainly did not do so, and of our letter-writers in uniform, his subsequent career was the most successful. He saw no contradiction in being intensely involved in American social life, business, and politics—and playing an active role in the German community. On the contrary, his involvement in ethnic institutions gave him the solid base that led to his election to the important position of city engineer in Buffalo. It is remarkable, however, that even a man who was so successful in American public life still found it necessary to emphasize proudly that this or that German American cultural event had compelled respect and even admiration from the Americans.[90] Isn't this somewhat reminiscent of claims that German military prowess would win American respect? At least it seems evident that people who are so proud of being respected are either in need of such respect or do not feel accepted enough that they can do without this reassurance.[91]

One final look at our thirty-six letter-writers in uniform provides some concrete evidence on the issue of "Americanization." Nine of them were killed in the war, and three became invalids. Of the twenty-four who survived more or less physically unscathed, two were subsequently elected to their state legislatures (in Indiana and Missouri). Six veterans turned to or, in most instances, returned to farming, and six others found employment in trade, as artisans, or

89. Keller (2001) rather emphatically denies the occurrence of general Americanization among Germans in the military. He even claims that after Chancellorsville, the rift grew still wider and was not to be healed for many years. Keller (2001), 37–38, 56, 58, 64, 85–86.

90. Krause (no. 22), July 22, 1883.

91. The issue of "respect from the Americans gained by special efforts made by the Germans" is often discussed in the NABS letters in the last three decades of the century.

as professionals. Carl Uterhard (no. 18), who had never intended to stay in the United States, went back to Germany; and the fate of four others is unknown. The majority of those who were able to achieve success, or at least "respectability," after the war did not take up anything new after they were mustered out. Instead, they went back to doing what they had learned or done before the war. These cases do not provide much evidence in favor of Americanization as a positive boost to subsequent civilian life, but they do not rule it out either.

Seven others, however, or almost a third of the survivors who remained in the United States, do not seem to have profited from "Americanization." Five privates who served in German as well as American regiments along with two officers in American regiments proved to be incapable of organizing their later lives.[92] They remained in poverty, on the margins of society. Individual circumstances or differences in ability and determination, of course, cannot be ignored, but the fact remains that for almost one-third of our military letter-writers, the "American dream" did not even begin to come true. This should at least raise some doubts about the notion that the "Americanization" of immigrant veterans resulted in widespread and successful integration into American life.

The arguments presented here do not lay claim to validity in all specific cases. The study of a few dozen individuals does not rule out the possibility that further study of a larger number could modify the results. Interpretation, too, is always subjective and can lead to misrepresentations. It is, however, safe to say that these arguments are based on solid, though limited, sources that reveal certain general tendencies. Fortunately, readers can form their own opinions about many of these issues by reading the actual letters in this volume.

92. Boffinger (no. 15); Gerstein (no. 34); Heck (Kamphoefner, Helbich, and Sommer [1991], 370–82); Heinzelmann (no. 20); Richter (no. 8); Rossi (no. 6); Treutlein (no. 27).

Letters

EASTERN THEATER

1. Otto Albrecht

Johann Albrecht, a farmer and tavern keeper in the village of Abbenrode (near Harzburg, Duchy of Braunschweig), had eight children, and at least four of them immigrated to the United States. The eldest son, Hermann, had left in 1855, and August and Otto, twins born in 1839, left in the fall of 1860. While Hermann Albrecht came into a considerable fortune in 1857, apparently by marriage to an American, and prospered as a manufacturer of various metal goods, Otto Albrecht remained a technical draftsman. Like his brother Hermann, he lived in Philadelphia; he married a German American around 1868 and died in 1933. Despite Otto's enthusiasm for the Republican cause, there is no evidence he fought for the Union.[1]

Philadelphia, November 11, 1860

[salutation missing]

[48 ll.: joy at finding an inexpensive substitute (military service in Braunschweig); he and his twin brother are working in brother Hermann's establishment; family; elections for governor and president; parades with groups carrying banners, flaming torches; music loud and off-key] There were speeches almost every evening; the Republican Party had put up a large octagonal pavilion especially for this, with a large speaker's platform and wooden benches all around. Of the German speakers, a man named Carl Schurz* has acquired a great reputation, he even drew loud applause from the Americans for his speeches in English, at least from his fellow party members, the Republicans. The Democratic Party, though, hates him all the more, especially the slaveholders. <u>Carl Schurz</u> came to America in 1849 [8 ll.: Schurz as 1848 revolutionary; imprisonment; escape; freed his teacher Gottfried Kinkel from Spandau prison]. After Schurz got his friend out of prison, they used false papers to escape to England, where Kinkel remained, and then Schurz came to the United States. He studied law here and set himself up as a

SOURCE NOTE: The way Albrecht handles the language, correctly, expressively, and with a respectable vocabulary, he must have had some schooling beyond the elementary level, probably either in preparation for or as part of his technical training. Not included here are three letters in the series and four letters by other siblings from the time after 1865.

1. KB Abbenrode, 1835, 1839; information provided by the donor; CD Philadelphia, 1862–82; MC 1860: Philadelphia/Pa., W. 17, #986 (Hermann); MC 1880: Philadelphia/Pa., e.d. 404, #18 (Hermann); MC 1900: Philadelphia/Pa., e.d. 708, #257 (Otto).

lawyer in the state of Wisconsin, where he was very successful, and he's now one of the most celebrated speakers in the United States [35 ll.: enormous torch-lit march before the election of the Republican candidate for governor, Andrew Curtin, with clubs wearing uniforms, fire brigade; paid for by contributions and "the big moneybags"; the losing party is not doing well]. The Democratic Party, likewise, spent several million dollars this time to buy votes in New York, a rich man named Astor alone gave one million. He has several hundred millions, and you can be sure he wouldn't part with anything unless he believed he could make 10 times more out of it; but this time the Democratic slaveholders with all their millions were soundly thrashed. The Republicans have elected Abraham Lincoln president; he will take office next March the 4th. This man shows how far you can get here: his father was a farmer and he himself worked on his father's farm until he was twenty, splitting logs that were used to build fences around the fields, which is why he now has the nickname rail splitter, used either in honor or in mockery, depending on the party. Then he studied law on his own and established himself as an attorney in the state of Illinois, where he soon gained a reputation for his genius and his upright nature. Later he got involved in politics, and now he's arrived at the position of the greatest honor here or anywhere else in the whole world. We'll see what his administration will be like in the next 4 years. AB. Lincoln is supposed to have the ugliest physiognomy to be found in the entire United States [14 ll.: correspondence; greetings].

Embracing you in spirit, Otto

2. Private Alexander Dupré, Emile Dupré, and Lottie Dupré

Emile Dupré (1833–66) did not leave Germany due to economic hardship, but the twenty-three-year-old may well have been dissatisfied because of his limited pros-

SOURCE NOTE: The letters of the Dupré brothers are similar in a number of ways. Both Emile and Alexander write grammatically correct German without a trace of local dialect (the Hanover and Braunschweig area is usually considered the place where High German and the local dialect are the same, or where "the best German is spoken"); both of them spell accurately, and both know how to express themselves clearly. But here the similarity ends. Emile writes more elegantly, has obviously more practice writing, and expresses himself in a measured, careful way; Alexander is more given to exaggeration and emotions. Whereas Emile's handwriting is mostly very small, extremely regular, and never changes, his younger brother's is rather erratic, sometimes changes within one letter, and looks different in different letters. Not included here are the letters in the series from the time before 1860 (five) and after 1865 (one), as well as several letters written in 1860 (six), 1861 (eight), 1862 (three), and 1864 (four).

pects at home: he was a merchant with no capital to start a business of his own. He also grew up in a family that did not regard national borders as insurmountable barriers.[1]

His father, Franz Christian Dupré (1792–1862), ended his career as one of the top revenue officials in the Duchy of Braunschweig, and his salary allowed the family a comfortable middle-class life. With seven children, however, luxury was out of the question.[2]

At the age of fifteen, Emile was sent to Mönchen-Gladbach to a secondary school that specialized in commercial training. Instead of Latin and Greek, the curriculum featured French and later English but above all mathematics and commercial calculation, and "continuous activity" was demanded of the students. Emile only stayed a little more than a year at the school and left shortly before he would have moved up into the graduating class. Immediately afterward, starting on April 1, 1850, he did one year of voluntary military service, which he completed as a sergeant in the Braunschweig militia. On September 1, 1851, Dupré started training as an apprentice with Lösener & Schoch, merchants in Magdeburg, a city some forty miles east of Braunschweig (annual fee 100 talers*).[3]

In the fall of 1854 he returned to Braunschweig, but despite intensive efforts, he was unable to find a position. The following spring he was working as an unpaid trainee for a company in Le Havre, but a short time later he found a job in Paris with an annual salary of 2,400 francs ($480), working for a company that looked after wealthy Americans who were traveling in Europe. There he seems to have remained until the end of 1856. In early 1857 he left for America with 300 talers in cash.[4] In 1858 he was living in New Orleans, had survived an attack of yellow fever, and was working in a saloon.[5]

According to family tradition, Alexander Dupré, born nine years after Emile, was the spoiled baby of the family who did not exactly live up to his parents' expectations. At the end of 1858, the seventeen-year-old had a job as a technical draftsman

1. His mother had spent much of her youth in St. Petersburg; her two sisters were married and were living there and in Moscow, and a cousin lived with her husband in New York. Family tree Baron Ludwig v. Müller u. Suzette, née Tielker (1758–1864), supplied by the donor; letters from the Seiffert Family, New York, to the Dupré Family, Braunschweig, December 16, 18, 1854, NABS.

2. Geheime Canzlei, personnel files Dupré, Ns. StA Wolfenbüttel, 2 A Neu Fb II D, Nr. 67; Braunschweig AB, 1846, 68, 71.

3. Letters from the principal Dr. Fricke to his mother, Friederike Dupré, October 21, 1848, November 21, 1848, March 25, 1850, NABS; Letter from Franz Dupré to the city magistrate of Braunschweig, April 6, 1857, StdA Braunschweig, D II 8 Nz 25/61, Nr. 14; letter from Franz Dupré to Friederike Dupré, September 7, 1851, NABS.

4. Letter from Franz Dupré to the city magistrate of Braunschweig, StdA Braunschweig, D II 8 Nz 25/61, Nr. 14; entry in the emigration files 1847–72, Braunschweig-Stadt (Polizeidirektion), Ns. StA Wolfenbüttel, 133 (Neu 2034). See also Emile's letter of January 29, 1860, NABS.

5. Letter from Franz Dupré to Friederike Dupré, August 14, 1858, NABS.

in a machine factory, and in the winter semester of 1859–60 he enrolled in mechanical engineering at the Collegium Carolinum,[6] but as early as the summer of 1860, his parents were seriously considering sending him to America. On May 15, 1861, he finally arrived in New York, but not without having spent all his money en route to Le Havre and running up debts.

In Emile's first letter after Alexander's arrival (June 8, 1861), he complains bitterly that there is no sign of improvement. Alexander's subsequent life is vividly depicted from the point of view of these two different letter-writers. The correspondence demonstrates one of the risks of using letters as historical sources: without Emile's account of his brother, one might well believe Alexander's fanciful reports.

In 1860 one out of eight New Yorkers were German-born, some 120,000. In 1855 more than half of the bakers, brewers, cigar makers, carpenters, locksmiths, shoemakers, tailors, and barbers in New York were German—between 53 and 61 percent. In the category of professions that would become increasingly important for Emile Dupré, however, Germans were relatively scarce. Of the 252 New York bankers and stockbrokers, only 18 were foreign, and only 4 were German.[7]

From a modern perspective, Emile Dupré's personality seems quite contradictory. On the one hand, it is clear that he was driven by ambition and worked extremely hard in his profession. On the other hand, he was highly sentimental and longed for a quiet, comfortable, domestic life—even though he was in the midst of hard-nosed New York. Nevertheless, he was very careful with his numbers, took only calculated risks, and had a good head for business. He valued trustworthiness and respectability, but these qualities do not mean than he never went beyond the letter of the law.

The German side of his personality is shown in his continuing interest in the arts and his cultivation of his mother tongue and native culture. At the same time, however, he was quite cosmopolitan and successfully integrated into American business life; if he had not been fully accepted by his American business partners, he would never have had such a successful career.

EMILE DUPRÉ

New York, November 21st, 1860 [. . .]

My dear mother,

[15 ll.: correspondence; his brother Alexander should learn English] As I wrote to you in one of my earlier letters, my contract here runs out on the first of January, and I cannot yet say for sure if I will be able to extend it for the next season.[8] I am trying very hard, and I am sometimes surprised to find myself still at my desk at midnight. I never used to be able to do things like

---

6. Alexander Dupré to Emile, December 1, 1858, NABS; *Die Matrikel des Collegium Carolinum* (1983), 101.

7. USC 1860.1, lviii, xxviii; Ernst (1949), 42–43, 214–17.

8. He was employed by the Vanderbilt steamship company.

Emile Dupré.
(Brigitte Leiß)

this, but now that I know what goal I am working toward, it is easy for me to do. I've even started to enjoy it. It is the first job where I earn more than I actually need and which would allow me to get married[. . . .] At any rate, I am determined to start a commissions and agency business, and even if I keep my job, I will be doing the groundwork for this.

In order to do this, however, I will need some capital [17 ll.: details about agency and commissions business]. If a European company agrees to do all its business here with me, then I am its <u>agent</u>. If they only send goods now and then I receive them on commission. Both arrangements work equally well. When I see that this job on the side is earning me more than my other job, I will give up the latter. If my company fires me, however, I will have to work that much harder to increase business. 2,000 talers* are about $1,450 in the currency over here, and this is the sum I am convinced would enable me to get started, because then I would be able to take small orders for domestic companies that turn a very nice profit [8 ll.: details]. Here you have to pay 6–7 percent interest, but I hope you can get me the same amount for 5 percent since I don't want to pay more [21 ll.: details; needs the capital quickly].

Now to my private life. The father of my bride is named Zophar Mills, and he is the head of R. M. Blackwell & Co.[9] Unfortunately, he does not approve of our engagement, and for now I will not be able to count on financial support from this source. That isn't the custom here anyway. If I get married I will have to rely on my own strength, as I have been doing all along. Mr. Mills belongs to the party that doesn't like foreigners,[10] and it is his political prejudice that turns him against me, he doesn't object to me as a person. If we lived in Europe, he might be able to keep me from marrying his daughter, but here in the land of freedom, parents can't block marriages. Charlotte [. . .], the one most directly involved has said yes, and that's the end of any objections [27 ll.: marriage; apartment; furniture; would like linens from Germany; greetings].

New York, February 1, 1861. [. . .]

My dear mother,

[42 ll.: correspondence; is married; family; friends; Charlotte (Lottie) can sing; has rented a piano; business] The political confusion here is having serious effects on business. By March 4 things will have been decided one way or the other. At any rate, things will improve—be it war or peace. No country in the world is as rich as the Union—every *Steamer* that arrives brings a million or more to our ports. Food is cheaper than ever—but as they say—when the jackass has it too good, etc.[11]—and that's the case with the Americans. Hopefully the states that have left the Union will reconsider and return—even if they don't, both the North and the South have a chance of making it on their own without having to resort to force. Love of the Fatherland, the great and

9. Mills is listed in the 1861 New York CD as co-owner with its namesake of R[obert]. M. Blackwell & Co.; he is listed as a merchant with $55,000 worth of property in MC 1860: New York/N.Y., W. 7, p. 96. He had a distinguished career as a volunteer fireman and president of its veterans' association, and he was honored in 1882 by having the city's second fireboat named after him. His death was front-page news in the *New York Times*, March 1, 1887, p. 1; see also *New York Times*, March 4, 1887, p. 3, December 19, 1882, p. 3, and April 24, 1898, p. IMS15.

10. Although the importance of the American Party, known as the Know Nothings, declined rapidly after 1856, and the young Republican Party also had nativist overtones, Dupré is probably referring to the former. Mills was prominently listed as a vice president selected at a citywide meeting for cooperation between the American and Republican Parties in the *New York Times*, October 22, 1858, p. 1.

11. The proverb continues, "he goes out on thin ice," roughly equivalent to "pride goes before a fall."

Page from Emile Dupré's letter of February 1, 1861,
with a sketch of his apartment. (Brigitte Leiß)

the powerful, only now seems to be awakening in the breast of the North, and the South will surely be given the guarantees they're asking for. [50 ll.: two-room apartment; sketch; three other neighbors (all Americans); domestic life; ice-skating in Central Park; bought $3,000 policy with Germania life insurance, greetings] from your loving son / Emile

New York, April 26th, 1861 [. . .]

Dear parents,

[. . .] As you probably read in your newspapers, our steamers have been commandeered by the government of the United States to be used for the war. For the last 3 weeks I have spent all my time at the docks or in the arsenals. The government has chartered 11 of our steamers that we are outfitting with war supplies, troops etc. and sending off. My regiment, the 71st light infantry, went to Washington last week by steamer[. . . .] After consulting with my friends, I stayed in New York, and my friend Henry Phillips went to the battlefield in my place and in my uniform.[12] I was also asked to take command of a German jaeger company, but I turned this down as well out of consideration of my wife. New York looks like an army camp. There are armed men everywhere, everyone carries a revolver, and we're living in an absolute torrent of commotion. Heaven knows how it will all turn out. Both sides are deadly serious and will probably have to wear each other out before they can even think of settling their differences or making peace. Business is terrible — only guns and more guns are in demand. Every now and then someone earns a fortune, and your little Mizel has also had some luck. If things don't get any worse, I think by the end of the year I'll be able to call the small sum of 8,000 talers* my own. I'm doing a lot of work on my own now, and I'm starting to trust my own abilities. And many of the most respected companies here are also placing their trust in me. The sum mentioned above is a commission for the completion of a splendid deal. On Strasbey's advice I asked a mutual friend to join in this venture, and he gets half the profit, but he has been a real boon to the operation. We're working on a second project that looks most promising. The first shipment of my champagne has arrived, and I've already sold it. Just now, one of our steamers has arrived with troops from Texas — a second one, the *Star of the West*, was captured by the South, and in the next few days we will be receiving compensation for it in gold from the government. The steamship company gets $1,600 for the use of the *Illinois* and $1,000 for

---

12. The 71 N.Y. State Militia Inf was recruited for three months and mustered out on July 30, 1861, after taking part in the battle of Bull Run. Henry S. Phillips (age 35) was mustered in as a private. Adjutant General, New York, Box 3073, RG 94, NatA.

the *Kill v. Kull* (per day, and you, dear father, can easily calculate what a profit we're making when I tell you that the costs of a steamer like the *Illinois* run about $400).

I just got an order to fill up another steamer with coal and food supplies— tomorrow it's taking a Scottish regiment to Washington.

[5 ll.: greetings] with all love / your / Emile.

ALEXANDER DUPRÉ

New York, May 16th, 1861

Four weeks now have already passed since I left the old home country, and a new world has opened itself up before my eyes [153 ll.: voyage; arrival; impressions]. Things look unbelievably warlike here, soldiers who've been signed up roam through the city, and I must pass on the news that A. v. Steinwehr, a relative of Prof. Schleiter's, is raising a German regiment.[13] It's already been inspected and will be leaving for Washington in the next few days. Emile helped a lot, and this morning I went to see Steinwehr at his headquarters, and he was very pleased to see me and now we're on a first-name basis, since the formal "*Sie*" sounds too distant. He looks very good, and he sends his warmest regards to you and the Schleiters. He is a colonel. Had I wanted to, I could easily have joined the regiment as a Captain of Engineers for 150 dollars a month and free board, but over here you can earn even more money in my line of business [21 ll.: friends; wants a letter; greetings; Emile will be rich soon; is in a rush; signature].

New York, June 6th, 1861

Dear parents,

[45 ll.: Emile's father-in-law has half a million dollars; Alexander is working as a draftsman for the Vanderbilt Line; family] It's easy to earn money here if you have some training. I'll probably take a job in Brocklyn as director of a sugar factory and mechanical engineer, where I'll get 4 dollars a day and free room and board. A great country, where everyone makes enough to get along, it's not like in Germany where good people hardly get enough to eat [35 ll.: wages; speaks good English; New York].

Every day troops march through here to Washington on their way to war, it will certainly be a bitter war [. . .] there is recruitment going on in every street, and there are still enough stupid people who sign up[. . . .]

---

13. Friends and neighbors from Braunschweig. In 1846 the Duprés, Professor Adolf Schleiter, and Second Lieutenant Adolph von Steinwehr all lived on the same street, Neuer Weg. AB Braunschweig, 1846, 117, 161. The regiment was the 29 N.Y. Inf.

As to my military service, I ask you, dear father, to have me registered as an emigrant; otherwise I'll send enough money in the meantime to pay for a substitute. I am certainly not going to play the soldier in Germany [20 ll.: family news; went to the theater with Emile; greetings; signature; financial matters].

New York, July 14, 1861

Dear parents,

[10 ll.: correspondence] I have taken the Navy exams in Brooklyn to become 1st assistant engineer and have passed them successfully. It was a risky business taking an exam in a foreign language, but fortune favors the brave. I am now prepared to enter the United States Service, as long as I don't have anything better to do. My *Appointment* from Washington, however, may be delayed for a few months, but *never mind*, the position is guaranteed and thus my future is taken care of, since my pay will be 1,200 dollars with rations, and I also get 10 Cts for every mile I travel on duty for the government. My rank is captain, and our uniforms will be provided by the government as soon as our orders to report have arrived [22 ll.: details; travels; address]. Emile is doing extremely well and will make a fortune even in wartime. He's now moved to Pensylvanien Avenue in Washington [18 ll.: family; has rejected an offer from the Vanderbilt Line; friends; Emile has "incredible influence"].

Steinwehr has not made a good name for himself, he owes everyone money and doesn't pay anyone back, even though they all have his signature. His behavior as colonel has also been less than good, since he left his regiment after only a week just because he had a toothache and came back to New York [118 ll.: details; apartment; daily schedule; climate; family; friends; greetings].

Your loving son / A. Dupré / *U.S. Engineer* [. . .]

Washington, August 15th, 1861

Dear parents,

[9 ll.: correspondence] I have lost my post in the Navy Yard because the order was given by the Secretary of the Navy that no Germans, only Americans, are allowed to serve as officers; the fact that this is nonsense is as clear as daylight, and someday the cowardly Americans will be happy to let German officers into their ranks. I am in Washington at the moment and I'm a captain in the Corps of Engineers, but I don't know how long I want to keep this post, since the world has never seen such a wretched way of fighting a war. Just imagine, a week ago Sunday there was a battle near Washington at Bull's

Run [Bull Run] where entire regiments just dropped their guns, swords, and revolvers, none of them were injured, and they came running back here as fast as they could. If the Confederate troops had taken advantage of their victory, they could have taken Washington without any trouble[. . . .] There's much too much corruption at the top. There's such cheating, treachery etc. that I firmly believe that in 4 weeks time Washington will no longer be in our possession. The president along with all the other ministers have already packed all their belongings [6 ll.: details]. Most of the officers are resigning because they don't want to serve under former saloonkeepers who know nothing about war. I have a good colonel, Albert Sigel, brother of Franz Sigel,* the *Hero in Missouri*, and we're going back to New York (*Neu York*) to enlist more companies.

[. . .] For example, my daily expenses, with my lodgings and everything, amount to 1½ dollars, about 2 talers,* and I don't have anything besides plain food and a small room where my orderly has to sleep too, but the fellow sticks to me like a leech and would give his life for me in a moment. He's also a German and comes from a place near Cassel, he was a schoolteacher there but he ran into hard times and enlisted, but he's well educated and a real giant of a fellow. Colonel Sigel and I are about 2 miles from Washington on a farm, since we still have to do a lot of things with the War Department, and we have to go down there every day to get them to give us various things.

I have also received an offer from the famous Lindner, who has many patents, to set up several workshops where his newly invented cannons will be made. He's offering me 5 dollars a day, I think that's more than one can earn in Germany [21 ll.: family; the heat].

First lieutenant von König was here with his colonel Betge who is from Braunschweig.[14] He claims to have been an officer, but there's no trace of it, nothing but connections, all humbug[. . . .]

They write so much in the newspapers about how capable the Union troops are, it's a disgrace that the newspapers lie so much, you just have to take a look at how the men are treated and what they get to eat. I may be a Union supporter, but giving the men *Kräckers* and water for 3 days and then marching them 200 miles through field and forest to capture a battery, and then they get beaten badly—that's not fun.

[4 ll.: correspondence] Your loving son / A. du Pré *Captain of the Pioneers*

14. Colonel Robert J. Betge was commander of the almost exclusively German 68 N.Y. Inf; König was also from Braunschweig.

EMILE AND LOTTIE DUPRÉ

[letterhead:] Emile Dupré
Iron Building, 320 Penn. Ave.
Washington, D.C., August 18, 1861

My dear mother,

You must have been wondering why you haven't had any sign of life from your children for so long, but things here have developed so quickly and un-expectedly that I have hardly even had the time to look after my business here[. . . .] As I wrote in one of my last letters, I had the good fortune in these dark times to pull off a real *coup* that will earn me several thousand during the course of the year. That was when I left my job with the Vanderbilt Line and started to work for myself. The current situation made me cast my eye on military supplies, & I had the good fortune to run across a very wealthy man who used my services, and I must have gained his trust because he sug-gested that he supply me with a <u>very</u> substantial amount of capital so I could establish myself here in Washington as a supplier to the army. Things were set up within a week, and I have been here now for a month. I have a very nice iron building where my store is located, and it's 140 foot long and 40 foot wide. This enormous space and the cellar are full of my goods, and besides the finest wines, fruit and groceries you can also buy shirts, shoes—in short, everything a soldier or an officer needs that is not supplied by the govern-ment. Although it's only been open for a short time, business is booming, and things look promising for the future.[15]

I employ five young men, 2 Negroes, I have two *Express* wagons of my own, and a charming one-horse carriage just for my own use. Charles and Theodor Spengler are two of the young men who work for me. The former is married to the girl who used to be Miss Strohmeyer. My little wife, of course, could not leave me alone, and she is here. I have rented lovely lodgings for her, a little

15. In the Washington CD the business first appears in 1862 as "Liquor Imports"; in 1863 Dupré could afford an advertisement. The imposing store in the Iron Building, built in 1851 (Goode [1979], 140), was centrally located on the main business street at the time on the north side of Pennsylvania Avenue between 9th and 10th Streets; today the site is occupied by the J. Edgar Hoover FBI Building (the house numbering was changed in 1867). There is some evi-dence that Dupré was not overly scrupulous in his dealings. On February 16, 1863, a government agent, "Col Baker, U.S. Detective," reported that he had found contraband goods on board the schooner *A. Sawyer* that were addressed to "E. De Pre"; Turner-Baker Papers, M-797, Roll 129, Baker #280, NatA. During the court-martial trial of Colonel Robert J. Betge (see Alexander Dupré's letter of August 1, 1861), the accused testified that the quartermaster of the regiment, Simon, had stolen 400 pairs of army boots "and sold them to a certain Emile Dupré in the city of Washington." Betge said he had spoken to Dupré and then had Simon arrested. Betge trial, RG 153, Court-Martial Case File, KK 407, NatA.

house that is completely furnished and surrounded by a small flower garden. The house has a *Veranda* that goes all the way around it and is covered with grapevines and wild roses. After lunch I usually sit with her for a while on the balcony, listening to the hummingbirds as they fly from flower to flower to sip honey. The whole thing seems like a wonderful dream to me. I am truly happy and in my element. As to Alexander, I don't have much to say that is positive, he has not behaved toward me like a true brother and has returned all my goodness with scandal [6 ll.: details]. Using my connections, I got him permission from the Navy Department to take his exams to become an *Engineer*. Shortly thereafter, he came to see me and told me he had passed the exams brilliantly, so well that they would offer him a job as Chief Engineer, but since he still had to wait until he was appointed, he asked for some money so he could go to Philadelphia to work in one of the factories there in the meantime. I had hardly been here for two days when he approached my partner and asked for money to come here, and then he followed me here and lied to me that he hadn't found work in Philadelphia, although he never went there. In order to speed up his appointment I went together with a very influential man to see the Minister of the Navy, who was very courteous. I told him Alex's story about the exams, and he said he would be glad to lend a hand. He sent someone to the archives to get the report of the examination commission so he could read it himself, but he couldn't find Alex's name mentioned at all. As a favor to me, he wrote to New York, and then he received the reply that Alex had completely failed the examination for 3rd *Assistent*. Of course this made me look like a complete idiot.[16] [12 ll.: Alexander was dismissed from his job in the Washington store because of impertinence; has refused a ticket back to Europe] I [. . .] hear he's selling cigars and liquor to the soldiers. Of course he'll forget everything he once learned, and so I ask you please to order him to return. I have already paid more than 100 dollars for him and had a lot of trouble, but I'd be happy to pay for his trip so he can be back under your supervision. Here he will come to a bad end [19 ll.: details; Lottie; greetings; signature].

[LOTTIE DUPRÉ continues in English:]

Please send for Alexander. For my sake. As he give much trouble to my husband. Good bye-dear Motha ˙

love to all—from your daughter / —Lottie—

---

16. There are no records of any of the military ranks or activities mentioned by Alexander in the military archives of the NatA.

Lottie Dupré née Mills. (Brigitte Leiß)

ALEXANDER DUPRÉ

Washington, Sept. 22nd, 1861

Dear parents,

Bowed down and punished by fate, I send these lines to you, beloved parents[. . . .] I have returned from the field without having been wounded or having had my limbs shot to pieces, but like so many thousands of others I have been smitten by typhus fever [21 ll.: on death's door; no mention of Emile's support]. So I lie here all alone [6 ll.: wants to come home]. I've been lying here like this for four weeks now. The fever comes and goes, I've lost almost all my strength, since I had to wait for my money until payday, and the United States is already bankrupt and is taking 3 percent from everyone who has more than $500.

[14 ll.: petition for release from the army approved] Your faithful son / A. Dupré / U.S. Adjt. & Engineer / 4th Brigade 5 Division. A.D.

EMILE AND LOTTIE DUPRÉ

[letterhead:] Emile Dupré
Iron Building, 320 Penn. Ave.
Washington, D.C., October 5, 1861

My dear Lina,

With a heavy heart I take up my pen to bring you, dear Lina, the sad news. One more of our brothers has departed this life for the hereafter. Alex died of typhus fever on Oct. 1st at 12:30 in the morning [4 ll.: details]. Alex, whose arrival I had been looking forward to so much, caused me much grief and distress. As you have probably heard from Braunschweig, two months ago I felt forced to offer him the choice, either I would pay for him to go back to Europe or he would have do without any more help from me. He chose the latter and worked for a while with some success, but then he became dissolute. I saw that this couldn't go on for long, and I wasn't mistaken, for shortly thereafter I heard that he had joined a German artillery regiment as a private. A few days later he came to see me and asked me for some money, which I refused him, because he had had a nice sum before, then he went into debt and hadn't even paid for his own food.

Three weeks ago his captain told me that Alex had taken ill with fever, and that he thought it would be better if he were moved from the camp to the city and put in a private house instead of an overcrowded hospital. I spoke with the sutler* of his regiment, whose family lives here in Washington, and asked him to take care of Alex and said that I would be willing to pay all the costs. They called a doctor, and every day I sent one of my young men to inquire after his condition [13 ll.: recovery; relapse; recovery]. The next day his landlady sent a message that I should come immediately. I went and found Alex semiconscious and with a high fever. I tried to cheer him up, and he promised me that he'd go back to Europe as soon as he got better. Worried by his condition, I called in the leading German doctor, Dr. Hansmann, who was not encouraging. The next day his fever got worse, and he lingered on in this state until the 1st, when he passed away into a better life[. . . .] My last remaining brother was gone. — All that was left was the mournful duty of giving his lifeless body a decent burial. I bought a mahogany coffin and a plot in "Glenwood-Cemtry," and we buried Alex there the following day [30 ll.: details, is also in poor health; correspondence; family; greetings; signature. October 6: 37 ll. by LOTTIE (in English)].

EMILE DUPRÉ

[letterhead:] Emile Dupré
Iron Building, 320 Penn. Ave.
Washington, D.C., November 24, 1861

Dear parents,

[28 ll.: thanks for letters; birthday wishes; present; details of his brother's death] I don't know either why he went into the army, probably because he thought he'd be an officer soon, and then he could lead a nice life like he'd seen the other men do [49 ll.: Alexander in America; health ("old throat complaint") has improved; plans to visit Germany in two years' time; family; Christmas; asks for tablecloths and sausages]. The Hamburg Line doesn't charge me for freight. At the beginning of the year I got them a contract with the U.S. postal service and thus an income of 90 to $100,000 a year, of which I get 10 percent that I share with Möhle, as long as the line keeps carrying the mail. At the moment I'm working on getting the contract renewed for a second year, and I have high hopes of *Success*[. . . .] Both of the young von König boys came by to see me yesterday. One is a captain and the other a lieutenant. They are both fine, which you should tell their family when you have the chance[. . . .] With love, your Emile Dupré

Washington, April 24, 1862

Dear parents,

[24 ll.: correspondence; family] — I'm also including my contribution toward your trip to the spa, and I would be most thankful if God, through this trip, may fortify and keep you for many years to come. Today I sent off an important shipment to the army in Yorktown. Hopefully the *Merrimac* won't take <u>my</u> goods away from me, as has happened in the past.

[. . .] I'll probably be staying only two or three more months here in the capital and then I'll move back to N.Y. I'll turn the company over to my two best clerks who will run it for me. Then I'll turn my attention to business in N.Y. [11 ll.: his wife is going to a spa in the North; she's expecting a baby]

Tomorrow I'm going to Chicago, Ill. on business, a trip of over 1,000 miles and by no means pleasant. Seven days on the train with only one day's rest is not a pleasure trip; especially on American trains.

May 8th, 1862

After writing this I had to break off to start the journey mentioned above. This was extremely interesting but very tiring. On my way back I went to Wheeling on the Ohio River to visit General John C. Fremont* and I arrived back here on the morning of May 2nd. Things don't look so much like war now here in Washington, since the army has moved forward. It looks like the rebels have suffered a lot in recent weeks, but I don't believe we'll have peace any time soon [12 ll.: wants to set up a gold and silver refinery in New York; asks for advice from Professor Farrentrap in Braunschweig; has more than 300,000 talers* of capital at his disposal]. Steinwehr has become a brigadier general, which you should tell his parents. V. König is a major and his brother Paul will be a captain soon.[17] People move up quickly through the ranks here, but when the war is over, school's out too, and that's the end of that, and the gentlemen who are now leading a grand life will go back to being laborers, servants, and barbers. That's how things are here in America, down at the bottom today and up at the top tomorrow. If you're sensible you can stay where you are, but most people here never think about the future, and they suffer a lot later on [7 ll.: family]. Emil Dupré

EMILE AND LOTTIE DUPRÉ

Washington D.C., June 19th, 1862

Dear mother,

[28 ll.: thanks; wishes; friends; gold refinery; spa at the seaside] My business here is doing very well, and I'm not giving it up, just turning it over to my best clerk to run. Although I've been hit hard a few times by the army, other shipments have been more successful and have covered my losses, and I'm making money [14 ll.: details].

The German troops drew fire last week and lost very badly.[18] Steinwehr is now a general, confirmed by the *Congress* and the *Senate*. He is fine, I saw him

17. This news was somewhat belated: Steinwehr was promoted on October 12, 1861. He and the von König brothers were acquaintances from Braunschweig.

18. Battle of Cross Keys, June 8, 1862.

after the battle. Louis Ahrens, the son of the lieutenant colonel, was wounded in the arm and he'll probably lose it, but he is safe, and you should tell his parents this, in case they may have heard rumors that were worse.[19] [19 ll.: family; hopes next year to be able to show Lottie "the beauties of our dear Fatherland"; signature. 37 ll. by LOTTIE (in English)]

EMILE DUPRÉ

Washington, September 17th, 1862
Sunday morning!

My dear mother,

[4 ll.: thanks for letters; Lottie] The last unsuccessful campaign in Virginia has brought the tumult of war much closer to us again. We had the rebels close to here, and some of the local families packed up all their belongings to go north. Under these circumstances I decided it would be better for my wife to stay in the North for the winter. At the beginning of October, she's going to stay with her aunt in Newark, in the state of New Jersey, where she will receive the best care during her confinement. On October 15 I will be relieved here by Speyer's brother-in-law for a couple of months, so that I can take over running the New York office[. . . .] A large number of our troops are now concentrated in this area, and that's increased my business significantly, and I have a lot to do. The commotion here has been beyond description. All the churches have been turned into hospitals and are overcrowded with the sick and the wounded. The ladies here have taken on the task of helping these unfortunate men. There really is nothing more terrible than a civil war like this one, where brother fights against brother, father against son. This war has already cost more than half a million lives as well as 15 hundred million dollars. Heaven alone knows where this will end. Everything is incredibly expensive, and the prices keep going up every day. A dozen eggs cost 39½ cents or 15 silbergroschen.

Most families are mourning the untimely loss of one or more loved ones, and still there's no talk of peace. Our government is unfortunately in the hand of incompetent men, and I wouldn't be at all surprised if the rebellion didn't force the North to recognize the South, despite all the clamor in the newspapers [47 ll.: friends; family; hopes to visit Germany; business; greetings; signature].

19. Ahrens received his discharge with the rank of captain in the 4 N.Y. Cav on April 27, 1863. *OAR*, 2:322.

New York, November 3rd, 1862

My dear mother,

[. . .] My stores in Washington and Alexandria Va are still in my name and still run the same way. I have given Mr. Speyer's brother-in-law, a young American, power to act and sign on behalf of the company and he is filling in for me [72 ll.: family; business; daily life; mother should come to visit; greetings]. As always, your loving / Emile / <u>Emile Dupré Esq</u> / <u>Washington</u> D.C. / <u>Iron Building, 320 Penna Avenue</u> / <u>via England</u> [. . .]

EMILE AND LOTTIE DUPRÉ

Washington D.C., March 28th, 1863

My dear mother,

Since I last wrote I've been with the army [23 ll.: financial matters; business; has given up the store in Washington]. König's brother, who used to be a sailor, is now Steinwehr's adjutant; even the president of the U.S. doesn't have any adjutants [43 ll.: business; family; friends]. Emile / My address is: Emile Dupré / Washington D.C., USA [22 ll. by LOTTIE (in English)]

EMILE DUPRÉ

New York, July 17th, 1863

My dear mother,

[33 ll.: opened a new company, Speyers & Dupré on July 1; business; family; friends; plans for trip to Germany] Please be so kind as to send me a *Document* in which you swear I am your only son and that you are a widow. It wouldn't hurt to add that one of your sons lost his life in the current war. This *Document* has to be certified by the American Consul over there. I'll swear then that you are partially dependent on income from my work, and that is how I will avoid military service. We've experienced terrible things these last 4 days [draft riots*]. They wanted to force the men into the army, then the mobs rose up, burned a lot of houses, and plundered and stole everything they could get their hands on. It cost a lot of lives. I know about things like that, and I just stayed at home. Among the injured, as usual, there were a lot of curious onlookers. Fortunately, the government won't be enforcing the draft for the time being, otherwise N.Y. might have experienced days even worse than in Paris at its worst [4 ll.: greetings; signature].

Dunn W. McKee, Hon., M C, h 391 C north
Dunn William, h D south n 8th west
Dunn William, blacksmith, h 33 Penn av
Dunn William H., salesman, bds 463 E north
Dunington James A., carpenter, h 4th east n G south
Dunscomb, Jane, wid Daniel, h 357 E north

DUPRE, EMILE
320 Penn. Ave., Iron Hall, Washington,
And 53 King St., Alexandria.

Fine Groceries, Segars, Liquors, &c. &c.

SUTLERS, OFFICERS, AND OTHERS SUPPLIED.

Du Puy Horatio A., storekeeper, h 109 H north
Durham James H., h Md av bet 2d and 3d east
Durity Geo. W., watchman, h P north n 14th west
Durity James R., undertaker, 303 Penn av, h 284 N Y av
Durham George G., soldier, h 70 East Capitol
Durkin Thomas, laborer, h 176 E south
Durnin Peter, stonecutter, h 255 Va av
Durr William, carpenter, bds 343 10th west
Duruz Jules, steward, h 227 H north
Dutcher J. C., nurse hospital, H north n 9th west
Duthie James, engraver, h 34 Missouri av
Dutrow David K., wholesale butter and produce dealer, 450 8th west
Dutton George W., butcher, 77 Centre and 46 Northern mkts, h 500 L north
Dutton Adeline, Mrs., photographer, 324 Penn av, h E south bet 6th and 7th west
Dutton M., clerk, h 243 B south
Dutton Thomas, messenger, h 243 B south
Dutton Thomas H., carpenter, h 324 8th west
Dutton William H. H., clerk, h 324 8th west
Duvall Amon, messenger, h 362 7th west
Duvall Andrew J. (Duvall & Brother), merchant tailor, 434 Penn av, h 421 5th west
Duvall Ann O., boardingh, 486 E north
Duvall Benj. H. (Duvall & Brother), merchant tailor, 434 Penn av, h 70 Indiana av
Duvall Edmund, blacksmith, h C south, n 4½ west
Duvall Edward S., clerk, bds 379 3d west
Duvall Eliza, wid Sam., boardingh, 159 Penn av
Duvall Enoch, laborer, h 386 L south
Duvall George W., policeman
Duvall H. C., baggagemaster, h 591 Mass av
Duvall Jessie, blacksmith, bds 446 L south
Duvall John (Bleyliss & Duvall), blacksmith, Mass av n 7th west, h 274 9th west
Duvall John, stonecutter, h 267 21st west
Duvall John W., blacksmith, bds 274 9th west
Duvall L., Mrs., dressmaker, 500 7th west
Duvall Marshall, plasterer, bds M south n 3d
Duvall Samuel, blacksmith, bds 274 9th west
Duvall Samuel, grocer, 208 I nth, h 112 Penn av
Duvall Sarah E., wid Eli, h 274 B north
Duvall W. T. S., clerk, h 379 3d west
Duvall Washington, blockmaker, h N south n 11th east
Duvall William T., h 379 3d west
Duvall Zachariah, clerk, h 486 E north

DUVALL & BROTHER (Benj. H. and Andrew J. Duvall), merchant tailors, 434 Penn av
Dux Emanuel, watchman, h 223 20th west
Dwenger George W., clerk, bds 231 G north
Dwyer Ann, wid Patrick, h 434 K south
Dwyer Hannah C., boardingh, 16 East Capitol
Dwyer Joe W., clerk, h 426 F north
Dyer Benj. F., carpenter, h 671 N J av
Dyer C. S., clerk, h 273 Vt av
DYER EDWARD C., wines, liquors, and segars, 256 Penn av, h 270 F north
Dyer J. T., bds 421 E north
Dyer John C., clerk, h 452 11th west
Dyer John W., clerk, h 125 H north
Dyer Kinsey, messenger, h 438 L north
Dyer Margaret, Miss, h 491 8th west
Dyer Mary, wid James, h 452 10th west
Dyer Wm. B., superintendent, h 313 13th west
Dykes Ann G., wid William A., h 664 7th east
Dykes Francis M., blacksmith, h 664 7th east
Dykes George T., master mate U S N, h 664 7th east
Dyre Wm. W. S., clerk, bds 166 N Y av
Dyser David, blacksmith, h 533 5th east
Dyser Jacob, provision store, 1st east cor East Capitol, h 533 5th east
Dysert William E., clerk, h 261 8th
Dyson Charles (col'd), huckster, 80 Centre and 45 Eastern mkts, h B south bet 11th and 12th west
Dyson Robert (col'd), h C south cor 3d west

E

Eades John P., gardener, h 86 20th west
Eagleston John, butcher, 54 Centre and Northern Liberty markets, h 10 4th west
Eagleston Josiah, butcher, Northern market, h 265 N Y av
Eakins Samuel, engineer, bds 563 12th west
Eakle Elias H., grocer, 3d west cor D north, h 10th east n B north
Eames Charles, machinist, bds M south n 3d
EAMES CHARLES, lawyer, 451 14th west
Earl Richard, h 190 14th west
Earl Robert (Earl & Son), liverystable, H north n 21st west, h 21st west n I north
Earl Robert, jr. (Earl & Son), liverystable, H north n 21st west, h 21st west n I north
Earl & Son (Robert and Robert, jr.), liverystable, H north bet 20th and 21st west
Early Robert, soldier, h 500 3d west
Earp John W., billiards, 11th west cor Penn av, h 495 11th west
Easby Mrs., wid William, bds 16 E Capitol
Easby Horatio N., lumberdealer, D north cor 26th west, h F north cor 20th west
East John, tailor, h 637 O north
Easter Ann (col'd), wid David, washing, h 218 2d west
Eastman Jno. R., aid Observatory, h 407 9th west
Eastman Norman, clerk, h 257 8th west
Easton Mary (col'd), washing, h 431½ I north
Easton Thomas, laborer, h 26th west n F north
Eaton Ann J., seamstress, h R north n 12th west
Eaton Alex. W., carpenter, h 2d east n K south
Eaton Allen W., clerk, h 358 11th west
Eaton William H., h 6th cor N north

Emile Dupré's entry in the 1863 Hutchinson's Washington and Georgetown Directory. (Washington, D.C.)

per Hamburg Mail *S.S. Germania*
N.Y., February 3rd, 1864

My dear mother,

[15 ll.: correspondence; family] Major General Hartsuff[20] and his wife spent 2 weeks visiting at our house [5 ll.: business]. We will start constructing our factory this month [35 ll.: will travel to Europe in May 1865; family; friends; greetings; signature].

New York, March 11, 1864

My dear mother,

[22 ll.: correspondence; family] Now you have war over there in Germany, too, that is attracting attention here.[21] Hopefully it will only be of short duration, because if England and France get involved, it will be bad for everyone. The Americans are hoping for a complication like that, due to their hatred of England, for then they could attack them with a lot of <u>neutral</u> privateers under German flags. In revenge for the neutral [ships] *Alabama, Florida, Rappahannock* etc. that burned our merchant ships. <u>Here</u>, chances for peace are looking bad, the government under Lincoln will never win the South back [21 ll.: has received a large government order for silver nitrate; elegant office furnishings]. I remain your loving / Emile

[letterhead:] Office of SPEYERS & DUPRÉ;
No. 29 PINE STREET, / Under 4th National Bank,
New York, July 28th, 1864

My dear mother,

[36 ll.: family; financial matters; strongly advises against buying American government bonds; business is good] Yesterday I bought myself a substitute for the army, a Negro, and now I am free for three years in case I should get called up. The president has called for another 500,000 recruits. It is unbelievable how many lives and how much money is being wasted here. The government is spending 3½ million a day [7 ll.: details; greetings]. Your Emile

New York, October 21st, 1864

My dear mother,

[5 ll.: has not written for a long time] Thanks to my efforts and good fortune, our business here has blossomed very quickly, and in one area in particu-

---

20. George Lucas Hartsuff, 1830–71, career officer (West Point, class of 1848) who was still a lieutenant when he lived in the same building as Dupré (letter of February 1, 1861); he advanced quickly after the war began and in 1863 became commander of the XXIII Corps. Warner (1964), 212–13.

21. The German-Danish War of 1864.

lar, brokerage, I am earning a lot of money. The only obstacle in the path to success was my partner, Mr. Speyer, who has a number of talents but not the ability to run an office and manage finances [5 ll.: details] and after a number of discussions back and forth our companies split up on the 18th. Speyers will continue here on his own. Mr. Kretz and I immediately moved into a much nicer *Office* and are already working as his competitors, but only in one area, namely brokerage, buying or selling for our clients at their own risk [15 ll.: details].

There was another reason why I took this step, namely my health[. . . .] In our new office, Kretz will take over all the paperwork so I only have to work away from home during the day, not like with Speyers where I had to work away from the office during the day and then in the office until late at night [14 ll.: family; greetings; signature].

Brooklyn, February 5th, 1865
Sunday evening

My dear mother,

[10 ll.: correspondence; family] We're living a quiet and retired life here, like always. My business is doing very well, and I've earned quite a bit of money in the last 3 months [16 ll.: details; family]. On May 1st we are going to move, probably into New York, because of my business [14 ll.: wants photographs of Braunschweig; friends; thoughts about the Old Country]. There are now rumors of peace here, this endless civil war may come to an end after all. Even though I don't believe there will be peace, it would probably make it easier for me to visit you. I probably won't be moving back to Europe. In the 10 years I've been here I've made a lot of dear friends, in other words I have found a second homeland. After a hard struggle I am finally able to see a quieter future up ahead, and perhaps more than that; who knows? I don't know if I could be happy over there in all that peace and quietude after living in such exciting times over here [9 ll.: family]. Your loving / Emile

The brokerage house Dupré & Kretz flourished: in the first half of 1865 Dupré's share of the profit was $14,800, and he spent money freely ("Mr. Steinway [from Braunschweig] is here at the moment, and I bought one of his pianos for $600"). The crowning moment of Dupré's career came in January 1866 when, after a vote of ninety-five to five, he became a life member of the Upper Board of Stock Brokers, the third German ever to achieve this honor. Only members could trade on the stock exchange for customers who paid brokerage fees of 0.8 percent. Dupré was not only proud and gratified; he also felt that his future was now secure and that he would be able to retire in a few years' time. But in September 1866, at the early age of thirty-three, after having complained about poor health and throat problems, he died of typhoid fever, like his brother Alexander before him. His widow and daughter visited the family in Germany at least twice, in 1868 and 1869.[22]

22. Emile Dupré (after the death of his mother) to his sister(s), May 5, 1865, November 11, 1865 (quotation), January 28, 1866, March 12, 1866, NABS; Robert Schultze, New York, to Dr. A. Bloom (Dupré's brother-in-law—with the news of Emile Dupré's death), September 29, 1866, NABS; entries in guest book Heinrich von Eynern, Rüdesheim, NABS.

3. Wesslau Family

The cabinetmaker Julius Wesslau, the Protestant son of a carpenter in Jüterbog, some fifty miles south of Berlin, emigrated in 1850, at the age of twenty-three. By 1853 he had opened a workshop in New York, and in 1856 he was running it together with his brother Karl, who was three years older. They soon specialized in making furniture, were apparently very successful, and employed more and more workers. In 1858 two younger sisters, Emilie and Marie, arrived in the United States and married German American craftsmen; four more brothers and sisters remained in Germany.[1]

JULIUS AND LISETTE WESSLAU

[Ne]w York, December 26, 1860

Dear parents,

We received your last letters and read the contents with great interest [6 ll.: family]. As for us, we are all well [4 ll.: birth of a son]. The business and political situation here in America, however, is less positive, and we have been hit very badly[. . . .] For a long time now there's been a big fight about slavery: in the South, where it is too hot for the white race of men to work, for centuries now the people have been buying black Negroes, and they grow cotton so extensively on their plantations that they now constitute the world market

SOURCE NOTE: The biography of the Wesslau brothers gives no indication of more than an elementary education, but that seems to have been quite solid. It would be difficult to pinpoint differences in their command of the language. They handle a large vocabulary well, make few spelling mistakes, and write in a lively, animated fashion. Even their handwriting is much alike—neat and regular, indicating that they had considerable practice in writing, presumably in their business. What appear to be serious lapses in grammar are in fact the results of putting the local (southern Brandenburg) dialect into writing. The Wesslau ladies write very similarly, though their spelling is a little weaker. Not included here are the letters in the series from before 1860 (two), as well as a letter dated June 4, 1864.

1. CD New York 1853/54; letters by Julius and Karl Wesslau, 1860–62, NABS.

in cotton. In the northern states slavery is seen as unjust, and they abolished it more than 50 years ago, and they don't want it to spread to the new, unsettled territories in America [5 ll.: eighteen states in the North, fifteen slave states in the South; Congress and the president]. For many years the presidents were of the southern party, but this fall the candidate of the northern states won. Now the southern states are claiming that their property and their lives are in danger, and they have cut themselves off from the Union. The effect this has had on business here can't be put into a few words, but business all over the country has collapsed. The South always bought its industrial goods from the North, and we can't continue to exist without them [4 ll.: the southern states refuse to pay bills, are preparing for war]. The North would have been well advised to stay out of things that are none of its business, and everyone in business hopes things will be settled, but now the ball has started to roll, and no one knows what will happen. It would be a real shame, though, if a country like this, which has no equal in the world in terms of wealth and riches, should be destroyed because of the willfulness of its politicians [4 ll.: European powers would be pleased]. In my opinion, too much freedom isn't always a good thing. It would be better for America if they had a set, more well regulated government with more protection of private property, where all the civil servants can't stuff their own pockets as much as they can during the short time they are in office. Our main business was with the South, and up to now we've lost about 600 dollars, and we may lose most of another 1,500 dollars, and we've let half of our workers go, and if things don't get better soon we'll have to send more away[. . . .] At any rate, it will take us a year at least to make up our losses.

January 3, 1861. Things are looking worse and worse, we'll probably have a civil war in a few days, or the government will have to permit a number of states to leave the Union peacefully, which is not very likely, and the northern states wouldn't like it either [12 ll.: war is probable if the United States breaks up; hopes for peace in Europe].

Your / loving son / Julius Wesslau

[LISETTE WESSLAU continues:]

Dear parents-in-law,

As I read in your last letters you are all quite well, which I was very pleased to hear, and what I can report about us is that on September 21st I gave birth to a son who gives us great pleasure. It all went very well, and I hope the good Lord will keep little Albert hale and hearty.

It is difficult to raise children here in the summer, the air in the city is very bad, and most children die [9 ll.: family; correspondence; greetings]. Your daughter Lisete Weßlau

JULIUS WESSLAU

New York, July 23rd, 1861

[salutation missing]

[4 ll.: correspondence] There's a very bloody civil war on here, and the day before yesterday we lost a big battle against the rebels, much like at Jena[2] [10 ll.: looking back at history; condemns "treason" committed by President James Buchanan]. This treachery kept swelling up more and more, then a government and armies were set up in the South, a real reign of terror that stole the property and lives of all the people who remained loyal to the legitimate government. The new president has called on all loyal citizens to save the country. This is difficult, since there were only about 12,000 soldiers here, all the money stolen and all the arms in rebel hands, but the North rose up to a man, and Neu York was like an army camp, with some 200,000 men marching out [4 ll.: the Union is stronger in terms of money and population]. This is the worst situation you can imagine. On the border of the rebel states, people are killing each other, there have been quite a number of Germans killed, especially in the state of Missouri[. . . .] In the state of Missouri the German soldiers have done well, attacking bands of rebels, and so they are hated by the slaveholder party. It's like this all over the country, with people destroying each other. When the soldiers went home, they were attacked and shot on the road, and many families who had spent years working to get good farms had to flee by night, their houses were set on fire and everything was stolen [7 ll.: disastrous situation; vandalism]. 3 days ago I still thought it might be possible to defeat the slaveholder party within 6 months, but losing this battle makes that very doubtful. There was great commotion here in the city, and everyone was very disheartened[. . . .]

Most of the men are in what you know as the militia, and you can well imagine what it's like when out of 800–1,000 riflemen only half are left, the effect this has on their families and the city. It is terrible that we don't have any seasoned officers and soldiers. Thousands have died, and we lost almost the entire artillery because the enemy was in too good a position and outnumbered us, 40,000 to 80,000.[3] They should have waited until they had more men and their soldiers were better trained[. . . .]

2. The battle in which Napoleon routed the Prussian army in 1806.

3. He is referring to the first major battle of the war, the first battle of Bull Run or Manassas (July 21, 1861). Wesslau's estimate of the number of troops and casualties involved are highly exaggerated. McPherson (1988), 344, 347. His numbers for New York City are also too high. The 625 Union dead had served in sixty different regiments, of which seven were from New York City. The three predominantly German regiments from New York City (8, 29, and 41 N.Y. Inf) lost a total of 203 men in military action during the entire war. *OAR*, vol. 2.

Business here is very bad, there's nothing to do. Even though more than thirty thousand men have left the city to go to war, there are as many people here as there are stars in the sky, and the workers are suffering badly. What a disaster, at least 50 thousand more men from here have to go to the war, and their families will have to be supported by the city, otherwise we'll have a riot here in Neu York. The South owes Neu York 200 million dollars, but not a penny has been paid or has been allowed to be paid, and therefore the best businesses are bankrupt. Half of our customers are bankrupt, and of course we have lost a lot because of that, we can't even tell how much will be left over, since our running expenses are high and we are earning very little. It is certainly easier to make money over here, but easy to lose it, too. But you needn't worry about us, we'll take care of ourselves. We can hold out until the spring, and if things still look as bad then, we can buy a farm to tide us over. Not, of course, in the area where the two sides are fighting. We still have a good reputation here and we could easily get credit, but we don't want to put any more into the business. In fact, we are doing much better than thousands of other businesses, but it hurts to lose so much money. Before the war started, we wouldn't have sold our business for 10 thousand dollars, and now it's not worth very much [10 ll.: his wife and child are out in the country; there's not much to do]. A lot of people are going back to Germany[. . . .] Some of our friends who are short of money have cut back on what they spend, so quite a few people are missing at social events, and we don't have as much fun as we used to [7 ll.: wishes; greetings; signature].

New York, May 14th, 1862

Dear parents,

[6 ll.: is sending letter and photograph with a friend who is going to Germany] We are all very well, and our little boy is quite tall for his age and clever, and he babbles in both German and English, walks quite well and gives us great pleasure. Almost all of the children speak English, and if they don't learn German at an early age, they won't want to speak German later on because it's not *mode (fashionable)*.

The war has been bitter for quite a while, but now it looks like the rebels will soon be defeated. The destruction of property, however, has been enormous, and when they have to retreat, towns and villages, bridges and railroads—everything of any value—is burned, and hatred runs strong, especially on the southern side [10 ll.: New Orleans taken; losses].

Business in Neu York has improved a lot, and we now have enough work to keep 24 men busy. When the war is over, wages will probably go higher than ever before, since so many men won't be returning [7 ll.: correspondence].

All the best / Your son / Julius Wesslau [. . .]

KARL WESSLAU

New York, May 14, 1862

Dear parents,

[4 ll.: positive developments] The last victories over the rebels have almost guaranteed that the whole country will be under one government again, and so business is picking up. In our line of business, there's a shortage of people even now, and wages are rising. When the war is over, labor will be in great demand and very expensive. We kept most of our workers on when times were bad, that cost us a lot of money and trouble, but now we have them when we need them, and I hope we'll be able to make up our losses. Over the years we've gotten so many customers that for now we won't be at a loss for sales [14 ll.: destruction in path of retreat; rebels can't hold out much longer]. Your son / Karl Weßlau [. . .]

JULIUS AND LISETTE WESSLAU

New York, October 26th, 1862

Dear parents,

[20 ll.: photographs; correspondence] Now they're going to call up men again here to fill up the army that's been reduced by half, even a bounty of $200 for a volunteer isn't enough, they need too many men. Now all the men between 18 and 45 have to draw lots, whoever is chosen has to go into the field or provide a substitute. This is not to the liking of the citizens and the businessmen, and especially not to my liking, and if I was unwilling to be treated like a piece of government property in Prussia, I am just as unwilling to do so here, at any rate there'll be a riot when they try it here in New York next week[. . . .] The country seems to be heading toward ruin at a fast clip, the army can't be paid, there's no money in the treasury even though they've borrowed 500 million dollars and more since last year.

The problem is the boundless corruption of the authorities, and no one can do anything about it. Contractors, suppliers, civil servants, officers, government officials, and their relatives all stuff their own pockets, since they only have their posts for a short time. Volunteers, too, sign up and get their 200 dollars bounty, then, since it takes a few weeks until the regiment is full, many of them run off to another regiment and get another 200 dollars, and so on till some of them have taken in 200 dollars a dozen times, and when the regiment finally moves out, they discover that they haven't even got half the number of men they paid for. In order to raise money for the war, every little thing is being taxed, so everything we need is more expensive. There's a business tax, too, and then 3 percent on everything we produce, that means about 600 dollars a year for our business. Many people might even be quite happy (?) to pay this, except for the fact that everyone knows that only a fraction of it gets to the government—the rest is spent to cover the cost of collecting it. All in all, politics here (which is responsible for all our woes) is much like the confusion of tongues at the tower of Babel, one person says one thing, another something different, the newspapers help fan the flames, and in the midst of this dreadful confusion, prosperity perishes, while men on both sides kill each other in the field. German against German, American against American, brother against brother, son against father. I've seen so many officers and generals buried, hundreds of fresh regiments march out of New York, and then a little while later I read that whole regiments have been reduced to little more than a company, thousands of cripples come back and so on.

[11 ll.: they didn't dare hold the draft in New York City] Our business has done rather well this year, and it is quite possible that we'll make up what we lost last year. Some of our friends have made a lot of money through the war, especially those who supply the army.

[. . .] If the war's over by next spring, I expect very good times in America, and anyone who feels like coming to America will be sure to find well-paid work, since we're already short of men, but I wouldn't advise it for a married man or anyone who isn't willing to work hard, and I certainly don't want to take any responsibility[. . . .] All the best / Your son / Julius Wesslau.

[LISETTE WESSLAU continues: 21 ll.: family; photographs; greetings; signature]

EMILIE WESSLAU

November 10, 1862

Dear parents,

[11 ll.: family; correspondence] Otherwise times are very hard, it's been 2 years now, earnings were cut in half, instead of being able to save some money as we used to, we had losses. Now there's more to do, but the prices are still bad[. . . .] A pound of coffee 34 cents, a pound of sugar 16 cents, in short all twice as much as before, nothing still costs the same. The same is true of material for clothing, especially cotton. And all the gold, silver, and copper has disappeared[. . . .] The worst part is the draft; it's decided by lottery which men under 46 have to go to war, since they can't get any more volunteers, today is the day they decide, and it can easily hit my husband or brothers[. . . .] With hugs and kisses for my dear parents / Your daughter / Emilie [. . .]

KARL, MARIE[?], AND EMILIE WESSLAU

New York, July 28, 1863

Dear parents,

[4 ll.: many new things] This spring, business took a lot of attention, there was more demand for work and labor than ever before. Part of the problem was that our paper money had an unstable value, and then for two years not much was done and a considerable number of workers had gone to the war. At the first sign of improvement in business during the winter, the workers started asking for higher wages. Wages fluctuate a lot over here, they're now twice as high as last year, a good cabinetmaker can earn 2½ dollars a day, a laborer 1½ dollars, instead of ¾ of a dollar before. It's very unpleasant for someone who needs workers when wages are so different and unstable, but from year to year it's becoming more common: demand sets the price. The demands of the workers are not always reasonable, so there are often bitter disputes. The dock workers, for example, demanded 2 dollars a day, and when the merchants didn't accept this, most of them just stopped working and ganged up together and used violence to force out the men who still wanted to work. Occasionally Negroes were employed there or hired as teamsters, and they took the brunt of all the violence of the rough mob that brutally mishandled anyone they could get their hands on. The police here are very good and usually know how to keep the peace, but it just wasn't possible to protect every single person. Even if things aren't that rough in every line of business, in particular for clerks and craftsmen, it is still irksome enough if you are affected—smashed windows, infamous accusations at workers' meetings, insults in the newspapers and other ridicule. And every time there's something that leads to a court case between workers and employers, there's never been a judge who has decided against the worker. All the civil servants here, except the police, are elected by the people, so it's in their own interest to pander to the prejudices and passions of the mobs. That's why there's no talk of moderation in either of the political parties, and it's this same ruthless party politics that has gotten us into this war. Here in the North, there's a large party that's against the current government, and it's often led to bloody resistance[....] The local Neu York militia, some 10,000 men strong, has been sent off to the war three times. At the same time, they called up new recruits, and this met with opposition here in the city, and a terrible mob uprising erupted [draft riots*]. There was only the police to keep the peace, and one small army unit left here to protect the docks, hardly enough to guard the most important buildings, so the mob ruled the city for 4 whole days and murdered and burned everything in sight. In Germany, especially in the big cities, there's riffraff too, but they're nothing like the low-down rabble here. These people committed every atrocity imaginable, for three nights in a row the city was lit up by the burning buildings.[4] Everyone thought the government here was really spineless, and the parties attacked it and made fun of it, but in the eyes of law-abiding citizens, its reputation has been restored. Through all the murder and arson they kept saying: we can let our citizens be murdered and our factories burned, but we will not give in to the mobs. The riots may well have cost 4–500 lives and will keep the prisons full for a long time.[5] We personally suffered no damage, some of the shops in our neighborhood were plundered, but most of the rioting was in other parts of the city. Now the city is so full of soldiers that a new outbreak is highly unlikely. When you see the soldiers here they make quite a strange sight: they don't look nearly as clean as in Germany, but tough and weathered. The war has already claimed many lives, and probably less than half of the troops that set out in the beginning are still alive [21 ll.: details]. Your son Karl Weßlau

[MARIE? WESSLAU continues:]

Dear parents,

[15 ll.: family] As far as everyday life in general goes, things here in America are wild and stormy. Thousands are killed or wounded in one battle, and as if that wasn't bad enough, riots broke out here in New York, where the rabble took over, life and property weren't safe, especially the poor Negroes were subject to merciless manhandling, so that it looked like the world was coming to an end—now things are quiet again, thanks to the government[. . . .]

[EMILIE WESSLAU continues:]

Dearest parents,

[15 ll.: family] The draft is taking place at the moment, and I am worried that they'll take my husband. If you pay 300 dollars, you're free for one round, but Bogenschneider doesn't want to part with any of his hard-earned money. The city fathers have approved 3 million dollars to buy out poor citizens and support their families, in order to relieve the harshness of the *Conscription* law, but the *Major* [mayor], a Republican, hasn't signed it yet, he's waiting until the men who have already been drawn have been sworn in, but then it'll be too late, then only the family can get the 300 dollars, the whole thing is very unfair [5 ll.: high prices; greetings]. Emilie

---

4. Wesslau is remarkably restrained here: he does not mention that it was primarily blacks who were murdered, the fact that most of the violent crimes were committed by the Irish, or that German Americans did not take part and even took action against the rioters.

5. According to the most careful calculations, there may have been as many as 150 deaths, but only 105 could be confirmed. Cook (1974).

KARL AND MARIE WESSLAU

New York, May 28th, 1864

Dear parents and brothers and sisters,

[6 ll.: family] There's not much chance at the moment of my having the time to visit you, because right now our business takes up all my time and attention, but maybe later I'll be able to find the time. The situation here in America is very peculiar. At the moment there are opportunities to earn money like never before, these are golden times for craftsmen, workers and soldiers, a laborer can support his family on 4 days of work a week; on the other hand the value of money is down by half, so the property-owning classes watch the value of their wealth just melt away. It is almost like free-for-all plundering, everyone takes whatever he can get for his services and labor, and it's clear that there can't be any talk of peace and contentment. The workers' demands for higher wages have been repeated every 2 to 3 months, but it hasn't always been possible to meet these demands in every line of business. So it happens frequently that certain businesses, like the machinists and piano builders, are shut down for months. Work stoppages on the part of the laborers have become so common that there's almost always one group of workers on strike[. . . .] The country seems to have become much richer because of the war, everybody is buying much more and much better things, like clothing, household goods, furniture etc. than before, and so much paper money has been printed and spent that everyone has his share. These are very good times for people in Germany who want to come over here, it's easy enough to find well-paid employment[. . . .] The government does all it can to encourage immigration, since the war has already cost so many lives that there's starting to be a shortage of men. All the foreigners who haven't declared their intention of becoming a citizen of the United States are exempt from military service [24 ll.: burdens and victims of the war; guerrilla warfare in the border areas]. In the North there are about 100,000 Negro soldiers who used to be slaves. The rebels refuse to recognize them as soldiers, and they murder all the prisoners and wounded they can get their hands on. Naturally, the Negroes exercise their right to retaliation and perhaps even more because the war is being fought in enemy territory. One of the main things about this war is the destruction and devastation. Wherever the army has been, not much is left that can be of use. In what used to be some of the richest areas, the government had to feed the people last winter to keep them from starving [17 ll.: devastation caused by the war; he himself is content; wishes].
Karl Weßlau

[MARIE WESSLAU continues: 16 ll.: correspondence; expresses sympathy on the death of brother-in-law Wilhelm; family; wishes; signature]

JULIUS WESSLAU

New York, December 1864

Dear parents,

[15 ll.: family; is content; the war is becoming increasingly barbaric; over a million dead[6]] Now I want to report what the situation is like here in New York. Up until about a month ago, work was plentiful and trade was good, but things have slowed down a lot now. The city has never had so many residents, because everyone who could get away from the countryside and from the South has been crowding into Neu York, partly to make big money and partly to avoid the draft, because the government hasn't dared hold a lottery here since the dreadful riots last summer. Twice they've said they were going to, but a lot of men are signing up voluntarily. So while in the field in the South the most horrible war is raging, here in Neujork it's one good time after another, at balls, the opera, theaters and other places. The main streets are clogged with fine and glittering ladies and gentlemen, and sometimes there are so many carriages it's dangerous to cross the street [13 ll.: wealth of the country is unlimited; details about raw materials, trade, entrepreneurial spirit]. A few years ago I wrote: we have everything we need to be happy, and what's happening now, everything is being destroyed, everyone is expecting the government to go bankrupt. Even though our business has made several thousand dollars this year, all the money we had is worth so much less. We had considerable sales this year, sometimes more than a thousand dollars a week and never less than 500.

[15 ll.: family; son Carl was born on July 6; hotels destroyed by arson; much crime]

The first thing I do every morning is look through the newspaper. Every day there are reports about battles, towns being destroyed, railroads, ships and other property, there are articles that curse the rogues in the government, one screams for peace, the next for war, and usually the rabble with nothing to lose screams the most about the government (they themselves elected). It is terribly sad but true that in New York there are more people who support the rebels than the government, but they are mostly riffraff. When I'm finished with the paper, business is waiting, and thus I am always kept so busy that I don't have enough peace and quiet to write more often—but I haven't forgotten the old homeland[. . . .]

Your son / Julius Wesslau

---

6. In fact, over half a million.

KARL, EMILIE, AND MARIE[?] WESSLAU

New York, December 14, 1864

Dear parents,

[14 ll.: memories of home; war] Up until now we haven't had to fight in the war ourselves, and we intend to stay out of it come what may, but we're still suffering plenty from its effects. They haven't mastered the art of raising men and money as well as in Europe. The businesses are saddled with having to pay most of the taxes, and they try, of course, to avoid this almost crushing burden [7 ll.: details]. Whenever they order a lottery, it affects all men 20 to 45. The younger ones haven't usually settled down yet, so when things look dangerous, they move to another address so they can't be found, and so this burden must be carried largely by the middle classes. Volunteers are being offered a lot of money now, last summer they were paying 7–800 dollars for one year of service. These recruits, of course, then run away as fast as possible, and they claim that not even half of the men who were paid ever end up in the army, and that's why there are never enough soldiers, and the compulsory draft remains a constant threat. Last spring and summer business was very good, the demand for things was almost unbelievable, and people paid almost any price [15 ll.: prices; wages; harvest]. The conditions for peace have been set by the North: abolition of slavery and reunification, the South only wants its independence. A compromise between these two positions is apparently impossible. If the war ends badly for us, national bankruptcy will be almost unavoidable, but if it ends badly for the South, all the rich and proud plantation owners will be completely ruined forever. The southern cavaliers (as they call themselves) are therefore doing their utmost to succeed. Every man aged 15–60 is subject to the draft, and only as few men as possible can stay home to run things. One man who escaped from Savannah told me: the most striking difference between a northern city and a southern one is that you see comparatively few cripples in the North. But at some point the war will have to come to an end, and maybe the worst is over already. As long as we're not personally affected, we'll be able to get through any difficulties[. . . .] Karl Weßlau

[EMILIE WESSLAU continues:]

Dear parents,

[4 ll.: correspondence; wishes] Here in America it looks like we can't expect anything good in the next few years, because there's still no hope of peace. The situation is still the same, the last lottery didn't affect any of our relatives, but now comes the next one. Food prices have tripled, clothing has gone up even more, but we still haven't suffered any want and are lucky to be so far away from where they're fighting, because everything there is being destroyed and burned, and even some of the rich have become beggars [11 ll.: details; her husband won't be writing: "he's not accustomed to it"; arson in New York hotels, allegedly by southerners].

Fondly, Emilie B.

[probably MARIE WESSLAU, Karl's wife, continues: 6 ll.: family; 30 ll.: a poem that begins:

> Memory, you gentle ray of sunshine,
> The heart of life doth measure.
> Upon our earth most precious wine,
> Our one and only—final treasure.]

KARL AND MARIE WESSLAU

New York, June 13, 1865

Dear parents,

[17 ll.: war has ended faster than expected; recruitment in New York City; enormous cost of the war] All in all, this war has been conducted with such violent emotions and such brutality that all the cruelty shown to Poland by the Russians pales in comparison. The rebels treated our prisoners so atrociously it borders on the unbelievable, almost 60,000 men died miserably, and those who were exchanged or freed at the end have only been rescued into a life of lingering infirmity. Only a few were murdered immediately, most of them had to slowly starve to death. So you can well imagine how often this was avenged, even though President Lincoln, with his gentle character, has forbidden retaliation [10 ll.: destruction caused by both armies in South Carolina; alleged rebel atrocities]. There has been a general amnesty for everyone except for the rebel president Jefferson Davis, who now has time to reflect upon matters in his lonely prison cell, and if they are magnanimous and let him escape the noose, that is more than he deserves.

It's hard to say what the effects of the war will be now, all the wealth of the South depends on the work of Negroes, and it's hard to tell to what extent they'll be willing to work if they aren't forced to [6 ll.: details; New York suffered no damage in the war]. Many people here have gotten rich quickly. During the war and because of the war, work was paid better than ever before, and it isn't very likely that wages will go down in the next few years. As far as our business goes, we did our best to make the most of the situation. At the beginning of the war we lost a lot of money, but in the last two years we've made up for our losses and more. Some of the outstanding bills of our southern customers that we had given up on have now been paid. Now we've taken some of our money out of the business and bought ourselves a house, 95 Attorny Street.[7] We're not living there now because it's not close enough to the workshop, and it doesn't bring in a lot of money either, but at least we can be sure we won't lose money on it. We'll probably buy another house soon that will bring in more. One of our friends, a sutler,* made such a fortune during the war that he wants to go back to Germany and live off his private income, and we want to buy his house [8 ll.: details; concern about his mother]. All my best wishes to everyone / Karl Weßlau

[MARIE WESSLAU continues:]

Dear parents,

[. . .] Yes, those were 4 difficult years. Many thousands of families bemoan and bewail their loved ones who fell on the battlefield or lost their lives miserably in the prison camps; life was a constant battle between fear and hope. The greatest concern was caused by the draft, the government demanded no more than 20,000 men from New Jork, and if the rebellion hadn't come to an end so quickly, it would have been safe to assume that every man, 18 to 40 years old, would have had to fight, because whoever drew a lot either had to go or provide a substitute (and you had to pay 800 to 1,000 dollars for one man for 3 years, and even then hardly anyone could be found)[. . . .] In the midst of the joy and triumph came the shattering news of the murder of Pres. Linkol [Lincoln] that had a terrible effect on everyone (I'll never forget the 15th of March [April] as long as I live). It was terribly sad to walk through the streets with all the flags on the public buildings at half-mast and almost all the buildings draped in black and white with all sorts of inspirational inscriptions. But the most impressive thing was the funeral procession (it cost 6,000 dollars just to build the funeral coach). I don't believe the death of any monarch has ever been as deeply mourned as that of <u>Pres. Linkol.</u>

[4 ll.: concern about her mother] Your / loving daughter / Marie Weßlau

JULIUS WESSLAU

New York, June 21st, 1865

Dear parents,

[4 ll.: correspondence; was spared from the draft] The war is finally over, and the power of the slaveholders has been completely destroyed, but the number of lives that it cost is beyond words, and the debts we are supposed to repay are most unpleasant and oppressive. For example, last year we sold about 40 thousand dollars worth of goods, and now we are supposed to report this and then we have to pay 6 percent in taxes, that's 2,400 dollars for the

---

7. Their house and workshop was on the East Side on Columbia Street, some 500 yards from the Williamsburg Bridge; Attorney Street ran parallel to it, about 500 yards to the west. In 1875 Julius moved to a house in a better part of town, on East 49th Street.

year. Anyone who doesn't agree that this is outrageous doesn't know the value of two thousand and four hundred dollars. If you don't report everything and it can be proved, then the tax collectors impose a fine of 10 to 20 thousand dollars without batting an eye, and a good many people we know have had to pay a hefty *Contribution*. In the four years of the war, there were a good many dramatic events, every morning you'd pick up the newspaper and read about things that could only happen in America, words can't describe the devastation, the furious hatred of the two sides, the heartbreak of relatives, the evilness of mankind. When the details come to light, mankind will look upon this tragedy with horror and unbelief. The movement of our armies was followed here with intense interest, and there were sad faces after a defeat and joy after every victory. Every day was like a holiday during the first half of April, but the rejoicing came to a sudden end on Good Friday, when the president was murdered by a rebel conspiracy. I can't begin to describe what a shattering effect this had here, and I have never seen or heard anything like what happened when his body was driven through New York, what an enormous procession it was in a metropolis like this, everyone was most deeply moved, and in the procession and in the entire city, with all its good and evil men, there was nothing but solemn silence. The rebellion is now over, but anyone who experienced it here will never forget it, just as we'll always remember the July riots in Neu York.—

[17 ll.: buying a house; income (see below)]

I remain / your loving son / J. Weßlau [. . .]

The last Wesslau letter in the collection is dated March 1, 1867. There is no reason to suspect that the brothers exaggerated their income or assets. In 1865 they bought one house in Manhattan for $6,000 and another for $16,800; in 1864 they earned $5,000; and they admitted, "people think we're rich, and maybe we are, if 40 thousand dollars means being rich. And if that's not enough, we hope to have more soon."[8] Karl Wesslau was listed in the New York City Directory until 1869, and Julius continued to be listed until 1894. Years earlier, however, Julius's two sons Albert and George had joined the business, and they not only expanded it (contracting, real estate), but they also continued to run it until World War II.[9]

8. This is confirmed by the 1870 census in which Julius listed $25,000 worth of property. This would put the brothers' joint worth at closer to $50,000, a twenty-fold increase since 1860. Letters of Julius Wesslau, June 21, 1865, March 1, 1867 (quotation), NABS; MC 1870: New York/N.Y., W. 13, e.d. 3, p. 110.

9. New York City CD. At age fifty-three, Julius was listed as retired in MC 1880: New York/N.Y., e.d. 538, p. 505D. His death is indicated by two real estate transactions of his executors that were reported in the *New York Times*, February 18, 1896, p. 15, and April 19, 1896, p. 14. One granddaughter married a Princeton graduate; another held her wedding at Delmonico's. *New York Times*, December 4, 1913, p. 9, June 9, 1916, p. 13.

4. Christoph Barthel, Anna-Katharina Odensaß, and Jacob Odensaß

It was probably the spring of 1847 when Christoph Barthel, a twenty-two-year-old Protestant cabinetmaker, immigrated to the United States, together with his younger brother, Johann Jost Barthel. They do not seem to have left Germany because they faced destitution or grinding poverty but rather because life in America offered hope of improving their economic situation. Their parents and brothers and sisters remained in Kirchhagen, a village near Kassel in Hesse. Shortly after their departure, their brother Heinrich took over the family farm, which prompted Christoph to ask for his share of the inheritance, so that he could set up his own business. By 1849 he had set up shop in Baltimore, Maryland, where many acquaintances from the Kassel area were living. However, he still appears as a cabinetmaker without property in the 1860 census.

Some time after 1850 their sister Anna-Katharina joined them, together with her husband, Jacob Odensaß, also of Kirchhagen. His mother-in-law had called Jacob a "good-for-nothing," and her daughter probably agreed. Their son Jacob, however, seems to have turned out well: he later supported his mother and wrote to the grandparents back in Kassel.[1]

The Barthel brothers must have been quite interested in politics. On March 17, 1848, Christoph and Johann Jost wrote that the newspapers had reported "that there is a great uprising in Germany, and France is already free, and all the Germans over here have decided to raise a large sum of money to send to the subjects, to help them hold out."[2] In 1863 Christoph and three other Germans organized a political club, the "Unionsverein," and he was characterized as "one of the most active German Republicans."[3]

JACOB ODENSASS

Baltimore, July 14th, 1861

Dear grandfather, godfather, godmother, and cousins,

[8 ll.: health] Dear relatives, I felt the urge to write to you once again, it may be the last time because our Promised Land is in a state of war, and it may turn out to be so for many years, though I definitely hope not. The rea-

SOURCE NOTE: Both Anna-Katharina Odensaß and her son Jacob are obviously not used to writing. The shape of their letters is very close to what their primer had prescribed; their capability of expressing themselves is quite restricted and their spelling erratic. One may conclude that their formal education stopped early, with little improvement afterward. Much the same can be said about Barthel, except that he must have done some writing after leaving school, and that his Hessian dialect is clearly recognizable in his phonetic spelling. Not included here are the letters in the series from before 1860 (three) and after 1865 (two), as well as one letter of 1863.

1. Information provided by the donor; letter of June 1863, NABS.
2. Letter of March 17, 1848, NABS.
3. Cunz (1948), 303–8. Several German Jews also figured prominently in this *Verein*.

son for this war is that the United States of N.A. have split up into the states with slavery and the states without slavery. The northern states are the ones without slavery, and the southern states are the ones with slavery.

This split happened because of the new election of the current *Presetent* [Lincoln] who got the majority in the northern states, and the northern states are against slavery and want to set all the slaves free, but naturally the southern states don't agree because of course they are their property, and that's why the southern states have left the Union to set up their own government and become independent, and now the northern states want to force them back into the Union, which is how the war came about.

I would have written to you earlier, but I failed to do so because we've been having such hard times in the last two years, and now it's reached rock bottom, with many thousands of people with no work and no food and there's nothing but starvation ahead for the winter [10 ll.: is working in a store for ten dollars a month].

When you get this letter and write back, which I really hope you'll do, then please write back as soon as you get this letter, because I don't know how long or how soon it'll be till they say—off to the battlefield.

(I also want to mention that Uncle Johann Bartel is in the army that's from Chicago, State of Illinois) [5 ll.: greetings] Jacob Odensaß

ANNA-KATHARINA ODENSASS

Baltimore County, December 12, 1864

Dear father and brothers and sisters,

Should this distant letter reach your eyes and find you well, I shall be most pleased. I am still well, thank the Lord.

Dear father, I wanted to let you know, although you may have already been aware of this, that Odensaß has been gone for a year, I cannot tell you if he is in the war or dead. I am living very happily here with my children, not a life of luxury, but Jakob is a big help [13 ll.: family].

Dear father, I don't have any particular news, except that the ongoing war continues to cause bloodshed and debts, according to the last calculation 1,740,690,489 dollars and 40 cents, or seventeen hundred and forty million, six hundred ninety thousand, four hundred sixty-nine dollars and 40 cents, and that father Abraham Linkoln, the *Presetent*, was elected for 4 more years on November 8, 1864. Also, my brother Christoph was elected a member of the legislature of the State of Maryland, which is a great honor to him and to all the Germans here, since he's the first German to hold this office [13 ll.: family; wishes; greetings; signature missing].

CHRISTOPH BARTHEL

[letterhead:] Legislature of Maryland, House of Delegates.

Annapolis, March 16, 1865

Dear father and brothers,

It has been a fairly long time since I last wrote, and I want to let you know about recent events.

I am presently sitting in the capitol building of the legislature of Maryland and writing this letter. I am the first German to have the honor of being elected to the Legislature of Maryland and, as you can well imagine, I am quite the envy of many people, due to this high and responsible position that I was elected to, by a majority of 6,000 votes in the 1st district of Baltimore,[4] because our name has become one of the most important and prominent ones among the Germans in Maryland, since I am the first German legislator of Maryland.

The calamitous *Repellion* is moving swiftly toward defeat, our fleet is now in command of all the ports. Genral Leutnand Grand [Grant], commander in chief of the whole army, is outside Richmond and is holding the rebel — General Lee in his iron grip, and General Sherman, the bold and unbeatable who since the fall has moved thousands of miles with his brave army through the heart of the rebellion, driving everything in front of him, is already on the other side of Richmond with a hundred thousand men, and thus our generals are moving in from all sides, and we have high hopes that the entire gang of thieves will soon be taken prisoner and the ringleaders hanged. They truly deserve this death, not just because of the horrible bloodbath and all they misery they have caused us, but also because of our prisoners whom they systematically starve to death. The men who survive prison camp and are exchanged and brought up here are nothing but skin and bones covered in a few filthy rags. The pen of history will balk at writing about all the cruelty and atrocious things these brutes have done to our prisoners. Although we have twice as many rebels in our prisons they haven't been mistreated in return, we treat them like humans according to generally recognized human rights [8 ll.: health; greetings; signature].

In 1880 Anna-Katharina Odensaß was seventy and living with her son Jacob and his family, who still lived in Baltimore even though he had become a farmer (in 1875 he bought thirty acres of land for $3,500).[5] Christoph Barthel died in 1885 in

4. The Republican candidate Barthel received 6,216 votes and his opponent less than 1,200 in the election of November 8, 1864. Governor (Election Returns) 1864, Baltimore City 1st District, Maryland StateA S108, MdHR 40, 132-2086, 2-50-1-29.

5. MC 1880: Baltimore/Md., e.d. 258, #65 and 66; letter of Anna-Katharina Odensaß, January 8, 1878, NABS.

Baltimore, after having worked not only as a cabinetmaker but also as an undertaker and saloonkeeper. In an obituary he was called "one of the best-known German American citizens of Baltimore," who had amassed a considerable fortune and taken on many honorary posts. Among other things, he was active in running the German orphanages and the German Workingmen's Sick Relief Union, and he was president of the German nursing home he had founded and generously supported throughout the years.[6]

6. Death certificate (copy in NABS); obituary in the *Baltimore Morning Star*, April 15, 1885.

5. Augustin Family

The Protestant tailor Albert Augustin (born ca. 1823) emigrated in the spring of 1857 from Mirow in the tiny state of Mecklenburg-Strelitz. The fact that he traveled second-class, not steerage, indicates that he was not completely without funds. His wife, Louise, also came from Mirow, and she must have emigrated shortly before or after Albert. They probably got married in the United States.

In 1860 the couple was running a saloon in Champaign, Illinois, and were listed as owning no property and only fifty dollars in cash assets. Shortly thereafter, their economic situation seems to have improved rapidly. The Augustins profited not only from economic recovery after the 1857 recession but also from the rapid growth of the town, starting in 1855 when a train station was built on the Illinois Central Railroad. German immigrants were probably not the main customers in the saloon: in 1860 only 11 percent of the residents in Champaign County were foreign-born, and only half of these were Germans.[1]

Champangen [Champaign] City / Champangen Conty / State of Illinois
Nord: Amerika
August 21, 1861
Death to the slave traders [handwritten "translation" of the letterhead]
Dear brother-in-law and all my brothers and sisters,
You've probably been wondering why we haven't written in such a long

SOURCE NOTE: The regular, legible, and almost elegant handwriting stands in stark contrast to the writer's handling of the language. The grammar is weak, the spelling bad, and the punctuation erratic. Thus, Albert Augustin seems to have enjoyed little schooling, but he is able to express what he wants to communicate clearly and in a lively, colorful fashion.

1. Information provided by the donor; HPL April 16, 1857; NYPL May 29, 1857; MC 1860: Champaign City, Champaign Co./Ill., #2628; USC 1860.1, 109; USC 1870.1, 307.

time. Our reasons have been good ones. Things have been going very badly for us here in this country, just like for thousands of our countrymen. Business has come to a standstill [18 ll.: recession; went hungry; had hardly any clothing] so why lure relatives over here, it doubles your trouble, 1st you lose your homeland, 2nd you can't speak the language, and then you come to a new country where even the most educated German is like a child in terms of the language and the customs. It's not easy to learn English, and it takes years to figure out all the tricks and traps in America. And so the Germans fall behind and stay there. I've studied day and night, and now I have the feeling I can speak English well enough and I'm familiar with the laws here and how they do business, but thousands of others, even though they've been here for 20 years, still have to take orders from coarse Irishmen and nasty Americans [18 ll.: people write home to Germany about their farms and homes, but they've really only got "wooden shacks" bought on credit; Germans often get cheated]. There's nothing worse than American moneylenders.

A horrible war has broken out between North and South America, and soldiers are being signed up every day to fight the South. There are 340,000 men in our army against the South, and there are a lot of German officers here, most of them Prussians. Almost everyone has been called to arms, God only knows how it will all turn out. We may all have to leave here, the enemy is 300 miles from this town where I live. If I should have to go fight or should die, please help my wife leave America, this I ask of you, your A. Augustin. But I don't think it will come to this, since there are still over 1 million good young able-bodied men in the United States. Many have died already, but every single citizen in America is willing to give his last drop of blood for freedom. Death and eternal damnation to the slave traders! I've seen it often enough how the poor slaves are sold away from their wives and children and beaten with a whip until their skin hangs in tatters.

Long live America's freedom, and may the slave traders be damned.

Enough of these remarks. I also want to tell you, my dears, how we're doing. We've been earning good money for a year now, and even have some to spare. I've given up my profession and we now have a saloon, our business is so good my dear wife and I have to work very hard from early in the morning until late at night. We started with the $50 you sent us, dear brother-in-law, and in the beginning we had lemonade, 1 *Box* of cigars, some cake and ½ *Berl* of Bavarian beer. Now I have 3 to 4 hundred dollars worth of goods in my house, liquor and cigars, all paid for, and a very nice saloon[. . . .] Our customers are almost entirely Americans, Louise speaks English pretty well and is a hard-working and clean saloonkeeper's wife. We've also built a small house where we live — its the custom here, you don't live in the same place you work [12 ll.: the first

Albert Augustin's letterhead, August 21, 1861, with a "translation" of its slogan.
(Dr. Gert Durchschlag)

two children died; daughter Rosa is in good health, as is Louise; offers to re-pay the fifty dollars; does his younger brother want to come over?]. Because if Louise had one of her brothers here, we'd do everything we could to help. Of course it'd have to be of his own free will. No one likes it here at first, but it's a big advantage if you have close relatives [44 ll.: details; family; photographs; greetings; signature; address].

[LOUISE AUGUSTIN continues:]

My dear brothers and sisters,

[21 ll.: wishes her brothers and sisters were in America; family; Rosa is six months old; greetings; signature]

The 1870 census gives a somewhat less optimistic picture of the Augustins' progress. Although still keeping a saloon, they listed only $400 of personal property and, despite talk of building a house, no real estate. Their daughter Rosa apparently did not survive childhood.[2] Ten years later, there was no trace of the family in the census.

2. MC 1870: Champaign City, Champaign Co./Ill., #526.

6. Corporal Robert Rossi

Emigrating had been quite a tradition in the Rossi family. Grandfather Guiseppe Rossi, who made optical instruments, left Como, Italy, to move to Stockholm. His son Joseph was the personal physician attending the Swedish royal family, but for reasons that are unclear, he was banished from Sweden in 1810 and then settled in Schwerin, the capital of Mecklenburg. His only son, Robert, was born there in 1831. Robert's father, private teachers, and the local secondary school all tried to educate him without any remarkable success, although Robert did manage to finish an apprenticeship as a clerk. He changed jobs frequently and then decided in 1858 to immigrate to America, "to come back in a few years hopefully as a millionaire."[1]

SOURCE NOTE: Rossi's position as company clerk shows at least that the officers of his company had confidence in his ability to write well in German and presumably fairly well in English. As to the former, his letters prove that this confidence was justified: spelling, punctuation, and grammar are impeccable, the vocabulary respectable, and no influence of his regional dialect can be traced in his High German. His handwriting looks irregular but betrays that he spends a considerable amount of time writing; similarly, his occasional attempts at being original in the handling of words and phrases do not really succeed, but he always gets his meaning across clearly. Not included here are the letters in the series from the time before 1860 (four) and after 1865 (eighteen), as well as two letters from 1860, one from 1861, and one from 1864.

1. Information provided by the donor; letter of Robert Rossi, July 10, 1858, NABS (quotation).

Robert Rossi.
(Dr. Friedhelm Zwickler)

It is unclear exactly why he joined the army. Perhaps it was because success still eluded him, but thirst for adventure or genuine idealistic fervor may also have played a role. On April 23, 1861, he signed up for two years as a volunteer in the German regiment commanded by Louis Blenker,* the 8th New York Infantry Volunteers. He became a bugler, and in September 1860 he was made a corporal, but as early as June 30, 1862, he resigned from the army on the grounds of nearsightedness.[2]

Camp Reach Mills, Aug. 6, 1861 / near Washington
My dear Elise,
    [4 ll.: birthday wishes] Fanny must have told you that I'm a soldier now, and she'll be sending you the letter I wrote to her. There isn't much chance

2. Muster Rolls, NatA, including medical certification of myopia.

to write letters here at camp, so I hope you don't mind getting news from me
like this.

[. . .] best wishes to Ludolph and you from your loving brother / <u>Robert</u>

Gooding's *farm* / in Virginia / December 8, 1861
My dear Elise,

[7 ll.: correspondence] The main thing is that I am doing very well, and
living in all this fresh air does me good. All my friends tell me that since I've
been in the army I've gotten much more hefty. I wanted to prove it to you with
a likeness taken in Washington, but it so happened [4 ll.: he gave it away]. I
sent one to Lina; when you go over there you can have a look at me dressed
up like a warrior! [5 ll.: correspondence] Anna is doing very well and wants
me to come see her in New York, which I shall do soon if it is possible. We've
been on picket duty for a week, but we're only supposed to be on the lookout, since the top general, as Blenker* told us recently, intends to wait until
the South attacks us, and if we wait for that to happen, I think we'll be waiting
for a long time. In our camp we have made preparations for the winter. We've
built a stove in almost every tent and since there is plenty of wood around,
we burn a lot of it to keep things warm[. . . .] Last week it was our Colonel
Wutschel's birthday and there was a small procession with torches and a sere-
nade in his honor. His wife came too and it was all very merry and pleasant.
He used to be the captain of our company and so we sent a delegation to con-
gratulate him, and I was one of them. He received us warmly and we quickly
drank several bottles of wine with him.[3] For a while now I've been earning a
few dollars on top of my pay by having the shop where I used to work send
me some goods that I sell again here at a small profit [4 ll.: wishes; greetings,
kisses]. from your loving brother / Robert / Corporal.

Camp Hunters Chapel, Virgin. / February 17th, 1862
My dear Elise,

[22 ll.: correspondence; weather; quiet Christmas celebrations] We made
punch both Christmas Eve and New Year's Eve and we spent the evening with
pleasant conversation and singing. On New Year's Eve at 12 o'clock we went
from tent to tent to wish everyone a Happy New Year, and we had a lot of
fun and didn't get to bed until around 3, all of us dutifully drunk[. . . .] In this
cold weather, the tents have become unpleasant in spite of the stoves we built,
so some of my closer friends and I decided to build a cabin, and we started
work on it immediately and have been living in it for quite a while. It is fitted

---

3. On Wutschel's drinking, see note 4.

out for 5 people: three beds made of thick twigs, with a table in the middle. Our guns, knapsacks, ammunition pouches, pipes and other useful things are hanging on the walls, and one of the walls has some shelves with our dishes, and there are newspapers, books, soap, cigar boxes—both full and empty— and the most useful thing of all, a small stove. It's so cozy in our little house that we're always glad to come back in even after a short absence. In the evening we read or play cards, sometimes we drink punch and while away the time as best we can. Since the weather has been so bad for so long, we don't have anything to do except our daily guard duty. I take care of the company's paperwork and don't have any other duties, but I often go along for drill and I always go along on outpost duty. All of the volunteer regiments will soon be suffering a heavy loss: a new law in Congress has determined that all the music corps will be eliminated since they cost too much money. You can well imagine how sad we are about this, since what good is the military without music? [19 ll.: war will probably be over soon; family; friends; greetings] and keep in fond remembrance / your loving brother / Robert

Hoboken, June 19th, 1863

Dear Elise,

[10 ll.: correspondence; birthday wishes] As you must have heard from Fanny, I was fortunate enough to be discharged from the army, and no one was happier than I was. On July 1 I left the regiment with two other friends who had the same good fortune, and I arrived safely in New York on the 3rd. You can well imagine how hard it was to leave so many friends and acquaintances, with whom I shared 14 months of toil, hunger, and travail as well as many a happy hour, but I took comfort in the hope that I would see them all again, which was indeed the case, since the entire regiment returned to N.Y. after their two years of duty. Neither my bride nor any of my friends knew anything about my return, and they were all most surprised and happy to see me again, uninjured. Anna was especially happy to have me back again. Even though I will never regret having been a soldier, nothing in the world could make me want to go through what I experienced again, and when a friend of mine says he wants to go, I advise against it as strongly as I can [23 ll.: a friend from his company is going to visit Elise in Berlin; photograph; greetings; signature].

Hoboken, October 18th, 1863

Dear Elise,

[35 ll.: family; got married August 1] The war is still going on, and there's no sign of things changing or getting any better[. . . .] In the last 2½ years that the war has now lasted, we have achieved little or nothing, except that the Mississippi is free[. . . .] It is at any rate the most peculiar war ever fought; instead of allowing the commanding officers to make the decisions, the men who ought to know best how to make this or that move, they receive their orders from Washington, and some of these orders are so absurd that any sensible person would know they are nonsense. Then, if they don't follow them, they are relieved of duty, no matter how capable they are (like, for example, Sigel,* Mc Clellan [George McClellan], Porter, etc.) and often they're replaced by people who know as much about military campaigns as a cow knows Spanish, but are willing tools of the administration. It's still like this, now for the third year, and it probably won't change until we have a new president (in two years' time) who will hopefully be a Democrat, because otherwise, things will just keep on like always! [10 ll.: friendly visit by European warships] Otherwise things here are very jolly, just like peacetime. Theater, concerts, and all the amusements are always crowded: everyone tries to have as good a time as possible [17 ll.: German theater; fiftieth anniversary celebrations in Leipzig (battle where allies defeated Napoleon); family]. Love and kisses from / your faithful brother / Robert

Hoboken, June 9th, 1864

My dear Elise,

[15 ll.: lives simply but is content; family] Some of the old members of the 8th Regiment have created a veteran's mutual aid association, called the Blenker*-Veterans' Association which I also belong to. Yesterday was the anniversary of the Battle of Cross-Keys where three years ago our regiment received its baptism of blood. This year the association held celebrations again, with speeches and singing, followed by dancing, and since the weather was so beautiful, the celebration went very well.[4] Now all hopes have been placed in the new commanding general Grant, who has had considerable good luck

---

4. It is not easy to understand how this battle could be commemorated with such festivities. At Cross Keys the regiment suffered almost half its casualties during its entire service: 43 dead and 143 wounded. This was primarily the fault of Colonel Francis Wutschel, who was obviously drunk and disregarded orders when he ordered the regiment to attack prematurely and in the face of heavy enemy fire. Afterward he reported sick and left his unit without leave. A few days later the officers in the regiment confronted him and offered him a choice: he could either resign or face court-martial proceedings. On June 18, 1862, the charge had been drawn up: the first specification referred to the fact that he was constantly drunk—the whole regiment called him a "boozer"—and the second was his having disobeyed orders to wait until the command to attack had been given. In the end, no court-martial was held, but Wutschel was dishonorably discharged on August 23, 1862. Attachment to Muster Rolls Francis Wutschel; Office of the Adjutant General 1862, W620, Box 154, RG 94, NatA. Also see Horstmann (no. 13), undated first letter.

in moving forward, driving the enemy back so that our troops are now said to be only a few miles from Richmond. [5 ll.: heavy losses; everyone hopes] that there will be peace soon so that the high prices we have to pay for everything will start to come down again. The war in Holstein seems to be almost over, judging from the news we've heard, and the whole world is anxious to see how the matter will be settled. Prussia and Austria will probably divide up the spoils [10 ll.: correspondence; greetings; signature].

Rossi and his wife Anna Pfeiffer from Cologne had four children; he died in New York in 1916. He worked as a bookseller, then became unemployed, and later worked for the post office, but he did persist in one thing—his applications for his veteran pension were always completed with meticulous care and imaginative creativity. He claimed that the war had not only caused him to become nearsighted but that he had also contracted rheumatism and malaria, leaving him permanently disabled in 1890. His efforts, however, were not particularly successful: when he died his pension only amounted to twenty-four dollars a month.[5]

5. Information provided by the donor; Pension File, NatA; letters written between December 19, 1864, and December 12, 1914, NABS.

7. Private Friedrich Schmalzried

Friedrich Schmalzried, born and baptized a Protestant in 1822, emigrated in the spring of 1849, together with his younger sister Katharina. He settled near Ann Arbor, Michigan, where his brother Conrad had taken up residence one year earlier. Nothing specific is known about their reasons for leaving Germany. Their father was quite a prosperous farmer in Münchingen near Stuttgart; the emigrants were able to take along several hundred guilders,* and they later inherited similar amounts of money. One plausible motive, given their circumstances, might have been a desire to buy land and improve their economic situation.

Conrad Schmalzried was obviously quite successful in this endeavor. In 1900 his five sons were living on debt-free farms in Carp Lake, Emmet County, in the northern tip of Michigan, and Conrad was living with the eldest. Katharina married and also seems to have had no regrets about emigrating. In 1853 Friedrich, however, had reportedly been ill for over a year, and in 1860 his father was distressed that he still

SOURCE NOTE: Schmalzried's handwriting looks like it is straight from a primer. It is very even, and he obviously does not write a lot. The spelling is clearly substandard, but his letters are still easy to read. His local Swabian dialect is less evident in his spelling than in his syntax. Not included here is one undated letter, as well as two letters from 1861.

had "no property" and was working as a "servant" for a wealthy German American farmer named Feldkamp in Saline, Washtenaw County, not far from where his brother and sister lived.[1]

The reasons why he volunteered in nearby Detroit on August 23, 1861, are fairly clear from his letter of September 10, 1861; political convictions do not seem to have played a role. He served in Company C, 1st Michigan Cavalry, a regiment with only a few German Americans.

Detroit, September 10, 1861

Dear friends,

I would be most delighted if my letter finds you in good health. I am also well, thank the Lord. You may well be angry at me that I've become a soldier now, but I wouldn't have done it if I hadn't been all alone, but after working for the *Farmers* by the year I was fed up with it, and business is down in these bad times. I've been breaking my back now for 5 years and know I've earned my wages honestly, but I was treated so rough and harsh it really hurt [4 ll.: details].[2] That made me sick of the whole thing, so I thought that if I'm so hardworking and decent and that's all the thanks I get, I might as well try this instead. It's not so bad here, they treat us right, and there's enough to eat and the pay is just as good as anywhere else[. . . .]

We don't know yet when we'll be moving out, we don't have any uniforms or anything. At any rate it'll take quite a while before we've learned enough to fight in a battle, and maybe by then the whole war will have dried up. Please send me some money—but only if you can really spare it. I only had a few dollars when I left, and it's tough to be here without any money, and we don't know yet when we're going to be paid.

[9 ll.: debts and outstanding payments]

Your brother / Friedrich Schmalzrid [14 ll.: address; will probably be in the camp for three more months; his brother should pick up his things at Feldkamp's]

1. Information provided by StdA Korntal-Münchingen; 1873 estate inventory of Friedrich Schmalzried Sr. and his first wife, StdA Korntal-Münchingen; MC 1900: Carp Lake, Emmet Co./Mich., e.d. 84, #156, 171–73; MC 1860: Washtenaw Co./Mich., Saline Twp., #593; letters by Friedrich Schmalzried Sr., November 20, 1853, June 5, 1854, January 30, 1858, January 4, 1861, NABS.

2. His employer, Feldkamp, was a thirty-year-old farmer who had emigrated from Prussia with his wife and two children. He also employed a sixteen-year-old serving girl and was quite well off: he possessed some $5,000 in property and assets. MC 1860: Washtenaw Co./Mich., Saline Twp., #593.

Camp Lyon, [September] 23, 186[1]

Dear brother and friends,

I received your letter on the 21st with the money and was very pleased indeed[. . . .] We get meals 3 times a day, and duties and drill aren't very strict, we still don't have any uniforms and the whole regiment has about 100 horses now, but they are kept out in the open and I haven't even touched them yet, I still don't know when we'll be leaving, some people say we're going to Waschington, others say Missouri, but no one knows anything definite. One thing is clear, though, it'll take at least 3 to 4 months before we're ready for battle, all [untrained] men and horses[. . . .] Commissioned as well as non-commissioned officers and soldiers, we all eat the same food from the same kitchen and sleep in the same camp. We're all equal here, and I also haven't heard a harsh word from anyone, everyone is very civilized[. . . .] I don't see why I shouldn't do my part to preserve the Union and freedom, if all these good-for-nothings do [33 ll.: has forgiven Feldkamp; family; advice on moral issues; pious exhortations; greetings; signature].

Camp Bradhent [Maryland], December 22, 1861

Dear friends and brothers and sisters,

I would be most delighted if my letter finds you in good health, I am also well, thank the Lord. I haven't been sick a day since I've become a soldier, and I hope the Lord will keep me in good health. We are here in a beautiful, healthy area about 2 miles *North* of Frederiktoun in Maryland. We're in General Bänks [Nathaniel P. Banks*] *Divission*, we left Washington on December 9 on horseback in true military style, and we camped for 4 nights out in the open. At night we made camp in the woods, and we tied our horses to the trees and made ourselves a nest out of leaves under a big tree, with our saddles as pillows and blankets and coats as covers, and a fire nearby. The food for the horses and for us followed behind us in wagons, we only had meals in the morning and in the evening, and then only hard bread and cold meat and lousy coffee—there were more than 60 wagons, each pulled by 6 mules and about 15 wagons with 2 or 4 horses. The whole column was 2 miles long, and on the last day our company was at the end[. . . .] We may be coming home soon—that's what everyone here seems to think—and at least we definitely believe we won't be getting into any battles. But who knows—I wish they'd fight a battle and put an end to things, even if I had to help. Staying in one place isn't any fun either, they keep us busy all day long. I don't know what to make of the whole business, the higher-ups don't have much determination, it's all humbug, all they want to do is stuff their own pockets—we get some, too, but not for free.

Headquarters ____ Reg't Co. C ____
Camp ____ 1861

With the hearts of the Patriotic
and the hands of the Brave,
we'll teach rebels to surrender.

Beginning of Friedrich Schmalzried's letter of November 11, 1861 (not included here), with a typical letterhead. Winfield Scott was general in chief of the Union army until November 1, 1861. (Michigan Historical Collection, University of Michigan, Ann Arbor)

[6 ll.: long horse ride] The next night the rebels found a hole where they could cross the *Riber*, and they wanted to get into our camp, because they thought we were still there and so they could do some shopping among our horses. There were about 800 rebels, but the soldiers who were posted there sent them home again in a hurry. Everywhere we go we hear we're the best-looking regiment that ever came through, at any rate our horses are quite good.

[11 ll.: family; friends] I can't complain here, it is really a strange life, but my superiors and comrades respect me fully, they all think I'm a good soldier and an honest man, no one treats me unfairly and that helps a lot.

[11 ll.: parade; wants to send a photograph] Maybe I'll have a chance soon, or maybe we'll come home ourselves soon, and then you can see all of me, although I don't look very nice because I haven't shaved since I left home [. . . .] It's so hard when they pass out so many letters to the men in the company and I have to go away empty-handed, and there's no one besides you that I can expect a letter from.

Best wishes to you all / I remain your faithful brother / Friedrich Schmalz-rid [6 ll.: correspondence]

Camp Bradhent, January 29, 1862

Dear brother and sisters,

I would be most delighted if my letter finds you in good health, I am also well, thank the Lord. Our soldier's life is really not very hard, because to be honest, we don't do anything at all. The normal duties we have here are feeding the horses and cooking for ourselves and chopping the wood we burn. The life of a soldier like we have here is the biggest humbug the world has ever seen, just so any *Humbuger* can stuff his own pockets. In any case I am quite content since we don't run any risk, though it wouldn't be much fun to go into battle with a regiment with horses like these, because most of them would either run off or fall into the hands of the enemy without our being able to stop them or to lead them when the shooting started [. . . .] A lot of our officers are gone, some have *Reseint* [resigned], some have left the army, and some are home on leave. Our colonel, our major and our captain have all gone home, but we certainly aren't pining for them—when you see men like that it makes you really proud to be a soldier. When we see our captain riding you can really see a true soldier, holding the reins in his left hand, the pommel with his right hand, with his mouth stuffed so full of tobacco that he chews on both sides and so on. They dragged us away from Detroit before we learned anything, and so now we move from one place to the next for no reason at all. We can't really complain because I've never had it so good since I came to America, but I think it's a sin to run up such costs.

[8 ll.: ready to march] Last week one company went off to catch deserters, there was one gone from our regiment, too, he sold his uniform and put on different clothes and got as far as Baltimor before he was caught [. . . .] 4 soldiers and a corporal from my company were sent to Frederig to get him, and I had to saddle my horse and send it along so that the first deserter from our regiment could be transported. I don't know yet what will happen to him, and I also don't know why he did it [15 ll.: should demand money from Feldkamp; hasn't shaved while a soldier; greetings; signature].

Waitplains [White Plains, Virginia] April 11, 1862

Dear brother,

I hope my letter finds you in good health. I was sick for a couple of days last week, my stomach was upset and I had a very bad time of it, but it's better now although I still feel a bit weak [. . . .] all my comrades did everything they could for me. It's really nice to know your comrades respect you [7 ll.: correspondence]. I still haven't seen any fighting yet. Our company ran into the rebels once, but they ran away. One man wasn't careful and got shot and later 7 others were taken prisoner, but it was entirely their own fault. I was with the major's escort in Winchester at the time, and it took me 5 days to get back to the company [. . . .] There's a rumor that much of the *Cavalry* will be disbanded since food for the horses is too hard to find. I hope it's true [12 ll.: friends; financial matters]. Friedrich Schmalzrid

Washington, June 10, 1862

Dear brother and friends,

[9 ll.: troop movements] We also did some hard marching and got close enough to the rebels, and so we gathered a large force together, and that sent Jaksan [Stonewall Jackson] off in another direction, so fast that he'll soon run out of breath. We feel quite good here, the beer tastes good, too. We're here to recover from all our hard work, and now we're resting on our laurels, but they're damned hard and when we don't get any hay or straw to put under them, our bones break [8 ll.: is sending a photograph; signature; correspondence].

Camp near Warronton [Warrenton] Virginien July 11, 1862

Dear brother,

[12 ll.: correspondence; ride from Washington to Fredericksburg and back] We had to escort 18 cannons, 150 extra horses, 150 wagons and 600 head of cattle from Washington to Warrenton, where we'll meet up with the rest of the regiment [. . . .] It will be a long time before this war is over. It's high time we had honest men as leaders instead of these traitors—it would be best if we had all the abolitionists as cannon fodder at Richmond, that would be the best thing for the country. *Nigger*[s] and nothing but *nigger*[s]—as soon as we're done here we're coming north, well armed, and we'll send the black abolitionists to the devil, along with their *Niger*[s].[3] They shouldn't think there's nothing but Republicans here in the army, not by a long shot[4] [5 ll. correspondence]. Friedrich Schmalzried

Camp near Washington / September 24, 1862

Dear brother,

[6 ll.: family] Things are in complete disorder in this regiment. The highest officer we have is the 3rd major, the colonel is dead, the lieutenant colonel has resigned, he's now a colonel in the 5th Cavalry, the first major was taken prisoner, the second wounded [4 ll.: Captain "Fischer" (James S. Fisher) wants to leave; First Lieutenant "Weh" (William Way)] then thought he'd be able to win all the laurels himself with his company, so he can become a major or something even better, but ever since we've been here in Washington he's been fishing around for a better-paid post, or maybe he's been in a whorehouse, but at least one thing is clear, they don't much like this *Pienuts Pedler* from Detroit.[5] He's only been in the camp once since we've been here [. . .] and then our 2nd lieutenant—now there's a real man. If his father weren't so rich he'd be too dumb to [approximately three-quarters of the page is torn off].

[7 ll.: cavalrymen without horses are digging trenches; approximately three-quarters of the page is torn off; correspondence]

Apuitang [Occoquan, Virginia] November 20, 1862

Dear brother,

[4 ll.: correspondence] There are only sick soldiers left in the camp, the others have all left. The first group is at the front near Culpepper, the 2nd near Aquitan, there's a *Cavallry Picket Lein* between the army and the *Infantry Picket Lein* near the fort on the Potomack. These pickets are there to catch deserters and stop all the *Contraband* [escaped slaves]. No one can pass our line unless they have a pass from General Heinzelman [Samuel Heintzelman]

---

3. Schmalzried uses the American epithet but treats it as a German word; italics indicate that the word (except its English plural) was taken over from the German original.

4. This attitude is not unusual for a Lutheran from rural Michigan, where the majority voted for the Democrats in 1860. Formisano (1971), esp. 180.

5. Captain James S. Fisher received his discharge on September 12, 1862; Captain William B. Way received his on November 12, 1862. *OAR*, 5:254.

or Mec Cleland [George McClellan]. We're on duty every 4 days, otherwise there's nothing for us to do. There are men from our regiment, from 1st Virginien and 2nd Pennßilvanien, we're all mixed up together, and the rest are being sent to various places, and a large number from my regiment have enlisted as regulars[. . . .]

We don't hear much about what is happening, but I wonder if they won't have had enough soon. I've already had enough for a long time. Michigan is and remains stupid, but the Republicans are making a big mistake if they think they've got the most in the army. When I get home again I'm going out into the wilderness so I don't have to see this humbug anymore. I've learned how to live there. Apples and cider are very hard to get here, but I wouldn't mind that if I could only get hold of some tobacco [17 ll. was ill; needs ten dollars because he has not been paid; greetings; signature].

> Camp near Wolf run schom [Wolf Run Shoals,
> Prince William County, Virginia]
> January 31, 1863

Dear brother,

I received your letter and was pleased to hear that you are well, I am also well, thank the Lord, but what upsets me the most is that father knows I am a soldier. He knows all about the soldier's life, and so he worries a lot, even though you can die in an accident at home [12 ll.: little hope the war will end soon; regiment]. That crummy old fogy of a colonel reported more than twice the number than we really have for the simple reason that he wants to stay in his *Ofes* [office]. When they find out the right number of able-bodied men we have, we won't have a major as a commander any more, you have to have 600 men and we don't even have 300, although there are some others who are of no use and never will be of any use, and our new doctor sends these idlers home as fast as he can. The old doctor kept them on in our new colonel's personal guard since they still counted then, but it won't be long before this humbug is found out, since every week one or more of them leaves. Since we've been here we've had 4 dead, 5 wounded, and I don't know how many sick, and it's like this at all the camps. It's not an unhealthy place—everyone looks as healthy as possible. I haven't seen any *Rebs* since I've been here—two of the wounded shot themselves[. . . .] I'd like to read the letter from Germany, but everything gets lost here. If I get home safely maybe I'll go to Germany—I don't want to become a *Jänke*, it's not such a proud thing to be a *Jänke*, they don't have much to recommend them, they're best suited to a loud fair together with a bull or a sheep [3 ll.: greetings; signature].

My horse is black with three white pasterns. He'll be 6 years old next spring and was sired in Redford, 13 miles from Detroit, at Conrad Ziegler's, from Kur-Hesse. I like him so much because he is German through and through — he doesn't like the *Jänge* either, and when one gets too close, he knocks him down with his long hind legs.

Anaples [Annapolis, Maryland]
February 22, 1863

Dear brother,

[. . .] I am well, thank the Lord, but I had bad times last week — the *Rebs* got their hands on me. On the 17th we went scouting from Union Mill to Brensville 50 men strong, and 3 miles this side of Brensville we split up into 3 groups.[6] One was to go to Wolfranschoh [Wolf Run Shoals], but they fell into a trap and 9 men and 1 lieutenant were captured. The other two groups took two different routes to Brensville, and all was quiet there, but after we'd gone 2 miles on our way back there they were lying in the thick low pines, and we had to go through a narrow pass. They let the vanguard and half the *Callum* through, then they started firing at us. The ones who were lucky enough to be in the front got through, and the *Rebs* lost 1 man, and we had 1 dead and 2 wounded, and our *Coward* of a captain was off and away — if he'd been a man he'd have turned back and not a single *Rebbel* would have gotten away from us, but there was no officer in sight. I was in the back letting my horse have something to drink, and when the firing started I was behind the *Rebs* and I wanted to ride through the woods behind them, and then I got knocked out of my saddle by a branch. My horse went wild because he was not with the other horses and heard the shooting. If I had gone 4 rods [approximately twenty yards] farther then I'd have been over a *Fenz* and the *Rebs* wouldn't have been able to follow me, but before I could get back up, a rebel was standing 10 feet away from me with a cocked pistol, and he called out to me to stop, and since any further resistance would have been pointless, I let go of my horse, and he ran off after the others like a shot. Six of our group were taken prisoner. The rebels put us up behind them on their horses, and we had to ride 25 miles to their camp. We were there for 2 days, the next day we went to Gordensville, the next day to Richmont on the train, then 3 days in Richmond, and now we're in Annaplis. I don't know how long we'll be here or where we'll be moved to. We've been treated well by the rebels wherever we've been, and they say we won't be *exschänt* [exchanged; see parole*] for 3 months. Don't answer until I write again, which I'll do as soon as I can send you the address.

All the best to you all / I remain your brother / Friedrich Schmalzrid

---

6. Union Mills and Brentsville, both in Prince William County, Virginia.

Annapolis, March 4, 1863. / Parolt [parole*] Camp

Dear brother,

[. . .] I really wish I could come home, and maybe I'll be able to, we're still waiting. They say the old parolees will be sent back to their own states. If this is the case then it would be very easy. This is the most miserable life I have ever seen, there are more than 3,000 men in the camp, some have been here almost 6 months. The people just lie around, no use to God and the world, they have nothing to do but cook their food and gather wood all day long. When the weather's nice they walk up and down alone or in groups and at night there's usually a *Feigt* [fight]. Then it's best to stay in your *Tent*. That's what happened last night—one man went out of his tent, he was so sick he could hardly talk, and then a *Rowdy* knocked him down and took away his *Revolver*, and then there was an uproar and the fellow fled into a *Tent*. Then they pulled him out of the *Tent* and there was great commotion. Then they found a *Suttler* [sutler*] *schop* where they found some whiskey, and they ripped it down and then it was such an awful mess that the guards turned out on horseback—several shots were fired and the poor cavalrymen were chased off. [5 ll.: friends] Since they're always threatening with the draft, I'm glad I enlisted so long ago, because I think I've survived the worst, and I wouldn't want to be in the *Infantry* for all the money in the world. I would much prefer to take up arms again, though, than be forced to lay them down, because if our men were to seriously get down to business, they could really accomplish something now. I've often heard the officers and soldiers there say how sick of this war they are. We were in their [the Confederates'] camp for 2 days, and we could clearly see what it's like, they only get flour and plain raw meat and not enough of either, and on top of that they have to cook themselves. Most of them have bad tents and poor clothing, the horses are in a miserable state and many don't even have one. If our heroes didn't send them fresh ones occasionally, since because of our stupidity and inexperience they get a good many horses and weapons, and if this weren't the case, I think the cavalry would collapse [17 ll.: correspondence; complains that he does not get any letters; greetings; signature].

Annapolis Camp Parolt, April 7, 1863

Dear brother and friends,

[. . .] I am also well, thank the Lord. I have a bad finger, there is some sort of worm inside, it hurts and always gets in the way [4 ll.: correspondence]. You may be expecting me to come home, but I don't think this will be the case. First of all, there's no *Furloh* here. You can get away, in fact it's easy to get away from here, but then it's a long way and you're always in danger of being picked up because the *Oder* [orders] are much stricter than they used to be, now that there's the draft. If one of those bastards were to give me any trouble,

I'd snuff out his life, because I hate those cowards more than an armed rebel, and then again it'd cost a lot of money and I'd have to come back. Much as I long to come home, I wish it was all over because when I come home, I want to stay there. Some get through safely and some get caught and get stuck in Fort MecHenry.[7] That's a worse hole than Lippi[8] in Richmond [27 ll.: boredom; no word about release; friends; address; greetings; signature].

Parolt Camp Annapolis / May 9, 1863

Dear brother,

[4 ll.: finger still painful] As far as I know we've been *Exchangt* too, though we're still here at the moment, and I can't say when we'll be leaving. The infantry had to go to Annapolis yesterday to guard rebel prisoners. I don't know what will happen to us. I only know one thing—if I'm still alive and well, I'll be coming home in 15 months [14 ll.: would rather be with his regiment—boredom; greetings; signature].

Fairfäx Court Hauß / May 19, 1863

Dear brother,

[. . .] Yesterday I got back to the regiment. Many are still back in Michigan, but they'll be returning soon. I can't do any duty yet[. . . .] I don't have a gun or a horse, just a bad finger, but I'm not in any great rush. I'm taking it easy. Things here are much the same, but instead of *Picket Guard* they have *Camp Guard* drill, *Inspekschen Dres Parade*, and the like. Last night I went along, too, and wanted to see a *Dreß Parade* again [23 ll.: details; needs a saddle and a bridle; greetings; signature].

A short time later, Friedrich Schmalzried was admitted to Mt. Pleasant Military Hospital in Washington. According to the casualty sheet, he died of diarrhea on June 28, 1863. And on that same day, Brigadier General George A. Custer (up until that time only a captain!), who later achieved such tragic fame in the West, took command of the 2nd Brigade, 3rd Division, to which Schmalzried's unit belonged.[9]

7. Fort McHenry near Baltimore, used as a prison by the Union army.

8. Libby Prison, notorious prison for Union officers in Richmond.

9. Casualty Sheet, June 28, 1863, Muster Rolls, NatA; Utley (1988), 21–22. In a letter of September 29, 1863, NABS, Friedrich Schmalzried Sr. wrote from Münchingen: "When I was reading the letter, I knew you had sad news to tell, and then I had to weep and could read no further. I had to cry out—oh, Friz! Did he have to lose his life in the war in America? If only he hadn't volunteered, he wouldn't have been to blame, but now it has happened, it is like what he himself wrote, that not even one hair may fall from our heads unless it be the will of God"; and "Dear Konrad, you must make sure we receive a death certificate, otherwise his property will not be released until he would have turned 70. They won't accept your letter. I think it has to come from the regiment or the hospital."

8. First Lieutenant Alphons Richter

The son of a lawyer and Prussian civil servant, Alphons Richter was born in 1836 in Neu-Berun, near Pleß (Silesia), attended school in Leobschütz, and began university studies (in Breslau?) together with his older brother, Edwin. Soon deep in debt, the two decided to emigrate, breaking into their father's desk to get the money they needed. Edwin became an officer in the English army and fell in the Crimean War. On March 1, 1857, Alphons sailed from Hamburg on the *Sir Isaac Newton*, bound for New York. In the passenger list he appears as a "clerk," and he arrived on April 24.

For the next four years, he worked as a sailor on American whaling ships, rounding the globe once via Cape of Good Hope and Cape Horn before heading back to New York. When he was unable to find a job to his liking, his solution was to join the 56th Infantry Volunteers, from Newburg, New York. He enlisted in June 1861, and in November the regiment marched off to Washington.[1]

Newburgh, August 4, 1861

Dear parents and sisters,

[. . .] But in these times of war I found no opportunity to secure a good position on a German ship[. . . .] I am courageously pursuing my goal of becoming a man, and since my ambition gives me no respite, I hope to satisfy it soon with a better position than the one I now hold.

I have enlisted in the American 10th Legion[2] for the duration of the war. I've been named 1st sergeant of the whole company and have been promised a promotion to lieutenant when we go to the theater of war. My path to glory is clear, and, with God's help, I want to follow it bravely. My motto is "either live or die like the son of good and righteous parents."

For the next two months, our camp will be in Newburg on the Hudson

SOURCE NOTE: It is not surprising that an educated young man who grew up in an upper-middle-class home writes German that is clear, correctly spelled, and free from local dialect influence. It is quite remarkable, however, that after only five years in the United States, there is such massive interference from English—not only technical terms, for which there are perfect German equivalents, but also basic conjunctions and prepositions. He uses, for example, "*wann*" ("when?") instead of "*als*" ("when"), or "*auf*" instead of "*von*," probably due to the fact that "*auf*" sounds so much like "of." Not included here are the letters in the series from the time after 1865 (nine) and the letter of November 20, 1862. For this series only transcripts of the original letters are available, but there are clear indications that the transcriber conscientiously avoided making any changes.

1. Information provided by the donor; NYPL, March 24, 1857; Muster Rolls, NatA; Pension File, NatA; *OAR*, 2:507.

2. Nickname of the 56 N.Y. Inf; only a few German names are listed in the unit. Dyer (1959 [1908]), 1425; *OAR*, 2:506–7.

River [32 ll.: correspondence; has no money for a birthday present for his father; has forgotten his German; address; signature].

                    Camp Newburgh, October 30 / 1861 / near Washington

Dear parents and sisters,

[. . .] Oh, how gladly would I rush home if I could. But I have raised my hand in oath to the laws of the Northern American States and I will remain true to my oath.

When this letter reaches you, I will be in the midst of battle. We have met the enemy and driven him back twice. He did not dare resist our fire. This skirmish led to my being made a lieutenant. I am sending you my portrait. I had it made after I received my sash and my saber. My new uniform wasn't finished yet. This is why I had it made in my sergeant's uniform.[3] [18 ll.: asks that letters be sent to Julius Goldberger in Brooklyn, who will forward them; family]

On my birthday, think of your son, who will do everything in his power to once again become your good son / Alphons Richter

                                        Washington, January 14, 1862

Dear parents,

[7 ll.: correspondence] My fever has abated, and I must report to you about my life.

The reason for my illness is the following:

On about Dec. 10 we marched toward the enemy camp. In the first attack, our right flank was pushed back, and I was on the left. The order then was issued that our regiment was to send out a company as skirmishers, and our company was to be used for this. The captain was commanding the 1st, and I the 2nd *Platone* because the 1st lieutenant had been shot. This command was gratifying for us, although the enemy pressed us hard. We bravely fought our way through the front line of the enemy's right flank. We then thought we had done our good deed for the day and we could rest a bit, but then we were called back to the regiment and told we were to storm the enemy camp, which was heavily defended by artillery. But I'll cut this short, since I think you won't find talk of killing and the dead at all amusing.

While we were in the midst of doing the job and confident of victory, we were attacked again by fresh new cavalry regiments, and 2 of them proved to

3. In fact, according to the records, Richter first served as a second lieutenant in May and June the following year, and he was officially promoted on October 3, 1862. On December 1, 1861, while still a first sergeant, he was reduced to the rank of private and sentenced to sixteen days of extra duty as a carpenter. Muster Rolls, NatA.

be a tough job for me [4 ll.: details]. But I did get a good gash on my forehead above my left eye. I collapsed from exhaustion and losing so much blood so quickly. After receiving a lot of friendly kicks from both horses and men, I lost consciousness, and when I awoke on about December 25th, I was in the hospital in Washington.

We won the battle, and so I can tolerate my illness better than if this were not the case[4] [35 ll.: family; weather; signature].

DIARY ENTRY[5]

On February 19, 1862 came the good news of the first and a significant Union victory, the seizure of the largest and strongest fortress in the South, Fort Donalson [Donelson].[6] There was great excitement all through the camp: bands were playing, cannons, pistols and rifles were shot off, and the soldiers were shouting hurrah till late at night. All the windows in our barracks were lit up brightly, and outside there were victory fires, made of old barrels and tar, burning all night.

With this great victory, hopes have risen among all unionists that this war, which has been so disastrous for America, will be over soon. I, too, share these hopes, although I am quite content with my current lot, because I won't be able to stay in the army in America.

New-Port News / York / Yorktown / Fortress Monroe / April 21, 1862
Dear parents,

I want to write a short note to let you know that I have not yet been shot dead, and I am hale and hearty again. The *Rebels* have once again sent me greetings in the form of their bullets, and I have replied in kind with the same bravery as before my injury. I have rejoined the 56th Regiment,[7] and since there were no officer posts available, I have had to make do with the rank of sergeant again, but only for a short time. Since our captain has left, and the colonel is <u>very</u> kindly disposed toward me, I will be an officer again before this letter reaches you [29 ll.: entrenchments; fighting; greetings; signature].

4. In the Muster Rolls, NatA, there is no mention of the fact that he was wounded; in the official documents there is no record of the skirmish or the death of a lieutenant. Dyer (1959 [1908]), 1425; *OAR*, 2:507.

5. A copy of the diary was sent to the parents together with the letter of November 20, 1862 (not included). In diary entries abridgments are only indicated when cuts have been made *within* a text printed here.

6. This victory on February 16, 1862, was important, but his superlatives are unjustified.

7. There is no record of his resignation or reenlistment.

DIARY ENTRY

Bloody Battle of Fair-Oaks
on May 30 [31], 1862

Due to an enemy cavalry attack, my friend Becker got cut off from our regiment and fell into the ranks—as I later learned—of the 55th Regiment, mostly Germans. They were completely surrounded, but they fought their way through with courage and joined us the following day. I had given him up for dead and wanted to send some men onto the battlefield to look for him among the dead and wounded when to my great joy I saw him coming toward me and we embraced.

DIARY ENTRY

[June 16, 1862]

The last thing our troops did before leaving Savage-Station was remarkable:

As soon as General Williams realized it would be impossible to save all the *Amunition* and *Baggage*, he gave orders that everything our men couldn't transport should be destroyed. The lieutenant who had to carry out the order loaded a train with all the shells and *Baggage*, set fire to it and sent the train down the track at full steam without an engineer.

The sight was magnificent: the powder and shells exploded as the locomotive raced along with incredible speed. The bridge across the river had been burned down, and the whole train plunged headfirst into the water. The locomotive exploded with a horrible thunderous crash, killing and wounding many of the rebels—I've never seen anything more marvelous!

DIARY ENTRY

Yorktown, September 6, 1862

I simply cannot believe how long this war is lasting. The government is getting 600,000 more men, and when we have more, I think, the outcome of the war will be clear. I must admit that despite all the troubles and hardship I have survived, I feel quite good. Oh, when I look back and remember all the dangers I have safely survived, shivers run through my bones, and my heart sinks when I think of all the handsome young men I have commanded, leading them on with high hopes of victory, and then after the battle was won, seeing them lying there dead and stiff all around me, never to wake again. Their last thoughts were always of home, their parents, brothers and sisters or wives. They never complained, speaking only the words: "Lieutenant, when you tell my wife (sister or parents) of my death, tell them I died for my country as a brave man, not one with a cowardly heart!"

I've had to write several of these death notices, and it was horrible to read the answers from a loving wife or parent, their concern and worry about their husband or son, and yet at the same time their pride that he had died a brave man, defending his country.

My friend Carl [Becker] and I have safely come through all the turmoil. A few times I was quite sick with colds and fever, and then I realized what a true friend Carl was. Under his care, I recovered more quickly than with the doctor's medicine. Now we've put up a small tent together and pass the time with conversation, enjoying the peace and quiet we've been lacking for so long. We get our rations raw, go hunting, and cook and prepare our own food to our own liking. We take turns cooking and washing our pots ourselves, one does the cooking and the other goes fishing or hunting. That is, when we have the time for it, which is not the case for me at all now that I have command of the company[8] because the captain lies wounded at home and the 1st lieutenant left to recruit more soldiers for us [64 ll.: details. September 14: describes the geography of Virginia, farming, fauna]. On our forays we found all the beautiful, large plantations had been abandoned by their white owners, here and there we found a few white residents, but many blacks. I had read about the blacks, but I'd never been able to imagine how slaves were treated, but now I've had unbelievably horrible experience with it.

One mother told us that 14 days before we came to the plantation, her master had sold her two children—and to different buyers: the daughter, 18 years old, for 800 talers,* the son, aged 22, for 1,200. Women are usually more expensive, if they're strong and healthy, than the men are. Marriage between slaves is unthinkable—the master just picks a girl and a boy from whom he expects numerous and healthy offspring and gives them a hut to live in as man and wife, and when he doesn't need the man anymore, he sells him and the girl has to live with someone else.

[54 ll.: describes an episode where Carl Becker, together with ten men, was searching a plantation for weapons—with no success; a "Creole girl" disclosed their location, was whipped after the soldiers left, her younger brother came to ask for help; Becker and his men returned and destroyed everything except what belonged to the slaves, burned the house, and took the plantation owner and his wife into custody]

The general was seized with anger when he heard the truth, and he sent the couple to the fort as punishment. Karl was praised for his behavior and good deed.

8. Not mentioned in the official records. In March 1863 and from June 7, 1863, to April 1864 he officially commanded Comp B as a first lieutenant, and in March and April 1864 he was also the regimental adjutant.

Oh, humanity! What has become of you in a country endowed by nature with such blessings!

We are truly glad to be fighting for the side that is trying to put an end to all these cruelties and destroy the slave trade.

Yorktown, October 11, 1862

Dear parents and sisters,

[51 ll.: correspondence; wants to come home for a visit after the war; repetition] We'll probably have peace soon, since the *Rebels* can't hold out much longer. They have very little to eat and almost no winter clothing. All the soldiers they could get are already in the army, whereas the North can send another ½ million into the field[. . . .] I don't care at all what happens. I am hale and hearty and ready for a *Fithing* battle anytime. But oh, with what sublime feelings would I go into battle, if I could draw my sword in defense of my own fatherland.

Day before yesterday I was in a hospital in Alexandria. What a terrible but also beautiful sight, to see 20,000 wounded soldiers lying there; one man without legs, the next without hands, yet another without ears and so on. But almost no one complains. If you ask someone: "What will you do after the war without a foot or an arm?" he answers laconically: "*Uncle Sam will provide for my!*" i.e. "The government will feed me." Everyone is willing to give his life to defend the country because he knows he'll be well taken care of in case of injury.

[23 ll.: correspondence; birthday wishes] Best regards from Charles, even though you don't know him personally. He is a flag bearer in my company, and I couldn't have found a better and braver man and friend among all the Germans in America. His mother can be proud to have such a son. May God grant that we can both come home for a visit together.

I wonder if any of my fellow pupils in Germany are already officers. I think they could earn a couple of epaulets quite quickly here, although not by studying hard but due to their actions, their honesty and courage [9 ll.: greetings; signature].

DIARY ENTRY

Yorktown, November 10, 1862

Our regiment was sent out immediately to see how strong the enemy was and if we couldn't dislodge them. My company, which is the left wing company, had to go out as *Skirmishers*, and we were bravely making our way through the woods when we suddenly came to a clearing and were attacked by enemy cavalry [. . . .] we had resisted the attack for 15 minutes, when our regiment rushed to our aid and the enemy took flight. I captured a captain, a lieutenant and a sergeant and two privates. Bullets from the enemy carbines came very close, but even though they tried, none of them could do me any harm with their sabers, because my men, who are all most kindly disposed toward me, gathered round me like a band of young lions and tigers and bravely defended me.

Port Royal in Süd-Carolina [. . .] January 30, 1863
[salutation missing]
[12 ll.: correspondence] On October 3rd, 1862, I was made 1st lieutenant, and in my next letter I will send you my picture and my commissions as a lieutenant, that is, if I come through this business safely [28 ll.: family; greetings; signature; address].

Island of St. Helena. Hilton Head / Süd-Karolina, March 2, 1863
Dearly beloved parents and sisters,
[43 ll.: correspondence; war] Charles and I live a rather isolated life. My socializing is almost completely restricted to him[9] because I am the only German lieutenant in the regiment and many are not well disposed toward me since I have passed them in advancement. My commission as 1st lieutenant has been backdated by the colonel to October 3rd.[10] In this manner I have passed by the others—me, the 4th lieutenant in the regiment! When 3 more have been promoted to captain, then my chances of a higher position are good. Charles and I, whenever possible, always go on *Picket* or guard duty together. Or, when we're not on duty, we go out in groups of 12, armed with pistols, to hunt alligators and snakes. There are large numbers of these here.

We don't have much to eat and we're living hand to mouth, because since we've been shipped around so often, things are all topsy-turvy. We haven't been paid now for 6 months because of being moved around all the time, and so we have to live on credit. My pay is 50 dollars a month, which is usually just

9. Carl Becker's mother wrote to Alphons Richter's mother: "Dear Madam, On the 5th of this month I received a dear letter and diary from my son in America, and I wanted to fulfill the wishes of our sons that I write to you. I am happy beyond words that our sons are helping each other like brothers in these difficult times that have been imposed upon them in order to improve their character and that have had the effect of teaching them the error of their ways. I also trust in God that we may see them again [. . . .] I have long forgiven him for the anguish he caused me [. . . .] I remain respectfully / yours very truly / Caroline Becker / née Humbert-Droz / Carolath, January 11 / 1863." NABS.

10. In fact he was promoted to first lieutenant on December 13, 1862, after having become a second lieutenant on October 3, 1862. It was common practice to backdate commissions. Muster Rolls, NatA.

enough to get by on since clothing for officers and food is horribly expensive [45 ll.: his savings have suffered because all of Carl's money was stolen and they had to buy food; war situation; greetings; signature].

Rockville City / S.C. May 28, 1863

Dearly beloved parents,

[26 ll.: correspondence; family] I have read in the newspapers that the Poles have risen up again to shake off the Russians. I hope they gain their freedom, the best right a nation can fight for. If Prussia moves against Russia, I wish I could have a hand in some battles for the well-being of my fatherland. Please write to me, dear Papa, and let me know if I can come home, even if only for a short time, without being bothered by the military authorities.[11]

I'm sending you my commission as a 2nd lieutenant. I have to keep my commission as 1st lieutenant here until I receive a higher one [55 ll.: fighting; has fallen off his horse and sprained his arm; fall of Vicksburg*; greetings; signature; address].

On May 29, 1864, First Lieutenant Richter was discharged as unfit for duty on the grounds of poor health, and he then set off with his friend Becker to look for gold in California. On his way back to Germany, according to his own report, his "friend" robbed him of all his money, and because of circumstances connected with the case, the authorities were looking for him. Using a false name, Richter fled to Texas, where in 1868 he married Elisabeth Phillips, a Scots-Irish sharecropper's daughter who was a single mother. The couple had seven children, and Richter worked as a day laborer, then as a tenant farmer, and probably as a farmer with a few acres of his own.[12] Up to the turn of the twentieth century he continued to complain about his poverty in letters to his parents and sisters, and he frequently begged for money — not always without success. Due to various afflictions caused by his military service (hemorrhoids, kidney and back problems) he received a modest pension: in 1870, twelve dollars a month, after 1875, twenty dollars, and finally thirty dollars at the end of his life. He died in 1929, after many years of needing nursing care, without a penny to his name.[13]

11. According to his emigration permission from Oppeln, July 25, 1857, Alphons Richter had lost his Prussian citizenship "due to emigration to America" (copy in NABS).

12. MC 1870: Lamar Co./Tex., Paris Pct. 3, #650 (wife); MC 1900: Johnson Co./Tex., Pct. 6, e.d. 65, p. 56; MC 1910: Johnson Co./Tex., Justice Pct. 6, e.d. 59, p. 56; MC 1920: Johnson Co./Tex., Justice Pct. 1, e.d. 34, p. 15B.

13. Information provided by the donor; letters from 1872 to 1904, copies in NABS; Pension File, NatA.

9. Corporal Wilhelm Albrecht

Wilhelm Albrecht was twenty-seven years old when he left Hamburg in early July 1861, on board the sailing ship *Louis Napoleon*. After an unusually long voyage, he landed in New York at the end of August and enlisted almost immediately in the Union army. It is quite possible that he had planned to join the army even before he left Europe: a barber by trade but apparently not by vocation, he had already served for longer than the required period in the Mecklenburg-Schwerin army, some 3,500 strong, and had become a sergeant. His letters certainly indicate that he was familiar with the craft of war and at times even relished it.[1] His almost exclusively German American artillery unit was deployed in Maryland, Virginia, and West Virginia, and during the entire war the unit lost a total of eighteen men (no officers)—seven killed by the enemy and eleven by disease.[2]

Albrecht grew up in Schwerin as the son of a master tailor, and it is highly unlikely that he had any secondary education, although his writing style, spelling, and handwriting indicate that he might have had some. At home in Schwerin, he left six brothers and sisters, all but one of them younger than he was. His letters are addressed to his siblings; in 1861 his parents were no longer alive.[3]

[May 1863]

[salutation missing]

Since I can't give you a detailed account of my brief but eventful time here in America, this excerpt from my diary may give you at least a superficial impression [93 ll.: sea voyage]. When we had entered Long Island Sound, a steamboat soon arrived which brought us quickly into New York harbor, and half an hour later we had landed in Castle Garden, a reception building for immigrants. After I had gotten my bearings a bit I looked around for a good opportunity, and there was no lack of that at the time, for as soon as you set foot in the country the recruiters come at you from all sides. Since

SOURCE NOTE: Albrecht is one of the unusual cases where the discrepancy between the degree of formal education and the quality of language is remarkable. This barber and soldier is most unlikely to have received more than an elementary education, but his German is that of a university graduate. In his regular and very tiny handwriting, he uses language that is not only impeccable in every respect but also highly sophisticated in terms of allusions and nuances—although his rather complicated and lengthy sentence constructions do not make for easy reading.

1. HPL, June 5, 1861; NYPL, August 27, 1861. He is clearly the same "noncommissioned officer Albrecht" listed in the Schwerin address books of 1859 and 1860 and the "Sergeant Albrecht" of the 1861 edition, residing at Werderstraße 135.

2. At first Baty B, 1 Batn, N.Y. LArt (also called Brickel's 1 Batn German LArt), after March 16, 1863, renamed 30 Baty N.Y. LArt; Dyer (1959 [1908]), 1387–88, 1402.

3. Information provided by the donor as well as Mecklenburgisches LHA Schwerin.

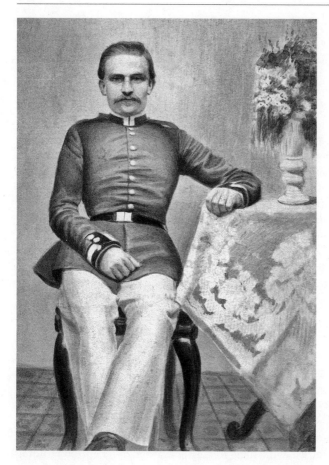

Wilhelm Albrecht.
(F. F. Brockmüller)

I didn't know the slightest thing about American recruiting tricks, I did the same thing as so many others, and I made a mistake. I signed up in a regiment that, as I unfortunately found out later, didn't suit me at all. There was no talk of bounties anywhere here, and if they had been promised to some of the soldiers here, they never received one. This regiment consisted mostly of Americans and Irishmen, which is why I didn't like it. They had wanted to promote me, and did in fact do so, against my own wishes, but since I couldn't speak English I didn't want to have a position of responsibility.[4] I didn't want this

4. Having arrived in New York on August 27 (NYPL), he signed on with the 59 N.Y. Inf only three days later, on August 30, 1861. By the end of October he had been transferred from Comp D to Comp C, so that all the Germans would be together in a company commanded by German officers, "a company of Germans." On November 27, 1861, he deserted in Washington; Muster Rolls, 59 N.Y. Inf, NatA.

then because of the language, and I haven't wanted it since then on principle. To put it briefly, I didn't want to have a position of responsibility, I wanted to stay free, at least as free as you can be as a soldier.[5] But unfortunately you're less free here in America than in any other country, because the arrogance in the German regiments borders on the incredible. There was no lack of opportunity for advancement, and in the infantry I certainly could have become an officer as well as anyone else, but when I saw that the men who were least fit for the job were being made officers, and the best men were either turning promotions down or maybe couldn't be promoted, I made up my mind to do without all such honors in these circumstances, and that is why I am only a common soldier[. . . .] In the eyes of an American I am worth as much as if I were an officer. But I'll continue. After I had spent almost 3 months with the regiment doing drill and parading—the latter carried out with greater precision than in Germany—we received the order to march to the theater of war. We went via Philadelphia and Baltimore to Washington. When I arrived there, I took leave to look around the town, but when I came back I found that the regiment had left unexpectedly, and I couldn't find out where they had gone. I didn't know what to do. Of course, I could have gone to the provost marshal's office and they would have taken me to my regiment immediately, but I decided to use this as an opportunity to do what I had wanted to do for a long time, namely to leave the regiment secretly. By chance, I met someone from Mecklenburg who encouraged me in my plans. He was serving in a German artillery regiment that was camped half a mile from Washington[. . . .] So I went along with this compatriot and signed on with this regiment. This wasn't a problem, given the confusion at the time, when all the troop units were still being put together. With regard to my oath to the state my conscience was clear, since I had never left the army, and the government doesn't care which uniform I wear[. . . .] This German artillery regiment consisted at the time of 3 rifled 20 [lb.] batteries with 4 gunners each and one 32 [lb.] howitzer battery. I signed up for the second battery, and I'm still with it, even though we were renamed a few weeks ago, i.e. the name of the battery.[6] I joined at the end of November 61.[7] Drilling was quite fun because it was new to me and a more pleasant diversion. I must admit that the drilling in both the battery and the regiment got so good that I can't remember ever having seen anything better, even in Germany [5 ll.: progress of the war].

---

5. On August 12, 1864, Albrecht was in fact promoted to the rank of corporal (Muster Rolls, 30 Baty N.Y. LArt, NatA), but he did not mention this in his last letter of August 22.

6. See note 2 above.

7. Officially on December 10, 1861, Muster Rolls, Baty B, 1 Batn, N.Y. LArt, NatA.

We spent the entire winter living in canvas tents, just like the round tents in Germany, right outside the capital Washington, which we visited frequently, of course. On March 10 the army began to move, commanded by the now famous General McClellan[. . . .] Our rations from now on consisted of 1 [lb.] of *Kräckers* a day (ship biscuits or what soldiers in Germany call iron rations). Beans with bacon or rice with salt beef for lunch and coffee in the morning and evening, without milk, of course. About twice a week—but sometimes not for 4 weeks—we had fresh beef, and this was all we had to eat for a whole year until the beginning of this year when we set up winter camp, and the food improved a bit [6 ll.: war situation]. I assume, of course, that you know from the newspapers that the southern or rather slave states have pulled out of the Union and are now fighting for their independence. This is why they are seen by the other states as rebels and treated as such, and they are trying and have been trying for 2 years now to force them back into the fold. It remains to be seen if this will ever be successful [14 ll.: troop movements; on March 27, 1862, embarked for Fort Monroe*; march to Yorktown]. We began preparations for a regular siege, since there were supposed to be 60–80,000 men in Yorktown.[8] The infantry had to work day and night on the earthworks and entrenchments. There were about 10 to 12 small forts built about 4,000 paces from the enemy fortifications, all connected by trenches and lying in the woods surrounding the enemy positions and hence hidden from their view. The one exception was one single fort in the middle of our position that was in an open field, and of course, this was where our battery was assigned. We took up position at the end of April with 6 and later 7 pieces and remained there until the enemy retreated (April 4) [May 3, 1862] without being relieved for even a single hour. But I will never forget this week. It was here that I as well as other men received my first baptism of fire, since when we arrived, our captain had the insolence to shoot off a few cannonballs (against orders), so they knew that the fortification out in the open was armed, and we became the target of all the enemy cannons that could reach us [40 ll.: details of caliber and ammunition; were also fired on at night; went for eight days with hardly any sleep; battery was not allowed to return fire; enemy retreat; troop movements]. After several unsuccessful attempts, we finally took up battle position around noon at Gaines Mill.[9] Here, in a small valley, the bloodiest scene of the whole war began a few hours later and unfolded in front of our eyes[. . . .] We were standing in the middle of the battle line with the light artillery to our right and left and saw the whole thing only too well. I should also mention that

8. In fact, approximately 15,000; Long and Long (1971), 193.
9. June 27, 1862, one of the Seven Days' battles.

about 28,000 of our men were fighting an enemy with three times more infantry.[10] Oh, and when you see how rashly these splendid regiments are thrown into the mêlée your heart simply bleeds. The fighting was almost exclusively with bayonets. [5 ll.: retreat of the Union troops "through the batteries":] so that these were now defenseless and exposed to the heaviest infantry fire. "Captain! If you even intend to save the battery, this is the time to do so" — said an old gunner from Baden to our captain. He said he didn't have the order yet. But then it came and we started to limber up. Under the heaviest rain of bullets from the infantry we succeeded in this, but we would not have gotten away if the courageous Zuaven [Zouaves] hadn't returned, seeing the danger we were in, and thrown themselves at the enemy. The batteries to our right and left were captured, but we escaped safely[. . . .] In yesterday's battle our battery lost 9 men, and every cannon was fired 96 times. This unlucky day was the first of the 6 bloody days during which the most heroic battles were fought by the Army of the Potomac on its retreat to the peninsula, and in which my battery was involved to a greater or lesser extent. In these unforgettable days, this truly splendid army was decimated by half[11] and the rest fled to the James River under the protective fire of the gunboats [41 ll.: march to Fredericksburg*; Alexandria; march to Maryland to meet Lee; Battle of Antietam; back to Fredericksburg]. The Rappa Hannock (river) flows here in a deep valley, and Fredricksburg is on the left bank of the river. The left bank was and still is held by the enemy, and we have the right bank. We stood on the steep bluffs on the right bank (Stafford Heights) with the order to shoot the next train that came out of the town. On the morning of the second day a train did come slowly along out of the town. We quickly shot off half a dozen rounds but the train continued slowly on its way. Angry, we were just about to try again when 2 adjutants galloped up at full speed with the order to hold fire immediately, because there were women and children in the train (just imagine how carelessly these orders are given). A short while later 2 more trains came along and then we could see only too clearly that this was true [5 ll.: details]. We then took up a better position on the heights directly across from the town, and this is where we've been for the last 5 months. The enemy has set up formidable fortifications against us on the hills on the other bank [8 ll.: commander had planned a frontal attack, which was absurd]. As usual we were positioned (thanks to the heavy caliber of our guns) on one of the highest hills above the

10. More correctly, 35,000 to 55,000; 4,000 Union troops were killed or wounded and 2,800 taken prisoner, and there were a total of 9,000 Confederate casualties. McPherson (1988), 467.

11. An estimate that is highly exaggerated. The Army of the Potomac lost approximately 10,000 of its 105,000 men in the Seven Days' battles, and Lee's army of 87,000 suffered twice the number of casualties. McPherson (1988), 464, 470–71.

place where the river was to be crossed so we could see very clearly the horrible scene that then unfolded at our feet. On December 10 the preparations for crossing the river were finally finished, and the commander decided the army should cross the river that very night [12 ll.: bridge building; bombardment of the town. On this day, they had moved 176 pieces, mostly heavy caliber, into position (to the right and left of us were rifled 32 [lb.] Parrott guns) and these now opened horrible fire on the poor town, while at the same time a Michigan regiment, under the protection of the thick powder smoke, crossed the river in boats and routed the enemy sharpshooters from the river bank. Then the bridges were completed and the whole army moved across the river during the night. We, of course, stayed put, because our guns commanded the entire battlefield and could easily reach the enemy's fortifications [4 ll.: attack was repulsed]. Yes, God knows it was horrible to see the soldiers marching boldly forward, only to be cut down by enemy artillery (Dec. 13). One of these regiments, the 7th N.Y. Steuben (only Germans), lost half its men and all its officers except for 3,[12] and things were much the same in all the other regiments [4 ll.: retreat on the third night]. This disaster cost us 12,000 of our best men, killed and wounded. The bridges were of course destroyed, and our battery has remained as usual in its old position. We've been here for almost 6 months now, and the pickets on both sides are on quite friendly terms with one another.[13]

[7 ll.: so many setbacks because Union troops are led so badly] The Northern armies are decidedly superior to those of the South, both in terms of numbers and equipment. The fact that we've had so little success is due to the exceptional bravery and tenacity of the southern troops, which of course can be attributed to their officers and especially their generals. If our generals were even half as much soldiers and military leaders as the enemy, the Union cause would be in a much better position today. There they promote the most competent officers, while here they try to stifle them. A fatal addiction to party politics paralyzes the force of the armies in the field. The leaders don't have a free enough hand, and instead they are commanded by the *Cabinette* in Washington [5 ll.: the war is ruining both sides]. As for me, I doubt very much we will ever be in a position to conquer the South by force [13 ll.: troop strength; battles]. I don't really care how it turns out. We are now so

12. The word "lost" includes the wounded and captured. During the two years the regiment served, eighty-eight soldiers and fourteen officers were killed (Dyer [1959 (1908)], 1408), nine of the officers at Fredericksburg.* *OAR*, 2:432–33.

13. This is an understatement: they did not shoot at the enemy, and soldiers used boats to cross the Rappahannock to trade coffee and salt from Union army supplies for tobacco from the South; Johnson and Buel (1987), 3:224.

deadened it's almost like we've been reduced to animals. It couldn't be otherwise since we've been in the field for almost two years now, with no mitigating
influences at all. I will close now, and if I am still alive I'll write more soon
[signature missing].

                                                            [finished August 22, 1864]
[salutation missing]
    [6 ll.: reference to the report on Fredericksburg] The current commander
of our army, Gen. Hooker, decided to attack the enemy that was still in its
strong position behind Fredricksburg. His planning was better than that of
his predecessor, Gen. Burnside, but he didn't know how to see it through. —I
don't intend to write a detailed description of the battle of Chancellorsville*
since I wasn't there because my battery remained in its old position on the
Rappahannock. [37 ll.: troop movements and fighting in the battle of Chancellorsville, especially in the Fredericksburg area. On May 3 the VI Corps
under General Sedgwick stormed Fredericksburg:] Nothing can be compared
to the joy we felt when we saw the glorious light artillery division of this
corps take the famous green hill where the best artillery of the South was
entrenched. (It was the Washington Artillery, unfortunately also German,
with which we had exchanged heavy fire many times.)[14] [11 ll.: analysis of the
battle of Chancellorsville] The whole thing had taken too long, and given that
amount of time it wouldn't even take the well-known military talents of the
enemy commander, Gen. Lee, to have seen through our general's plans. Due
to a number of unfortunate coincidences, the whole thing, as usual, was a disaster, and once again all the blood was shed for naught.
    [21 ll.: on the death of Confederate general Stonewall Jackson; troop move-
ments] Since some of our cannons had cracked again, they took them away
and gave us 12 [lb.] pieces. I can't say how unhappy and angry we were to
lose our dear 20 [lb.]ers [18 ll.: troop movements; Martinsburg, Virginia]. We
stayed here all summer long to defend the Baltimore-Ohio line. Our camp
was on quite a high hill with the pretty little town spread out below. This was
the beginning of a time in my life as a soldier that couldn't have been more
pleasant for any soldier in the field. We stayed here for the hottest 3 months
of the summer. We only saw the enemy when 2 pieces had to accompany the
cavalry on its larger patrols, which were frequent[. . . .] So here we tried to
while away the time as best we could. Many of the young men expressed an in-

    14. The Washington Battalion (its official name), recruited in New Orleans, was a famous
elite unit, but only 167 of its 1,039 men and a few of the officers had been born abroad. Bergeron
(1989), 14-17, 24-26; Lonn (2002 [1940]), 208-9.

terest in starting a four-part singing group in the battery, which was of course
warmly received. I was chosen as the leader, and I've done my best to put
together some passable singing, and I must confess that we have all been very
satisfied with the results and have spent many a happy hour singing. We also
set up an area for gymnastics in order to pass the time as well as possible.
At the end of October we were sent to Marylands High[t]s (*Mariland Höhe*)
and we spent the whole winter there. We set things up as well as we could as
soldiers in the field. In particular we practiced our singing so much that we
had many happy hours, and no civilian singing group could have had a better
time. We built a nice clubhouse with all the basics, beautifully decorated with
German and American flags and all sorts of things. The best thing was that
we subscribed to 8 of the best German American newspapers and magazines,
and one of them was the *Leipziger Gartenlaube*[15] from Germany. We also had
several English* papers, and so we were able to follow not only the events
in America but also what was happening in Europe and particularly in Germany. We also had a song festival, and what we liked the best was when we
went on a singing tour in November to the battlefield at Antitam with about
20 singers. The road there was really bad, but since we were on horseback it
didn't matter much. We were warmly received and entertained by the *Lady's*
in the nearby town of Sharpsburg, who had never heard anything like this before[. . . .] On April 2nd, 1864, we received marching orders, and in the most
horrible weather we were sent by train to Cumberland, where we stayed for 14
days, and then from there on a difficult march through the mountains back to
Martinsburg. An expedition force was being organized here under the command of Gen. Sigel* (the well-known German) to march up the Shannandoh
[Shenandoah] Valley. We were also assigned to this corps; it was about 10,000
strong.[16] We marched off at the end of April. This is the most beautiful part
of Virginia, and it was wonderful to march through this valley with spring
breezes wafting through the air[. . . .] We were in good spirits and had high
hopes that our expedition would be a success. We were supposed to destroy
the railroads that went west to Richmond, and since we were under the command of the popular and beloved Sigel, we felt confident we would accomplish great deeds [4 ll.: advance; encounter with the enemy; battery sent to
the front]. We galloped 7 miles forward on the road before we met with the
enemy.[17] Here, aside from one other battery, we found only cavalry fighting

15. A very popular weekly paper published from 1863 to 1943 that contained educational
articles providing light, sentimental, family entertainment.

16. More correctly, 6,500; McPherson (1988), 724.

17. Battle of New Market,* May 15, 1864.

the enemy. We went as far forward as possible in order to ensure the success of our smooth 12 [pounders]. But after only about 10 minutes a huge mass of infantry appeared in front of our line and began to advance on our battery. At this point our cavalry turned around and retreated. Now we were in a very tight spot, but we limbered up under the hail of about 4,000 guns and reached our next line. We wanted to set up our guns here, but then this line started to falter, too, and then there was no more chance of the infantry and cavalry holding this line either. Under a terrible storm of bullets, everyone retreated in total disarray. Then General Sigel called another battery and us back. We set up our guns and brought the enemy to a halt with our heavy fire. Then our troops were able to cross back over the Shannandoh, which hadn't looked possible at the start. In short, the battle was lost, we left the enemy 2 of our cannons and 2 ammunition wagons that either had their wheels shot to pieces or their horses killed. We all felt sorry for Sigel, since shortly thereafter he was relieved of his command and has probably ruined a career that had been so promising. We also lost 10 men[. . . .] In early May we advanced again under the command of Gen. Hunter. At Pied Mount there was a bloody battle[18] in which our battery had the opportunity to distinguish itself with glory, and I think I am quite correct in saying that without us, the battle wouldn't have been won. I have seen many horrible things in this war, but I have never seen such dreadful devastation and mutilation as was caused by our cannonballs among the rebels hidden in the woods. We made quite a name for our battery there, and that is why all the troops now greet us with great respect. Among the troops we are now called the Pied. Mount Battery. The rebels were completely routed and fled into the mountains. We marched on. During the entire march, whenever we appeared, our troops received us with jubilant cheers. It is true, it fills a soldier's heart with joy when he knows he has done his duty and that this is appreciated by his comrades. Then we went to Staunton, a major railroad *Depot*, destroyed 50 miles of the railroad [13 ll.: battle of Lynchburg, June 17-18, 1864]. But now our line of retreat through the Shannandoh valley was cut off, and we were forced to retreat through the wilderness of the West Virginia mountains where there are no paths[. . . .] This retreat, I think, was much like the French army's retreat from Russia, except that we didn't suffer from the cold but from the heat, and I think it isn't difficult to decide which is worse. Every day about 500 men were left lying on the road, totally exhausted from hunger and thirst, who fell into the hands of the enemy cavalry that was following at our heels. And the horrendous number of horses and mules, wagons and supplies that were lost cannot even be calculated. The en-

18. Piedmont, June 5, 1864.

tire campaign in West Virginia had failed again. During this campaign we had covered 1,500 miles, and you can imagine our condition when we returned, after living off tree bark for 3–4 days at a time and never any chance of sleep [31 ll.: withdrawal from the Shenandoah Valley; pessimistic about war situation; greetings; correspondence; signature].

Harpers Ferri, August 22, 1864

Dear brothers and sisters,

Let me tell you about something else besides this endless slaughtering and murdering. There is so much I wanted to say, but now that I want to write it I can't think of anything[. . . .] I also can't say much that's positive, the conditions here in this country are now as wretched as they can possibly be. It affects the soldiers the most. Paper money, and that's all there is here, is almost worthless, and food prices sky high[. . . .] You can imagine what it's like if I tell you that people are offering us 5–10 cents for one cracker (*Schiffszwieback*) that otherwise wouldn't be worth a cent. On top of that they haven't paid us in 8 months, and so you can imagine that we are still suffering from deprivation. I am only happy about one thing, that my time will soon be up. On December 10th of this year I will have served 3 years with my battery and hopefully then my suffering will be over. I hope that on that day I will go home, and then by Christmas I'll be a human being again, which we can't be as soldiers. Last fall the bounties for volunteers willing to reenlist were so high that many of my comrades were enticed into signing up for another 3 years, but I didn't let myself be taken in, neither by the good life we had at the time nor the good money (almost 1,000 talers*) being offered. What good is all the money in the world when I have to risk my life all the time for it? And on top of that, I would ruin my health, because no one can hold out for 6 years, it's bad enough after three. I want to at least try and see if I can't do better in civilian life, and at any rate I am not afraid I won't be able to survive because I've made friends and connections that will be of great use. If nothing else works out, I'll be a barber again, for this is one of the best trades in America. I used to dislike this trade, but I've gotten over that, or will have to get over it, because the word now is just make money [15 ll.: correspondence; greetings]. Think of me with only half the love I feel for you, and I will thank you forever / Your William

This is the last direct sign of life we have of the letter-writer. His unit remained in and around Harpers Ferry until January 1865,[19] but he was mustered out at the end of his three years of service, as he had announced, on December 18, 1864.[20] When

19. Dyer (1959 [1908]), 1402.
20. Muster Rolls, 30 Baty N.Y. LArt, NatA.

he left the army, he was neither wounded nor seriously ill. But after December 1864, there is no more evidence, direct or indirect, about his subsequent life.

10. Carl Hermanns

Carl Hermanns, the son of a Lutheran farmer from Hamberg in the Rhine Province (now part of Burscheid, near Cologne) completed his training as a teacher in Elberfeld and must have had intense exposure to liberal ideas while there. According to family tradition, the twenty-six-year-old emigrated, together with a friend and colleagues, because he did not want his work to be dependent on throne or altar. This claim is borne out by numerous references in his letters.[1]

After arriving in New York in March 1857, he first worked on a farm outside the city; by November 1858, he had already spent several months in Savannah, Georgia, working as a teacher in his own school. Having returned to New York, he again found employment as a teacher and married the daughter of a German immigrant, with whom he was to have three children. By early 1860, he had established himself in Philadelphia as a "teacher of German and French." His expectations of life in America seem to have been fulfilled, as is confirmed by his repeated exhortations to his sister Laura to come over as well.[2]

Philadelphia, April 12, 1862

Dear brother-in-law and sister,

[12 ll.: family] Man's lot on earth, after all, is hard work and struggle, and you at least are in a better position than so many farmers here who have lost all the crops they have worked so hard to grow, and sometimes they've even lost their houses and farms, everything they had. Wherever war rears its head, the farmers are always hit hard. War seems to be everywhere now: in America, Asia, Africa and in Europe it seems to be raging the most. The news from Germany doesn't sound peaceful at all. Of course, there are still many evils among men, and they can only be eliminated by war, and then it always has its

SOURCE NOTE: Hermanns's writing is what one would expect of a teacher: the handwriting is neat and regular, showing that he was used to a lot of writing. His German is always correct, his vocabulary is extensive, and he writes in a style that is lively but not flamboyant. Not included here are the letters in the series from the time before 1860 (six) and after 1865 (six). No letters have been preserved from the time between May 1859 and April 1862.

1. Information provided by the donor.

2. Letters of July 4, 1857, November 28, 1858, and May 10, 1859, NABS; MC 1860: Philadelphia/Pa., W. 13, p. 905.

good sides as well. First the power of princes and priests must be abolished, because where they rule, they hinder the free development and education of the people. I have nothing more to do with those preachers, I don't attend any church or allow my children to be baptized, and therefore I am much freer and happier and will make sure that my children grow up to be good and decent and hardworking, without all that religious fraud and deception. And because I do it this way and keep the Bible out of the school as well, my school is filling up, since people agree that what the church teaches is not a religion that can bring peace to man and heaven to earth. Being good and loving <u>all</u> men as brothers is the religion that God approves of and that should prevail on earth, and this religion shall be my guiding light.

As you will see from my letter to my parents, I am doing quite well despite these sad times of war. I have been in good health, have both hands full with all my work, and therefore I make a good living. I delight in my family and am held in high regard by everyone I come in contact with, and that is all I desire. The two classes in my school are enough to support me and leave me time to devote myself to my family, that is why I don't want to expand [20 ll.: family; friends].

I hope that your are well and will write to me soon, and give my best to <u>everyone</u>, especially Julchen / Your brother, brother-in-law, and uncle / C Hermanns [4 ll.: correspondence]

Philadelphia, April 12, 1862

Dear parents,

[40 ll.: family; his school; income and costs; his brother-in-law and his business] The war is still going on and causing misery and suffering beyond words in this beautiful country where in times of peace, everyone could live happily. The North clearly has the superior strength, and if things were being conducted in an honest manner, then we would soon have peace. But the men who are at the top and who collect all the millions don't want to turn their men loose, and they are dragging the war out like a lawyer does a court case. The Germans are always the ones who are the most honest and fight the best, and the bravest fighter of all is the German General Major Sigel,* who has vaulted his way up from the rank of colonel to this high position. It's been five years now that I've been in America, and when I see my school, my lovely house, my loving wife and my two beautiful children and then think about my situation back in Germany: I should be truly satisfied, and I am satisfied, and my happiness would be complete if you were here, too. I look at your picture everyday, but that's not good enough.

Hoping to hear from your soon, with hugs and kisses to <u>all</u>
Your loving son and brother / C Hermanns / [8 ll.: mail; address]

Philadelphia, August 5, 1862

Dear parents,

[37 ll.: school; family] The school fees are coming in well; the only problem is that all the money is paper money. All the coins have vanished, even the smallest copper coins, which means are forced to use postage stamps for money. Many saloonkeepers have even had their own paper money printed. This lack of money has been caused by this wretched war, which still hasn't come to an end even though no one wants to be a soldier anymore. And since they can't find any more volunteers, they're moving on to *Conskription*, and many fathers are being torn away from their families. Since I am not a citizen yet, I am not in any danger, and as a teacher I would probably be spared. So don't worry about me. If I were in danger I would rather return to Germany than go to war here for these cheats and politicians. Lawyers and politicians are ruining this wonderful country, where everyone could otherwise live happily[. . . .] They say the harvest has seldom been so abundant, but the war has destroyed everything and stolen the hands that should gather it in, and all this misery has been caused by the lazy idlers who profit from it. If they were stood up in front of the cannons, then the war would certainly be over soon, but the people are letting themselves be tricked [6 ll.: questions about the harvest]. Hoping to hear from you soon, our best to <u>all</u> / especially from / your obedient son / C Hermanns [. . .]

After the letter of August 5, 1862, there is a gap in the correspondence—until December 9, 1873, when Carl Hermanns, then in Stuttgart, wrote to his brother who had inherited the family farm. When or why he left America is unknown. At any rate, in 1881 he and his wife returned to Philadelphia, where his two sons were living. Here he founded another German American school that was slow getting started, but by the third year it was attracting a considerable number of students. In September 1883, however, Carl Hermanns died unexpectedly while taking a walk in Fairmont Park—whether he died of natural causes or was the victim of an assault was never resolved.[3]

The radical opinions he expressed during the Civil War changed little as he grew older. He wrote about "lazy parasites," called out "down with the godly," and urged others to "become Social Democrats." A stop, he argued, should be put to the

3. Letters written by one of his sons, Otto Hermanns, Philadelphia, March 8, 1881, October 4, 1881, NABS.

"thievery" of "throne and pulpit."[4] These exhortations sound somewhat repetitive and schematic, more like the complaints of someone who is powerless than a serious call for action, but at least one son adopted Carl Hermanns's political views and considered himself a "Social Democrat."[5]

4. Carl Hermanns from Stuttgart, August 8, 1877, December 29, 1878, NABS.
5. Letter of Otto Hermanns, March 8, 1881, NABS.

11. Caroline Eversmeier

Caroline Eversmeier (née Neuer), born in 1824 in Eberbach/Baden and the daughter of a wood turner, lived a life in Germany that was on the fringe of society. Released from police custody in December 1850, she was picked up and punished six times in the next year and a half for "shirking and being dissolute" and then was finally put in jail.[1] As happened frequently, though secretly, in several German states, she was given the choice of remaining incarcerated indefinitely or immigrating to America, with her passage paid by the authorities. She opted to leave and received 45 guilders* from her hometown of Eberbach plus 76.31 guilders from the state of Baden to defray costs; together with four other inmates, she sailed on March 31, 1853.[2] By then her three sisters were already living in Algeria. In the United States she was apparently more successful in establishing herself. She married a hack driver from Hanover who was listed in the 1860 census with fifty dollars in assets but no property.[3] Aside from the letter of 1863, no information is available about her subsequent life.

[Baltimore, July 9, 1863]
[salutation missing]

Once again I take my pen in hand to write to you, dearest sister. It has been 9 years since I left my parental home, and during this time I have written 2–3 times to Eberbach and never received an answer.

As for me, I am well, thank the Lord, and I hope that my few lines find you as happy, hale and hearty as I am, for I have put my trust in God and He

SOURCE NOTE: Caroline Eversmeier's handwriting is unpracticed and irregular, her spelling, grammar, and punctuation are chaotic, and her vocabulary is quite limited—but despite considerable interference from her local Baden dialect, her writing is easily understood.

1. Letter from the Eberbach district authorities to the town council, June 15, 1852, StdA Eberbach/Neckar.
2. A file on payments to detainees unlikely to reform, GLA Ka 236/8640.
3. MC 1860: Baltimore/Md., W. 2, #894.

has not forsaken me. I was only an outcast in my own homeland, but here in a faraway country there are people who still have feelings, and after misfortune and unwarranted suffering, great joy will come to pass. If you were only here with me, you could live as happily as I do. I was all alone when I arrived here, but I met good people from Bruchsall on the ship, a girl and her uncle, Mr. Rullmann, who took me along to her brother's house where right from the start I got paid 5 talers* a month. I worked there for about a year and then I met my husband. We got married in 1854 on the 17th of December, and we've been living a happy life and are as pleased as punch. [16 ll.: asks for news of her sisters; correspondence] Dear sisters, I want to let you know that I don't know when my husband will have to go to war, and then I will be all alone. I don't have any children, and every day there are so many men being slaughtered, on some days 10 to 20 to 30 to 40 thousand men, they're taking one man after the next [9 ll.: correspondence; address].

I remain your loving / sister Charlotte Karolina / Eversmeier

[Attached is a letter to the town council in Eberbach, requesting that her letter be forwarded; note: address unknown]

12. Dünnebacke Family

Of the six children of the owner of the farm Haus Marpe near Niedermarpe (in the Sauerland, southern Westphalia) who lived to adulthood, the two youngest immigrated to the United States. Johann, born in 1813, left Germany in 1836, and nine years later he was joined by his brother Joseph, born in 1818, who emigrated together with his wife, Maria Franziska. An uncle was already living in Detroit with his seven children, but the two brothers decided to settle in the country. Johann's farm in Clinton County, Michigan, was valued at $3,000 in 1860, and Joseph's farm nearby was worth $1,600. In 1850 the respective values had been $800 and $200 — the brothers were not doing badly.[1]

In Clinton County, which usually voted Republican, there were relatively few Germans: 5 percent at the most, but perhaps 10 percent if the second generation

SOURCE NOTE: The Dünnebackes' spelling is rather chaotic, their punctuation is quite weak, and their writing style is awkward. They certainly belong to the group of immigrants for whom writing is hard and time-consuming work, since they do it so rarely. Some local dialect shows through. Not included here are the letters in the series from the time before 1860 (eight) and after 1865 (one).

1. Dünnebacke (1938), 90, 89; letter by Friedrich Dünnebacke of July 25, 1858(?), NABS; MC 1860: Clinton Co./Mich., Westphalia Twp., #406, #539; MC 1850: Clinton Co./Mich., Westphalia Twp., #58, #96.

is included.[2] One reason for Joseph Dünnebacke's disapproval of the war may have been religious: all of his letters show how important the Catholic Church was to him, and one of his daughters entered a convent.

JOSEPH DÜNNEBACKE

Dalles [Dallas, Clinton County, Michigan], May 3, 1862
[. . .] Dear brother-in-law Ernst,

[30 ll.: correspondence; family; one of his five children has died at the age of twenty months] The harvest this year was about average, but we still have those confounded weevils, small worms in the wheat, and I have no idea when they'll go away. Grain prices are also not the best: a bushel of wheat brings in 80 to 90 cents, corn 30 to 40 cents, and the potatoes are rotting.

Oats are worth almost nothing at all, fat hogs and cattle fetch only half the normal price. On the other hand, the goods from the store, sugar, coffee, tea and calico—indeed anything made of cotton cloth—have doubled in price. Who is to blame? Unfortunately the Abolonisten [Abolitionists], which include a lot of European 48ers. They did a lot to get this war going, like in the Senate in Wasington where the higher-ups refuse to give in to each other even a little bit; they also can't agree about southern slavery. That's why 11 southern, most of them slave states, have withdrawn from the Union and set up their own government with President Jeferson Dävis [Jefferson Davis] at the head. The states that left are South Carolina, Georgia, Alabama, North Carolina, Misisippi, Louisiana, Tennessee, Arkansas, Florida, Texas, Virginia, and the following 3 Maryland, Centucky, Missouri, were half and half, but more for the South than for the North. Now just imagine, our government in Waßigtenn, that is the North, has 6 times a hundred thousand men, and they say the South has 4 times a hundred thousand men, that's a million all together, and every common soldier in the North gets 13 dollars a month plus rations, and the officers get even more than in Germany, and they're all volunteers.

They've already had 4 big battles, the North lost the first one but in the others the South was beaten, and the North has already captured 4 cities. Now you can well imagine what all of this is costing, they've already run up 5 to 6 hundred million dollars in debt, and if this goes on much longer, then oh, dear! Now they're saying they want to finish off the South in 2 months! This much is certain, the South must lose, but in such a short time—that's another

2. Estimates based on USC 1870.1, 169, 313; and USC 1860.1, 269, 238, 247.

matter. One good thing is that the war is so far away from us. We also finished our steeple last year, it hadn't been completely built and it cost about 100 dollars, but what is even more exciting is that we have bought an organ that cost 457 dollars and a few cents. It isn't very big and only has 6 registers, but these are expensive items here. We also have a good parish schoolteacher and a fine organist as well [7 ll.: correspondence] And we remain your loving Joseph Dünnebacke Maria Frannzisca Anna Maria Johannes

Write back soon

MARIA AND JOSEPH DÜNNEBACKE

Dalas, August 3, 1864

[salutation missing]

[45 ll.: family; daughter Anna Maria, age seventeen, "is working for an American [. . .] 6 hours from here, so she can learn more than what she knows from life at home." Johannes, age fourteen, "was still attending the English* school last winter"; bad wheat harvest; clothing expensive, but also grain and livestock; wishes] Dear sister Theresia, I wanted to send you an extra letter, but it's hard for me, but I imagine you will also have a chance to read this one. I'll stop here and let someone else tell you the rest of the news and remain your loving daughter and sister

Maria Franzisca Dünnebacke

So, that's about it in terms of family matters. What should I write about now? Should I write about the war? It will no doubt make me very angry, but I'll try. At least in our war, which has been raging now for 3 years and destroying everything, we've now reached the point where we were back at the beginning. The northern army is now about 660,000 strong, certainly a fine army if only the scoundrels in Washington would lead them better and make better use of them. When they have good generals like Me Klellen [McClellan] and others, then they make too much progress and really hit the South hard, so then they are recalled and inexperienced men are put in their place [from here on about one-third of the right side of the page is missing, about twenty letters per line]

all because the war must be [drawn out?]

so that the bigwigs and all their relatives [twenty letters]

can stuff their own pockets [twenty letters]

War is about nothing but money [twenty letters]

[23 ll. without the last twenty letters of each line: enormous war debts; describes the draft where the lots in a barrel were drawn by a child; he had to take part in 1862, although the "smallest lie" could have gotten him out of it, but the "whole business was too disgusting." End of letter missing].

In 1870 Joseph Dünnebacke's farm had risen in value to $3,000. His brother Johann had died in the meantime, and his farm, now run by his widow and three adult children, was valued at $10,000. Joseph Dünnebacke passed away in 1899.[3]

3. MC 1870: Clinton Co./Mich., Dallas Twp., #238; MC 1870: Clinton Co./Mich., Westphalia Twp., #199; information provided by the donor.

13. Captain August Horstmann

About 1856, three years after his older brother Albert (who became a farmer in Texas), August Horstmann left Germany and moved to St. Louis. Nothing is known about his reasons for emigrating. Born in 1835, he had grown up with four brothers and sisters in Schweiburg, a town of about 1,400 inhabitants in the Grand Duchy of Oldenburg, where his father was a teacher, as well as the sexton and organist of the Protestant church.

His letters indicate that he received more than just an elementary education, and in nearby Varel he probably had commercial training. In 1859 and 1860, at any rate, he was working as a salesman or agent in St. Louis. In August 1861 he signed on for three years' duty with the 45th New York Infantry Volunteers, the "5th German Rifles," a unit that was almost exclusively German American. The regiment was first deployed in Virginia and fought in the battles of Cross Keys, Groveton, Bull Run, Chancellorsville,* and finally Gettysburg.* In the fall of 1863 it was transferred to the South and stationed in Tennessee until the spring, when it took part in Sherman's Atlanta campaign; it was then ordered to Nashville on July 6, 1864. In the meantime, August Horstmann had had a brilliant career: he was made a corporal on December 18, 1861; and on June 15, 1862, he became a sergeant and regimental clerk. He was subsequently promoted to second lieutenant (February 7, 1863), first lieutenant and adjutant on the regimental staff (May 3, 1863), and finally captain (May 1865).[1]

[fragment of a letter written shortly before June 16, 1862]
[salutation missing: to his parents]

Because the damn'd flying dutchmen are behind me; I would not care for all the Yankes (that means because the damned flying Dutchmen / the Germans

SOURCE NOTE: With his clear and concise phrases, Horstmann conveys a great amount of information in a few lines. He does so in High German without any flaws in spelling, punctuation, or grammar.

1. Information provided by the donor; emigration permission for Albert Horstmann April 27, 1853, Ns. StA Oldenburg, Best. 70, Nr. 6144 Litr. H. KI; *OAR*, 2:489; Dyer (1959 [1908]), 1420–21; Muster Rolls, NatA.

are called *dutchmen* here / I wouldn't care about all the Americans). And indeed the enemy has tremendous respect for German soldiers, so that even the farmers come running from all directions to see the flying dutchmen, as they call our division. General Frémont* is well aware of this & only has Germans on his staff, & our division & specifically our brigade, the 1st, is always given preferential treatment & is always out in front. On Pentecost Sunday on June 8 we set out early to take up the chase. The road through the woods and fields was bad enough but then about midday we ran into the enemy about 8 miles from Harrisonburg. They were posted in the woods on steep hills [battle of Cross Keys]. The artillery immediately opened fire & our 1st brigade marched toward the enemy in battle formation. The other 4 brigades were still far behind & could join us only one after another. The Garibaldi Guard N.Y. chased the enemy out of the woods and moved on toward their main position, with the 27 Regt Pa skirmishing on the left; the De Kalb Regt NY in the center, then ours, the 45 Regt N.Y., & the 8 Regt. N.Y. Blenker's* Jäger on the left.[2] But the whole battle plan and any chance of winning the battle was foiled by the precipitous actions of Colonel Wutschel from 8 Regt.[3] Long before the battle was supposed to begin & without having any reserves behind him, this officer gave his regiment the command to attack (rumor has it he was drunk, & he now faces court-martial). They beat back the enemy pickets, and then they started singing *"Hinaus in die Ferne"* [a German hiking song] etc. and went straight into a bayonet attack, & it was uphill and over three fences, until after the last *Fence* on the other side of the hill, they met up with 7 enemy regiments hidden in the woods. They were received so warmly by the enemy that 4 regiments were firing on this 1, & 3 more were standing by with their bayonets poised. What must those 7 enemy regiments have thought when they saw a single regiment storming at them with their bayonets at charge and singing at the same time. The outcome could easily be predicted, the 8th Regt. met its doom and a terrible hail of bullets fell on them from a distance of only 50 paces, so that in no time at all, more than 300 were lying dead and wounded in the field in the midst of the enemy position.[4] Our regiment, which according to the battle plan & battle orders was to have led the attack, was quickly sent to their aid. We marched double-time through the

2. The 1st Brigade (commander: Brigadier General Stahel), 1st Div. (Brigadier General Louis Blenker*), Mountain Dept. (Major General John C. Frémont) consisted of the 8, 39 (Garibaldi Guard), 41 (De Kalb), and 45 N.Y. Inf; the 2 N.Y. Ind. Baty; 27 Pa. Inf; and Baty C, 1 W.V. LArt. Apart from the last mentioned unit and the 39 N.Y. Inf, which was only predominantly German American, all of these units were almost exclusively German American.

3. Letter-writer Robert Rossi (no. 6) also served in this unit.

4. Casualties amounted to 220, including 43 dead. Colonel Wutschel was dishonorably discharged. For details, see Rossi (no. 6).

fields, meadows, & woods, & then up the dangerous hill; but the fate of the 8th Regt. had already been sealed. We were almost at the top of the hill when suddenly there was such a torrential hail of bullets that we had to stop & get down on one knee and mount our sword bayonets so we could meet an onslaught of the enemy we could not see yet, in case they attacked. Our skirmishers, who were farther up the hill in a barn, were fighting with the enemy, & our Colonel G. von Amsberg, who was higher up surveying the position of the enemy, decided that this single-handed attack was foolhardy and ordered a retreat, after our regiment had suffered 38 dead & wounded [7 ll.: details; that night the enemy pulled back]. The battlefield of the Feast of Pentecost was horrible. More than 500 enemy corpses were heaped in 2 big piles. And 2–300 of our men.—Our total casualties, dead, wounded & missing amounted to ca. 700.[5] Enemy losses must have been twice as high, judging by the number of their dead. Hundreds of dead horses were strewn all over the field, which made it a scene that was sickening and sad to behold. Our artillery in particular had had a dreadful impact & many of the corpses were ripped apart so badly you couldn't distinguish friend or foe. Some had both legs shot off, others were blown apart in the middle, others were lying there with no heads. Arms and legs were scattered everywhere. This is war!? [31 ll.: marching; the Shenandoah Valley; Union must be preserved; situation in other theaters; England and France]

As for me, despite all the horrible hardships, despite hunger, rain, & sore feet, I am healthier & stronger than ever & this life of war does me good. My only wish is that I could see you again; if this can be fulfilled, in the near or more distant future, then I will be happy & content. But even if I should die in the fight for freedom & the preservation of the Union of this, my adopted homeland, then you should not be too concerned, for many brave sons of the German fatherland have already died on the field of honor, & many more besides me will fall!—Much the same as it is in Germany, the free and industrious people of the North are fighting against the lazy and haughty Junker spirit of the South. But down with the aristocracy who are lacking only in titles, and may industrious and free men revive the glorious soil of the South. Immigration & opening up the South to free labor is the only way to prevent civil war from returning.—

[. . .] I remain / your dearest loving son /

Aug. Horstmann

On June 16, early in the morning:

I've just been made a *Sergeant Major*, the same as an *Oberwachtmeister* at home, and thus transferred to the regimental staff.—Soon I'll be a *Lieutenant*.

---

5. Dead, 114; total casualties, 684 (Confederates, 288). Boatner (1959), 211.

Stafford Court House, Va, January 11th, 1863

Dearest parents,

When I returned yesterday from Washington, where I was attending to regimental affairs for a week, I received your letter of December 1862 [12 ll.: family].

If I am not hit by any of the many unfortunate events of the war, I will be leaving the military this year, whether the war is over or not; because I fear a change in the politics here that will take away my desire to continue to risk my life and my good health in chasing a phantom.—I'll become an officer this month and then at the appropriate time I will resign. Even though tremendous efforts are being made at present, I fear this country and its great institutions are falling victim to the ambition & self-interest of the politicians. The rebels in the South have too many friends in the North, and their intentions are becoming more and more obvious; and it wouldn't surprise me if this war were to end in a complete revolution [9 ll.: fighting in Virginia without success]. The 5-day New Year's battle near Murfreesboro [Stones River] in Tennessee brought better results, where our German[6] General Rosencranz [Rosecrans*] beat the southerners completely. More of these successes in the West will do more to end the war than this never-ending campaign in Virginia[. . . .] I spent Christmas and New Year's in such a way that I don't even know when they were. Nothing at all, not the slightest festivity, no joyful shooting in the air, no punch, no beer or wine, and no change in the bill of fare to remind us that these otherwise so richly celebrated days had gone by. No one even wished anyone else a Merry Christmas, and most of the men were more in the mood for cursing. With salted bacon, *Cracker* and *Caffee*, camping in the snow etc. you can't expect much else. I lay down early on my bed of fir sprigs with my blankets wrapped around me, observed the moon and the stars for a while and sent them on their way with greetings to my friends, and then I went to sleep.—

[4 ll.: greetings] Your loving son / Aug. Horstmann [. . .]

Headquarters 45th Regt. N.Y. Volunteers
Bivouac near Potomac Creek Bridge, Va., February 11, 1863

Dear parents,

[6 ll.: little change] This entire winter campaign does not seem to be having any results; except that the incredible strain and misery of the soldiers is being doubled. Many more soldiers succumb from suffering and deprivation than from all the many, many bloody but indecisive battles, and it would be better if the two armies just met head to head and kept fighting until one of the two

6. Rosecrans was actually born in Ohio, on September 6, 1819. Warner (1964), 410.

armies, or both of them, were completely destroyed [16 ll.: some ladies in Oldenburg have apparently sent bandages; asks for their names].

I can also report that since the 7th of February I've been a [2nd] *Lieutenant* in the 45th Regt. NY.V. and will soon be appointed regimental *Adjudant*. I hope this does not displease you, and I am sure I will not be a disgrace to the post.—

This position of honor also means a significant change in pecuniary terms, in that my current salary amounts to one hundred and five dollars a month and as *Adjudant* it will rise to one hundred and thirty.—

As an adjutant I have already received a fine horse, and it looks like I've "gotten up on my high horse."—

Hoping to hear from you again soon, I send my best to you and my friends & relatives / yours sincerely / Aug. Horstmann [28 ll.: address; his brother Wilhelm (born 1845, apparently a seaman) should contact him when he is in New York; photographs; correspondence]

Headquarters 45th Regt. N.Y. Vol. Inf.
September 18, 1863

Dearest parents.

[7 ll.: correspondence] I would very much like to come to see you for a few weeks to refresh my memories of the happy years of my childhood; but that will have to be postponed for a while. Higher duties keep me here at the moment! The freedom of the oppressed and the equality of human rights must first be fought for here! To us the war is a war of sacred principles, a war that should deal the fatal blow to slavery and bow down the necks of the southern aristocracy.

[12 ll.: outrage at position of England and France; if they dare support the South openly, they will regret it] The free states have risen to such power and self-confidence that they defy the whole world; and all attempts to overthrow this republic or to destroy it would come to naught [20 ll.: Union victories at Gettysburg,* Vicksburg,* Port Hudson*]. The last decisive battle will be fought in southern Virginia or in northern North Carolina, and when we have won it, the entire South with its cavaliers and slavery will be lying at our feet, and the curse of tyranny will be revenged.—

[24 ll.: attack on Charleston, "where this horrible war was hatched"— wishes that "this cursed nest will be leveled to the ground"; developments in Virginia and Mexico]

In my last letter of July I mentioned that I wanted to resign from the army and become a partner in a large import business in New York. My resignation was turned down, however, and so the association with the New York business has gone up in smoke. But it doesn't matter, I will just stay in the army for my 3 years; I will see this war, that I've been in from the beginning, through to the end. A month ago I was supposed to become *General Adjudant* with the rank of captain with *General Major* Schurz*; but my colonel objected. He absolutely didn't want to let me go because he wants to make me his own *General Adjudant*, since he will soon be promoted to *General* soon.[7] That was fine with me because I don't want to leave the regiment in which I marched out as a private and have moved up through all the ranks. If possible, I will also return home with the rest of my regiment.—

[9 ll.: correspondence] Your most loving son / Aug. Horstmann [. . .]

Headquarters 45th Regt. N.Y. Vol.
Inf. Lookout Valley, Ga. [near Chattanooga] November 13, 1863
Dearest parents,

[27 ll.: family] Do you still get the weekly *Belletristische Journal*, the *New York Criminal Zeitung** regularly? I subscribed to it for you in August and paid for 1 year in advance. This paper is the best one in America because of its accurate reporting of events. In particular, the *"Panorama des Freiheitskrieges"* [war for freedom] should be of interest—you can follow the history of this glorious war and rely pretty much on what it says [25 ll.: details; march to Chattanooga, Tennessee; on November 28, in the evening, the enemy attacked a division of the XII Corps: beginning of the battle of Wauhatchie, Tennessee, one of the few night battles of the war]. In an instant the 11th *Corps* was on its feet and rushed to the aid of the *Division* in trouble. Our regiment—the first one ready, marched forward on the double, fanning out into a chain of skirmishers. And thus we stormed forward through the night with our brigade behind us in a column [16 ll.: firing on the flanks—nothing of the enemy could be seen but their muzzle flash; bayonet attack; enemy retreat]. During the first attack by the enemy, I was at the far left end of the skirmishing chain, directly in front of the enemy line. As usual, I was riding my white stallion, which made an excellent target in the darkness, and so I attracted a considerable amount of enemy fire. Never before have the bullets flown so close; to the right and to the left shots whizzed by, to the right, to the left and in front of me the lead bullets hit the earth, showering my stallion and me with mud. Two bullets ripped through my coat, making nice little round holes in it, but as if by a miracle I remained completely unharmed in body and soul [7 ll.: victory about 2 o'clock in the morning; entire chain of hills in front of the

---

7. Georg von Amsberg received his discharge on January 22, 1864, still a colonel. *OAR*, 2:489 (as "van Arnsburg").

enemy's position in the mountains taken]. There is nothing in war more horrible than a life-and-death struggle at night; when you can't even see friend or foe, let alone tell them apart; when you can't see what you're stepping on or getting into. Thus the 143 Regt. N.Y. Vol. fired on our regiment [. . .], they thought we were the enemy since the enemy's bullets flew through our lines and hit the 143 Regt. because they were standing behind us. Another regiment, the 2nd *Division* of the 11th *Corps* was marching up the hill and saw a regiment in a line across the edge of the woods. The former kept on marching until it occurred to the commanding officer to ask "what regiment is that." The answer was "the 43rd Regt Alabama!" You can imagine the surprise when suddenly 2 regiments who are enemies are so close to each other that they could shake hands if they were friends. The commander on our side wasn't taken aback, however, he gave the order "*Front*" and at the same time "*Charge Bayonet*" & "*forward.*" In less than 1 minute the enemy regiment, paralyzed by shock and with no time to defend itself, was dislodged, and those who didn't fall were taken prisoner. Since that bloody night we've dug ourselves into the positions we captured and have been exposed to continuous artillery fire from the enemy; but we have learned not to pay any heed to the southern artillery because they don't do us any harm [8 ll.: every night entire groups of southern soldiers desert to the Union army; greetings; signature].

> Headquarters 45th Regt. N.Y. Vol. / Lookout Valley,
> Tenn. December 22,
> 1863

Dearest parents,

[11 ll.: Christmas wishes; is in good health] On Sunday and on Christmas Day my coffee with a bit of hard bread (a kind of ship's biscuit) and a piece of bacon will taste better to me than a roll with butter and honey. We are certainly going through "hard times" these days: we're camping on rocks, sleeping on blocks of wood, eating *Zwieback* that has to be cut into pieces with an axe, and working with iron and steel—and occasionally the other side works on us, too, with their iron and steel. You might think that officers should have a better life, but my dear parents! the field puts an end to all preferential treatment and we are all plain soldiers who share all the hardships and privations.

[69 ll.: describes the battles near Orchard Knob, Tunnel Hill, and Missionary Ridge, Tennessee, November 23–25, 1863; march to Knoxville—150 miles in six days—and back to Chattanooga; in winter quarters in Lookout Valley on December 17; marches were very grueling] Our shoes were soon completely worn out so that half the men were marching on the frozen and stony ground in their bare feet; and since we had no connections to the rear or front and no baggage *Train* at all, no rations were given out the whole time, and we had to feed ourselves on whatever corn & cornmeal we could get our hands on. The unbelievable resilience of human life, when supported by firm will and good intentions, astounded me at times, and it is with legitimate pride that I believe I can claim that the American volunteer army needn't be afraid of standing up to the best European army.

[20 ll.: is the *Criminal-Zeitung* still arriving regularly? Friends; home becomes more precious from afar]

With all my best to you and my brothers and sisters, I remain your loving son / Aug. Horstmann [6 ll.: address; greetings]

Headquarters 45 Regt. N.Y. Vet. Vol. / Bridgeport Ala, April 27, 1864
Dearest parents,

Having said goodbye to the whirl of amusements, feasts, from the wine, the lovely ladies, and all human society, we arrived out here in the desert a few days ago, where the war has destroyed everything, leaving only wasteland behind. We have returned here to continue the destruction and take it further and further[. . . .]

In the city of New York, we were treated to the most lavish reception probably ever given a regiment returning home, and all the festivities and being besieged by invitations to the all the different circles of New York society meant that for us warriors, the pleasures of life reached the greatest heights. But this frenzy was short-lived and is no more! [. . .] Within a few days, we were 1,500 miles away from New York, one of the greatest and most pleasure-hungry cities in the world, which our entire regiment calls home, and we've now been transferred to the wooded hills of northern Alabama, western Georgia, & southwestern Tennessee, where the only people we see are our own soldiers, and there's nothing to do except our military duties, where in April the southern sun burns us up during the day, and the nights leave us stiff with cold, and where there are no friendly female creatures at our sides to weave rosy wreaths into life on earth [19 ll.: was sick for three weeks; after eleven battles, expecting more of them that will decide the war].

I wish I had news of Albert, because he is living in a bad area,[8] and the way the people in the South have been ravaged by this endless, grueling war is frightful, and if you haven't seen this misery with your own eyes, it's absolutely impossible to imagine. No field has been planted, and the wealthy

8. High Hill, Fayette Co., Tex. In fact, Albert Horstmann seems to have done quite well: from 1860 to 1870 the value of his land increased more than five times, to $8,000. MC 1860: Plum Grove, Fayette Co./Tex., #339; MC 1870: High Hill, Fayette Co./Tex., #414. There is no record of his having served in the military.

people who live near our lines have to beg for their bread and their livelihood and are being supplied with army rations from the United States *Government.* Here in Bridgeport alone, more than 4,000 rations a day are being handed out to the proud people in the area so they won't starve. In order to get hold of coffee, sugar and other luxury items, the women here who used to be so proud even stoop to brazen fornication with our men; and I've often been an eye-witness to incidents and acts that have filled me with the deepest disgust but also a certain pity for these degenerated people. — This is the horrible pun-ishment for their treason, and fate is taking wretched revenge on these people who were misled by the politicians and their own interests and participated in the rebellion [24 ll.: family; friends; end of letter missing].

Headquarters 45th Regt. N.Y.V.V. / Nashville, Tenn., July 16, 1864
Dear parents,

[48 ll.: dreams about a photograph of his parents; the South at its end; the 45th is taking part in Sherman's march to Atlanta, got as far as the Chatta-hoochee River, about twelve miles from Atlanta] On the 7th of July, our regi-ment was sent back to Nashville Tenn. to guard the capital city of Tennessee and the *Capitol.* As a reward for our 3 years of hard duty in the field, we've been put in a garrison, and another regiment that has more men and has never seen fire has taken our place in the field. Your concern about me in terms of enemy fire, therefore, should be over for the time being, because we will probably stay here in the garrison and not be sent back to the army, since our regiment has shrunk so much we wouldn't be much use in a battle[9] [14 ll.: Sherman's march; Atlanta has fallen].

You rebuke me for having signed up for another three years? Dear par-ents! Men of principle do not put up with 3 long years of the greatest hard-ships imaginable — without receiving some kind of reward, being able to see either the successful or unsuccessful outcome of their efforts. He who fights for ideals and principles cannot stop halfway! This is the opinion of our gov-ernment, of the people here, and I share it! Believe me, this war will be fought to the end, the rebellion will be defeated, slavery abolished, equal rights estab-lished in all America, and then finally "your Maximilian,* Emperor of Mexico owing to Napoleon's grace, will be sent packing." — And until this happens, war will not cease.

I also had another good reason to remain in the regiment, namely: at the

9. The regiment suffered losses that included a total of 47 killed (including five officers, 3 of whom died at Chancellorsville* alone) and 107 who died of disease, as well as several hundred more who were discharged due to illness and injury, taken prisoner, or who deserted. Dyer (1959 [1908]), 1421; *OAR,* 2:489.

time when the regiment was given the opportunity to extend its duty for another 3 years, our soldiers agreed to do so on the condition that the officers would also stay on, because they didn't want to have strangers as their officers. It was then only natural that we agreed, so as not to rob the government of the service of an entire regiment of veteran soldiers [2 ll.: details: end of letter missing].

Headquarters Co H, 45th Regt. NYVO Inf. / Stevenson, Ala, June 23, 1865
Dearest parents,

[57 ll.: situation in Mexico; declaration in favor of Maximilian's expulsion, Monroe Doctrine and democracy] It almost seems as if the European peoples and governments still can't or don't want to understand or realize that in our republic the people themselves actually rule, and that the government, elected by the people, only does or doesn't do what is stipulated by the will and opinion of the majority of the people. Because of the fact that our people determine what the government should do, it appears certain that the Empire of Mexico must come to an end, either by persuasion or by means of force similar to the way this unnatural empire came into being [4 ll.: no European soldiers would be in Mexico if the Civil War had not happened]. We republicans, who in the last 4 years have fought thousands of battles against the largest revolution and rebellion the world has ever seen, were forced to sit by and watch while the thieves took over and divided up the defenseless spoils [6 ll.: the United States is not afraid of France]. The terrible war that threatened to destroy our union has only served to make our nation strong and invincible; and if Europe wants to be honorable, it can take the policies of the United States in the last 4 years as a shining example [14 ll.: overwhelming victory; Union volunteer units have been disbanded, with a few exceptions]. Our regiment is still in service; but I have taken my discharge, and in a few days I'll be free to pursue my own interests. I don't intend to make the military my goal in life, because I cannot stand life in the garrison, so I am resigning since I have done my duty with regard to the enemy, and at the moment I see no prospect that the regiment will be used in active duty.

Louisville Ky, July 10, 1865. — 3 weeks ago I had to interrupt my letter because the reorganization and discharge of part of the troops also affected our regiment. I took advantage of the opportunity to leave the army and asked for immediate discharge because different regiments that had been reduced to small numbers were being combined, put together and consolidated.[10] In

10. This description is not quite accurate. According to the records, Horstmann did not leave voluntarily but became a supernumerary officer and was hence discharged when the 45

such a situation every officer has the right to leave the army, because no officer here can be forced to serve in any regiment except the one he was sworn into. This was most convenient for me, since I still had almost 3 years left to serve because I was recently sworn in—in May—as a captain in Co H for 3 more years. I am very happy to be free of garrison duty—which deadens body and soul—and on July 30 I left the Co & regiment and have closed the book on an entire life. These last 4 years have been so rich with memories of a turbulent, dangerous, difficult life—they are worth millions. On Aug. 15, 1861, I joined the regiment as a private, and after I had risen through all the ranks I left on June 30, 1865, as a captain. I saw the beginning of the 45th NY Regt. since I was one of the first soldiers to enroll, and I've seen the end of the 45th NY Vet Regt., because I was practically the last to leave when the regiments were consolidated and the rest of the regiment received a different name [53 ll.: looks back on twenty-two battles, hardship, misery; Mexico; new job in Louisville; family]. Mr. Albers wrote me that many of my letters have been published in the Varel newspaper. I am sorry this happened without my knowledge,[11] because if I had known about it, I could have written my letters accordingly, to make them suitable for publication. If the people in Varel and the editor of the newspaper enjoy reading my correspondence, I would be happy to write about the situation and events in America, as long as the censors and the police over there allow it, since as you well know I am very free with my speech [16 ll.: details; family; greetings; signature].

After his discharge, Horstmann became the manager of a sizable business in Louisville, Kentucky. In 1866 he married Amalie Gies, a twenty-two-year-old from Marburg, and the couple had six children. In 1870 he was listed as the owner of a cigar shop with $5,000 in real estate and $1,000 in cash assets, and he employed a domestic servant who lived with the family. In 1880 he was listed as a wholesale merchant, but a short time later he must have returned to St. Louis, where he worked as a wine and liquor merchant. At some point he visited his parents in Germany, but the exact date is unknown. He died in 1892. His widow continued to receive his war pension: twelve dollars a month at first, but forty dollars a month by the time of her death in 1928.[12]

---

and the 58 N.Y. Inf were combined. Order June 29, 1865, Regt. Books 45 N.Y. Inf, Order Book, Comp H, NatA.

11. Horstmann's description of the battles of Chancellorsville* and Gettysburg* appeared in the local paper *Der Gemeinnützige* (Varel) on July 29 and September 5, 1863. Although he claims not to have known about this, the style of the letters is markedly different from his private letters; there is no trace of "free speech" or criticism in the published letters.

12. MC 1870: Louisville/Ky., W. 4, #406; MC 1880: Louisville/Ky., e.d. 104, #415; CD St. Louis 1883–92; Pension File, NatA.

14. Private Wilhelm Hoffmann

Wilhelm Hoffmann was born around 1828 in one of the six villages named Giers-dorf that were listed in Silesia at the time. He was either a cabinetmaker or wood carver by trade, and he arrived in New York on May 23, 1857, on the sailing ship *Amalie* from Bremen, settling in Columbia, Lancaster County, Pennsylvania.

In September 1861 he was in New York, where he volunteered and signed up for three years' military service. He served as a bugler in the 54th New York Infantry Volunteers, which consisted almost exclusively of German immigrants and German Americans. The regiment was deployed in Virginia until the summer of 1863.[1]

Philadelphia / November 22nd, 1862

My dear mother, dear brothers and sisters,

If these lines reach you, my dear ones, in good health, I shall be very pleased indeed. I am still in good health, thank the Lord, despite the fact that I have been under so much fire. There was such a storm of cannonballs that my dear comrades both to my left and my right were felled by the shots. This horrible battle lasted from August 29th until 11 o'clock in the morning on August 30. The regiment I was in had 1,800 men, and no more than 13 survived.[2]

I've been wanting to write to you for a long time, but I haven't had the chance since almost the whole time up to now I've either been in battles or marching, and we hardly get enough time to eat our daily bread to satisfy our hunger. We've been starved and especially parched so much in this hor-rible heat that almost more men have died of hunger and thirst than in battle. Sometimes we would have paid more than a dollar for one slice of bread if we could have gotten one. A war as horrible as this one has never been fought in the entire world. How many family fathers have been victims of this terrible war, and now the wives and children have to starve because their providers gave their lives for liberty, or so they say. I therefore advise all my German friends never to set foot in this country, for sorrow and misery await all those

SOURCE NOTE: Hoffmann's German is simple in vocabulary and structure but quite adequate to describe events and express feelings. There are occasional lapses in spelling and punctuation, but even after five years in America, there is no interference from English and just one untranslatable word: "loafers."

1. Muster Rolls, 54 N.Y. Inf, NatA; Glazier and Filby (1989), 2:62.

2. The second battle of Manassas, which he is referring to here, involved heavy losses, but his numbers are completely unrealistic. No regiment had more than 1,200 men; perhaps he means the 2nd Brigade (3rd Div., I Corps), which consisted of four regiments, including his own; its casualties amounted to 46 killed, 274 wounded, and 5 missing. Johnson and Buel (1987), 2:497. During the entire war, 40 men in his regiment were killed. Dyer (1959 [1908]), 1425.

who expect to find the streets paved with gold. In my opinion the war will last another 3 to 4 years, and during this time I don't advise anyone from Germany to come over here, at least not if he values his life, because every immigrant, after he's been here in this country for a few weeks, finds he can't get by unless he becomes a soldier. Business is so bad here no one can earn his daily bread, no matter how hard he works. This is true for everyone now, not just the humble and poor. If someone who's rich and well-to-do comes over here, then he can live lavishly and very well for 3 or 4 months, but that's as long as his money will last here, no matter how much money he has, because this country is <u>now</u> made up of nothing but swindlers and rogues. When an immigrant arrives in New York, his own compatriots, who have largely become professional swindlers, will cheat him so badly that like I said before, all his money will be gone in 3 to 4 months. These swindlers (here in America they're called *Loofer* [loafers]) come on board the ships when they arrive in Neu Jork harbor and meet their dear compatriots when they're still on the ship [5 ll.: details]. The immigrant follows his dear compatriot, naturally, because he would of course never believe a compatriot to be capable of such a thing, and he can't see into everyone's heart, but then good night, compatriot! The *Loofer* won't let him go until he's gotten his hands on not only his money but also the gold watch and chain the rich compatriot, of course, was wearing. If trickery doesn't work, then he steals it, naturally, but he just has to have it. Normally, after an immigrant has been in the country for 3 to 4 months, no matter if he's rich or poor, he shows up in rags, poor as a church mouse, at the recruitment office, ready to sacrifice the last thing he has, namely his life, for this country. Yes, I must admit [letter breaks off].

Hoffmann was taken prisoner near Gettysburg* on July 1, 1863, the first day of the battle. He was held in Richmond until the end of July 1863, then released on parole* and officially exchanged on September 23. From August 1863 to May 1864, however, he remained in parole camp near Annapolis and spent most of this time in the hospital. In October 1864 he was mustered out at the end of his term of service. Hoffmann died one year later in Lancaster, Pennsylvania.[3]

3. Muster Rolls, 54 N.Y. Inf, NatA (letter-writer Knoebel [no. 17] was captured on the same day); marginal note written on the letter, NABS.

15. First Lieutenant Peter Boffinger

Peter Boffinger, born in 1826 in Ehingen near Ulm and a weaver who was apparently quite well off, emigrated in 1853; he "ran away from home," according to the entry in the town records. According to family tradition, he left the country because his wife Johanna, whose marital status was listed in the files as "deserted" until her death in 1856, had taken a lover.[1]

Once in the United States, Boffinger bought land in Portsmouth Township, Bay County, Michigan, where a sizable number of German immigrants had already settled: in both the 1860 and 1864 presidential elections, a large majority voted for Lincoln. Unlike many other German Catholics who were highly skeptical of the war, however, Boffinger joined the army as a volunteer. As early as August 15, 1861, he went to Fort Wayne, some 120 miles away, and signed up for three years. There were only a few Germans in his regiment, the 5th Michigan Infantry Volunteers, and this makes his army career all the more remarkable. He was promoted to sergeant in 1862, in 1863 he made first sergeant, in 1864 he became a second lieutenant and later that year probably first lieutenant. In early 1864 he was sent back to Michigan on recruitment duty. Boffinger's unit fought in many battles in the eastern theater, losing a total of 16 officers and 247 soldiers (and another 191 who died of disease), an unusually high casualty rate. Only 5 Union regiments (out of 850) reported more soldiers killed.[2]

Camp near Fredricksburg, Virginia
December 24th, 1862

Beloved sister,

You must forgive me for not writing earlier, but here in the field it hasn't been possible. I received your last letter, and I am sorry that your situation is

SOURCE NOTE: Boffinger's handwriting is regular, easily readable, and self-confident, and his language is straightforward, correct, and expressive, suggesting that he had a formal education beyond the elementary level.

1. Letter from StdA Ehingen, August 24, 1992; Inventar und Realtheilung Friedrich Boffinger from April 24, 1840, StdA Ehingen, Jur B 74; Inventar und Realtheilung Johanna, née Fuchs, deserted by Peter Boffinger, from February 23, 1856, StdA Ehingen, Jur B 152; information provided by the donor.

2. Handwritten note that Peter Boffinger owned "the eastern half of lot No 586 Block No 147 in Wm. Daylisch Division in the village of Portsmouth in Bay County," NABS; Schem (1869-74), 9:48; Burnham (1955), 516; Dyer (1959 [1908]), 1283-84; Muster Rolls and various health certificates, etc., NatA; only *Record of Service of Michigan Volunteers* (1905), 5:15, contains a reference to "1st Lt." not otherwise mentioned in the archives; on casualties see Dyer (1959 [1908]), 40-45.

| B | 5 | Mich. |

Peter Boffinger
2 Lt., Co. K, 5 Reg't Michigan Infantry.
Appears on

Company Muster Roll
for _July & aug_, 1864
Present or absent _Absent_
Stoppage, $ 100 for
Due Gov't, $ 100 for

Remarks: *Promoted from 1st Serg't to 2nd Lt. July 16/64 Entitled to $100 old bounty $10.49 due him for clothing. Absent sick at division Hosp'l. since Aug. 20/64.*

Book mark:

(358)

Boyd. Copyist.

| B | 5 | Mich |

Peter Boffinger
2 Lt., Co. K, 5 Reg't Michigan Infantry.
Appears on

Company Muster Roll
for _Mch & Apl_, 186
Present or absent
Stoppage, $ 100 for
Due Gov't, $ 100 for

Remarks: *Mustered out Feby 6/65 on Surgeon's Certificate of Disability*

Book mark:

(358)

WM Jackson Copyist.

August 1864 and April 1865 Muster Roll entries for Peter Boffinger, noting his promotion, illness, and discharge. (National Archives, Washington, D.C.)

not more satisfactory, but at the moment I am not in a position to lend you a helping hand, because our government, so it seems, is short of funds and keeps us waiting for our money.

Up to now I've been hale and hearty and have escaped all danger, and I hope I'll continue to be so lucky, but there are still 20 months before my service is over, and it doesn't look like the war will be over soon, even though both sides are trying their hardest. What we lack are good leaders for such large armies. We have almost two times a hundred thousand men, and then there are three more armies of a similar size in the field, not counting the war fleet that has 389 ships and about 3,000 heavy cannons.

On the 13th of this month we attacked the main position of the enemy, but we were beaten and we lost more than 10,000 dead and wounded.[3] I was close enough to the fighting, and comrades fell to my left and right, our regiment lost over one third of its men, and we're now back where we were before [where] we'll probably stay for the winter.—Since Sept. 18th I've been *Comp.* sergeant [this] is a tiresome job because I have to get rations, clothing, etc. for my men, and there's a lot of paperwork, but I get 7 dollars more a month and the prospect of a position as lieutenant, but it's almost too difficult for me [33 ll.: attached is an exact description of the land he owns, in case anything happens to him; greetings to friends; often sees a friend from school who is in the same brigade; signature, address; notes in English and German about his land].

Boffinger had already been wounded on May 31, 1862, at Fair Oaks, and at Gettysburg* he received a serious head injury. This, in combination with sickness and exhaustion, led to his being mustered out in February 1865, after having reenlisted in July 1864. He moved to St. Louis, where he worked as a laborer in various trades until he died, penniless, in 1907. In 1896 he was classified as a disabled veteran and received a monthly pension of twelve dollars. In 1869, 1872, and 1880 he married German Americans: his first wife in the United States died one year after the wedding; the second one left him after only six weeks; and he deserted the third after his first pension check arrived in 1890. According to affidavits in support of his pension application, he must have been a trial to his wives and children—violent and stingy. Due to his complicated family circumstances, his last wife did not receive a widow's pension.[4]

3. The battle of Fredericksburg*: 1,284 killed, 9,600 wounded, and 1,769 missing. Johnson and Buel (1987), 3:147.

4. Muster Rolls, NatA; Pension File, NatA. MC 1870: St. Louis/Mo., W. 4, Subd. 9, #488, lists him as a laborer in an oil mill with $100 to his name; MC 1880: St. Louis/Mo., e.d. 67, p. 512A, lists him simply as a laborer.

16. Sergeant Wilhelm Francksen

According to family tradition, Wilhelm Francksen, born in 1831 in Hollwarden (Butjadingen) at the mouth of the Weser River, was a "drop out." The son of one of the wealthiest farmers in the village, he studied law in Göttingen and Heidelberg but never took his final exams, and he emigrated in late 1861.[1] His brother inherited the family farm. The family's image of him finds some support in the letters: Francksen mentions a drinking problem, and there are passages indicating that he was occasionally somewhat out of touch with reality.

It is not clear why Francksen enlisted in the army. He volunteered in Milwaukee in June 1862 and was assigned to Company D of the 26th Wisconsin Infantry Volunteers. This regiment, raised the previous September, consisted almost exclusively of Germans or German Americans. It was attached to the XI Army Corps, also predominantly German, of the Army of the Potomac in October 1862. The commander of his company was named Schueler, the regiment was commanded by Winkler, the division was led by Brigadier General Carl Schurz,* and the entire corps was under the command of Major General Franz Sigel.*

The regiment remained in reserve at Antietam and Fredericksburg* and did not have contact with the enemy, but it suffered heavy losses at Chancellorsville* (26 killed, 126 wounded), as well as in the battle of Gettysburg,* where apart from the 20 killed and 55 missing, 134 men were wounded. Wilhelm Francksen, now a sergeant, was in the thick of the action.[2]

Mayvill, Wiscons., March 9, 1862

Dear father,

I just received your letter of February 2 [11 ll.: boarding house; journey]. The reason I haven't written for so long has to do with the situation here. The war and the winter made business slow down. I was advised not to become a soldier, even by people who had been soldiers themselves or still were. I could always have decided to take up an ax, but only as a last resort [6 ll.: new job]. If L[ogemann] thinks working means hard physical labor with a lot of sweat, that would make sense in his case, because he wouldn't be any good at any-

SOURCE NOTE: Francksen may not have finished his law degree, but his German is truly elegant, precise, and nuanced. The suspicion that it may have been embellished—for this series only transcripts of the original letters are available—seems unfounded in view of his articulate use of language and the occasional mistakes that can be found. Despite the short time he had spent in America, he occasionally throws in a few English words like "sutler," "creek," and "smart." One undated letter is not included here.

1. Information provided by the donor; NYPL, *Herzogin von Brabant*, November 23, 1861 (here Francksen traveled in cabin class but is listed as a farmer).

2. Pension File, NatA; *OAR* 7:201–2; Dyer (1959 [1908]), 318–20, 1624.

thing else here. I can do better[. . . .] You don't have to learn any particular profession here: today you are this, tomorrow that, depending on what you want to do and where the money is[. . . .] I am also starting to feel more at ease here than in Jeverland and in Butjadingen. I am working, but not slaving away, am earning money and have no expenses. If you think learning how to be a merchant would only be Greek to me, that's only because you have no idea what things are like over here. I skipped doing an apprenticeship; I started as a clerk for 300 dollars, and now I can acquire more knowledge of the business, get some experience, and to make better use of both, become a bit more fluent in English[. . . .] But that doesn't mean I'll stay in trade, I might become a schoolteacher, pastor, lawyer or even a druggist, butcher or something else completely different. The most important thing is that I become an American, this means first I have to get to know the country and the people.

[10 ll.: does not expect money] With a good wage, I can play the gentleman over here better than in Jeverland with hard work and expensive room and board. [6 ll.: training in Germany; signature missing].

Madison, Wiscons., August 4, 186[2][3]

Dear father,

[. . .] When I was in Mayville, I was very pleased to receive your last letters from home and from Ruhwarden, and from time to time, if you have the time and the inclination, please write to me again. You have no idea how pleasant it is to receive letters with news from the old homeland; because here there's no feeling of being at home, no matter how long you live here, because here there's no *Gemütlichkeit*, without which Germans can't even imagine feeling at home. An unmarried man can easily make his way and even lead a life of material luxury, but he must make do without distractions of a higher sort like in Germany. But for what you call family life over there, all the prerequisites are lacking. Marriage is a business proposition, the children are free citizens of the United States and they want to be treated accordingly by parents and teachers. So they grow up wild, and when the boys have grown up, they are coarse, ignorant louts, more or less well trained, depending on their money, but without any general education, and in particular with no respect for au-

---

3. In the German edition of this volume (Helbich and Kamphoefner [2002]), this letter was dated August 4, 1861, and placed before the preceding one. However, a subsequently discovered passenger list entry and internal evidence suggest that the 1861 date on this letter was an error on the part of the writer or transcriber. Moreover, his date of enlistment indicates that Francksen was already in the army by this time, but apparently he hesitated to tell his parents; Pension Files, NatA.

thority or sense of morality. The only thing they learn is how to make money, and the Americans have surpassed all other nations in that.

[37 ll.: quality of goods; women; earning money; cleanliness; cheats everywhere] On top of all this, in terms of the law, the situation here is at about the same level as it was in Germany in the Middle Ages, although for different reasons. In Europe at that time, laws and rights were undeveloped and imperfect; here, by contrast, we have laws originally written by the founders of the *Constitution* for men who were highly developed, but when they are applied to nothing but scoundrels and cheats there are bound to be serious problems. So now what usually counts is might is right, depending on how much money someone has or the number of his supporters among the riffraff; or in some situations just physical force, either with his fist or a gun. America is rotten, through and through. Maybe it will be better after the war that is hanging over the country heavily at the moment and probably will not come to an end for quite a while. The South is stronger than they thought at the beginning, it has become incredibly powerful, and our armies have recently suffered one defeat after the next, so that the North now feels compelled to make a supreme effort to prevent the worst. It has therefore been decided to send another 300,000 men into the field as quickly as possible. The state of Wisconsin has raised 5 more regiments, and the governor has issued a call for men to join the army and also indicated that there will soon be general conscription that will affect all men between 18 and 45 years of age. I don't know whether they will use lots or impressment. But at any rate they will have to resort to drastic measures, because I don't think it is very likely that 5,000 men will volunteer now in the middle of the harvest. The recruitment law that's now in effect is also flawed and wrong, and besides that, people here don't seem to me to be very enthusiastic about it at all. Most of the men who've already gone off to war thought they could bring it to an end quickly. They wanted to make some easy money and then rest on their laurels. They now feel they were completely misled. Others went because they were truly patriotic; but they've cooled off as well. The multitude of obvious errors made by some of the generals, mistrust of the government, and in particular one fact that affects everyone, that when they are in the field the soldiers, for whose rations the nation pays a sum that is more than sufficient, are completely at the mercy of swindlers and cheats who unscrupulously stuff their own pockets with the money the soldiers should be getting [end of letter missing].

Camp near Stafford, Virginia, March 1, 1863

My dear father,

[15 ll.: marches] We marched 13 miles in 2 days, moving forward slowly with frequent stops because our wagons could not proceed. Completely drenched and frozen to the bone, we arrived where we were to be posted on the 2nd afternoon, made a fire and put up our little cotton tents, after we had brushed the snow off the ground in a makeshift fashion. Then we toiled to make a cup of coffee, and gulped it down along with a few *Crackers*, a hard wheat bread, a kind of ship's biscuit, and a piece of salt pork, and finally 2–3 men cowered together, tightly wrapped in *Blanketts*—woolen covers—under the small linen roof, pressed close together to keep at least a little warm. The next morning snow was piled high on the tent, and our joints were stiff from lying on the damp ground. During the day the order came to build some sturdy, warm huts, and so we started cutting down trees and dragging them back, through the woods, without any paths, which gave us no end of trouble. We also had to cook our own food and get hold of wood and water for this. We were bustling around like ants in an anthill. A few days later a little town had grown out of this wasteland, consisting of good huts made out of raw tree logs, with chimneys, a fireplace and comfortable places to sleep. The soldier in the field is quite inventive, as was demonstrated by the construction and the furnishing of our little houses. Some of them were so delightful and cutely made, I would have liked to wrap one of them up and send it to you as a curio. The tree trunks were fit very skillfully together, the joints were filled out with green moss, there was a porch in front of the hut with green firs, cedars and wild laurel, with red berries with moss and colorful stones in front. Inside, too, everything was very clean and tastefully furnished: a fireplace, seats, a little table, with the beds in the back, 2 bunk beds, each one for 2 men[. . . .] On special days the streets were nicely swept and fresh greenery brought back from the woods [11 ll.: soldier's pay; shopping spree; trip]. Every regiment here has a sutler,* who makes a lot of money when things go well. But he also has to provide credit when the regiment doesn't have any money, and the paymaster sometimes keeps us waiting for 5–6 months. He also runs the risk of having his goods taken by the enemy when they're on the way or if there's a quick retreat. And he also has to be good at bribery, giving the right officials 100 dollars or more when he wants to get a load of goods through to the army from Washington. Of course all these costs are passed on to the soldiers, and even though we are paid a lot we can hardly save anything, if we want to live at all decently, and you can't blame us for wanting to do that, since we don't know how long our lamps will keep on burning. I don't spend any money myself on drink; I don't even drink the whiskey rations that I get, and I think that when I am out of the military I will have finally conquered my old fondness of liquor. But I do spend money to add a bit of variety to what we get to eat. For almost 9 months now I've had bean soup with bacon one day and rice soup with beef the next, at least when we weren't moving. When we're marching we don't even get that, and we have to make do for weeks on end with coffee,

Crackers, and salt meat, and some of the time we didn't even have that. So it is not surprising that your stomach gets excited when it's offered something different. You also lose heart and strength when you're living like this, and the hardships caused by the changes in the weather are also already having an effect on me. I have rheumatism in my right leg and I am racked with a terrible cold [24 ll.: package; paper money; prices; climate]. I would be happy if this humbug were over soon, and the entire Potomac Army thinks the same. We were supposed to cross the Rappahanoc River at Marie Church, where we were camped, since the enemy had dug in on the other bank. But it didn't work. The pontoons couldn't be let down into the water, entire regiments had to make roads, and even the lightest artillery couldn't move forward as it got stuck in the mud. It was terrible—nothing but mud everywhere. The enemy stood on the other bank and watched and laughed at us. The pickets—the outposts—held up signs making fun of our expedition and offering to help us cross the river [9 ll.: on February 5 orders for a night march; snowstorm; rain; difficult march; a foot of snow where they halted in the woods]. That night was wretched, we were lying half in the water and the mud [6 ll.: flooding prevented marching any further; new camp]. Now our new town is finished, it's nicer than the other one. It's on a mountain between a *Creak*—stream— and the woods. We have firewood and water nearby, and the train station isn't far away, so we always have enough supplies. There are also enough sutlers around and there's no lack of tobacco. The only thing is our duty is a bit hard. Every 2 days we have picket and guard duty; but as a sergeant it's my turn only every 14 days [7 ll.: his father's birthday; weather]. A few days ago our corps was reviewed by the current commanding general, Hooker. He has taken over the position from Burnside, who resigned his command after the unfortunate battle of Frederiksburg [Fredericksburg*]. Heaven knows what Hooker has planned for us next spring[. . . .] But all in all I am quite content: I have my food, and some money, and no worries. I'm not plagued by debt, or by work, and duty is quite tolerable. There are not many distractions, but we have some fun every now and then. The future, however, is a bit uncertain, but for what sorry mortal is this not the case?! I won't be wearing my uniform any longer than I have to, since a free civilian position seems to me to be preferable, but my time as a soldier will not hurt my future life as a civilian, since I don't have any skills to unlearn or forget. As an unmarried man I will easily find a position, even though times will be very bad in America. But the Americans don't deserve anything better! Greed, lust for power and the spoils system have completely ruined these people. Perhaps this war will make them a bit better and smarter? Justice does not preside in the courts here, instead public opinion does, that means the will of the mob; here you can't be respected for living a clean life, people only look up to you if you know how to make a lot of money, no matter how you do it. The more you cheat your neighbor, the *smarter* you are. Public officials are elected not because they are worthy and deserving, instead each party tries to beat the others through intrigue and the most brazen vote buying, and some candidates have to spend their entire fortune to get a position. If he manages to get one, he can then easily find ways to make twice as much as he spent, i.e. he cheats the state and the people and takes bribes. Here everyone has the same rights, but you only win in court if you can spend a lot of money. A poor man can't even start a court case. Here there are officially no classes, but whereas in Germany you are at least on good terms with the members of your own class, here you're enemies with everyone; no one looks out for anyone else, unless he thinks he has something to gain from it. They are selfish and suspicious to the highest degree, and if they give or donate something it's not to help anyone else but themselves: to make a name for themselves. They know nothing about *Gemütlichkeit* or community festivities, and that is terrible. Horse racing and cockfights are for the rich, and they've taken that over from England. The common man, if he wants something special, goes to a saloon, drinks a lot, and pays for drinks for other people who have to drink with him but don't have anything to do with him otherwise, and it usually leads to killing and murder [7 ll.: American leisure activities]. Nearly everyone reads a newspaper here, but only the papers from their own party, in which all the facts are colored or changed according to the party line and that contain nothing but lies and poison aimed at the other parties. Thus honest Germans soon grow sick of public life. You make sure that you get along yourself and with a few good friends, and you leave in peace the arrogant *Yankees* who think the Germans are only good enough to work for them, but otherwise pay them less respect than a Negro. And yet it is the Germans who have done the most to cultivate America.

[49 ll.: family; technological progress in Germany; European politics; military situation; no prospects of peace; currency devaluation] Gold is now at 173, so one dollar of our money is only worth 57 cents. Even copper pennies get an 18-cent premium on the dollar. At the moment I have no chance of being promoted. And you are wrong: officers here aren't any higher except in terms of their duty, and their money doesn't go any further than ours. And anyway you have to be content with what you have. Everything's a swindle here [2 ll.: greetings; signature].

Gettysburg,* September 29, 1863

Dear aunt,

Your letter was sent to me recently by A. Meinecke. I had just sent a few lines to Theodor, and they apparently arrived safely. I would write more, but

I still have to lie on my back. So I hold the paper with one hand and my pen in the other, and you can imagine how uncomfortable and tiring this is. Otherwise I am recovering, thank the Lord, and my wound is healing well.

The wound on the right side of my neck, where the bullet went in, has healed already, but on the left side there is still a 1½ inch hole; but a month ago it was 3 times bigger. I can now move my legs, which were completely numb and lame at the beginning, but there's no strength in them. I can also bend my back a little bit, but I can't sit up yet. Two pieces of bone came out of the wound. All in all, I'm getting stronger and more cheerful every day, and I feel quite well. Most of the time I spend reading, and I still enjoy smoking my pipe just as much as ever. Our beds are good, we have enough clothing and linen, and 3 times a day I can buy all sorts of good things. Last week we had a festivity organized by the people around here, a so-called *Picknick*. All the tents were decorated, there was a very good lunch: oyster soup, stuffed poultry etc. and so much cake, ice cream, fruit etc. that we had enough for 2 days. A band was playing the whole time. In the afternoon there were all sorts of contests: footraces, wheelbarrow races, sack races, Blind Man's Bluff etc. where there were prizes of 2–10 dollars. Attached to the top of a greased pole there was a 10-dollar bill and 60 days of leave. Everyone who could walk had a wonderful time. And even for us in our beds it was a pleasant diversion, and we were entertained by the noise outside[. . . .] When the weather is good, this is a good place to be, but it isn't when there is rain or a storm, and our tents have often threatened to blow down on our heads. Hopefully the hospital will be taken down and we will be taken to Philadelphia or Harrisburg. I've been lying here for three months now, and who knows when I will be able to walk again. The Meineckes wanted me to come to Milwaukee, but I can't get any leave at the moment, and I can't even think of traveling, since it would have to be done lying down, and the trip is too long for that.[4] If I can go later I will take some leave, even if the trip costs 50–60 dollars, there and back. What I would like the most would be a discharge. Times are hard now here, and you can't earn a lot of money, but I would get by somehow. I am sick of the soldier's life, and I can hardly hope to get through 2 more years of all the danger; because our corps is always at the front, and in the last two battles I fought in, we had the worst positions. There are so few of our Company D left that they were consolidated with Company F. Our regiment, last

4. Presumably the family of George Meinecke, a physician born in Oldenburg; his daughter Agnes may be the person referred to above who forwarded the aunt's letter. MC 1860: Milwaukee/Wisc., W. 7, #1014. On problems of caring for the wounded at Gettysburg in general see Patterson (1997).

year 1,000 men strong, has fewer than 500 left [13 ll.: details; health; family; end of letter missing].

Baltimore, Maryland, November 3, 1863

Dear aunt,

[6 ll.: correspondence; family] More than a week ago I was moved from Gettysburg to a hospital in this city. A special railroad car was built to transport the wounded, and it was nicely fitted out; you see there's a railroad between Gettysburg and here. The car has 30 beds hung on springs, 15 on each side, in three levels. There is also a *Sopha* and an armchair that can be made into beds. And so we started off on our journey at 1 o'clock, hoping to get dinner in Baltimore. But it was on a Friday, and as you know: a bad day for traveling. Halfway there, we were thrown out of our berths by a hard jolt, then the train stood still. A cart full of stones from our train had fallen on the tracks and smashed apart. We were lucky to have escaped without injury. But until the obstruction could be cleared away it was night, and we had to lie still. Our car contained a small supply of drugs and a well-stocked kitchen. Our doctor made us a good cup of coffee and brought us what he could find in a small store he had found nearby, pretzels, cake etc. The doctor also had liquor and wine[. . . .] At 10½ a freight train came and took us along; but it went so slowly and kept stopping all the time. The doctor turned down the lights and nestled himself into the *Sopha*[. . . .] At 7¼ we stopped again 4 miles from here. A coal train had jumped track in front of the bridge. One car had crashed down some 40 feet on the right and another on the left and the rest of the train had run across the bridge and damaged the entire track on it. That then had to be repaired, and we lay at anchor again until the afternoon, together with a lot of other trains. So our trip took 24 instead of 4 hours, and we only arrived at dinnertime on Sunday. I thanked the Lord that I had the trip behind me and was out of the Gettysburg tent hospital, because we suffered a great deal from the weather. We were lying practically out in the open. The hospital here, Mc.Keims-Hospital, consists of 2-story wooden huts. In each room there are 25–30 men. It is on a hill, and out the window I can see the big beautiful city that I would like to take a look at, but I am still tied to my bed. My wound is healing well, but my legs are still lame; I can only sit up if I prop myself up with my hands. But I seem to be generally improving. With God's help, I will hopefully come through. From lying in the cold, drafty tent and from all the hardships in the field, I've developed all sorts of rheumatism, and even here where it's warm I'm in a lot of pain and I can't move my arms properly.—We have it good here. We can be quite content with the beds and the food, and the city supplies us with various extras we can buy. I spend a few cents every

Wilhelm Francksen's certificate of disability for discharge. (National Archives, Washington, D.C.)

day on things to eat, apples 2 cents or *Grothe* [Low German: *groschen*] apiece, cake, torte, etc. They come by every day selling things, but it is all quite expensive. The cheapest thing is oysters. You get a small container full, 1 can, for 35 cents. I also have to have my tobacco and a newspaper and every now and then a book to read. So I don't end up saving any money, but I think I should make my life as comfortable as possible here, so I don't get bored and disgruntled, since this is the 5th month now that I've been lying on my back [5 ll.: details]. If I could walk a bit, I would wander down to the harbor. There are always ships from Bremen there. Every Sunday and in the afternoons the *Ambulancen*—hospital wagons—come and take the cripples for a drive. But I would have to be carried to the wagon and that is too much for me. I concentrate on being patient and hope to have a longer vacation when I am better. Then I will go to Milwaukee to see my friend Adolf [5 ll.: has a booming business and an eighty-acre farm] and now he's built himself a house in Milwaukee, in the most elegant part of town. I will of course stay with him, and when I am out of the army, he'll probably find me some kind of suitable job [24 ll.: prospects; family]. I often think about things over there and I wonder if I'll ever get around to seeing old Butjadingen again. It would be nice if sometime in the future I could live on the old familiar soil again [5 ll.: details; greetings; signature].

Baltimore, Maryland, December 1, 1863.
Dear Theodor,

[12 ll.: correspondence; family] My wound still hasn't healed completely, but I am recovering well. I still don't have any strength in my legs, but every day I sit up in bed for a while, and I hope I'll be able to walk a bit soon. As of today I've been lying in bed for 5 months. Here in this hospital we have it quite good. One of the orderlies here in the room is a Low German: John Tietjen from a place near Bremerhaven. He is a good fellow and does what he can for me. He only likes real "Low Germans," as he calls the people from our area. He can't stand High Germans and Americans. Having a friend like that is worth a lot here, because the Americans always tend to discriminate against Germans. They think the immigrants are only good enough to work for them, and they cheat them whenever they can. With John I can also speak some decent dialect. English is still not too easy for me. I just hope we can stay together for a while. I won't be leaving the hospital for quite some time, and will no doubt spend Christmas here[. . . .] When I am well again and the war is over, then I hope to have some good times, and God willing, to see you all again, happy and healthy [8 ll.: war situation; greetings; signature].

After spending months in various hospitals, Francksen received his disability discharge from the army in February 1864. The physicians certified that his legs had been partially paralyzed due to an injury in the lower part of his neck. There are only a few brief hints of what happened after the last letter. In 1871 he was apparently in Germany, from where he applied for a war pension, although it is unknown if it was successful. According to family tradition, he died in Chicago in 1876, but a document dated September 1878 indicates that he (or possibly his widow) submitted another pension application.[5]

5. Information provided by the donor; Pension File, NatA.

17. First Lieutenant Emil Cornelius Knoebel

Anton Knoebel, a tailor in Kirchhofen near Freiburg in Baden, had five children—and four of them emigrated in the 1850s, most probably to escape a life of bitter poverty. Among them was Cornelius Knoebel, who was nineteen years old when he left in 1853. He arrived in New York in January 1854 and went on to Pittsburgh, where his two older brothers had been living for about three years. Cornelius apparently left Germany not only for economic reasons: he also wanted to avoid military service, and the letter of March 19, 1863, indicates he had gotten into some kind of trouble. In 1857 he finished an apprenticeship—probably with a watchmaker, like his two brothers.[1]

As early as April 20, 1861, Knoebel volunteered for three months, then on August 24 he signed up for three years with a predominantly German regiment, initially called the 35th, later the 74th, Pennsylvania Infantry Volunteers, under the command of the former Prussian staff officer Alexander von Schimmelfennig, who later rose to the rank of major general. Knoebel advanced rapidly: in 1861 he was promoted to corporal and sergeant, in 1862 to first sergeant, second lieutenant, and then first lieutenant. For two months at the end of 1863 and from January to September 1864 he was the commander of Company D, after the company commander, Captain Henry Krauseneck, had been tried by court-martial and found guilty of cowardice in the face of the enemy (at Gettysburg*).[2]

November 27, 1862

[salutation missing]

On May 10th we left our camp, which we had occupied for the entire winter and had only consisted of tents. Then our long-standing wish was ful-

SOURCE NOTE: For a person with the small amount of schooling that Knoebel probably had, the quality of his German is amazingly good. A touch of local Baden dialect is present, but it flavors rather than mars his writing. In this series, only one transcript of an original letter, that of March 19, 1863, is available. The other three have been taken from Priesner (1981), 221–24, and 225–31. A comparison of the original transcript with the published letters indicates that in the letters of November 27, 1862, January 22, 1864, and May 19, 1864, the spelling and grammar were standardized, significant cuts were made, and the language was simplified and edited.

1. Information provided by the Kath. Pfarramt Kirchhofen; Priesner (1981), 220; Knoebel's letters of December 6, 1854, and December 2, 1856, excerpts in Priesner (1981), 221; Glazier and Filby (1989), 6:253. His older brother Heinrich (born in 1823), who immigrated either in 1850 or before, was listed in the 1860 census with total assets worth $8,000, and in 1870, with assets worth $16,000. MC 1860: Allegheny Co./Pa., Pittsburgh, W. 3, p. 213; MC 1870: Allegheny Co./Pa., Pittsburgh, W. 3, #186, #188.

2. *History of Pennsylvania Volunteers* (1872), 2:52; Muster Rolls, NatA; Krauseneck trial, February 1–3, 1864, RG 94, Court-Martials, Box 588, No. P-2935 VS 1864, NatA. Citizens petitioned the president, and instead of being discharged, Krauseneck was mustered out on May 24, 1864; *OAR* 3:890.

filled: we marched toward the enemy, but we didn't come into contact for a long time because they rapidly retreated to Richmond, the capital of Virginia. In the meantime we had to survive an equally difficult battle with nature and the weather. We had heavy, continuous rain, sometimes snow, and bottomless muddy roads that hardly supported the foot soldiers, let alone the artillery. For a total of 68 days we slept without tents, out in the open with no shelter, day and night, in the snow, rain and storms. Drenched to the bone and completely frozen, exhausted from marching, we had to sleep sitting by the fire, and one time had to make do behind a wall of rock with 18 inches of snow on the ground. In order to get wood, we tore up all the fences, of which there are many here, and used them to feed a fire that was as long as the entire front line of the company. We weren't given anything to eat, or damned little. At dawn a few men went to a nearby farmer, drove a steer into camp and shot it dead. We were often forced to forage food on our own because the roads were so bad, the quartermaster wasn't able to bring us provisions fast enough. For months we marched around Virginia ignorant of where and what for. In one town named Sperriville, we stayed for about two months. On the 7th of August we had to leave unexpectedly[. . . .] The battle had started while we were still ten miles away. At 11 o'clock at night we finally arrived at the battlefield, completely exhausted from the 24-hour march.[3] Large numbers of the wounded were being carried past us. Our troops, who had fought bravely, had only been able to hold their ground by taking heavy losses. The next day there was no fighting; the wounded were rescued and the dead were buried. Then on the third day, the enemy was exhausted. When we went across the battlefield, we saw hundreds of graves. The most terrible sight, though, was in the woods, where the enemy had dragged 200 corpses into one pile and tied a note to the foot of one of the unfortunates asking us to bury them. But we did not have the time. We marched about ten miles that day and then rested for a few days.

[39 ll.: description of the battle of Freeman's Ford, August 22, 1862: retreat; swimming across the torrential Rappahannock; reinforcements halted the enemy]

When our regiment was assembled again, it was discovered that we had lost a total of 61 killed and wounded, and all within a very short time. We also lost the brigadier general Bohlen.[4] We stayed there all night. Later we heard that we had been facing an enemy four times our strength. Without knowing it, we had done more than we had thought: we'd saved an entire army from de-

3. The regiment was at Hunter's Chapel, Virginia, until May 10, and at Sperryville from July 10 to August 8; it marched approximately forty miles in twenty-four hours and participated in the battle of Cedar Mountain, August 9, 1862. *History of Pennsylvania Volunteers* (1872), 2:894.

4. Schimmelfennig, up to that time commander of the 74th, then took over command of the brigade.

struction. The enemy had gotten ahead of us, and one day later we would have been surrounded.[5] But because of the bold attack General Sigel* ordered our brigade to make, the entire enemy army received orders to withdraw, and so the next day we got ahead of them[. . . .]

In the long hot battle that was fought, under the command of General Sigel, we fought back the enemy, inflicting much heavier losses than we received.[6] Piles of enemy dead lay all around. On the next day, the battle continued with renewed intensity; due to treason we were defeated and had to retreat[7] [signature missing].

Stafford Court Hause Va. / March 19th, 1863

Dear father and brother,

I received your kind but not so comforting letter of January 12th in the midst of the fray but in good health [41 ll.: correspondence; father seriously ill; would like to come home, where he had experienced good times and terrible times (for which he was to blame); reflections on life]. Since you got my last letter I haven't been in any danger, we were close to it one time, but the weather got in the way, it rained the whole night and all the next day (when the attack was to take place) thus making any operation impossible.

[8 ll.: crossing the Rappahannock] Winter campaigns, of course, are very hard, many men succumb to the severe hardships that accompany campaigns like that. As for me, I am always in good health, thanks to my strong constitution. Also, on February 24 I received my commission as a first lieutenant, which—as you can easily imagine—certainly did not make me angry. Wait! I almost forgot something, give my regards to Ludwig Schemmer—and ask him if he's recovered now, hiding behind his mother's apron strings, from the shock he got last fall from the draft? That was the reason for his voyage, besides spreading the most terrible lies about this country, about a country that gave him a free home, a free homeland, but instead of defending it and supporting it like a free citizen should, his cowardice got the better of him and drove him home behind the stove, where he spread lies that even reached our camp.

[21 ll.: details about this "hero from Güntersthal" (approximately six miles from Kirchhofen); is ashamed "that this coward is a countryman of mine"; greetings; signature]

5. A claim that cannot be corroborated by any other sources.

6. The second battle of Manassas, August 28–29, 1862.

7. Rather than treason, the Union defeat was mainly attributable to rivalry between commanders, although General Fitz-John Porter was court-martialed and cashiered for ignoring an order to attack on August 29. McPherson (1988), 528–32.

The address is / C. Knoebel / *in care of* / Henry Knoebel / No. 35. Diamond Alley / Pittsburgh / Pa.

January 22, 1864

[salutation missing]

I have been through a period of time that was filled with danger, hardship, and adventure. Of the two large battles I took part in, the last one was the largest and bloodiest in this war. It lasted for two days and was fought near the town of Gettisburg [Gettysburg*] in the state of Pennsylvania. Our army was about 85,000 strong, the enemy perhaps 10 to 15,000 men stronger. When the enemy army had been beaten, it had been reduced to 5,500 to 6,000 men.[8] The 1st of July was the first day of the battle. As we were approaching Gettisburg, we received the order to double-time through the town. Consequently, we went through it and out into the open field. Our regiment was sent forward as skirmishers and met with artillery fire with bombs and cannonballs. One cannonball went by so close to my head that the pressure almost knocked me down to the ground and did knock my cap off my head. For about an hour we were under heavy artillery fire, then when the enemy infantry attacked, with its superior numbers and such vehemence, we were forced to retreat. Another attempt to hold the line had to be abandoned because the enemy threatened to surround us. We went into the town, where on both sides of us the window-panes were crashing down into the streets and cannonballs were ripping off parts of the houses. Then, all of a sudden, we found ourselves completely cut off by the enemy, and so we had to surrender as prisoners of war. Never in my life will I forget the feeling when I had to give up my saber.[9] As prisoners, we were brought a mile away behind the town. As we walked across the battle-field we could see the terrible effects of our artillery fire. The dead lay in piles everywhere, there were even two field guns lying stripped on the ground[. . . .] On the 4th of July we could see that the enemy had been defeated. They started a hurried retreat. They left behind thousands of wounded men. Every barn, every house, every stable was filled with the wounded, and hundreds of them were lying in the woods; without any medical help and all alone, aban-doned to their sad fate. Since the rebels had to retreat so quickly, they couldn't take proper care of their prisoners. We had no glorious days. The rain was pouring down in buckets, so that the mountain streams turned into torrential rivers. We were completely starved and tired to death. But on we went with no

8. Union: 85,000; Confederates: 65,000. Losses: 23,000 (Union); 20,500 (Confederate). Long and Long (1971), 378.

9. The regiment's losses that day included fifty-one killed and wounded, as well as fifty-two missing, one of whom was obviously Knoebel.

rest or respite, up hill and down dale, into the dark night, because the enemy was being chased by our cavalry and light artillery and had to move quickly to get out of imminent danger by daybreak. This haste proved to be to our advantage. It was on the 6th of July, toward evening, when we marched into a large mountain range. The rain continued to pour. Starving, drenched, and tired to death from all the hardship, so that I was ready to drop, I made the desperate decision to escape, despite the danger of being shot. I put my plan into effect on the night of July 6th to 7th, under cover of darkness. Three of us, with another officer and a common soldier, crept through the woods[. . . .] Then, all of our deprivations and hardships were forgotten. Up the mountain we went, in good spirits and with a sprightly step, until we were about a mile away from the road and felt somewhat safe [18 ll.: slept like a log in the mountains; the next day they went on with the help of a compass; rested at a farm, good food; stayed with another farmer for three days, until July 10]. Now we felt safe and were very glad to have escaped imprisonment. Because our prisoners are treated horribly, even cruelly, by the rebel government. Hundreds have already died in prison from hunger and deprivation, and they died a more horrible death than the heroes who met their death on the battlefield. All the officers who were taken prisoner in the battle I was captured in are still languishing from want. They probably won't be exchanged until this accursed rebellion has been crushed.

Without any further mishaps, we met up with our regiment again on July 16th, where we were met with loud cheers [5 ll.: march to Virginia].

On August 8th we were quickly sent by railroad to Washington, the capital of America, and there we boarded a steamer and went several hundred miles south, to South Carolina, where we set up camp on a small island right on the coast of the Atlantic Ocean.[10] We are still here, near Charleston, the main hideout of the rebels. We're enjoying the best respite here, except for when we make a foray. Here on the coast, in the southern climate, life is wonderful [5 ll.: details about the pleasant climate; greetings; signature missing].

May 19, 1864

[salutation missing]

[95 ll.: concern about his ill father; traveling to Europe would use up all his savings he needs to use as capital for setting himself up in business; description of the battle of the Wilderness and Spotsylvania, May 5–12, 1864] Last I heard, the enemy is retreating everywhere, which has been made difficult by the destruction of the railroads. General Sigel* played a decisive part

---

10. Folly Island, South Carolina; *History of Pennsylvania Volunteers* (1872), 2:894.

in that. He now has an important new command; he will no doubt add new laurels to his earlier ones.[11] My men and I are several hundred miles from the theater of war. We only hear what is happening there about a week later, if we are lucky. We're camped in beautiful, warm South Carolina, where our duties are not without danger, but we have more rest and tents that are more comfortably furnished than the fighting troops in Virginia do. In four months my term of service will be up, and by then the war might also be over. Because our army has surrounded the main forces of the enemy with an iron ring; every day the ring gets tighter, and hence our might is increasing. Soon the decisive pressure will have been exerted, enough to cause the proud and misguided cotton princes and slaveholders to heave a final sigh and nestle at the feet of the conquerors. That is the punishment they deserve; for never has so much blood been shed like in this war—for such a wretched principle like the one the southerners have fought for. They—the monsters—are not content to maul the blacks with their whips and sell husbands off from wives and mothers from their children. They are depraved, defying the most sacred goods of humanity [signature missing].

This is the last direct sign of life we have of Knoebel. The regiment was sent back to Virginia in August 1864, where he was mustered out on September 16, 1864, three weeks after his term of service ended.[12]

11. Dept. of West Virginia, appointed on March 10, 1864, removed from command on May 21, 1864, after the battle of New Market* and two days after the date of this letter.

12. Muster Rolls, 74 Pa. Inf, NatA.

18. Surgeon Carl Uterhard

Carl Uterhard, born in 1835 in Parchim (Mecklenburg) and raised in Rostock, is an unusual case compared with the other letter-writers in this volume, perhaps most similar to Heinrich Stähler (no. 51). He traveled to the United States with the inten-

SOURCE NOTE: Uterhard has a command of the language one would expect of an upper-middle-class man with a medical school degree, but even for someone with his upbringing and education, the imaginative use and fluency of his words and phrases, as well as the vividness of his descriptions, are impressive. His occasional lapses in spelling are better characterized as an individualistic rejection of the pedantry of small minds, not as mistakes. For this series, only transcripts of the original letters are available, but there is no indication that any significant changes were made. Not included here are several letters in the series written in 1863 (five), 1864 (two), as well as one undated letter and one fragment.

tion of returning to Germany, and after the end of the Civil War, he did in fact go
back. But the inclusion of his letters here seems justified by the fact that many immigrants came to the United States intending to stay "forever" and then went back,
and others intended to stay for only a few months or years but never returned to
Germany. There is no sharp dividing line between permanent emigrants, long-term
visitors, and returning migrants. The American authorities made no distinction,
either, when they approved a veteran's pension for Uterhard's widow; and two of his
sons, an orchestra conductor and a doctor, immigrated to the United States in the
twentieth century.[1]

Carl Uterhard studied in Jena, Copenhagen, and Rostock, where he did his dis-
sertation on a complicated case of typhoid and was awarded his doctorate in June
1861. In 1861 and 1863 he published two medical monographs he had translated: one
from Danish, on syphilis, and one from English, on surgical techniques. After a year
of working in private practice, he was excited by the possibility of gaining firsthand
medical experience on the battlefield.[2] He set sail from Cardiff, Wales, as a guest of
the captain on the *Johann Keppler*, a sailing ship from Mecklenburg that transported
coal. After a six-week voyage, the ship arrived in New York on February 20, 1863.[3]
Only one week later, on February 27, Uterhard took the medical board examinations
required by the military, and on March 6 he received notice that he had passed and
was to report to the 119th New York Infantry Volunteers. This unit, formed in New
York City in September 1862, was about half German, and it was initially assigned
to the predominantly German XI Army Corps (2nd Brigade, 3rd Division).[4]

TO HIS MOTHER

                                   [New York] Saturday, February 21 [1863]
[salutation missing]

[26 ll.: arrival in the harbor] Our trip lasted 43 days. The harbor pilot
brought some newspapers along, and these reassured me that the war was still
raging away. I had often thought to myself that perhaps they had made peace

---

1. Information provided by the donor; Pension File, NatA.

2. On December 31, 1862, he wrote to his mother from Cardiff: "but thousands go into battle
and come back from them unscathed, so why should I—as a doctor—not have the same hopes,
especially since doctors, who are not inexpensive and can't even be recruited now for money, are
only exposed to minimal danger. And the main thing is, I can get my hands on the sick and the
wounded and learn from this; so don't think about the dangers." NABS.

3. Information provided by the donor; *Biographisches Lexikon* (1962 [1929]), 5:685; Pension
File, NatA; obituary in *Warnemünder Zeitung*, March [19?], 1895; NYPL.

4. Muster Rolls, NatA; Dyer (1959 [1908]), 1451–52; *OAR* 2:615–16. Of the ten companies in
the 119 N.Y. Inf, five were approximately 90 percent German, two about 50 percent, and three
about 5 percent. Regt. Books, Desc. Books, NatA.

Carl Uterhard,
ca. 1873. (Klaus
Ohlerich)

during our voyage [12 ll.: captain's hospitality]. If I were to describe the impression I have of the American people, after reading the papers the pilot brought us, it would be negative, nothing but boasting and conceit in every regard, and unfortunately the people in my profession are the worst, so that in America I am often ashamed to be called a doctor. But more about this another time.

Your Carl.

Saturday, February 28

[salutation missing]

[4 ll.: has returned from Albany, New York] You see, I had found out in the first few days that for over a year now, they have only been admitting doctors into the army who have taken the exams set by a commission in Albany. This was bad news for me, since I couldn't find out anything about what the exam would be like. At first I had wanted to spend another three to four weeks preparing [5 ll.: time too short, medical books too expensive], and so I decided to travel to Albany that very afternoon to take the exam. The train left at 10:30 in the evening [63 ll.: train trip; asked a colleague about the exam]. He just said that I could answer the questions in German, and that I had to be at the arsenal at 9 o'clock, where I would find my questions. So I betook myself there, finally found the right man who was to supervise me and who gave me 16 English questions, paper etc. I couldn't understand some parts of the questions because of the English formulations, no dictionary to be had, the monitor an Anglo American to the bone so I couldn't ask him anything, and so I just had to start writing anyway. All 16 questions had to be answered. In Germany we would have had 14 days to answer them, and I was in despair at first. I wrote from 9 to 3 o'clock in the afternoon, without even getting up from my chair [39 ll.: results uncertain; return trip; description of New York].

March 6th, Friday

[. . .] Yesterday the reply from the Surgeon General in Albany finally arrived. I opened the letter with not a little trepidation, but it said that I had passed my exams and that I would immediately receive my commission as a surgeon in the 119th regiment [6 ll.: details]. All I have been able to find out is that it belongs to the so-called Potomac Army under General Siegel [Sigel*] (a German) and is posted near Falmouth [11 ll.: Washington; pay]. But at any rate, it will be enough for me to live on in reasonable comfort here [93 ll.: paper money; Germans in New York (are all saloonkeepers or waitresses); friends; amazement at seeing steam-powered elevators; greetings; signature].

Washington, March 18, 1863

Dear Marie and dear Mama,

At the moment I am in the city where the president of the United States resides, in Washington, as a surgeon in the 119th regiment, in full uniform [18 ll.: train trip]. All the men who traveled with me were officers and soldiers going to join up with the army. Generals, colonels, captains, common soldiers, all mixed together in the only class of wagon that American railroads have. There isn't as much distance between the officers and the soldiers as back home. The soldiers are just as much like *Gentlemen* as the generals are. This time my lucky star led me to a German hotel, "New Yorker Hotel," that was overflowing with military men-Germans [17 ll.: Washington]. The city life here, the hustle and bustle, is more impressive than in London and New York; the city is teeming with soldiers who have come here to join the army like me or are here on leave[. . . .] In the hospitals here there are supposed to be about fifty thousand wounded. On the sidewalks it's hard to get through the crowds, crossing the streets is dangerous due to the countless wagons on their way to the army. The dirt and mud they have here is indescribable[. . . .] Because of this, all the ladies walk around in knee boots made for men [11 ll.: had to borrow money]. You see, I had to buy all my own equipment, and even though I'm going into the field with only one suit, it still cost a lot; my sword with its straps and sash for 25 dollars; my uniform, dark blue trousers with a gold cord along the outer seam, blue vest with yellow buttons, dark blue coat with gold stripes on the shoulder for 30 dollars, hat for 7 dollars; small suitcase 8 dollars etc. All the equipment I'll be taking into the field weighs less than 10 pounds, and I can easily carry it in a leather suitcase. They don't deliver extra baggage. You just have to learn to make do with less [6 ll.: address; pay as of the day he took the exams]. I don't know yet exactly how much it is, but I think 160–170 talers* a month in your money, but I heard that unfortunately I get nothing for free. I have to provision myself, buy my own horse and take care of my own orderly. That sounds like a lot of money, but in America it's nothing [88 ll.: others had to wait longer for a position; adventure in dangerous New York; March 22: on the way to the regiment, he missed the stop, then wanted to take the train back, but it didn't stop:] so I took my belongings, threw them into a car, and, at full speed, in one giant leap that could have cost my life, I jumped onto it as well. I fell down, but I was inside the car, and could ride along—I jumped off in Brookstation with the same alacrity [20 ll.: adventurous march on foot to meet up with the regiment; signature missing].

TO CAPTAIN JANTZEN[5]

Washington, March 18, 1863

My dear captain,

[69 ll.: describes his experiences; asks him to send some things] What I would like to have is the following: two volumes, bound in black, with the title: *Spezielle Pathologie* [special pathology] by Dr. Niemeyer, one volume with a brown binding: *Arzneimittellehre* [pharmaceutical handbook] by Oesterlen, two volumes with new bindings: *Anatomische Chirurgie* [anatomical surgery] by Roser, two pairs of boots and a pair of shoes, and my woolen blanket [30 ll.: details; greetings; signature].

March 22, 63

My dear captain,

[21 ll.: experiences; address] I am the only doctor here in the regiment, the *acting Surgeon*. Every morning I see 40 to 50 of the sick, and I also have to visit a hospital and the officers who are sick; everything has to be written down and reported to the brigade. So you can imagine what things are like around here. I have a druggist and a surgeon and two orderlies on my staff, a small tent with a stove is my home, with a tree stump for a chair and a crate turned upside down for a desk. I get 114 dollars a month and fodder for my horse, which I have to buy myself[. . . .] My rank in my regiment is captain. Tomorrow our regiment is going on picket duty and will stay away for three days and nights, out in the open. I have to go along, unfortunately, but I think an ambulance wagon will be going along that I can slip into at night [5 ll.: correspondence].

Your faithful friend, C. Uterhart.

TO HIS MOTHER

March 23, 63

[salutation missing]

[. . .] I am very busy here, I work from 7 in the morning until late at night because I am the only doctor in the regiment, and we have a large number of sick men. When the regiment was recruited, they took anything, the old, the weak, the sick—and now, of course, they can't take the extremely strenuous war conditions. We are about 500 strong, and every morning I have 50 to 60 on the sick list, but every week men are discharged who are no longer of any use, and there's no end to it. We have 14-year-old boys in our regiment who aren't even strong enough to carry a gun [5 ll.: camp life]. I'm living near the hospital tent in a fairly large tent, together with the so-called *Stewart*.

---

5. Captain of the ship *Johann Keppler*, on which Uterhard had crossed the Atlantic.

The latter is the regiment's druggist, who prepares the medicine I prescribe. We have both requisitioned stretchers from the hospital, which we sleep on, wrapped in new woolen blankets, also taken from the same source [15 ll.: furnishings; iron stove; details]. It is cold lying here at night, I often have to get up and walk around in order to warm up a bit. As soon as it gets light, I am wide-awake due to the cold, and I get up and make a fire. The officers [. . .] have to see to their own food [9 ll.: he gets free (bad) food from the hospital]. The first two nights I stayed with the regiment's adjutant and ate and drank with him, the colonel (Colonel Peisser), and the lieutenant colonel.[6] They keep their own black cook, but he doesn't seem to understand much of his trade, at least they aren't living much better than we are, but more expensively[. . . .] I gave one of the hospital orderlies the honor of becoming my orderly and servant; he used to be a tailor, and that's why I chose him for this privileged position [72 ll.: still does not have a horse; experiences. March 25: spent the night on picket duty; rain. March 27: daily life; visited a German doctor in the neighboring regiment; details; signature missing].

Camp near Stafford House Virginia / XI Army Corps, 2nd Brigade,
3rd Division / Army of the Potomac. / April 6th, 1863
My dear Marie and Mama,

[31 ll.: weather; rumors] But don't be shocked when I write you that I also have lice. There are millions of these creatures living in our camp, and if you manage to give these irksome visitors the slip by means of an energetic cleansing, you just pick up some new ones a few days later [60 ll.: experiences; a "new doctor, an Englishman*";[7] Uterhard has more time off; details. April 11:] But instead of resting up from our hardships, as we had hoped, our regiment received the order to get ready within an hour for a large review of our entire army corps that was going to be held by Präsident Lincoln in Broock Station, four miles (eng.) away from our camp. The colonel lent me a horse from one of the regiment wagons and some spurs, and so I set off with our regiment in full array [8 ll.: 20,000 men in the parade]. Finally the batteries thundered, and we saw a large number of men on horseback riding down a wooded hill—it was Lincoln, surrounded by hundreds of staff officers. Amid the sound of the trumpets and drums and the deafening thunder of the cannon, he rode along the front line of each regiment, hat in hand. He was dressed simply, in black, wore a black hat, long hair, quite scrawny, and

6. Elias Peissner fell at Chancellorsville* on May 2, 1863, Lieutenant Colonel Edward F. Lloyd one year later at Resaca, Georgia; *OAR*, 2:615.

7. Assistant Surgeon Henry Ayme, whose predecessor, Charles Brueninghausen, was mustered out on February 23, 1863. *OAR*, 2:615.

he looked more unkempt than impressively noble. Our chief surgeon, myself, the captain, and an adjutant halted behind the front line of our regiment and the entire procession passed by right in front of us. Later, Lincoln took up position on a nearby hill where the United States flag was flying, and every regiment had to march by in front of him. We were almost the last regiment and didn't get back to camp until late afternoon [14 ll.: hungry; heat; bought a revolver]. I don't want to stay forever in America, I've never seen such a country of swindling. It's all humbug here—another time I'll write to you about wartime swindle [62 ll.: ready to march; sent the sick back; provisions for a week; bought a horse for seventy dollars; went riding with his friend Dr. Haerl from the 58th New York Infantry]. I do want to write you one piece of news, though. I have bought myself a *Nigger*. I give him 100 dollars a year to be my servant, wash, clean, cook for me, take care of my horse, etc. If he is loyal and good, I will bring him with me to Europe [21 ll.: correspondence; family; greetings].

May 17th, 63.

[. . .] I'm afraid the newspaper report about the unfortunate battle at Chancellorsville,* in which our army corps played a major role, will have filled you with concern about me [8 ll.: is unscathed]. It was the first battle I was in, but it was enough. I never, not for even a moment, had any feeling of fear for my own life, despite the heaviest rain of bullets, because such massive slaughtering of one's fellow human beings does not permit any concern for one's own small self to arise. But upon sober reflection, one realizes what madness it is to put one's life in such danger. Those who are shot and die immediately are the lucky ones; those who are wounded and left behind on the battlefield are the most unfortunate men in the world. Hundreds of our men starved on the battlefield, died of thirst—or of madness brought on by the scorching rays of the sun burning straight down on them. Hundreds burned to death in the woods, when the grass and the underbrush, desiccated by the sun, chanced to catch fire. Hundreds died in the teeming and overcrowded hospitals, where we could hardly help those poor souls, we had no bandages, nothing to eat, nothing to drink. Doing the most strenuous work while hungry and parched left us doctors so weak and faint that we were in despair. We had a hard, hard time of it, and I hope to God I never get into such a situation again. I can't understand how I managed as well as I did [11 ll.: several days without food and drink]. During the last night it poured down with rain, and since I was only wrapped in a blanket, under God's great sky, lying on the ground with my boots for a pillow, I woke up in the morning, soaked from head to toe, with no coffee to quench my thirst, no crust of bread to still my hunger [5 ll.: details]. Then our regiment discovered some piglets that the farmers had chased into the woods, and immediately a wild hunt began. I killed one with my revolver, and immediately cooked myself a piece of meat that made one of the best meals I have ever had, even though I devoured it half-raw [34 ll.: beginning of the battle of Chancellorsville, defeat of his XI Corps]. Then all of a sudden we heard a rustle in the woods behind us, we were struck by bullets, and then thousands of men suddenly dashed out of the woods, fleeing wildly, trying to reach the woods on the other side [8 ll.: was swept along by the fleeing cavalry and artillery; finally I:] caught my breath and managed to get to the other side of the road, where some regiments were still standing in battle formation, trying to stop the men from fleeing and ready to receive the enemy. The generals and officers struck the soldiers with their sabers to get them to stop running, but they just kept on fleeing. I rode back toward the enemy to look for my regiment, but I couldn't find it, because after having been attacked four times, with the colonel killed and 128 men lost, it had withdrawn from the advancing enemy. I was now about 200 paces away from the enemy, and [. . .] so I turned around and galloped back to our battery as fast as I could, because I thought I would be safest there for the moment. There were 8 cannon there maintaining a steady, terrible barrage of fire aimed at the enemy coming out of the woods and preventing them from making an advance[. . . .] But then we saw large numbers of enemy artillery come rattling out of the woods, and they took up position and directed horrendous fire at our battery. The first shots already killed a large number of artillerymen; the battery turned around, broke away, and I went with them as fast as I could toward the woods about 500 paces away. Then the enemy artillery aimed its devastating fire on everyone who was fleeing, and I saw that almost all of the officers who had been riding near me had been shot off their horses. So I jumped off and ran, leading my horse toward the woods on the double. Right in front of the woods I met my chief surgeon and our druggist [8 ll.: flight; finally:] we got to the road: 40 to 50 of the wounded had dragged themselves to a log cabin there, so we stopped together with some other doctors and started to bandage them up. I had finished bandaging three men and was just about to cut a bullet out of the back of a fourth, when suddenly the rebels, close on the heels of our men, stormed toward our house, spreading death with their shots. Our men turned around while they were fleeing and shot back at the rebels who were bearing down on them. We lay down flat on the ground, trying to stay out of the crossfire we were in. Finally the rebels advanced so far that we were no longer in any danger from the shots of our own men, but then the rebels stormed at us, although when they saw we were doctors, they called out *All right* and pressed on. Every now and then a rebel officer came riding up, and so bit by bit we lost everything

we owned—my horse, my bag, my coat which had my revolver in it, everything gone to the devil. Finally a noble enemy colonel came by who gave us
some guards, but they couldn't do anything but try to protect our lives, which
were to be seriously endangered two more times [34 ll.: Union cavalry attack;
prisoners were marched with guards to Chancellorsville, under fire from their
own troops; two doctors seriously injured]. We were prisoners for two weeks
and had to survive hard, hard times. From early morning to late at night the
most strenuous work [13 ll.: taking care of the wounded] all in all we have
about 1,500 wounded here. All these men were wounded in the short three-
or four-hour battle of Chancellorsville on the evening of May 2nd, and even
more were killed. Seven thousand prisoners and 30 cannon were captured by
the enemy. The dead and wounded were lying around as thick as turnips in the
field [9 ll.: suffering of the wounded on the battlefield]. Those poor fellows—
a day and a night of solid rain drove all those who could not be put somewhere
inside almost to despair—their bloodcurdling wails filled the air. Those who
died were fortunate, and we could not be of much help, because we were in
enemy territory and were prisoners, we had nothing, not even the bandages
we needed to dress the wounds. We suffered from such hunger and thirst we
all thought we would die. Every day we hoped our ambulances would arrive
to get us and the wounded, but we always hoped in vain. On the eighth day a
wagon from our side finally did arrive, waving a flag of truce for protection,
and they brought us flour, *Crackers*, bandages, milk, and liquor. On the 14th
day the long-awaited ambulances finally crossed the Rapahannoc. On the fif-
teenth we packed up our entire hospital into about 130 ambulances and departed from enemy territory [20 ll.: good bed and free food at the Sanitary
Commission; back with his regiment; had been thought dead]. As for me, I
hope I will never again come under fire as a physician, and I will make sure
by staying thousands of paces away from the fighting. Now I know all about
this swindle. I can resign any time I want to—I signed up for 3 years of service, but I can leave the army any time if want to resign, like some doctors do
every day, because the hardships are too strenuous. All my belongings that I
lost, including my horse, and my Negro, who is also gone [13 ll.: will be paid
for; correspondence; address; signature missing].

      May 27, 1863 / Headquarters of the 119th Rg. near Brookes / station
Dear Mama,
      [8 ll.: correspondence; has recovered] As luck would have it, I immedi-
ately found a good servant, who cooks for me at my own expense [5 ll.: hospital food is too bad]. In the beginning I didn't have a servant, and then I had
quite a lazy Negro, at my own expense and who soon thereafter was killed or

taken prisoner in that memorable battle. Now I know all about the American swindle system and have requisitioned a man as a hospital orderly who works just for me. Our expenses amount to eight dollars a month, but we live well [4 ll.: details]. Milk, fruit soups and other delicacies are sent to the hospital for the sick. Before the battle, whenever deliveries of this kind arrived, the chief surgeon had them brought to his tent and then consumed them with his friends. Since the battle, now that he is aware that I know him a bit better, I've been choosing what I need for my own use first. Unbelievable amounts of money are being spent on things to nurse the sick and the wounded, but no patient ever sees any of it. Large shipments of *Whiskey*, for example, are sent to the sick soldiers every month, but the respective regimental doctors drink it all with their friends. I always did as much as I could for the sick, and before the battle I never took any of these things for myself, but now I have come so far as to take some of the things, though sparingly, that the regimental surgeon would otherwise consume himself. My regimental doctor was in charge of the hospital that we set up in enemy territory, but he behaved so badly that some of the doctors who were with me in the same hospital have had him called up for court-martial: he is charged with incessant drunkenness and incompetence in his operating. I don't know how he is going to get out of this. I think he will probably be discharged. I have promised him I won't discredit him, although I could easily do so. I wouldn't refrain from doing this if we weren't in the same regiment. He is deeply hated in the regiment. We often don't see each other for weeks, he doesn't take care of anything. I do all the paperwork, and if I need his signature, I send the papers to him. I think I will not be staying at my post much longer than Michaelmas [September 29], because then I intend to take some leave and go to Washington, take various examinations and, if I pass them, get a position as a chief surgeon. Then you don't have any superior officer, you can do what you like, with the rank of a major and 160 or 170 dollars a month. The only catch is that I probably won't have learned as much English as is required, since the examinations in Washington are written in English. In the two weeks as a prisoner, when I was together with American doctors, I learned more than the entire time before, I was really quite fluent. Here I've forgotten it all again, because I only associate with Germans.—I don't have much hope of being promoted, since the Americans loathe all the Germans and slight them whenever they can. In the report that the *Medical Director* of our entire corps sent to the war secretary in Washington about the activities of the doctors after the battle of Chancellorsville, Dr. Armstrong, chief surgeon of our brigade, and I were the only doctors who were highly praised and most warmly commended—I happened to read a copy of the report at General Howard's—but I think that Armstrong, who is English,* will be made division surgeon and I, a German, will be forgotten. This doesn't offend me, I am not ambitious, but I would like the higher pay and the complete freedom of the position [8 ll.: wants to buy a horse. May 30:] Our army has been significantly reduced due to the last five-day battle [Chancellorsville*], and in addition, no one has even a penny's worth of trust and respect for the generals, but great respect for the courage of the enemy. Every soldier can see that the colonels and generals are only interested in making as much money as possible [letter breaks off].

June 3rd, 1863

[19 ll.: correspondence; friends] Before I forget, I want to write you a few words of reassurance about how the doctors are positioned in battles. The ones who are ordered to stay with their regiment follow along behind the soldiers at a reasonable distance of 400–800 paces. This doesn't guarantee absolute safety, of course, but the guns, cannonballs, and shrapnel don't fly as close as they did to me at the beginning, inexperienced as I was, when I took part in my first battle. In addition, doctors wear a green silk sash over their shoulders. In the last battle, mine was in my suitcase, but that won't happen again because now I wear it almost day and night, since I never think it is safe here even for a moment. For this reason, I bought myself a horse two days ago, a splendid horse [30 ll.: June 5: prepared to march. June 6: false alarm]. Today Captain v. Borries left our regiment and went home.[8] He was a great swindler, took money away from the men in his company in the nastiest way, until finally he was advised by his superiors to take his leave. I have now been here for a little over two months, and in this time we've lost twelve officers, including one colonel and one captain killed, 2 officers seriously wounded, three captains who'd had enough of this swindle of a war, and several officers. Our regiment consists of 376 men at the moment, divided into 10 companies. Each company is supposed to have one captain and two officers, but we only have a total of three captains and 7 or eight officers. The situation looks much the same in all the other regiments, and it's even worse in many of them. The 58th regiment is 180 strong, that means 18 in each company. It is clear that regiments like this cannot win a battle, as we will find out in the near future. My chief surgeon is up for court-martial today, and I am curious to see if he manages to get by[9] [35 ll.: heat; friends. June 16 or 17: gorgeous fields and woods; skirmishes; signature missing].

---

8. Captain Otto Van [von] Borries was mustered out on June 6, 1863. *OAR*, 2:615.
9. Surgeon James D. Hewett was dishonorably discharged on June 14, 1863. *OAR*, 2:616.

June 26th, 63

My dear Mama,

[74 ll.: camp; mail service; skirmishes; snakes; was allowed to stay in a house in Jefferson, Maryland, for the night. June 27:] My hosts were only an old maid who was hard of hearing, an older slave woman and two black men: the last three looked more like apes than human beings. The funny thing was that these blacks decided they really liked me and did everything they could for me, against the wishes and despite the admonitions of their old mistress. I had just caught the first whiff of my lunch being cooked when the general call to march was sounded, and I hastily ran back to my regiment. Our entire army—I think we must be 15 or 20,000 men strong-marched through the little town [Jefferson] with music playing. It was raining, and the wagons could hardly get through the deep mud, which is why our procession took several hours. My blacks shouted out when they saw me ride by. In the afternoon, soaked to the skin, we marched through Midd[l]etown, a somewhat larger town, and here all the maidens were dressed in white, threw us flowers, waved Union flags and white handkerchiefs. In return, we beat our drums mightily, shouted out the occasional *Hurrah*, rewarded the little ladies with a gallant salute, and set up camp about half a German mile [2.2 U.S. miles] away from the town in a wet field of clover [47 ll.: needs a pair of glasses, can't get one. July 3: to Frederick; romantic area; to Emmetsburg]. It is interesting to watch how busy everyone is when camp is being set up. From the colonel down to the lowliest kitchen help, everyone is as busy as possible, especially when it's like it is here, with heavy rain falling from the skies, and the need to prepare some kind of shelter and then something warm to eat [6 ll.: they cut branches to put up tents, fetch water and firewood, make a fire to dry out]. A large number of the men descend on the nearest farm, like a bird of prey on its quarry, to buy or steal hay, straw, and if possible delicacies like bread, milk, or eggs. Then the men sit around all the fires and take care of their needs: one cooks bacon, another makes coffee, the third one soup, a fourth man eggs, a fifth one an unplucked chicken, the sixth a stolen pig, etc. [42 ll.: marching orders; took care of the wounded; got separated from his regiment; battle (Gettysburg*) begins]. I went over to the hospital for our corps that was located on the hill to the right of the town in a German church. [4 ll.: shots, heard shouts; "the enemy":] was 20 paces away, chasing our men. I didn't want to be taken prisoner and wanted to mount my horse, but my horse shied at the shots and all the shouting [4 ll.: the horse bolted, his orderly stopped it and rode off]. At the same moment I was taken prisoner, but I didn't lose anything, because all my money and belongings were on my horse. Our men were hit hard, but they repositioned themselves behind the town. Our colonel has apparently been killed, along with our major, two captains, our adjutant is either severely wounded or dead, a large number of soldiers are lying in the various hospitals here, where the mess is the same as it was at Chancellorsville*: nothing to eat, no bandages and a lot of work to do [22 ll.: caught in friendly fire. July 5:] The enemy retreated during the night, and in the morning our troops came in, and we were rescued[. . . .] / Your Carl.

July 10th / between Booneslong *and*
Hagerstown near Antietam Creek

[salutation missing]

[18 ll.: military situation; expects another battle] In the last battle near Gettysburg,* which I described to you only very roughly, our regiment suffered horrendous losses. All of the close friends I had among the officers were killed or mortally wounded, out of 16 officers we only have six left. I had to muster all my strength not to cry when I got back to the regiment, there were so many missing who had been dear to me. Our regiment has been reduced from 300 men to 140, and we lost a flag [49 ll.: troop movements. July 29: is sick, being looked after by his orderly]. My route took me through the little town of Jefferson, where I wrote you that I stayed with an old woman and her slave. They recognized me immediately and, best of all, they instantly invited me to lunch [8 ll.: details]. The first afternoon we were lucky, we stopped at a large mill that was owned by a rebel captain. As soon as we found this out, the building was plundered, and we got our hands on a hundred barrels of flour and a lot of grain to feed the horses with. Meyer got hold of about 15 lbs. of flour, and this, prepared in a multitude of ways, was our sole nourishment for the next few days [76 ll.: pancakes and dumplings—stomach revolted; marching in the heat and the rain. August 5: friends; correspondence]. On the 3rd of September it will have been one year since I left Warnemünde. The time has just flown [4 ll.: climate]. I have experienced more in this one year than in my entire life before. I never thought I could endure all the things I've been through, but all in all, it has agreed with me quite well [6 ll.: expenses]. But here in America everyone is so self-centered, and it's really quite contagious. When there is a starving man lying on the side of the road and an American goes by with his pockets full, he won't even give him a crust of bread [34 ll.: compensation for his horse, clothing; will be paid soon; greetings; signature].

Weaverville, near Warrenton Junction / August 20, 1863
Camp of the 119 N.Y.V.R. 2 Brig. 3 Div. / XI Corp / Potom. Army

My dear Mama,

[12 ll.: correspondence] Here they have a special way of celebrating days of significance, they drink liquor. From the generals down to the common soldiers, they all drink liquor to celebrate happy events or to suppress miserable memories. They don't drink it out of glasses, but from the bottle, and get alarmingly intoxicated as a result. Every day, dozens of officers are dishonorably discharged without pay because they drink themselves into oblivion. A few days ago our regiment lost an officer this way, a Bavarian named Brunner, who was otherwise a good and decent officer, but then he got drunk, and after he had insulted our brigadier general Chrysanowsky [Kryzanowski*] he went to our division general Carl Schurz* and said the classic words: Kiss my ---. Brunner named me as a witness at his court-martial; he wanted me to testify that he often suffers from temporary insanity. He had hoped this excuse would get him out of it. I naturally told the court that I couldn't swear to it, but it was nevertheless possible. They gave him a dishonorable discharge and took away all his pay.[10] Many of our officers have had to leave the army because they ruined their health by drinking liquor[. . . .] In the other regiments the situation is even worse than in ours, because the colonels usually set a bad example. The colonel we have now, the former Lieutenant Colonel Lockmann, doesn't drink, and on this issue we get along well together, because I don't drink either, at least not liquor[. . . .] In the field it is hard to come by liquor, but the *Medical Department* has the best supplies, we get a good number of bottles for the patients delivered every month. We don't need much for the patients, and Dr. Ayme, my colleague, and I don't drink, and as long as we have even one drop, the gentlemen officers come by in the morning and keep on begging until they get their morning shot of liquor from us. America is full of contradictions; it is undoubtedly the country where people drink the most, yet it also has the largest associations of people intent upon never letting a drop touch their lips [80 ll.: details; alcohol extremely expensive. August 21: heat; hardships]. The best thing, though, was that my colleague and I, along with a former officer, a well-educated young man who is a common soldier here, regularly had lunch at a nearby *Farm* for 25 Cts. [. . .], and we liked the family a lot. It included, you see, three young, grown-up, warm-blooded daughters, and our amiability served to mitigate the hatred they had otherwise harbored against every Union soldier [11 ll.: general call to march while they were drinking coffee; rushed back to camp]. We quickly packed and saddled our horses, and everything that couldn't be taken along in the rush was burned, on orders from the commanding officer. Among other

10. In hearings held on August 10 and 12, 1863, an eight-member court pronounced Frederick Brunner guilty of the offense described above. He was not, however, dishonorably discharged but reduced to the rank of private. RG 153, Brunner trial, NN 131, Files 1809–1994, NatA. One year later he was promoted to first lieutenant again. *OAR*, 2:615.

things, our beautiful hospital tent, worth 2 to 300 dollars, met this fate and was burned, because it would have taken too long to pack it up [4 ll.: departure in the evening]. I hate these night marches from the bottom of my heart, and on these marches I have frequently been driven almost to despair, as have many others, not believing I would live to see the next day. How I have managed not to drown, fall off my horse, or get run over by the artillery and baggage wagons, I have no idea [158 ll.: met up with a German friend serving with the cavalry. August 22: details about weekly expenses; forays to secure furnishings for the tents in Weaverville. August 27: war situation after the fall of Vicksburg*; greetings; signature].

                   Bridgeport on the Tenessee River, Alabama / October 9, 63.
[salutation missing]
     [6 ll.: address; location of Bridgeport] The area here is one of the most beautiful in the world. We are camped in a valley basin, several miles wide, surrounded by densely wooded hills. The Tenessee River, where we are camped, is almost as wide as our Warnow River in Rostock, a majestic river that flows very quickly, like all mountain streams [25 ll.: rivers; bridge building typically American—shoddy]. And you can tell how little the American government cares about soldiers breaking their necks by the fact that on our trip, out of our two divisions of five to six thousand men, 25 men died before we arrived. The poor fellows had all crept onto the top of the railroad cars, because they were packed like sardines inside them, but if they were then overcome by sleep, they fell off and either broke their necks or were run over. Every night we lost a few, but during the whole trip nothing was done to remedy this dreadful grievance, and 25 men paid for it with death [6 ll.: chaotic organization of the trip; officers had to get their own food]. No one knew how long the train would stop, sometimes it stopped for a quarter of an hour, sometimes for hours, but no one dared get off, because we didn't know for sure [16 ll.: enjoyed city life during stops in Indianapolis and Louisville]. In Nashville we arrived in the morning in the pouring rain and got a good breakfast in the city, but as luck would have it, our train had already left when we came running back as fast as we could to the train station, stomachs full but soaked to the skin. About 40 officers had been left behind, of every rank, from colonel down to 2nd lieutenant. They attached another car for the 40 of us to another train that was about to leave, but it had been used to transport horses earlier, and the droppings were ankle-deep [35 ll.: thirty hours in horse manure, hungry; rumors; baggage was delivered later]. The baggage had been thrown out of the cars and lay in a huge heap next to the railroad. Many of the suitcases had come open and their motley contents were scattered all over

the ground. Hundreds of soldiers and officers were busy trying to take whatever they could get their hands on. Hundreds of men who had never owned anything managed to equip themselves with a complete set of clothes. Hundreds of other men lost everything they had. Almost all of General Schurz's* things were stolen; I saw him wandering around, cursing and yelling at people, while he was looking for his garment bag and other belongings.[11] [208 ll.: details; prices in the market near the camp; a German baker and photographer are earning enormous amounts of money; guarding the railroad line to Nashville; flora. October 17:] At the moment my ambition is aroused, or at least my desire for a regimental surgeon's salary, and I am busy applying for such a position. Promotions are to be expected; a large number of black regiments are being formed here, and all of us have been asked to apply for posts in them. I sent in my papers and am curious to see if I will be successful[. . . .] I also think it would be interesting to associate with the blacks for a while, to get to know the race; and in addition it pays 2,400 talers,* or 1,800 dollars with fodder for two horses; you also get the rank of a major[12] [18 ll.: asks for two fever thermometers; friends; greetings; signature].

Chattanooga, October [November] 26, 63. / Corps Hospital *of the* XI Corps [salutation missing]

[100 ll.: description of the battles of Chattanooga and Lookout Mountain, November 23–25, 1863] Then it was our turn to move forward into the fray, and arrayed in tight columns, we poured down into the valley, into the thick of the enemy cannonballs and bombs. In case of battle, my orders were to carry out operations in our corps hospital, and as the corps moved into the firing, I received the order to go to my assigned position. This was the first time I received such a command, in Chancellorville [Chancellorsville*] I had to be in the thick of the battle, stand there like any other soldier and be taken prisoner, and it was the same at Gettysburg.* I must admit I breathed more easily after I reached the corps hospital, which was on our right wing, close to Chattanooga, on a hill that afforded us a clear view of the battlefield [37 ll.: further fighting, storming of Lookout Mountain]. Finally a gust of wind dispersed the fog, revealing a sight that caused us to cry out a lively *Hurrah*. Way up in the mountains, we saw our flag at the front of one of the regiments, and fighting at every step, they were moving forward slowly in one long battle line [46 ll.: artillery fire; mountain taken by storm, 2,000 prisoners; the Ameri-

---

11. Most historians view this railroad operation much more positively than Uterhard; see Clark (2001).

12. On the motivations of Germans to become officers of the U.S. Colored Troops, and their relations with these troops in general, see Öfele (2004), 83–112.

cans can be proud of this victory; recovery of the wounded without wagons: terrain too steep; battle of Missionary Ridge, November 25, 1863]. On Friday the 26th we doctors received orders to report to our corps; all the sick were to be sent by steamship [. . .] to Nashville. So at midday we left, some eight to ten doctors and about 80 men we had used as orderlies [letter interrupted in mid-sentence; continues below:]

December 3, 63 / Landon on the Tenessee / East Tenessee in the hospital went to find our corps. We hiked over the Mission Ridges, and on the roads we found many, many wounded rebels lying there, and since they had no tents, no blankets, no food, they had to suffer endlessly. Ambulances, wagons, and men from our side were combing the woods in all directions, looking for the wounded, but there were so many of them that quite a few had to lie there on the battlefield for many days. On our way we came upon a small farmhouse that was full of corn and flour, and since our horses had had nothing to eat the whole time we had been in the hospital, we raided it. The woman cried bitterly when we took her corn, but our need was too great. I was obliged, as were many other men, to pull my horse along behind me, it was so weak from 4 days of fasting. So, even though I felt sorry about it, I took half a sack [letter breaks off].

Lookout Mountain Valley, January 7, 64, Teness.
My dear Mama,
[21 ll.: address; correspondence] I was just about to go to Nashville, the capital of Tennessee, to take the exams there [32 ll.: details; is waiting for leave; daily life; Christmas]. But to get back to the exams, I know I will have a very hard time with the exams in English. I will have a week of tough examinations, and 27 out of 30 doctors have failed with flying colors. But I am still going to do it, since I'd like to stroll around Nashville for a few days, and because it won't bother me if I fail due to the fact that I don't understand enough English [104 ll.: correspondence; financial matters; family; horses are suffering from privation]. The fact that I wasn't made chief surgeon from the very beginning is only because of my ignorance of how things work here. Once you are already in the army, it is difficult to be promoted, because everything in Washington depends on your *Connexionen*. Those with good *Connexionen* there become generals, even if they are imbeciles. My *Connexionen* don't amount to much, I have only myself to thank for what I have achieved and may yet achieve [20 ll.: financial matters; greetings; signature].

Nashville, January 20, 64 / Tennessee

My dear Mama,

[76 ll.: Nashville. January 25: exams over; satisfied with written papers; terrified of the oral exams because of the language] On the third evening I was called in and things went well with two of the men—they repeated their questions or reformulated them when I didn't understand and tried their best to understand my English [6 ll.: communication with the third examiner was difficult]. Then the president asked a few questions. The last three questions were: how long do you cook beans to make sure they're done? How long do you cook potatoes? Do you think it is humbug when a doctor asks a patient to show him his tongue all the time? I answered—certainly, and the exams came to an end amid laughter [10 ll.: has a good feeling]. It wasn't all that terribly difficult; I think that anyone who took his exams in Germany and hasn't forgotten too much can pass. They really only ask things a practicing physician ought to know.

[57 ll.: complains about Nashville: all the taverns closed on military orders; expensive—room and board costs $1.50 a day; everything very dirty; very cold winter; soldiers are freezing to death; war situation] How are Uncle Fritz and his children? There are thousands of cute little mulattos like them, no blacker than Martha, Carlchen etc., running around here in Nashville. They should never come to America, since the Americans won't live together with descendants of the black race. I am firmly convinced that when the war is over, all the Negroes and mulattos will have to leave the country, or there will be another war of extermination. More next time. / Your Carl [. . .]

March 1864.

My dear Mama,

[24 ll.: uneventful camp life on the Tennessee River] Our military goal here is to keep the enemy from destroying some important railroad bridges both above and below Schell [Shell] Mound. Some of them span the Tennessee River, others go across *Bäche—Creeks—*and some span rocky gorges [7 ll.: details]. The rebels haven't exchanged any prisoners for months now, instead they let them starve to death in their prisons [51 ll.: details; nature. March 1: correspondence; camp life; rain; good food]. In the evening I usually go over to brigade headquarters and play a game of chess with the general[13] or one of the staff officers. In the morning I usually go for a ride in the hills and woods or pay a call on someone who is sick, which occasionally happens here. Re-

13. In early March, the commander of the 2nd Brigade, 3rd Div., Army of the Cumberland was Colonel John T. Lockman, 119 N.Y. Inf. Dyer (1959 [1908]), 456; *OAR,* 2:615.

cently, I happened to deliver a baby[. . . .] Later in the day, all of our officers get together at the colonel's and place bets, and many a hundred-dollar bill changes hands [51 ll.: he doesn't participate—hates gambling; needs a new horse; has already had four in one year: one captured, one shot, one stolen, one "worn out"; family; German-Danish War:] I am extremely glad that I am not there at the moment, since I probably would have joined in, without being very enthusiastic about either the Prussian or the Austrian cause [24 ll.: family; greetings; signature].

                                            Georgia, May 11, 64.
[salutation missing]
    [16 ll.: marches; shots fired by pickets] As is almost always the case in these situations, some chicken heart or another who is on picket duty is misled by his anxiety into thinking that an innocent tree is the advancing enemy. He calls out, but the latter of course has good reason to remain silent, and so he shoots. The pickets at his side are then startled by the shot and think they have nothing better to do than start shooting [147 ll.: everything is quiet; marching orders the next midday; battle of Dug's Gap (May 8, 1864); marches; battle preparations. May 20: battle of Resaca; heavy losses].

                    May 31, 64. Dallas Gap in Georgia near Atlanta
My dear Mama,
    [12 ll.: fighting; exhaustion] Our corps, which has come under fire three times this month (on May 8 at Dug's Gap or Rocky faced Mountain, May 13 and 14 and 15 at Resaca and starting on May 24 here at Dallas Gap) has already lost more than 5,000 men, and we have gained nothing by it[. . . .] As soon as we move into a camp where I can sort out my things, I want to leave the field forces, even if I am offered 10 positions as a regimental surgeon. I have had enough good luck, and I only hope it doesn't desert me during the time I have left in our decimated regiment. We only have about 96 soldiers able to carry a musket and 3 officers left. I am thinking of taking a job for half a year as a civilian surgeon in some military hospital in New York, Philadelphia, or Washington, so that I can get to know something about life in America. With regard to Heinrich,[14] I would be the last person to recommend joining the army as an officer or a soldier [33 ll.: details]. My life in this field campaign is a hundred times better than it was before. Having learned from experience, I have set things up so well that I seldom run into any difficulties. I have a good saddle horse and a good packhorse that always carries a week's worth of

---

14. Uterhard's brother, then living in India.

Provision on its back, and I have 5 men in my *Department* who are solely responsible for looking after me, their superior officer, when we march — one fetches water, another makes a fire, the 3rd cooks, the 4th takes care of the horses, the 5th sets up the tent. So you see, in this regard I'm not suffering very much; in fact I'm the best off of all the officers, most of whom don't even get one servant. We doctors, once we know how things work, can take some liberties [36 ll.: food monotonous but sufficient; Heinrich should not become a soldier under any circumstances; hundreds of thousands have been killed; family; greetings; signature].

Georgia, near the Chattahochee River / July 10th, 1864.

My dear Mama,

[8 ll.: hardships] Since I last wrote, we have been leading the same life the entire time, without any respite. We fight every day and only advance a little. The rains stopped after a while, and relentless heat has set in[. . . .] It is probably an average of 27° in the shade[15] in the middle of the day, and when you imagine that we have to march in such heat, you won't find it strange that the men go down like flies in the hot rays of the sun [13 ll.: most difficult campaign up to now; family; pay overdue]. I am now absolutely determined to leave the war and am only waiting for payday, since I obviously cannot leave without any money. As a doctor, it is infinitely difficult to get away, because there is a lack of doctors in the field [6 ll.: colonel offered him a position as a regimental surgeon but is prepared to let him go:] since I've been on duty with the regiment for 16 months now without a break, whereas my colleague has been on sick leave for many months [25 ll.: family; greetings; signature].

DIARY ENTRY [enclosed in letter of July 10, 1864]

June 12, 1864

[29 ll.: rain, storm; soldiers camping for days on end in the rain without any shelter] Scurvy, with only a very few exceptions a disease that has been largely unknown in our regiment, is starting to become more evident. Along with poor nutrition, dampness seems to be one of its main causes. [104 ll.: no remedy for scurvy; June 14: camp life; wants to get away as soon as possible; June 15: setting up camp; fighting on the march to Atlanta; Methodist sermon; June 16:] The call came to fall in, and general orders were read out to every regiment, that the previous day our right or left wing had made great gains, Fort Darling near Richmond had been captured, and the *Govern-*

15. Reaumur scale, equal to 93° Fahrenheit.

ment was making a considerable profit with cotton captured from the South. We knew immediately that there would be a battle, since before battles they always send out some proclamations about gains that have been made, to encourage the soldiers [55 ll.: reports of successes usually exaggerated; many in the regiment wounded by sharpshooters and artillery; June 17:] On the morning of the 16th I saw the wounded in our hospital, a total of 16. All were seriously hurt, several were mortally wounded [6 ll.: details]. When I wrote the casualty report on this morning, I had 13 dead and 30 seriously wounded. We went into battle with 120 muskets and lost 47 of this number within two days. There may also be some more who haven't been found yet [44 ll.: description of the battle; endless hardships: under fire for days on end, in the rain and without sleep]. Our brigade was quite fortunate during the fighting on the 20th. Our regiment was behind strong fortifications (*Riflepits*) and only lost two men, one of whom, a poor German, was so unlucky as to be shot in both knees, and he will probably lose both legs [39 ll.: further fighting and marches].

July 31, 64 / near Atlanta, Georgia.

My dear Mama,

[47 ll.: family] The heat makes you so weak you can hardly move your limbs. We've been camped now for almost a week in front of Atlanta, only a few English miles away from here, and are besieging it. Our cannon thunder day and night at the strong fortifications, and our heavy artillery are shooting off a continuous stream of heavy bombs into the city, which you can see clearly from every hill. And the rebels pay us back in their own coin [34 ll.: getting used to constant danger; fighting; losses; war situation; greetings; signature].

Atlanta, September 5, 64

My dear Mama,

[34 ll.: address; request for discharge denied; Atlanta has fallen, troops exhausted] Maybe also that the American people will elect McClellen president and that then there will be peace. A conservative estimate puts the cost of this campaign at 100,000 lives. Our corps left Look out Mountain with 30,000 man and now has only 10,000 muskets, our brigade used to have 3,000 men and now has 600, our regiment suffered 100 dead and wounded, i.e. more than half the men [10 ll.: no pay for eight months, exorbitant prices]. We are now camped as far away from Atlanta as Bramow is from Rostock [approximately two miles], on the south side of the city, and every day ten men from our regiment get passes to go into town. Of course, I can go anytime I like, but

I don't do so because I haven't got a penny in my pocket, and my clothing, after four months spent camped in the field, does not look especially elegant [5 ll.: Atlanta; when they marched in, bivouacked in the street]. In the dark, I happened to run into a German family with whom I ate dinner. Judging by the appearance of their home, they are extremely well off. Of course I didn't have any money to pay them, so I very politely thanked the lady of the house, and took off to pick out my spot on the road for the night. I found it a bit embarrassing, and I doubt very much if I will visit them again [10 ll.: hunger was too great; family; greetings; signature].

October 2, 64, Atlanta, Ga.

My dear Mama,

[11 ll.: correspondence] We are still in the same *Camp* as before, when I sent my letter of Sept. 4th to you. All the people have been driven out of Atlanta, and there are only a few families and some blacks sitting around, so the only diversion provided by the nearby city is the empty houses. We seldom go into town [5 ll.: is living in a large tent, furnished fairly well; books from Atlanta]. I am now busily learning Spanish from a French grammar book, and when I get tired of that, I go into the fields and the woods and over here, I find an animal that interests me, and over there a flower that captivates me with its beauty and blaze of color [20 ll.: likes the South; repetitions; November 4: election, Lincoln against McClellan]. I don't care at all, I basically don't like America very much, despite the incredible advantages it has over other countries. The people here are a very strange, broad-minded breed, they call cheating and swindling being smart, and everyone tries hard to be smart [17 ll.: family; greetings; signature].

end of 1864

My dear Mama,

[5 ll.: correspondence] I was offered a position in Nashville as a surgeon in a heavy artillery regiment stationed there, with the rank of a major and 1,800 dollars pay and two horses. This evening I decided to accept it [11 ll.: winter is approaching; Nashville better than living in camp]. Here in the field, where we haven't received any money for 10 months, my clothing is a real sight[. . . .] I have sewn over some of the seams two or three times, and I have darned many a hole made by thorns in the woods or caused by wear and tear. My hat is full of holes, and otherwise all I have is a simple pair of army trousers and heavy army shoes and a broken pair of glasses. In Nashville I will throw the whole kit and caboodle into the fire and equip myself from head to toe with new clothing [4 ll.: details]. Day after tomorrow I'll be traveling the 300 miles to Nashville to take over my regiment of 12 or 1,500 men [37 ll.: preparations for the trip; greetings; signature].

Nashville, November 20, 64 / (November 6, Atlanta)
My dear Mama,
[94 ll.: arduous journey; arrival in Nashville] I finally had to report to the authorities and go to a regiment that is camped about a half a mile from Nashville. The commander is a German, many of the officers are German,[16] and the Americans also seem to have a fairly good lifestyle, so I am content. My quarters are very nice, we have a mess hall, and when I want anything, I just have to give the order. I'm living here like in paradise, have a good bed and every comfort I can imagine. We will be staying here the whole winter. I am the only one here (as a doctor) and so I have a lot of work to do, but this will improve in time [8 ll.: correspondence; address; asks for two more fever thermometers; signature missing].

December 3, 64, Nashv. Tenn. / Headqt. 9th U.S.C. Arty. (*heavy*)
My dear Mama,
[24 ll.: threatened by the enemy; moved into the town] There are quite a few gunboats lying in the Cumberland River to protect the town, and their screaming steam—here I was interrupted, a drunk (white) cavalryman wounded our sutler* with a stone, and received a few saber thrusts in return, and so I patched up what foolishness and dissipation had caused. Given the large number of soldiers here, there are scenes every day that usually end in bloodshed. Every day some three, four (yesterday as many as eighteen) men are shot or stabbed to death on the streets. In terms of safety, London is a thousand times better than Nashville; everyone has his six-shooter in his pocket, and you hardly go out alone at night in the city. In particular, there are frequent incidents between black and white soldiers, and every evening one group murders a few of the other, as if they just can't wait until they end up in Hell [35 ll.: daily life; bought a horse; address; signature].

December 15, 64. Nashville, Tenn.
My dear Mama,
[70 ll.: correspondence; photographs; is well; daily life; cold weather] I am content with my position in the regiment. I get along very well with the

16. The commander was Major Eduard Grosskopf. Besides the letter-writer, three of the other sixteen officers serving in November 1864 had German names: Captain Anton Kilp, First Lieutenant Alexander Thener, and First Lieutenant Joseph Diehl. *OAR*, 8:156.

blacks; they are usually good-natured people, easy to lead with kindness. They are by nature somewhat lazy but willing to do any service. The men I have in my *Department* are great fellows and completely devoted to me; they'd go through fire and water for me. Along with a picture of me, I will send you a portrait of the one who is my favorite and who I want to promote to sergeant at Christmas. I am sure you will like his face. I am quite an important person here, a major, the same rank as the commander of the regiment, a German whose family wants to live with us in the *Camp.*—I have every imaginable comfort here. Under my command I have half a dozen blacks, a six-horse transport wagon, a two-horse ambulance [. . .] a mule. Everything provided by the regiment; I also have a beautiful black stallion of my own [26 ll.: details; correspondence; greetings; address; signature missing].

January 8, 1865
Nashville, Tenness. / 9th U.S. Col. Arty. (*heavy*)

My dear Mama,

[48 ll.: journey; duties; equipment; Christmas] I am very busy during the day, I have about 70 patients who take up a lot of time, and there is a lot of paperwork connected with my position, and on top of that I have had the honor of being named a member of the examination commission in Nashville for regimental doctors, physicians, and pharmacists. This position means a lot of work and inconvenience given the distance to the city and condition [letter breaks off].

March 11, 1865 / Nashville, Tennessee

My dear Mama,

[68 ll.: correspondence; new camp outside the city; flooding] This flood caused the true character of the Yankees to be revealed again for what it is. Hundreds of course were in danger of drowning, and many were working with boats to save them—but only for money. No one could get into a boat without making a deal first, and of course it got more and more expensive. Some people paid hundreds of dollars for their rescue. In this country people often speculate and make a profit on the misfortunes of their fellow men. It is even the custom here with the physicians. They don't write up their bills at New Year's or get paid a fee without submitting bills like they do at home. Here, they either get paid in cash for every consultation or they make a contract. Then of course they paint the case as black as possible so as to raise the price, and then when they've agreed on the price of the treatment, half is paid in advance, and the other half when the doctor has fulfilled his promises—of course he often has to abandon all hope of getting the second half [12 ll.:

weather]. This summer I think I will put in a large kitchen garden, or rather I have already started. I have staked out the borders of the patch, and on Monday I will have it plowed and dug, planks put down, and then it will be seeded and planted—whether for ourselves or for other people, of course, we don't know. We're planting cabbage, onions, potatoes, turnips, peas, beans, tomatoes, melons, and some root vegetables I don't know the names of. I think it will be interesting, and also extremely healthy for me to eat fresh vegetables I've known only by name for the last two years. I am also thinking seriously about getting a cow[. . . .] Up to now we've been living on artificial milk: milk thickened with sugar and hermetically sealed in tin cans. We get it delivered to the hospital from the government or the Sanitary Commission [28 ll.: details about food; gets along well with regimental commander; greetings; signature].[17]

After he returned to Germany, Uterhard applied his extensive experience to working as a surgeon in a Mecklenburg dragoon regiment in the war against Austria in 1866, then again as chief of medical staff at the hospital in Ludwigslust, Mecklenburg, during the Franco-Prussian War of 1870–71. In between these assignments, he completed his double qualifications in pathology and surgery and published a series of articles on surgical techniques. From 1873 to 1878, working some of the time as a ship's doctor on English vessels, he sailed the seas to Africa and Australia; he then got married and opened his own practice in Warnemünde, where he died in 1895.[18]

17. On May 5, 1865, Uterhard was transferred to the 18 Colo. Inf, but for various reasons he did not report for service. On September 6, 1865, he applied for a discharge in order to return to Germany to attend to family matters, which was granted only ten days later, on September 16. Muster Rolls, NatA; War Department, Special Orders [printed] No. 31, 498, RG 94, NatA.

18. Obituary, in *Warnemünder Zeitung*, March [19?], 1895; information provided by the donor; *Biographisches Lexikon* (1962 [1929]), 5:685.

19. Johann Philipp Heubach

Johann Philipp Heubach, born in 1825 in Steinach (Thuringia), had inherited a mill, but he must have become involved in the democratic agitation preceding the revolution in 1848–49 because he fled his tiny principality of Sachsen-Meiningen to avoid prosecution by the local authorities. On his way to Bremen, the port from which he

SOURCE NOTE: When Heubach wrote the first letter printed here, he had not spoken or read much German for fourteen years. It shows in his limited vocabulary, rusty idioms, idiosyncratic spelling, and chaotic punctuation. Not included here are the letters in the series from the time before 1860 (two) and after 1865 (four) and the letter of January 18, 1865.

sailed to New York in August 1849, he changed his first names to "Georg Christian," probably to avoid detection.

After three years on the East Coast and in the Midwest, he moved to California in 1852. He soon gave up digging for gold and began to accumulate a considerable amount of money as a carpenter, miller, mill builder, and the owner of a mill. He then moved back to Missouri (in 1866) and invested most of his money in land.[1]

Rock Creek Mühl [Mill], July 1/63

Most dearly beloved brothers and sisters,

I must take up my pen again and let you know that I am still alive[. . . .]

I've been in California for 10 years now, and it looks like I will spend the rest of my life here.

California is the most beautiful and richest land in the world. Nothing can top it in terms of riches and climate—the pleasant sunshine keeps us very warm every day [7 ll.: climate; poverty and wealth in California]. But I must admit that anyone who wants to work can always put some money away [5 ll.: wages; prices; many job possibilities].

My dear brothers and sisters, when the war is over that is now going on in the eastern states, I will come to visit you. Here in California they only want to make money, that's everyone's ambition.

[15 ll.: family; trust in God; correspondence, greetings]

Geo C Heubach

My address / Geo C. Heubach

Rock Creek P.O. / Butte County / California

You must forgive me for my spelling mistakes, I haven't written any German in 14 years and haven't read much.

[no date; according to the contents: July 1863]

[salutation missing]

I just heard by *Telegraph* that the Union armies have won one of the biggest battles that has ever taken place on earth, South against North [Gettysburg*], and 100,000 men have already been shot on both sides, and entire regiments have been blown apart, down to the last man. Such bravery is hard to find anywhere. The southern armies marched into Pennsylvania and wanted to continue the fighting there, where there are a lot of Germans, but they didn't succeed, and the Germans fought bravely. It is praiseworthy that there

1. NYPL, October 1, 1849; letters by Kurt Hayn, Steinach town chronicler, of 1991 and 1992, NABS; donor Robert Eichhorn, correspondence 1982–89, NABS; letters by Georg Christian Heubach, 1849–76, NABS. According to MC 1870: Maryville, Nodaway Co./Mo., Polk Twp., #566, Heubach's property in Missouri was worth $12,000.

are many Germans in the northern army and also a lot of generals and other officers who are distinguishing themselves. If the North keeps this up, we'll soon have peace.

The South is already worn out.

As I see in the papers, the Poles are holding on bravely, and it looks like the Prussians will be taught a lesson because they are suppressing freedom in Germany and Poland [14 ll.: rumors of war in Europe; plans to visit Germany; greetings; signature].

Rock Creek Mühl, Oct. 20/63

Most dearly beloved brothers and sisters,

[51 ll.: family; is earning $124 a month with board and a saddle horse; can save $120 a month] Dear brother, you want to know if I am well off or not, (I am.) I have more money than I ever could have expected to have in Germany, I also have some of the [----------] *precious Metal* that the world worships, so don't worry about me, dear brother [11 ll.: trust in God; greetings; signature].

Rock Creek Mills, Dec. 24/63

Dear brothers and sisters,

[41 ll.: hard times in the first years in the United States; family; will stay in America] If I had stayed poor I would have been lost to you forever, and I couldn't write what was untrue, and I was ashamed of being poor, and that is why I didn't write to you in those first years [7 ll.: greetings; signature].

Rock Creek Mill, Febr. 10/64.

Dear brothers and sisters,

[59 ll.: went by oxcart from Missouri to California in 1852; no social life in America] The Germans are only here to make money [. . .] more and more, that's their motto, and so sometimes they lose everything. I know very well that when the middle and the poor classes in Germany manage to make a living they are satisfied, because they have no other prospects, and the ones who don't know any better are the happy ones! But here it is different, the poor get rich if they work hard, and the rich get poor if they are lazy, here you're paid according to what you do.

I have now gotten used to American life, I've learned the language, to read and write it, so there's nothing I miss as far as that goes. I like to read books and newspapers, and sometimes I get out my *Instrument* and take photographs, I learned this in California. I'll send you a sample [25 ll.: details about the mill he is running; would like to visit Germany soon; greetings; signature].

Rock Creek, May 13/64

Dear brother,

[20 ll.: being free of guild restrictions is good, but "in Germany it will never get any better," no matter if it is a monarchy or a republic] It is the country that makes for freedom?—where workers are needed, and when that's the case, they get high wages and necessarily become wealthy if they work hard and are thrifty [14 ll.: a free country; transcontinental railroad; his brother does not read newspapers—doesn't know what is happening in the world]. That is Germany's misfortune, that so many people do the same. I am ashamed to say that Germany is still living in the 14th century compared to America. I can judge it, I have been in this country long enough, and you can tell the difference when you see someone recently [arrived] from Germany. The United States are far in advance of the Old World in every way, in art and science, in learning and in machines, and in every other way you can imagine, they're a lesson for all [25 ll.: American character; reads newspapers from all over the world; does not want to live in Germany again; greetings; signature].

In Maryville, Nodaway County, Missouri, where in 1870 less than 2 percent of the settlers were German-speaking, Heubach built and ran a large new mill. He married an Austrian woman, and in 1880 they were listed with a daughter who was ten years old. In 1873 he was one of the founders of the local Masonic lodge, and according to the courthouse records, he was still alive in 1888.[2]

2. *Nodaway County, Missouri* (1910), 1:332, 335; MC 1870: Maryville, Nodaway Co./Mo., Polk Twp., #566; MC 1880: Nodaway Co./Mo., Polk Twp., e.d. 263, #143; *History of Nodaway County, Missouri* (1882), 1:280; Nodaway Co. Deed Book 90, p. 127, December 28, 1888, Nodaway Co. Courthouse, Maryville, Mo.

20. Corporal Jakob Heinzelmann

In November 1841, about two years before the birth of his own son Gustav, Pastor Keppler christened Jakob Heinzelmann in Lombach, a village near Freudenstadt, Baden, in southwest Germany. The son of a farmer from nearby Sulzbach, Heinzelmann apparently was apprenticed to a blacksmith. Nothing is known about the reasons for his emigration or the details of his passage, but on September 3, 1862,

SOURCE NOTE: Heinzelmann's German is almost unadulterated Swabian dialect in its spelling, use of idioms, and syntax, with some interference from High German and English. A German-speaker from a different region has to stop and think about the meaning of a word occasionally, but despite Heinzelmann's rather limited vocabulary, he can make himself understood.

he enlisted in Buffalo, New York, for three years. He served in the same regiment (116th New York Infantry Volunteers) as Albert Krause (no. 22), but in a different unit (Company G, in which about half of the soldiers were German-speakers).[1]

For about a year starting in June 1863, the 116th Infantry was deployed together with the 14th New York Cavalry (Gustav Keppler's [no. 21] unit) in various campaigns of the XIX Army Corps, from the siege of Port Hudson* until the Red River campaign. Three of our letter-writers, therefore, ended up taking part in the same action and describing some of the same events, a fact that is statistically quite improbable.

Frankling, January 23, 1864[2]

Dear parents and brothers and sisters,

I take up my pen with joy for a second time to let you know that I am well and still alive, because since I wrote you the last letter things have been quiet and we haven't had any more battles. We marched for two days back toward Neworlians, and those were two hard days because it had just rained very heavily, and so we had to go through mud and mire that came up almost above our knees, and it was very cold as well, and we had a bit of snow, the first snow in 50 years. We spent the night in a sugar factory because the ground was too wet to lie on, and there were no boards that we could use to set up our linen houses[3] [5 ll.: weather]. I also met one of Pastor Kaapler's sons,[4] he is in the 14th Neuiorger Gabalri [New York Cavalry] regiment, but he is not with his regiment, he is one of our colonel's orderlies and hasn't been in any battles. I didn't recognize him, nor he me, even though we've met up every day now for 4 months[. . . .] I could tell from the way he spoke he was a Swabian, and so I thought I'd just have to ask him where he was from. I asked him where he was from in Germany, and he answered that he was a Swabian, and I said I knew someone who was supposed to be from there, and he said he came from Oberndorf, and I said that's not far from where I come from, Loßburg near Freudenstadt, and he said then you must know my old man, Pastor Kabler, and I said what? he can't be your real father, because he didn't have a boy who was that old when he was in Lombag—for with his beard he looked like a thirty-year-old man. I could hardly believe he is even younger than me. I said I would never have thought he was a pastor's son; I had thought to myself when I first

1. Landeskirchliches Archiv Stuttgart, KB 2114, STV 2171, Lombach; Taufbuch 1841, No. 72; Muster Rolls, NatA.
2. See Krause (no. 22), January 22, 1864.
3. See ibid., January 10, 1864.
4. See Keppler (no. 21).

saw him that he was just another stuffy farmhand from Germany. It made him happier than anything in the world to meet an old acquaintance from his old homeland, and then he immediately asked me what the tavern keeper's daughters were doing, and if they were still single, because he was really stuck on the youngest one, and he said if his father and mother knew that he had to lead this dog's life here, his mother would die of heartache [-----------]. I answered back that I wasn't like that, letting people wait so long, if I didn't write for 2 years then after 4 years I'd be sure to, and he said his parents must think he is no longer alive, and that he was in Boston first and from there he went to Neuorg [New York] where all his belongings were stolen, his suitcase with all his clothes, and he also ran out of money and then he got fed up, and so then he went in and got himself signed up in the city of Neuorg. He said he'd earned 40 to 50 dollars a month when he was working as a baker, and he was really fed up with the soldier's life, and every day he said he thought about the good times he'd had in Germany, eating and drinking things he liked, and here he couldn't even get a good drink of water, and even his dog would have refused to eat the food here, the beans and the rice and the hard *Gräker* [crackers] you get[. . . .]

I told him if I'd had it as good in Germany as he had, I would have deserted a long time ago, but he doesn't want to do that because he hasn't been through any hardships yet like I have, in battles and everything. If the cannonballs, grenades and case shot and bullets ever get as close to him as they did to me, then he will think, if only I were in Germany, sitting behind a wine barrel in the tavern keeper's cellar [. . .] because he doesn't have to do very much besides deliver whatever messages there are, back and forth, or sometimes ride behind the colonel when he rides out, so just wait until he goes somewhere where bombs or shells are bursting over his head. [11 ll.: details; describes artillery on ships and in fortifications] we also have gunboats made of solid iron that float almost completely underwater, with a round tower in the middle, that are powered back and forth by steam engines, with cannon on them, and this tower is covered with flat iron plates so it can't be shot through at all [. . .] they're also made so they can sink wooden gunboats, because they are sharp and pointed on both sides so they can ram the wooden boats and make a hole in them that's 7 to 8 feet wide [8 ll.: details]. That's where we were supposed to make an attack from the water and take Säbein Päs [Sabine Pass] last September, on the Täxas border, but we had to go back to Neuorlians where we almost died of thirst because we ran out of drinking water, if a gunboat that luckily happened to meet up with us on the Golf of Mexigo hadn't helped us out—Dear parents, I must close my letter now, because this piece of paper is too small and time is too short. Gustaf Kapler sends many greetings to the tavern keeper, and when he gets a chance, he will visit them. Write back soon Comp. G 116th Reg. N.Y.V. / Neworlians. Lo.

1864.
Grandcore [Grand Ecore, Louisiana] April 18.

Most esteemed Pastor,

It is with joy that I take up my pen to reply to your esteemed letter that you sent to me; I received your letter on the evening of April 6, but on the morning of the seventh we marched on, and so I did not have time to write immediately, but on the same evening I tried to find your son, but the cavalry had already left. Now he is back with his regiment again, and I had to be patient and wait until I had an opportunity to meet with him again. On the 8th we had a fierce battle,[5] the cavalry was chasing the enemy all morning, but then enemy reinforcements arrived, and they beat our cavalry back, and then I saw your son, but I couldn't leave my ranks because our infantry had to advance, and I only had enough time to ask him if he had received the letter you wrote to me or not, since when I received it I went over to his regiment that same evening, and I gave the letter to the soldier in his company who has taken his place as an *oderly* [orderly], and this man gave it to a *Scherschante* [sergeant], and the *Scherschant* gave the letter to his lieutenant, but unfortunately this lieutenant was captured,[6] and the letter never reached your son, and I am very sorry about that. We in the infantry had another fierce battle that same day, but we held our ground, but at 12 o'clock at night we set off and marched 18 miles or 6 hours back to blessend [Pleasant] Hill, where we set up our battle lines in the morning. The enemy followed us, and at 9 o'clock in the morning we had another fierce battle, but we fought off every attack made by the enemy, and the field was strewn with dead and wounded men. Nightfall ended the battle, and enemy losses were 5 times more than ours. You can't imagine the sound of the moaning of the wounded men who had to lie on the field all night. We took all of the men who weren't wounded too badly along with us, and the seriously wounded were carried into a house, and we left some surgeons there to take care of them. Both friend and foe were there, all the men who were seriously wounded were together. That same night our army withdrew, because we didn't have anything more to eat, and we had to march back to our supply ships that were in a big river, called the red reber [Red River]. The plan our general had made was foiled, however, because our

5. Near Sabine Crossroads, Louisiana; see Keppler (no. 21), April 15, 1864.
6. First Lieutenant Charles Brewster and Second Lieutenant Peter R. Biegel were listed as missing as of "April 1864." *OAR*, 2:342.

ships couldn't go any further, since the enemy had drawn off the water from the river to disrupt our shipping, and the water wasn't deep enough to advance with our gunboats. We will probably go back to New Orleans or Franklin or a town near the Missisippi and stay there until the water rises again. Most esteemed Pastor, I never thought I would have another opportunity to write to you or to see your son again, but thanks be to the Lord, He protected us both. It did take a lot of effort to find your son again, and for 5 days I went over to his regiment 2 times a day, but every time he was out on picket duty or scouting, and so I soon lost all hope of seeing him again, until yesterday, the 17th, I found him there. His comrades had told me the first time I went over to his regiment that he'd been taken prisoner, and so I went to see his captain, and he said he had sent him out with a detachment of 40 men and would be back in 1 or 2 days, but it was very close, he almost didn't return, because the entire detachment was surrounded by the enemy, but they successfully fought their way through. I went to see him again today, and as long as we are here, I can visit him every day, and so I will be able to send you news of him, and if anything should happen to him, I will let you know. With this, I will close my letter, in the hopes that when these lines reach you, you will be as well as I am now, and I remain, most respectfully, your friend Jacob Heinzelmann.

One more request: would you be so kind as to tell my parents that you have heard from me, because I have already written 2 letters and have not received any reply from them [35 ll. money matters; correspondence; asks for photographs of his parents].

And now I shall close, with many thousands of best wishes, and I remain your faithful friend Jacob Heinzelmann. All the best to my parents and brothers and sisters and friends and acquaintances [4 ll. address].

Heinzelmann was listed as missing in action twice after battles in the summer of 1863. In the spring of 1864, when his company had shrunk to forty-four men, he became a corporal and served until June 1865. During the last months of the war, his company was stationed near New Orleans, and after it was over, he moved into the city. One year after he was mustered out, he married Mary Weitzel, born in Württemberg, who was apparently employed as a domestic servant. By 1880, the couple had five children. He seems to have remained a laborer and never accumulated any property. According to his death certificate, he committed suicide in 1887 by ingesting rat poison. His widow received a modest war pension and lived in New Orleans until 1928.[7]

7. Muster Rolls, NatA; Pension File, NatA; MC 1880: New Orleans/La., W. 9, e.d. 62, #638, Jacob "Heinsman." Although he is listed in the 1880 census as Swiss, the names of his wife and children are the same as those in the pension file.

21. Private Gustav Keppler

Gustav Keppler, born in Lombach and raised in Fluorn (both near Freudenstadt, Baden, in southwest Germany), was the son of a pastor. He completed an apprenticeship as a baker in the city of Ludwigsburg, but before he turned nineteen, he sailed from Hamburg to New York on the steamship *Saxonia*. In the letters there are indications of a possible rift with his father or some youthful transgression, but he may well have emigrated primarily for economic reasons.

Keppler quickly found work in New York, but he soon moved to Boston to start working in a better job. In Boston, however, he became seriously ill, and having returned to New York, he suffered a series of further blows (detailed in the letter of July 28, 1864). In April 1863 he enlisted for three years with the 14th New York Cavalry, a regiment that was predominantly American and Irish with only a few German-speakers. Keppler's unit was first deployed in the siege of Port Hudson.* This last Confederate stronghold on the Mississippi surrendered on July 9, 1863, leaving the entire river in Union control—and the Confederacy cut in two. The unit remained in Louisiana, took part in the inglorious Red River campaign (March–May 1864), and was then stationed in Baton Rouge until January 1865. During the last four months of 1863, Keppler was assigned as an orderly to the commander of the 116th New York Infantry, the regiment in which Heinzelmann (no. 20) and Krause (no. 22) served; in July 1864 he was listed as company clerk.[1]

New york, June 14, 1862

Dearest parents and brothers,

You have no doubt been waiting for a long time for a letter from me, about how I got here and how I was received and if I immediately got a job? I will answer these questions for you one after another! [54 ll.: irritation with other passengers and lack of morals on the ship; steerage was filthy; the food terrible; arrival in "Kesselgarten" (Castle Garden); visited acquaintances in New York].

The next day we ran all around trying to find jobs, but didn't get one, and the next day was the same, and then I also went to see Wolf, who really took me under his wing, but he was very ill, and so he couldn't go around with me,

SOURCE NOTE: Despite the widespread opinion that in the nineteenth century, the Protestant parsonage was the incubator of the German intellectual elite, Keppler's writing is quite unremarkable: straightforward in style, with a limited vocabulary, quite a number of spelling and grammar mistakes, some influence from his regional dialect, and consistent problems with the spelling of English words and names.

1. Information provided by the donor; HPL *Saxonia*, NABS; letters of June 14 and August 3, 1862, NABS; Dyer (1959 [1908]), 1379; *OAR*, 2:342; Muster Rolls, NatA.

Gustav Keppler
and wife Beate
(parents of
Gustav Keppler,
no. 21), with one
of their four sons.
(Paul Elwert)

but he did send someone else along [12 ll.: advertisements for bakers in the newspaper, including a job in the Bowery] and so I'll be staying here with him for now, because I liked the man and his store the best. They are Low Germans, unfortunately, but they also speak High German, I don't know yet what my salary is, I start on Monday [7 ll.: greetings].

I'll be getting 20 talers* a month for now. If Bertha Rose wants to come over here, there are still plenty of jobs for women at 10 to 16 dollars a month, and they don't get to do hardly any work [6 ll.: his hours are from 6 A.M. to midnight; an acquaintance has probably been killed in the war; signature missing].

Boston, August 3, 1862

Dearest parents and brothers,

[8 ll.: correspondence] At the moment I am here in Boston, as you will have just read, working in a pastry shop owned by Mstr. Georg. Fira, and it is very pleasant here, because I am my own boss, and all I do is decorate cakes. There are 10 other people working here, but I usually don't have any contact with them [14 ll.: details; is earning forty-eight dollars a month plus room and board].

I want to learn the English language before I move any further inland. Living here is very expensive, and silver and gold are extremely rare; everything is paid in paper money. We don't feel the effects of the war here very much; the only thing they are afraid of here is that despite the enormous sum of 1,200 dollars per man, they won't be able to get enough men and then they'd end up closing down businesses, and this would probably set off a revolution. There are certainly enough sick and wounded men around here, and it makes you shudder sometimes to see men like that. Schultheiße's son is also said to be wounded and on his way back to Germany, he apparently spent some time at Wolf's—please write and tell me if this is true, because I haven't seen him myself, I didn't have the time [65 ll.: considerable expenses due to his severe illness; family; gossip; greetings; signature; Staiger's son is working for a butcher].

Neckar toss [Natchitoches] April 15/65 [= 64] / State Louisiana
Dearest parents and brothers,

For a long time I'd been waiting and waiting for a letter from you, but always in vain, until four days ago when I saw a man from Losburg, whom I met when I was an *Ortele* [orderly] at Brigade *Hedquater*. He had written to his family back home and heard that a letter for me had arrived. But I was unsuccessful in my attempts to get hold of it, because I am no longer an *Ortele* but was sent back to my regiment, and it was transferred to another division, and so he couldn't give it to me himself anymore, and he had to send it along with someone else, a lieutenant, but in our two-day battle at Schivport [Shreveport],[2] where we lost 1,600 men along with all of our supply wagons and 16 pieces, the lieutenant fell in the battle and the letter was lost.[3]

As I see from the letter sent to Mstr. Heinzelmann, you haven't received any of my letters.

I have sent 3 letters to you since I've been in the army, and I sent one to you before I left Boston to go to New York.

In this letter, I don't want to spend any more time making excuses, because

2. Shreveport, Louisiana, was the nearest town and the objective of the Red River campaign, but the battle mentioned here is known as the battle of Sabine Cross Roads (April 8, 1864) and Pleasant Hill (April 9), lost by the Union.

3. Casualties were somewhat higher: 2,235 of the approximately 12,000 Federal troops, including those listed as taken prisoner or missing. Long and Long (1971), 482. About the lieutenant, see Heinzelmann (no. 20), note 6.

I don't have much time, for we are not safe here for even a minute, we never know if we have to saddle up or not. We're in the saddle almost all day and night, and our duty is very difficult, we are surrounded by the enemy. We are about 250 miles from Neuorleans, in the middle of the woods. But we will probably withdraw to Neuorleans or Fränklin, and at any rate go back to Alexandria. Bänks [Banks*], who is our commander, has been completely defeated; it was a terrible retreat, we had nothing to eat for ourselves or our horses for 3 days, we marched day and night with everything all mixed up in a mess—infantry, cavalry, *Nigger*[s],[4] mules, horses, wagons. You can't even imagine how horrible it was, the battlefield was strewn with dead and wounded. Our captain was wounded twice, but he kept on trying to get us through as best he could. I think our captain is the best officer in our regiment, he is a German, a Bavarian. His name is [Julius P.] Merklein, he looks after his men very well, but the other officers are absolutely useless, and when a battle begins, they all disappear.

I think the fellow from Losburg will be writing again too, and then we can send our letters off together. He certainly went to all kinds of trouble to locate me.

[. . .] Meanwhile, I once again beg your forgiveness for everything, and at any rate I think this will be a good lesson for me, since it certainly isn't pleasant being a soldier in America. Since I've been in the field, I haven't had anything to sleep on but the bare ground, during the day it's unbearably hot, at night it's bitterly cold and foggy, with no change of clothes until they almost fall off your body, and then there's an appalling number of lice and fleas, *Muskitos*, so-called *Holzböcke* [wood ticks] that bite terribly. On some days, nothing to eat. Water to drink that frogs and toads are swimming around in and that stinks terribly, and if you have money you can't even get a wine glass full of beer, no matter how hard you try. 1–2 dollars for a piece of bread like a rock, 2–3 dollars for a bottle of wine, 3–4 dollars for a packet of tobacco, ½–1 dollar for the worst kind, so bad not even a peasant farmer over there would smoke it [signature missing].

Beten [Baton] Rouge, July 28, 1864

You will be receiving my portrait along with a strand of my hair soon, but that doesn't mean you need to wait to answer this letter, because I am longing to hear from you!

Dearest parents and brothers,

4. The German equivalent of Negro, "*Neger*," sounds similar to the American racial epithet, but most writers make the distinction. Keppler uses the American epithet but treats it as a German word; italics indicate that the word (except its plural form) was taken over from the German original.

Finally after waiting for so long, I received your kind letter, in which I learned that you are so worried about me, and so I want to send you news as fast as possible and answer the questions you asked me.

We are now 8 miles from Beten Rouge, in the middle of woods, swamps, and wilderness in a small *Fort* or *Festung* [Highland Stockade] where we don't even have enough space to tether our horses decently, in heat that is almost unbearable. Our duty here is to drive out the so-called *Guerillas* or bands of robbers, and there are many of them here. Otherwise things here are fairly good, but we have almost no time off, and we are never allowed to leave the *Camp* and go into town, because it seems that our *Cornel* is afraid that since we just got paid for the last six months, most of the men would run off, and so he doesn't give anyone a pass. But if I can manage it, I will go into Beten-rouge either tonight or tomorrow night and have my picture taken and then send you my portrait.

Heinzelmann is not here with me any longer. I think his regiment has been moved to the Potomak,[5] but I don't know for sure, since we don't find out anything here, not even what is happening around us. We can't get any news-papers[. . . .]

When I arrived in New orleans I didn't have any clothes except an old pair of pants and a shirt and a cap, my hair was so long it hung down to my shoulders, my beard looked pretty wild, and I was armed with a rusty old saber, 2 pistols, and a carbine. I didn't have a horse anymore, since on the retreat from Alexandria I lost a total of 5, 2 got shot and 3 died of starvation. That's what it looked like for most of the men in our regiment, and many were even worse off. Half of our regiment were wounded and lying in the hospital or dead. Our company lost one lieutenant, and our captain was wounded and is now lying sick in New York. Compared to the other companies we lost the fewest men, and we were under the heaviest fire.

Now I want to start answering your questions, since I don't have too much space left.

1. Under what conditions did I enlist? I went and enlisted only when I had no other choice. First of all, I lost my suitcase with all my clothes, when it was stolen from Dutts Express company [7 ll.: details; went to court]. I lost the case, and I had to pay 45 dollars in costs. I'd had 70 dollars when I left Boston, but that money was gone by then, since it had been 4 weeks, and so I ran up some debts, but then I couldn't get another job. I didn't have any clothes ex-cept for 2 shirts and one suit[. . . .] I looked for a job and found one working

---

5. The 116 N.Y. Inf was in fact ordered to Fortress Monroe,* Virginia, and then transferred to Washington on July 12. Dyer (1959 [1908]), 1450.

for a baker, but then after I had been working for him for almost a month, he went bankrupt and didn't pay me, and so I had to pay for my room and board during this time with my own money. So I didn't know what else to do except escape, and I enlisted with the 14th New York *Cavalerie* Regiment, having been promised that when I signed up I would get 175 dollars *Bounty*, but then they didn't keep their word. If I had received the money at that point, I would have paid off all my debts, but then we were kept on an island for 8 weeks and then, when we were leaving the state of N.Y., we were paid 75 dollars on the boat and told we would get 100 dollars when we had done our time, and from then on we were supposed to get 26 dollars every second month, which also wasn't true, since the first time we had to wait for more than 6 months, and then we only got paid for 4 months, with credit for the other 2 months. Now we get more, 16 dollars a month and more *Bounty* as well, but you have to pay 2 and ½ dollars in paper money for one gold dollar, and everything is terribly expensive, and usually by the time you have paid for what you really need, all your money is gone [23 ll.: his parents should refer his creditors to him; greetings; signature].

Betenrouge [Baton Rouge], September 30, 1864

Dear parents and brothers,

I don't know if you got my last letter that I sent to you via our *Suttler* [sutler*], which is what you call a *Marketendner*, because I never saw him again. Where we were at the time, about 8 miles from here in a *Fort*, we were attacked that same evening by the rebels, and things happened at such an incredible speed that our regiment was almost completely destroyed. There are now only perhaps 100 men left in our entire regiment.

I lost all my money that night, since we had just been paid the day before. I didn't think I had any chance of being saved that night, because we were completely surrounded and my horse was dead, so I took our lieutenant's horse, who had run off through the woods when the shouting started. I wasn't wearing anything except pants, shirt, and boots, with no hat and nothing but a saber and two pistols that were in the holsters on the saddle, and we had to fight our way through, saber in hand. 15 men from my company were able to escape in this manner, but we had to fight fiercely until we were through. Eight of the 15 were wounded, and one died a couple of hours later—he was shot 10 times, 5 shotgun wounds and 5 bullet wounds. The others have now pretty much recovered.[6]

6. Highland Stockade, July 29, 1864. This description of a crushing defeat conflicts with the official account of the encounter as an "affair" with two men from the 14 N.Y. Cav (the only unit involved) wounded. Dyer (1959 [1908]), 585, 755.

That same night I caught a terrible chill that has kept me tied to my bed ever since. I came down with so-called *Schwamm* fever,[7] and I felt terribly hot, but I was ice-cold to the touch, and so badly swollen I couldn't move. I was taken to our regiment's hospital where a German surgeon helped me. He took special care of me, and now I am quite a bit better. The doctor promised me I would get the first furlough to N. York that he could grant, so please be so kind as to write me as soon as you can. I can't write very much this time yet, because my fingers are too weak and heavy. So now I will close. I also want to write to Heinzelmann when I am feeling a little better; he wrote to me yesterday that he is in Virginia with his regiment. I lost his letter along with your letter when I lost my money. He wrote that Otto sends his best. In this place where we are at the moment, the water is really terrible, and 100 times now I have wished I had a good glass of your water, I'd gladly pay 1 dollar for one, because whoever doesn't get killed by the rebels, and they are certainly fierce enough, dies from the water. Every day you can see hundreds of soldiers buried around here, maybe 50 of them were shot, the rest just died from other causes. You can't get anything for money here anymore, because everything is closed and all the people have fled.

If I ever get to N. York I will write <u>more</u>! and the details. / So for now, fare well, with all the very best from your / most dearly loving son Gustav / Keppler [. . .]

Beten Rouge, November 19, 1864.

Dearest parents and brothers,

[11 ll.: correspondence; repetition of letter of September 9, 1864; prospects of furlough to New York:] but that's impossible now, because we've been almost completely cut off from any railroad connections by the rebels, so that it is even difficult to send off any letters. Our troops are about 12,000 strong here, half-starved soldiers who have lost all their will to fight because we only get half rations of food. No one has any money, neither officers nor soldiers. Our regiment filed a petition, it's only 80 strong now, to get paid for what we lost during the last raid, but they didn't do anything; they even charged us for our clothes, which means that many men will lose a lot of money from their next pay, whenever it comes in, and I myself will have to forfeit about 2 to 3 months' worth. I am now in the general hospital, but conditions here are absolutely miserable. You only get ½ enough to eat, and then it is such wretched food that at home even the dogs wouldn't eat it, and if you

7. Keppler turns the common term "swamp fever" (malaria) into a German word that sounds very similar: "*Schwamm Fieber*" (sponge or fungus fever).

don't carry it with you all day long, it gets snatched by half-starved men who look like they've risen up out of their graves. If we get paid again I will send you a bank draft, and then could you please send me a scarf to put around my neck and a knitted cap like I used to wear when I was a boy? I would have bought one here a long time ago, but there is nothing more to be had here, there's nothing but piles of rubble and houses in ruins. For 20 miles around, there are no people here. We had to burn everything because of the *Guerillas*. And it's not even a regular war that's being fought here, it is nothing but marauding around. The *Guerillas* are absolutely ruthless with us, like we are with them. If they catch you, they strip you and tie you up from the next best tree. If you aren't really on the alert during picket duty, they have various ways of catching you. They sneak up to you at night and throw a noose or nets around you. They don't usually shoot you at your post, because then the rest of the men might get away, but when they've captured the pickets and taken them away, then they ride through the rest as fast as their horses can carry them. These men are usually asleep, and so they kill and rob as many as they can, and then they ride back into the woods, and it is very dangerous to follow them there. Our side does things that are just as horrible—when they find a *guerilla* hideout, I've seen high officers do inhuman things, like ordering the men to throw fire inside it before the men could come out, and then when some did come out half burned, they laughed out loud at the sight and then tied them to their horses, so that they had to run while we rode, and afterward they were all hanged.

I am now much better but still terribly weak, since there's nothing to help yourself along with here. If you know where Carl Staiger is in New Orleans, please write and tell me, because when we get some money I want to write and ask him if he can't get some wine or a good bottle of *Wisky/Schnapps/* and send it to me. This is what the doctors prescribe for me but I can't get hold of any. It is truly ridiculous here in this hospital; they prescribe all sorts of things, chicken soup, pancakes, eggs, wine, milk, etc., but I believe if you were to stay here an entire year, all you'd ever see is ship biscuit that's so hard you can't even chew it and salt beef. Drugs are very rare here. I'm just glad I don't need much more medication, because the doctors here tend to cure you to death instead of making you better, and in Germany no village barber would even let these regimental surgeons be his helpers. Recently, our old captain, who came back from New York last week, gave me a grand letter from our brigadier general that said that the horse I was riding when we were attacked is now my own property, due to my courageous action. I was very pleased, and the captain brought me a bottle of wine, which costs 1–3 dollars here. He is a very beautiful American racehorse, worth perhaps 7–800 dollars, but I can't ride him yet, I am still too weak. I have him here with me at the hospital, the general gave orders that a *Nigger* should feed him and look after him. From what I heard today, troops to relieve us will be arriving from New Orleans this week or next, and then I hope things will improve. I also received an offer to become a noncommissioned officer or *Corporal*, not general, from our captain, but I turned it down, because the job means too much trouble. It is much better to be a private here than to have a particular position, because there are too many different types of people in the regiments. I think I'll be back with my regiment in 2 weeks' time. We're supposed to get 800 fresh men next week, since there will be another foray soon, and I want to see if this horse can accompany me longer than my other ones. I've already lost 5 horses and 2 mules, and three of the horses belonged to me since I caught them myself on farms [6 ll.: correspondence; climate]. When it's windy here and snowing, you can hear music from the woods all night long—made by big frogs and other animals. In our little tents it is so terribly cold that you can hardly sleep at night. I hadn't slept in a bed or a house for 2 years until I came to this hospital, and the first time it was strange to be lying in a bed, and I couldn't sleep at all. I spent the whole night thinking about you[. . . .]

As far as what dear father said about the fresh air in America goes, I freely admit that it was my own fault, due to thoughtlessness, and maybe even negligence, but I think my biggest failing was my <u>foolhardiness</u> and <u>thoughtlessness</u>, combined with a bit of bad luck, but had I not become so despondent and had I stuck to the truth, I could have made up for it in a short period of time. But I think that these 2 years have brought about a major transformation in me, both spiritually and physically. I've even been told several times by our officers that I am far too serious. I am all on my own, I have very little contact with the others who are mostly Irishmen of the most uncultivated class. There were 2 men in the company that I could associate with, but one died of fever and the other got shot in the backside, and since they couldn't get the bullet out, he was declared unfit. He'd been a merchant in Switzerland, but he went bankrupt and ended up in the army here. When he was shot, we were riding next to one another, and then first my horse got hit in the head by a shell that exploded in front of us, and less than 5 minutes later, I was lying right under my horse. He called out, Keppler, help me! My horse and I have been shot— and at that point his horse collapsed. I pulled him free and gave him a drink of water, and then, because the hail of bullets was so terrible, I carried him over and put him down in a ditch behind a bush. I had to run around for at least 2 hours before I found an ambulance, and then they didn't want to take him because they were overloaded. As far as I have heard, he is now a clerk in an office in Washington [11 ll.: greetings; signature; November 29: the regiment is being transferred].

New Orleans, Dec. 14 / 1864

Dearest parents and brothers,

I have sent you 3 letters recently, but I haven't been able to receive any answer up to now, because I keep being moved from one place to another, and my regiment has a hard a time knowing where I am, and I don't know where they are. So now that I am supposed to be moved to New York, I have asked Karl Staiger, who's done very well here—he has a two-story house,[8] to forward any letters etc. that arrive from you, and I will always write and tell him where I am. For the last 3 days I've been here in Sct Louis Hospital where things are a bit better than in Beten Rouge, but still absolutely wretched. We don't even have the most basic clothes we need to keep ourselves warm, there are now 1,600 patients in this hospital, and there are 6 hospitals here that are just as full. I'm expecting to be sent to N.Y. any day now, because the doctors say I'll never be able to get rid of my fever in this climate. It's not so bad anymore, and on good days I can go out, but it's hard for me to walk because I am terribly weak, and there's nothing we can do to help ourselves along because they already owe our regiment 8 months' pay, and we can't get any money until we are back with our regiment, and when we do get back, then it can still take several months until we get paid. I have 3 months to recover, and if I don't get better then I'll be discharged, and if I can manage it, I will make sure that I don't have to go back. And when I get my discharge, then I'll get 282 talers* including my enlistment money, and I should be able to make a new start. And so in case grandfather or you could spare a few dollars at the moment so that I would have some money when I get to N.Y., I would appreciate it very much, and then I would pay you back as soon as possible. Don't worry about me if you don't have any to spare, even without money things should work out.

I am being treated by a very good surgeon here, Doctor Struve is his name, he is German and he's been very good to me from the very first day, and I am feeling much better since he started treating me, he gives me completely different drugs. I am losing all my hair, but he says it will grow back quickly when I'm up north. The only problem is the food, which is better than before but doesn't agree with me. In the morning, we get half a bowl of cabbage

8. Dr. Staiger's prosperity may have been exaggerated: in 1860 he recorded only $800 of property, none of it real estate. In 1870 his widow and two sons were down to $200, living next door to a chambermaid. MC 1860: New Orleans/La., W. 4, p. 170; MC 1870: New Orleans/La., W. 4, p. 778.

and a cup of coffee made from corn and two small pieces of bread, and if I eat this I get diarrhea immediately, so all I eat in the morning is two mouthfuls of dry bread. I'm not much better off at lunch—2 times a week I can eat something, because there's *Soupe* and a piece of fresh meat, but the other days there's salt beef and sour beans, which I must not eat, because they make me swell up with gas too much. In the evening there's bad tea and bread, that's all I can eat here.

Doctor Struve asked me several times whether I didn't have any friends here who could send me something. I told him I had no one, and then he had his orderly bring me potatoes and a piece of roast veal, and he gave me a glass of *Schnaps. Wisky.* He also gave me a pass so I could go and have lunch once with Staiger, who had invited me over, and we had roast goose *Soupe,* and then roast veal and salad, and afterward I drank good coffee with milk and two beers. Lord, did that taste good! Then I had to come back home because they said we were leaving for N.Y. that evening, which wasn't the case. He also bought me some tobacco and gave it to me together with a pipe. But I am not allowed to smoke much. When I found out where he lived, I sent a *Nigger* to him with a message, and he came immediately and was very pleased to see me. I asked him to write to you, since I didn't know if I would have a chance to do so.[9] [7 ll.: greetings] Your / most dearly loving / son / and brother / Gustav Keppler

On December 16, 1864, the transfer to New York finally began. Keppler and 202 other wounded and invalid soldiers were brought on board the paddle steamer *North America,* a fairly new boat that the U.S. government had chartered for $475 a day. At 5 P.M. the ship left New Orleans, with a forty-four-member crew, fifteen passengers, and an assistant surgeon to look after the patients. About midday on December 22, the ship sprang a leak during a storm off the coast of Cape Hatteras, North Carolina; three hours later the water reached the engines and put them out; by 7 P.M. the water in the hull was twelve feet deep, and the captain left the ship in the last lifeboat; and six hours later, the *North America* sank.

9. "New Orleans. De. 14th, 1864. / Most esteemed Pastor, / Alerted by a message from your son Gustav, I went to see him in St. Louis Hospital in New Orleans, where I found him convalescing from 5 months of malaria that he had contracted in Baton Rouge, La. He is now improving and was about to be sent to New York with other convalescents. He told me that he didn't like the soldier's life, but he still has 1 year to serve, and so in New York he will probably be reassigned back to the Gulf. The fact that soldiers have no money is well known. On top of this, it is the case that in the U.S. they are often not paid for 7–8 months, so that soldiers who do not receive any money from home live wretchedly. / Your Gustav asked me to write to you because he is expecting a bank draft from you [20 ll.: details; address]. Respectfully yours / C. Staiger, M.D."

Waiting to drown for twelve long hours, or at least until the water reached the bedridden — it is hard to imagine a more horrible death for these soldiers. Only a handful were saved. The fact that there were only eight lifeboats may not have been unusual, but it is scandalous that the sixty-two persons who were saved included forty-two of the crew, all of the passengers, and even the surgeon who had been assigned to supervise the transfer of the patients. Apart from two sailors, all of the 197 victims were wounded or invalid soldiers, Keppler among them.

Contemporaries, of course, also noticed this imbalance. The surgeon general demanded that the assistant surgeon be given a dishonorable discharge or at least that the case be investigated. On orders from the president, the Adjutant General's Office appointed a four-member military court of inquiry in March 1865; three of the judges held the rank of general, and the hearing was to be held in Trenton, New Jersey.

Both of these investigations were apparently quashed, however, as were so many others after the end of the war. After the confusion and the horrors of war, attention now became focused on making a fresh start. There is no trace in the National Archives of any results of an investigation or trial. Many questions have remained open ever since, and it is unlikely that they will ever be answered.[10]

10. RG 92, 8w2A, Box 3, 1403, NatA; Enlisted Branch Letters Received, 130-100-1865, Box 290 (Steamer *North America*), RG 94, 9w3, R23, c. 31, pp. 13, 409, NatA.

22. Sergeant Albert Krause

In the early 1840s Albert's father August Krause came into possession of Polnisch-Konopath, a large manor in the Prussian district of Schwedt, near the Vistula River, now part of Poland. His son attended grammar school in the provincial capital of Bromberg and then probably studied at a trade school in Berlin to become a draftsman. When Albert left Germany in the early summer of 1861, he was twenty years old. He may well have emigrated to avoid serving in the Prussian army, but economic reasons probably also played a role: his father's estate was in financial

SOURCE NOTE: For a graduate of a Prussian secondary school, Krause's written German is quite unexceptional. Spelling or punctuation errors are very rare, his grammar is impeccable, there is no influence of his local dialect, and his vocabulary is extensive. He handles the language with great ease, and his descriptions are almost as precise as his drawings, but he is not one to use flowery or particularly colorful expressions. Except for the letters of July 27, 1861, October 9, 1862, May 10, 1863, May 26, 1864, and four pages of the letter of February 27, 1863, for which handwritten copies have been used, this series is based on typed copies. A comparison of the copies with the original letters that have been preserved, however, indicates that they are highly reliable. Not included here are the letters in the series from the time after 1865 (four) and some of the letters from 1863 (two) and 1864 (two).

difficulties and would soon be lost. His relations with his father also seem to have been somewhat strained; one year after he left, he wrote, "you see, dear father, that at least I haven't been a disgrace to you here in America."[1]

Krause sailed from Hamburg on the *Gellert* and arrived in mid-July 1861 at the immigration center on Grosse Isle in the St. Lawrence River. After spending a week in quarantine due to an outbreak of smallpox on board, he went to Quebec and then took a train to Ottawa the following day. In late 1861 he turned his back on neutral Canada and settled across the border in Buffalo, New York.[2]

Quebeck, Wednesday the 27th of July, 1861.
Dear parents and brothers and sisters,

[259 ll.: embarkation; sea voyage; arrival; quarantine; train trip to Ottawa; job plans] On Saturday night an English* farmer came by and really wanted to have me, and I didn't want to at first. But he coaxed me into it and I signed a *Contract* with him. I get free room and board, laundry, and 10 dollars for the first month, and in return I'm supposed to help him in his fields. You see, I have a plan that I intend to carry out, and it must be advantageous. I want to become a *Farmer*, and when the *Farm* is running fairly well, then I'll set up a repair shop for farm machinery[. . . .] If I'm working for the *Farmer*, I'll learn English quickly, become familiar with farming here, the machines here, and with the 10 dollars, I should be able to set up my own farm after 2 years at the most. Maybe you, dear father, can send me 50 dollars, too, and I'll build a house on the *Farm* and furnish it a bit, and after one year all of you, my dear ones, can come over and run the farm, and I, for my part, will set up a factory on it. When the war is over, then something like this ought to be very profitable. After the war everything here will improve, and then I'll have the advantage of already knowing the language and the situation[. . . .] My address:

Mr. Albert Krause / in care of Jame Gleeson / Poowers post office
West-Osgoode / West Canada-West / in Amerika

Camp Chapin near Baltimore (Maryland), / September 11th, 1862
Most dearly beloved parents and brothers and sisters,

[6 ll.: correspondence] In my last letter from Buffalo I told you that business there was fairly good, whereas in Canada business was very bad, and that I was in the United States militia[. . . .] The situation still looks very bad in Canada, and it keeps getting worse. Here in Maryland and farther south in

1. Information provided by the donor; letter of September 11, 1862, NABS.
2. Letters of July 27, 1861, September 11, 1862, NABS.

the United States business has also slowed down, and in the rebel states everything is down, but in the North for some lines of business, there's plenty of work, and here and there they can't even get enough people. Up until 4 weeks ago I also had a good job in a machine factory and earned more than a teacher or a store clerk in Canada.

As you have probably read in the newspapers, the militia has been called up here, and as a result, I have become a soldier.[3] I've been wearing the little blue jacket for four weeks, and I am now with our regiment, the 116 N.Y.V., in a camp 4 miles from Baltimore (M) in the middle of a beautiful forest, ready to march to Washington and beyond when the next *Order* comes. — The new Buffalo-Regiment No. 116 N.Y.U.S.V. is under the command of the best general in the North, the German General Siegel [Sigel*], half the men are Germans, and they are in best fighting spirits[4] [20 ll.: address; coworker in Buffalo, Felix Rose, is his best friend].[5] When I come back from the war, I believe I won't need to be afraid to set up my own establishment and provide you with a living [16 ll.: in case he dies, Rose will settle his affairs; has eighty-two dollars in savings].

Enthusiasm for the war is great; in no other country in today's world could it reach such heights. Everyone is following the flag, everyone tries to be useful. The voluntary contributions of the citizens are tremendous — thousands of them give to the government[. . . .] In Buffalo there are several rich people who give 25 dollars, 50 dollars and so forth to every soldier in a regiment in which one of their children or friends has lost their lives — everyone makes his contribution. The ladies also do a lot; they collect money for the wounded and the sick, and they feed the soldiers. The whole time we were in Buffalo, the ladies of the aristocracy fed us personally at their own expense. Cake, fruit,

3. How Krause ended up in the army is unclear for two reasons. Despite the impression he gives, he could hardly have been called up against his will, since he had only been in the country for less than a year. It is also unknown if he enlisted after he had lost his well-paid job, or if he quit in order to join the army.

4. Krause's regiment belonged to the VIII Corps, while Sigel commanded the XI Corps. Dyer (1959 [1908]), 318, 339–40. Heinzelmann's (no. 20) Comp G and Comp H consisted of about 50 percent German-speakers, but in Krause's Comp D only 30 percent were Germans, and in all the other companies, the percentage was much lower. Of the seventy-four officers who served in the regiment, only six had names that were clearly German. Regt. Books, 116 N.Y. Inf, Desc. Books, NatA; *OAR*, 2:611.

5. According to his daughter Milla Fieberg, the "best friend" (also mentioned in letters of September 11 and October 9, 1862) "robbed him of all his clothes & family relics that he left by them and all his money, even his last salary so that when he returned to B. [Buffalo] he had only the soldiers' clothes that he had on his body." Undated, handwritten note signed by Milla Fieberg, NABS.

and everything the human heart might desire was available, and the ladies themselves did the serving. — When we left town almost the entire population was at the train station, each one with a flag in hand; there were flags waving in all the windows, the entire town was a sea of flags, and with many damp eyes of farewell, the *Hurrahs* resounded in the air until the ground shook[. . . .] The ladies rode along beside us for miles on each side of the train in open carriages with flags in their hands, drawn by swift steeds flying along, saluting and waving flags the whole time. During the entire trip through the state of N.Y. and Pennsylvania, everywhere we stopped we received a similar reception and were given whatever we wanted. No one accepted any payment. (*I wouldn't ask anything from a soldier — ich werde doch nichts vom Soldaten verlangen*) was the reply, when you asked what this or that cost. The ladies came to the stops and gave us something to drink and washed the sweat off our faces and hands — they did the same when they came along while we were marching in the heat with our knapsacks[. . . .] On top of this, during the parade in Buffalo every soldier in the regiment received something handmade by the daughters of the town aristocracy under the age of 10, and they presented them in person; I got a soldier's pin cushion. The power of the Union is immense, and the South would have been defeated long ago, if we had had better commanders and the government hadn't been so weakened by the factions; still, England or France shouldn't even think of tangling with us [4 ll.: great hatred of both — England would have made a great mistake].

As far as I am concerned, I am off to the fire filled with courage and enthusiasm. The United States have taken me in, I have earned a living here, and why shouldn't I defend them, since they are in danger, with my flesh and blood?!

I don't want to go back to Germany, especially Prussia — I have tasted freedom, and it tastes too good to trade it again for a dungeon. I don't think I could take it there for even one day, I would feel too miserable. — Long live freedom! [8 ll.: family; correspondence; greetings].

I am writing these lines on a tree stump in the woods. We don't have any ink, pencil is our only writing implement, but we can write the address in the captain's tent with his ink. We also have very little free time, we have to drill hard and in ¼ of an hour I go on guard duty, so please excuse my hurried and chaotic writing.

Things are strict in the army, but only when we're on duty. Afterward, the general is just like the common soldier; he eats with him, smokes and takes snuff with the same tobacco out of the same box. They don't stand on ceremony here; if you want to speak to an officer, you talk to him like a comrade, depending on how well you know him personally. A soldier just puts his hand on an officer's shoulder and lights his pipe on the latter's cigar, without asking permission, and if he turns away, you take his arm and turn him around again so you can talk to him. In Germany this would be considered impossible, but despite this, when we are on duty or drilling, discipline is just as good here as in Prussia [9 ll.: family; signature; postscript].

[October 9, 1862]

Most dearly beloved parents and brothers and sisters,

[14 ll.: correspondence] We are still in the same camp near Baltimore and have to drill very hard, so that we have very little free time. I am writing this when I have a few hours off from *"Guard" (Wache)* duty, but my train of thought keeps getting interrupted by frequent calls to "fall in." [54 ll.: family; consolation for his father who is in financial difficulties; photograph].

Dear father, you want to know how I hope to make a living, what plans I have? To be perfectly honest, I am not quite sure myself [18 ll.: large choice of professions; does not know enough about it; frequent change of profession is customary in the United States].

I can't decide between mechanical engineering and farming; but what I would really like is to become a *Farmer*. A farmer here lives the happiest and the most independent of lives; he is the king on his own property [10 ll.: details]. Before I became a soldier, I had wanted to work for some time in agricultural factories in Milwaukee, Chicago, and St. Louis. Now my plans have been thwarted a bit, but if all goes well, I will reach my goal even more quickly [69 ll.: is full of confidence; compared to one year ago he has a place to live (at Rose's) and savings; family; after the war his brothers and sisters should come over]. How has my political situation in Germany developed? Did they ask about me again at the next mustering for the army? Did they declare me an outlaw? What is [Gave] doing? Did he get in touch with you again because of the money I owe him?—Reassure him that I will never forget my debts to him and that he will get his money back! [90 ll.: details; correspondence; encourages his brothers and sisters to emigrate; climate; family] There is one interesting thing about our camp; it lies in the quiet of an old oak grove, on the side of a hill with a small stream at the bottom[. . . .] Our tents are made of white *Cotton* and set up in nice straight rows, a pleasant sight, particularly to the European eye. The camp is especially pretty in the evening, when the lights are burning in the tents.—We have to drill very hard: from 5 to 7 in the morning, then from 9 to 12, and after lunch from 2 until it gets dark, which happens around 6 o'clock here now [22 ll.: laundry, keeping things tidy, and cleaning weapons takes a lot of time; correspondence; greetings; signature; date].

[February 27, 1863]

Most dearly beloved parents and brothers and sisters,

[37 ll.: correspondence, family] Dear aunt, I was most pleased to receive your letter. There is little chance of peace any time soon. I have also thought about returning to Europe when I have some means—but it will depend on the circumstances. I am a Union soldier, and no power on earth could force me to fight for the slaveholders! It is very doubtful, however, that we will win. But slavery will come to an end sooner or later, after this business that has given it the deathblow, and so it is in the interest of the common good, no matter how it ends for the two sides. No matter what, it is good that I have done my part—shame and disgrace be on those who deal in human flesh!

Here in Baton Rouge we don't get many newspapers, and the ones that are brought in from the North by sea to New Orleans are at least two weeks old, so it often happens that we only find out what our own army on the Potomac is doing some 3, 4, or even 5 or 6 weeks later. In the Army of the Potomac they have small tin stoves in their tents, but here it is never so cold that we need them.

[35 ll.: temperatures; encouraging and admonishing messages to each of his brothers and sisters] As for me, I am still hale and hearty, healthier and stronger than ever, so that all the harmful effects of a foreign climate and an irregular life marked by all manner of deprivations, which have claimed the lives of hundreds, thousands of my comrades, have not affected me [5 ll.: details].

But my eyes are very weak—looking at the white paper is such a strain that after writing 5–6 lines everything swims before my eyes, and I have to stop writing for a few minutes [7 ll.: greetings to numerous acquaintances].

Albert / Camp Banks near Baton Rouge La. February 27th, 1863

[February 27, 1863]

Dear parents and brothers and sisters,

[. . .] We remained in Camp "Belger" near Baltimore until November 6. On the night of the 5th to the 6th we received marching orders and the command to prepare for a sea expedition [6 ll.: march to the Chesapeake Bay]. Hungry and half-frozen—it had turned quite wintry cold for the first time— we had to wait for about another two hours for the small steamer *"Robert Morris"* that was supposed to take us out to a large magnificent oceangoing ship, the *"Atlantic."* Finally it arrived, and we went on board [7 ll.: had to stand on deck for twenty-four hours in the snow during a storm]. Finally we were transferred to the other ship. The *"Atlantic"* is a first-class steamship, the likes of which seldom ply the ocean. Before she was chartered by the government as a transport ship, she sailed between New York and England carrying the mail. She is fitted out with every luxury. On the 1st deck, occupied by the officers, everything is furnished most elegantly. Pastry shop—ice containers—ballroom with a pianoforte[. . . .] Our company had to squeeze into a small section on the second deck. We were [. . .] forced to lie down on the floor, and then it was so crowded there was no place to walk in between the rows. The men lying at the far end walked all over our things, our bedding [. . .] and us [. . .] with their snowy, dirty boots. And on top of all this, there's the disgusting American habit of chewing tobacco, accompanied by spitting out the juice. High-class and low-class, everyone chews tobacco [7 ll.: details]. After we had taken off our knapsacks and put them down, that is on the floor in the dirt, we were given warm bean soup and bread. Oh, how good it tasted! Never had I been so plagued by hunger. The rest of that day and all the next day, all of the things belonging to the regiment, the tents, ammunition, etc. and drinking water were loaded. There were about 1,300 men on board, our entire 116th regiment and three companies from the 114th. On the morning of the 9th we weighed anchor, but we ran aground about 14 miles from Baltimore, and we remained there until the 11th, and despite all the efforts of the engine and all sorts of different attempts, we didn't budge an inch [53 ll.: the *Atlantic* had to be unloaded, soldiers and equipment were put on smaller steamboats; on the 12th they boarded the ship farther out at sea, sailed south that evening; weather; dolphins]. In the late morning we approached the coast that had always been off in the distance to our right, first the coast of "Maryland," then "Virginia," and at about 12 noon we dropped our anchor under the protection of the strong fort "Monroe" [Fortress Monroe*] in the mouth of the "James River."

Here we were at the spot that had seen the bloodiest fighting in this war [. . . .] We were floating on the waters where the famous battle between our "*Monitor*" and the enemy "*Merrimac*" took place, which then forced the latter to commit suicide [48 ll.: graves; shipwrecks; Fortress Monroe; ships; war situation; destination of the expedition unknown]. With troop movements like these, there is the strictest silence on the part of the government about the destination, in order to prevent spies from sending information to the enemy. Our officers, even the colonel and the general, were no better informed in this regard. The sealed orders were not given to them, but to the captains of the ships, so that even they could only determine from one place to the next where we would be stopping.

[18 ll.: went ashore to wash, do laundry, drill, clean their weapons, look for oysters; shellfish of all sizes] In the evening a small steamboat brought us back out to the *Atlantic*, and this embarking and disembarking went on every day for 4 weeks, except when the weather was bad. The point of this was to give us a chance to clean things thoroughly during the day, without our having to sleep at night on the ground, which is always damp in the South. This may well have helped preserve the health and even the lives of many of our comrades, even though 3 men died and we left 150 sick behind when we sailed from Fortress Monroe.

[23 ll.: details of his stay; pay for the time from August 13 to October 1] I received 21 dollars and 20 cents. And then you should have seen how lively camp life became among the soldiers! The whole ground looked like a European market, everyone wanted to buy something, and soon the few stores there were empty. I sent 15 dollars to Buffalo, and I kept the rest for unforeseen events [6 ll.: visited Hampton, completely destroyed]. No white person has stayed behind or is to be found anywhere, all you see are dirty blacks on the run who have taken up residence here and there, under a piece of sailcloth or canvas, in the corners of what, until recently, used to be splendid houses [50 ll.: detailed description of a new ironclad ship nearby—improved version of the *Monitor*].

Almost every day, when we got back to the "*Atlantic*", we saw new ships arriving: warships and transport ships with troops on board. Finally, on December 4th, everything was ready for the upcoming expedition. The weather was nice and warm. At 10 o'clock in the morning we weighed anchor, hoisted the flags, and headed out to sea. The flotilla consisted of 18 steamships, one of which was a war frigate [141 ll.: description of the ocean voyage; storm, seasickness; sailed around Florida; fish, sea birds].

On December 10th we witnessed a sad event, a funeral at sea. One of our comrades had died the day before and was to find his grave in the depths of the waters that evening. On the top deck of the ship, with the flags lowered to half-mast, the chaplain made a solemn speech to the entire crew. The deceased was sewn up in a blanket, his feet weighted down with iron, and lay surrounded by the men, who were all deeply moved. They had put him on a plank that rested half over the railing, and when the chaplain said "Amen," two of the attending sailors lifted up the end of the plank on which the deceased was lying. He slipped down and sank immediately into the depths of the ocean. The flags were raised again, and we departed from this sad spot, deeply moved—once again, death had robbed us of one of our comrades.—

After a voyage that went quite quickly, we finally arrived at Schip-Island [Ship Island] on the 12th. Schip-Island is an island that is 7 miles long and only ½ a mile wide. It lies in a bay that is formed by the shores of the Mississippi, which extends far out into the ocean, and the coast of the state of Mississippi, the state to which it belongs. The island is nothing more than a *Sandbank* that has risen up from the sea [23 ll.: strategic importance of the island]. We stayed on board the *Atlantic* the whole next day, and in the afternoon of the 14th we were put ashore in small boats. We set up camp ½ a mile from the Fort [. . .] yet that same day [27 ll.: details about the island; temperatures].

For Christmas on December 25th, our colonel provided us with some entertainment—he reduced himself and all the other officers to the rank of common soldier, while we elected a colonel and the other regimental officers from our own ranks. The latter exchanged uniforms with their superiors, and then the demoted officers and we had to treat them with the same respect we always show our superiors. It was only a simple thing, but it gave rise to all sorts of fun and amusing jokes, and many of the men who are usually very quiet and serious brightened up for a day. We didn't have to do any of the jobs normally done by the common soldiers. That day the officers had to fetch water from the well, chop wood, make the fires, use spades, rakes, and brooms to clean the paths in front of our tents and stand guard [14 ll.: unpopular officers were given a rough time; details].

On the 28th, after a two-week stay on the island, we received the *Order* to break camp. It was afternoon before we had moved all the tents, cooking equipment etc. through the deep sand to the dock. At 4 o'clock in the afternoon we went on board the "*North Star*" and headed southwest toward the Mississippi delta [51 ll.: impressions of the Mississippi; shipwrecks, deserted plantations; bright glow in the distance]. It was New Orleans that lay before us, and we dropped anchor. The next morning we weighed the latter again and sailed past the Crescent City [20 ll.: elegant city, now dead; disembarked 5 miles north of New Orleans]. We finished unloading about noon, and that same day we set up our new camp, Camp "Love," half a mile from the river and 4 miles from New Orleans near the town of Charleston [6 ll.: camp was below the water level of the Mississippi]. Here it rained so often, and the water drained off so poorly due to the low level of the land, that everything immediately got so muddy that when you left the tent, you sank into the mud up to your ankles. Despite all our scraping and scouring, the claylike mud stuck most firmly to our shoes and was an unwelcome guest in our linen houses, in which 6 men were housed, and we only had just enough space to lie down right next to one another [5 ll.: mud in the tent].

The sick men were a bit better off. The place we were camped belonged to a rich plantation. When our war ships arrived in the year 1861, the owner, a rebel, had abandoned it and made off up the river, taking his wife and children and all his possessions with him. We used this beautiful empty house as a hospital, and the men who were sick, and there were rapidly increasing numbers of them due to the unhealthy location of the camp, had a better chance of convalescing in these dry rooms than in the hospital tents that were just as damp.

[52 ll.: many properties deserted and confiscated; soldiers profit from the poverty: large food markets on both sides of the camp, prices dirt cheap; visited New Orleans] Almost all the citizens are more devoted to the South than the North, and they can only be made to obey by the use of force. Everywhere I went and could be seen, people stared at me in my *Yankee*-soldier uniform with hostile, wary eyes. This is particularly true of the rich, wealthy residents. The proletarians and the poorer classes favor the North. These people have suffered terribly under the rule of the South, as business has gone way down. Before Buttler [Butler*] arrived, a barrel of flour cost 40 dollars, and even for that you couldn't get hold of one [9 ll.: arrival of Union troops prevented mass starvation; details]. If things are this bad in the rest of the South, I cannot understand how they can keep on with the war?! It seems that only the incompetence of our officers is to blame for the fact that we, who have an abundance of everything, have not yet been able to force the "South" back into obedience! — But will this ever happen? —

Buttler has more or less secured the city for our side. There are soldiers with small cannon stationed strategically on several streets, and heavy artillery in the large squares so that, together with the ships, the city is covered in all directions.

[65 ll.: weather; February 3: transported by ship to Baton Rouge; city is a pitiable sight; new camp two miles away] Our pickets are posted only one mile away. We are right near the enemy, and fighting can break out any time. The pickets exchange fire almost daily, and often 2–3 companies from each regiment (we have about 30,000 men here outside of Baton Rouge) are sent to help them in case there's a raid.

On February 13th our regiment went on a sortie. Five miles beyond the picket line we still hadn't met the enemy, and so we were able to fill 50 wagons that we had brought along with grain and other things without being disturbed, and we brought them safely back to the camp. On February 13th, when I was on *Picketguard "Vorpostenwache"* for the first time, a detachment of enemy cavalry tried to surprise us. Our cavalry, still riding around about half a mile beyond the picket line, stopped them and skirmished with them [28 ll.: enemy withdrawal; no Union losses; temperatures; correspondence].

Your son and brother / Albert Krause Camp Banks near Baton Rouge, Louisiana. February 27th, 1863 [. . .]

[May 10, 1863]

Dearly beloved parents and brothers and sisters,

[12 ll.: correspondence; photograph; family; messages to each sibling; greetings to friends; more and more troops arriving from New Orleans] On

March 2nd, General Banks* arrived from New Orleans to *Revue* the troops stationed here. A large open area, right in front of our camp, was designated as the place where the General would review the troops at 10 o'clock in the morning [10 ll.: details].

I estimated our numbers at about 25–30 thousand men, and every soldier was reassured by the awareness of our strength, should we be attacked by the enemy [14 ll.: speculations about the goal of the operation; fleet had also been enlarged; probably an attack on Port Hudson, Louisiana*].

On the 10th of March small portable tents for use while away from camp were distributed among the troops, and the large ones, in which 6 men had been sleeping, were taken down, rolled up, and sent to Baton Rouge, so we were ready to march at any time.

These small portable tents consist of two square pieces of cotton that are the same size, with buttons and buttonholes on each side. Two sides are then buttoned together at the top, and the other four corners are fastened to the ground with small wooden pegs, and then the tent is propped up with two sticks that you can find anywhere. A tent like this is 6 feet wide, 6 feet long, and about 3½ feet high, with just enough space for two men, and it's supposed to keep off the heavy dew that falls here at night.

Using the other buttons and buttonholes, a number of these tents can be put together into one long one, big enough for as many men as there are pieces of cotton. On the march, the tents can be put up in 2–3 minutes and taken down even more quickly. —

Our camp now looked completely different. On the morning of March 14th we started off toward Port Hudson. As long as the sun remained below the horizon, marching was quite pleasant, but when it rose in the firmament it got very hot, and marching became strenuous. The sweat was pouring down from our foreheads over our faces. Our underclothes were soaked with sweat. And on top of this was the incredible dust. The ground was very dry (it hadn't rained for a long time), and with the sun burning down, the marching soldiers kicked up so much dust that you couldn't see a man 12–15 paces away, and a thick layer collected, especially in our noses and eye sockets, on our faces that were gleaming with sweat. We looked like Moors. —

On both sides along the way we saw lots of knapsacks, blankets, clothing, boots, etc. This proved to us that significant forces were marching ahead of us: those sluggish and reckless soldiers were too lazy to carry their things and just threw them away. I say they were reckless because every soldier here knows how much you need your woolen blanket, when after a hot day it turns bitterly cold at night. And the thing you have to be most careful about, even in the greatest summer heat, is not catching a cold. —

Sketch by Albert Krause, "small portable tent," in letter of May 10, 1863.
(Gerhard and Ingborg Krause)

About 11 o'clock in the morning, after we had covered about 12 miles, we set up our camp about 1½ miles from the Mississippi River. Soldiers show the most activity when it's time to set up their tents: some go looking for sticks, others look for boards so they don't have to sleep on the bare ground, and others look around for fresh meat. No house, no home is safe from the soldiers. — For the sake of a couple of boards, the most beautiful houses are often ripped down and razed to the ground, and the fences surrounding the rich fields are fed to the flames [8 ll.: this seems barbaric, but the soldiers do not want to sleep on the ground and get sick]. But most of these beautiful plantations had been abandoned by their owners, who were well-known rebels, as soon as our armies approached. Any owner who stays on his property and swears an oath of allegiance is given some guards to keep the soldiers from destroying it [44 ll.: eyewitness account of the spectacular incident involving the U.S. warship *Mississippi*: having run aground at Port Hudson, it was abandoned and set on fire, but then it suddenly broke free and started drifting down the river, cannon exploding, until it came close to Krause, when the powder magazine exploded].[6]

Half an hour after this affair, things on the road became extremely busy. Wagons rattled and cavalry rode by[. . . .] Soon we realized that they were all rushing back to Baton Rouge, and that we were in the midst of a retreat. It was now time for us to be relieved, and I was surprised that no one came to relieve us or order us back to the regiment.

We waited until 11 o'clock, and then it was clear to us that the guard officer, in his haste, had forgotten about us. But we couldn't leave our post just like that. I put one of my comrades in charge of the post and went down the road, hoping to find a superior officer who could tell me what I should do. I met up with our division General "Auger" [Major General Christopher C. Augur] and told him about our situation. He was astounded to hear about the negligence of our guard officer, and he gave me the order to evacuate our post and attempt to catch up with our regiment, which had left before dawn, as quickly as possible. After a brisk march, we caught up with our regiment about 5 o'clock in the afternoon [7 ll.: camped 5 miles from Baton Rouge]. I had not even rested for half an hour, however, when it started to pour down rain. Within a few minutes, we had a foot of water in the tent, and on top of this, a storm that suddenly came up blew our tent down. Drenched to the bone from head to toe, our clothes completely soaked, my tent mate and I were standing there, completely helpless [16 ll.: orders to withdraw]. We walked with our knapsacks until we reached the main road from Baton Rouge-Port Hud-

6. See Johnson and Buel (1987), 3:566.

son, loaded them onto the baggage wagons that were waiting there and then marched double time to B.R. [. . .] After we reached B.R. we were immediately put on board a steamship on the Mississippi and off we went—none of us knew—where to?

In the afternoon we went on a reconnaissance expedition into the nearby woods. We marched about ½ a mile through the swamps, where the water came up to our knees and several of our men fell into deep holes or flat into the water when they tripped over tree trunks they couldn't see in the water.

We caught about 20 guerrillas and then went back the same way we had come, getting wet all over again, and returned by the evening [26 ll.: camp is right on the river; war fleet could be seen, including the *Essex*; description of the ironclad; bombardment of Port Hudson].

That same evening, a group of about 100 Negroes who had run away from their masters came up to us, and every day we were camped there, hundreds of these slaves arrived, many of whom had walked 10–100 miles to get their freedom [8 ll.: right outside the camp, slave catchers caught two young slaves; the man was ripped to pieces by the dogs:] One of our patrols heard the noise and arrived just in time to save the girl from a similar death, and they took these barbaric men prisoner [42 ll.: marches, expeditions on March 19, 20; his comrades killed a nine-foot snake with two young rabbits in its stomach].

We had heard that 6 miles northwest of the camp there was a plantation in the woods where sizable reserves of tobacco were stored. The smokers in our company immediately decided to avail themselves of this noble herb. I decided to join in. The property had also been abandoned by its owner. After everyone had appropriated a sufficient amount of tobacco, we went up on the flat roof of the house to get a clear view of the area. Then we realized that there was an enemy *Signalcorps* [7 ll.: description of the signal system with flags] near the river bank, concealed so that it could[n't] be seen from our camp, busily working away, telegraphing everything that was happening in our camp to the Fort across the river. It consisted of a captain, 2 lieutenants and 6 privates[. . . .]

They were so busy that they didn't notice us until we had come very close. We moved forward out of the bushes into the open and ordered them to surrender. They didn't hesitate—9 men against more than 50 of us: there was nothing they could do—and they had to surrender their weapons and come with us [45 ll.: prisoners sent to Baton Rouge; Krause's regiment also transferred back to the camp there (February 22); unsuccessful attack on Port Hudson*]. All the soldiers, including myself, agree that we, the ground troops alone, had been strong enough to take P.H., and that our failure was only the fault of the cowardice or sluggishness of our higher officers, who don't care— how long the war keeps on [40 ll.: to improve the defense of Baton Rouge, a five-mile ring of trees around the city was cut down by April 4; then the main army was transferred, leaving only four regiments behind—including the 116th].

Most of the men have hammered together a rectangular box and then put up their tent as a roof. Ours is one of the best-made ones, and it looks much like no. 3 in the sketch above. The drawing on the right shows the inside of our house, looking in from the door. On the two side walls and across the back wall, we have built bunk beds, so that two men sleep on each side, making a total of 6. Along the back wall, where the number 3 is written, is my bed. Our knapsacks serve as pillows. With things set up like this, life is endurable, everyone has his own space where he can sleep at night, and when it rains, he can keep his things dry and clean [22 ll.: troop movements; speculations; payment].

On April 28th, 20 men from our company, including myself, escorted a number of wagons to an abandoned plantation [9] miles down the river, to get the supplies stored there: sugar, feed, corn etc. [. . . .] This plantation, by far the richest, had belonged to a German who is now a colonel in the rebel army, serving in P.H.[7] After we had filled all the wagons, we returned by the evening, without being challenged!

On Saturday, May 2nd, our picket lines were briefly startled when they saw 6–7 thousand cavalry coming from P.H.—But they were even more surprised when they realized they were Union soldiers!

General Grant, the commander at Vicsburg [Vicksburg*] had sent two cavalry regiments to destroy the Vicsburg-Jackson and Jackson New Orleans railroad lines. They had completed their task, but then the rebels cut them off, and in order to avoid being taken prisoner, they had the daring idea of cutting across to Baton Rouge. We heard our first news about the North from them. They took a number of prisoners, who were given parole* near [Natchez?], destroyed the enemy food supplies there, then went on to destroy the Port Hudson Clinton railroad, rode around Port Hudson, took 800 prisoners— enemy cavalrymen who were camped between here and P.H.—and arrived here from Tenesee after riding for 14 days, accompanied by several thousand escaped slaves, each of whom had stolen 1 or 2 horses from their masters.—

They (troops from the state of Illinois) had had a strenuous march and had gone hungry for 48 hours. Covered in dust, nothing but skin and bones just

7. Charles A. Kock, who was also the Hamburg consul in New Orleans, owned two adjacent sugar plantations: "Belle Alliance" and "St. Emma." Before the war, these were worth $800,000 and were worked by 314 slaves. Information provided by Dr. Andrea Mehrländer, based on Kock Papers (1813–69), Southern Historical Collection, University of North Carolina Library, Chapel Hill.

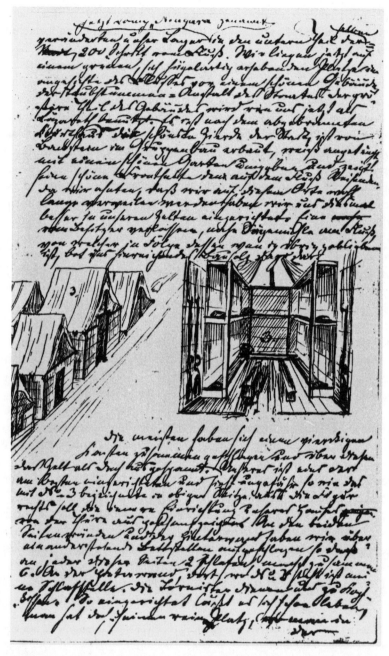

Sketch by Albert Krause, views of quarters, in letter of May 10, 1863.
(Gerhard and Ingborg Krause)

like their horses, we felt sorry for them and admired them, and those great boys from the West were greeted with one "*Hurrah*" after another. Almost everyone ran into their tents and got some bread or something else we now had more than enough of, and gave it to them, and they accepted with gratitude.[8]

We took over their prisoners immediately and put them under guard, while our company cooks quickly prepared them something warm to eat. Others asked for permission to stand guard and look after the horses that night, so that all of them could enjoy an undisturbed and good night of sleep under the protection of our picket line [20 ll.: Camp Niagara, near the river, had facilities for laundry and bathing—important for maintaining health; fewer sick men than in Camp Banks; heat; new campaign to take Port Hudson has begun].

Albert Krause. May 10th, 1863. / Camp Niagara Baton Rouge La.

[July 17, 1863]

Dearest parents and brothers and sisters,

[21 ll.: correspondence; address] Since May 20th we've been living a life of nothing but bivouacs, with continuous fighting and the hardest marches. On that day we left Baton Rouge for Port Hudson, and 4 miles from Port Hudson, on "Port Hudson Plain," we engaged the rebels, who outnumbered us two to one, in a hard battle with 3 bayonet attacks, beating them so badly that they withdrew into the Fort, having suffered heavy losses. It was here in these bayonet attacks that our regiment made a name for itself in Banks's* Army. In the confusion, 4 regiments, all from Massachusetts, had dropped their weapons and were fleeing, and it was only the steadfastness and vehemence of the bayonet attack made by the 116th Reg N.Y.S.V. that could turn the day around into a glorious victory. Our regiment of the 116th N.Y.S.V is made up of more than ⅔ Germans[9]—new proof that the German can fight for freedom. This battle took place on May 21st. On May 25th we had completely surrounded Port Hudson. On May 27th and June 14th we tried to storm the fort, but we were beaten back with heavy losses[. . . .] The bombs, shells, and shrapnel, together with the small arms fire of the enemy, ripped entire limbs off our best soldiers—it was horrible. My place in the regiment is third man from the flag-bearer. Three flag-bearers fell, and the flag itself, hit by

8. Grierson's* Raid from La Grange, Tennessee, to Baton Rouge, made by the 6 and 7 Ill. Cav, April 17–May 2, 1863. Dyer (1959 [1908]), 1024; Faust (1986), 326; McPherson (1988), 628. See also Böpple (no. 39), 7 Ill. Cav.

9. See n. 4.

shrapnel, is in tatters [4 ll.: details] but still, even though our regiment lost ⅔ of its men in these two attacks, I wasn't hurt in the slightest.[10] The most intense preparations were then made for a third attack, and this time the fortress would have been taken without a doubt [6 ll.: constant bombardment; 800 cannon on land; eight warships]. Our trenches and battery fortifications had advanced to within 500 paces of the enemy fort, and almost all the enemy cannon had been taken out by our heaviest crossfire.—On top of this, we had received a large number of cotton bales, and we were supposed to use these as protection by rolling them forward in a new attack. The attack was planned for July the 8th. But the enemy found out about this, and since they had no hope of being able to ward off this attack, they sent an intermediary over about midnight the night before the planned attack to negotiate a surrender. The negotiations lasted all day on July the 8th, and we marched into the fort on the 9th. The soldiers stood in neat rows and lay down their weapons—the sign of surrender. We captured about circa 60 more good cannon, more than 12,000 muskets, and took 6,000 prisoners. The bombardments had wrought massive destruction—almost all the cannon on the ramparts were shot to bits, the houses demolished, and the air was filled with the revolting smell of dead horses-mules-cattle, and everything else[. . . .] The United States flag was raised amid the thunder of our cannon on land and water and a chorus of our own Hurrahs [6 ll.: was sent by ship to Donaldsonville that same day; new victorious battle on July 13].

When we left Baton Rouge, our regiment still had 900 men. After these 4 larger-scale engagements—the first three were real battles, because more than 6,000 of our men were involved—it has been reduced to only 200 men who are able to fight, and yet I am still completely unscathed [22 ll.: after the division of the South into two parts, peace is near; successes on other fronts as well].—Here in the field; ready to march off somewhere at any moment, taking nothing along—since May 20 we've been on light marching orders, taking only a couple of things along, our guns, ammunition, bread bags, and water bottles, since we left our knapsacks back in Baton Rouge—with nothing to write with and always drenched in sweat by the southern sun that burns

10. These figures are hardly exaggerated. The 14,000 Federals who made the attacks on May 21 and June 14 suffered a total of more than 4,000 casualties, which included 406 dead, while the rebels suffered losses of only 282. During its service in the entire Civil War, the 116th lost a total of seven officers, including two who died of illness; four of the five who fell were killed in the attacks on Port Hudson. Krause's company, which had included seventy-six privates at the end of October 1862, was reduced to fifty-five on May 16, 1863, and only thirty-five on August 3, 1863. Long and Long (1971), 359, 366; Dyer (1959 [1908]), 747; *OAR*, 2:611; Regt. Books, 116 N.Y. Inf, Morning Reports, NatA.

straight down on us—life is not good; it is unbearably hard [16 ll.: family; greetings]. Fare well! / Albert Krause

Camp near Donaldson Ville La, July the 17th, 1863 [5 ll.: address]

[August 19, 1863]

Dearly beloved mother and brothers and sisters,

[114 ll.: death of his father; his brother Aurel's plans: he should avoid the navy, would lose his freedom] I am in a much better situation here, serving the state in a free country, where being subordinated to a superior cannot be compared to the situation in a monarchy. If you are treated unfairly here, you can complain and [. . .] you can immediately report your superior, but still there are innumerable cases like the one I mentioned above.

We are under martial law [4 ll.: this was inevitable]. The first condition of martial law is obedience, and that is already enough to offer the smooth-talkers and swindlers a wide-open field of opportunity for their talents.

Flatterers receive positions, promotions, get passes and leave, when they ask for it, much more easily that those who disdain to achieve their goals in such a base manner.

I see and notice things like this every day. But it doesn't affect me much—except that I despise these people, but I leave them alone, I do my duty, and if I am treated unfairly, then I complain or shrug it off. And I can also do this more easily than Aurel, because I didn't choose the military as a profession, I didn't seek my future happiness in a military career, I only became a soldier in order to defend a principle that is well justified in the eyes of the entire civilized world, and when this goal has been fully achieved, that will be enough for me, that will be recompense enough for my trials and tribulations [11 ll.: ingratiation is also a problem outside government service, but then one can always leave].

I think the best thing would be for Aurelius to come over here. In a year's time, I hope to have a permanent job in Buffalo and to be able to find him a position immediately. If he wants to learn a trade, become a merchant or take up a profession like surveying, engineering, etc., then the training here is less fraught with difficulties than over there in Germany[. . . .] Here they operate on the principle that all work deserves appropriate payment, and even an apprentice who lends a helping hand, even if he doesn't understand the business yet, has to be paid [. . .] accordingly[11] [23 ll.: details].

---

11. The implicit reference is to the traditional European system where an apprentice only receives room and board, and the master can demand a considerable amount of money for taking him on as an apprentice.

I don't mean to say that Aurelius should necessarily stay here in America forever—I don't even want to do that, and I have planned to visit you in the next year or two—but I think it is much easier to get ahead at the start over here than it is over there[. . . .] In the meantime I suppose he should go to school for another year and make sure he does not fail to become somewhat familiar with English grammar, if he gets the chance, for this will be most useful, even if he sticks to his decision to become a sailor [62 ll.: his father's estate; family; signature].

[August 19/22, 1863]

Dear sister Elise,

[168 ll.: correspondence; repetition of events at Port Hudson*; regiment received a new flag from the city of Buffalo, embroidered by the local ladies; the surrender of Port Hudson] Then we had a pleasant conversation with the prisoners, we exchanged reports of our mutual sufferings, and we made a special point of providing them with coffee, which the southern army hadn't had since January, as well as bread and meat—they had been living off mule meat recently—which they took eagerly and which we have more than enough of. You never would have thought that these people who were chatting so peacefully could have been shooting at each other the day before yesterday [30 ll.: more descriptions of military campaigns; back to Camp Niagara; correspondence; photographs; his eyes have gotten worse; messages to each of his siblings; greetings to friends].

Your son and brother Albert / Fort Williams *near* Baton Rouge La. August 19th, 1863.

We just received marching orders; it seems we're off to Mobile, Alabama [. . . .] May God keep you well, please write soon. / Your loving brother Albert. / Camp Fort Williams, August 22, 1863

December 25, 1863 [postmark: January 2, 1864]

Dearly beloved mother and brothers and sisters,

[54 ll.: Christmas; family; correspondence] We are still camped here near New Iberia, but our duty is very strenuous. Most of the troops have already gone from here to Rio Grande, Texas, so that every third day it is our turn to do picket duty. We also make frequent expeditions to capture the numerous guerrillas[. . . .] In the evening I occasionally write articles, and I've sent a few to New York to the editors of the local *Kriminalzeitung* [*Criminalzeitung**]; they were well received,[12] and now I get every issue sent to me regularly. The

---

12. Two of Krause's texts (with no byline) could be found: "Vom Kriegsschauplatz" [from the front], *New Yorker Criminal-Zeitung und Belletristisches Journal*, December 11, 1863, and February 12, 1864. They are similar to the campaign descriptions in the letters and remarkably open

New York Kriminalzeitung is the best American newspaper, it doesn't belong to either the Democratic or the Republican Party and is therefore much better than the usual American *"Newspapers"*!

[24 ll.: is sending a copy (probably the issue published December 11, 1863); troop movements; greetings; correspondence]

Our former Captain Higgins has advanced to lieutenant colonel, and our First Lieutenant Seymore [E. W. Seymour] is now captain of the company. But letters to the old address care of Captain Higgins still reach me just as well. / Albert

> *Camp near* Franklin La, January 10, 1864
> [postmark: New Orleans, January 22, 1864]

Dearly beloved mother and brothers and sisters,

[23 ll.: correspondence; left New Iberia on January 7; snow very unusual in Louisiana; melts in the midday sun:] so that at times we were wading through water that was knee-deep[. . . .] The artillery horses were the worst off; the wheels of the heavy gun carriages cut very deeply into the black marshland, so that in especially difficult spots, it became necessary to unharness the horses, and then we all worked together to pull each separate piece through these pools or swamp holes. About 3 o'clock in the afternoon we finally reached the small town of La Fayette; it was dead quiet, windows and shutters closed, and not one white person, either male or female, to be seen, only a few Negroes who watched us with curious eyes. We stopped 2 miles beyond La Fayette and spent the night in a sugar plantation deserted by its owner. Our regiment chose the sugar refining building as its quarters,[13] and after I had dried my clothes and in particular my shoes in front of one of the numerous fires, I went to sleep in one of the troughs where the Negroes used to stir the syrup. It was the best night of sleep I ever had, and why not? Since we left Baton Rouge, it was the first night I had spent indoors, except for the times when we were on board various ships! [39 ll.: march to the camp near Franklin; family; greetings, signature].

> Camp "Emory" *Near* Franklin La. / March 2, 1864
> [postmark: New Orleans, March 11, 1864]

Dearly beloved mother and brothers and sisters,

[49 ll.: correspondence; photographs; spring; alligators] I am enclosing 2 issues of the *New Yorker Kriminalzeitung*.* In one of them, under the headline

---

in their criticism of Union strategy and of specific individuals: "General Franklin has become unpopular with the troops [. . .] only a few men still think highly of him" (December 11).

13. See also the letter by Heinzelmann (no. 20), January 23, 1864.

"*Inländische Korrespondenz*" [domestic correspondence] there is a short article of mine.[14] The rest might be of interest to the mayor, to see what people here think about the Prussian situation [31 ll.: destination of the upcoming march unknown; messages to his siblings; greetings].

Your truly loving son and brother Albert

Camp near Morganzia [Morganza, Louisiana] [Bend?] *on the* Mississippi—
River, May 26th, 1864.

Dearly beloved mother and brothers and sisters,

[4 ll.: correspondence] On March 15, we left Franklin, passing Opelousas, Alexandria, and Natchi Toches on our way to Shreveport La, where the rebels had strongly fortified themselves. We are all, including myself, still so exhausted from the strains of this march, and as a consequence my mind is still so confused, that at the moment I am unable to give you, my dear ones, a clear picture of this campaign. Suffice it to say that the expedition was a failure [17 ll.: descriptions of Sabine Cross Roads and Pleasant Hill].

We finally left Grandécore La. on the morning of April 22nd and marched straight through to Cloutierville, 45 miles away. This was the hardest march we had ever made. Suffocating southern heat and scorching sun, as well as dust so thick you couldn't see a comrade 4 paces away, sapped our energy completely. And despite this, we were only granted 3 hours of rest. We were awakened early on the 23rd, and fighting with the enemy broke out immediately. Our regiment had to skirmish in the woods until midday. The ground was marshy and most of the time we were up to our hips in water, and as we got more and more tired, we ran the risk of losing our balance and falling over the tree roots and tree branches into the water, all the while being greeted by with thick clusters of grapeshot, canister, and shrapnel. Around 4 o'clock we had chased off the enemy, and a pontoon bridge was put across the river. That was the battle of "Cane river-crossing" or "Pine Bluff crossing." On April 25th we arrived in Alexandria [7 ll.: May 14: marched off; fighting]. On the 22nd we arrived here at the Mississippi[. . . .] Put on half rations, we had to march almost the whole time from Pleasant Hill La in the greatest heat, day and night, and still manage to fight small skirmishes every day. Those who are familiar with this country and the sun here can easily imagine what this was like, and they won't be surprised that the army, at the moment, is incapable of any further action. And although I am one of the hardiest, I have been weakened so much by the excessive strain that I find it difficult even to write, and I will need 3 to 4 weeks before I have recovered some of

14. Krause's report of February 12, 1864; see n. 12.

my strength [33 ll.: thinking and writing are also hampered; correspondence; photographs; greetings; signature].

Camp *near* Cedar Creek Va., October 31, 1864

Dearest mother and brothers and sisters,

[21 ll.: correspondence] From my letter of August 9,[15] you know that our corps was transferred from Louisiana to the state of Virginia, to the Shenandoah Valley, and I am sure you have read in the newspapers about the great success of the army in this valley against the rebels. General Sheridan, who is in command here, has won four large battles in the last month [3 ll.: Winchester, Fisher's Hill, New Market*, Cedar Creek]. In all of these battles, our regiment was in the front, coming under the heaviest fire, and at Cedar Creek our flag was the first to be raised over the fortifications we had won back [87 ll.: he is healthy; details of the battles; army correspondence]. Your truly loving son and brother Albert

Camp near Newton in The Shenandoah-Valley Va. December 1, 1864

Dearly beloved mother and brothers and sisters,

[18 ll.: correspondence; family] Whether we'll be staying here this winter or not? These are questions we ask ourselves all the time [8 ll.: details]. The presidential election for the next 4 years was on November 8[. . . .] Lincoln was reelected by a majority larger than ever before, and the traitors were defeated [5 ll.: "traitorous governors," like Horatio Seymour of New York, were also defeated]. The government is now in a position to gather together the largest force ever in the spring—to finish off the rebellion—long live freedom! [6 ll.: season's greetings]. This will be the 4th Christmas that I haven't been able to celebrate with you. All alone in a strange country, surrounded by strangers who speak a foreign language, so it is like music to my ears when I occasionally hear a few familiar, German, good, pithy words (otherwise all the Germans here speak English, even among themselves) [43 ll.: good wishes; messages to his siblings; greetings, signature].

Camp Sheridan *near* Stevens Depot Va. / February *the* 1st, 1865

Dear mother and brothers and sisters,

[5 ll.: correspondence] We have left our camp near Newtown and have moved nearer to our supply of provisions for the winter, and everyone here thinks that we will remain here quietly in winter quarters until the begin-

15. This letter is not included here; its 68 ll. describe his departure by ship, July 2, and arrival in Washington on July 13; various marches; correspondence; greetings; signature.

ning of the spring campaign [19 ll.: groups of three to four soldiers have built wooden huts with a tent as a roof and a "fireplace"—protection against the snow, up to a foot high, and the northerly winds; details].

I am enclosing the resolutions passed by the business community in Buffalo, in recognition of our courage, that they wrote and had printed on the occasion of a visit paid by our colonel when he was on leave; perhaps you will find it interesting[16] [39 ll.: assessment of war situation; rebellions]. There is talk of setting the Negroes free and letting them fight for their independence [11 ll.: would not do the South any good because the blacks would desert]. By the way, the massive desertion of slaves across our lines, following the public announcement of this plan in the South, leaves no room for doubt as to the opinion and patriotism of the majority of the Negroes. At the same time, this measure is sowing discord among the traitors themselves—between the majority, who grew up with prejudices against slaves and still cannot imagine an existence without them, and another, not insignificant group of more sensible men, who think it is better to return to the Union. The latter calculate that this way it would be a lot cheaper to get rid of their slaves, that they wouldn't need to be shot to death for their emancipation [33 ll.: the South is faltering; greetings; signature].

On June 8, 1865, Sergeant Krause (who never wrote home about either of his two promotions) was mustered out in Washington. He returned to Buffalo and started looking for a job: six weeks later, he found employment as a technical draftsman. On October 23, 1865, he became a United States citizen. In one his letters, he mentioned that he was in very poor health and that this was an aftereffect of the war. Nevertheless, he managed to work not only for various employers but also independently in his own office, making a decent living.[17]

In 1870, however, he was still without property, renting rooms from a well-to-do teacher from Hesse-Darmstadt.[18] Then his career took off: the technical draftsman became an engineer or civil engineer, and then he became the assistant head of the Buffalo city engineer's office (1874–77). After working for a few years as a self-employed civil engineer (1884–87), he was elected Buffalo's city engineer—a very prominent position, especially given the size of the city, which had grown from 155,000 in 1880 to 256,000 in 1890. Krause continued to be enthusiastic about the United States, although less so as the years went on, and he was a member of the veteran's association, the Grand Army of the Republic (GAR), but he often spoke

16. A translation was also enclosed: "in gratitude and recognition of the 116 N.Y. Inf; pride of the citizens of Buffalo in the regiment; respect for the colonel—he should be promoted."

17. Letters of August 27 and December 31, 1865, NABS.

18. MC 1870: Buffalo/N.Y., W. 4, #469.

with pride of his German background and remained a staunch member of several German American associations as well.[19]

In 1872 Krause married a nineteen-year-old woman who had emigrated from Austria in 1860. The couple had four children, and both of the sons later became civil engineers.[20] It seems Krause never fully recovered his health. In 1904, at the age of sixty-three, he applied for a war pension, on the grounds of being partially "unable to earn a support" due to "age disability." He received a monthly pension of twenty-four dollars, until he died of pneumonia in 1913, at the age of seventy-two.[21]

19. Letter of July 22, 1883, NABS; obituary in *Buffalo Courier*, December 29, 1913.
20. MC 1880: Buffalo/N.Y., e.d. 145, #144; MC 1900: Buffalo/N.Y., e.d. 137, #145.
21. Pension File, NatA.

23. Christian Härring

Christian Härring, born January 13, 1824, in Bietigheim in Württemberg, was a shoemaker, like his father before him. By 1850 only four of the original nine Härring children were still alive, and all but one, Charlotte (born in 1826), immigrated to the United States in the early 1850s. Louise was the first to cross the ocean, in 1852, and a year later she got married in Philadelphia to a clothmaker from a village twelve miles from her hometown. Her younger brother August left Germany in 1853, and in 1854 letter-writer Christian followed.

The only information we have about Christian Härring's subsequent life is provided by this one letter and the census records. By 1860 he was married to an Irish immigrant; the couple had no children and very limited means—no property and $100 in cash. The 1870 census found him in similar circumstances in an Irish neighborhood of Salem, New Jersey.[1]

Wilmington August 30, 1863

Dear parents and sister,

[8 ll.: correspondence; he writes too seldom:] I want to tell you why— over there, you know enough about this war here in America, and that's the cause of it all. Why? well, we keep thinking we can see an end to this war, and then one thing after another happens and gets put into the history book;

SOURCE NOTE: For a man who probably had very little schooling, Härring writes surprisingly sophisticated German without any noticeable influence from his native Swabian dialect. It is also surprising that there are very few spelling errors in his letter.

1. KB (ev.) Bietigheim; information provided by the donor; MC 1860: New Castle Co./Del., Wilmington, W. 2, #815; MC 1870: Salem Co./N.J., Salem City, p. 181.

first we thought the southern rebels would win, and then it was the northern rebels again—there's not much difference in the description, which means: it depends on how you see it—the rebels in the South are fighting for their property and their constitutional rights! The rebels in the North are fighting for, what?—I don't quite know what to say, it is clear that the rich are fighting to make a lot of money, and the poor—to make a living or to lose their lives, or even worse, to be crippled for life! Times were really bad when the war broke out, business slowed down completely, and so for the workers there was no other way to earn a living except to enlist. And others who didn't have to make their living as laborers found it a good opportunity to play the role of an officer, and so it went, nothing but a competition to raise one regiment after the next, just to make money.—But this has changed somewhat now that the war has lasted more than 2 years. Some of the poor men have distinguished themselves a bit with their military experience, and so now some of the common soldiers are being made into officers, and now they've started the first draft, for 20 to 35-year-olds, and a second draft for 35 to 45-year-olds is being planned, because the volunteer regiments have really been decimated and need to be filled up again. This is starting to get unpleasant for those who have a good job or those who have to leave their families behind and can't say, I'll be home again soon, because these battles are tremendous: 20,000 to 40,000 have fallen in some of these battles, and you can say that one million and 500,000[2] men have already fallen, and it seems that this is just the beginning. It is hard to imagine, but I'll try to give you at least an idea of it: enormous hospitals have been set up everywhere and are still being set up, and they are filled with many thousands of men who cannot even imagine being able to take care of themselves in the future, and there are so many men limping around in the cities on crutches and walking sticks that when you see all this, it is truly dreadful. But there are still enough men who go into this wretched slaughter gladly, just to make money, because a new law was passed that every man who is drafted can buy himself off when he pays 300 dollars or pays for a substitute, but now the substitutes are becoming rare in some places, and so they cost 4, 5, and 600 dollars, and so now everyone who can somehow raise the 300 dollars pays this sum to the government [. . .] and now they're also setting up regiments of Negroes or blacks, which adds a new force to the field, fighting alongside the white troops, so that the war and the money making can continue for several more years. The southern *Präsitent* has also made a law that from now on all the blacks, the slaves and the free blacks, have

2. The official fatality numbers for the entire war: 110,100 (USA), 94,000 (CSA) were killed; 224,580 (USA), 164,000 (CSA) died of disease. McPherson (1982), 384, 488.

to serve in the army, and there are more than 4 million slaves, not counting the free blacks, and that will be a mighty force against the North, so there's not much chance of an end to the war any time soon. But dear parents, don't fret and worry so much about me, because we have gotten quite used to the war, and as long as the fighting doesn't move up here near where we are, we are not affected. There's enough work for anyone who wants to work, and they pay good wages, too. Everything is more expensive than before, but you can still have a good life. Even though you can't save very much at the moment, you can make a good living. America is very large, and it is growing enough so you don't die hungry. But you don't see any gold or silver and hardly any copper anymore, that's all disappeared, for one dollar in gold you have to pay an extra 75 cents [8 ll.: details].

I could write more about this baneful business, but to keep this letter from getting too heavy, I will turn to our family affairs [28 ll.: brother August died of "consumption" in May, after a long illness]. Dear sister, you mention in your letter that you would so much like to return to America, that you can't get it out of your head, so why don't you see to it that you all come over together? My wife and I both wish that we were all living together and working together, and then we would certainly be able to enjoy a wonderful life, free of care[3] [17 ll.: has suffered financial setbacks due to doctors' bills for his bad hand and for August, but he can take her in if she pays for her own passage; family; his dog Prinz drowned, but Hecktor—"my only joy in America"—is well; greetings; signature].

3. Louise had returned to Germany in 1858 because her husband was ill. After his death in 1859, she moved back to Bietigheim.

24. Barbara Pack and Nikolaus Pack

When the Catholic miner Nikolaus Pack left Schiffweiler in the Saar region in 1853, he was already forty-three years old. He emigrated together with his wife and seven children, obviously hoping to earn more money in the United States. He worked in his old trade in the coal mines near Pittsburgh, Pennsylvania. In 1860 he listed real estate worth $900—probably a small house. By 1870 he had moved up to a position

SOURCE NOTE: Only a transcript of this letter is available, and it seems safe to assume that Joseph Scheben, who collected and transcribed emigrant letters in the 1930s, standardized at least the spelling and punctuation. Therefore, what remains to be said of Pack's language, for example his flowery and pungent imagery, can be gleaned from the English version as well.

as a gardener and claimed $2,500 in property, but his children remained miners and laborers.[1]

                              Mt Oliver [Pennsylvania], October 12, 1863

Dear brother-in-law and sister-in-law,

We have waited so long to write to you for the following reason. We wanted to write to you the truth about how the American war would end. But we couldn't wait until it was over. We know the beginning, but only the Good Lord knows the future.

The cause of this war is basically a nice present from Europe that the dear 48ers, those heroes of freedom who have broken with God and their respective monarchs, have brought into this beautiful country. The main cause was the excessive pride of the entire American people. The Good Lord had blessed them with an abundance of everything, food, good food and cheap besides. There were no empty stomachs, and where there are no empty stomachs, there are no cool heads. Arrogance took the upper hand in opulence and showy dress. This brothers' war between the North and the South is a punishment from the Lord. Thousands upon thousands from our side as well as the South's have already shed their blood, and the situation is still just the same as it was at the beginning. The Negroes are still not free and are just as black as they ever were, and the mark of Cham will not be washed from them.[2]

The despots in Europe are also stoking this fire mightily, and why, this is clearly obvious. Engelland, that godless place, the home of all rebellions, the refuge of all murderers and vagabonds, with the head of its beautiful government adorned with the diadem of a woman, and as many freemasons as trees in the forest. The splendid tract society, which sends out millions and millions of copies every year throughout the world,[3] will have to come and pull the chestnuts out of the fire that the North and South have scraped together (*never meyd*). And that schemer Napoléon, who has stolen into Mexico but

---

1. Information provided by the donor and the archivist Friedrich Denne (Schiffweiler) from the rk. Pfarramt Schiffweiler; MC 1860: Allegheny Co./Pa., Mt. Olivier, Lower St. Clair Twp., #723; MC 1870: Allegheny Co./Pa., Mt. Olivier, Lower St. Clair Twp., #201; MC 1880: Allegheny Co./Pa., e.d. 67, #83; MC 1900: Allegheny Co./Pa., e.d. 455, #271.

2. Noah's curse on his son Ham (Genesis 9:18–27) was ideologically exploited in various ways. Here, Ham was seen as the progenitor of the black race and the enslavement of the Canaanites as the origin of slavery. Fredrickson (1971), 60–61, 87–89.

3. From the 1830s on, the American Tract Society, an arm of evangelical Protestantism, published five pages annually for every inhabitant of the United States, crusading against slavery, "popery," and liquor, as well as promoting individual conversion.

hasn't taken hold of it yet[. . . .] And Emperor Alexander of Russia has 5 warships in the port of New York at the moment, ready to help us. The polar bear should go to Poland and do justice to them first, before putting its paws on American territory. The whole world is up in arms, and it's come to the point that everyone wants to give the orders, but no one wants to obey.

Our government has done something in this respect that no heathen monarch has ever done. This summer, men from 21 to 35 years of age were conscripted as soldiers; whoever was chosen had to go or send a man in his place or pay 300 dollars. No exceptions were made for priests. One of our priests was chosen, too. Five men wanted to go in his place, but he would [hear] none of it. He said: no, the shepherd must give his life for his flock, not the flock for the shepherd. A collection was taken up for him, and 500 dollars were raised for him, and for 350 dollars he got a Negro; and the parish also collected 450 dollars for new robes for the acolytes and a chasuble that were used for the first time on the 1st Sunday after Michaelmas. The man who brings you this letter can tell you more, I don't have enough time [6 ll.: son Konrad got married on October 8, 1863; family].

We here, thanks be to the Lord, have not seen anything of the war, and business is booming so much that there's a shortage of workers. Many rolling mills can only work one shift, due to the lack of men, and most of *Fäktorien* [factories] as well. Wages have gone up in all lines of business, and the coal diggers who used to get 1½ cents a bushel now get 4 cents for digging, and so everywhere it's gone up the same.

Food is not that expensive. A hundredweight of white flour costs 3½ dollars, pork and beef cost 6–7 cents a pound.

As far as clothing is concerned, it's gone up by half, and cotton is three times more expensive, since there's no cotton coming from the South.

All of us here send our very best, your faithful friends to the end / Nikolaus Pak. Barbara Stein [wife]

Nikolaus Pack's son Jacob was born in 1842 and became a coal digger like his father. He volunteered for military service (for a bounty of $300) in Pittsburgh on February 12, 1864. He served in the 116th Pennsylvania Infantry, and on June 15, 1864, he was listed as missing in action near Petersburg, Virginia, and was presumably killed. His father died in 1886.[4]

4. MC 1860: Allegheny Co./Pa., Mt. Olivier, Lower St. Clair Twp., #723; Muster Rolls, 116 Pa. Inf, NatA (Jacob Pack); information provided by the donor.

Muster Roll entries for Jacob Pack, son of Nikolaus Pack.
(National Archives, Washington, D.C.)

25. Matthias Leclerc

Not much more is known about the life of Matthias Leclerc than what is in his few surviving letters. Born in 1822 in Vallendar near Koblenz on the Rhine, this son of a linen weaver seems to have made a living trading goods—apparently across the border as well—until in his own words he became "slovenly," started drinking and neglecting his work. By 1862, the forty-year-old was financially ruined and found himself faced with a choice either "to put a bullet through my head or choose Ammerika." He opted for the latter, probably leaving considerable debts behind.

Once in the United States, as Leclerc wrote in 1864, he stopped drinking and became "a responsible person" again, earning more money than he needed to live a decent life. He worked for more than a year with a man who had apparently emigrated from the Koblenz area some time earlier, (Carl?) Lammersdorf, then opened a store together with a watchmaker. When that enterprise went bankrupt, he ended up working in Washington, D.C., as a mason—the trade he had probably learned in his youth.[1]

Washington, October 2, 1864

Most esteemed Cousin Simmon,

[88 ll.: reasons for his emigration; money matters; family; life in America] You get the news from the newspapers, but that's nothing but press prattle, the war or rather this brothers' war is so horrible at the moment it is hard to believe. The northern government has mustered up a colossal army and the human slaughter is terrible. Now they can't get any soldiers for 3 years anymore, so they're recruiting them for 1 year. A man gets 1,000 to 1,500 dollars for 1 year and 16 dollars a month pay plus 48 dollars for clothing plus food. When I was working for Lammersdorf, I had a chance to see what it's like to be a soldier here, and you couldn't get me to be one for 100,000 dollars unless I was fed up with life, which isn't the case. Here in the *Cämp* or *Lager*, the soldiers get meat 2 times a day, as much as they want. A whole loaf of bread, 2 lbs. of fine white bread, coffee, tea, sugar, vinegar, salt, pepper, syrup, but when they're marching—and oh, what marches—not so much can be taken

SOURCE NOTE: Perhaps Leclerc's business went bankrupt because there were too many misunderstandings. He is one of the very few letter-writers in this volume whose use of the local dialect, defective grammar, atrocious spelling, and incongruous punctuation combine to make the reader stop, think, and wonder what the writer wants to say every two or three lines. In most cases the meaning can be deciphered, but it requires considerable patience. Not included here is one letter from after 1865.

1. Information provided by the donor; Matthias Leclerc to Simon Leclerc, October 2, 1864, February 15, 1865, NABS.

along, and they get *Kräker* and salt pork, thick slabs of bacon, salted with salt-peter so it can withstand the great heat, since normal salt doesn't keep meat well enough. That will give you an idea of what this heat is like. And then they march day and night, and whoever falls behind is lost. I've taken part, too. Then the soldiers throw away everything, blankets, coats, they only keep their bullets and guns, and now especially this time of year the days are ter-ribly hot and the nights are cold, and there is thick fog in the woods at night. This is now causing terrible fever, since they drink the water wherever they can find it, and this causes diarrhea, and it just runs down their pants, and they get more exhausted than you can even imagine. The more water you drink, the worse it gets, and the upshot is you're a wreck. The ones who stay well have to meet the enemy, and then there's so much shooting that entire regiments disappear in no time, I've seen it in the last 1½ years on the battlefield since I left Carl. I've been going to the hospitals near Washington, because I had a *Rekomantazion* [recommendation] for a *Pass* so I have access to all the *Forts* & hospitals. A while ago, after the battle in the Wiltniss [Wilderness] I saw 13 cadavers being carried to the morgue in one night, and two men were busy with a stretcher that was covered with a sheet, bringing nothing but arms and legs that two other men were packing—as if it were normal meat—in large crates. Then they nailed them shut and took them away on wagons. I got sick to my stomach twice, what with the great heat, the millions of flies and the stench, but I wanted to see it. Later on I could watch without shuddering, that's just the way it is. And I think there are more than 25 hospitals in and around Washington, and in every one there are roughly 5,000, would you be-lieve, five thousand beds. And you must bear in mind that these wounded men have been transported more than 200 miles (English), partly by water, rail-road, and ambulances, and often by wagon when there aren't enough ambu-lances, although they have a large supply. So this will give you at least a small picture of what things are like here. The government is spending 2½ million dollars a day. Hard to believe, but it's true [10 ll.: prices; chances to earn some money; letter breaks off].

Washington, February 15, 65

Dear Cousin Simmon,

[137 ll.: family; money matters; is earning a lot; his English has improved; is working as a mason in the waterworks from 7 A.M. to 6 P.M.] when I tell you 2 to 3 kinds of meat for breakfast, coffee, sugar, two kinds of fine white bread, eggs, etc., and the same for lunch and tea in the evening, you can see how we live here. And at home, the poor workmen, living like dogs. Every poor young person who likes to work and who knows he can only survive by working should save every penny to pay for his passage and then not hesitate for one minute to come over here, not to stay in Ney jork, but to move out into the countryside [22 ll.: workmen need to learn new things but are well paid; prices]. You can easily get beaten up with a blackjack and have your pockets emptied, that happens all the time here, but it's not as bad as it was before the war, because the war has drained off a lot of these characters. A while ago there were rumors of peace, but nothing came of it, and the war will be fought even more intensely in the spring. That means there's great demand for human flesh, and anyone who hates to work can take up the brilliant career of a soldier, for which he gets a 1,000 dollar bounty [15 ll.: repetition of letter of October 2, 1864, about soldiers and corpses; it takes four to six days to transport the wounded to the hospitals]. As valuable as these soldiers are, they are simply squandered in the horrible fire of the weapons of war. No questions are asked when a regiment with 2,000 men goes into *Bättel* and comes back with a few hundred men. It is hard to believe how bitterly this war is being fought. And on top of this there are all the *Curillers* [guerrillas], like in Spain; they raze everything to the ground, but they can't expect any mercy, either, when they get caught by our soldiers, they are hung on the next best tree. There's no telling yet when this war will come to an end. The two sides are too angry with each other; but the slave question, I think, has been decided. Sooner or later America will have no more slaves, freedom takes its course with great strides. And it is good that it stops, I have seen this shameful stain on America in Virginia, and it is dreadful. Now the South is turning the Negroes into soldiers, and we'll have to wait and see what happens. Yesterday I was in the Senate where Bräsident Lincoln was reelected. I am very interested in listening to the debates. What a ruler by divine right does over there, the people do here [61 ll.: description of the weather, fauna, hunting, and women (who spend the whole day in rocking chairs); public laundries; taxes; greetings; signature].

In 1867 Matthias Leclerc reported he had opened his own masonry business, had a "fairly good command" of English, and enjoyed listening to congressional debates. But he also seems to have returned to some of his old habits: in 1870 he ordered butter and eggs from a farmer he knew in Indiana, saying he could sell them for a good price, but the farmer then complained that he had been paid only $50 of the $325 he was due. In 1870 Lelerc was listed for the first and last time in the Washington city directory, with the occupation of bricklayer. On October 4, 1875, he apparently wrote one more letter from Washington, but there are no other traces of his subsequent life.[2]

2. Matthias Leclerc to Simon Leclerc, November 17, 1867, as well as Christopher Kirsch to Simon Leclerc, March 17, 1876, NABS; Washington CD 1870.

26. Private August Strohsahl
(alias Henry Johnson, alias August Warner)

The letter-writer was born in 1846 in Cuxhaven, near Hamburg, the son of a shoemaker who had a workshop in Midlum on the Ems River. August Strohsahl, probably a trained cook, ended up in California in 1864, after a series of long sea voyages.[1]

Benicia [California], November 4, 1864.

Dear parents and brothers and sisters,

I must finally take up my pen again and write you a few lines. I received your last letter of October 12th, 1863, when I was in Singapore in Nov[. . . .] From there to Honkong, and from there to San Franzisko in California, where I jumped ship from the *Diana* because I had to work so hard, and as you know I only got $5 a month. After I ran away I signed up on board an American ship, the *St. Charles*, and I was to get 20 dollars a month in gold, and we were supposed to go to Hamburg, and I would have been paid 120 dollars. But my luck didn't hold [5 ll.: shipwreck; back to San Francisco] and since I couldn't get work on any ship or on [--] land, therefore there was nothing I could do but become a soldier. I get $16 a month, I signed up for only one year, and the reason that times are so bad here is because there's been no rain this season, but now it is raining a lot and there's more work. They are already paying 40 dollars a month for farmworkers here. I've been a soldier now for 1½ months and the year will be over soon. I am, thank the Lord, always hale and hearty, and I hope you are, too. As soon as I am out of the army, I want to stay in California and be a true and faithful help to you.

[. . .] One more thing, don't worry, there's no war out here and I don't have to fight.

[. . .] I must close now, dear parents [because I] don't know what else to write, but you know that I have been on every continent and already speak and read English well, and I'm learning to write it[. . . .]

I remain / your faithful son / August.

SOURCE NOTE: As far as can be judged from a few lines, Strohsahl's writing meets what one would expect of a person with little formal education: limited in vocabulary and deficient in spelling, though easily readable. Not included here is one letter from the time after 1865 as well as the letter of September 12, 1865.

1. Information provided by the donor; HPL; Taufregister Amt Ritzebüttel 1846, StA Hamburg Abt. II; Fach 12, Vol. A.

In September 1865 Strohsahl wrote from San Francisco that he had been mustered out on July 1. The last surviving letter from August 1867 indicates that his life continued to be quite an adventure: he wrote that he was engaged to a wealthy American whose father disapproved of the relationship and attacked him, whereupon Strohsahl shot and wounded him. Then, under an assumed name, he fled halfway across the continent, fought with Indians and so on, and finally returned to the San Francisco Bay area, where he was intending to rent some land the following year.[2]

According to the archives, however, his life was even more adventurous. He used a false name—Henry Johnson—when he signed up for the military duty mentioned in the letter printed herein, and from October 1864 to July 1, 1865, he served in Company B, 6th California Infantry. On October 2, 1866, he signed up again as a regular soldier, this time for a term of five years and under his real name. He served in Company B, 8th Cavalry, U.S. Army, but three months later on January 2, 1867, he deserted the unit, taking along his uniform, arms, and horse, and leaving behind approximately $200 in debts.[3]

In 1870 he was living in Story County, Iowa, under the name of August Warner, supposedly born in California. In 1872 he got married, and he subsequently had at least four children. He supported the family by working both as a farmer and a painter, and he lived to be eighty years old.[4]

2. Letters of September 12, 1865, and August 11, 1867, NABS.

3. Muster Rolls, Henry Johnson (6 Calif. Inf) and August Strohsahl (8 Cav U.S. Army); Adjutant General's Office, Enlistment Papers: U.S. Army, Box 753, August Strohsahl, RG 94, NatA.

4. August Warner, Pension File, NatA; MC 1870: Story Co./Iowa, Washington Twp., #5; MC 1880: Story Co./Iowa, Union Twp., #4; MC 1900: Story Co./Iowa, Indian Creek Twp., #10. Proof of his various identities is clear (copies in NABS) but not of sufficient consequence to include here.

27. Petty Officer Eduard Treutlein (alias Edward Smith)

Eduard Treutlein was born in 1838 at Ittenschwand in the Black Forest, where his father, Josef Treutlein, was a teacher. For the sake of his children's education, the father requested a transfer first to Wieblingen and then to Neuenheim, two villages close to Heidelberg. Eduard started middle school on a vocational track, but when

SOURCE NOTE: Treutlein's German is sometimes a little awkward, and he certainly has not had much practice writing, but he manages to compose gripping descriptions of blockade-runner chases and battles. The misspellings seem to stem primarily from lack of concentration. His Heidelberg dialect is not noticeable, but there is some influence from English on his vocabulary. Not included here are the letters in the series from the time before 1860 (thirteen) and after 1865 (fourteen), as well as two letters from 1860, one from 1862, and two from 1865.

he was fourteen he switched to grammar school, which meant he had to catch up on several years of Latin. A mediocre student, this proved to be a difficult task, and in 1857, now almost twenty years old, Eduard still had two years of school left. He gave up on the idea of graduating and went to Bremen to sign on as a sailor.

Having arrived in Bremen in December 1857, it took him until the following April to get a job on a sailing ship, despite his great physical strength that was so admired by his family. After about a year spent as an ordinary seaman on the North Sea and the Baltic, he arrived in Buenos Aires in the summer of 1859 and then sailed on to become acquainted with most of the major ports in Asia and the Americas.[1] On April 10, 1864, he disembarked once again in New York; less than a week later, on April 16, he signed on in Boston as a volunteer (15th Massachusetts Infantry Volunteers). One month later his transfer application to the U.S. Navy was approved.[2]

Norfolk in Virginia, December 7th, 1864.

Dear grandmother,

[29 ll.: correspondence; family; sending 215 fl. to grandmother; lost his papers in Cape Town, also the addresses of his relatives in the United States] I left China with the firm intention of paying a visit to Germany, but when I arrived in New York I felt so estranged that after a 6-day visit I went to Boston and joined the army [21 ll.: transfer to the navy; daily life at sea, in greater detail in the letter of May 5, 1865]. I am pretty much out of danger, don't worry about me. I volunteered for 3 years and still have 29 months to go, and if my situation at home improves, I will see what I can do. I must say that it has often pained me very much that I have been so slighted by you, and I couldn't understand why I couldn't even receive one letter from one of my brothers. Even if my father refuses to write, once my letters arrived, they could have found out my address. But so God will. If my parents are ashamed of me, they will never hear from me again [18 ll.: correspondence; family; greetings; signature].

My name is now: / Edward Smith; send your letters to: / Joseph Todt, East Berlin / Adams County, Pennsylvania [. . .]

Norfolk in Virginia, February 27th, 1865.

Dearest brother,

[210 ll.: sailed in 1861 from New York to Cape Town, jumped ship upon arrival; March 2, from Fortress Monroe*: brought back on board in chains,

1. Information and documents provided by the donor and Treutlein's letters of 1858–64, NABS.

2. Muster Rolls, Army and Navy, for Edward Smith, NatA.

escaped again, stayed one year in South Africa, arrived in Hong Kong in the summer of 1862; March 3: served as a sailor in East Asia, arrived in New York in early April 1864] The *Santiago* is about the fastest steamship, and has been a terror to all the *blokade runners*. We chased many of them, and most of them had to dump their loads of cotton overboard to save themselves, and we captured 2 English steamers with valuable loads of cotton on board. (*A. D. Vance* and *Lucy*). My share of the prize money is about 900 talers* [7 ll.: unsuccessful attempt to take Fort Fisher,* North Carolina, on December 25, 1864 (in greater detail in letter of May 7, 1865)]. But on January 15th we started another surprise attack from water and land, and we took the fort that evening about 9 o'clock. There were 2,000 sailors on land to help the soldiers storm the fort, including 45 volunteers from our ship, and I was one of them. After a fight that lasted about 10 minutes, we sailors were pushed back, having lost about 400 men, but it gave the soldiers the *Chance* to enter from the other side and take the fort at 9 o'clock in the evening, after a 6-hour battle. The soldiers lost about 1,000 men; on board we had 1 dead and 9 seriously wounded, 2 of whom have since died.[3] Now we are pretty much out of danger, since there's little more for the sailors to do. I think the war will be over soon [34 ll.: Union victories; family; sending money; greetings].

Your brother and son / Edward Treutlein (Smith).

NB. I now go by the name of Smith, because no English or American person can ever get my real name through their head. In your next letter, please write all the details and all about the political and social situation in Germany[. . . .] Yesterday I was promoted to *petit officer*, as the boatswain in the 2nd *Cutter*. Please excuse the choppiness of this letter, but it is hard to write in the midst of 150 men. / Your brother [. . .]

U.S. Steamer *Santiago da Cuba* / in Washington, May 7, 1865.
Dearest parents,

[29 ll.: family; is sending money; exchange rate; joined the 15th Massachusetts Infantry] That same day I received my $38 bounty and, along with about 40 other volunteers who had enlisted the same day, I was taken to Gallop's Island, which is about 8 miles from Boston at the entrance to the bay. This was the *Rendez-vous* for recruits from Boston, where they are trained before being sent to their various regiments in the field, most of which have been chopped to pieces. There we did our daily 1-2, 1-2, etc. but without guns, across the

---

3. The figure of 1,000 includes wounded; combined fatalities in the army (4,700 strong) and navy amounted to 266. With the capture of the fort the Union shut down Wilmington, the last important blockade-running port on the coast. Long and Long (1971), 624–25; McPherson (1988), 819–20.

grass behind our barracks (19 in number, each for 120 men). We also had to do some work with our picks and shovels every day, improving the paths between the barracks, cutting turf etc., to make us familiar with this work as well, which is necessary when raising fortifications etc. etc. But we had 6–7 hours off every day, enough good food to eat, and were treated well in every respect. Finally the paymaster came and paid every fresh recruit $325. As soon as I had the money in my pocket, I sent a request to the War Department, together with many other sailors, asking to be transferred to the fleet. In the meantime, 2 others and I had become the cooks for *No 12 Barrak*, and we had an excellent time of it. The 3 of us had our own cookhouse, nothing to do with all the drilling, and we could do things at our own pace. We had to look after 3 tables; the 1st one for 120 men, the 2nd for 3 corporals [and] sergeants, and in our cookhouse, the 3rd one where 2 *non comissioned* officers [---] and 1 regimental clerk had their meals. After a month's stay here, our request was finally approved by the War Department, and on May 17th we sailors lined up (85 in number) and marched on board a steamer and were taken to Boston to the *recieving ship "Ohio."* There we had to take a simple test of our seaman's knowledge, and except for 2 or 3 men, we all passed. The *Ohio* is an old battleship with 72 cannon that is anchored in the *Navy Yard* and is the same thing for sailors as Gallop's Island is for soldiers. I didn't like it very much there, because there were more than 700 men on board and hardly enough space for 500. I soon had a great desire to escape from this tangled cluster of men.

After a 3-week stay I was finally assigned to the gunboat "*Santiago de Cuba,*" which was anchored in the same *Yard* at the time and had been thoroughly overhauled after she had returned from a 3-year crusade. She had taken 14 valuable ships as prizes and had an excellent reputation [15 ll.: details]. The *Santiago de Cuba* used to be a mail steamer between New-[York?] and Havanna, but at the outbreak of the war it was bought by the government and armed with 11 cannon[. . . .] All of us, of course, were happy to have gotten such a good ship. We stayed for a while at anchor, were divided into watches, everyone received his special duty at the cannon, the boats, the sails, etc. etc., and then we trained hard every day. It went on like this for about 3 weeks, until our captain (Glison) [Oliver S. Glisson] received papers from the *Secretary of the navy* assigning us to the *North Atlantic* [----] *squadron*[. . . .] [We] were ordered to the blockade of Wilmington [North Carolina], which is the main place where arms, *Amunition*, ham, clothing, etc. etc. are imported and traded for [---] cotton. This trade is usually done by English steamers, and they make enormous sums with it when they go from Nassau to Wilmington and arrive back safely. Our fleet outside of Wilmington consisted of about 35 ships, with the slower ships guarding the two entrances to Cape Fear River and the

Eduard Treutlein's *Santiago de Cuba*. (Prints and Photographs Division, Library of Congress, Washington, D.C.)

fastest ones sailing back and forth some 100 and more miles out at sea to spot the *blokade runners* that had slipped through [the] inner *blokade* under cover of darkness. Having spotted them at daybreak, their job was to chase [---] and capture or destroy them if possible. We were also assigned to this squadron, to the great joy of our crew and of our captain, who is a distinguished officer and a real father to us [4 ll.: from Boston to Wilmington; first action]. (Wilmington is 15 miles up Cape Fear River, which has two entrances [that] are defended by 2 strong fortresses and many batteries.) There were lookouts dressed in white on top of both masts, able to spot any ship some 15–20 miles away. And of course they kept their eyes peeled as best they could, because the first man to report a *blokaderunner* that gets caught receives $50 on top of his share. On Saturday morning [. . .] we were all on the foredeck and everyone was hoping we would discover a steamer, in order to find out how well we could match up to these English *Steamers* built specially for this purpose [7 ll.: at dawn on Sunday a ship was spotted:] 4 bells rang in the engine room, the fire men stoked up the fire, whistles of steam started to hiss, the wheels started turning faster and faster, and in 5 minutes our noble *Steamer* was flying across the smooth surface of the sea [27 ll.: it was only a sailing ship; but shortly thereafter a steamer:] Finally we could see the low, white, but very long hull of our enemy. Black smoke was billowing out of her 2 smokestacks, and the poor thing seemed to want to head down into the depths under her own steam; she was jumping up and down so much and breaking through the sea, even though the water was as smooth as a mirror[. . . .] Our enemy seemed to be counting on their superior speed and so disregarded us and stubbornly kept on course as if we were nothing at all [7 ll.: bombardment]. Crossing our course would have meant certain destruction, and so in no time they turned tail[. . . .] One shell after another and also [---] were sent after them, trying to cripple them, but to no avail. We did get somewhat closer and closer, but evening put an end to the chase, and they disappeared into the darkness. We've had 26 chases like this in all since I've been on board, and we've caught 2 steamers and forced 8 or 10 to throw most of their cotton overboard in order to save themselves. We chased one of them for 28 straight hours, day and night, a matter of life and death, but she too disappeared the 2nd night. We usually fished the cotton out of the sea and sold it. All together we made $52,000 on the various batches. I can't tell you how exciting these chases are, but I think the feelings are much the same as those of a man sitting at a gaming table, playing for high stakes. This is what it was like most of the time. Every 3 weeks we went to Norfolk in Virginia to take on more coal, where we usually spent a week, got our letters, sent other ones off, etc. etc. and then started off on another 3-week crusade[. . . .] And then one time we arrived in Norfolk and were quite astounded to meet up with a number of large warships that were covered with thick heavy chains on the outside, where the engines are [6 ll.: ordered to Fortress Monroe,* arriving on December 11, 1864]. Several ironclad ships had also appeared and everyone suspected that an attack on Fort Fisher* was being planned. The next morning (Dec. 12th) the admiral's ship signaled the entire fleet to raise anchor, and within a half hour a fleet of more than 60 ships, all steamers, set out to sea. The *new Ironsides* and 2 *monitors* were with us, one of which we had to take in tow because the ocean near Hatteras was very rough. But the next day we all arrived safely in Beauford, where all the ships were to assemble. This was also where the army transports with 7,000 soldiers under General Butler* and General Weitzel (German)[4] also assembled [80 ll.: ship deployments; beginning of the attack; description of ships, cannon; bombardment; fort in flames; own casualties; continuation of the battle on December 25, 1864]. About 10'clock our division was ordered to leave, with our ship as the flagship, to assist the landing of the troops, since

---

4. Son of German immigrants, born in Cincinnati in 1835. See Warner (1964), 548–49.

at 3 o'clock an attack from the land was supposed to be attempted[. . . .] The *Transports* dropped anchor right behind us, and then all the ships sent off their boats to land the troops. There were about 300 boats that were filled in no time, in between the ships and the land. Our boat, the one I was in, had the honor of serving Butler and Weitzel, and Weitzel[,] one of his adjutants, and an *aid de camp* were the first to embark. At [a signal], all the boats started rowing toward land, and we were on the end, on the farthest right wing, the first to land, and grabbing our boat flag from the boat, sabers in our right hands and revolvers in our left, we raced to storm the sand batteries. It only took an instant, and our flag was the first to fly on top of one of the batteries. Behind it we found a company from the 42nd North Carolina Regiment with one lieutenant and a captain who were on picket duty, who immediately surrendered unconditionally [9 ll.: General Weitzel approached to within 400 yards of the fort]. General Weitzel got back into our boat and we went back to Butler, who had stayed on [land]; General Weitzel had only seen 2 cannon destroyed and was of the opinion that the fort was still undamaged. But he still wanted to storm it, because he thought it could be taken. Butler, however, said there was no point and gave orders for the troops to return to the ships. You can hardly imagine the commotion among the soldiers. They were cursing and swearing and did not want to get back on board the transports [28 ll.: withdrawal; everyone blamed General Butler for the failure].[5] In the meantime, another *Expedition* was prepared, with 5,000 more men under General Terry. On January 13th we arrived unexpectedly at Fort Fisher again, with increased numbers, and while part of the fleet started to bombard the fort, the others took charge of landing the troops, but this time with provisions and artillery, under the command of our captain, because according to General Grant's *Plan* this place had to be taken no matter what[. . . .] There were also several thousand Negro soldiers who marched across the spit of land where Fort Fisher is located, which is only an hour wide, to Cape Fear River, where they surprised a steamer, captured it and took one battery with 2 field pieces and all the men prisoner [83 ll.: detailed version of the description in the letter of March 3 (Fort Fisher); his ship ordered to Baltimore on March 23; pleasure voyage made by the secretary of the navy and high officers]. We had a very nice trip to Havana, Matanzas and returned to Charleston on April 14 [5 ll.: anniversary of the capitulation of Fort Sumter]. That evening there were fireworks on all the warships assembled there, and no one suspected that at the same time that assassin was plotting to kill our president, and that at 10 o'clock he would carry out his devilish plan down to the letter. We only learned of

---

5. As did General Grant and President Lincoln, who relieved him of his command.

this when we arrived at Fortress Monroe, and then we left immediately with our party for Washington. If there was ever a ruling person for whom I had esteem, affection, and respect, then for Abr. Lincoln. I wish Germany could someday have a man like that! The Americans didn't appreciate what they had in him until he was taken away. But with this dirty trick, the [---]bers of the revolution have put a noose around their own necks, from which they will surely swing. All the friends of the rebels must fear for their lives now, and in the last few days many have paid with their lives for their joy at Lincoln's murder. Richmond has now fallen, Gen. Lee has surrendered to Grant and Johnson [Johnston] to Sherman [79 ll.: anchored at Washington; uncertain when he will be mustered out; family; asks for several hundred guilders* for his grandmother that he will repay when the exchange rate improves; signature; correspondence].

A few weeks after the end of the war, Treutlein went on a ten-day furlough. He never returned to the ship, leading to the entry in his files "deserted on May 19, 1865," which was deleted the following year.

In late 1865 Treutlein moved to Litchfield, Illinois (sixty miles east of St. Louis), where he successively opened a butcher's shop, then had to give it up, ran a saloon for a while, then sold it, was unemployed for months, worked for a brief time in a mill and then for a farmer as a harvest hand, ran a grocery store, then rented a mill, but had to give it up, became a teacher in a Catholic school, transferred to another school, and then became unemployed again—all in the course of twelve years and within fifty miles or so of Litchfield. In 1880 he was a teacher in St. Rose, Illinois.

During this time, the daughter of German immigrants whom Treutlein had married in 1866 bore him eight children, before dying in childbirth in 1881. From then on, little information about his life is available. In 1900, now sixty-two years old, Treutlein was working in Denver, Colorado, as a tamales vendor and boarding with his employer. After a stroke in 1903, he was in the Denver County Hospital—paralyzed on one side, deaf, and blind. Here he remained until at least 1907, the last time he is mentioned. None of his children apparently felt in a position to support him.[6]

Eduard Treutlein's extensive letters between 1868 and 1872 provide evidence of the development of the political attitudes of this Catholic immigrant and his opinion of German and Anglo Americans. Before the 1868 presidential election he favored Ulysses S. Grant, who he said was supported by "all the educated property holders, all the sanctimonious religious fanatics, and most of the Germans." Three years later, his feelings on Grant were summed up by the observation that Grant's reelection would be as bad as electing a Democrat. Grant had managed to unite the

6. Muster Rolls, Volunteer Navy (Edward Smith), NatA; letters of Eduard Treutlein, Peter Treutlein (nephew), and Georg Ballweg (uncle), 1866–77, NABS; MC 1880: St. Rose, Clinton Co./Ill., e.d. 77, #95; MC 1900: Arapahoe Co./Colo., Denver, W. 1, e.d. 5, #94; letter of Henny Coolidge (daughter), November 30, 1907, NABS.

German Americans just like the French declaration of war in 1870 had united the German people, and "if the Republicans want to win, they will have to give in to the Germans and prevent Grant's nomination." Treutlein made several exhilarated comments about the founding of the German Empire; for example, "The Latin race is played out, and the Germans are now the main factor in Europe, and in 2 to 3 generations they will be so in America, too."[7]

Although he expressed loyalty to the Union during the war, his criticism of the United States became increasingly biting thereafter.[8] The Germans were no longer willing to become Americanized just like that, and the Anglos "are doing everything in their power to keep the Germans under their thumbs." For the Americans, "the almighty dollar is [. . .] the only final purpose." Corruption was blossoming at all levels, and the spoils system was a disaster, he thought: "I just wonder where they came up with the word *honor*; for such a thing does not even exist here." The dreary Sundays were terrible, the newspapers were filled with crime and murder, the clergymen and physicians were all charlatans—and in every way the Germans were better and did things better.[9] Eduard Treutlein had adopted almost the entire catalog of anti-American clichés held by Germans in America and expressed them with a bluntness rarely found in print. He had failed economically and in social life, and he was culturally estranged from Anglo America: the life of this German sailor was anything but a success story, and it certainly cannot be seen as an example of successful "Americanization" through his experience in the Civil War.

7. Letters of Eduard Treutlein, October 22, 1868, and January 5, 1871, NABS.

8. As early as the summer of 1865 he reported, with no trace of disapproval, about a relative in Abbotsville, Pennsylvania, who had earned a lot of money as a shoemaker with his three sons. Then, when the war broke out, all three sons had "to flee, to save themselves from military service, and they went to the West to Indiana, Illinois, Missouri, Minnesota, etc. etc., from one state to the next, to avoid being put on the citizens' lists." That had cost the father $1,800. Undated letter, about July 1865, NABS.

9. Letter of May 26, 1871, NABS.

28. Jakob Kessler

Jakob Kessler was born in 1844 in Eberbach on the Neckar River, a few miles upstream from Heidelberg. An illegitimate child christened as a Protestant, he was raised by foster parents after the death of his mother in 1848. In 1864 he immigrated to the United States without permission from his home state of Baden.[1] Aside from the following letter, no information about his life is available.

SOURCE NOTE: Little can be said on the basis of so little, but for a writer who probably did not have much education, his spelling and grammar are surprisingly correct.

1. Information provided by the donor; KB (ev.) Eberbach.

New York, February 24, 1865.

Most honorable Mayor,

Once again must I trouble you with a small matter. My nephew, little Fritz, wants to send a small present to his mother for Easter: 30.00 guilders* are from him, and I have added 5 guilders for my sister Sophie. The exchange rates are improving every day, so now it is easier to send remittances than it used to be. Gold is at 150 now; 4 months ago it was still 250–70.

There are still no significant events on the war front to report, the general opinion here is that the war will be largely over in 5–6 months. The rebels are losing one important place after another, and very little hope remains that during the spring campaign they will be able to turn the fortunes of war around in their favor.

The leaders of the rebels have begun to realize this themselves, and everyone is trying to put the blame on someone else for the failure of their plans. They are quarrelling with each other now, the surest sign that the rebellion will soon fall apart. By the end of the war, we will have run up enormous debts (4,000 million dollars), but we don't owe anything to anyone, except the Germans, about 100 million. The vast resources of this country, the rapid increase in population will make it much easier to pay back this debt.

They have calculated that if the hardworking white population plants cotton in the South instead of the Negroes, they will be able to produce such large amounts that a 5-cent tax per pound will pay the interest on our debt.

I will be writing to you again soon about another matter, and will send you further reports.

With the best wishes to you and your family,

Your faithful / J. Kessler

[attachment: receipt by Lisetta and Sophia Keßler of April 11, 1865]

29. Victor Klausmeyer

Victor Klausmeyer was born on December 17, 1828, in Bühne (Westphalia), where his father was apparently a Catholic school teacher. He left Germany in early 1851.[1] During his first years in America he held a succession of jobs: first he worked in farming ("my original line of business"), then in a sugar refinery, on the railroad, as

SOURCE NOTE: Klausmeyer's writing is consistently critical, nuanced, and facetious, and he wields all the language tools necessary for such a brilliant tour de force. In other words, he writes like a bright college graduate. Not included here is one letter in the series from before 1860.

1. Listed as "Clausmann" in NYPL, *Heydorn*, May 15, 1851.

a canal worker, in a wire factory, and finally in a paper factory. In between jobs, he was often unemployed for several months.[2]

When the war broke out, he was living in Baltimore, Maryland. By the end of the war he was living and working in Washington, D.C., where he had found a job at the War Department.

[ca. April 4, 1865]

[salutation and start of letter missing]

[11 ll.: unclear due to lack of context; about brawls and justice of the peace] Since the capture and *Evacuation* of Richmond and Petersburg, the whole country has been in an uproar; the lampposts were drunk and the cobblestones shook. Today in particular it was like all hell had been let loose. It poured down rain from seven o'clock yesterday evening until tonight, 8 o'clock, but even that couldn't stop the celebrations. Then you just put on your impermeable [raincoat] and off you go to walk the streets. Speeches were made by some of our most distinguished men, several tons of powder were shot off, church bells rang, associations paraded by in congratulation, and everything was very harmonious. All the *Departements* had the day off, and you couldn't even see the houses, there were so many flags and banners. The rebellion is on its last legs, and whoever the Confederacy owes money to will just end up sitting on their debts. The most honorable English creditors will go home with a long nose and astonishment on their faces. We won't pay a *Goddam Cent*. All we have left to deal with is one more major stronghold, the seaside town of Mobile. The small armies that still hang around in various places we will chew up one after the next, depending on our appetite. Then it's off to Mexico. Maxle [Maximilian*] has to be swept out. One Brazilian monarch is enough for this continent. And all of this is happening without my taking part. I was lucky enough not to get drafted. I was conscripted here in Washington, but since I only live in this city on a temporary basis and still want to be considered a citizen and a voter in Maryland, they had to let me go again; and in Baltimore my lot wasn't drawn. But that was fine with me, because as you know I am not a *Fighting character*, and someone has to stay home and do the yelling, and so I joined the latter group. On that score I am a *Quäcker* [Quaker]; they don't fight either, and since it is much more pleasant to clench your fist in your pocket than to look for a new bed every evening in the woods and the swamps, I preferred the first option. It also cost me quite some money at home, because we owe our crippled and sick defenders or the widows and orphans left behind an indelible debt, and honor and patrio-

2. Letter to his brothers and sisters, Trenton, N.J., March 24, 1854, NABS.

Victor Klausmeyer.
(John Klausmeyer)

tism are always good ways to entice money out of our pockets. But in exchange we will get back a vast and united fatherland, where you don't need any passports or border guards. The golden age that our Black Republicans have always been prophesying will damn well soon be here. At the moment, though, we're still in the black age, because the *Negroe* comes first, and much of our politics revolves around him. But *Sambo* is fitting in with the new system of things in an admirable manner. The arguments of those people who used to claim that the Negro is unfit for education and not receptive to higher pleasures find their strongest contrary evidence in the many strong men who keep pouring into all branches of industry every day. And the fellows are even intelligent [5 ll.: one made a counterfeit treasury note, was only found out by chance]. So you see when the *Amalgamation* or *Misengenation* is taken up more seriously, i.e. when every white man gets a Negro woman to marry, and the white women marry ambitious black bucks, there's a good chance we'll become a stronger breed. Period.

[19 ll.: petroleum is in widespread use; also other wonders taken out of the earth; if his brother Wilhelm comes, he will take good care of him] Hopefully he won't attract as much bad luck here as I did, because not only did I frequently have bad luck, I also got cheated. He can come anytime, for what Dina writes me about the *Circular* from the Very Reverend Bishop of Paderborn is not true. Those were secessionist stories. If you are not a citizen of the United States, you are not subject to conscription, and you can't become a citizen in less than five years. I admit there are some clumsy oafs who got fooled by recruitment officers. That's their own fault. Should watch out. There are enough Germans here in the country, particularly in the port cities, who can tell you how things work. When Wilh. comes, he should sail to Baltimore and take along the address of Karl Wiener, and he will inform me of his arrival immediately [12 ll.: greetings; signature; best wishes for his brother Joseph and family].

[between April 15 and 28, 1865]

[salutation and start of letter missing]

[57 ll.: describes 1860 election and candidates; secession of South Carolina; had Democratic president James Buchanan (in office until March 4, 1861) taken firm action, he could have suppressed the rebellion, but as it was:] it was easy for the leaders in the South to win over many of the people to their plans. All they did was scream: the North wants to take away your slaves, set them free and make them your equals. Given the well-known ignorance of most of the people in the South, it was naturally easy to make them fear for their independence or even their lives. But to tell the truth, the Rep. Party was also screaming to no end about what they would do if they got control of things. And that's why people thought they had to calm down the northern Democrats by electing a conservative like Lincoln. The South would never have seceded so rashly if they hadn't [19 ll.: counted on (1) support from northern Democrats, (2) a shift in the position held by the New England states that processed cotton, (3) the neutrality of the northwestern states, (4) help from Great Britain and France].

From the reasons listed above you can well imagine, my dear boy, that we were in a difficult position at the beginning of the war. But the North was inspired by infinite enthusiasm to regain the lost states. There were no longer two branches of democracy. The Douglas Democrats, now the war-Democrats, joined up with the Republicans and called themselves unionists (only the Breckinridge people are still opposed to the war to this day, because as <u>good Christians</u> they don't want to spill their brothers' blood, and hence they are called Copperheads*). The South had been preparing for this war for years. Most of the officers in the regular U.S. Army were from the South, and when it came to a fight, they went over to their brothers [6 ll.: South made off with weapons, forts, some 12–15,000 men from the army, and a fleet of sixty ships]. And the people in the North gladly made the greatest sacrifices. Today we have more than two million soldiers in arms, an experienced army, even if it isn't as splendid as yours, but it can fight. We have more than six hundred warships [. . .] we also have a small batch of debts, but what is 2,000,000,000 (only two thousand million) for a country like America? [9 ll.: infinite resources; finances]

But back to our war. I mentioned earlier that the government had not been planning to get rid of slavery; their program was only to prevent this blot on a free country from spreading any further; and then, admittedly, gradually eliminate it. Even in the first years of the war, none of the leading politicians thought of supporting abolition. The purpose of the war, then as now, was the restoration of the Union [8 ll.: Lincoln wants the Union, with or without slavery].

April 28th [. . .] When during the course of the war it became increasingly apparent that slavery was a great or even the most important support to the rebellion, they made sure the slaves had as many chances as possible to leave their *Masters*. Everywhere our army appeared, men, women, and children followed—like a herd of black sheep. The women and children were sent north, and if there was work for them, they were put to work, and if not, they were fed at Uncle Sam's expense. The men were put to use by the army, as teamsters, building fortifications, etc. [4 ll.: the slaves see the Union soldiers as liberators]. Since we ended up with a very large number of blacks, we decided it was more practical to arm the men for whose liberation the white man was shedding his blood. So Congress ordered the formation of black regiments, and it turned out that the woolheads streamed into the ranks with joy [3 ll.: approximately 100,000 blacks in the army and navy]. And they usually make good soldiers; fight like devils. Under a law passed by Congress, they can only be led by white officers, the highest rank they can make is sergeant; but we do have a few cases where they have become officers. Some of them are even regimental surgeons. From the start there were serious problems with these woolheads as prisoners, because the South didn't regard them as prisoners of war but as recovered property [16 ll.: Union government put an end to massacres like at Fort Pillow, "where they were slaughtered like sheep," and arranged for the exchange of prisoners; confiscation of rebel leaders' property; reports on events of the war until:] the time when you receive the *Criminal-Ztg.* [*Criminalzeitung**]; for this can give you, as I mentioned in my previous letters, an accurate summary and insight into our current position, and it is also just as good in its criticism. In one of my earlier letters, if I am not mistaken, I told you how often bad, incompetent generals were retained in command, long after their incompetence was proved. This was a purely political move, because these men usually had a good reputation as [------]men and had many supporters, had also done a lot to bring the current government to power, and so the government didn't want to put noses out of joint, despite their blunders [44 ll.: Lincoln is also subject to such pressure, until public opinion forces him to dismiss someone for grave errors; examples: General Banks* (Red River campaign),[3] General Butler* (Fort Fisher*);[4] southern Maryland still had slavery at the start of the war]. Of course the slaveholding section sympathized with the South, and was only prevented from seceding by the firmness of the governor at the time, Governor Hicks, and the opposition of the northern, nonslaveholding part of the state. The bitterness on both sides was dreadful. After the bombardment of Fort Sumter on the 12th and 13th of April '61, President Lincoln called for 75,000 volunteers to defend the stars and stripes. When the first contingent, the 6th Massachusetts Volunteers, marched through Baltimore, they were met by the rabble in Baltimore, who had been stirred up by the steady incitements made by a few brilliant secessionists into such a belligerent mood that they started to exchange goods with these defenders of their country—with cobblestones and bricks as their main weapons. But gun stores were also broken into, pistols, muskets, and even sabers were taken, and a real good fight was well underway. The men from Massachusetts did quite well, lashing out in all directions, and several idlers ran up against their bayonets and bullets. About twenty men fell on both sides. This was on April 19th, '61, a day never to be forgotten. I was working in another part of town that day and only saw the blood on the next day. If ever a town looked like war, it was Baltimore on the three or four days after this sad event. Everyone armed to the teeth, barricades on every corner, running that never stopped, day and night. But then the situation changed. We were surrounded on all sides, and the North swore that Balto. must be burned down. But then, through the persuasion of patriotic, moderate men, things calmed down [53 ll.: a week later, the same regiment marched through peacefully; political generals, like Democrat George McClellan, who made the Army of

3. See letters by Heinzelmann (no. 20), April 18, 1864, Keppler (no. 21), April 15, 1864, and Krause (no. 22), May 26, 1864.
    4. See Treutlein's (no. 27) letter of May 7, 1865.

the Potomac strong, was constantly under pressure from political enemies, and dismissed because of his excessive caution (on November 7, 1862), became 1864 Democratic presidential nominee; goal of the divided Democrats was to maintain slavery]. With the reelection of Ab. Lincoln on November 10th last year, the American people, the loyal voters of the North, gave the best possible answer to what it thinks of the Copperheads* and democracy gone awry [66 ll.: at the start of the war, no general in the field had a free hand— "kitchen and cabinet generals" ran operations from afar, via the president; grave errors; Grant ignored orders from Washington at Vicksburg* with success, and now Lincoln has permitted the generals to give orders, in particular Grant, the only one who had beaten Lee].

Long before you receive these lines, you will have already read the terrible news of the murder of our beloved President Lincoln. I don't need to tell you how this plunged the whole country into grief and commotion. A cry of horror and anger swept through the whole country, and even the smallest incident could have led to all the rebel prisoners and rebel-sympathizers having to pay for this crime with their own blood. But I haven't heard of any cases at all where any prisoners were harmed [5 ll.: southern sympathizers attacked in the North, some killed].

Served them right. Why didn't that rabble move to secession-land and underscore their words with their deeds? It is true that we have rights, guaranteed by the *Constitution*, to free opinion and speech as well as a free press, but traitors who rejoice at the assassination of the first citizen of the republic, the best of the patriots, a man who was full of love for those entrusted to him—such traitors cannot be tolerated [41 ll.: refers to *Criminalzeitung**; details of assassination]. You say the *Zeitung* is too democratic for you, but it is based on pure democratic republican principles and has always remained true to them [4 ll.: details on the press].

We are now winding things up. The expenditures of the War Department are supposed to be reduced as quickly and as much as possible. From yesterday to tomorrow night, at least five thousand government employees will be dismissed. I will most probably be one of the lucky ones, and then I'll go to Balto., take myself a wife and then live off my wife for awhile [15 ll.: family; greetings]. Victor

P.S. Baltimore, May 8th '65

I've been in Balto. for three days now. I was one of the ones who [-------
-----] a dismissal during the cutbacks at the War Department. I am getting married this evening, and I will soon be sending you a picture of my [---]. I don't know yet if I will be staying here. Business is slow here at the moment but will hopefully be picking up soon.

[18 ll.: family; signature; his brother Wilhelm still welcome; details; money matters; address]

The bride at the wedding mentioned above was four years younger than Victor Klausmeyer, a young widow with two small children who was apparently a pianist from Alsace. The couple had three more children. Klausmeyer was one of the founders of the German Fire Insurance Company of Baltimore, and starting in 1866, he worked as one of its agents. The business was obviously quite successful: the 1870 census lists him with real estate worth $2,800.

That a *German* insurance company could flourish was primarily due to the fact that a good quarter of the population of Baltimore were Germans of the first and second generations. No fewer than three of the eight local daily newspapers were in German ("*Correspondent*," "*Staatszeitung*," and "*Wecker*"). When Klausmeyer died on December 8, 1889, both the English and the German papers reported that the Catholic funeral of this highly respected citizen had been well attended.[5]

5. Information provided by the donor; MC 1870: Baltimore Co./Md., Baltimore, W. 3, #1215; MC 1880: Baltimore Co./Md., Baltimore, e.d. 28, #143; Obituaries, December 9, 1889, NABS; Schem (1869–81), vol. 2, s.v. "Baltimore."

30. Kaspar Herbst and Agatha Herbst

Kaspar Herbst was the fifth of eleven children and was born in Altstadt, near Rottweil in Württemberg, in 1802. In 1849, now a widower with three children, he married Agatha Efinger, who was twenty-one years younger and the daughter of a tailor from the nearby village of Aixheim. The family immigrated to the United States in 1852, in the midst of one of the largest waves of immigration in the nineteenth century.[1] Without making any stops along the way, they moved to northern Pennsylvania, near the shores of Lake Erie. Herbst probably had some experience as a farmer, and it is likely that he crossed the Atlantic with at least some means. In the 1860 census, at any rate, he was listed as a farmer with four more children and real property worth $2,000, plus $800 in personal assets; in 1870 his assets were valued at $6,000 and $1,000, respectively.[2]

SOURCE NOTE: Herbst's spelling in German is not quite as bad as it is in English, where he mangles words or names, but almost. But this is not what makes his writing hard to understand; instead, it is his use of stilted, old-fashioned language, perhaps the result of his intense interest in reading religious tracts.

1. The parents and four children sailed from Le Havre on the *Eastern Queen* and arrived in New York on May 10, 1852. NYPL.

2. MC 1860: Erie Co./Pa., Fairview Twp., #757; MC 1870: Erie Co./Pa., Fairview Twp., #20.

Kaspar Herbst's case is already unusual since he left Germany at the advanced age of fifty (most emigrants were under forty), but even more remarkable is the fact that he was the only one of the letter-writers in this collection to convert from Catholicism and become a Protestant. It seems that right after he arrived, he became a member of St. Jacobus Evangelisch-Unierte Kirche in Fairview Township.[3]

[Fairview, July 15, 1865]

Dearest parents,

[47 ll.: property dispute with his brother Melchior in Germany; transfers his claim to his parents] As for emigrating, which you once dreamed of, this is my opinion: [. . .] only those people emigrate to America who are ready for it[. . . .] They are not afraid of the great ocean, nor of the war. But the war is over now, the South is bowed down, their weapons taken away from them. Everyone who wanted to stay in the country had to swear loyalty to the Union, all those who did not want to swear had to leave the country and give up their property.[4] Their *Presetent* Schäff Devesen [Jefferson Davis] is being held prisoner on an island in the sea, tied to a column in chains like a mad dog, day and night, out in the open. He is being guarded by a regiment of soldiers, and under pain of death, no one is allowed to talk to him. He has to stand there mute, he's not allowed to bark. For nourishment, he is given 3 *Krekis* [crackers] a day[. . . .] Now and then he also gets some soup fit for dogs. For refreshment he is given water from the stinking rain puddles, and this is how he must wait out his slow death by starvation.[5] He'll be paid in the same coin, what he did to soldiers taken prisoner will be done to him [25 ll.: inflation during the war]. We were pretty much spared from this dreadful war. Andreas was at risk twice, the 1st time he wasn't quite old enough and got off, the 2nd time his high number kept him free, but we do have to help pay the war costs, and they are already higher than the [country's] income. There will be painful aftereffects for a long time—you can well imagine, what with so many thousands of invalids who have to live without arms and legs, and the country has to support them as long as they live [41 ll.: health; family; money matters].

3. Compelling evidence from a commemorative plaque in Fairview and Kaspar Herbst's gravestone; the congregation is now known as St. James Lutheran Church.

4. Unclear statement; this tended to be true for the Confederacy, but not for the Union during the war. Afterward, no former Confederates were forced to leave.

5. This description reflects rumors that made the rounds at the time, but it is—to put it mildly—incorrect. Davis was briefly put in chains when he arrived at Fortress Monroe,* Virginia, and his prison was located on a peninsula, but the rest is fantasy. He was released without trial in May 1867. Long and Long (1971), 687, 689.

I remember those times—if someone had offered to give me all of America as a present, I would never have left Germany. But later I was ready to give up my homeland completely and, full of courage, seek a new one in America. I [. . .] am thankful to the Lord for this, [. . .] that with our steady work and the Lord's help we are now living in a nicer home than in Germany. Imagine how pleasant and convenient it is to have your fields near your house, all in one piece, how much easier it is here, compared to over there [6 ll.: details]. Our northern General Scherrmann [Sherman] went through the state of Virginien [Virginia] with his army from one town to the next, and burned down everything he came across. All the woods were cut down and burned so they could march through with all those thousands of soldiers, cavalry, wagons, and incredibly heavy cannon [4 ll.: description of an enormous cannonball:] it was with cannonballs like this that our General Kränd [Grant] bombarded the city of Richmond, where the southern *Presentent* was entrenched[. . . .] For two years General Grant lay in front of Richmond, until he could overcome this nest of rebels and drive them out [6 ll.: details]. The northerners entered Richmond, the southerners lay down their weapons and asked for *Barton* [pardon]. Their *Presentent* along with his ministers all got away. A cavalry regiment had to chase them more than 100 miles before they caught him, the president. He was dressed up as a woman when they got him[6] [47 ll.: details; prices; suffering and destruction in Virginia; conscription]. No one has to become a citizen if he doesn't want to, he can move around freely. Citizenship only costs one dollar. But I haven't noticed even one dollar's worth of benefit since I became a citizen, on the contrary, I took a loss with the draft, which my son Andreas was subject to[. . . .] Those who didn't want to go themselves could send another man as a replacement. They tried to buy, [. . .] whoever wasn't able to pay for or couldn't get hold of a man—for they were rare—had to go himself [15 ll.: details]. The last ones drafted, scared to death, paid 12 to 15 hundred talers* and even more for a man. There were even cases where they turned over ownership of their homesteads, including their houses and fields, to some man who went to the war in their place [23 ll.: hardships and misery of marches during the war]. So now this war is over, slavery defeated, the rich fellows in the South now have to pay their workers, the poor Negroes used to have to work for them for free [16 ll.: northern migrants are taking possession of deserted rebel properties]. You said you thought the murder of

6. Many things have been confused in this section. Sherman systematically destroyed Georgia, not Virginia, and it was because of a "scorched earth" strategy, not the need to move heavy artillery. Grant was commander in chief, but he did not "lie" in front of Richmond; instead, he conducted a mobile campaign. The rumor about the women's clothing may have arisen from the fact that Davis was wearing a raincoat and scarf when he was taken prisoner.

President Linkols [Lincoln] would cause great commotion and change; but everything has stayed much the same and continued on its course.

The *Fizen-Presentent* [vice president], Andreas Tschanzen [Andrew Johnson] is his name, followed right in the footsteps of Linkols. At the beginning of the war, he was a rich plantation owner, in earlier years a tailor by trade [7 ll.: details]. The loss of Linkols is actually not that great; for 25 thousand dollars in gold as a yearly salary you can get a lot of presidents, for a salary like that somebody else can issue orders, too. He didn't do much else besides that, and in the government there are still the ministers and a governor from every state.[7] Lincoln himself never took a gun in hand to win freedom for the slaves; that rough task was up to his poor underlings[. . . .] Linkoln would certainly still be alive if he hadn't gone to the pleasure-theater on Holy Good Friday. He should have stayed home with his wife, contemplating Our Redeemer [4 ll.: details]. But I can't talk like this here in America, because Linkoln was a god to most of them, they know no other god than the president. They don't hold it against him that he went to the theater on Good Friday.

[70 ll.: comments on godless America; religious prophecies; wartime fate of a neighbor as an example; emigration; correspondence] We are wondering if your dreams of emigrating would not come true if you got the money all at once, or at least a good portion of it.

We would love to give you a fresh drink of our *Seider* [cider] every day, and apple butter to spread on your bread. We have enough of both every day [4 ll.: family].

I am and remain your faithful son until / death do us part—
Kaspar Herbst.

And I remain your eternally / loving daughter Agatha Efiner.

Far well! / Fairview, July 15th, <u>1865</u> [25 ll.: additional details on the property dispute and Lincoln's assassination]

All that is known about Kaspar Herbst after this time, besides his census entries, is that he died in Fairview on October 2, 1886.

---

7. Another of the many misunderstandings: Herbst confuses the federal and state levels of government.

31. Müller Family

Heinrich Müller was born in 1830 in Stade, near Hamburg. A road paver by trade, he left Germany in the summer of 1857, and he must have had some means, since he traveled second class and still had some cash reserves when he was in New York. Although he arrived in the middle of an economic recession, he immediately found work in his trade, but then he chose to work as a sales clerk in various stores. His reports about America and how he was faring were positive on the whole, but he also warned, "don't believe the people who visit Germany with their nice clothes and polished boots, that they're all rich, when they are here they hardly have sleeves in their jackets."[1]

He describes his work, local festivities, and the fate of the unemployed, but he makes no mention of larger political issues—except that he obviously had nothing against African Americans: "almost nothing but blacks come in where I work, and they are easier to deal with than the whites."[2]

No letters from the war years have survived. The following letter reports about this time; it is also his last letter and the last trace of his life.

New York, July 25, 1865

Dear parents, brother, and sisters,

I hope you are all in good health, I am always quite hale and hearty. Dear parents, you probably already know that I am married, I have a very good wife and two beautiful children [9 ll.: details]. I am very fine and I hope you are too, but I do have to work hard. I have now agreed to do cobblestones, 100 miles from New Jork, I earn 4½ dollars a day there, and when I work in New York I earn 13 dollars a day. Dear parents, I have made a lot of money, but I have also had bad luck. When the great civil war broke out I had a *Grosristor* [grocery store] or *kaufman laden*, but business was so bad I couldn't keep it up. I lost a lot of money on that, and then I was drafted and was supposed to go to war, but to keep my wife and children from misery, I ran away and went deep into the countryside, and they didn't get me. That was a terrible war, several hundred thousand had to sacrifice their lives, and so many cripples, you see young men who have lost both arms, and some of them both legs. It was

SOURCE NOTE: The short text shows a limited vocabulary, weak and sometimes bizarre spelling, deficient grammar, and some interference from English, but the writer still manages to get across what he wants to say. Not included here are the letters in the series from the time before 1860 (five).

1. KB (ev.), Stade, St. Wilhelmi; letter of September 15, 1857, NABS.
2. Letter of October 27, 1858, NABS.

a good thing that I was married, otherwise I wouldn't be alive any more, but my wife and children held me back.

Now it's all over, the soldiers are all coming back. I've always had enough money but I am not rich by any means. Soon I will start up another store and hope that my luck will be better. Dear parents, my wife is from Germany, from the Principality of Waldeck.

This is a picture of the funeral of our good *Pressedend* Abraham Likoln [Lincoln] who freed the whole country from terrible slavery, and when it was all over, he was murdered by an [assassin's?] hand, but they all got their just reward, four have been hanged and one was shot like a dog and thrown into the deepest waters.

[at least 1 line missing] not to write, all the best from my wife and children. We remain your faithful

children Hinry Miller, Friderricke Miller and best regards from Anna Miller to her grandfather and grandmother

Dear brother, write me back soon

Address Hinry Miller 210.5 Street / New Jork

WESTERN THEATER

32. Surgeon Magnus Brucker

Considering the fact that he was a doctor and a Forty-eighter, Magnus Brucker's background was remarkably humble. When he was born in 1828, his father was listed as a day laborer, and his mother was illiterate. His hometown of Haslach, in Baden in southwest Germany, was the county seat, but it was relatively small (1,670 inhabitants), somewhat isolated, and almost exclusively Catholic.[1] Scholarships probably helped Brucker complete his secondary education in Heidelberg and study medicine in Strasbourg. He must have been actively involved in the Revolution of 1848; after its failure, he fled via Italy to the United States in 1849.[2]

In the early 1850s Brucker opened a medical practice in Troy, Indiana, a village with a population of about 400 on the Ohio River. In November 1855 he married Elizabeth Meyers, who had emigrated from Bavaria with her parents. A daughter, Flora, was born in 1858, and a son, Karl, followed two years later. Before the war Brucker had acquired considerable social standing in the community but little wealth. In 1860 his assets were listed at $500, but he had already been elected to the town council, and in 1861 he became a member of the Indiana House of Representatives.[3]

More typical of a Forty-eighter than his social background were Brucker's religious and political beliefs. He tended toward free thought, the word "God" never

SOURCE NOTE: Brucker's German is grammatically and idiomatically correct, but his spelling is quite bad though not hopeless. He writes without frills in a factual, straightforward manner. We do not need to guess about his education: he finished preparatory school and graduated in medicine. After a dozen years in America, English interference is quite noticeable and of various kinds. There are German words for English phrases like "*im besten Spirit.*" Sometimes it is hard to decide whether he has coined a hybrid or misspelled an English word, like "marsh" for "march" (German: "*Marsch*"); and since no similar German word exists, "Warf" is simply a misspelling. He uses "Railroad" (as well as "*Eisenbahn*"), "attack," "Cristmass," "River," "Riflepits," "Charge," "Shells," and quite a few other English words when he either does not know the German equivalent or the English word comes to mind more quickly from the context—and it seems worth noting that he obviously was sure his German-born wife would understand. Not included here are the letters in the series from the years 1860 (one), 1861 (one), 1862 (twenty-three), 1863 (twenty-nine), 1864 (nineteen), and 1865 (three), as well as eleven from the years after 1865.

1. KB (rk.) Haslach; *Beiträge zur Statistik* (1855), 1:149. The originals of the Brucker letters are located in the Brucker Papers, Indiana Historical Society, Indianapolis.

2. *Biographical Sketches* (1861), 86–87; *History of Warrick, Spencer, and Perry Counties* (1885), 172–73.

3. MC 1860: Perry Co./Ind., Troy Twp., #933; MC 1870: Perry Co./Ind., Tell City Twp., #720; *Biographical Directory of the Indiana General Assembly* (1980), 43; Pension File, NatA.

appears in his letters, and he was a Freemason. Even before the war he was an active Republican; his county, Perry, was one of the few in southern Indiana that voted for Lincoln. A good half of the county's population were of foreign birth or parentage, and 65 percent of these were German or Swiss.[4] Brucker's Republican views became more radical during the course of the war, as is shown in his letter of September 18, 1864, which also reveals that many of his neighbors sympathized with the Democrats or even the South.

Brucker served as an assistant surgeon in the Union army, but not together with friends and neighbors as was usually the case. It is possible that a company of the 53rd Indiana Infantry was recruited from his neighborhood. But on March 21, 1862, he joined the 23rd Indiana Infantry, a regiment that had already been formed the previous July. In this unit Germans made up a small minority: only about a dozen of the over 100 officers had German names.[5]

Indianapolis, March 19th, 1862

Dear wife,

As you already know, I was cheated out of my post as regimental surgeon, our regiment was disbanded and Colonel Mansfeld betrayed me in order to get a post for his son.[6] I've been promised another post, but I haven't received one yet. I would have come home, but I don't have much money. I can't sell any horses since no one will give me anything for them. The government owes me $414 and in order to collect this money I'll be staying here until an order is issued to the treasurer to pay [8 ll.: is sending a box]. I am hale and hearty and hope that you and my family are too. Write back soon.

My best to you, your father and mother and my friends

your / M. Brucker med. D[r.] / *care of* M. Ommonogger / Union Hall

Pittsburgh *4 miles in the Wood* / April 10th, 1862

Dear wife,

Finally I have a bit of time to write, you will have heard about the bloody battle [Shiloh*], you can get more details from the newspapers. My regiment

---

4. *Biographical Directory of the Indiana General Assembly* (1980), 43; USC 1870.1, 124, 128, 309, 353. The Bruckers were married by a Lutheran, not a Catholic, clergyman. Their son Victor did become a Catholic priest, but he was only two years old when his father died. Pension File, NatA; letter of Hulda Davis, June 22, 1987, Brucker Papers.

5. The regiment was recruited in New Albany, a small town on the Ohio River about sixty miles upstream from Brucker's home. Muster Rolls, NatA; Dyer (1959 [1908]), 1128; *Report of the Adjutant General of Indiana* (1865), 2:220–28.

6. A Fielding Mansfield was a major in the three-month and colonel in the one-year 54 Ind. Inf. *OAR*, 6:117, 418.

lost 8 men and 42 wounded, my hospital was surrounded by the enemy 3 times while being set up, all of our wounded have now been taken to the river. The 32 Regt Col. Willich had about 300 dead and wounded, I treated many of them. Morton Battery, Captain Bär [Behr] lost all its cannon but one, Bär is dead. I saw Leut. Col. 24 Rgt. Garby about half an hour before he died, Veach Col. 25 is slightly injured, of the people from our area I've only heard about [Ada?] Williams—he was injured, 2 times in the arm and his stomach was grazed.[7] I think the Wittmann boy is dead—it is impossible to find out anything since the battlefield was about 6 miles long and completely strewn with bodies. I treated about 400—according to our estimates there are about 10,000 to 12,000 dead and wounded, our division fought brilliantly and in particular our Brigade General Walace. On Monday we were on the right wing[. . . .] I was bandaging the first casualty, a man from 1 Nebraska, the shells were flying by and whistling over my head, small-arms fire could be heard all day, like hail falling on a shingled roof. Both sides fought unbelievably bitterly. We held the battlefield, through the help of General Buel [Buell], but our losses seem to me as bad as those of the enemy. Our Colonel fought like a devil, our L. Colonel Anthony had a horse shot dead out from under him[. . . .]

Fare well / M. Brucker *Surgeon* / 23 Regt. Ind. Volt. Col. Sanderson Lew. Wallaces Brigade. Tenessee. / Brucker

Camp near Monterey / Tenessee May 24th / 1862

Dear wife,

Today I finally received a letter from you, the one from April 14th. I am so glad that all are well. I had been expecting a little newcomer to the family by now, but that doesn't seem to have happened yet. If Dr. Rapp has good serum taken from a healthy child you can have the children vaccinated [5 ll.: instructions]. I am fine, we are presently in the rear in *Reserve*, our *front* lines are fighting every day. Corinth hasn't been taken yet. You can find out more in the newspapers, since we don't even know what is happening 4 *miles* from here. We are on the right wing, our army is spread out in a line of about 15 *Miles*. Corinth is half surrounded by our troops. I think when the battle is over, peace will be made soon, since it will be impossible for the rebels to

---

7. The predominantly German 32 Ind. Inf was commanded by Colonel (as of 1862, General) August (von) Willich (1810–78), a former Prussian officer, Marxist revolutionary, and Forty-eighter. Brucker's casualty figures are exaggerated; the brigade, consisting of four regiments, suffered a total of 247 casualties. "Bär" refers to Captain Fr. Behr; about half of the 6 Ind. Baty under his command were Germans. "Garby" refers to Lieutenant Colonel John Gerber, "Veach" to James C. Veatch (as of April 28, 1862, brigadier general). Kaufmann (1911), 272–73; Warner (1964), 565–66; Johnson and Buel (1987), 1:538; *OAR*, 6:26.

hold out any longer. Governor Morton of Indiana[8] was here and visited us, we received a splendid regimental flag from the citizens of New Albany Ind. as a present and in recognition of our bravery in the battle *of Shiloh* [8 ll.: financial matters; horse]. *Mayor* [Major] Davis and I have to ride behind the regiment when we march [14 ll.: organization of the military; greetings; signature; address].

Camp near Monterey / June *1st*, 1862

Dear wife,

I was happy to learn in a letter from Mr. Weber that you have given birth to a baby girl. I hope you are both well, I'll send the name for the child later[9] [. . . .] I will send some money as soon as I have a chance to do so safely, if you are really in need, sell one of the better notes, or collect them. By the way, every *Store* will lend you money, I hope I still have that much *Credit* in Troy. If people are impertinent, take them to court.

Corinth was abandoned by the enemy today, about 6,000 prisoners were taken and many weapons captured. Tomorrow we will break camp too, and move farther south. Where we're going I don't know yet, whether toward Memphis or Mobile. I don't think the enemy can do much more to us; it is very hot here and water is getting scarce, we will have a lot of hardships to bear. The health of the regiment is good, this evening I only excused 34 from the *marsh*, sometimes I've had to excuse more than a hundred and leave them behind when marching orders came. As long as I've been with the regiment only two men have died on me, both were half dead before I started treating them. Our regiment is still one of the strongest in the field. We still have over 800 men, today we'll be marching for the first time with our new flag—it is the most attractive in the whole *Division*. Our boys are in the best of spirits, they have money, new trousers and jackets, and the 23rd regiment will add to its fame when it has a new opportunity to meet the rebels. On my prescription they get a drink of whiskey twice a day when marching and when it rains. I had to fight a lot to get that through, our chaplain and the Methodists were against it. We can also buy some beer from time to time, as well as other things that are great delicacies for us, for example stinky smoked herring, sharp cheese, sardines, *Oisters*, lemons, dates, oranges etc., but all at a horrendous price. I got a new tent today, put on a clean shirt that I washed myself yesterday, and

8. The Republican Oliver Morton was one of the most effective governors in the North, despite strong Democratic opposition in the legislature. Faust (1986), 513-14.

9. His daughter Theresa was born on May 22, 1862; letter of Hulda Davis, June 22, 1987, Brucker Papers. Alderich Weber was a merchant from Bavaria. MC 1860: Perry Co./Ind., Troy Twp., #450.

my bed has a clean pillowcase. I put everything in order in my private tent, and then came the marching orders, which is always a lot of work for me, first examining the people to see who's not fit, and then all that packing [4 ll.: details; end of letter missing].

Camp near Bolivar Tenessee / June 16th, 1862

Dear wife,

[4 ll.: correspondence] Yesterday I turned in my *Resingnation* to General Hallek [Halleck], but I doubt it will be accepted, at any rate if it is accepted it will still take another month. Nothing is to be heard from the enemy, enemy deserters come through here and take the oath of loyalty, then we let them go on their way[. . . .] In our area there are enemy *Guerillas* who go from plantation to plantation and burn the *Cotton*, tobacco, and anything else they can find, they are all on horseback and hard to catch [6 ll.: correspondence; greetings, signature; address].

Camp near Bolivare / Tenessee / August 2nd

Dear wife,

Finally I got a whole lot of letters, the last one of the 17th of *July*, in which you told me that you and the youngest child were not well; I hope that you and the baby are better when you get this letter, put yourself under a doctor's care and hopefully you will improve. Much as I regret it, I can't come home now, no matter how much I would like to see you even if it were only for a few hours, but no leave is being given to officers and my request for discharge from the army was turned down because I am needed. Maybe I can arrange it that I am allowed to bring some of the sick in our *Division* to the *General Hospital* in Evansville or New Albany, and then it would be easy for me to spend a few days at home. If I leave without permission I might lose three months of my pay, since next month we will be paid for 4 months[. . . .] Last week we had some small skirmishes but they weren't important, the enemy retreated again, and our entrenchments are almost finished, which will enable us to defy even a superior enemy. T. Austin has come back to the regiment, but he doesn't do a thing and wants to apply for his discharge, which wouldn't give me more recognition but would increase my pay. Under my direction the regiment is healthy, and the regiment is satisfied with me, and they are demanding that I stay[10] [14 ll.: address; greetings; signature; financial arrangements].

10. Surgeon Thomas R. Austin left the regiment on September 17, 1862; before this date he spent several months in a hospital in Paducah, Kentucky. Brucker complained in a letter of July 3, 1862, that he was doing the work of both a surgeon and an assistant for only an assistant's pay. In a

Magnus Brucker's letterhead, July 27, 1862 (letter not included here).
(Brucker Papers, Indiana Historical Society, Indianapolis, Ind.)

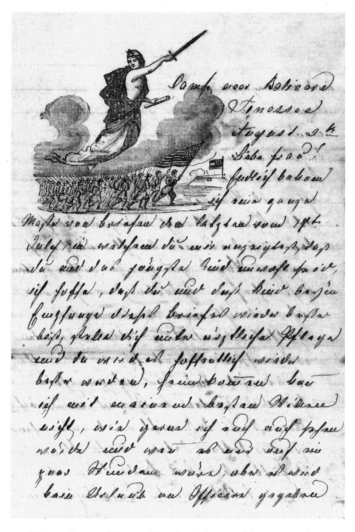

Illustration on Magnus Brucker's letter of August 2, 1862.
(Brucker Papers, Indiana Historical Society, Indianapolis, Ind.)

Bolivare Tenessee, September / 10th, 1862

Dear wife,

I received your letter of August 30th, and I am very sad to hear that you are not well, but if it isn't anything more than a fever that you get every day, this will be easy to treat [16 ll.: medical advice]. On the subject of being afraid, up until now there hasn't been any danger in our immediate area, the *Guerillas* who are on the lower Ohio are too weak to cross the river, since they would all be captured,[11] but a woman with children has nothing to fear anyway, since on both sides women and children are protected by officers and soldiers, the only thing to be perhaps afraid of are thieves and vagabonds, but we're at the mercy of those rascals even in peacetime. If one breaks in at night, shoot him to pieces. Make sure the rifles and pistols are well loaded, there's no place for fearfulness and timidity in these times. If my duty and circumstances permitted, I would have come home long ago, since there are perhaps only a few who love their family more than I do[. . . .] I won't be applying for a discharge as long as I stay healthy and as long as good fortune continues to desert our side, like at the moment in Virginia and Kentucky. I will stay until the rebels have been beaten back so that they are put off from marching to the Ohio River for good, and that will happen shortly. Still, even if the southern-minded in Troy are cheering for the fall of the Union, it will not fall and must not fall. The advantage that they have gained over individual units of northern troops I hope will make a great impression on the North, because we've been too forgiving and considerate and too slow on our side up to now. It wasn't the fault of our army that more hasn't happened yet, the soldiers are courageous and seek every opportunity to fight the enemy, but they haven't been allowed to. With hungry stomachs they have had to guard rebel property so that no soldier could take even one ear of corn. Of course soon when the fellows in Washington are up to their neck in trouble, they will come to their senses a bit and give other orders. If the government can't come up with some other plan in its strategy, even I say it would be better to just let them go and make peace. The only way to overcome the South, like I have said before, requires

---

letter of September 26, 1862, his commander passed along the "unanimous wish of the regiment" that Brucker be appointed surgeon, a request that was only granted on January 15, 1863, but took effect retroactively as from September 18, 1862. Military correspondence, Brucker Papers; Muster Rolls, NatA.

11. Confederate advances in Kentucky in August 1862 caused great agitation north of the Ohio River. On September 5–6 Governor Morton ordered militias to be formed in southern Indiana. Cincinnati and Louisville also felt threatened. Faust (1986), 414–15; Long and Long (1971), 262–65.

enormous sacrifice, the only way is to take away all their workforce, namely the Negroes, destroy everything they need to live, or use it ourselves, otherwise they will keep getting stronger behind our backs, because we can fight big battles to conquer for a short time, but not for good, and by occupying so many places with our troops we're weakening our army, and then the enemy comes out in force and descends upon parts of our army and wipes them out. And what the enemy doesn't do, disease accomplishes—the whole thing could be over if the war had been conducted seriously, our army was large enough at the beginning.

I myself am fine, I have a lot to do, have 80 patients in the hospital and nothing but beans, rice, and bacon to feed them, you can't buy anything for 20 *Miles* around and since the *Railroad* has been burned out we can't get anything from Columbus, not even an onion, let alone cabbage and lettuce, haven't eaten any vegetables for 4 weeks. Our pockets are full of money, but we can't buy anything with it, so my dearest wish is to get away from here [10 ll.: speculations about next deployment]. I have about 200 dollars, money that I don't need, but I don't know if I should send it or not, you and your father are so apprehensive, but it would be damned awful if the rebels were to catch me, the fellows would have far too good a time if they found the money on me and I won't allow that. Give my best to your father and mother, Mr. Weber and Heinze and tell Mr. Weber he should write me the news from Troy and Tell City [signature missing].

Bolivare Tenessee, September 29th, 1862

Dear wife,

Today I was confidently expecting a letter, but I didn't receive one, everyone in the whole regiment got one, so don't try to save paper and do write more often, because I am always uneasy about the well-being of my family. You are no longer in any danger from the enemy, the enemy is retreating, the Spencer County Home Guard did well at Owennsburg,[12] in particular young Schwind. His brother is presently here with the 25th Regiment, as is a Cannelton[13] company from the 53rd. *Regt.* I saw that the 60th Regiment, which the Spencer County boys are in, has been taken prisoner. They will now be allowed to go home. I am glad about that, they did their best in Munfords-

12. Spencer is the next county west of Perry County, where Troy is located. On September 19–20 its Home Guard took part in a skirmish with the 12 Ky. Cav in Owensburg, leaving two dead and eighteen wounded. Dyer (1959 [1908]), 732.

13. Cannelton was a neighboring town of approximately 2,200 inhabitants on the Ohio River about seven miles upstream from Troy. USC 1870.1, 128.

ville Ky. but they couldn't withstand the enemy's superior force any longer.[14] [16 ll.: is well; march to Iuka; signature; address; greetings].

Bolivare Tenessee October 18th, 1862

Dear wife,

[6 ll.: correspondence] As regards Mr. Weber's conjecture that I could come home any time if I wanted to, I can only reply that he is wrong. If I had an <u>honorable</u> opportunity to come home I would do so, but my chances of getting leave are as slim as any other soldier's. And if I were to just leave my post, especially since I am all alone here with the regiment, I would be treated as a *Deseteur* and dishonorably discharged, and I don't want that to happen, and on top of all this the war can't last much longer, the rebels must be and are getting hit badly everywhere, I hope they'll be beaten out of Kentucky in about a week, when they get to us we will teach them a lesson, like we recently did to Prise [Price] Van Dorn and Lowell, they've lost all interest in trying anything with us again. General Veach came to see me yesterday, he has recovered, was only grazed. As for the cold, I had to put up with that at home, too, on my *County* tours. If we set up winter quarters here it won't matter at all, because if we stay here I have a good room here with a fireplace and a good bed and enough wood and enough people to chop it, I also have enough clothing[. . . .] As regards sending things with Karl Schmuk [. . .] I will arrange it that Schmuk can remain at home for a while, because I can do this for other people, but not for myself [8 ll.: greetings; signature; address].

Holly Springs Miss November 30th, 1862

Dear wife,

I still have not received any letters from you since I left Troy[15] [8 ll.: march route] today our *Advanc* had a small *attack*, but the rebels have retreated, we heard the cannon all afternoon, probably they will give us a battle on the Talahachee River about 10 *Miles* from here, but we now have about 80,000 men and there is no doubt that we will beat them back[. . . .] My regiment is in very good health, I now have an *assistent Surgeon*, and as a result I won't have to do so much work, he is a young doctor from Barnsville, Harrison County, Indiana.[16] The 25th and 53rd regiments are in *front* of us about 1 mile ahead, the boys from Troy and surroundings are in good health, the regiments camped

---

14. In the siege and capture of Munfordsville about 4,000 Union soldiers were taken prisoner, including the 60 Ind. Inf. Dyer (1959 [1908]), 732.

15. On October 28, 1862, Brucker was sent to Columbus, Kentucky, to get medical supplies, and he was thus able to visit his family. Muster Rolls, NatA.

16. Assistant surgeon Spencer Ayrn mustered in on September 26, 1862.

with us last night, Col. Williams stayed with me. Write to me at least twice a week, you have no idea how a person longs for letters in the field [12 ll.: correspondence; greetings; signature; address].

Hospital 23rd Regiment in the / *Field near* Jackna Missisippi
December 19th, 1862

Dear wife,

My regiment is still on this side of the river about 15 *Miles* south of Oxford, Missisippi, I don't know how long we'll be staying here. I received your letter in which you let me know that you had the children vaccinated, and I hope that when you get this letter the pain will have completely disappeared without any bad aftereffects. If circumstances permitted, I would love to come home and live with my family, for life here in the field is not the most pleasant, but given the current situation, there's nothing to be done. I and my fate are entangled in this ill-fated war, like thousands and thousands of my fellow citizens. I don't like it at all that I can't be with you this *Cristmass* nor will I be able to give you any Christmas presents, the paymaster still hasn't come, and even if he were to come, you can't buy anything here. Buy the children something they will enjoy. Enclosed is a piece of silk, make it into a *Christmass Gift* for Flora Bella. It comes from the battlefield of Iuka, where it was found, I haven't got anything else[. . . .] The weather last week was fairly cold but quite pleasant during the day, the army's state of health leaves nothing to be desired[. . . .] If our troops in Virginia and East Tenessee had better luck, we would be finished here with our part, our army *Corps* hasn't lost a battle yet, and the rebels don't like having anything to do with us[. . . .] I see from the newspapers that the 49th Regiment passed through Troy on its way to Memphis, they will probably join up with our army. It would be good to see the Troy boys, the 53rd with the Cannolton Company is only a mile from here, the 25th is still in Lagrange. Give my best to your father and mother as well as Mr. Weber and write again soon / to your loving

M. Brucker [. . .]

Dear Flora Bella,

I am sending you your *Chrismass gift*, stay well and be a good girl, your loving father / M. Brucker

Steamer Continental / Memphis Tenessee / February 21st, 1863

Dear wife,

I received your letter of February 12th today, and I am pleased that you received the money, unfortunately you said that Flora and the *Baby* are ill, spend all the money you need if it is necessary for the children [16 ll.: medical advice;

is sending money and a package]. Today or tomorrow we'll be going down the river, we don't yet know ourselves where we are going, the whole division is on the boats. Resignations from doctors are not being accepted, so I have to remain, and you must bow to the inevitable like many thousands of women. I hope that the war will be decided soon, and then I can return home in honor. If it weren't for you and the children I would be very happy with my current post, since the practice in Troy is a poor one and hard work [10 ll.: greetings; signature; address].

Lack [Lake] Providence Louisiana / March 8th, 1863
Dear wife,

[. . .] It is quite warm and it's been raining a lot, but few men are sick, we don't know anything about the enemy since we hardly get any newspapers and no letters, the whole countryside is under water and next week we will probably let the Missisippii River run into the lake and then in my opinion all the neighboring *Countys* will be flooded, the Missisippii is 17 feet higher than the water in the lake. We cut through the woods in the water up to a mile from Bayou Baxter, as soon as we bring the steamboats from the Missisippii to the Waschhita River, we will have to go to Fort Hudson [Port Hudson*] on the Missisippi to help General Banks,* but it will still take quite a while, because the whole project is badly planned and poorly led. I don't believe that we'll have enough water so we can use the steamboats, since the land is too flat and the water spreads out on all sides.

I got sick on the first of March with vomiting, diarrhea and cramps, but I am better now, just a bit weak, but I have been doing my rounds for three days now, my horse is sick too and I fear I will lose it, these are things, by the way, that happen every day, but it is unpleasant when it happens to yourself [6 ll.: greetings; signature; address].

In the field on the banks of the Big / Blak River, May 5th, 1863
Dear wife,

We left Miliken Bend April 25th and reached Richmond the same evening, on the 30th we reached the landing across from Grand Gulf after taking a large detour on land around Viksburg [Vicksburg*], went to the other side of the Missisippi and met the enemy by Tomsons Hill 2 *Miles* south of Port Gibson Mississippi. We beat the enemy, took about 1,000 prisoners and captured 2 cannon. The battle lasted the entire day, the 1st of May, it was a horrible May Day celebration, my regiment had 4 killed and 23 wounded, some of these will die. Mr. Kinley and Charles Schmack are uninjured as well as all the boys from our area, on the 2nd we reached Port Gibson, a beautiful town.

On the 3rd we pursued the enemy and yesterday we had another small skirmish in which 4 were wounded, yesterday evening we reached the *River*, but we couldn't prevent the bridge over the river from being destroyed, we have to build a bridge, and the enemy will try to prevent us[. . . .] I have no idea what will happen next, but I firmly believe we will succeed. We have to attack Viksburg from the rear, because of our *Manouver* the rebels had to leave Grand Gulf.

I feel fine but am very tired, we've been marching all day and half the night by now, don't have any tents and wagons with us, and we eat what we find and sleep out in the open, it is very warm and all the trees are in bloom, magnolia trees as high as a house [6 ll.: met some friends]. I had a lot to do, during the battle I had command of the *Brigade* and was busy until late at night, had the Surgeons from our regiment, from the 20th Illionois, from the 31st Illionois, 45th Illionois, 124th Illionois under me and I had all the responsibility [6 ll.: greetings; signature; address].

Camp near Viksburg [Vicksburg*] / July 4th, 1863

Dear wife,

[4 ll.: relief at recovery of children] Today we celebrated the 4th of July by taking Viksburg my regiment was the 2nd into the city, today at 2 o'clock I let my horse drink from the Missisippi at the *Warf* in Viksburg. You can get the details from the newspapers. The siege lasted 47 days, my regiment has had 200 killed and injured since we crossed the river.[17] We captured everything, about 25,000 men, all the cannon and all the muskets. It was a glorious 4th of July, one I won't forget it as long as I live [10 ll.: greetings; signature; address].

Hebron, miss December 25th

Dear wife,

[10 ll.: correspondence; sending money] I am pleased that you are well, I would have sent something for Karl and Flora, but there was no opportunity, and also you can't get anything here suitable for *Chrismass gifs*.

I spent quite a pleasant Christmas Day yesterday, was invited to *Dinner* by Mayor [Major] Ferguson and it was excellent, *Roast Pig Türky*[,] *Oisters Cakes* and *Pays* [pies] and champagne wine, and *Ladis* were also there. Mrs. Davis, the Colonel's *wife* and a Mrs. Miller from New Albany came to visit the *Camp* with their children. The whole regiment was in good spirits, since we had

---

17. This seems somewhat exaggerated: the total number of casualties suffered by all five regiments of his brigade at Vicksburg was only 483, including 69 dead. Johnson and Buel (1987), 3:548.

given the soldiers beer and *Wiskey* as a Christmas present and that made them all lively. I had a lot to do last week and will also be busy in the coming week, since I have to write the reports and bulletins for the *Surgeon General* in Washington. I also have to examine all the people who have signed on for another 3 years, and this together with the tasks which the post as Brigade Surgeon requires will leave me little free time until after New Year's [. . .] otherwise things are fairly quiet, except for our pickets who tease each other from time to time by shooting at each other for fun [9 ll.: correspondence; greetings; signature; address].

Hebron Miss, March 5th 1864

Dear wife,

[12 ll.: postal service restored after long march towards Mobile] I think my regiment has the requisite number of veterans and will then have the right to a 30-day leave, and so I hope to get leave if I am not sent somewhere else first,[18] but there is already talk of another *Expedition* to the Redriver and I have been assigned to the *Operations* staff by the *Medical Director* on *Order* of General McPherson, a post of honor with great responsibility. However, if my regiment goes home and the rest of the 17th Army Corps goes on an *Expedition*, this might keep me from coming. I will send the money for your father when I get the next chance or bring it myself [13 ll.: instructions; greetings; signature; address].

Decatur Alabama on the / Tenessee River / May 26th, 1864

Dear wife,

[. . .] We arrived here this evening and we'll be crossing the river tomorrow on a pontoon bridge, up to here there is a railroad connection with Louisville and Nashville, the railroad bridge over the river has been destroyed, so there's no connection on the other side. After this letter you won't be getting any more for a while, since we aren't leaving any railroad connections intact behind us. It will take us about 15 to 20 days until we meet up with the railroad line to the east that's taking General Scherman forward. Since Sherman is advancing quickly, it is possible that we will only meet up with the main army when we get near Atlanta Georgia, which is about 200 *Miles* from here. The countryside here is very rich and densely settled. The roads are quite good but very dusty. The rebel General forest [Forrest*] is near here with about 5,000 men, but I don't believe that he wants to take us on. I am doing well,

18. Indeed, both Brucker and the regiment received a month's leave and returned on April 29. Dyer (1959 [1908]), 1128; letter of April 30, 1864, NABS.

apart from a bit of diarrhea. We don't have anything to eat but meat and hard
bread, you can't get any vegetables, and black coffee and water to drink [8 ll.:
greetings; signature; address].

Bigshandy [Big Shanty, Cobb County] Ga., June 17th, 1864
Dear wife,

I received your letter of June 2nd and was sorry to learn that Flora and
Theresia are ill[. . . .] It was right to have the children vaccinated but you
should still be very cautious, don't let in any visitors and don't make any visits
yourself, because even the vaccination does not always protect you from getting smallpox. As for me, I am fine, have a lot to do, up until this morning
I've had 38 wounded and 48 sick in the Division Hospital. My regiment has
had two killed and 4 wounded up to now, 2 more will probably die. The regiments I'm in *charge* of are the 23rd Indiana, 12th Wisconsin, 53rd Ind., 32nd
Illonois, 11th Iowa, 16th Iowa, 15th Iowa, 13th Iowa, all *Batteries and Pioneer
Corps* that belong to the 4th Division[. . . .] We are fighting every day and
often all night long, our troops have taken the first line of the enemy *Riflepits*,
we've taken about 1,500 prisoners up to now, we are on the left wing, I can't
say with any certainty what is happening along the entire line, the enemy has
an excellent *Position* on Lost Mountain and we are at the foot of the mountain
[8 ll.: greetings; signature; address].

Riflepits near Atlanta Ga., August 19th / 1864
Dear wife,

As for me I am fine, we are still in front of the fortifications around Atlanta
and have skirmishes day and night. My regiment has lost no more men recently, we haven't had any new wounded, except for Louis Gillmann, his parents live on Crooket Creek, but his wound is not dangerous and I think he'll
be fit for duty again soon. The Cannelton Company in the 53rd Indiana has
had very bad luck, there are only 10 men left, last night another one was shot
dead, by the name of Baid, his family live somewhere behind Cannelton on
Deer Creek. The rebel Weekler [Wheeler] destroyed the railroad between
here and Dalton, but it has been repaired already [6 ll.: wishes; signature; ad-
dress].

Riflepits near Atlanta Ga. / August 21st, 1864
Dear wife,

Today I received your letter of August 9th and the letters from my dear
daughter Flora Bella and from my little fellow Karl. I am pleased that you
are fine and that you have recovered. I am fairly well informed about what is

happening in Indiana, and I believe that if the government doesn't step up its action we'll soon have the war at home amongst ourselves. That the *Guerillas* have had the nerve to cross the *River* and they aren't being stopped, that they can keep marching just like that—I can't explain that, unless the people are pleased by this and happy to see them. Otherwise our people would certainly be strong enough to stop them, particularly if they have guns and ammunition like our other citizens. Not much is happening here, a few wounded and once in a while one killed, cannon and muskets are firing day and night, I am in the *Center* and my Division is 100 *Yards* from the main enemy position[. . . .] General Osterhaus* has gone off with 12,000 *Cavallery* in order to free our soldiers who are being held prisoner somewhere to the south, the prisoners were in Macon, Georgia, but then they were transported somewhere else. I hope that Osterhaus finds them and is able to free them.[19] General Stoneman and General McCook also left to try the same thing, but they were not successful, Stoneman was taken prisoner. I hope that we will soon take Atlanta and think our work will be finished then and that the campaign will be over when we take the city. If the Copperheads* keep making such progress in Indiana, Ohio, Illinois, then our government will have to call back the army to use it against the traitors in the North, and that will mean irreparable damage to the United States. The people in the North have no idea what a civil war means, otherwise they would act more sensibly [9 ll.: greetings; signature; address].

South of Jonesborrow, September 4th / 1864

Dear wife,

[. . .] We left the north side of Atlanta during the night so that the enemy couldn't see us moving and marched along the Stantoweeroad west from Atlanta, two days later we reached the Lagrange & Atlanta *Railroad*, or rather the Montgomery *Railroad*, destroyed it at Fairburn *station*, built some trenches, and the next morning we marched forward and found the enemy, beat them, took many prisoners. We extended our line across the Macon *Railroad*, thereby cutting off the enemy army that was still in Atlanta. Schofeld with the 23rd Corps was left behind and the 20th Corps guarded our wagons on the north side of the Chattahoochee River, we only had a few wagons with us. And then we went forward in our line of battle, my Corps, the 17th, at the front[. . . .] We beat down everything in our path and forced the rebel General Hood to leave Atlanta. There were plenty of dead and wounded, and I

19. In the notorious prison camp at Andersonville, Georgia, 33,000 Union prisoners were packed together, out in the open, into a space averaging thirty-four square feet per man, and 29 percent died. McPherson (1988), 755, 796, 802.

was in more danger myself than ever before. I was riding with General Blair,*
our *Corps Comander*, near Flint River to look for a good and secure place for
a *Hospital*, the enemy made a Charge and the shots flew around us like hail,
General Sherman arrived at the same time with his *Body Gard*, the enemy discovered him and sent *Shells* thick as snowflakes at us, I jumped off my horse
and found a big tree to protect myself until our *Artillery* was able to quiet
down the enemy. Today we are near Laffaieteville, across from the enemy, but
now that Atlanta is in our hands I don't think we will be moving forward,
and I don't believe we'll have another battle, unless the enemy attacks us. We
will probably retreat, the *Army of the* Tenessee to Aestpoint [East Point], the
Cumberland Army to Atlanta and Decatur. I am well and hope to be coming
home soon, either they will make peace or I will press for my *Resignnation*.[20] I
don't have any money because I haven't gotten any money since we arrived in
New Albany, it is already 8 months that the government owes us [8 ll.: greetings; signature; address].

Atlanta Ga. September 18th, 1864

Dear wife,

[. . .] The money Charles Schmuck gave you he borrowed from the men
in the regiment, and I will pay it back as soon as the paymaster comes, use it
as you best see fit. I hope we will be paid soon for at least two months, then
I'll send you some money as soon as I have a chance. I don't think it is a good
idea for you and the children to go to Saint Louis [15 ll.: details]. I'll come
home, and then when things have quieted down, then you can go, and I will
accompany you. If wood costs 3 dollars a *Lot* then you will have to pay that,
just like other people, things in Troy aren't any more expensive than anywhere
else. If you don't have any money in Troy you can still get everything you
need, but not in a strange place, you have enough notes on hand and enough
credit in every *Store* to stave off every need. As for the population of Troy, you
don't need to worry if they are Democrats or Republicans, and even if they
are Butternuts[21] or loyals, you have enough space to stay away from them and
there's no need at all for you to have much contact with them. As far as the
population of Troy goes, I don't care one bit what they think of me or if they

20. On July 14, 1864, Brucker had applied to be discharged at the same time that the regiment's term of service was to end on July 27, 1864, obviously without success. Military correspondence, Brucker Papers.

21. "Butternuts," named after their homespun clothes dyed with the oil from walnut hulls,
were backwoods inhabitants of the southern Midwest, mostly Democratic in their views, and
frequently southern in terms of their descent and even their loyalties. McPherson (1988), 31,
493, 593.

call me *Blak Republicaner Abolitionist, Lincolnit* or *Yankee Vandal* like the rebels call us, *blak* or white. I am satisfied with myself and am doing my duty as a citizen of this republic, and it is the duty of every good citizen to support the government elected by the majority of the people, even if he does not agree with all of its decrees. If it weren't for the cowardly traitors in the North, the revolution would have been suppressed a long time ago, and time will tell and history will worship and honor the names of those who bled, fought and died for the *Republic* just as much as it will damn the cowardly traitors, especially those in the North. A curse will fall on these wretched people who sow the seeds of civil war in the North, just as it has already fallen on the southern traitors, who started the war without cause. They are fleeing from one place to the next, their houses have been burned down and deserted and we, their enemy, feed their women and children, otherwise they would starve to death. Hundreds of rebels come to our lines every day and explain they were forced to fight against their old Union, where they had lived happily and without complaint. They have all been cured of their illusions and realize they were wrong. I was in Atlanta today, it is a very beautiful place, full of riches and wealth before the war, but now it's been destroyed, not by us but by the enemy, there are women and half-naked children begging in the streets for something to eat, and all of this for the sake of a few ambitious Negro-breeders, since most of the population doesn't have Negroes and *Sclavery* is the bane of the free white working man. They may call me a *Blakabolitionist* in Troy, but before the outbreak of the war I was opposed to the *agitation* of the northern *fanatics*, even though I despised *Sclavery* like I do now, realizing it is incompatible with a free *Republic*, because I was afraid of a civil war and because I thought that in time and given the progress of culture and civilization, this damnable institution would die out of its own accord over time. This opinion led me to support the *Crittenten compromise*[22] in the Indiana *Legislature*, but the South, or more precisely a few corrupt southern politicians, didn't want to settle the matter amicably [. . .] and even now the South is not willing to accept any peace terms to settle things and so there's nothing we can do except <u>destroy their armies</u> and then dictate peace terms, prohibit *Sclavery* in all parts of the United States, in order to end the quarrel once and for all, and to open up this country for free labor and to keep it free for our children and our children's

---

22. Proposal made in 1860 by Kentucky senator John J. Crittenden, which included the following "unamendable" constitutional amendments: the national government would be prohibited from interfering with slavery in the states where it already existed; slavery would be prohibited in territories north of 36° 30′ but permitted south of that line in all U.S. territories held at the time or later acquired. McPherson (1988), 252–53.

children[. . . .] <u>The army will keep on fighting despite the traitors at home</u> [7 ll.: details]. I have spent more time writing this letter than I had intended, you can let Mr. Weber read it, I make no secret of my opinions and am not ashamed of holding them. If you want to go and stay with your father, that's fine with me [13 ll.: details; greetings; signature; address].

Gailsville [Gaylesville] Alabama, October / 23rd, 1864

Dear wife,

Today, Sunday, we have a day of rest. We have been pursuing the enemy day and night, the enemy is camped about 6 Miles from here, but I don't believe they will offer us a battle because we are too strong[. . . .] We will keep on pursuing the enemy and try to capture or destroy the rebel army under General Hood, in order to bring this thing to an end. We capture some men every day, and if this chase keeps up for a while, there won't be much left of the rebel army in the southwest. We are presently in north Alabama [. . .] we had to stop here since our people don't have any shoes any more, and the horses don't have any horseshoes, and the stony ground makes it impossible to march without shoes[. . . .] I am still well, even though we spend every day and night out in the open, we don't have any tents with us and we eat what we find, since wagons would only hinder us from moving forward quickly. I will be pleased to see some of our *Coper heads* [Copperheads*] here in the field soon, for there won't be many who will spend 1,500 dollars for a substitute, like Specht and Leistner were able to do in Santafee.[23] What do the *Buternuts* have to say about the election results—our party won, Governor Morton was elected even though no one in Troy voted for him, and President Lincoln will also be elected just as safely with more votes than last time [7 ll.: greetings; signature; address].

10 Miles from Savannah near Fort Mc
Allister at the 4th Division Hospital / December 15th, 1864

Dear wife,

A lot of time has passed without my having heard from you or you from me. We left Akworth on the night of November 12th, arrived in Marietta on the 13th, left Atlanta on the 15th, crossed the Amulgee River on a *Ponton* bridge on the night of the 18th, passed Montesella [Monticello] at 4 o'clock in the after-

23. Both were Germans from neighboring counties: John Specht, a merchant with assets of $10,000, and George Lestner, a farmer with assets of $2,375. MC 1860: Spencer Co./Ind., Clay Twp., #460; Huff Twp., #752.

noon and made camp 5 *Miles* to the south, went through Hillsboro at 11 o'clock in the morning on the 20th and reached Gordon on the 2nd, reached Irvington [Irwinton] and the railroad *station* No. 15 on the 23rd. Had a skirmish at the Oconee River railroad bridge, lost one man from our regiment, crossed the river on a *Pontoon* bridge in the evening on the 26th. Early in the morning on December 1st we crossed the Ogheechee River on a *Pontoon* bridge near *Railroadstation No. 10* near Midville, Burke County, Ga. December 2nd we camped on Governor Brown's Plantation,[24] reached Millen at the junction of the Augusta and Savannah and Macon railroads. On the 2nd we reached *station No. 5* about 55 *Miles* from Savannah, on the 5th we reached *station No. 4½*, the enemy had good fortifications, we outflanked them and they left without a fight, on the 8th we left camp 31 *Miles* from Savannah, *camped* on the night of the 8th to the 9th 24 *Miles* from Savannah, on December 8th we reached the railroad *station* 4 *Miles* from Savannah at the junction of the Savannah and Charleston railroads, found the enemy strongly entrenched and the entire countryside under water, there was fighting every day, we had to move farther on toward the sea and have already taken Fort Mc.Allister, which is near Warsaw Sound and controls the Ogheechee River, which we need to reestablish our connection to the north. It is very unclear how long it will take before we capture Savannah, read the newspapers about our *Expedition*, they will give you more details than I am able to [12 ll.: financial matters; greetings; signature; address].

Near Savannah on the Ogechee River
December 17th [or 19th], 1864

Dear wife,

[9 ll.: correspondence; provisions] We took about 200 prisoners and 32 cannon at the capture of Fort Mc. Allister, our lines are now open and we will soon be able to besiege Savannah, we have destroyed all the railroads for a hundred *Miles* around, and the enemy knows it's helpless since we went through the richest part, right through the middle of the state of Georgia, and destroyed the only railroad the enemy still had running from south to north, burned down all the mills, all the machines needed to work the cotton, and we've been living off the land since we left Atlanta, driving all the herds along with us, taking thousands of horses and mules, and the enemy hasn't been able to stop us, and if Savannah falls before the rains start we will probably go from Savannah to Charleston which is about 100 *Miles* from here, and

24. Joseph E. Brown (1821–95), Confederate governor of Georgia. Boatner (1959), 91–92.

if that falls too, then an end to the war can soon be expected [18 ll.: sending money; medical advice for the parents-in-law; greetings; signature; address].

                               Savannah Ga., December 22nd / 1864

Dear wife,

Yesterday afternoon we entered the town. After heavy bombardment from our side, the enemy left its defenses and fortifications in the night of the 20th to the 21st, on a *Pontoon* bridge across the Savannah River, and went north of the town, leaving it at our mercy. The town is very beautiful, one of the prettiest I have seen yet, but it's so crowded with people we haven't been able to get hold of one of the houses for our *Division Hospital*, and so the *Hospital* is still in tents that we have put up on the edge of town. What will happen to the people here and their property is still unknown, and General Shermann [Sherman] will probably wait for orders from Washington on how to proceed. Up to now everything has been strictly guarded, otherwise the soldiers would destroy and steal everything. Under General Hardee the enemy left town so quickly even the people living here didn't know anything about it. They had to leave everything behind, couldn't even spike the cannon, and they didn't have enough time to destroy their own bridge, they tried to burn their gunboats on the river, but we saved two of them. If they had waited until the next morning we would have taken them all prisoner. The river from here on is no longer navigable, the rebels have sunk stones and large ships and there are many *Torpedos* [mines] in the shipping channel, but I think that we will be able to clear out all these obstacles soon so that larger ships will be able to get here from the sea, and then the army will be supplied again with everything it needs [5 ll.: mild, healthy climate] but we won't be allowed to rest here, since before we even got here there was talk of another *Company* and a long march, maybe to Charleston in South Carolina or even to Richmond, Virginia. I wish I could be with you and the children for Christmas and New Year's, if the money gets there in time you should buy something for the children. In hopes that you and the children are well when this letter reaches you, I wish you a merry Christmas and a happy New Year and remain your loving / husband

Magnus Brucker *Surgeon* 23rd Regt.
Indiana Vols. *first Brigade* 4th Division
17th *Army Corps* Savannah Ga.

As Brucker suspected, his regiment continued its campaign into South and North Carolina, where it was located at the end of the war. Brucker himself, however, was no longer in the field. His term of service ended on March 28, 1865, and with Union victory imminent, he left the army. His regiment suffered a total of 217 deaths. Two-thirds were victims of disease, despite all the efforts of their doctor—the same percentage as in the Union army as a whole.[25]

Magnus Brucker returned to his medical practice in Troy, and in 1866 he was reelected to the legislature. While the Republicans during this era are generally regarded as having been subservient to the interests of big business, Brucker retained his concern for social reform. In a letter of March 1, 1867, he wrote, "my law, which does not permit children under 16 years of age to work longer than ten hours a day (I introduced the *Bill* because of the Cannelton *Cotton* Factory) passed the House on the 27th." Magnus Brucker died on October 28, 1874, at the age of only forty-six. The cause of his death was chronic diarrhea that, according to doctors' certificates, he had contracted during the war.[26]

25. Dyer (1959 [1908]), 1128; McPherson (1988), 487. However, according to some conflicting figures in the *Report of the Adjutant General of Indiana* (1865), 2:288, only 179 out of 524 deaths were caused by disease, which would speak more highly of the doctors.

26. Muster Rolls, NatA; Pension File, NatA; *Biographical Directory of the Indiana General Assembly* (1980), 43.

33. Monn Family

The tailor Christian Monn, age thirty-two, and his wife Barbara, née Schwarz, arrived in St. Clair County, Michigan, in November 1853, one year after Barbara's brother, the enterprising Jacob Schwarz, had settled there.[1] None of them had good things to say about conditions at home, although their village Blaubeuren was not as hard hit by emigration as other areas of Württemberg.[2] The Monns must have arrived with very little money, since Schwarz had to "immediately advance more than 100 guilders.*" With this help from his brother-in-law and as "the only tailor

SOURCE NOTE: Christian's handwriting is very different from Barbara's. His is quite irregular and variable, while hers is more impressive—straight, regular, and more easily legible. Considering the fact that neither of them had any secondary schooling, their German is quite acceptable, with hardly any influence from the local dialect. Typical of immigrants who have lived in a mixed community for a decade, Barbara uses English words, but she spells them according to German rules. Not included here are the letters in the series from the time before 1860 (five) and after 1865 (twenty-one).

1. On his arrival in New York on August 25, 1852, Schwarz was listed as a machinist. Later he was employed in shipbuilding and mill construction. NYPL, *Agnes*. The Monns seem to have sailed on the *Fortitude*, which arrived from Le Havre on November 15, 1853.

2. Hippel (1984), 194–97. Schwarz wrote on January 25, 1854, "I'd rather have one American citizenship than 25 in Blaubeuren, because in America you can amount to something"; NABS.

in town," Monn was able to establish himself relatively quickly in his old trade.[3] In 1857, however, he was not yet self-employed, and in 1860 the couple still rented rooms from an American. In terms of their religious and political affiliations, the Monns continued to be Lutherans and remained — like most Michigan Lutherans, but unlike their American neighbors — somewhat reserved about the Republican Party.[4] Monn did write in a letter of February 9, 1857, "We know about things in Germany as much as you do or even more, we read enough newspapers," but he had little of substance to say about American politics: "Last fall a new president was elected for 4 years. We also had the right to vote, every 4 years a new president is elected. We received our citizenship papers last fall."[5]

CHRISTIAN MONN

Newport, December 9, 1863

God be with you!

Dear brother and sister-in-law and children?

[26 ll. has received and sent photographs; waived his inheritance rights; friends] The war just keeps going on and on, they've called up the 18 to 35-year-olds twice here now, the unmarried men are fleeing to England — right across the water from Newport here is England, half of the *River* is northern and the other half is *Brittisch* and they don't get sent back.[6] And so of course it hits fathers with 3 to 4 children, and a man like that can't go or everything would fall apart, so he has to pay for a substitute and this costs $300. So it costs you everything you have. The war won't come to an end until there's no more men and money and a new president is elected, we have a Republican at the moment. We haven't had any riots yet but everything is unbelievably expensive. You don't see any gold and silver any more, just paper money from 5 cents to one dollar. Newport could still turn out to be a good place, they are presently drilling salt, 800–1,000 feet deep till they can tap the sea, it's done with a steam engine. Business is very bad, the war is mostly to blame for this [32 ll.: health; correspondence; greetings and encouragement to emigrate]. And I also wish you happy holidays, and if your throats are parched then come unto me and I will refresh you with a good glass of beer. Mine is excellent[. . . .] Your friend / and brother-in-law, / Christian Monn [. . .]

3. Joint letter of January 1, 1854, NABS.

4. MC 1860: St. Clair Co./Mich., Cottrellville Twp., #412. On the Lutherans, see the Gerstein series (no. 34). In 1860 56 percent of the vote in St. Clair County went to Lincoln. Burnham (1955), 530.

5. Probably only "first papers."

6. The St. Clair River marks the Canadian border.

BARBARA AND ROBERT MONN

Newport, March 18, 1865

God be with you!

Dear brother, brother-in-law, sister-in-law and children,

[23 ll.: correspondence; nephew is a "foreman" in the salt works; congratulations on confirmation] So now we have our old president again, because all the papers say that since he started the war he should also bring it to an end. They're still calling up soldiers—if only that at least would stop. There's nothing left but poor people. If you can't go yourself you have to buy a soldier for not less than 500–700 dollars and that's hard for a poor man. My Christian was called up 2 years ago, but because of his bad teeth and a stiff finger on his right hand he got off, there's no cloud without a silver lining. We don't know anything about Traugott, if it hits him then Jacob will buy him off.[7] The northerners just want to take one more fortress away from the South, so it will be over soon, everyone's waiting for it anxiously. [19 ll.: weather; salt and oil drilling; shipbuilding; prices; appearance in photographs]. Our boys, thank God, are also well, they never lack for good food and the occasional beer; we often said to Robert when we were sitting at the table and eating, Robert, you wouldn't have food like this in Germany, and he said, yes, in Germany they are poor, I wouldn't want to live there. Here it is 10 degrees better than the old home country and we aren't strangers here anymore, we're already old Newporters. They want to make Newport into a *Sitte* [city], or in German a *Stadt*,[8] but the costs are too high at the moment since every resident has to make a *Seidwog* [sidewalk] as long as his house and *Lott*, but the boards are so expensive. Then the court has to build a prison. We're right in the middle of Newport in a lovely spot, we can see all the big boats and *Wesel* [vessels] go by. On the other side is England [12 ll.: religion; correspondence]. As for us, we are healthy, thank the Lord, our business is always good, of course it's better in the summer than in the winter. More people from outside will be coming when the boats are running again, otherwise we haven't seen any fellow countrymen or friends, nor have we read any names we know in the newspaper lists of war deaths. The war has swept away all the gold and silver money, so I can't please you, Jacob, with a gold dollar for your confirmation, but when we write again we will send one [15 ll.: requests; greetings].

Fare well and be in good health!

7. Their brother-in-law wrote on February 12, 1865, "None of us have to do military service, I'm too old and Traugott [his son] is still too young, and I hope there will be peace soon, it's already lasted long enough"; NABS.

8. The name was apparently changed to Marine City. There is also a Newport in Monroe County, but it is not the one mentioned here.

I remain your faithful sister Barbara Monn / next time Christian will write to
you himself [6 ll.: greetings; postscript by ROBERT MONN]

The Monns never showed much interest in politics, but a change in their attitude
to political parties is evident in a letter of March 12, 1877: "now we have another
Republican as president, the Democrats are evil, they wanted to bring in the Pope,
but thank God it didn't come to that."

Brother-in-law Schwarz prospered in the postwar economy; in 1873 his assets
were estimated to be $8,000–$9,000. The Monns fared less well. Toward the end
of the war they had opened a saloon, and Christian is listed in the 1870 census as a
saloonkeeper with assets of $800. The next year they wrote, "our business is really
very slow, but our life here is very pleasant, there are 20 saloons here, all German."
By 1880 Monn had gone back to working as a tailor, an increasingly outdated profession. Barbara Monn then reported in 1887, "Christian's business is cleaning clothes,
we always turn a good profit." Even the crisis year of 1893 did not shatter her trust
in America: "be patient until next spring, things will get better then. I wish your
boys were here and didn't have to be soldiers." Four months later she passed away;
her husband had preceded her two years earlier.[9]

9. Letters of February 8, 1871, February 4, 1873, March 12, 1877, July 21, 1887, and August 29,
1893, NABS; MC 1870: St. Clair Co./Mich., Marine City, #87; MC 1880: St. Clair Co./Mich.,
e.d. 373, #189; information provided by the donor.

34. Private Dietrich Gerstein

The name Dietrich Gerstein is not to be found in any of the standard works on
the Forty-eighters, but his career is at least as typical of this group as is the success

SOURCE NOTE: Gerstein liked to call himself and his relatives in Germany "well-educated
people," and he certainly was, even though he was denied his secondary school diploma, mainly
for political reasons. He was well read in German literature, certainly knew Latin and French,
probably some Greek, and at least after a few years in America he got along smoothly with
English, even though he claimed to dislike it heartily. So, not unexpectedly, his German, including the spelling, is infallibly correct without local dialect interference, and he handles the language masterfully and sometimes dramatically. In accordance with his reserve toward English, at
least until the late 1860s he does not let it intrude. When a word was written in Latin script, it sig-
nifies that he felt it was a foreign word. "Conscription" appears in German script, meaning that
he uses the German word in an American context. The verb "*fouragiren*" (Latin script) might
look like it had been taken over from the English word "to forage," but it is certainly derived from
the French "*fourrager*," which was used in Germany at the time. True, he uses "*Yankee*," but in a
pejorative sense, and there is nothing like a German equivalent. And when there is an equivalent
and he still uses the English term, for example, when he writes about "*bounties*," he hastens to

story of Carl Schurz.* Gerstein was born in Westphalia in 1828 and grew up in a
well-to-do family. His mother died in 1841, which threw him off course, but despite
moving and changing schools three times, he would have received his secondary
school diploma and gone on to university "if the 1848 revolution hadn't broken out
the following year."[1]

Gerstein's revolutionary activities seem, in retrospect, more adventurous than
subversive. He was expelled from school because of a petition against compulsory
prayers, and he then set off with the volunteer corps to Schleswig-Holstein. When
he arrived, however, the fighting had already abated. Back in Dortmund, he was arrested during a street riot on December 3, 1848, and detained while awaiting his trial
for eight months. Finally acquitted (he was more a spectator than a participant),
he was denied the right to take his final exams due to his republican leanings, and
this severely reduced his chances of ever having any kind of career. Like many other
wayward sons, he turned to America.[2]

With 250 talers* he emigrated in 1850, bought forty acres of land, and tried to
hew a farm in the forests of Michigan, where the Indians who still lived nearby
occasionally came visiting. In June 1853 he entered into an unequal and occasionally stormy marriage with Karolina Huß, the daughter of an artisan. By 1860 he
had cleared fifteen acres, and from this and some other jobs on the side, he barely
managed to feed his family. Nevertheless, he regarded newspapers as a necessity,
not a luxury, and he remained very well informed about politics in America and
Germany.[3]

Hinterwald [backwoods], September 10, 1856

Dear sister,

[242 ll.: death of his eldest daughter; economic problems on the farm;
statement to the effect that he had received a total of 2,100 talers* from Ger-
many] I'd like to know where you get your ideas about our life and our party
system, at any rate some things you know nothing about, and you are partly
wrong about others, so hear the words of your wise little brother who will en-
lighten you.

---

provide a rare, five-syllable German term: *"Vergütungsgelder."* Not included here are the letters
in the series from the time before 1860 (nine) and after 1865 (thirty-eight), as well as the letters
of January 1861, March 4, 1863, and February 10, 1864.

1. Gerstein (1934), 53, 163–72, based primarily on letters written by Dietrich Gerstein to his
nephew, the author. For more details see Helbich (2002).

2. Gerstein (1934), 53, 163–72.

3. MC 1860: Tuscola Co./Mich., Denmark Twp., #203; as well as MCA 1860. His farm was
listed as worth $400.

Dietrich Gerstein and wife Karolina née Huß. (Klaus Gerstein)

Many people are trying to bring about the fall of the Union, or rather its separation into a South and a North, and these people are in the party with the better principles, since they realize that the South will not abolish slavery and even wants to exert all its influence to have slavery introduced in [other] territories, and free labor and slavery just don't go together. The better elements of the nation belong to this newly established party of black Republicans, who have, however, recently been joined by the Know-Nothings (who admittedly are in favor of extending the length of time that immigrants have to wait before they can become citizens), since the Know-Nothings had no other chance of winning. The other party consists of the slaveholders, the Irish (Catholics), the bulk of the German riffraff, certainly all the Catholics, and everyone who is entangled in the Bible and believes the Negroes are the descendants of Ham—who as is well known behaved a bit inelegantly toward his father—and therefore must atone for the impropriety of their ancestor by being American slaves. My dear neighbors, the <u>Old Lutherans</u> (the mere word is a disgrace) also belong to this glorious party, but I do not reproach them for anything more than incredible stupidity, for they know not what they do, so forgive them, O Divine Being. A rational German is in a difficult position, beset on the one hand by slavery and its corruption of everything, all morality, the shameless impudence of Christian preachers, etc. and, on the other hand, by the <u>probable</u> infringement of immigrant rights [17 ll.: more on politics; greetings; signature; correspondence]. My address Blumfield / Saginaw County / Michigan / United States of America

February 15, 1860

Dear brother,

[526 ll.: farm life; financial problems; "Latin farmers"*; his marriage; visit from Indians] Old [John] Brown has been hanged, as you probably know. The 350,000 slaveholders are in triumph at their victory over an old man and his 20 followers and the fact that their divine institution continues to exist. Indeed, the fear felt by the slavery men about this business reveals only too clearly how wretched slavery actually is. This is having dire consequences, things are in ferment, and the squires in the South are so frightened that they keep coming up with one stupid idea after the next. Now they are driving out all the people from the South who are suspected of being Republicans.[4] And what will the North have to say about this? Pay them back in the same coin? Well, then there will be civil war, the horizon will darken, there will be terrible thunder, and where will it all end? It is very likely that the Union will be split, but what kind of government will the South have then? The South cannot survive on its own, and I am convinced it would rather become part of Russia than free its slaves. The North, on the other hand, can stand on its own and will survive, since the overwhelming majority of its inhabitants are Republicans.[5] Of course then it would be necessary to drive out the northern Democrats and send them south, and then I would also be rid of my dear neighbors, the Old Lutherans. Isn't it curious to see all the pious people voting for slavery? Of course they prove from the Bible that slavery is a divine institution, but even the Catholics who want nothing to do with the Bible are wild for slavery, especially that dumbest and most beastly of all nations, the Irish.[6] Why do the Irish priests encourage people to emigrate to the United States? Well, the republic is a thorn in Rome's flesh, and if they send all the religious riffraff in the whole world over here, then when the next revolution comes, along with the slavery of the South, there will be a good chance of subjugating the North as well. The Pope with his cohorts is clever indeed, but he may well have miscalculated, for the Republicans are on the alert because they know what to expect from the spread of Catholicism [11 ll.: comparison with France]. Some two thousand newspapers, written free of restraint, keep the people informed about what has happened and what is to be hoped and feared in the near future. You can find newspapers even out to the edge of settle-

4. See Ruff (no. 48).

5. In the 1860 presidential election, two-thirds of the vote in Tuscola County, Michigan, went to Lincoln. Burnham (1955), 532.

6. Frankenmuth, a settlement founded in 1845 by conservative Franconian Old Lutherans, was located less than six miles away from Gerstein's farm. According to Catholic tradition at the time, only priests could instruct the laity in the Bible.

ment, and thus people who are politically well educated. Every man belongs to a party, has a well-founded opinion about our political situation and can explain his views as clearly as the top *Senatas* in Waschingston. Here again, I have to exclude the Catholics and the Old Lutherans, my neighbors. Those people don't read any papers, they let their preachers do their thinking for them. Thanks to the press and the most rational and liberal institutions in our counties and towns, the republican way of life has taken hold of the people, and no comparison you care to make with France, Rome or a Greek republic fits the United States [7 ll.: details]. Next fall there will be the largest election campaign we have ever had in the United States, I think blood will flow, and what happens after that—the future will tell. The Republicans will vote for Seward, that old soldier in the fight against slavery, that champion of right, light and freedom. The Democrats, on the other hand, are still looking for some hog thief whom they can elect for president [63 ll.: financial difficulties; German politics; hunting stories; signature missing].

Christmas, 1862

Dear Ludwig,

[105 ll.: details about sending package; birth of a daughter] What has been and is now my duty, dear Ludwig? To leave my family, put aside everything and join rank and file with a pack of riffraff that is truly, I am not exaggerating, the scum of humanity—or to do my duty as the father of my family and just watch this battle, a battle more momentous in its stakes than any fought before. For now I am still watching, because I think that a time will come when better men enter the fray, and the fact that justice and freedom are being defended at the moment by these other people is simply due to the good pay they receive and the lack of serious danger up until now. When one side gets serious, the other side runs away, that's the rule. In fact, the Europeans can see in this war what a high level of culture the Americans have attained— they hate spilling human blood so much, so they simply kill men who are only wounded or sick and helpless, since they would only be a burden to themselves and to others and on top of that would cost the government money. If that is not humane, I don't know what is. Soon the battle will become more serious: for when the 700,000 men have been turned into soldiers a bit more, the fun will be over[. . . .] I think it is high time to write a pamphlet on *Malheurika*.[7] The immediate effects of the war for us farmers, although they have not been ruinous up to now, are anything but gratifying [. . .] everything we have to

7. A play on words, well known to Germans at the time: a blend of "*Malheur*," the French word for bad luck or disaster widely used in nineteenth-century Germany, and "America."

sell is cheap, and everything we need to buy is expensive, especially cotton cloth. Supplies of wheat, corn etc. in the central states were and still remain so abundant that no one feels obliged to look for grain and meat in places like Michigan that are so far away from the battlefield. So we have to sell cheap, as usual, but on the other hand it is clear that due to the greater transport distance, we have to pay more and more for imported things than in the eastern and southern states. Cotton, coffee, tea, sugar, tobacco, spices etc. and even almost all our boots and shoes, everything comes from New-York, 1,000 miles away, but this part of the country doesn't send anything back but boards and barrel staves. We have, however, started to produce salt, and although not much of it is exported, our wood has become more valuable, since the salt works use an incredible amount of wood.

The only thing a sensible person can do in a situation like this is to only buy what is absolutely necessary and to make do with other things instead. This is why, for example, I haven't had any coffee for a long time now[. . . .] Corn comes closest to it, that's why at my house I always ask "wouldn't you like a cup of coffee or rather corn? Thanks a lot, but I'm drinking barley at the moment." We don't buy any sugar, and only occasionally tea, spices, salt and pepper [65 ll.: $105 gratefully received; neighbor Karl Post has given up his farm].

Father's views on the war aren't all that far off base, since the union of the North and the South is an unnatural one [14 ll.: both separation from the South and conquering it endanger the republic]. A third possibility would be to conquer the South and then gradually ease out slavery, since the sudden abolition of slavery would plunge these states into abject misery. At any rate it is a fact that most of the slaves are treated like beasts and, if let free, they would just behave like beasts. Since the slaves hardly ever see white men working, they think freedom is the same thing as idleness, and the time would come when I would rather be living with the Tartars or in Poland than here [61 ll.: children; Indians; deaths and suicides of German neighbors; greetings; signature].

[Begun] October [1], 1862

Dear brother,

[42 ll.: lost letters?; financial and health problems]

1 January 1863 [continued on same page]

[68 ll.: military draft; duties to nation and family] In connection with Lina and the Bible, it occurs to me that Lina wrote to me about slavery in a letter, saying that slavery is against the Bible and thus cannot be defended. I wish that

Lina could challenge the countless Christian clergy in the South to account for their actions, and she would find that these same clerics use the Bible to prove that slavery is a divine institution that the wicked hands of the Republican robbers and murderers want to do away with [5 ll.: details]. In truth, even though I learned as a child that God is extremely long-suffering, one could say that his patience has worn thin, and he has resorted to fire and brimstone to bring our southern brothers to reason.

But the South stays sunny like always, and while we have to make a terrible effort to bring in our harvest, the South harvests twice with ease, thanks to those people with wool on their heads. Enough of this, it is too disgusting, I just wanted to ask Lina to keep her Bible away from a rational man like me.

As far as our war goes, I have not yet lost all hope that we will beat the South, although the treachery and disgraceful profiteering on the northern side and the fanaticism of the women on the southern side seem to be giving victory to the South and then it's *adieu* to the republic. If this republic is actually lost, mankind's struggle for freedom will be pointless for years to come, since the moral defeat of the entire liberal party will be so severe that it will be unable to rise again any time soon. You can say what you like, but Christianity must fall before republics can endure: Christianity is the religion of the monarchs, and even if German writers in particular have proposed that Christianity can be compatible with freedom, making explicit reference to these dis-United States, this is nothing but a big mistake. The four to five hundred Christian sects who would like to devour each other have to preach freedom and tolerance for this very same reason[. . . .] Even the Catholics, who are certainly the least tolerant of the sectarians, drivel on about freedom and tolerance, although here in the North they are all Democrats and generally take sides with the South on the slavery question[. . . .] Our southern so-called Democrats only want and cannot want anything but a despotic aristocratic oligarchy, and our northern Democrats would prefer them to win rather than the increasingly dominant radicals. The Catholic religion has always been in its core the Christian sect that is the most dangerous to freedom, and it is totally impossible to be a good Catholic and a good republican at the same time [107 ll.: war taxes; financial matters; greetings; signature].

August 1, 1863

Dear brother,

Thirst, my dear Ludwig, thirst is the only thing a sensible man can have in this terrible heat [6 ll.: details]. What is the nature of this thirst that drives the masses to do great things? Is it thirst for fame and honor, thirst to make justice prevail, thirst for collecting riches, or thirst for wine, or even, disgusting to mention, thirst for beer and liquor? Let us begin with the last point and say that quenching one's thirst with beer and cheap spirits is the main reason why the crude masses storm into battle, and then we've hit the nail on the head. I'll throw our officers into a better category, since they don't want to quench their thirst with beer and liquor but with champagne[. . . .]

Sad, how sad, that the means to reach a noble end are often so ignoble [6 ll.: details]. This rebellion must be defeated, even if it costs the life of the last white man in the South, and the sunny South is settled with free colored people. What will happen to our great armies after they have defeated or destroyed the rebellion, I'm not so sure. I think they'll be sent to Mexico to expel the French [Maximilian*], and then there will be hundreds of thousands of *soi-disant* [so-called] men fewer, and the air will be that much fresher. Once our slaveholders have been destroyed, the colored people freed, and about a million of our northern scum have been slaughtered, then I hope rational men will be able to live in this country and things will improve. Dear brother: a riot in Detroit, the absolutely abominable barbarity of the mobs in New-York [draft riots*] must have opened your eyes a bit as to the true nature of the northern Democrats, supporters of the South[. . . .] I assure you, Rome and its black hangmen has its hand in the game, and its purpose is to destroy the republic at any price and [establish] an absolute monarchy. Physical and spiritual slavery—don't they go together nicely—and how clearly evident it is at every turn what the Roman priests are trying to achieve. Recently, the editor of a Roman Catholic church newspaper was arrested because he directly called for the murder of A. Lincoln[. . . .] You may not yet know that all our church newspapers that follow the orthodox position here defend slavery, not just our *Alt-Lutheraner*, a paper published in the nineteenth century in America, the freest of republics, and which Luther, in his time, would have spit at.[8] Therefore, and you can count on this, you really can't compare our government with that of Nero. Now and then drastic measures have to be introduced, and they can easily be described by foreign papers as despotic, but in fact they aren't, since up to now, in all of history, there has never been a government which has shown greater tolerance and indulgence of the most insolent attacks on its authority than Abraham Lincoln's. In truth, when I ponder the whole thing, I am almost ready to believe in the so-called Providence of history, because if this man, whom circumstances have assigned the most diffi-

---

8. The correct title was *"Der Lutheraner,"* published by the conservative Missouri Synod, which insisted that slavery was compatible with the Bible. Gerstein ignores, however, the close connections between other Protestant groups and the antislavery movement. Schafer (1971), 56–57; McPherson (1988), 8, 88–91.

cult post in the world, should actually make a mistake, then take into account that in view of the given circumstances, in a country so torn apart by so many parties, only a God could conclude his term of office without being accused of having made a grievous error by the judgment of history. Just compare our administration with J. Davis's wretched despotism. Is there freedom of the press in the South? Not as much as in Russia. Is there freedom of speech in the South? On the gallows, if you dare to be a unionist.[9] So come to the North and see the impudence with which the Democratic newspapers support the South, how here in the North, despite the Emancipation Proclamation, Democrats assert the legality of slavery, how they say all the Negroes should be killed, etc., and you would surely change your views [10 ll.: details]. I would be sorry, Ludwig, if you were to cling to your opinion with the obstinacy typical of the Gerstein family [35 ll.: military service; farming]. Almost all the single men who work full-time for other people are gone, and the married farmers either don't work for wages or ask for wages that no one can possibly pay [5 ll.: details]. For laborers here, in fact, times have never been better than they are now, even though they have to pay dearly for things, our merchants are getting rich, our suppliers and the speculators even richer, our officers are making money like hay, and our common soldiers are <u>boozing and carousing with the womenfolk</u>, as a Swiss fellow told me who was discharged because of a wound. All in all, the North is increasing in wealth, despite the fact that we are running up debts of about 1,000 million dollars a year. Now the question is whether we will suffer later on under the burden of this debt like England did, for example. I don't think so, since we are so rich in land[. . . .] The population in England can hardly grow, and hence their debt must always be shouldered by the same number of people, whereas we can certainly count on the fact that once we have defeated the Rebels, which is now beyond doubt unless there is foreign interference, our population may have reached about 100 million people by 1900.[10] And so the pressure of our debt burden per person will become lighter every year. Then look at the countless numbers of the poor in England, whereas we have no poor people, or at least none that have to be fed by the government [20 ll.: thanks for money; family and friends in Germany]. I am indeed surprised that none of my previous friends and acquaintances have been dispersed to America. Have they all really turned out that well? Strange: only one black sheep in the family and it had to be me [70 ll.:

9. Even before the war, freedom of speech and the press were denied to opponents of slavery. Eaton (1966), 249–56. On the fate of a number of Union supporters in the South see Cramer and Simon (no. 55).

10. Not until the decade 1910–20 did the population of the United States reach 100 million.

family; child labor among German settlers; financial matters. Early November: family; harvest]. The draft is over and it hit one man in Richville. We paid his commutation fee, which cost me 10 dollars. Of the 300,000 men who have been called up for January we have to provide four from our sparsely populated township,[11] and in order to pay the fees for these people we are having a war rally on December 5th. It's always pay, pay, and I can't get out of it because if I did and got called up myself, no one would do anything for my family.

[9 ll.: "this never-ending money business"] All the best to you and yours from your brother Ditz.

> Camp East Saginaw, September 28th, 1864
> Balance thine account with heaven
> Thy sand is run![12]

Dear brother,

From the above you can see where I am and in what guise[. . . .] What made me take this calamitous step was conscription. It was possible that I might not be called up this time, but since it was highly unlikely that I would be spared this bitter cup, I decided it was better to volunteer, so I could at least make a bit of money. Oh, what a role money plays in this life after all!

Our regiment is not full yet, but I doubt we will be here for another week. Then it's off to Detroit for 2–3 weeks, after that we will probably be broken in and trained enough to do our tricks in the sunny South.

Our company, Tuscola Co. Volunteers, is full, and more than 80 out of the hundred men are married, hunters and backwoodsmen, by and large. Nice cannon fodder indeed, men aged 25–45. We also have some old men and boys in the company, not surprising given the circumstances caused by this disastrous war.

We have recently had considerable success in the field, and in my opinion when the 500,000 men we have now do their duty reasonably well, the South will be crushed. But there are still a number of ifs and buts, and we didn't enlist for three years for nothing.

Yes, Ludwig, I assure you it is very hard to leave behind everything you cherish for a second time and to set out toward a destiny completely unknown. But, when this business is over, I will have my peace, and perhaps I'll find it even earlier [10 ll.: family; address; greetings; signature].

---

11. In 1860 Denmark Township had a population of only 309. USC 1860.1, 265.
12. From Friedrich Schiller's *William Tell*, Act IV, Scene 3.

Cowen, April 28th, 1865, Cumberland Mountains

Dear Ludwig,

[10 ll.: correspondence] As you can see from the heading, I'm still in the same place and am leading a truly ghastly lazy life because there is only one thing I have to do, every two hours from 12 noon to midnight: tell a soldier to relieve the guard. There are virtually no formalities and the whole changing of the guard business is carried out with true Christian republican simplicity, a simplicity which actually shouldn't be tolerated from a military standpoint, in the midst of an agitated enemy population, although I like it myself, since there's nothing I hate more than silly Prussian drills. We have defeated the South, it doesn't matter how, and that's what counts, since now we will be free of slavery, an evil which before long would have corrupted men and circumstances to such an extent that it would have been out of the question to maintain our republican constitution [5 ll.: details]. This southern cotton aristocracy, however, is the worst the world has ever seen, but stamping out slavery will deal it a fatal blow, even if the aristocracy tries with all its devious schemes to win back in peace what was taken from it by the sword. But I don't want to go on and on with arguments about slavery and aristocracy in this country, but tell you instead the simple tale of battle and hardship that you seem to want to hear [9 ll.: too much hubbub to be able to write].

We left Saginaw, as I think I mentioned in my last letter, on October 6th and traveled via Indianopolis to Nashville, where we had about 10 days of horrendously strenuous guard duty. Around this time, the commanding general of the Cumberland Army, Sherman, started his march from Atlanta in Georgia to South Carolina, and General Hood, the commander of the southern army in this area, instead of following Sherman, turned towards Decatar [Decatur] in Alabama in order to invade Tenessee from there[. . . .] This would have forced Sherman to turn back from his march which was so destructive for the South. One fine evening, on about October the 20th, we were loaded back on the train and went south to an insignificant place named Stevenson, where the railroad coming from Nashville meets the major railroad line running from the Mississippi to Richmond. This is when a misunderstanding occurred that almost ended in catastrophe for us. The *Conducteur* on the train, a traitor, sent us east toward Chattanooga instead of west to Decatar in Alabama, a misunderstanding that could have cost many men their lives, if there hadn't been a sensible man on the train, and this sensible person was me. In Nashville, I had bought a good map of the southern states and despite the fact that I was armed with this, I still had to work hard to convince that lummox of a captain, a real *Yankee*, that we were going the wrong way.[13] Finally he caught on, and then he went to the colonel. Then we turned around immediately and arrived about 9 o'clock in the morning in Decatar, and then marched across the pontoon bridge over the Tennessee and right into cannon fire to defend a small *Fort* that was engaged in a fierce gun battle with the enemy. Tired, or rather sleepy, hungry and thirsty we lay there in a small trench, expecting to be overrun by forces 50 times stronger than we were, while cannon balls, shells, and musket balls struck up a song above our heads that I shall never forget [7 ll.: details]. The arrival of our regiment at just the right time, all the prisoners said, prevented this place which was very important at the time, from being captured,[14] together with the 700 men and their very important provisions. When you consider the incredible ignorance of our *Yankee* officers, it is hardly surprising that such misunderstandings occur, like when we went west instead of east, and the *Condukteur* justified his actions by claiming that he believed we were supposed to go to the Decatar near Atlanta in Georgia. In short, our arrival saved the day, and after that reinforcements arrived day and night, and so we were able to beat off Hood's attacks[. . . .] We stayed in this Decatar for about a month, and I assure you it was one of the worst months of my existence, we suffered so miserably. After that, one fine evening we were loaded onto the train and rushed to Murfreesboro, a fort 30 miles from Nashville, since it seemed that Hood was going to send a detachment of his army to take this fort. We didn't have to lie in wait for long, and Forest [Forrest*] drove a wedge between Nashville and Murfreesboro, thereby cutting off our food supplies, destroying bridges and railroads and laying siege to us very effectively. You see we weren't well supplied with food, and the ¼ ration of cornmeal that we got we had to forage ourselves, which usually meant fighting. I can't remember having ever been so hungry as in that hole [34 ll.: a narrow escape]. This constant fighting and starving went on for about 4 weeks, and if the battle of Nashville hadn't gone so well for us, we would have had to make our way north or else surrender. At Murfreesboro we only had one day of heavy fighting, where we thrashed

13. Probably Alson Greenfield, a New York native from Vassar, Michigan, Gerstein's superior officer. *Record of Service of Michigan Volunteers* (1905), 29:1. In a letter from around 1908, Gerstein repeats the entire story and adds, "The fact that the officers in our regiment tried to cover up the whole thing is hardly surprising, given the *Yankees'* deep-seated hatred of the Germans, and that is why I never got any recognition, since it would have been impossible to admit that the damned German had shown the regiment the right way[. . . .] If a battle was won, the *Yankees* did it, and if a battle was lost, it was the Germans' fault." Gerstein was one of four Germans in his company. Regt. Books, 29 Mich. Inf, Desc. Books, NatA.

14. The 29 Mich. Inf met its first test against an enemy three times its size "with the coolness of veterans." *Record of Service of Michigan Volunteers* (1905), 29:1.

Mr. Forrest soundly, who didn't bother us any more[. . . .] Christmas Eve we were loaded back onto the train, and after a short stop in Anderson, a small place on the Alabama border, we were stationed in small units along the railroad, and I am in Cowan, a small town on the northern side of a spur of the Cumberland Mountains. The war is over, and my estimates turned out to be more accurate than the ones in your rebel newspapers, and we are all longing to get back to work in our own family circles [7 ll.: considering a trip to Germany].

I must stop writing, dear Lutz, since the rats, as big as little pigs, keep running around my legs and I find this most annoying. / All the best to your wife, brothers and sisters, father, etc. / Farewell. Your faithful brother Ditz.

Sunday, December 16th, 1865
Home, sweet home!

Dear brother,

[6 ll.: correspondence] The fact that I managed to get back home again and even in good health doesn't mean that I am any less unhappy, for all of my expectations have been dashed. At least the war has ended well, but I don't like the current political situation; I had hoped my wife would be a bit more reasonable, but she is more of a battle-axe than ever; I had hoped to have made good progress with my financial situation, but this too has come to naught [7 ll.: doomed to misfortune]. I had hoped for 300 dollars more than I got, and then I thought I would come to visit you, but up to now we haven't received the money, although we may get it sometime next year [6 ll.: cannot visit Germany]. I am really sick of life here in primitive, frozen Michigan, and I assure you this country isn't good enough to make me forget about Germany; I'd like to move south, but up to now the situation has been too dangerous to move with a wife and children, for you can't imagine the hatred the southern white population feels against us[. . . .] The best thing for new immigrants would be to move to the South, because there it is really easy to make a good living.

Oh, what a tedious, boring, monotonous life we have here in our woods, nothing but hard work and no rest, no pleasure. Work, eat, drink, sleep, that's the story of the people who live here, indeed, you can't really call this life fit for humans [31 ll.: marital problems and overexertion]. I am now as full of disgust, loathing and contempt as the scorpions in the South are of poison, and if I knew of any place where better people lived than here, I would set off immediately, that's for sure. In Germany, the people are really dreadful trash, but you don't ever really get to know them, since they are kept in their place by force [8 ll.: details]. All truly human, rational freedom is absurd on this earth, as long as ignorance and greed are the driving forces behind the masses. This republic has managed this time, with the most enormous sacrifice, to escape the ruin brought upon it by ignorance and greed, but will it succeed again the next time, or do you think this edifice stands eternal? [18 ll.: problems and worries; asks them to bear with him; greetings; signature].

                                                      mid March, 1866

Dear Ludwig,

[131 ll.: balance of monetary account; considering moving] As things stand we now have yet another civil war, and it's a civil war in the true sense of the word, and it will be difficult for the republic to withstand this storm [30 ll.: "our politicians' thirst for power"].

So the King of Prussia has again deigned to send the representatives home, he certainly has the power to do so and thus the right as well.[15] On the one hand, this parliament business of yours is absolutely ridiculous, on the other hand, very serious and saddening. The fact that one person can keep spitting in the face of 20 million fellow men, without fear of reprisal, is indeed ridiculous, and the fact that these 20 million keep patiently putting up with this insult is very sad. It seems that freedom is making great progress everywhere [11 ll.: correspondence]. When Carl XII, after the first engagement he encountered, said that the whistling of the bullets was the sweetest music he had ever heard, then I don't share his opinion[16] [. . .] and every time a cannonball flew right over my head, I automatically made a bow, a strange weakness came over me every time[. . . .] The only advantage I have had from my life as a soldier is that my health has improved. I used to suffer so badly from rheumatism that in recent years I was in bed for four weeks every spring, bent double and crying out with pain. In the South it was root, hog, or die, and for a few months I had unusual strange pains, and then my rheumatism vanished, so to speak, and I am glad of that [15 ll.: brother-in-law's suicide; greetings; signature].

                                                   Early January, 1867

[salutation missing]

[140 ll.: correspondence; financial dispute] Since in your letter you don't know how and what to insult me about, you also reproach me for having gone to the South, and I want to justify my actions. In the first two years of our war, the government made do with volunteers, and when no one was willing to be

15. As a result of a continuing fight with the crown about power over the military budget, the Prussian parliament was dissolved early, on February 22, 1866. Pflanze (1990), 318–28.

16. Charles XII, king of Sweden from 1697 to 1718 and leader of its military forces in the Nordic War of 1700–1721.

killed of his own free will anymore, they introduced the draft, but any man who was drafted could buy himself a substitute or he could pay $300 and then he was free as well. So the government got money, but not many men, and the ones that it got were the riffraff who couldn't raise the $300. So the government changed the draft law, and that was in early 1864, and then each *Township*, depending on the number of able-bodied men, had to provide a certain number of men by a particular date, otherwise they were drafted, and they had to go unless they found substitutes, which was always permitted, or else flee to Canada, California, England, etc. Some 200,000 deserted to Canada alone. So then came the July 1864 call for 500,000 men, and our *Town* had to provide 7 men, but we only had 20 men in our *Township* who could bear arms, and the situation was dire. All sorts of *bounties* were promised to those who volunteered to help fill our *quota*. What could we do? If we didn't come up with our 7 men, they were going to draw lots, and those men not only wouldn't receive a bounty, but there would be no monthly wage for their wives and children, nor would their widows get a pension if they died in battle. All things considered, with my bones full of gout, along with this horrible shrew breathing down my neck, plus the prospects of being drafted, I decided to go, since this would mean I was providing for my family, whereas if I didn't go, I ran the risk of being drafted, in which case I would have left my family in penury. Does this justify my having left my family to go to the South, or should I have done what one of my brothers-in-law did? He ran off to California and made money there while his wife and child moved in with my wife, meaning that I as an honest soldier was feeding two families, while the deserter only had to provide for himself [12 ll.: his military service was easier than his life as a civilian]. Our *Townships* have fulfilled their obligations to us, the bounties were paid, and the women received their pay every month, depending on the number of children they had, my wife received $9 a month, but our state Michigan, as well as the government of the United States, have not fulfilled their obligations, which means that we received $300 less than we were promised, and the loss of this amount has annoyed me.

As far as my rheumatism goes, I seem to be rid of it [. . .] but first I must explain to the subservient vassal of limited intelligence that you can't get rid of gout on a march from Westphalia to Hesse, but you might if you marched from Westphalia to Algiers[17] [6 ll.: details].

In your letter you also keep harping on the fact that I subscribe to several newspapers, whereas you only permit yourself to share one newspaper with two others, and you call out—man cannot live on politics alone! I must say,

17. The former was a distance of about 100 miles, the latter at least 1,000 as the crow flies.

I never thought it possible that a man in your position could know so little about the nature of this republic.[18] It is my goddamned sacred duty and obligation to take several papers, for if I don't, I don't know what is happening in this country, what kind of feeling will I have when I approach the ballot box and cast my vote? Or should I relinquish my most sacred right as a citizen and not vote? If every man who belongs to the working classes, and here there are also more of these men than there are wealthy men, were to abstain from politics or not want to vote, we'd have an oligarchy overnight and then monarchy, and I have an overpowering aversion to monarchy[. . . .] There are certainly many things here that I object to, but they are not the fault of our constitution, rather they are due to the fact that too many subservient vassals of limited intelligence come over here [. . .] and the most tasteless behavior committed in the name of equality is the product of a false interpretation of freedom, and that's why even Heine was somewhat horrified by this country, which he liked to refer to as an enormous pigsty of freedom, filled with impudent louts drunk on equality, and right he was, indeed.[19] The dough in this country still needs a tremendous amount of kneading before it can make a decent pastry, that's for sure [32 ll.: "would-be novelists" working as journalists; financial dispute; end missing].

Richville, December 15, 1869

Dear brother,

[85 ll.: explains his long silence; suicide of a friend; emigration plans of two younger relatives] For whom it is good to emigrate and for whom it is not, that is the question. It is certainly clear that the truly well educated must necessarily feel miserable here, for what fields of activity are open to them? High officials? Those people are nothing but money-grubbers, and what lengths they have to go to in order to attain such a post. *He is running for an office, er läuft für ein Amt.* Doesn't the phrase running for an office say it all? If you look at the incredible fraud in all branches of our administration you can see what kind of people most of our civil servants are.

So, assuming that the well-educated man has money and wants to speculate with it—*O weh*, our Polish Jews could learn a lot from the Americans[. . . .] So what else is there? Working as a craftsman won't do, since he knows no craft. Day laborer? Strange taste!—Newspaper editor? That might work, and you can even earn a living at it, but first you have to sell your soul to the devil. A preacher, perhaps—yes, that might work, but then I am reminded of a speech

18. His brother had been a judge in the district court since 1858.
19. A reference to Heinrich Heine, "Jetzt wohin?" (ca. 1845); Briegleb (1975), 6(1):101–2.

by Carl Heinzen[20] who said if anyone is too stupid and too incompetent for any other employment, he must don the cloth[. . . .] So there's nothing left but to become a farmer, for then you don't have to waste your talents, degrade yourself, you don't have to make a pact with Satan [. . .] but out of a thousand cases, 999 of the well educated will end up being poor, poor devils, no matter what. And one more thing—when we came back from the South, having made free men of the Negroes, there was a saying among the farmers—yes, now we've freed the Negroes, and we're going back to be our own Negroes [284 ll.: differences between Germans and Americans; farming problems; financial dispute with German relatives; greetings; signature].

The following decades saw little change in the dilemma of the well-educated German in America. Gerstein never made more than a modest living from farming.[21] His strained relationship with his wife and children hardly improved over time. The only people he felt he could talk to as intellectual equals were his relatives in Germany.[22] Political differences, continuing financial disputes, and long stretches of affronted silence did nothing to change this. Even after the death of his brother Ludwig in 1894, Gerstein continued to pour out his heart (and vent his spleen) in long letters to other relatives.

Gerstein also remained true to his political convictions his whole life long. As late as 1908 he wrote, "I only regret that it will still take some time until Germany becomes a republic." In America he remained a staunch republican, and even in his last letter his attitudes toward religion had hardly softened: "let me tell you, it is high time for a different kind of religion, one based on science and reason." Dietrich Gerstein died on December 16, 1916, at the age of eighty-eight. He summed up his own life as follows: "I have cleared some 200 acres of land for cultivation, a decent piece of work. I support myself and my large family [nine children survived] from the land I carved out of the wilderness with great effort, and I can say: I have not lived in vain, and the results of my labor can never be erased."[23]

20. Journalist and Forty-eighter Karl Peter Heinzen, born in Grevenbroich in 1809 and died in Boston in 1880, was a German American radical who called for a democracy that was anticlerical and antiauthoritarian as well as technically and socially progressive. Wittke (1945).

21. According to the 1870 census Gerstein had cleared his entire farm of forty acres, but in 1878 he sold it and bought another of the same size. In 1880 it was only partially cleared and had an estimated value of $2,000—the same amount his first farm had been worth ten years earlier. MC 1870: Tuscola Co./Mich., Denmark Twp., #119; MCA 1870, 1880.

22. His daughter Sophie said the same in a letter to German relatives of June 8, 1894, NABS.

23. Undated letters, ca. 1908 and 1915, to Ludwig Gerstein, NABS; MC 1880: Tuscola Co./Mich., e.d. 399, #220; Gerstein (1934), 53, 172.

35. Corporal Ludwig Wilhelm Kühner and Private Karl Friedrich Kühner

By the time that sixteen-year-old Ludwig Kühner and his twenty-three-year-old brother Karl Friedrich left Baden in 1851 for the United States, emigration from the area had already become a mass phenomenon. But unlike so many of their countrymen, the Kühners did not leave to escape a life of poverty. Their father had been the mayor of Unterschefflenz, a village of 867 souls. After the deaths of their parents in 1848 and 1849, however, there were not many ties remaining to the Old Country. In addition, Karl Friedrich left behind a child born out of wedlock, and he either paid to be released from military service in Baden or simply deserted.[1]

Karl Kühner may have fled from responsibility but not into uncertainty. The Kühners' ultimate destination, a village named Thompson in northern Ohio, already boasted a small number of settlers from Schefflenz and nearby villages, including one family named Kühner. As a sister-in-law wrote in 1885, "where brother-in-law Ludwig lives, there are nothing but Germans for 3 or 4 miles and a schoolhouse where things are lively and just like at home."[2]

By 1860 both brothers had married and started families. Ludwig became a farmer, and Karl Friedrich combined his work as a cabinetmaker with farming. The settlements in which they lived, Thompson, Madison, and Trumbull, Ohio, were only a couple of miles apart.[3] Except for this small island of German settlers, how-

SOURCE NOTE: The handwriting of the two Kühner brothers is remarkably similar, very regular and slanted to the right, with Karl's being more slanted than Ludwig's. Their schoolmaster would have liked their handwriting, but he would have found their German far from perfect. Ludwig's first letter is basically a phonetic rendering of his local Alemannic dialect, and while this recedes in time, it is replaced by an increasing number of German Americanisms. Karl Friedrich's letters, by contrast, show increasing interference from English. Not included here are the letters in the series from the time before 1860 (five) and after 1865 (two).

1. *Beiträge zur Statistik* (1855), 1:187–88; *Beiträge zur Statistik* (1857), 5:28–29; KB (ev.) Unterschefflenz, which also provides the information about their emigration. The unmarried miller's daughter Karolina Frei gave birth to a child on February 10, 1849; no father was named, but the child was christened Karl Friedrich August. On March 14, 1851, Karl F. Kühner wrote to his brother from the Badenese garrison in Rastatt: "I'd rather have a bullet through my head than that woman as a wife," and "if it is not the case that I can make my fortune in Baden then America is not too far away for me. I'd rather die than stay here for two more years of military service." After his religious conversion (see note 4), Karl sent word via his brother in a letter (October 26, 1856, NABS) to the woman, now married, that he was now "determined to pay to have the child sent over to him so he could take on the role of his father"; however, this did not happen.

2. Emigration information in KB (ev.) Unterschefflenz; letter of Christina Kühner, Domson [Thompson, Ohio], January 25, 1885, NABS. A man named Georg Kühner emigrated with a large group of people from Schefflenz in 1847, and in 1870 he was Ludwig Kühner's closest neighbor.

3. In the mid-1850s the brothers moved from Albany, New York, to Ohio. Charles was listed in MC 1860: Lake Co./Ohio, Madison Twp., #421, as a cabinetmaker owning $1,500 worth of real estate, probably a farm; in MC 1880: Ashtabula Co./Ohio, Trumbell Twp., #227, he is only

ever, this area was dominated—as was all of northeastern Ohio—by New England-
ers and their descendants, making it a stronghold of abolitionists and Republicans.
The Kühners were obviously well integrated in their Yankee environment: before
the war, Ludwig had already changed his name to Louis Keener. He was married by
a pastor named Collins, probably a Baptist who had also rebaptized Karl Friedrich.
Considering their social environment, it is not surprising that both brothers enlisted
in Anglo American units before the end of 1861.[4]

LUDWIG KÜHNER

Thompson, December 22, 1861

Dear brother,

[. . .] You have already heard, I'm sure, that we are involved in a war. Our
area has not yet suffered much because the war is being fought in the slave
states that are far away. Most of the young men and the men who are unmarried have signed up as volunteers to defend our liberty. My brother Karl
Friedrich, three of my wife's brothers, and I have also signed up, we weren't
drafted, nor were we tempted by money or the excitement. It is hard to leave
your wife and children behind and march into battle, but there's nothing else
we can do if we want to preserve freedom for ourselves and our children. I'm
in the artillery and will be mustered in on December 27th, brother Karl Friedrich is in the cavalry and was mustered in two weeks ago.[5] My brothers-in-law
are in the infantry. Our government now has six times one hundred and fifty
thousand volunteer soldiers. We're committed for three years or until the war
is over. The reason for this war is slavery. America has 32 states, 19 free states
and 13 slave states. The slave states always got the majority in the presidential elections because many of the free states voted for them, but a year ago
back in the last election, the free states got their president. Then the 9 sepa-

---

listed as a farmer. MC 1870: Geauga Co./Ohio, #158, lists Ludwig as a farmer worth $3,900, but
according to the letter of December 22, 1861 (NABS), he also worked as a cooper. When the
brothers joined the army, both listed their occupation as "farmer." Muster Rolls, NatA.

4. Only 2 percent of the population of Geauga Co. was German; 80 percent voted for Lincoln. USC 1870.1 318, 368; Burnham (1955), 684. According to the Pension File, NatA, Ludwig
got married on November 11, 1854, to Ohio-born Caroline L. Baur. In Ludwig's letter of October 26, 1856 (NABS), he writes that Karl Friedrich "had himself baptized together with his wife
and joined our congregation," which seems to indicate they both had become Baptists.

5. Louis W. Keener enlisted in the 15 Ind. Baty, Ohio LArt on November 3, 1861, and
Charles F. Keener joined Comp L, 6 Ohio Cav, on October 16, 1861. They were the only soldiers with German names in their respective units. *Official Roster of the Soldiers of the State of Ohio*
(1886–95), 10:565–69, 11:357–61.

rated from the Union States and took up arms against the government, raided the arsenals and took over the forts in their states, elected a president and named themselves the southern independent Confederacy, and they sent representatives to other countries to convince them that they should help them and recognize their independence, but up to now they haven't accomplished anything. People are afraid that England might help them, and then the war would go on for a long time, but if they don't get any help, then the war will be over in six months or a year and slavery will be abolished. Freedom and slavery can't exist side by side, one of the two will be abolished.[6] I hope that right prevails. As far as the farm goes, everything is fine. A lot of the potatoes rotted this fall, my wife and children will be living with my in-laws as long as I'm in the army. My brother-in-law Kristian will feed my livestock this winter and plant my fields next year if I'm still away [24 ll.: cooper trade; drilling for oil; family; greetings, signature].

Thompson, February 24 / 1865

Dear brother,

[. . .] Dear brothers and sisters, with a heart that is grateful to God I want to let you know that after three long years of war I have returned home safe and sound[. . . .] I think I have done my duty and will be staying home now.[7] I think the war will be over soon, we beat the South in every battle last year and have taken many cities away from them, they have all the white men they have in the field, and now they want make their slaves into soldiers,[8] but the slaves know well enough that the North is their friend and defect to us. We have a lot of black soldiers who used to be slaves, they make good soldiers. Last year I was with General Scherman [Sherman] in the state of Georgia, brother Karl Friedrich is also home again, he has also served his time [11 ll.: parents-in-law; farming]. You've probably heard the presidential election went well last fall, the old one has been elected for another 4 years, which was a hard blow for the rebels, they wanted Meklellen [McClellan] to be elected. Three men from the South came up recently to see if they could make peace, our *Präsitänd* said if they lay down their arms and surrender they can have peace, and

6. This statement is highly reminiscent of Lincoln's 1858 "house divided" speech, where he claimed, "this government cannot endure, permanently half slave and half free." McPherson (1988), 179.

7. Ludwig was mustered out at the end of his three years of service on November 10, 1864. Muster Rolls, NatA.

8. In February 1865 Confederate president Jefferson Davis spoke out in favor of enlisting slaves, and on February 18 General Robert E. Lee agreed, but it was not put into practice before the end of the war. McPherson (1988), 834–37.

also slavery will no longer be tolerated, it must stop.[9] The *Präsitänd* and the people are determined to fight until they give up, the North doesn't want to conquer the South, just bring it back into the Union and under the government in Waschington.

I'd really like to spend some time with you. I'd be able to tell you a lot, but I wouldn't like to live in Germany again [13 ll.: economic prospects; greetings, signature].

Thompson, November 4th, 1867

Dear brother,

[38 ll.: correspondence; building a house; family; religious exhortations] Peace has been restored fairly well in terms of politics, the southern states still don't have any representatives in Congress in Waschington for now, they're still under military rule. The Congress has set them conditions, and when they accept them their representatives will be admitted, and they'll have all their civil rights again. One of the conditions is that they accept their former slaves as citizens and grant them full rights, you can see the Lord's hand in this past war [37 ll.: friends; money matters]. I am happy the war in Germany has turned out so well and that it is now almost united. I hope that Baden Wirtenberg [Württemberg] and Bavaria will also join Prussia, they've learned a lot from America in terms of law-making. Otherwise, I don't know what else to write about, I will close this letter with many greetings, all the best from your loving brother / Ludwig W. Kühner / all the best from my wife / to you all [. . .]

KARL FRIEDRICH KÜHNER

Trumbel, October 22, 1870

Dear brother Gottlieb,

[30 ll.: correspondence; farming; Franco-Prussian War] All the Germans in America who love Germany feel like I do about the homeland we left. My thoughts are with you day and night[. . . .] If I didn't have a family here, I would have joined the glorious German army a long time ago, without money and for no pay. If it were not any farther away than Neujork, I would have long since joined a cavalry regiment, with or without a family[. . . .] I wish to God I could fight at your side and be with you through all the joys and sorrows of camp life. If I get my hands on any Americans from Neu England who are fighting in the French army, I'll put them to the sword.

9. On January 31, 1865, Congress passed the Thirteenth Amendment to end slavery and sent the measure to the state legislatures for ratification. McPherson (1988), 839.

I want to describe these people to you in more detail. Many of them are the sons of rich parents who took to their heels to get out of fighting in our war. The rest are swindlers, horse thieves, highway robbers, nothing but riffraff who've escaped the arm of the law and settled down in France, many of them intending to fight against Germany's sons. And their mothers and fathers are now outfitting French ships in Boston and Neujork with arms and ammunition against Germany. But all these people are from the Neu England states Massaschusets, Vermont, Coneticut, and Maine. Ohio, Neujork, Pensilvanie, Indiana, or Illinois wouldn't stoop so low and anger their German fellow citizens. Our *Präsident* Gränt [Grant] is also a French-loving sheepheaded idiot, especially since the German soldiers helped him win his victories in our war, and if you ever get your hands on our ambassador in Paris, Mr. Waschburn, then throw stones at him because this wretch has behaved horribly toward the Germans in Paris[10] [5 ll.: correspondence; greetings]. Karl Friedrich Kühner

Karl Kühner's big talk and enthusiasm for the war appear rather paradoxical given his less than distinguished record in the Civil War: during most of his term of service, he was absent, either taken prisoner or sick and in the hospital.[11] Ludwig's experience was quite different—and not only because he was in the artillery instead of the cavalry. He served in the west and took part in the most important and successful campaigns at Vicksburg* and Atlanta. Except for one month of leave, there are no absences noted on his military record. On March 30, 1864, he was promoted to corporal. After the capture of Atlanta, Ludwig was content to be discharged at the end of his service.[12]

According to his pension application, Ludwig did not return home from the war unscathed. He complained of lung problems that repeatedly incapacitated him for longer periods of time. This did not prevent him, however, from becoming a successful farmer or living to the age of seventy-six.[13] His brother Karl indulged his love of Germany at least to the extent of visiting his old homeland in 1878. He died in 1886, at the age of fifty-seven.[14]

10. Grant's government sold arms to French agents until Carl Schurz* successfully protested against this breach of U.S. neutrality. Trefousse (1982), 178–79.

11. Muster Rolls, NatA; Boatner (1959), 870; Dyer (1959 [1908]), 1476–77.

12. Muster Rolls, NatA; Dyer (1959 [1908]), 1492.

13. Pension File, NatA.

14. Letter of Karl Kühner, December 31, 1879, NABS; Pension File, NatA.

36. Johann (John) Dieden

John Dieden left Germany in 1848 at the age of twelve, together with his stepfather, Johann Herting. The month of their departure is more significant than the year: they left in March, before the beginning of any revolutionary activity. The family were members of the Catholic establishment in the village of Ebernburg in the Palatinate, and they probably left for America for business reasons.[1]

Their destination was Chicago, where an uncle had already become quite prosperous.[2] John, as the boy referred to himself even in the first surviving letter from 1853, adapted quickly to his new environment. After working for half a year as a baker's apprentice, he peddled dry goods until 1853, when his supplier, an American merchant, gave the seventeen year old a job as a *"Clerk i.e. Ladendiener."* Dieden was bilingual, diligent, and had a good head for business, qualities that were obviously in great demand in a city with a large German immigrant population. When in 1856 he moved to a new job in a larger shop, his new employer had "2,500 circulars printed up for our German customers."[3]

Being German, American, and Catholic caused Dieden no conflict of loyalties. His letters show evidence of his pride in his new country ("America is still in its childhood[. . . .] The enormous steps forward it has taken so far, however, are

SOURCE NOTE: Dieden's German is grammatically and idiomatically correct; his spelling, however, is rather erratic, though certainly not to the point of impairing comprehension. There is no clear influence of a local dialect or of English, even though he was clearly fluent in the latter and had been living in America for half of his twenty-four years, when he wrote the first letter printed here. We know little about his formal schooling, but he clearly went beyond the elementary level and was not only interested but also well versed in politics, both American and German. His use of the language is at times flowery and somewhat stilted but occasionally quite original and creative. Not included here are the letters in the series from the years before 1860 (thirty-four) and after 1865 (seven), as well as two letters from 1863.

1. The stepfather (usually called "father" in the letters) crossed the Atlantic again in the same year to fetch the rest of the family, which indicates they had sufficient financial resources. Dieden's grandfather Schmidt had been the local mayor, and he was a clock manufacturer and the owner of a brickworks. Letter of May 3, 1867, NABS. Dieden's cousin and addressee Christian Dieden was a senior teacher and secretary to the mayor. Letter of May 30, 1856, NABS. Ebernburg itself had fewer than 600 inhabitants, but it was only four miles away from the Prussian county seat of Kreuznach. Neumann (1883), 238, 623, 802.

2. Jacob Dieden had started out in the late 1830s as a canal worker, and by 1855 he had become a merchant with assets of about $30,000. Letter of August 10, 1855, NABS. This appears to be confirmed by MC 1870: Cook Co./Ill., Chicago, W. 15, #4043, where he lists $31,000 in assets.

3. Letters of May 26, 1854, September 20, 1856, NABS. When the shop's owner cut his staff by half after a fire, only Dieden and one other German employee out of the six Germans were retained. Letter of January 14, 1858, NABS. The owner, merchant Jefferson Shay, was listed in 1860 with assets of $18,000. MC 1860: Cook Co./Ill., Chicago, W. 2, #825. In the 1850s Chicago's German population more than quadrupled from 5,000 to 22,000, finally reaching some 20 percent of the city's population. Keil and Jentz (1988), 4–5.

gigantic"), as well as his exuberant enthusiasm on the occasion of the Schillerfest or the "laying of the cornerstone for the German House in Chicago."[4] Political disagreements were common between Republicans and Catholics, but Dieden, like many Germans in Chicago, remained fully loyal to both groups. On May 18, 1858, he looked back and summarized what had led to the "urban civil war" in Chicago that broke out in 1855 "under the government of the *Knonothing* [Know Nothing] Mayor Boon":

> The causes of this uprising [. . .]: 1st the *Knownothings* had made a law which required every saloonkeeper to buy a *License* (*Patent*) for 300^{00} instead of 50^{00}, and 2nd they wanted to keep the foreign-born out of public office. The foreign-born and particularly the Germans, who by the way make up some 30,000–35,000 in Chicago, didn't like these laws and expressed their disapproval in public [. . .] and 3 months after the *Knonothing Mayor* took office, the *License* was reduced not to 50^{00} but at least to 100^{00}, and similarly in other cases. The following year, 1856, a democratic *Mayor* named Dyer was elected.[5]

Finally, in 1857, despite violent conflicts between German Republicans and Irish (Catholic) Democrats,[6] the Republican Party experienced a major victory, one that was subsequently confirmed in the 1858 election, much to the satisfaction of John Dieden: "The result [of the 1858 election] is a happy one, almost the entire *rep. Ticket* has been elected, the *Mayor*—is an American—, the city *marshall* is a German (Jacob Rehm), the city *clerk* is a German, there are five Germans on the Council [. . .] and all in all the Germans are well represented, even the guard on the Wellstreet Bridge, where like I say there's never been a German, is a German—he is named John Herting."[7]

Chicago, March 15th, 1860

Dearly beloved cousin (Christian Dieden)
My dear friend and brother,
[49 ll.: correspondence; European war; relations between Germany and France] They say the French are proud, but I believe the Americans beat the rest of world in this respect, when they say "*I am an American*" it means as much to them as when in Germany someone says: I am a "count" or a "baron."
The Germans in the United States, as I wrote earlier, have been winning more and more honor and fame in the last several years [5 ll.: because of German cultural organizations] and since the revolution in Germany in 1848, the

---

4. Letters of August 10, 1855, July 25, 1859, NABS.
5. Letter of May 18, 1858, NABS.
6. Bergquist (1971), 220–23, estimates that at least 75 percent of Chicago's Germans were Republicans; this would include many more Catholics than in other places.
7. Letter of May 18, 1858, NABS.

Photo and signature of
Johann (John) Dieden
in frontispiece of his
copybook.
(William S. Bailey)

position of the Germans in the United States has really improved remarkably, since in that year many intelligent and educated people left the old fatherland, and many of them had to leave because of their rulers. And despite all the efforts of the educated Germans to promote Germanness here, there still are some who, as soon as they have become a bit used to things, want to throw off everything that's German, probably just because they don't want to be a *Dutshman*—I can't imagine any other reason unless they'd been thieves back home or something like that.

[44 ll.: language difficulties experienced by people from various nations; Americanization of the Germans]

The hanging of an American captain named "John Brown," mainly because he wanted to free the Negroes, has been causing great commotion in the United States. He died with the most heroic disregard for death, and said on his way to the scaffold that in dying he would accomplish more than if left alive, and his words have already been confirmed by events.

Johann Dieden with his second wife Catherine and daughters Agnes, Catherine, and Anna in the early 1870s, in front of the house at 362 N. Wells Street, Chicago, that he purchased during the Civil War and where he resided the rest of his life. (William S. Bailey)

[18 ll.: Schiller anniversary; is sending newspapers] The newspapers may tell you a lot, but I also want to tell you one thing, namely that the Republican state *convention* was held in *Chicago*—5th St. This is the second-greatest honor the city has received, namely this—and the National Exhibition of the United States of America [10 ll.: reports about friends; greetings]. John Dieden. / (abridged)[8]

Chicago, November 29th, 1860.

Dearly beloved cousin, (Christian Dieden)
My dear friend and brother,
　　[75 ll.: allegorical account of courting his bride compared to moving up through a military career to the rank of general] Now I think, my dear fellow, you must have understood me by now, namely that my army is a German-French lady and the harbor is the harbor of holy matrimony[9] [5 ll.: details].

My choice, beloved cousin, in this holy state is a satisfactory one, my wife can wash and iron, mend and sew, cook and bake, knit and embroider, in-

8. The Dieden series has been preserved only in his own copies, sometimes abridged, of the letters he sent.
　　9. John Dieden married Maria Franziska Schott on August 30, 1860. A man named Gustavius Schott, presumably the father of Dieden's bride, appears as a druggist in CD Chicago, 1858.

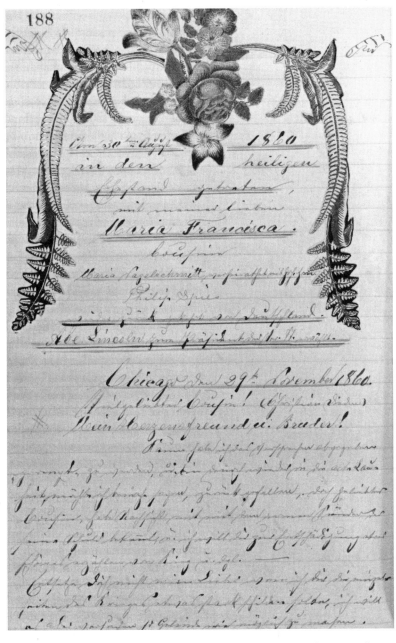

Page from Johann Dieden's copybook, with a "table of contents"
to letter of November 29, 1860, including his marriage on August 30
and Lincoln's election. (William S. Bailey)

deed do all women's work and—be a lady as well—you can take her anywhere you want (as they say in an American proverb)—and she's never out
of place [19 ll.: correspondence; a friend has returned from Germany]. The
presidential election is also over, but there are still dark clouds hanging over
the political horizon. A. Lincoln, the man of freedom, the enemy of slavery,
the man of equal rights, has been elected our president for the next four years.
The southern states, where the actual slavery is, are so bitter about this that
a few days after his election, one of these states, i.e. south carolina, broke off
from the Union—others have threatened to do the same. I have sent you some
magazines that contain information about various things and also a portrait
of Abe Lincoln.

I close, my dear fellow, with thousands of greetings to you and your dear
wife, from my dear Maria Francisca and your cousin / Johan Dieden.

Chicago, *May* 31st, 1862

Dearly beloved cousin (Christian Dieden)
My dear friend and brother,
[42 ll.: correspondence; thanks for books sent as wedding present] You
see, my dear fellow, all in all they don't distinguish between different German
nationalities in a foreign land, here there are no Prussians, Austrians, Bavari-
ans, Hanoverians, or Hessians anymore—but only Germans. In earlier letters
I already pointed out how the Americans are so prone to misjudge the shy, un-
demanding, modest outward appearance of the Germans, but this gives rise
to another comparison and this time the Germans are at a disadvantage. The
Germans, on average, have a terrible habit of criticizing what someone knows
or does [6 ll.: details]. The Americans, on the other hand, praise everything
or speak respectfully about these things[. . . .] They don't distinguish between
a student and a journeyman, not even in terms of clothing, or between a phar-
macist, doctor, lawyer and the like and a shoemaker or carpenter or farmer
etc. [6 ll.: all that counts is talent].

For example, look at the current president of the United States of America.
He was a *farmer* or *Ackersmann*, or look at the great Stephan A. Douglas—
who is certainly not unknown to you—he used to be a carpenter and was still
one of the greatest and most influential American statesmen, his influence was
so strong that a party was formed, called the Douglas-*Democratie*, and it attracted not just a few lawyers and other scholars but hundreds[. . . .] Also—
one of the former presidents was a tailor[10] before, what matters isn't whether

10. Here Dieden apparently confuses the name of President Zachary Taylor with his occupation; in fact, Taylor was a former general and wealthy plantation owner.

someone is a carpenter or a tailor but is the man capable or not? I believe it wouldn't hurt some of the German states if instead of one of their petty sovereigns on the throne they had a carpenter or tailor or farmer like our current president A. Lincoln[. . . .]

There are various opinions about Prussian politics and Napoleon III over here in America [14 ll.: lack of German unification]. Look at England's strength and France's power, and why couldn't Germany be just as powerful on its own? It's bigger than France or that little bit of England, and yet look how the proud Americans reacted to England's lion's roar, letting Mason and Slidell[11] go immediately. Wouldn't the same thing have happened had it been France? But what would they have done had it involved one of the individual German states? Especially one of the small ones. And aren't they Germans as well? I believe, my dear fellow, that Prussian bread may be hard to chew, but if it's a matter of turning Germany into an empire, to give it power, honor and glory, and if this is only possible when Prussia rules, then I would rather submit to the spiked helmet than be a servant of Napoleon III [33 ll.: details; family and friends].

I have passed on your essay "How to recognize the true calling to be a teacher" to the Catholic press. I have already sent you some issues of their publication. Let me close with many thousands of greetings from all of us but especially from your cousin John Dieden.

Chicago, July 26th, 1862.

Dearly beloved cousin (Christian Dieden)
My dear friend and brother,

[8 ll.: correspondence] You know, my dear fellow, what a hideous civil war America is entangled in, thousands of families have been thrown into misery and thousands more may meet a similar fate, before there is peace again in the United States.

The war—what a terrible word when it actually happens—is getting worse and more vicious every day. The rebels have now mobilized everyone they can —youths from 18 up to men of 45—all have to be soldiers, whether they want to or not, and the rebels now have an enormous army in the field, even though the South has hardly half the population of the North, that goes without saying [22 ll.: McClellan's offensive against Richmond (Seven Days' battles)].

Now, in order to bring this disastrous war to an end as quickly as possible,

---

11. The Confederate envoys James Mason and John Slidell caused a diplomatic crisis when they were arrested by the U.S. Navy on the British steamer *Trent*. Six weeks later they were released after a compromise was reached with the British. McPherson (1988), 389-91.

the president of the United States has called up another 300,000 men, which means an army all in all of 800,000 men, and hopefully enough to end the war quickly.

Of these aforementioned 300,000 men, Illinois has to supply 29 regiments or 29,000 men. The five times one hundred thousand men—including more than 90,000 Germans, according to the latest newspaper reports—are all volunteers, man for man, but if the new 300,000 men can't be mustered in the given time, there will have to be a lottery—or in other words compulsory conscription. This has already happened in St. Louis and in the whole state of Missouri [6 ll.: because it is a slave state]. When the president of the United States issued the first call for volunteers, it was the Germans in particular that saved the state of Misouri for the Union. Sigel,* Börnstein etc. set up the first regiments, nothing but Germans, some 4,000–5,000 men, while the Americans did very little, and most of them were even in favor of *Secession* [9 ll.: Chicago very cooperative]. 6 young men from my employer's shop rushed to arms as volunteers, five of them joined the ranks at the first call to arms, among them 2 Germans—one, an educated gentleman (Wilhelm Tinger) was a Hanoverian and spoke Dutch, French, and English as well as German. He joined the army as a private, and American soil drank his blood about half a year ago.

[18 ll.: large war rally] <u>Up to now in America it hasn't been the custom to have ladies as store clerks, but now several merchants have hired young ladies instead of the young men who are going to war</u>. My proprietor has also hired <u>two</u> and wants to take on another five as soon as he can find the right ones. Apparently we won't have to have a lottery in Illinois, but if it turns out that we do, I hope God will direct my and my wife's destiny to the best—I'm not in the best of health, either, but I am ready to take musket in hand should it be the will of God [6 ll.: farewell; greetings, signature].

Chicago, September 28th, 1862

Dearly beloved cousin (Christian Dieden)
My dear friend and brother,
[21 ll.: threat of conscription; sending newspapers] Did you get the Chicago Thelegraph from June 19th? On Sep. 20th 62[. . . .] I sent you more newspapers, containing your article mentioned above, along with an illustrated newspaper with a picture of General Franz Siegel [Sigel*] at the 2nd battle of Bull Run, giving commands for a bayonet attack against the attacking rebels, while the entire Union army was fleeing or had already run away. What do you think of this schoolmaster Siegel? [16 ll.: newspaper reports and local German festivities]. Up until now we haven't noticed much improvement, on the contrary, aside from the civil war with the South, our West has seen the hor-

rors of Indian atrocities—a horrible massacre in and around New Ulm[. . . .] Many, very many Germans fell victim there to the unexpected and murderous tomahawks of the wild beasts. New or Neu-Ulm is a colony mainly consisting of Germans and also founded by same. That's the way it is, my dear fellow—over there you're under the yoke, but over here you're exposed to all kinds of danger [71 ll.: has had a daughter; activities in four Catholic clubs; is sending a picture of the family and one of General Sigel; Catholic weekly paper wants more essays. Concluded February 15, 1863: brother Nikolaus's wedding]. Thousands of greetings from all of us, especially from my dear wife and your devoted / cousin / Johan Dieden / (abridged)

Chicago, [begun] March 31st, 1865

Dearly beloved cousin (Christian Dieden)
My dear friend and brother,
   [202 ll.: excuses "in jest and in earnest" for his long silence; writing activities; daily work; illness; debts from buying a house; birth of his second daughter] The first thing to report is my change in employment—I left yesterday April 15th, 1865 [. . .] in order to start work tomorrow April 17th in the business run by my father. I'm a partner together with my three brothers Nickolaus, Anton, and Wilhelm Anselm.—

   This business is not *Drygoods*, which I have been in for the last twelve years, but rather spices together with flour. Father is giving us the business partly for free, we only have to pay part of the cost.[12] [13 ll.: wages, family].

   With the help of Providence the murderous civil war has finally come to an end, at least it looks like it, but then just when the nation was about to dock safely in the harbor of peace it had to make the greatest sacrifice of the entire war. Yesterday, on April 16th, the long-suffering, high-minded president A. Lincoln fell victim to southern assassins in Washington, the capital[. . . .] The entire nation is draped in mourning, almost every house hung in black and white. The hearts of the different parties in the North, however, have melted into one—the newspapers I sent you give a detailed report.—

   [. . .] Many thousands of greetings to you and yours from your devoted cousin Joh. Dieden. / abridged

In the decade following the war, Dieden's stepfather served three terms on the Chicago city council, and his youngest brother became a member of the Illinois

---

12. According to a letter of January 21, 1866, the stepfather only asked for one-third of the actual value. According to MC 1860: Cook Co./Ill., Chicago, W. 7, #1003, Herting had $20,000 in assets; none were listed for John. In MC 1870: Cook Co./Ill., Chicago, W. 18, #1734, Dieden appears as a "wholesale and retail grocer" with assets of $5,000.

Page from Johann Dieden's copybook, with a "table of contents" to letter begun on March 31, 1865, with references to the birth of a daughter and Lincoln's assassination. (William S. Bailey)

state legislature at the age of twenty-five. John Dieden's only political office was as chairman of the board that supervised hospitals and facilities for the mentally ill and indigent in Chicago and Cook County, a position that he filled from 1873 to 1876. In 1873, angered by the passage of Republican blue laws, the family—together with many other Germans in Chicago—had left the Republican Party to become Democrats.[13]

Dieden's career as a successful and versatile businessman continued in the years after the war. Aside from his partnership with his brothers, he also worked as an insurance agent and even ran a saloon for a number of years. In his private life he was less fortunate. He was widowed twice in the course of eight years, and in 1875 he married for the third time. He died in 1887 at the early age of fifty-one.[14]

13. Andreas (1885), 2:764–66; Andreas (1886), 3:163, 399–400; Pierce (1957), 340–45. In the Great Chicago Fire of 1871 Dieden's brother lost $20,000 and the father a quarter of a million dollars. The latter was one of the seven leading citizens nominated to the emergency relief committee.

14. CD Chicago, 1865–90; information from descendants in the United States, NABS. In MC 1880: Cook Co./Ill., e.d. 180, #17, Dieden appears as a "saloon keeper." All three of Dieden's wives had German names.

37. Private Paul Petasch

Traces of all the usual reasons for joining the military—lack of money, hope for economic improvement, pure thirst for adventure, as well as opposition to slavery—can be found in the case of Paul Petasch. Nevertheless, one gets the impression that pure chance played a major role.

Petasch was born on August 12, 1842, in Dresden. His father had studied theology, worked as a language teacher, and later became a school principal in Dresden. It is unknown whether Paul attended his father's school, but it is clear that he had at least some secondary education. The death of his mother in September 1858 at the age of forty-five was already a major blow, but the subsequent loss of his father in May 1861 brought Petasch far more serious economic difficulties. Within three months, Paul had broken off his apprenticeship as a clerk and set sail for America, together with his twenty-year-old comrade Frank Riedel. In the American pas-

SOURCE NOTE: Petasch's command of English was and remained poor, in contrast to his German. He not only writes neatly and flawlessly but also constantly toys with the language, juggling metaphors and playfully constructing lively phrases. One senses echoes of witty mealtime conversations in a closely knit, educated family, where simple straightforward expression would be considered rather dull.

senger lists, both are referred to as merchants, but this probably reflected future ambitions rather than current circumstances.[1]

[October 27, 1861]

The Epistle of Paul to the Petasch family, Mr. Pochmann and all of his other friends!

Up to now you certainly haven't heard much from me, I admit it myself, so pull up the old round table where we used to fight over who got the most food and listen to what can happen to a fellow in good old America. You last heard from me in New York and now you must think, from what I said in my letter, that I went to Canada[. . . .] But instead of going to Canada, Riedel and I got on the immigrant train, and—imagine the miracle—only 7 days later I was in Chicago [24 ll.: train trip]. My first stop was the German Society, whose premises you can only enter in complete awe of *egalité, fraternité* and *liberté*—and in order to stay out of trouble not only do you have to take off your merchant boots at the door, but your trousers and jacket as well. So I crept in barefoot, and after quite a long wait I was asked what I wanted. Want, I thought, have to have would be more like it. I chose an intermediate form and answered: I am in grave need of work. What was your occupation? I was a merchant! Then I can't find any work for you. In desperation I thought, keep your mouth shut, and sat down quietly on a bench to wait, since it was up to him to find some job for me after all. And when he saw that there was no other way to get rid of me—what do you know—he suddenly gave me a letter addressed to *Mr. Tompson Smith, Dement Station, Ogle County, Illinois* and said I would find work there.

"*Dement Station*" rang out in the car, the train stopped, and, startled out of sweet railway slumber, I grab hold of my bag and jump out, the train pulls off and once again I'm left in the middle of the flat prairie at 2 in the morning [6 ll.: looked for work on farms]. More than a month has now passed since that day, and during this time I've learned to plow, groom horses, dig potatoes and many another task requiring honest sweat[. . . .] But last Sunday when I asked for my $6 wages, the scoundrel had the gall to answer my request: "*Please to pay me my wages*" with "*I would not please to pay ya a cent.*"[2] So I told

1. Information provided by the donor; KB (ev.) Dresden, Dreikönigsgemeinde; NYPL, *Atlantic*, September 2, 1861. Since the Saxon military later tried to call up Riedel for conscription, it is probable that both men emigrated without official permission.

2. Tompson Smith (if this was his employer) was a twenty-three-year-old farmer born in Canada with $3,700 worth of property, who had no apparent need to be stingy. MC 1860: Ogle Co./Ill., Dement, #1270.

Envelope of Paul Petasch's letter of October 27, 1861. The inscription reads,
"Death to traitors," and Petasch has added, "*but life to you.*" (Gerlind Voermanek)

him he was a dirty bastard and have since taken my case to a justice of the
peace. Now, there's no lack of work here offered by good people who actually
pay, though you certainly do have to find out ahead of time what they're like,
but it doesn't suit me at all to sit around the whole winter on a lonely farm,
cut off from everything.

So now I've spent a number of days making my way from one farm to the
next, sometimes sleeping in a barn, or in a bed, or not at all, until at last this
past Wednesday here in Dement there was a so-called *warmeeting. Scheiße!*
(here they say *cheat* [shit]), I thought, it can't be all that dangerous, rode down
with a farmer and wanted to enlist in the army, like we'd been told to do at
the end of the meeting, when a soldier came up and signed me up for his regiment. The next day he picked me up at the farm [. . .] and after I'd been with
him to see several of his friends, we traveled together to Chicago.[3] Then after
we'd hiked through the whole city, we finally reached the soldiers' barracks.
As a recruit I was treated to roast pork, coffee and bread, and after a sound
sleep on my bale of hay, the captain came up to me, shook my hand, and in
the open field had me swear to defend the Union against all its enemies. During the whole oath that the captain spoke, I only had to hold up my hand.

3. The 55 Ill. Inf included men of various nationalities from across northern Illinois, although
the main recruitment centers for Petasch's Comp B were DeKalb and Ogle Counties. Ogle
County was strongly Republican, voting 70 percent for Lincoln, and had only twenty-five black
inhabitants. *Story of the 55th* (1887), 91, 473–75; Burnham (1955), 384; USC 1860.1, 98.

That afternoon I drilled in my black coat and farmer's straw hat, since there's a shortage of clothes at the moment. The wage of a common soldier here is $13 *a month* and after 3 years $100 and 160 acres of land that you can pick out wherever you like. 13 × 12 = 156 = 468 + 100 = 568 + 160 acres of land—like a real *Western Farmer*! Adieu for today and maybe for a long time[. . . .] And one more thing. If Riedel's mother asks about my letters, make sure you tell her I only write very short letters and that I just said I was getting along very well, and that is the case.

Fare well, perhaps forever / Your Paul / Dement, 27th October 1861.

Paduca, Kentucky, Feb. 3rd, 1862

Dear brothers and sisters,

The last time I spoke with you I had come over to visit you. Today you should come and visit me here in Paducah, where I'm sitting in a German saloon, surrounded by nothing but Germans, trying to put my experiences down on paper as quickly as possible[. . . .] Last you heard from me I was a young recruit in Chicago. We spent 1½ months in that city, during which time I spent 3 weeks in the hospital. The reason for this was as follows: I was put on guard duty even though I was half sick, and then it got incredibly cold during the night. In the guardhouse there were 110 half-frozen soldiers lying around, one stove no bigger than a kettle, with no hay to sleep on, no chair to sit on, the boards freshly whitewashed, and on top of this a heavy snowstorm blowing in from Lake Michigan, enough to make even your ribs chatter. When my watch was over I stumbled back into my bed on legs that shivered and shook, then I lay there for several hours, half dumb with my teeth chattering, until the doctor had me taken to the hospital. Soon afterward, my throat swelled almost completely shut. For 10 days I was unable to eat anything and lived exclusively on tea. The medicine they gave me was so harsh that my tongue was soon so numb and black that I could pinch off whole pieces of it with my fingernails. I was also cut 5 times and cauterized and then, only halfway recovered but with the deepest respect for American medicine, I was released and declared healthy[. . . .] Finally after another 5 weeks—"Marching orders." Here I will remain silent and let another speak for me. I'm sending you a copy of a letter about this march that appeared in one of Chicago's best newspapers [74 ll.: text in English].

Since then I've stood guard only 4 German miles [ca. 18 U.S. miles] from the line of fire. Surrounded on all sides by *Secesh* inhabitants, I got lost one time. It was in the woods during the night, when a storm was blowing unusually hard through the sturdy oak and beech trees, and I was wandering around with my loaded gun through swamps and swollen streams, wearing only shoes on my feet, through bottomless mud holes, and once I had fought my way through and was safe on the other side, then I tripped over some fallen trees and piles of thorns. I just can't tell you what it was like. 6 other men got lost the same way. After 4 hours I happened to find the barracks and was met by the guard on duty. He immediately sent someone else off to my post and let me dry my shoes, trousers and socks by the dying fire. Give my best to everyone I know, Madame Schneider, the Mueller & Wolf families and thank Mr. Pochman for me for having put me through my paces on his favorite topic, that of far-fetched ideas. / Fare well, Your Paul

TO FRANK RIEDEL[4]

Chicago, Dec. 11th, 61.

[. . .] I was just lying in my bed suffering from a horrible headache and a stiff neck [. . .] when the Sergeant ordered me to either go on duty or go see the doctor like the day before. I didn't want to do either one, especially the latter, for the simple reason that the doctor told me himself that he couldn't understand much German.[5] It turned into quite a scene, with the whole company taking part and having their say, and I am flattered to be able to say that quite a lot was said in my defense. You know that my temper is quite hot, and so it happened that despite my miserable condition I jumped up, quickly got dressed and went up to my opponents and told them they shouldn't go on so much about freedom—when you send a sick man out on picket duty just because the doctor can't understand him, then you have less freedom here than the lowest secessionist's *Nigger*. And now I'm going to show you that my will power is even greater than your ugliness: I'm going on duty. This performance won me many friends, but I came down with a dangerous cold. I had to stand guard that day for 11 instead of the normal 8 hours and in the most miserable weather. Heavy rain had turned the ground into a morass so bad that I can only compare it to the road to Clark's house the first time we went to see that hypocrite.[6] In the guardhouse there was a stove no bigger than a water kettle, and 110 frozen soldiers asking each other if they could just have

4. These texts were excerpted and copied by Riedel; the originals are unavailable, and the original length is unknown.

5. Among the regiment's forty-five officers and noncommissioned officers there were only two Germans, along with one Swede, five Irishmen, and one Englishman. *Story of the 55th* (1887), 37.

6. Probably the Connecticut-born "preacher" Anson Clark of Dement. MC 1860: Ogle Co./Ill., Dement, #1231.

a *"smell of the stove."* There wasn't even any hay to sleep on, but *plenty* of lice on the whitewashed boards[. . . .]

St. Louis, Dec. 30th, 61.

[. . .] Our captain is the meanest and most drunkardly, low-down person that you can imagine on God's earth. Last night he came into our barracks, completely drunk, with a loaded pistol in his right hand, and wanted to shoot one of his enemies. To the great joy of all of his soldiers he was discharged[. . . .][7]

Paducah, Kentucky, Dec. 30th, 61

[. . .] We should be able to do something for Arthur. I must openly admit, however, that I don't think much of going to America now in these difficult times and in the stormy season, although even in the worst of times I could never yearn for my heavy German yoke[. . . .]

Paducah, Feb. 5th, 62.

[. . .] This morning at 8 o'clock I was sent over to General Smith's house to load some things. The job itself would have been quite boring, but then the general's adjutant gave me a most valuable book, an English translation of Plutarch, as a present.[8] Having been issued better weapons, we are now supposed to join the march to Columbus. So in the course of the next 4 weeks I will probably have something to report about the smell of gunpowder. As soon as we leave here I will send you the book—but until then let me soothe my soul in its lofty colonnades and lift my cup, filled from a fresh spring, up to my dry mouth to quench my thirsty lungs. Nothing has come of my chances for the gunboats, because everyone has to take an exam that I, of course, am unable to pass. I close this letter amid the cheers of troops marching into battle.

April 28th [1862] / Evansville[9]

Dear brother and sisters and relatives,

[. . .] just wanted to report that I was wounded on the 6th of April in a battle near Pittsburg Landing [Shiloh*] by one bullet above my right knee and one farther down below, but not very dangerously. For 36 hours I lay helpless on the battlefield. A week later I was brought to the Marine Hospital in Evans-

7. Probably Captain Thomas B. Mackey, who resigned on December 28, 1861. *OAR*, 11:307.

8. Probably the *Lives of Noble Grecians and Romans* by the first-century Greek moralist, which was translated into English in the seventeenth century by John Dryden.

9. It cannot be determined whether Petasch wrote this letter himself or dictated it.

ville. In this hospital I got to know one of the most highly respected ladies of the town who has provided me with the best care and attention.

Last Saturday this same Madame Lister came to fetch me, in that she had me brought to her own house. Since then I have had the best attention, and in Mr. Lister, [who] is writing [over?] this letter, I have truly found a new father and mother.

Fare well / all my dear ones / address Sam Lister / Evansville / Ind

ALEXANDER LEMCKE TO PAUL PETASCH'S SISTER
[letterhead:] Office of Evansville Gas Light Company,
Evansville, Ind., May 8th, 1862

Dear Madam,

It is my sad duty to introduce myself to you by letter with news that will bring you great sorrow. It concerns your brother Mr. Paul Petasch who arrived here about 4 weeks ago with other wounded soldiers and was put into one of our hospitals. One of the many citizens who visit the hospitals to care for sick and wounded soldiers was a Mrs. Lister, a wealthy American lady who was interested in your brother Paul and had him taken to her home so she could look after him. Several friends and I took him to the Lister family home, sat up with him at night, and learned the following from your brother: upon his arrival in this country, he set off for Chicago and seems to have had difficulties finding employment, because he enlisted in the army fighting for the American Union. After they had trained for a while in Chicago, the regiment (the 55th Illinois Regiment) was ordered to Tennessee and took part in the bloody battle at Pittsburg Landing[. . . .] Your brother was sent along as a skirmisher and was incapacitated by a shot in the leg, above the knee, on Sunday morning, 12 o'clock. The battled lasted Sunday and Monday, and it was Monday evening before Paul and the other wounded were brought to the boat that brought him here to the hospital.

His wound was quite serious, but it improved significantly, to the satisfaction of the doctors who treated him. It seems, however, that the privations and strain of war, which are worse in this country than elsewhere, the weather is too changeable and damp, caused him to develop a high fever along with traumatic fever, and it developed into typhoid or nerve fever a week ago. The doctors did everything they could to keep your brother alive, but despite this and the tender care provided by Mrs. Lister, who was fond of your brother Paul and treated him like her own child, he died on Tuesday, the 6th of May at 5:30 in the afternoon. On the last day he was fairly quiet and occasionally conscious and it seemed like he was not in much pain.

Several of us, young Germans who got to know your brother while he was

ill, buried him yesterday afternoon at 3 o'clock and, together with the Lister
family, we paid him the last honors as he was laid to rest[10] [12 ll.: grave; assets].

     With sympathy and sorrow at the death of a man so young and so promis-
ing, I remain yours respectfully / Alexander Lemcke [. . .]

Victory at Shiloh* came at a high price. This was particularly true for Petasch's
unit, the 55th Illinois, which occupied an exposed position in the front line. For
two hours they held on, outnumbered by the enemy four to one, and only began
an orderly retreat when they ran out of ammunition. Petasch also demonstrated
the valor of a true veteran, as his superior officer mentioned in his casualty report:
"Made every shot tell until taken from the field." His Company B was the first to
come under fire, and it suffered the heaviest casualties of the entire 55th, a regiment
in which over half its troops were listed as dead, wounded, or missing—the second
highest casualty rate among all the Union regiments in the battle. As the chronicle
of the unit reports, the 55th Illinois suffered half of all the casualties it incurred
during the entire war on that one day, within three hours.[11] The romantic illusions
of war, held by Petasch and many on both sides at the outset of the conflict, died in
the rain and mud at Shiloh.[12]

     10. The Listers had immigrated from England at least twenty years earlier and lived in rented
quarters (obviously above their means) with another family. Mr. Lister was a bookseller with assets of only $300, but they employed three servants, and their two young daughters were listed as
"ladies." Letter-writer Lemcke was a "trader" from Hamburg. MC 1860: Vanderburg Co./Ind.,
Evansville, #15, #1191.
     11. *Story of the 55th* (1887), 70-102, 125, 473-75, 519; Hicken (1991), 60-61, 70; Military File,
P. Petasch, NatA.
     12. McPherson (1982), 229.

38. Second Lieutenant Friedrich Martens

In the spring of 1857 nineteen-year-old Friedrich Martens left his home in the village of Delve in Ditmarschen, near the Danish border, and traveled steerage to
America. He probably wanted to avoid serving in the military, although the economic situation of his family may also have played a role in his decision to leave. His
early letters also clearly indicate a certain thirst for adventure.[1]

SOURCE NOTE: Martens's spelling is frequently weak, and so is his grammar at times, though
neither makes quick comprehension of his letters difficult. In terms of style, however, he is not
only well versed in stereotypical metaphors but also uses quite original turns of phrase. Besides
using well-known literary quotations, he also describes war experiences by drawing convincingly
on historical precedent. Not included here are six letters in the series from the time before 1860.
     1. HPL and NYPL, *Donau*, April 1–May 4, 1857; letter of May 17, 1857, NABS.

Martens came from a family of small landholders, encumbered with debts, who possessed more intelligence than property. In one letter he wrote about the son of the local agriculture administrator in Delve, also an immigrant, noting that in Germany "he was looked up to, and I was dirt on the street in his eyes, and here it's the other way around, because here nothing counts but education." His own education cannot have been very systematic, although in addition to lessons in the local village school, he received private instruction from the deacon. Martens's occasional errors in spelling and grammar stand out in stark contrast to his quotations from Heine and Schiller.[2]

A dense network of fellow countrymen surrounded Martens both on the way to America and after his arrival in Joliet, Illinois. In the passenger lists he appears as a "painter," and within three days he had found a job with a painting company, Dorn and Schott, whose owners both had origins in the same area as Martens.[3]

As a result of the economic recession at the time, Dorn and Schott went bankrupt in October 1857. Martens first went to work for an American as a bartender, but he soon went together with a partner and opened his own saloon. He also seems to have worked for a while as a teacher. When the war broke out, he was living in Peoria, about a hundred miles south of Joliet.[4]

Despite all the upheaval, Martens never regretted his decision to immigrate. After less than a year in the United States, he wrote that he was spending most of his free time studying American history. His interest in politics, too, began quite early: he had figured out exactly how much time it would take before he could vote in local elections or become a U.S. citizen.

Before the Civil War, Martens was an enthusiastic supporter of the northern Democrats and their candidate from Illinois, Stephen A. Douglas. He wrote with great excitement about Douglas's election to the Senate in 1858, not even mentioning the name of his opponent, Abraham Lincoln. Looking forward to the election in 1860, he wrote that Douglas would have to become president "or else there will be trouble." It is quite remarkable, therefore, that when Lincoln issued his call for troops at the beginning of the war, Martens volunteered that same day.[5]

2. Information provided by the donor; letter of April 18, 1858, NABS.

3. MC 1860, Will Co./Ill., #2958, #3748; CD 1859/60, Will Co./Ill. These sources describe Dorn and Schott as "painters"; later directories list them as "house and sign painters." Landesarchiv Schleswig 415/5471, Volkszählung Delve 1845, No. 11 (father's place of birth); HPL.

4. Letters of October 28, 1857, April 18, 1858, September 24, 1858, November 16-17, 1858, November 20, 1859, and June 15, 1861, NABS. Joliet was almost ten times the size of Delve; Peoria twice the size of Joliet. In 1860 one-quarter of the residents of Peoria County were foreign-born; one-third of these were Germans, the largest group of immigrants. The arrival of a half dozen Forty-eighters in Peoria had led to a proliferation of German institutions, in particular a *Turnverein* [Turner*]. Already in the 1860 election campaign, competition existed between German newspapers supporting the two parties. USC 1860.1, 98-103; USC 1870.1, 118-21, 352; Brandel (1901); Arndt and Olson (1965), 95, 100-102.

5. Letters of September 24, 1858, November 16-17, 1858, and June 15, 1861, NABS.

His behavior can perhaps be partly explained by the fact that Martens did not share the racial anxieties of other Democrats (in Joliet and Peoria, less than 2 percent of the population was black). Six months after his arrival, he casually mentioned a "Negro friend." When he was looking for work, he did not hesitate to ask a mulatto about the job market in New Orleans. A year later he added to a letter, "if neighbors, gossips, and tittle-tattlers happen to ask about me, you can tell them I'm well and hope to marry a rich black woman. Ha, ha, ha." A Lutheran Protestant, Martens did not think much of the Irish, the main supporters of the Democratic Party. In one letter apparently written while tending bar, he excused himself with the following: "I can write better; I'm being interrupted too much by these Irishmen who are drinking themselves into Purgatory."[6]

Martens first joined Company E, 6th Illinois Infantry, a unit that contained some twenty Turners* and a dozen other Germans from Peoria. When their three-month term expired, Martens signed on with the 17th Missouri Infantry, also a Turner regiment. Considering the fact that the Turners were usually among the better educated—and that Martens was not a Turner—his rapid advancement as an officer is quite remarkable. His skills in English no doubt helped.[7]

Martens and the 17th Missouri Infantry, at times under the command of the German generals Franz Sigel* and Peter Osterhaus,* were involved in the most important campaigns in the western theater. Among other things, they fought in the battle of Pea Ridge, Arkansas, which secured Missouri for the Union in early 1862, and in the summer of 1863 they took part in the siege and capture of Vicksburg.*[8]

Joliet, September 24, 1858

Most dearly beloved parents,

[. . .] You write in your letter that I should be a schoolteacher again this winter, *no Sir* I like variety [15 ll.: earns more as a waiter].

We're already in a war, party against party because of the election in 1860. We Democrats have a man at the top who's no dummy, a first-class speaker and the best statesman you could find, and he should and he must become president in 1860, and if the Republicans and the *Know nothinger* or Know Nothings attack us we'll get out the long barrels; but plenty of water will flow under the bridge by then.—

This fall I will be voting for the first time for *County* officials, since I've been living for 1½ years in the same *County* (great honor) [64 ll.: is healthy; correspondence; greetings, signature, address].

6. Letters of October 28, 1857, and September 24, 1858, NABS.
7. Brandel (1901), 24; Kaufmann (1911), 188; letter of October 28, 1857, NABS.
8. Additional details are provided by the letters of a German officer in the 12 Mo. Inf, another unit in the same brigade, published in English translation by Hess (1983). On Sigel and Osterhaus see ibid., 9–11, 14–15; and Dyer (1959 [1908]), 497–98, 541–43.

[letterhead] Second Brigade, Sixth Division, Seventh Regiment,
ILLINOIS VOLUNTEER MILITIA / Camp Defiance,
Cairo, Ill., June 15, 1861

My dear ones,

[12 ll.: sorrow on the death of a cousin] As you probably already know, a civil war has broken out in this free country. I don't have the space or the time to explain all about the cause, only this much: the states that are rebelling are slave states, and they want slavery to be expanded, but the northern states are against this, and so it's civil war! I also followed the drums when the first call to arms went out through the land. All volunteers, 250,000 men have taken up arms against the rebels, and if the government had wanted a million men they would have been there.

I've been in the field for 9 weeks now, life is very bad. Haven't been out of my clothes for 9 weeks, a little bit of straw for a bed, bread and meat for food, and on top of it the great heat doesn't make it any more pleasant. But it's a sacred cause, and so we don't feel the hardship.

My dear ones, it is not impossible that this might be my last letter, and if it is my last one, then take comfort, for I assure you that I will consider myself lucky should I breathe my last on the field of honor [5 ll.: details].

But on the other hand, you also know that not every bullet hits its mark, so there's no reason why I shouldn't return home. We are now at the Missippi, across from the enemy, and we've only engaged them once and only a few were killed. I didn't quiver!

How long the war will last depends on the circumstances, but it won't stop until the last traitor to freedom is lying at our feet, begging for mercy! [9 ll.: greetings; signature; address].

Peoria, August 24, 1861.

My dear ones,

[12 ll.: correspondence] Your son is a soldier! *Yes*, parents, your son is a soldier in America.—and the fact that this letter is being written in Peoria is because I took a week of leave to take care of some business. As you have probably already read in the newspapers, a revolution has broken out in this beautiful free country, and it is of such dimensions that all our forces must be roused to secure freedom, to crush the revolution.

We now have 400,000 men in the field, and our enemy has almost as many. But I must tell you briefly about the main cause of this horrible war; as you know, in our southern states, slavery exists in all its atrociousness, so in order to crush and stamp this out, last fall the northern men elected a president from the party with an antislavery policy, and then they passed some laws that were not to the advantage of the slaveholders, and the revolution began. Now,

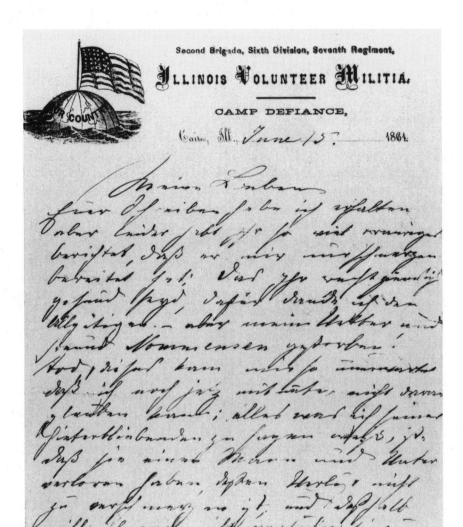

Beginning of Friedrich Martens's letter of June 15, 1861. Like the other letterheads included here, this one was privately printed, not issued by the U.S. Army. (Ingo Wichmann)

father, I'd like to know what you'd think of a son who stayed at home when the enemy was at the door, making war on freedom, suppressing the freedom we paid so dearly for. Would I still be worthy of living in this land, enjoying this freedom, if I were not also willing to fight for this freedom, and if need be, to die for it? Oh, I know my freedom-loving father, I know he will say I am right, for now he finally has a true reason to be proud of his son! And dear father, if it please the dear Lord to let me die on the <u>field of honor</u>, then you must also have enough strength to comfort my dear mother, and you will tell her and anyone else that your son couldn't have died a better death!

I also want to tell you that in the North no one is forced to become a soldier, instead the entire enormous army consists of volunteers, more evidence that the cause we're fighting for must be sacred! I signed up the first day, 4 months ago, and am now a *sergeant*. I've been in two battles where much blood was shed, but not every bullet hits its mark. —

Tonight I have to travel back to my post, and this is more than 400 English miles from here in Missouri [5 ll.: mail arrangements]. Keep me in your prayers, the Almighty will surely hear them. Give everyone my best[. . . .] Teach my nephew to hate tyrants, abhor oppressors and teach him to love and venerate freedom, true freedom, for our Germany must someday be free as well, and who knows whether he may need to play his part to make it free. Oh, truly God liveth, and God does not want slaves but free men. God does not appoint a government to oppress the people, but to rule them wisely! Once again, my best wishes to all from your son / Fr. Martens

Camp Schadt near Lebenon.[9] February 3/ 1862.
Most dearly beloved parents,

I received your kind letter of Oct 5th/61 last night, and from this you can see that our mail service is not the best [23 ll.: correspondence; family; health].

And now, sister and brother-in-law, I want to have a word with you, and it is a very serious word, do everything you can to make your child into a man, keep his spirit fresh and don't make it into the spirit of a slave [5 ll.: details].

My father says, among other things, Oh, soldier, that word cost us many tears. Well, it's possible that it cost you tears, and that proves to me that you still love me: but that is <u>all</u>. Look, you seem to have a poor understanding of the situation here, otherwise you certainly wouldn't talk like that, no, don't you know that when we cried, it was tears of joy; for we weren't forced to fol-

---

9. Lebanon, Missouri, a town about halfway between Rolla and Springfield. The camp was probably named after Lieutenant Colonel Otto Schadt, a former Prussian officer then in command of the 12 Mo. Inf; Hess (1983), 7.

low the drums, we did it voluntarily. Now, though, I am quite miserable, and our campaign reminds me of 1812,[10] many, many will not be returning home to their loved ones, instead they'll be crossing over to the great army where the Lord God will assign them good quarters; for He also loves a true soldier.

Yes, father! Your son is shaping up well, and if you could see me you wouldn't recognize me, healthy and strong and with a full beard, I look like a little rebel-eater, and as far as courage goes, I can say that I know the words fear or coward only from dictionaries, that's why the people want me to do so much.

Last week I passed my exam, and in the next few days I'll have *Epaulets* on my shoulders.

Now I must close, because due to all my comrades' questions and chattering I can't write a decent letter at the moment. The weather is very bitter, and the soldiers are suffering a great, great deal.

If you, my dear father, take an interest in this disastrous war, then I want to admit something I don't want to say out loud here. There's more treason here than in any other war, and when the government runs out of *Credit*, then we'll have to make a shameful peace.

(This war will be the downfall of a great nation.)

It may be that my bones will be bleaching by the end of this war, if so, then remember the words above.

Adieu for now [8 ll.: correspondence]. Fr. Martens Serg

Camp near Batesville. Arcansas. June 12, 1862

My dear ones,

[. . .] These lines are proof that I am still alive, and in terms of my health, I am doing fairly well, although the hard marches of that truly terrible winter campaign and now the horrible heat in these southern states have bad effects on every man (more on some, on others less)!

From the newspapers you probably know roughly how the war is progressing, and so I don't want to go into that in detail, but I do have to note that you people over there in civilized Europe can't possibly have any idea of the dreadful atrocities this war has produced. One example:

Last week two companies from our regiment were ordered to provide cover for a wagon train that had to go out to get fodder for the horses. Not very far from *Camp*, they were attacked by a large horde of rebels and were instantly surrounded. Our men fought like lions, but for naught, they were bound to lose to such a superior force. The ones who were still alive wanted to give

---

10. A reference to Napoleon's disastrous campaign against Russia.

themselves up, but they received as an answer: we don't want any prisoners, and they massacred everyone just before we arrived. We saw our comrades lying there <u>slaughtered</u>, and shouting out "*to hell with them rascals*" we closed in on them. Our colonel ordered some good maneuvers, and this time the enemy was surrounded, and so well that none of them could escape. But I don't want to write any more about it, you don't know how sweet revenge can be, and so you wouldn't understand how I can justify retaliation that was so appalling.[11]

Schiller said: the most fearsome of the fearsome,

that is man![12]

and this is very true. If you provoke a man to the limit, he becomes a tiger.

I have no idea how long this horrible war can continue, but hopefully it will come to an end soon. Oh, this poor country, how much it has suffered already. The heaps of debts, the fates that have been devastated, the large number of men this war has devoured, they are great. I am not exaggerating when I say that up to now the death toll runs to almost 150,000, for the battlefield claims many victims, but the hospitals even more.

Yours truly has made some progress with regard to position. I've been a lieutenant for a few weeks now, and as such I'm in a bit better shape, and the officers' pay in america is quite good, too. A lieutenant, for example, gets $105 a month or in Hamburg [currency] 4,375 marks a year; that is certainly a large amount of money, but I still will be leaving the army as soon as I can do so with honor, because otherwise my business will suffer too much [10 ll.: greetings; signature; address].

Camp Helena State of Arkansas / September *the* 24th, 1862

My dear ones,

[. . .] Since I last wrote I've been quite well the entire time, and no enemy lead has come too close, and this is more than many other soldiers can say, and if I should have such a merciful Lord next year as I did this year, then I believe I will reach old age. —

From the newspapers you probably know that the war continues to rage and threatens to turn this country into what Germany was after the end of the Thirty Years' War: a wasteland. According to the latest figures, three times one hundred thousand men have already fallen victim, and there is no end in

11. This was the skirmish at Searcy Landing, Arkansas, on May 19, 1862. According to two eyewitnesses, the rebels "barbarically hacked and shot at the wounded," shouting, "Damn you, we want no prisoners." *OR*, 1:13, 69–79. The 17 Mo. Inf suffered its worst losses in this skirmish: fifteen killed and twenty-six wounded. *OAR*, 8:102–3.

12. Taken from Friedrich Schiller, "Das Lied von der Glocke"; see von Wiese (n.d.), 4:188–200.

sight, instead it looks like it is turning into a war of devastation. Europeans have no idea what these rebels' hatred is like, in fact it's gone beyond hate, it's fanaticism; for example in the last battles the rebels took many prisoners, and as unbelievable as it may sound to you, they brutally murdered most of these prisoners!

After what I wrote above you can well imagine we would rather die sword in hand than be taken prisoner.

And there's more than enough to complain about how sluggish this government is in running things. If our government were taking this seriously, it would have the means at its disposal to crush this rebellion within four months.

Anyway, I'll see how things look next spring (that is, if I am still alive by then). If there is still no end to this disastrous war in sight, then I will give my commission back to the government and come back to Germany.

But let's hope that by then a new spirit will be sweeping through our *Capitol*, and if we can't suffocate this viper of a revolution, at least we should be able to pull out its poison fangs!

[15 ll.: longs to see them again; advice on bringing up children] I flatter myself that I have now become a man, but what battles did I have to fight to get there, how hard did I have to fight to avoid falling victim to all the temptations the depraved world offers to young, inexperienced men. Of course now I believe I have won, and Hell itself is not in a position to lead me astray, for I am clad in armor, and this armor is the fact that I want to be and remain an honorable man for the rest of my life.

Now I will close, keep your son in fond memory, forgive me for all the unnecessary trouble I caused you as a foolish young man, and if you receive the tidings that your youngest child has died on the field of honor then weep, yes—weep your fill, but after you have done that, then unite in a prayer of praise to the good Helmsman of the world, and thank Him that He gave you a son who was man enough to fight for a sacred cause and to die. I remain with all respect your thankful son

Fr. Marten Lieutenant. / *Commanding Company D 17th Regiment Missouri Volunter Infantry.*

Camp Steele Missip. December *the* 3rd, 1862.
Most dearly beloved parents,

[16 ll.: health; family] Now a few things about our current situation. The war continues to rage.

Thousands upon thousands are falling as victims, on the one side as men who were prepared to die for freedom, on the other side as men who became fanatics, since we didn't want to believe that slavery is a godly institution.

I would like to claim that we will have peace by the spring. The South is worn to death. But before it admits this, more blood will flow than has already been shed, this winter the clashes will be horrible. But as they say

Dead ist the gate to salvation

so there's no grumbling.

The weather here is pleasant today—even too warm, but fresh enough to be healthy.

Strange, every time I write to you I would like to sing along with Heine: I cannot determine the meaning of sorrow that fills my breast,[13] etc. Sometimes I think it's homesickness, although I'm too old for that, but who knows!

[22 ll.: looks forward to seeing them again; Christmas and New Year's greetings]

I haven't been promoted any further, but I don't mind very much, because the pay of a captain isn't much more than that of a lieutenant [7 ll.: greetings and exhortations; signature].

Peoria Ill. September *the* 19th, 1863.

My dear ones,

This time I have the pleasure of writing to you from Peoria. I have left the army. Due to the tremendous hardships that I endured, my health was so bad that I applied for my discharge, and on August 23rd my application was approved. Thanks to Providence, I was very lucky, I faced the enemy in eight fierce battles and I was never wounded. Now I have recovered almost completely, and I have made enough money to take it easy for a while.

We will have finished off the rebellion soon, and I hope that slavery will come to an end as well.

[7 ll.: family] Now, dear parents, you don't need to lose any more sleep over me, for I am in safety. I can well imagine you have had some sleepless nights in the last couple of years, but take comfort in the fact that I was fighting for a good cause.

My best wishes to all from your / most loving son / Friedrich Martens [8 ll.: address]

After his discharge,[14] Martens may have visited his old home, but if he did, then it was only for a short time. Less than six months later, he got married in the Peoria Lutheran church to Louise Bachmann, who had emigrated from Hanover in 1856 and was probably a sister of Wilhelm Bachmann, the man whom Martens gave as

13. Heinrich Heine's "The Homecoming," Draper (1982), 77; for German original see Briegleb (1968), 1:107. Set to music in 1838, the poem is better known, probably also by Martens, as the Lorelei song.

14. Muster Rolls, 17 Mo. Inf, NatA; letter of September 19, 1863, NABS.

his contact during the war. For the rest of his working life, Martens was a house and sign painter in Peoria, often working together with an American partner. When his wife died around 1900, he retired, and he spent his last eighteen years living in a home for disabled Union veterans in Danville, Illinois.[15]

15. Pension File, NatA; CD Peoria, 1882/83–1901/2. Bachmann appears in MC 1860: Peoria Co./Ill., Peoria, W. 1, #478. Interestingly, Bachmann owned a German bookstore; neither Martens nor his future wife were living in his household in 1860. MC 1870: Peoria Co./Ill., Peoria, W. 1, #267; MC 1880: Peoria Co./Ill., e.d. 220, #76; MC 1900: Peoria Co./Ill., e.d. 86, #126; MC 1900: Vermillion Co./Ill., Danville Twp., National Home for Disabled Volunteer Soldiers; MC 1910: Vermillion Co./Ill., Danville Twp., e.d. 134, #43.

39. Private David Böpple and Family

David Böpple and Magdalena Metzger came from Heumaden and Nellingen, two neighboring villages on the Neckar River, a few miles upstream from Stuttgart. They married in February 1860, shortly before they emigrated. They did not take much of a fortune along with them, since Böpple brought to the marriage only his clothing, a silver watch, and 100 guilders* for the passage, and his wife received only 200 guilders in cash along with her trousseau. The couple arrived in New York in May 1860 and probably traveled straight on to relatives in Shelbyville, Illinois. Böpple, who is listed in the German records only as a blacksmith, combined his trade with farming once he settled in the United States. Although he was not forced to join the army by the draft or severe economic plight (he took along his own horse), Böpple joined the 7th Illinois Cavalry in August 1862. There are no traces of idealistic motivation in the letters; instead, it seems that the good pay in the army was the deciding factor.[1]

SOURCE NOTE: The Böpples write very much alike: simple German with limited vocabulary and erratic spelling. For persons with little formal education, however, there are remarkably few traces of the Swabian dialect they grew up with. Not included here is one letter in the series from the time after 1865 and one undated fragment.

1. GA Heumaden, Inventuren und Teilungen, Bd. 39, Nr. 90; HPL, *Teutonia*, April 21, 1860; NYPL, May 8, 1860. One reason for emigrating was that although his father owned eighteen plots of land, none was as large as half an acre; ibid., Bd. 50, Nr. 5. The 1860 census, taken June 29, shows them without property, sharing a house with a Metzger family, and lists David's occupation as a farmhand. MC 1860, Shelby Co./Ill., S. Div., #500. Shelby County was predominantly Democratic, voting for Douglas by a two-thirds margin in 1860. Burnham (1955), 386. For Böpple's service record see Muster Rolls, Pension File, NatA.

David Böpple
and wife
Magdalena.
(Emma Klein)

MAGDALENA BÖPPLE

Schelbewill Illinois, December 8, 1863

Dearest mother-in-law and brothers-in-law,

[. . .] My dear husband was sick for a month last summer, he had dysentery, but now he is well again, thank the Lord. I get a letter from him every week.

Dear mother-in-law, you thought my dear husband was long since dead and I hadn't wanted to tell you, I would have written immediately if he had died, but our dear Lord has kept him [----] healthy up to now, and I think He will [----] continue to do so if we ask Him, He will not desert us.

[12 ll.: is sending photographs, also of her husband in uniform] The pay varies a lot, too, the infantry gets 13 dollars, and the cavalry gets 25 dollars if they have their own horses. David has his own horse and he gets 25 dollars a month. He's already sent quite a lot of money home, and he can make more money in the war than he can at home. I myself would much rather have my husband than the money, but I think this wretched war will be over in the spring, and they say when they've fought 3 or 4 more battles then it will be decided, either for the southern side or for the northern. This regiment that David is in has never been in a big battle, all the soldiers in the regiment have their own horses, and so they are always in the back. Most of the time they have to go out at night and find the enemy positions, where they are and how many men there are, but otherwise he doesn't have a lot to do, and they've never been in a big battle.[2]

Dearest mother-in-law and brothers-in-law, I also want to write you about the harvest [14 ll.: details]. I still have one cow, one mare and one foal, I have to pay 25 dollars to feed the mare and the foal this winter. David doesn't want to sell the mare, she'll have another foal in the spring, she's a pretty mare, and I'd like to sell my cow if I can get 12 dollars for her.

Cotton, too, is so expensive that you can't buy it, cotton print costs 20 to 25 cents, it only cost 10 to 12 cents before the war, and cotton thread that used to cost 1½ dollars a package now costs 5 dollars, pretty much everything you want to buy now costs twice the price.

Dear mother-in-law I would send you a Christmas present if things weren't so uncertain [9 ll.: wants to hear from them soon].

Dear brother-in-law Heinrich, I want to ask you not to leave your old mother alone, since as you wrote, the two of you are living together all alone. I wouldn't like to hear that her children have left her all alone in her old age, but when the war here is over then we can see each other again, if we're still alive and well, because at the moment Ammericka is no place for you. I'd rather be in Germany than here[. . . .] All the best to you from me and best wishes from David, too, and next time he has to write to you as well.

[. . .] Johann Georg Böpple / David Böpple and Magdalena Böpple [. . .]

DAVID BÖPPLE

Pana, January 15, 1871.[3]

Greetings and God's blessing to you all, especially to you, dear mother,

[43 ll.: correspondence; health; farming, prices; earnings] I can't refrain from writing a few lines about this, although my wife doesn't want me to, but I want to anyway, since you know that I was in the war for 3 years and the government gave every soldier 100 dollars, and then the government decided that since millions of acres are lying fallow, they would give every soldier who got an honorable discharge 160 acres or *Morgen*, and they can choose the land they want. It doesn't cost anything but the registration fee.

But my wife doesn't want to move away from here, she says we've built a

2. Magdalena either did not know or neglected to write that Böpple took part in one of the most daring forays of the war, Grierson's* Raid. David's letter of 1868 (NABS), not included here, makes no mention of the war.

3. Pana is in Christian County, about fifteen miles from Shelbyville, but the Böpples were still living in Shelby County.

school and a church and a nice farm here, and she doesn't ever want to leave [5 ll.: details]. But I think I'm the stronger of the two of us and I'll win.

[7 ll.: children] Rosine just doesn't understand why I don't take her to Germany, she wants to see her grandmother[. . . .] She is of course still a child; if she knew what the difference is between America and Germany, she'd never want to go to Germany or at least not want to go to stay there. I myself never want to go back to Germany again.

[25 ll.: promises to send photograph; has slaughtered a lot of livestock; power of attorney; greetings; signature; address; will provide for his mother]

Women are often stronger than they seem: Böpple never took advantage of the government's offer of free land. Through the turn of the century, he lived as a farmer in the same township in Illinois. He also "recruited" two brothers-in-law from Germany, who were living with him in 1880. David Böpple died in 1912 at the age of seventy-six. In his last years he also received a veteran's pension, and in his application there is an affidavit from his comrade W. A. Cooke, who noted, "there was not a better soldier wore the Blue than Boepple."[4]

4. MC 1870: Shelby Co./Ill., Tower Hill Twp., #49; MC 1880: Shelby Co./Ill., e.d. 201, #39; MC 1900: Shelby Co./Ill., e.d. 129, #118; affidavit of March 3, 1891, Pension File, NatA.

40. Christian Bönsel

Christian Bönsel took the unusual step of immigrating to the United States in the middle of the Civil War, but he must have known about the risks. He left in 1862, probably on the advice of a cousin, Heinrich Jöckel, who had come back to Germany to visit. An entire group of immigrants sailed together, including Jöckel's parents—Bönsel's godfather, also named Heinrich Jöckel, and his wife—and some other friends.[1] Avoiding the army did not play a role in his decision to leave, since Bönsel had finished his military service in 1859. Economic considerations no doubt were important: his brother and sister also had to leave their home village of Lanzenheim. This village of approximately 500 inhabitants, where Bönsel's

SOURCE NOTE: Along with numerous misspellings, some of them so serious a German reader has to stop and figure out which word the writer had in mind, Bönsel's use of language is awkward, and many of his sentences are incomplete. Still, he is able to convey his messages and feelings. Not included here are the letters in the series from the time before 1860 (one) and after 1865 (twenty-nine), other letters from 1862 (one), 1864 (one), and 1865 (two), and three that are undated.

1. NYPL, *Ottilie*, July 5, 1862; undated letter by Bönsel and the Jöckels, ca. November 1862, NABS.

father was a shoemaker, was located in a poor mountainous region, the Vogelsberg, in Hesse.[2]

Heinrich Jöckel led the group to Arenzville, Cass County, Illinois, where he had probably lived before. Bönsel, who had said he was a carpenter when he arrived, first worked as a hired hand for various German farmers. In early 1864 he moved to Chandlersville, some fifteen miles away, where he started a wagon-making shop together with his cousin Jöckel. The world he lived in was strongly influenced by the local German immigrants, in particular his old friends from Hesse.[3]

Arenzville, July 12th, 1863

Dear parents and brothers and sisters,

[12 ll.: correspondence; health; work; relatives] These are sad times here, you can earn a lot of money now here, business is good since there aren't many men. A lot of them are in the war, and now they want to draft all those who are citizens because the ones who already went will all be shot dead soon. It is bad here with the war, it costs over a thousand white men for one black man, and no one knows what all will happen because there's too much cheating in the war, they make a lot of money on it and kill all the men. You've probably heard about it in Germany, what things are like here. Dear parents and brothers and sisters, you don't need to worry about me, if the Good Lord keeps me healthy everything will be fine, and I don't need to go to war and I won't go either, and things are the same all over the world, and the Good Lord is everywhere. I've already been away for a year, time goes very quickly [23 ll.: he is doing well; description of farming]. America is a country where the workers are still well paid, but now that's being ruined, everything is expensive but you can still make more money than in Germany. But you have to work hard. It's a free country here, if you don't work, you don't have anything, but the young and healthy like to travel. I don't advise anyone to come over now, times are too bad, because as you know, when there's a war, things are in a bad state. Please write me if Hergehainer has written yet and where he is, and about everyone who left and are now in the war, if they're still alive. I can't write much about the war since you don't see much out here in the country, since the farmers live all spread out [6 ll.: friends].

2. Letter from the army camp in Friedberg, May 15, 1859, NABS; Neumann (1883), 666; KB (ev.) Engelrod, Hs. StA DA. In a letter from Offenbach, August 16, 1863, NABS, his brother Georg writes about their sister in the Wetterau.

3. Some 22 percent of the population of Cass County was German; Arenzville and Chandlersville were two of the townships with the largest number of German settlers. USC 1870.1, 307, 351; Schem (1871), 3:80.

The address is, Christian Bönzel Arenzville
Cess Kaundi [Cass County] St. Illinois Nord amerika
but in Latin letters
[19 ll.: health; exhortations; greetings; signature. Back of the page: 28 ll.:
postscript from godfather Jöckel]

Chantlervelle, January 29, 1865

Dear parents and brothers and sisters,

[5 ll.: correspondence] Times are bitter now because of the war, everything
is very expensive and the men all have to go to war. They aren't getting any
volunteers any more and so they're drawing lots. Johannes Jökel's name was
also drawn, but he is still at home, he is sick. Now they're drawing lots again
for three times one hundred thousand men. The war has cost many lives, there
are already more than two million dead,[4] and it's not over yet, and no one can
say what all will happen. Dear parents, you don't need to worry about me, I
have suffered no want, and I also haven't yet regretted that I am here, because
I don't have to go to war. I asked the German consul, since I am not a citizen yet, that makes me free. You can make a lot of money now if you want to
be a soldier, a thousand dollars for a year. But the money doesn't tempt me,
what good is money when I'm dead. If I had to go to war I would come back
to Germany. I don't want to give my life for the Negro. America was a good
country, where workers could still earn something, but it's all being ruined by
the war [26 ll.: prices; working conditions; friends].

Dear brother, you wrote me that if I wanted to come I shouldn't wait much
longer, but I can't come now because I would lose too much money. To cross
the sea you have to pay in gold and all we have now here is paper money; if
you want to get gold here you have to pay two dollars of paper money for one
dollar in gold. When the war is over, if I am still single then I'll come back to
Germany for a visit [15 ll.: religious consolations; friends; greetings].

> A time of great trouble and chill,
> Hangs over this mighty land,
> Their own blood they do spill,
> The citizens upon their hand,
> To raise the Negro up on high,
> They plunge us into slavery,
> High taxes, costly times,
> Eat away at people's lives,

4. He has confused the number killed with the size of the entire Union army; a total of
620,000 soldiers died in the Civil War. McPherson (1988), 854.

And instead of making peace,
To end this horrible fight,
Their own lives they will cease,
Finding even suicide right,
Peace will come to this nation,
Only through Mck Clellan and Pendleton.[5]

Christian Bönsel [. . .]

Chandlersielle, July 23, 1866

Dear parents and brothers and sisters,

[27 ll.: correspondence; friends; is considering a visit to Germany; expressions of sympathy on the death of a brother] Dear brother, I want to write to you about the news here, how things are. The war is over, more soldiers are coming home every day. It certainly cost enough lives; the South gave up since they couldn't do any more, and on April 14th someone shot our president. He was in a theater and someone shot him there. They caught him and shot him, too, and on June 30th three men and a woman were hanged who had gotten together, they'd wanted to shoot the president, and they have taken the southern president prisoner, they say he'll be hanged as well, we now have a new president.

Dear brother,

Please write me how the harvest turned out. We're having a good year [. . .] but everything is still very expensive, and the war is over now and the wages are also high. Heinrich and I have a lot of work, we now make new wagons, here they make wagons quicker here than in Germany and they are still better made here, we have nice, good wood to work with. Everything here is different from Germany and faster. You also have to work hard here, but if you're careful with your money, you can certainly earn a lot [end of letter missing].

The advantages of life in America are also evident in Bönsel's next letter of March 17, 1867: "As I have heard from other letters, things look bad over there, what with the Prussians, all the men now have to serve and what with all those debts on top of it. You could be working for the Prussians your whole life long, I wouldn't like that. I am pleased that the Good Lord led me to another land; I have never regretted that I am here."[6]

5. This bit of doggerel was probably related to the Democratic election campaign the previous fall. George Pendleton was McClellan's vice presidential running mate. In 1860 55 percent of the vote in Cass County went to the Democrats, and in later elections a majority of the residents voted Democratic. McPherson (1988), 772, 803–5; Burnham (1955), 370.

6. Letter of March 17, 1867, NABS; Bönsel's home state of Hesse-Kassel was annexed by Prussia in 1866.

In March 1867 Bönsel got married; his wife, Katherina Wahl, came from a neighboring village and had sailed to America on the same ship as her husband. Bönsel spent the rest of his life in Chandlersville working as a wagon-maker, and later he also sold agricultural implements. When he died in 1901 at the age of sixty-three, he had been an elder in the Lutheran church for many years.[7]

7. Undated letter, ca. 1867, NABS; NYPL; MC 1870: Cass Co./Ill., Chandlersville Twp., #3; MC 1880: Cass Co./Ill., W. 18, #129; MC 1900: Cass Co./Ill., e.d. 9, #176; letter by J. Eichenauer with the news of Bönsel's death, ca. 1901, NABS.

41. Sergeant Ferdinand Krieger

Ferdinand Krieger's background can be reconstructed with some degree of certainty. In the late fall of 1850, Friedrich Wilhelm *August* Krieger immigrated to New York; he was a druggist's assistant and the son of a druggist, then deceased, who lived in Rodenkirchen, Oldenburg. August received permission to emigrate from his uncle and guardian, Wilhelm Hayssen, whose son Wilhelm also traveled with him. August must have been the letter-writer's brother, and Hayssen the father of the addressee of the letter included here. August apparently soon moved on to Wisconsin (his traveling companion had arrived there by the end of 1851), and in 1854 Ferdinand, now fifteen, left for Wisconsin together with two other companions from Oldenburg.[1] Judging from his handwriting and his subsequent occupations, Ferdinand must have had some commercial training. In 1860 he was working as a clerk for an Oldenburger storekeeper in Milwaukee, but his contact address during the war was the village of Kiel, about fifty miles north of the city. Shortly before he joined the army, he visited his mother in Germany, a sign that he was doing well financially. In August 1862 he volunteered in Milwaukee; in the muster rolls of the 24th Wisconsin Infantry he is listed as a merchant.[2]

Camp on Stone River [Stones River] near Murfreesboro
Tennessie, February 7th, 1863.

Dear friend,

[10 ll.: correspondence] You've probably known for a long time that I am a soldier, and now I want to report to you about our life. We left Milwaukee on

SOURCE NOTE: Commercial training and a fluent writing style seem to be two sides of the same coin. Krieger's large vocabulary allows him to express himself with great nuance, although his spelling is quite erratic. Not included here are two letters in the series from the time after 1865.

1. Ns. StA Oldenburg, Best. 70 (Amt Rodenkirchen), Nr. 6013, 6140, 6144; NYPL, *Juno*, April 19, 1854.

2. MC 1860: Milwaukee/Wisc., W. 7, #331; letter of February 7, 1863, abridged, NABS; letter of March 14, 1866, NABS; Muster Rolls, NatA.

September 5, 62, went from there by train to Louisville in the state of Kentucky. This town was threatened by the rebels, but so many Union troops were massed there that they didn't try to attack. Instead they turned toward Cincinnaty[. . . .] But we'd gotten there first, too, and they didn't dare to attack and withdrew back to Kentucky. We traveled by steamboat down the Ohio River, beautiful that time of year, and after a two-day trip, we were back in Louisville. After we had been there for about 14 days, our entire army took off to chase the enemy, and after an extremely strenuous march, we caught up with them near Perryville.[3] Here there was a terrible battle, and the first one in my life that I took part in. You can perhaps imagine what it was like when I tell you that we put on our uniforms for the first time on September 1, and then took part in this battle on October 8th, how much we knew about drilling. We hadn't learned a thing, so to speak. But still our regiment did very well. Even though the bullets came as thick as raindrops, no one decided to take to his *Yankee*-heels, like Uncle Janssen in Strohausen always says, instead [we] all did a decent job of using our weapons.

Toward evening the enemy had to retreat and we were the victors. The next day I went to look at the battlefield, but I can't possibly describe it to you. Piles of bodies were lying around, some of them ripped to pieces, some of them hit by musket balls where you could hardly see a wound, and countless wounded. Spiked cannon with their wheels chopped apart by an ax, horses, trees, cannonballs, guns, cartridges all mixed up in a mess. The *Farmer*-houses were all filled with the wounded, it was horrible to see, there was an entire pile of arms and legs that had been cut off, more than 200, I believe. But enough of these horrors. The enemy had fled through the Cumberland Mountains to Verginien. We marched off to West Kentucky and then due south. We passed by the famous Mammoth Cave, the largest stalactite cave in the world. And so it went on through Kentucky. In early November we got to the Tennessee border and a short time later to the capital Nashville, which had been strongly fortified by our troops in '61 and was still in our possession. We stayed here until Christmas Day, when the rainy season started that our General Rosenkranz [Rosecrans*] had been waiting for. So on Christmas Day, of all days, we received our marching orders, and off we went. The rain was terrible, we always had to push forward through the thickest mud, pressing the enemy pickets to retreat in front of us. Finally, about 4 miles from Murfreesboro, they held their ground. This town is 33 miles from Nashville. On the 30th, the day before New Year's Eve, the battle began. During the day we only had

3. The battle of Perryville on October 8, 1862, though not decisive, turned back a Confederate invasion of Kentucky that had reached to within thirty-five miles of Louisville. One-third of the Union soldiers were raw recruits like Krieger. McPherson (1988), 517–22.

to provide cover for our batteries, but still we had 23 killed. We were lying on our stomachs all the time, either in front of the batteries or behind them, and one of my comrades got his head blown off by a cannonball so that his brains splattered on our things. That night we had to sleep lying down in battle formation in a small grove. But the next morning, it was hardly dawn, the enemy came back to attack us, 5 regiments one after another. We met them with a full volley and caused many of them to bite the dust, but many a brave man from our regiment had to give his life as well, the rebels were all drunk and fought like tigers. After half an hour we were relieved, but we still had 250 dead to mourn. And so it continued until January 3rd, when finally the enemy was forced to retreat.[4] Now we're camped 2 miles south of Murfreesboro, but every day you can hear the damned 80 lb. contrabasses warning that another battle is near. Right after the battle I was promoted to corporal. In the next battle I'll make general when it's over, everybody's becoming a general these days [12 ll.: about "young ladies" in Oldenburg]. If I manage to survive this war safely, then I'm definitely going to come back to Germany to find a wife, compared with the German girls, the girls here are like a counterfeit taler* next to a real one.

[7 ll.: greetings and inquiries] Please excuse my bad handwriting, I am sitting here in my tent, in a cotton state, with my paper on a board, and my comrades are making such a racket[. . . .] Give my best to all my friends and relatives / from your / old friend

Ferd. Krieger [5 ll.: inquiries]

The 24th Wisconsin Infantry took part in Sherman's entire Atlanta campaign, but Krieger was shot in the ribs in June and spent the summer and fall of 1864 recovering in Nashville. He returned to his regiment just in time for the battles of Franklin and Nashville. In February 1865 he became a sergeant, and four months later he was mustered out in Nashville.[5]

In the spring of 1866 Krieger went to Cardiff, Wales, to visit his brother Max, who was probably a merchant or employed in the shipping trade. Ferdinand's experiences in America had left a deep impression on him, as is evident from his letter of April 27, 1866:

"Oh Germany, how far behind America you are." But take comfort in the fact that Germany is not alone; even England, despite its boastful citizens, is no match for America. I always say there is only one America, but I have to

---

4. The casualty rate of the battle of Stones River was the highest in the entire war: Union losses came to 31 percent and Confederates losses to 33 percent of those engaged. The 24 Wisc. Inf reported sixteen killed, forty-three wounded, and eighty-five missing. McPherson (1982), 311; *OAR*, 7:199.

5. Muster Rolls, NatA.

suffer a lot for this. When we get together in the evening, all the local stick-in-the-muds attack me and start talking politics [. . .] because first of all I know the Americans in and out, and secondly I know that John Bull and Brother Jonathan don't exactly regard each other as schoolmates and old friends[. . . .] I admit this doesn't make me any friends, but I will not betray my convictions even if I make an enemy out of everyone in Europe.

Given his opinions, it is hardly surprising that Krieger returned to America. In 1869 he and his Oldenburg bride left for Kiel, Wisconsin, where his brother was a farmer. He opened a general store that was already valued at $3,500 in 1870. At the turn of the century, he was still living in the same place and working in the same line of business.[6]

6. MC 1890: Veterans' Census, Manitowoc Co./Wisc., Schleswig Twp., #9; MC 1870: Manitowoc Co./Wisc., #110, #201; MC 1880: Manitowoc Co./Wisc., e.d. 77, #298; MC 1900: Manitowoc Co./Wisc., e.d. 68, #179. Since the Kriegers cannot be found in the 1869 passenger lists, it is unclear whether they got married in Germany and then emigrated to America together; however, MC 1900 shows that his wife emigrated in 1869, the same year they married.

42. Private Franz Schorse

Only the outlines of Franz Schorse's life before his emigration and the outbreak of the Civil War can be reconstructed. He was born on July 10, 1844, in Rühle, Holzminden County, Duchy of Braunschweig, where his father was a pastor. His father later took a position in nearby Mahlum, where his mother died in 1858. These two villages, with populations of 679 and 469, respectively, were small and insignificant, but Franz Schorse obviously had a solid elementary education and also learned to play the piano, organ, and violin.[1]

In 1861 sixteen-year-old Franz Schorse left for Milwaukee, where several acquaintances were already living. His decision to emigrate was hardly motivated by poverty but rather by ambition and a thirst for adventure, and while he was en route to America, the war broke out. After his arrival he worked for several months as a clerk; on December 31, 1861, he joined the army. In Chicago he took his place in Company C of the 61st Illinois Infantry, a predominantly Anglo American unit. The company received its baptism of fire at Shiloh, Tennessee,* in April 1862 and

SOURCE NOTE: There is little more to be said about Schorse's writing than the fact that there are few spelling and no grammatical errors, and that his High German is lively, precise, and almost elegant.

1. Konfirmationsliste 1858, Nr. 6, KB (ev.) Mahlum, Ns. StA Wolfenbüttel; information provided by the donor; Kleinau (1968), 493, 392–93.

took part in the main campaigns of the western army up to the siege of Vicksburg.*[2] Schorse wrote his only surviving letter about the war on the same day the fortress on the Mississippi capitulated.

Snyder's Bluff *near* Vicksburg, Miss. June [July] 4th, 1863.[3]

Dear father,

I received your letter of May 14 yesterday, at exactly the same time that Pemberton raised the white flag in Vicksburg.* Because it was already late in the day, however, Genrl. Grant sent in a message that the official surrender would be this morning. So at 8 o'clock this morning, on the day of the celebrations in honor of the "Constitution of the United States of Amerika,"[4] Grant's troops marched into the city of Vicksburg, where 20,000 rebels surrendered their weapons. So when you say, "the work of the army is coming to naught," then leave us out, because now we have taken Fort Donelson and Henry with 15,000 men, Island *No.* 10 with 3,000, and now Vicksburg with 20,000. Genrl. Grant's skill has been remarkably apparent in the last weeks. But before I write about that I want to tell you how we got here. You've probably heard the story of the last battles; and also that Johnson [Johnston] was on his way, although too late, to rescue his friends in Vicksburg. And that meant the rear of our army wasn't strong enough to stave off J., if he had wanted to throw his entire *Force* at one spot in order to make a gap that Pemberton could have used to fight his way out.[5] And so on the night before May 31st we got our marching orders [10 ll.: details].

To give you a detailed picture of the march to Vicksburg, I am sending you an excerpt from my diary [81 ll.: in English].

2. Pension File, NatA; NYPL, *Johann Lange*, September 23, 1857 (Otto Schorse); CD Milwaukee, 1858/59–1860/61. According to the Pension File, NatA, his future brother-in-law H. Simmerling also lived in Milwaukee before the war; Schorse's sisters Rosalie and Paulina arrived from Bremen aboard the *America* on September 11, 1865, NYPL. *Report of the Adjutant General of Illinois* (1901), 4:234–37, 241–43.

3. Although dated June 4, 1863, the letter must have been written on July 4.

4. Schorse has obviously confused the Constitution with the Declaration of Independence, which was signed on July 4, 1776.

5. After Vicksburg was captured, John C. Pemberton, born in Philadelphia, was accused of treason, but his defeat resulted more from the mediocre leadership and contradictory commands he received from Johnston and Jefferson Davis. Boatner (1959), 441, 631; McPherson (1988), 629–36.

July 5th

General Engelmann[6] just read out the report about the capture of Vicksburg: 31,000 prisoners (including the sick and those wounded in earlier battles), along with 1 lieutenant general (Pemberton) and 16 major and brigadier generals; 54 heavy cannon (11–13 inch), a large number of smaller artillery pieces and almost 50,000 muskets. —

But I'll go back to my story of our trip, before I say any more about today. On the day when we received important news about Jahnston [Johnston]: we had been at Chicasaw Bayou (small river) for a few hours when we got orders to go to Sartatia [Satartia, Mississippi], 40 miles up the river. So then all the wagons and provisions that we had unloaded had to be put back on the same boats[. . . .] Around noon on the 4th we came in sight of Sartatia, which the rebels abandoned as soon as they saw our boats. We put in for a landing and followed at their heels. We tried to lure them into an open fight and unleashed our battery at them, but they fired at us with 5 cannon while they retreated. There was also a lively skirmish before we could drive them out of their best position, the village of Mechanicksville, where we thought they'd return with reinforcements. But instead they continued to retreat, and so our cavalry chased after them and took 75 prisoners. After we had set up solid pickets, we made camp for the night by putting dried grass and leaves on the ground[. . . .] The commander of the division was Genrl. Kimball. He learned on June 5th that Johnson was approaching with a large force to attack Grant's rear. Since we were the outpost that was closest to Johnson, we withdrew to Haines Bluff. At 9 o'clock in the morning of the 6th, we started to march double-time; by 11 o'clock more than 100 men were lying by the side of the road, almost 50 of them hit by heat stroke and the rest collapsed from exhaustion. A healthy soldier was left with each one, to lift them into the hospital wagons; and thanks to the activity of our doctors only 10 men died without having seen Haines Bluff. The only thing that helps is putting leaves in your cap so the sun doesn't burn through as much, put up with your thirst as long as you can hold out, don't talk a lot and breathe through your nose. When the sun was about to go down, half of the regiments were behind us, since they had stopped to rest. They caught up with us, though, when we stopped in a large cornfield to pick cornstalks to make our beds. We got out some good ham from the provision wagon and made some strong coffee. We enjoyed a

6. General Adolf Engelmann (1825–90) came with his father, a political refugee of the early 1830s, to live in Belleville, Illinois. He served in the Mexican War, and in 1848 he went back to fight in Schleswig-Holstein. In the Civil War he started off as a lieutenant colonel and then colonel in the 43 Ill. Inf, later brevet brigadier general.

rest until 3 o'clock in the morning, but then we didn't even have time to eat, instead we stuck some *Krakers* in our *Havresack*. That day the march wasn't so hard, because the day before we had come farther than we needed to. By the middle of the day we were 3 miles away from where we were supposed to be positioned, and we had enough time for a rest. After we had been sitting in the shade for about 15 minutes, the biggest and strongest fellow in our company, who was sitting next to me, suddenly went white as a corpse and fell backwards, seemingly dead[. . . .] We brought him some water, poured it on his head, especially on his temples, rubbed the pulse in his arms to warm them up, and after about a quarter of an hour we noticed that he had improved, and we turned him over to the doctors for care. When we got to our post in the evening and fresh pork was sizzling on the fire, good old Henry arrived as well, completely recovered from his faint. On the 11th another division arrived by boat, they were camped to the west of us and they started making strong fortifications on the highest point in the row of hills [11 ll.: details]. On the south slope of these hills there are large fortifications pointing south, surrounded by riflepits. They are well stocked with cannon so big you can stick your head in them, and 50 of them we captured from the rebels; they had them close to the river in order to shoot at our gunboats, not expecting an attack from the rear. That's why it was so easy for General Sherman during the last battles at Vicksburg* to slip in from the rear. On the 14th we marched to Snyder's Bluff to make space for the 2 divisions sent by Rosencrans [Rosecrans*]. These divisions were the first New-York, Rhode Island, Vermont, Massachusetts, and Pensylvania regiments we'd had in our army [6 ll.: digging entrenchments]. The entire job took 8 days, and many came down sick, and then all the troops except our division marched on to help Sherman to make a trench 15 miles wide (long) all the way down to the Big Black *river*. They finished this in time, before Johnston could get there with his 25,000 men; so he found that the way to Vicksburg was blocked. If he attacked, our 40,000 men could quickly reassemble, and Grant could send another 25,000 men. That's why it was impossible for him.

At the same time he had to listen to the continuous bombardment of Vicksburg, which we could clearly hear in Sartatia (40 miles away). One boom after another, with the sound of a vast number of smaller guns playing in between, all night long and through the morning. The heavy mortars woke me up several times during the night. They had been free to keep bombarding them since the end of May, since the army had dug in all around Vicksburg so Pemberton couldn't break out, and they dug new trenches when they moved in closer. When they reached the bluffs where the rebels had their fortifications, they rolled logs in front of them until they were less than 20 paces from

the enemy works. Then the cannon were too high to hit them and when anyone with a gun could be seen, he became the target of a couple dozen sharpshooters in the background. This way it became difficult to even send spies
to Johnston. Grat [Grant] threatened to blow up a *Fort* the day before the
surrender. But this was not necessary, hunger was enough to force the humiliating act. Women and children had been asking Pemberton to surrender for
weeks, and they even stooped to snatching bread and ham out of the hands
of our men who were passing it out. The prisoners look like corpses. But I
don't need to describe the suffering caused by a siege, you know enough about
it from books [15 ll.: correspondence; greetings]. from / your / loving son
Franz / didn't you know a teacher named Benecke from Blankenburg?[7]

The confident tone of the letter is misleading; Franz Schorse had already suffered an
injury and would be plagued by its aftereffects for the rest of his life. Shortly after
he was mustered out in March 1865, one brother-in-law, Heinrich Simmerling from
Milwaukee, who had known him before the war, said that Franz looked "entirely
changed in appearance" and was, in his opinion, "out of his mind." Otto Sontag, a
future brother-in-law, also reported that Schorse seemed to be "very nervous and
excitable, complained about pain in his head." Because he was unable to do any
physical work, several office jobs were arranged, the last one by Sontag in Winona,
Minnesota, but to no avail. Schorse himself admitted that he sometimes resorted
to alcohol to numb his pain. In June 1872 his relatives felt compelled to have him
committed to a hospital for the mentally ill. He was institutionalized for the next
eleven years, until he had improved enough to be released in March 1883.[8]

It remains unclear whether Schorse's ailment had physical or psychological
causes.[9] Like so many pension applicants, he complained of rheumatism and pain
that he claimed had been caused by the strains of the war and constantly living
outdoors in bad weather. In a letter of 1882, however, he wrote that he had been
wounded in the afternoon on April 6, 1862, in the battle of Shiloh*: "a bullet
bounced off a tree and hit me in the back of the head, and it was a terrific blow." For
a long time afterward, he had been dizzy. Despite this, Captain Benecke, who later
attested to Schorse's injury, recommended him in 1864 for promotion to lieutenant

7. Probably the father of his comrade, Captain Louis Benecke, who later provided an affidavit
as part of Schorse's pension application.

8. Pension File, NatA, affidavits from 1882 to 1884; Rochester State Hospital Case Books,
Minnesota StateA; MC 1880: Olmstead Co./Minn., e.d. 217, #26. In MC 1870: Winona Co./
Minn., St. Charles City, #61, Schorse appears as a store clerk living in the household of C. Him-
stedt, a merchant and store owner born in Braunschweig. Otto Sontag, a grain dealer from
Braunschweig who married Schorse's sister Rosalie, lived just down the street (#80). Rosalie was
listed in the Rochester files as Schorse's next of kin.

9. The psychological aftereffects of the Civil War have not been thoroughly studied, but
Dean (1997) provides an excellent start. See also Marten (2001).

in the 49th Missouri Infantry, but Schorse turned this down. In the mental hospital his condition was diagnosed as "chronic mania" caused by "intemperance"; no physical symptoms were noted. There is also no mention of his injury in his military record. This much is clear: the inexperienced troops of the 61st Illinois Infantry were in the front line when the surprise Confederate attack began on the first morning of the battle of Shiloh. They held the line for an hour and a quarter and were the last regiment to withdraw. The commanders of Schorse's division and brigade were both taken prisoner, along with one of the three colonels in his brigade; a second one was wounded.[10]

In 1884 Schorse filed an appeal to have the negative decision about his pension reviewed; that is the last sign of life we have. Nothing indicates he ever received a war pension. In the 1890s these applications began to be treated more generously, but Franz Schorse was probably dead by then.[11]

10. Letter from Schorse to Louis Benecke, August 15, 1882, Benecke Family Papers, WHMC; Pension File, NatA; *Report of the Adjutant General of Illinois*, 4:241–43; Johnson and Buel (1987), 1:502–3, 538; Hicken (1991), 56–57, 65–66. The Rochester State Hospital Case Books note explicitly, "Accompanying bodily disorder, none."

11. Schorse does not appear in MC MN 1885, Winona Co., where his brother-in-law Otto Sontag and family are listed; he also does not appear in the 1890 Veterans Census for Minnesota.

43. Bernhard Buschmann

Bernhard Buschmann was not particularly interested in the Union cause for three reasons: he had arrived in the United States only a short time before the war, he was Catholic, and he had settled in a rural area, outside the influence of the big cities and their more liberal press. Buschmann, born in 1838, came from a medium-sized but heavily indebted farm in Ostbevern, in the ultra-Catholic Münsterland of Westphalia. Although he was supposed to inherit the family farm, in 1861 he left for America in secret, to avoid the impending threat of being drafted into the Prussian army.[1] He settled in southeast Iowa, not far from the Mississippi River, and took up a familiar life as a farmhand.

SOURCE NOTE: Judging from his writing, Buschmann picked up quite a bit of arithmetic, but he did not learn much about language at school. His sentences are endless, and his spelling follows no recognizable rules; however, his descriptions are lively and sometimes quite witty. Not included here is one letter in the series from the time after 1865 and two undated letters.

1. Information provided by the donor. The farm consisted of about thirty-five acres, but it had a mortgage of 1,500 talers.*

[Burlington, October 28, 1863]

Dear mother, sister and brother-in-law,

More than two years have passed now since I last saw you and spoke to you [10 ll.: correspondence; family; weather]. The wheat turned out well, and everything is very expensive, also clothing is almost twice as expensive as it used to be, but that's because of the war, and no one knows how long it will last. The war makes everything expensive, but it also makes land cheap, now I could get a nice *Bauerrei, Fahrm,* for eight hundred dollars that otherwise wouldn't sell for less than thirteen to fourteen hundred dollars. Fine soil and fine meadows and fine pastures and fine timber. A lot of people here who know their way around are advising me to do this, and if I had all my money here I could pay for it directly, because if you sent it to me, I would get it paid out in gold, and then I could have it exchanged into paper money, and then for one dollar I'd get one and a half, and you can pay in paper money just as well as with gold.[2] I won't be getting married until I am twenty-eight or thirty, but I may never get the chance again to buy something for that price, and I'll have to find a home here anyway since you can't hire out when you're old here, the farmers pay very good money, and so they like to get a lot of work in return [29 ll.: wants his settlement; is healthy; advice on emigration; greetings; signature; date].

You write that young people are so bad in keeping up their faith, but it's not all that bad, I ride to church every Sunday, I don't need to walk, I'm just as Catholic here as I was at home.

[probably 1864]

Dear mother, sister, and brother-in-law

I received your letter and see that people over there are making up all sorts of stories, because I've never heard anything about what you wrote, that people who don't own any land have to work with the slaves, and so you don't need to worry about me in this regard because on March 16th I signed on for a year with a farmer who pays 160 dollars, that's 220 talers* in your money. I am 1 hour away from the church, but he has to lend me a horse every Sunday, and I haven't walked there yet. You write that the war is costing so many lives, which is not a lie, it has cost a terrific number of lives, but all the men who died went voluntarily, men who didn't want to work but were just loafing around and who weren't worth much more than a bullet, but no one knows how many

---

2. Buschmann's mother had bequeathed him 500 talers, but only on the condition that he return to Germany. He did finally get the money, but only after the turn of the century. Information provided by the donor.

good men it will still cost, because the war may go on for a long time. I don't believe the war will take my life, though, because if you're not a citizen then you don't have to go, and I'll make sure I wait a long time before becoming a citizen. Where I am it's just like at home when there was a war in Baden or Holstein, you never noticed it at all, and it's like that here too.[3] I've often listened for it, but I've never been able to hear a cannon shot, I often imagined I did, but it was always thunder, since it started to rain right afterwards. I'm about two hundred hours away.

Now I want to write you about how I've been. Instead of this letter you could have gotten a death notice [8 ll.: had a throat infection that killed many others]. But once again I had luck, since they didn't want me in Heaven yet, they're getting enough fellows like me who have been shot to death, and so they passed me by this time [5 ll.: weather]. And you, dear sister, wanted to know if I also go dancing, I'll tell you about it, I do go dancing but I don't like it half as much as in Germany. I know how to do the dances all right, but you have to take a girl with you, and they are so lazy here, they won't walk for even half an hour, instead you have to get a wagon and pick them up[. . . .] I haven't been to a dance since last year on the 4th of July, although there's a ball almost every month, but the 4th of July is a big holiday here, but not a Catholic one, it's just that no one works and there are large balls, and I think if I stay healthy I'll go to a ball again this year [14 ll.: friends; would like to give them a subscription to a newspaper; greetings; signature missing].

Kanosha, June 15th, 1865

Dearest mother, sister, brother-in-law, and mother-in-law,

[15 ll.: correspondence; church attendance; employment] I've been working here for one year and three months, and on April first I signed up for another eight months for 26 dollars a month and fodder for my horse, which makes 208 dollars all together for the eight months. But wages will be going down soon, because the war will be over soon, and then all the men will be coming back [42 ll.: farming; American womenfolk; end of letter missing].

Buschmann's letter of 1865 was probably written from Kenosha, Wisconsin, about 180 miles east of the Iowa border, because later that year he married a woman from Wisconsin who was the daughter of Bavarian immigrants. The young couple first rented a small farm in northwest Iowa; after 1870 they bought a farm in the same area, and they were still living there in 1900, free of debt. According to the census, he was the father of fifteen children; thirteen were still alive in 1900, and

3. Holstein and Baden, both sites of conflict during 1848, were 200–300 miles from Buschmann's home.

seven of them still lived at home. Bernhard Buschmann died in 1910 at the age of seventy-two.[4]

4. MC 1870: Winneshick Co./Iowa, Washington Twp., #262; MC 1880: Winneshick Co./ Iowa, Military Twp., #93; MC 1900: Winneshick Co./Iowa, e.d. 138, #239. In 1870 no real property was listed. According to MC 1900, Buschmann had immigrated in 1858, but he contradicts this in his first letter; MC 1910: Winneshick Co./Iowa, e.d. 161, p. 14, says 1860.

44. Lieutenant Colonel Conrad Weinrich

Conrad Weinrich came to the United States in 1837 when he was ten years old, together with his widowed mother and four brothers and sisters. They took up residence in Missouri, where the three eldest children had already settled with the Giessen Emigration Society from Hesse in 1834. Besides the fact that they came from the same area—the family lived in Alten Buseck, some six miles northeast of Giessen—the Weinrichs had little in common with the educated, well-to-do members of the society. Conrad's father had made a modest living as a shoemaker before he died in 1832, shortly before his youngest child was born. The family probably had little more than the money they needed for their passage.[1]

Conrad Weinrich had little opportunity for schooling after his arrival in America. He grew up in St. Charles County, an area of Missouri with one of the heaviest concentrations of German settlers, where Germans soon rivaled the Anglo Americans in numbers. A German weekly newspaper was founded in 1852, and soon afterward its editor, Arnold Krekel, was elected to the Missouri legislature. Krekel at first supported the position of the Free Soil Democrats, who were opposed to the extension of slavery, but in 1860 he became a Republican. While more than half of the Anglo Americans in St. Charles County were slaveholders, only 3 percent of the Germans owned slaves. In the New Melle precinct, where the Weinrichs lived, a

SOURCE NOTE: There is a stark contrast between the fact that Weinrich cites a historic battle twenty-four years after having left Germany at the age of ten, and the sort of spelling that betrays a very deficient elementary schooling and sometimes makes it difficult to understand what he says. His frequent use of English terms seems normal after a quarter century, and his German is simple and straightforward. Not included here are the letters in the series from the time before 1860 (seven) and after 1865 (thirty-one), as well one letter from 1860 and two from 1865. For part of the letter of April 12, 1865, only a transcript is available. Since Conrad Weinrich was the great-great-grandfather of Walter Kamphoefner, more background research had previously been conducted on him than is typical for the other letter-writers in this volume.

1. *Portrait and Biographical Record of St. Charles* (1895); Kamphoefner (1987), 100–101; KB (ev.) Alten Buseck, where the brother of Friedrich Münch, leader of the Giessen Society, was the pastor from 1820 to 1829; St. Louis Marriages, Book 3, March 22, 1846, St. Louis City Hall, St. Louis, Mo.

53 percent majority voted for Lincoln, but in five Anglo American precincts in the same county, Lincoln received between 0 and 4 percent of the vote.[2]

Conrad Weinrich took an active role in the Republican movement. In the meantime he had married and become the father of three children, and he ran a flourishing business as a blacksmith, employing several journeymen. He had learned his trade in St. Louis, where he had worked for a year in an oil factory and then for his brother-in-law, August Hill, one of the family members to whom these letters are addressed. In 1851 Weinrich came into his own business in New Melle by marrying the young widow of a local blacksmith.[3]

Weinrich's active support for the Union cause, despite his family responsibilities, can be seen as the self-defense of a German unionist who was threatened by American neighbors of southern background and convictions. There had already been several incidents of violence and intimidation during the 1860 election campaign, and there were even more in February 1861, running up to the special election held to decide whether Missouri would remain in the Union. Soon afterward, Weinrich and other Germans in St. Charles County began to organize and train Union militiamen, under the leadership of Arnold Krekel.

February the 20th, 1861

Dear brother-in-law, sister & brother and sister-in-law and friends,

[9 ll.: family; health] On Monday we had a regular *Figth* and the Americans fell like the French at the battle of Leipzig.[4] But now our lives aren't safe for a minute, we have night patrols and have armed ourselves as well as we can. And we will hold them off as long as possible (fair is fair). Today there were another 30 Americans here, armed to the teeth, but they must have gotten wind that the coast wasn't clear, but never mind, we are in the right.[5]

---

2. *Portrait and Biographical Record of St. Charles* (1895), 371; Kamphoefner (1987), 94–95, 111, 116, 130; Kamphoefner (1981), 91–92.

3. *Portrait and Biographical Record of St. Charles* (1895), 371; KB (ev.) Röhrenfurth; St. Paul's Lutheran parish register, New Melle/Mo.

4. Where the German forces and their allies decisively defeated Napoleon's army in 1813. Note that Weinrich uses "Americans" to mean "Anglo Americans," whom he equates with secessionists.

5. The *St. Charles Demokrat* reported this incident on February 28, 1861, in more detail: "On the last days of the election, the friends of both *Tickets*: for or against the Union, had been working harder than ever for the cause [. . .] and the men, fired up with drink, got caught up in a kind of '*fighting*' state. A certain Mason, about whose character no one can sing hymns of praise [. . .] got into an argument and started a fight with several others. He must have come out on the short end, because [. . .] during the fight his trousers were ripped off and he had to flee [. . .] dressed only in his shirt. A German rode after him with a club, but an American followed behind and shot at the German with a *Revolver*[. . . .] On Friday the news arrived here that [. . .] about 50–60

Please write again soon / Our best regards to all of you / your brother-in-law / Conrad Weinrich

Don't tell anybody there about the battle[. . . .]

                                                    New Melle, July the 26th, 1861
Dear brother and sister, brother-in-law, and sister-in-law,

[. . .] Dear sister, you write that you haven't seen or heard anything of us in these troubled times, but you shouldn't hold it against us, because times are more troubled here than where you are, and that everything is very cheap, that's the case here, too, but now there's no money around, I think the secessionists have buried it all, and if it ever sprouts and bears fruit we'll harvest it in bushels.

[5 ll.: could not locate a wagon maker for Heinrich] Heinrich also wanted to know if we'd gotten U.S. arms. We didn't have them yet at the time, but a week ago we received 80 pieces in Cotlevill [Cottleville] and another company got 40, that makes 120 in our area, and in Cotlevill 60 and in St Peters 60, that makes 220 altogether, apart from St. Charles where they received 100. Mr. A Krekel is the commander of the Union Guard of St. Charles County. Last Saturday 400 men from the Union Guard assembled with Capt Woodson near Dr [T]alley's. Capt Heine's Comp was drilling with U.S. weapons, and then the *Fire eaters* came and wanted to take them away, but they got a hot *Brackfeest* [breakfast] instead with *Muskets, Rifles,* & *Shottgunns.* They'd gotten 400 men together, but if they'd had 1,000 we still would have beaten them up all right. I don't know what will happen now. Some 4–500 secessionists have gotten together in Lincoln County and are after our hides, but I don't think these guys have any *Spunch,* we are ready *anny time.*

Please write again soon about what is new with you, because I can't get away now and I'm on my own in the *Shop.* Tomorrow I'm going to Augusta again for a *Meeting.* / Your brother and brother-in-law / Conrad Weinrich

---

Americans, armed with rifles and the like [. . .] were approaching to take revenge on the people in New Melle. During the night a special message arrived for the sheriff. Having arrived in New Melle, he rode forward to meet the men [Americans] coming from Wentzville, but it was a difficult task to dissuade them from their unauthorized, illegal plan. The Germans in New Melle had holed up in several houses in such a way that if it had come to an attack, the Americans would have been caught in a murderous crossfire." Conrad Weinrich and two others, the newspaper reported, were arrested and released on bail; those who were actually involved in the fighting were able to escape. One week later, New Melle was reported to be almost empty; all the shops were closed, and many residents had moved away. *St. Charles Demokrat,* March 7, 1861, April 18, 1861. More background on St. Charles County during the war is provided by Ehlmann (2004), 80–147.

New Melle, November 16th, 1862

Dear brother, brother-in-law, sister, and sister-in-law,

[10 ll.: family; health] You'll probably want to know how it was on my war campaign and where we were. So, on Sept. the 9th we went to Wentzvill, and then from there to Flinthill, where we gave the *Sisesch* [secesh] and Charles [S]ack, too, a good going-over. On the 12th we went from there to Warrenton, on the 14th from there to High Hill in Montgomery Co., that's where A[-] Bigelow, a strong *Sisesch*, lives. On the 15th to Martinsburg on the N.M.R.R. [North Missouri Railroad], on the 16th we arrived in Mexico in Audrian Co., on the 17th we left to go to Paris but we only got there on the 18th. Paris is a pretty little country town in Monroe Co. about 150 miles from St. Louis. We stayed in this area for 4 weeks and patrolled through the whole county as well as the neighboring counties and searched through all the main towns, from Paris to Santafee, Florida, Klinton, Midlegrove, Madison, Shellbiny, Dogwalk, Granvill and Longbranch, and from there back to Mexico through Calloway Co and Fullton, the headquarters of the *Sisesch* in North Missouri, and on October 15 we came back home. The entire time we got nothing from the government but a couple of barrels of *Krakers* and some coffee. All the rest, like horses and all our equipment, except for our clothing, we had to take from the *Sisesch*, because there was no other way to get anything. We had our food and drink provided by the *Sisesch*, when we found some, and when they didn't want to cook for us, we threatened to take everything away from them and cook for ourselves, but then they livened up and cooked what we wanted to have[6] [10 ll.: family celebration; greetings; signature].

New Melle, April the 12th / 65

Dear sister,

[28 ll.: family and relatives] Last week, after the capture of Richmond and yesterday, after Gen'l Lee and his whole army capitulated, our anvils had to take the place of the cannons, we shot off 15 dollars' worth of gunpowder from my anvil, and the good old barley juice was not forgotten either, but it does help you forget about some things, it was a wonderful day [12 ll.: greetings; signature; is thinking about coming for a visit].

6. On August 9, 1862, Colonel Arnold Krekel received instructions not to weigh down his campaign through the rebel areas in Missouri by taking along provisions but to take his supplies from the rebels (*OR* I, 13:551). From September 9 to 26, 1862, Weinrich was on active duty as a captain, Comp H, 27 Enrolled Missouri Militia. Before that he served in the Home Guard, and later he was in the 75 Mounted Inf, Enrolled Missouri Militia, where he reached the rank of lieutenant colonel. *History of St. Charles* (1885), 373; Muster Rolls, 27 Enrolled Missouri Militia, Missouri StateA.

Although the South had capitulated, Conrad Weinrich remained true to the larger cause. On September 17, 1866, he wrote, "Perhaps I will also run as a candidate to be elected to the legislature." One of the most important tasks of this session was to determine the legal status of freed slaves—a controversial question, as was reported in the St. Louis *Anzeiger des Westens*: "Mr. Weinrich from New Melle, the radical candidate for the legislature [. . .] is said to have recently told some gentlemen that he regards the Negro as quite his equal in political and social terms. He also remarked that if four of his five daughters were to marry white men, and one married a Negro, he would treat his black son-in-law just like the white husbands of his other daughters."[7]

This was printed in an antiradical paper and is perhaps exaggerated, but if it were intended to damage the candidate in the eyes of his countrymen, it completely misfired. Weinrich reported shortly after the election, "I have been elected to the state legislature, and we elected the entire *Radical Ticket* without exception, and the conservatives are hanging their heads. I heard that 2 days after the election, the barbers in St Charles were charging double the price to shave a conservative, because their faces are so long now."[8]

Loyalty to the union and energetic activism were obviously more important to the local German voters than higher education. Weinrich's candidacy, however, also profited from the fact that rebels were not allowed to vote. He did not write much about his activities in the legislature, but he staunchly defended the interests of his countrymen: "The Sunday laws have been made even worse again, but I hope that the bill won't pass the Senate. The Sunday bigots and temperance supporters are hard at work here, but I hope they won't get far with their absurd bigotry."[9]

Although Weinrich took little legislative initiative, the voters were pleased enough with him to elect him for a second term. One of his few actions, however, confirms his radical reputation: when the new regulations for the state university were being drawn up, there was a motion to delete a clause that prohibited discrimination based on race or gender. In a futile attempt to save the clause, Weinrich demanded a roll-call vote.[10]

After two terms of office, he withdrew from the legislature and ran (unsuccessfully) for a county office. He then turned his attention to his farm and vineyard— he had already turned over most of the responsibility for the blacksmith shop to his son-in-law Fritz Kamphoefner. Long after Weinrich retired, he still remained true

7. *Anzeiger des Westens*, November 1, 1866.

8. Letter of November 29, 1866, NABS.

9. Foner (1988), 42; letter of January 20, 1868, NABS.

10. *Journal of the House, Missouri* (1870), 379. Weinrich's efforts for the civil rights of blacks did not always enjoy the support of his fellow immigrants. In 1868 the Republican presidential candidate carried New Melle by a 72 percent margin, but only 39 percent of the voters supported a referendum to grant voting rights to blacks. Nonetheless, in two neighboring German precincts that went 97 percent and 71 percent Republican, black suffrage gained majorities of 74 percent and 68 percent, respectively. *St. Charles Demokrat*, November 11, 1868.

to his political principles. On November 2, 1890, he wrote, "*Well*, next Tuesday is the election, and we hope the entire Republican *Tiket* gets elected. I am an election judge here." Conrad Weinrich died in New Melle on August 25, 1904.[11]

11. *St. Charles Demokrat*, September 29, October 6, November 7, 1870; letters of February 2, 1876, September 3, 1873, December 26, 1874, NABS; St. Paul's Lutheran parish register, New Melle/Mo.

45. First Lieutenant Karl Adolph Frick and Alwine Frick

Karl Adolph Frick was one of the small category of emigrants who saw emigration as an economic venture. He did not leave his home because he had experienced or feared economic setbacks; instead, he was drawn to the New World by the hope of potential profit. He was born in 1835 in Lahr, Baden, a town of 7,000 inhabitants. His father was in the tanning and leather trade and prominent enough to be a member of the town council. Adolph probably attended secondary or commercial school until he was fifteen, then spent two years as a clerk in France and made his way to America via Le Havre in the spring of 1854.[1]

In the first surviving letter of March 1856 from Cincinnati, it is already clear that Frick had a good head for business. Two years after his arrival, in early 1857, he moved to Missouri, bought land sixty miles west of St. Louis, and opened a store that was obviously the main business in the village of Campbellton.[2] The following year he became the local postmaster and married Alwine Vitt, the daughter of a well-to-do farmer who had emigrated from southern Westphalia in 1853.[3] Politics

SOURCE NOTE: The handwriting of Alwine and Adolph Frick could hardly be more different, yet their writing style is very similar. Her handwriting is small, regular, constant, and easily legible; his is rather flamboyant, changing, and irregular. Though one might imagine the businessman would have had considerable practice writing, the structure of his phrases is remarkably undisciplined, with subjects that dangle or change in mid-sentence. His wife, however, is equally freewheeling in her style. They both write clearly; Adolph's rare spelling and grammar mistakes reflect the Allemanic dialect spoken where he was born, whereas Alwine's writing shows little, if any, influence from her local dialect. Not included here are the letters in the series from the time before 1860 (one) and after 1865 (six), as well as one letter each from 1860, 1862, and 1864 and two undated letters.

1. Neumann (1883), 654; GLA Ka 360 Lahr Zg 1935-11/2221; NYPL, *Hansa*, April 20, 1854. The motivational distinctions for emigration are based on Marschalck (1973), 52, 71. According to a biographical sketch in *History of Franklin* (1888), 748–49, Frick attended a "college."

2. Letter of March 9, 1856, NABS; the last letter from Cincinnati is dated May 8, 1857, NABS. According to *History of Franklin* (1888), 749, Frick spent two years in Cincinnati, but the date of his arrival in Missouri is unclear.

3. Letter of December 1858, NABS; *History of Franklin* (1888), 749; MC 1860: Franklin

are seldom mentioned in the letters before 1860, but Frick was at least an active member of the local *Turnverein*. Like many other Turners,* in terms of his religious views he was something of a freethinker.[4]

Although he probably got along well in the English-speaking world, most of the customers in his store were Germans: one-quarter of the whites in Franklin County were German-speaking immigrants. There were a significant number of slaves, almost 9 percent of the population.[5] Not surprisingly, given his association with the Turner movement and his familiarity with city life, Frick was a Republican: in 1860, in the first election after he was naturalized, he voted for Lincoln, who placed third out of four in the county with 24 percent of the votes.[6]

Frick did not take part in the war from the very beginning, but as the fighting spread from St. Louis through the rest of Missouri, he volunteered for the Franklin County Home Guards, a militia unit, on June 13, 1861. Since he was made a captain, it is highly likely that he helped organize the company. Perhaps his connections with the Turners played a role: they formed the core of the unionist movement in St. Louis, and the 17th Missouri Infantry, in which he briefly served, was also a Turner regiment. For family and business reasons, however, Frick soon returned to his local militia.[7] Although there were no major battles fought in Missouri after 1861, guerrilla warfare was more savage there than anywhere else, affecting Frick's area as well. This is one reason why he and many Germans in Missouri hoped for more a radical approach than Lincoln's and even attempted to nominate another presidential candidate in 1864.[8]

Co./Mo., Boeff Twp., #59 (Vitt), #63 (Frick), according to which Vitt had assets of about $10,000, and the Fricks $6,800; Woodruff (1969), 87, 93.

4. Although Frick was baptized as a Protestant, no mention is made in his letters or his biographical sketch of having belonged to a church congregation; neither his marriage nor his burial were conducted by a Christian minister. Letter of November 19, 1857, NABS; Kaufmann (1911), 584; Ueberhorst (1978), 48–49; obituary of April 27, 1906, from unidentified newspaper clipping in the Washington Historical Society, Washington, Mo.

5. USC 1860.1, 286, 291; USC 1870.1, 189, 315, 362; as well as hand counts from MC 1860: Franklin Co./Mo.

6. Arndt and Olson (1965), 240–41, 246, 279–80; *History of Franklin* (1888), 243, 749; Kamphoefner (1981), 95.

7. According to the Muster Rolls, Franklin County Home Guards and 54 Enrolled Missouri Militia, Missouri StateA, Frick served as captain, Comp D, Franklin County Home Guards, from June 16 to September 13, 1861, and then as first lieutenant, Comp D, 54 Enrolled Missouri Militia, sworn in and in active service from August 15 to December 31, 1862, and again from April 23 to May 26, 1863. According to *History of Franklin* (1888), 749, he served briefly in 1861 as an officer in the 17 Mo. Inf, but since he does not appear in *OAR*, 7:102–3, he probably was never sworn in, as his wife indicates in her letter of May 11, 1862, NABS. One of the initiators of the *Turnverein* founded in 1859 in Washington, Missouri, Francis Wilhelmi, became a major in the 17 Mo. Inf; another, Robert Reichard, was an officer in Frick's militia regiment. *History of Franklin* (1888), 245, 255–56, 309.

8. For details on the radical anti-Lincoln movement, see Nagler (1984).

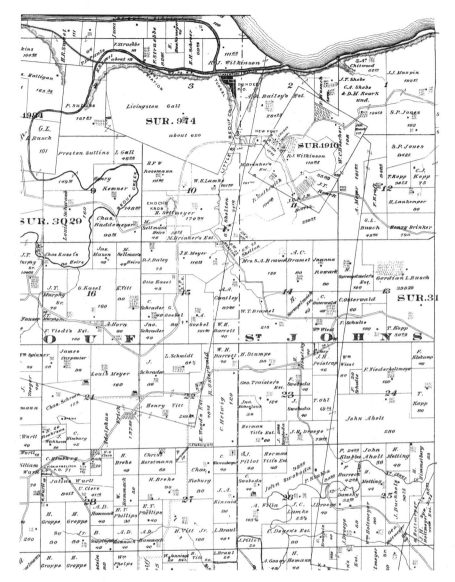

1878 Plat Book of the Campbellton area, showing Adolph Frick's farm in Section 21. (Used by permission, State Historical Society of Missouri, Columbia)

ADOLPH AND ALWINE FRICK

[1861?]

[salutation missing]

[19 ll.: from ALWINE FRICK (beginning of letter missing): children; would like her mother-in-law to visit; greetings; signature]

[ADOLPH FRICK continues:]

Dear mother and sisters,

[. . .] We are now living in a civil war. Our state as well as Wirginen [Virginia] are the main places where the war is spreading the most. It isn't a war where two powers fight to win a piece of land, instead it's about freedom or slavery, and as you can well imagine, dear mother, I support the cause of freedom with all my might and am *Captain* in a company which my three brothers-in-law also belong to.

At the moment we are posted about 5 miles (*engl*), 1½ hours, from home at a railroad bridge to keep the connection open between two armies, since several bridges have been burned down. We haven't had any trouble yet, but I can't say when we'll be moved.

On the 5th or 6th of August we are expecting a battle between the United States troops and the rebels, I hope our troops will be victorious again, which in this state has always been the case [8 ll.: population figures in slave and free states; greetings; signature].

Campbellten Franklin County Mo
May 11, 1862

Dear mother and sisters,

[. . .] As soon as I get the money for my service in the United States army, about 600 dollars, we will send you some, we should have been paid a long time ago now, I'm expecting it any day. I haven't been able to send anything recently because since the beginning of this perfidious revolution against the best government in the world, business has been very bad, and we can't collect any money. But since we have started winning everywhere, it's gotten a bit better, and I hope the war will be over by the winter. Here in Missouri it's pretty much over, except for the gangs of bandits which prowl through the countryside, murdering peaceful citizens who support the government and destroying their property. Just last week we had another one of these incidents in our area and felt compelled to call out a company again.

At the start of the revolution I signed up for three months of duty and commanded a company. When the time was up, I let myself get talked into another 3 years, but since I was supposed to go several hundred miles away from home with the army, leaving my wife and family to their own devices, I soon applied for a discharge. The pay you get as a *Captain* is quite good, 150 dollars per month, but putting your life and your family in danger costs more than what you get to protect them.

The duty I now have is just here in the area, and I hope it won't turn out that we have to move, for it is safe to say that two-thirds of the state of Missouri has been completely destroyed and we have suffered a lot.

The main thing it's about is the Negro question, the black people who are certainly human beings, just black instead of white, but who are treated like animals and sold at will, which any civilized human being must be against. A Negro used to bring 1,000 to 1,500 hundred dollars, depending on stature and age, and so there are people here who have 30 to 40 Negroes. In the southern states a man often has 2 to 3 hundred in his possession, and it's a money matter that this war is about. Our party wants to free the Negroes and give them enough land so they can feed themselves, since the slave trade is the most abominable thing there can be in a civilized nation—parents are torn from children, man from wife, and sold, never to see each other again. [6 ll.: financial matters; greetings] Adolphus Frick

[ALWINE FRICK continues:]
Dearly beloved mother-in-law and sisters-in-law,

[19 ll.: correspondence; financial matters; hope for Union victory] Adolph also did three months' service with the militia, and signed up afterward for three years in a company, since all the men in Missouri from 18–45 were going to be forced to join the army, but this turned out to be just a rumor, as we later found out, used to drum up a lot of volunteers. But Adolph got out again, by chance, since he hadn't yet been sworn in. At the same time my youngest brother signed up for three years or as long as the war lasts, since that was the only way to join up. He is still a soldier, but he hasn't been in battle yet. Oh! It was a terrible time when I was separated from Adolph in such a painful and uncertain manner and way, since you had to be prepared for the worst[. . . .] Business is bad because of the blockade, foreign trade has come to a standstill. In the South, where they didn't have enormous stockpiles of food, things are dire, because so many things can't be grown down there because of the incredible heat. In the North, everything is so cheap that the farmers don't want to sell anything because the prices are so bad, and many things are just being stored or used to feed the animals [16 ll.: their own harvest; correspondence; signature].

Campbellten Franklin County Mo
Sept. 29, 1862

[. . .]

Dear mother and sisters,

[17 ll.: correspondence; is sending money] I still haven't gotten my money from the government since they are running up enormous debts. They estimate the cost of the war, just for our side, at 1,500 million up to now, and unfortunately nothing has been accomplished as yet, on the contrary, the bandits and rebels are making headway in their devilish undertaking. But I hope that things will get better now, since another 6 times a hundred thousand men have been conscripted by the government, and the president has taken strong steps to crush the rebellion with all his might. For example, on September 22, a proclamation was made whereby in all the states that are in rebellion against the government as of January 1, 1863, all the slaves will be free. This will certainly deal the deathblow to these states, since they were the backbone of the rebels, doing their work at home and raising their crops while their owners went off to war.

For slavery is the sole cause of this disastrous war.

I am also back in the military, since here in Missouri all men ages 18 to 45 have to take up arms. I could have gotten off because I am the postmaster and already serve the government. But my previous company didn't want to let me off, and so I'm back in charge again. It is possible that we'll have to move out, but if the next battle some 30 to 35 to 40 hours from here goes well, I hope we'll be staying here to defend our property.

I also didn't want to beg off, because it is a shame for any man who can bear arms to desert his adopted fatherland, which always offers help and protection.

I am firmly convinced that before another year goes by we will have crushed the rebellion, and our republic, which is a home to any exile, will stand on a new firm base, more glorious than ever before. And then it may even be possible to think about freeing Germany, because that would only be feasible from this *Contingent* [continent].

As soon as we have freed our country from the curse of slavery, other countries can be taken care of [8 ll.: is sending newspapers; financial matters; greetings] Adolphus Frick

[10 ll.: food is cheap; hopes the family can come over after the war. ALWINE FRICK continues: 58 ll.: daughter Bertha was born; rebels stronger again; financial matters; correspondence]

ADOLPH FRICK

Cambellten Mo Dec 20, 1862

Dear mother and sisters,

[35 ll.: financial matters; family; little contact with fellow immigrants from Baden] As I see in your letter, opinion over there seems to be against the North and our government, but how could it be otherwise, since the newspapers in Germany have to write what the monarchs want, and the free republic of America has long been a thorn in the side of the European monarchs. But we are strong enough to uphold it, even if the European monarchs are craving to introduce their tyranny over here. I can well imagine that Mr. Eimer says the North will lose, because he has enjoyed too much southern sun and <u>blackness</u>, which has probably turned him into a Knight of the Golden Circle.[9] Our motto is that all men are born equal, whether black or white. I see no reason why August Aberle should write such bad things about our government, he's probably become a <u>Democrat</u> too [end of letter missing].

ADOLPH AND ALWINE FRICK

Cambellton, Feb. 28, 1863

Dearly beloved sister-in-law,

[14 ll.: correspondence; climate; defends Adolph in a financial matter; business; greetings] Alwine Frick

[ADOLPH FRICK continues:]

Campbellton Mo. Feb. 28, 1863

Dear sister Ida,

[14 ll.: correspondence] Things are not very pleasant at the moment, the war is raging here in full force, but I hope that we will soon crush those traitors to their fatherland. It's actually quite a strange story—the Germans, almost without exception, support the legitimate government and fight for its honor. The Americans who are slaveholders are the enemies of the government, they don't want to set their slaves free and just want to exploit other humans, that is blacks, because they don't regard them as human beings but as animals. You would certainly be amazed, dear Ida, to see how these poor black people are treated—no shoes in the winter and only a few old rags to wear—a terrible sight.

And then they're driven by white men with whips in their hands and often terribly mistreated and also poorly fed and so there are black families with 4 to

9. The "Knights of the Golden Circle" was a secret organization of Confederate sympathizers, especially in southern Ohio and Indiana. McPherson (1988), 560, 599.

5 children where the mother and father are torn apart and sold off thousands of miles away.

This is what our government can't stand to see any more[. . . .]

After all, all men are born equal. And that is the cause of this terrible war, and you will certainly agree we are in the right, along with our government that is the best in the world [15 ll.: correspondence; financial matters; greetings; signature].

ALWINE FRICK

Campellton, April 30th, 1863

Dearest mother-in-law,

[7 ll.: correspondence] A week ago yesterday in the middle of the night we suddenly got orders that the militia, everyone aged 18–45, had to move out, and Adolph had to leave immediately and command the troops; he hasn't been home since, except for two nights.

Yesterday, the 29th of April, the whole regiment moved out, they're stationed along a stretch of the railroad in order to clean out the bandits in the area, because once the woods have greened up again, they turn up everywhere. A few days ago a very nasty bandit named August Dolle was caught by the military, and he'll be hanged. He had plagued our neighborhood and was supported by the secessionists, for in times of war, no country is safe from such riffraff.[10] Everything is now so bleak and lonely, for all the men are gone; I am now alone with the children, I've only got only my sister who is fifteen and one workman who's 17, and I have a lot to do. My good father is a great help, but he is very busy because my sister-in-law, where he usually lives, also has three small children and is alone except for one serving girl. It's enough to break your heart when you think about these times and how painful it is to be separated. Adolph always comforts me and says they'll be back soon, for the militia has only been called out for 30 days—Oh, if I were never to see Adolph again, I would totally despair, for he is such a good man. God grant that I may soon embrace him again, safe and sound [63 ll.: correspondence; family; financial matters; signature. Letter to sister-in-law Bertha: correspondence; financial matters; greetings; signature].

10. August Dolle had murdered two Union soldiers on their way home. He was apprehended and was supposed to stand trial, but he was executed by the Franklin County militia. Dolle had emigrated from France (probably Alsace) before 1850 with his parents and was married to an American. *History of Franklin* (1888), 246; MC 1850: Franklin Co./Mo., #1362; MC 1860: Franklin Co./Mo., Boeff Twp., #424.

ADOLPH FRICK

Campbellten [M]o. July 8 [1863]

Dear mother and sisters,

[10 ll.: financial matters] I am now back home from the army, but I don't know when I'll have to leave again with my company. The Union has fought very important victorious battles this week, first Vicksburg,* where the main fortress of the rebels has fallen with twenty thousand men and a hundred cannon, and second the main battle that was fought at Getisburg [Gettysburg*] where so many men were lost, some 4 to 5 thousand killed and wounded on each side. It was a major defeat for the rebellion [. . .] just one or two more of such successful battles and the worthless rebellion will be stripped of all its forces, its army destroyed.[11] I was well paid for my last duty, 190 dollars a month, and I think we'll be paid in the next few days, along with my 400 dollars from before [16 ll.: good harvest; family; greetings; signature].

ADOLPH AND ALWINE FRICK

Campbellton, Franklin County Mo., March 6, 1864

Dearly beloved mother and sisters,

[15 ll.: correspondence; financial matters] We are now facing bad times since on March 10 there'll be a draft for another 5 times a hundred thousand men and it affects the age groups 20 to 45 which I fall into, too. If I am picked, which I certainly hope won't happen, then I will have to buy myself off, which will cost me about 3 to 4 hundred dollars, since I have no desire to take part anymore. I am still a *Captain* in the militia, but there's not much danger in that, since we're only used here in the state if there's an emergency [22 ll.: business is going well; family; greetings]. Adolphus Frick

[ALWINE FRICK continues:]

Dearly beloved mother-in-law,

[29 ll.: correspondence; destruction caused by the war; birth of daughter Elise; family] Help is hard to find here, both girls and men; you have to pay 7 to 10 dollars a month for a serving girl and a good workman costs 10 to 15 dollars a month. White workmen are very scarce here, they're almost all colored. We've also had one for almost a year now, and he's quite a decent man. Up to now Negroes haven't been forced to join the army, but they are now starting to use more of them, since there aren't enough whites to sacrifice for their freedom [14 ll.: hard winter; greetings; signature].

11. Confederate casualties at Gettysburg amounted to 28,000 killed, wounded or missing, as opposed to 23,000 Union casualties. McPherson (1988), 636, 664.

[. . .] Campbellten Mo. November 29th, 1864

Dear mother and sisters,

[8 ll.: death of daughter Klara of diphtheria] And then, as if things weren't bad enough, on October 1 there was a rebel attack in our area under Prise [Price]. There were about twenty thousand of them, and you can imagine, dear mother, that we had no hope of resisting. I was in command of a company of the militia and we had about 500 men altogether but we were far outnumbered and were forced to retreat. We were surrounded on all sides except for the Missouri River (as wide as the Rhein) in front of us. Part of one of our companies, after putting up a stiff fight, was captured and then murdered most horribly. We were lucky to have seized two steamboats and so we could cross the river, but the second one was almost captured by the rebels because it got stuck on a sandbank[. . . .] Four days later we came back with our boats, since then we had the Union army giving us cover at least from the back, but it was too late, the rebels had already retreated.

In the evening we landed in Washingten, 9 miles or 3 hours away from home, but I was most uneasy and had to find out what had happened to my wife and children, and so I rode home yet that night. At least I found my family well to my relief, although they had fled from my house to a neighbor's, an Englishman,* but my store goods, especially cloth, had all been stolen and plundered and everything in the house turned upside down. My losses in the store amount to about one thousand five hundred dollars—I also lost 3 very good horses worth 6 hundred dollars and some other things. All in all, my losses come to at least two thousand dollars. The rebel army was defeated in the upper part of the state and it was broken up and several thousand men were captured[. . . .][12]

However, about four hours from here, where the rebels camped, almost everything has been destroyed, many families torn apart and a large number with no roof over their heads, no food, no clothing. It is really a shame that after three years of murderous war it has come to this. I only hope that new measures will be introduced, because things can't go on like this. I think Missouri will be a free state within two months, because we have elected a good governor for the state. Lincoln was elected as president of the United States for another 4 years. Although he wasn't my choice, for I don't believe Lincoln

12. General Sterling Price marched into southern Missouri with 12,000 men in late September 1864, but he was deflected from his original objective, St. Louis, and plundered his way through the state along the south bank of the Missouri River until defeated by Union troops near Kansas City in the last week of October. Although he recruited thousands of men along the way, he left the state with fewer than 6,000 soldiers. The Germans suffered in particular during his rampage. McPherson (1988), 787–88.

is the man to end this civil war[13] [35 ll.: correspondence; financial matters; family; signature; is sending newspapers].

[ALWINE FRICK continues?:][14]

Dearly beloved mother and sister-in-law,

[30 ll.: correspondence; Klara's death] Then the rebels, Commander Price, Marmeduke and Shelby went on a rampage through Missouri, stealing and plundering everything they could get their hands on; especially men's wares and horses.

You don't see any of the latter any more, except for a few they didn't find and various starving animals they left behind. The militia was called up two days before they came through, but they hadn't all assembled when the enemy invaded, badly outnumbering them. At the beginning they were thought to be just a small detachment of a few hundred men, but as it was our troops had to retreat, and they all got away safely, orderly, across the river[. . . .] All the men who had to stay behind went and hid in the woods, since anyone they found they forced to join their army or killed them in cold blood. It was a time of fear and trembling. Many women and children also fled into the woods, since they thought everyone would be murdered and everything burned down. Others thought it was wiser to stay in their houses; which was the best thing to do, since the women and children were treated well, all in all, but they did steal everything, often even children's clothes that were of no use to them at all, and they only did it out of revenge or to give them to their consorts. In our area they were more moderate, for they were in a great hurry and probably thought their pursuers were too close. We would have been spared from the robbers, if they hadn't cut all the railroad connections, by burning down the bridges, ripping up the tracks and cutting the telegraph wires, which hindered our army considerably [7 ll.: much worse elsewhere]. We also spent four days with a neighbor, because we would have been in more danger in our house. They searched the neighbor's house, too, but they didn't find anything. Our losses amount to about 1,500 dollars. We didn't have any time to pack anything away except what we hurriedly packed onto the wagon. Fortunately, we didn't have much[. . . .] Oh, how I feared for Adolph; and what joy, when I could embrace him, safe and sound, in my arms once again, and the children, when they saw their Papa again; for without Adolph all my happiness would have been destroyed. Oh, may the Heavens grant that these desperate times

13. Frick's wording leaves it unclear whether he thought Lincoln was too "radical" or not radical enough, but his enthusiasm for the radical gubernatorial candidate, Thomas Fletcher, shows that the latter was the case. As he expected, a Missouri convention (chaired by a German) abolished slavery in January 1865. Foner (1988), 41, 43.

14. It is unclear whether the two letters belong together.

never return, and that this entire war be over soon [14 ll.: details; greetings; signature].

Campbellten Mo., April 4, 1865

Dear mother and sisters,

[11 ll.: financial matters] Because the capital of the rebels, Richmond, has been taken by our troops, and the main army of the rebels under General Lee, about eighty thousand men, almost all taken prisoner. And so the rebels only have small gangs of bandits and little armies left, and we will surely have true peace in a few months. Things were delayed, secondly, because our barn burned down on December 23, which caused me a loss of 500 dollars alone on feed, not counting the building[. . . .] Furthermore, on January 14 I was drafted into the army, but I got off because of my teeth. I had already spent 100 dollars, however, to pay for a substitute, and that money was gone. My business did so well this winter I was so busy I didn't know what to do [30 ll.: correspondence; promises to meet his financial obligations; signature. ALWINE FRICK continues: 26 ll.: correspondence; financial matters; end of letter missing].

ADOLPH FRICK

Campbellton Mo. July 11, 1865

Dear mother and sisters,

[18 ll.: correspondence; financial matters] As you know, dear mother, the shameful 4-year war is over now that the rebellion with its armies/bandits have been destroyed, I can't call it anything else but that.

But not without great sacrifice, from which many families will never recover.

Our President Lincoln has also become a victim of these murderers. Although he didn't always do what I thought he should, I am sorry for him because he did do a number of good things. He was too lenient toward the rebels and that was the death of him, and this is what the people in the Union accused him of, too. If he had acted decisively at the beginning, the rebellion would never have reached such dimensions and many a life would not have been lost.

Our current President Johson [Johnson] (a journeyman tailor) seemed to be more decisive earlier, but he's still not strict enough by far with this riffraff, because he pardons them too quickly.[15]

15. President Andrew Johnson was in fact a tailor, and radical circles criticized him for his leniency toward the South. Foner (1988), 176, 183–84, 190–92.

And so I hope that now at least, after 4 years of war when our lives were in such danger and we suffered such great losses, we'll be able to live in peace and quiet, and our business will be able to grow, for in these times you could never tell what disaster the next day would bring [35 ll.: is sending money; harvest; family; signature].

Campbellton Franklin County Mo, December 9th, 1865

Dear mother and sisters,

[40 ll.: correspondence; is sending money, family] We now have peace, but unfortunately the cost of the war still has to be paid for, and it's really severe; my taxes now amount to circa (100) one hundred dollars a year, and that's certainly enough, although I'd have been happy enough to pay if it'd helped things.

But all the loss of life and money seems to have been for nothing. The rebels have gotten back all their rights and have all been pardoned and given (public) office, and so it won't be many years until we'll be singing the same old song again.

There's just something rotten in the state of Denmark and with our tailor. He is not the man who can patch up this tattered and torn pair of trousers properly, namely thoroughly.

He is, as bad word has it, too seldom sober [30 ll.: hopes to come back to Germany; greetings; signature; correspondence].

ADOLPH AND ALWINE FRICK

Campbellten Franklin County Missouri
March 23rd, 1866

Dear mother & sisters,

[36 ll.: financial matters; sister Bertha should come to America; family] Our political situation is unfortunately not taking shape like every patriot expected. Our current President Johnsen is a traitor to the loyal people of the Union, and so it looks like all the great sacrifice made in the 4-year war in terms of men and money will have been for naught.

The southern traitors, supported by President Johnsen, are holding up their heads as proudly as ever and don't tolerate any northern emigrants in their states. The slaveholders don't have anyone to work for them, because their slaves don't want to work for them without pay, but these slaveholders make promises but then they don't pay.

So they are trying to get workers from Germany by sending agents to Germany with very attractive offers, but people should beware and not sign any *Condrakte* [contracts]. Anyone who comes over here can still find enough work for good pay[16] [20 ll.: recommends immigrating to Missouri; correspondence; signature. ALWINE FRICK continues: 29 ll.: is pregnant; family; cold winter; greetings].

Although Adolph Frick only served for a short time in the militia, he suffered considerable losses in the Civil War, in particular due to General Sterling Price and his raid: from 1860 to 1870 the total value of Frick's assets shrank from $6,800 to $3,200. Shortly after the war, he gave up his store, keeping only his position as postmaster, and turned his attention to farming and livestock trading. He seems to have been quite successful and well respected: in 1874 he owned almost 200 acres of land and had become a notary public, and in 1886 he became a justice of the peace. Not surprisingly, Adolph Frick continued to be an "active Republican" for the rest of his life.[17]

16. For more details on immigrant recruitment and contract labor law, see Schöberl (1990), 39–41, 66–68, 94, 145–51.

17. MC 1870: Franklin Co./Mo., Lyon Twp., #398; MC 1880: Franklin Co./ Mo., Lyon Twp., #11; MC 1900: Franklin Co./Mo., e.d. 32, #10; *History of Franklin* (1888), 749. Adolph Frick died on April 20, 1906; obituary of April 27, 1906. In 1910 his wife Alwine was living in the home of one of their daughters: MC 1910: Franklin Co./Mo., Boeff Twp., #184.

46. Private Georg Bauer

Most of what we know about Georg Bauer, who emigrated from Baden in 1853, we learn from his brother Johann, an assiduous letter-writer who followed him to America the next year. Shortly thereafter, both of them settled on farms near Kirksville in northern Missouri, an area where Germans were a tiny minority and that boasted "10 Union men to every rebel," according to Johann Bauer in 1867. Before the outbreak of the war, Georg had converted to Methodism, married an American wife, fathered a child, and settled down with his family on a rather substantial farm. Johann Bauer had become a fervent Republican as early as 1856, and his brother Georg presumably had similar political views. Johann was exempt from military

SOURCE NOTE: This one short letter fragment does not permit a precise and reliable analysis of Bauer's German writing, but it is fairly certain that his schooling was only elementary. The structure of his extremely long sentences is loose and somewhat chaotic, his vocabulary is limited, his grammar and orthography shaky, though not so bad as to hamper comprehension. His German is slightly colored by his local Baden dialect. English interferes a couple of times (number instead of *Nummer*), but the writer spells American states correctly and is clearly more familiar with terms like Union army, rebels, or president than with the German equivalents he is struggling to find.

service; he was unmarried, but he had a glass eye; Georg, by contrast, volunteered for the Union infantry on July 15, 1861, despite the fact that he was leaving behind a small child and a pregnant wife.[1]

[Memphis, end of 1863][2]

My dear parents, brothers and sisters and friends [. . .],

[probably pp. 5–6 of a longer letter] It is also sometimes the case in our army that a man is a soldier with a wife and children at home and times are hard, but the problem is nothing but foolhardiness. The soldiers in the United States get 13 dollars a month, 42 dollars a year for clothing, enough to eat, paid out almost every 4 months, but before they send the money home to the wife and children to buy food and clothes, they play cards and drink, and in a short time, all the money is boozed up and completely wasted, and the family gets nothing. But thank God, in our free states there are still compassionate people back at home who help poor families, give them food when some foolhardy, shabby father, so to speak, doesn't send anything to his wife and children, so at least the children, thank God, are taken care of[. . . .] I am still in the same place where I was when I wrote to you the last time, the place here is a town in enemy territory in the state of Tennessee, the name is Memphis, there are about 20,000 soldiers here. It's been fairly quiet here all summer long, this summer three fortresses were captured from the enemy. There are 34 states in America, 20 free and 14 slave states, most of the people in the slave states want to set up their own government, but they've been losing every year and every day since the war started, the united army, which is called the *Union Army* in English, has taken away from the enemy, who are called *Rebels* here, Maryland, Missouri, Kentucky, Tennessee, Arkansas, most of Mississippi, most of Louisiana, the western part of Virginia, and we have soldiers in other towns in all the other slave states, so you can see that the *Rebels*, the enemy, are losing every day.

[. . .] I believe that before the year is out, the enemy will no longer have a single state, maybe not even one town, and I believe that when the war is

1. Background information and letters by Johann Bauer in Kamphoefner, Helbich, and Sommer (1991), 149–81; letter of Johann Bauer, February 2, 1867; telephone interview with Johann Bauer's granddaughter Lola Bell, December 1993; Muster Rolls, Comp D, 21 Mo. Inf, Pension Files, NatA. Georg Bauer owned a farm worth $1,600; MC 1860: Scotland Co./Mo., Sand Hill Twp., #912.

2. A note in the margin contains best wishes for the new year; one of the captured fortresses mentioned below refers to Vicksburg* in 1863. Bauer's term of enlistment, mentioned below as lasting eight more months, ended in July 1864.

Georg Bauer.
(Catherine Nulliner)

over, times will be better than we had before the war started, no more slaves, and freedom for all. We have about 600,000 men in the field. My time is up in 8 months, with God's grace, may He keep me healthy, and should I be in another battle, I hope His hand will guide me safely through, that I may have the great joy of returning home to my wife and children. Because this summer time will be up for about 300,000 soldiers, the ruler called *President* in English has called up another 300,000 men, those who volunteer for three years get 302 dollars extra when their time is up, and 13 dollars a month, and an old soldier who signs up for another three years gets 402 dollars when his time is up and 15 dollars a month. Every state has its quota to fill, and the ruler (*President*) gave the citizens 2 months' time to volunteer, when the two months are up and a state hasn't filled its share of the 300,000 men, then they'll be called up in that state, the 20-year-olds to 40-year-olds, and they only get 13 dollars a month and nothing extra. That's the difference here between volunteer soldiers and drafted ones. The war must be fought, whether you like it or not, the government must be supported and obeyed, if we must drive the enemy into the sea [8 ll.: correspondence]. I remain your faithful son, Johann Georg Bauer.

Georg Bauer's subsequent fate was reported by his brother Johann in his letter of February 19, 1865:

> Our son & brother George sleeps or rather is no longer of this world. He died on June 22nd in the army hospital in Memphis, Tennesse, patiently & devoted to God[. . . .] His letters were always a great comfort & it put my mind to rest that in the army, where such horrible godlessness reigns, he had always sought to serve God & to be prepared when the Lord called him[. . . .] The next thing to cause you worry & concern will no doubt be his wife and 2 children; but here we can take comfort. God himself said specifically in His own words that he is a Provider for widows and orphans[. . . .] Every family that has lost its father in the army is guaranteed by law half his pay until the eldest child is independent. George's wife gets this & his bounty as long as she remains a widow [. . .] so you don't need to worry about her as far as this is concerned.

When Bauer died, he had only twenty-three days left in his term of service.[3]

3. Letter of Johann Bauer, February 19, 1865, NABS.

47. Private Ludwig Müller (Louis W. Miller)

In the spring of 1853, eighteen-year-old Ludwig Müller left Massenheim, a village a few miles outside of Frankfurt, and moved to Missouri where some of his acquaintances lived. His family was obviously not impoverished since his brother later became the village mayor and treasurer of a local charitable institution. Once in Missouri, Ludwig immediately started work as a tailor, so he probably had done an apprenticeship in Germany. In his first letter he reported that the pastor was teaching him English after church, and from 1856 on he always signed his letters "Louis Miller." He soon left his friends in the "wilderness" and settled near Cape Girardeau, a port town on the Mississippi about 120 miles south of St. Louis. In July 1860 he married Caroline Essig from Bavaria, and together with his brother-in-law

SOURCE NOTE: Müller writes very simple German, with spelling that is irregular and reveals that he is fighting a running battle against his local Hessian dialect, which he cannot entirely suppress. Not included here are the letters in the series from the time before 1860 (nine) and after 1865 (six), as well as four undated letters.

he leased a "grocery," which at the time could have meant either a store or a tavern.[1] He was, so to speak, right on the border as tension between the North and South became more acute.

Cape Girardeau Mo / January 8th, 1865.
from Louis W. Miller

Beloved father, brothers and sisters,

[9 ll.: health; apologies for long silence] Now I want to describe to you the world history of America for the year 1860, in the month of November, when we had an election here for the *Presetend* of America, and since the one *pardie* lost they went to war.

America now has 35 states (or in German *Kreise* [districts]) of which there are 13 states that belong to South America and besides that also have black slaves; they wanted these 13 states to become a *Reboblick* [republic] and called it the *Confederat* states. The others are called the *Federal* states and they didn't want to allow the others to leave the United States and so it came to war.

I support the old laws, the *Federal* states that have been winning the whole time, and I hope they will be victorious. This state Missouri where I live is also counted as one of these 13 states. There were also a lot of people who sided with the *Confederal* states, they set up companies and regiments of soldiers.

I couldn't stay any longer in my home town, Jackson, where I lived, so on September 12, 1861, I moved away from there to the town of Cape Girardeau where it was much safer, but business was bad and there was no money around until the new paper money came out.[2]

The town of Cape Girardeau ran the risk, day after day, of being attacked by the *Confederat* army. So they called up soldiers, but all of them were volunteers—until last year, when they started drafting people like they do in Germany. They can't get enough volunteers anymore to crush the *Rebelgion* [rebellion].

[7 ll.: apologies for his long silence]

In the year 1861, on the 11th of October, I signed up with the artillery here in Cape Girardeau for three years, to crush the *Rebelgion*, but I didn't think it

---

1. Background information and additional excerpts from his letters are in Heil (1979), 3–12; MC 1860: Cape Girardeau Co./Mo., Jackson Twp., #1268–69. The brother-in-law is listed with $1,000 in assets, Müller with none.

2. In the 1860 election Lincoln received only 10 percent of the vote in the county, the least of the four candidates. Burnham (1955), 574. Germans comprised 33 percent of the nonslave population in Cape Girardeau, compared with only 15 percent in Jackson Township. Hand tallies from MC 1860.

would take that long, since everybody thought it would be over in a year, and then we would come home again. But the three years are over, and it still hasn't come to an end. On December 20, 1864 I came back home to my dear wife, safe and sound.[3] On May 14, 1862, we left Cape Girardeau with 6 cannon in one *Battery*, 4 of them six-pounders and 2 twelve-pound howitzers, and from then on I didn't see my dear wife until last year in April, and we already had a daughter, too[. . . .] This child lived to be 13 months and 11 days old before the Good Lord took her away from us[. . . .]

In these three years I was in 4 big battles, apart from little skirmishes, but the Good Lord protected me.

The first battle was on April 6 and 7, 1862.

The second was on October 3–4, 1862.

The third one started on May 1, 1863, and ended on the 4th of July. The town we wanted to take was about 20 to 25 hours [i.e., marching distance] away, and we fought every day until the enemy pulled back into the town, and then it came to a siege for 47 days. Then they didn't have anything to eat anymore, and they surrendered with 32 thousand prisoners.[4]

The fourth battle was this last summer, it lasted until September 2nd, until they took the town they wanted.[5]

When I was on my way home, the *Confederal* were beaten badly on December 15th, and on December 21 the *Confedral* also had to give up a seaport.[6]

People think it is possible that the war will come to an end this year.

[7 ll. greetings:] I remain your faithful / son / Louis W. Miller

Dear father, give my best to all my friends and acquaintances.

Cape Girardeau Mo, February 18, 1866.

Dear father and brothers and sisters,

[15 ll.: health; waives his share of an inheritance (800 fl.)] Dear brother John, now I want to write you a few lines. You wrote that you haven't given up on the idea of coming to America, and you wrote that you are thinking of giving up the tailor business and that you think you might volunteer for the army. Dear brother, let me write you my opinion about this. Do not do this and do not join the army. I could tell you all about it, and brother Konrad can

3. Miller spent three years as a private in Baty F, 2 Ill. LArt. Muster Rolls, NatA. For a primary and secondary account of a sister battery in the same regiment, see Brown (2000).

4. These were the battles of Shiloh,* Corinth, and Vicksburg.* McPherson (1988), 409–13, 522–23, 629–37.

5. Atlanta; McPherson (1982), 429–36.

6. This refers to the battle of Nashville and the occupation of Savannah. McPherson (1982), 463–66.

also tell you all about it, but you wouldn't find out what it's really like until you were in it, just like me. If I had to serve again, no one could get me to sign up voluntarily, and for me it wasn't nearly as bad as in Germany [27 ll.: advice on emigration; signature].

After the war, Müller started another saloon that he ran with obvious success. In 1870 he was already listed with assets of $2,000. He expanded his business several times; later he sold not only beer and wine but also oysters. In addition, he was a partner in a bank and helped start a brewery. His death in 1892 was noted not only in the German-language newspaper, the Jackson *Deutscher Volksfreund*, but also by a lengthy obituary in the English-language *Cape Girardeau Democrat*. He had been an enthusiastic member of the Union army veteran's association, the Grand Army of the Republic, and the local chapter led his lengthy funeral procession.[7]

7. Heil (1979), 9–12; MC 1870: Cape Girardeau Co./Mo., W. 1, #154; Jackson *Deutscher Volksfreund*, April 6, 1892; *Cape Girardeau Democrat*, April 5, 1892; Pension File, NatA.

48. Private Carl Anton (Charles) Ruff

Carl Anton Ruff was born in 1832 in Hohenzollern-Hechingen, an enclave within Württemberg that became part of Prussia in 1849. He grew up in a wealthy Catholic family; his father was a high-ranking treasury official, and Carl and his three brothers studied at the universities of Tübingen and Freiburg. Carl, at least, did not graduate, and because of some unknown transgression, he left for the United States in the mid-1850s. The events leading up to his enlistment are described in the only letter that has survived.[1]

St. Louis, Mo. January the 12th, 1865

Dearest mother and brothers and sisters,

Not having heard from you, my dearest ones, for such a long time — not even the slightest news — plunged me into a mood that sometimes bordered on melancholy, and only a firm faith in God and my hopes that you, my dearest ones, were faring well were able to sustain me in this dry, self-serving

SOURCE NOTE: As one would expect from a man with his background, Ruff writes impeccable German, without a trace of local dialect or interference from English.

1. Information provided by the donor. In a short note sent together with a photograph, his mother was addressed as "*Frau Finanz-Räthin.*" On October 19, 1854, a man named Charles Ruff, a twenty-year-old farmer from Württemberg, arrived from Le Havre in New Orleans on the *Mulhouse* (NOPL).

Carl Anton Ruff.
(Lisa Winkelmann)

America [7 ll.: inquiries about family and acquaintances]. One thing pains me, that my dear, magnanimous father is no longer alive,[2] that I cannot tell him how much I regret my youthful imprudence, and how hard I intend to work to make up to you for what I have done, should God the Almighty grant me the chance[. . . .] But now I want to tell you briefly about my experiences up to now. After living here for three years and playing music in Cousin Sauter's *Band*, the best in St. Louis, I was overcome by my old thirst for adventure when I heard about the American South from some other friends. Despite Sauter's contrary suggestions that I should stay in St. Louis and go into trade, I took up the offer of a very profitable engagement with a *Concert-Troupe* touring various southern states, where we made money to burn and lived like kings. Then I settled in New-Orleans and lived there for two years and saved up quite a fortune. Ten dollars a night for a ball (25 guilders*) and $25.00 a week at the theater. I was well on my way to financial independence, to coming

2. His father died on July 16, 1857, so Carl must have emigrated before this time.

home to find one of our pretty and easygoing Prussian Swabians (it's hard to find women here who are any good) and to being the happiest man alive. But then, what the devil, this most dreadful of rebellions broke loose. That of the "slaveholders" of the South, who want to expand slavery and make themselves as rich as Croesus through the sweat of those poor black devils. This was completely against my strong sense of justice, my deepest convictions, and carried away by all this, I spoke up one evening in a public café, and this led to my immediate arrest. I was charged with being an enemy of the South. A friend of mine (musician) saved me, but *all* of my money in the bank was confiscated (I had given my things to him earlier). After New Orleans was taken, I traveled to Havanna and from there to many different islands in the West Indies, and then back to New York, spent ½ a year there, then on to Buffalo, Toledo, Chicago, Milwaukee, and now I am back again in old St. Louis. The tale of all the special events of my life, all these dangers (bombardments, explosions, being in danger of drowning or being shot) would take up 28 pages. Then last summer, to take revenge on these wretched rebels and to do my part in the fight for freedom, I enlisted in the 41st Missouri-Vol. regiment, mostly "Teutons." Businesses are suffering, all the big ones, and practically all the clerks, and I didn't want to be fiddling in some dive, either. God has helped me up until now, and He will continue to do so. And I've already made 1st lieut., that happens more quickly over here. I don't need to be a citizen, either, and I would like to ask dear Gustav or Constantin to send me a new passport with their next letter, so I can avoid conscription here next year, since I am still a Prussian and want to remain one. *Liberté, égalité, fraternité, c'est toute la plaque* [that's all we need]—My friend Sauter is very well and living happily. Perhaps I will be someday, too. I have collected a lot of experience, knowledge of the language, etc. [Ensels?] will get rich here.

And now my dearest ones, farewell. I send you many greetings and kisses from afar. If I am still alive in 2 years time, we will see one another again. I'll come back.

[. . .] your eternally loving

son and brother / Charles A. Rouff, *Prof. of Music, care / of* Professor Severin Robert Sauter, St. Louis, Missouri, U.S. *of* North America

[in the margin:] More soon, did you get my *Daguerrotype*?

Ruff is stretching the truth in this letter. One Charles Ruff did enlist in the 41st Missouri Infantry on August 13, 1864, but he was never promoted and remained a private until he was mustered out in July 1865. This seems to be a case of "self-promotion."[3]

3. Muster Rolls, 41 Mo. Inf, Comp G, NatA; Lonn (1951), 109.

First page of Carl Anton Ruff's letter of January 12, 1865, showing a view of St. Louis from across the river and small illustrations of public and commercial buildings. (Lisa Winkelmann)

Apart from the entries in the muster rolls, Ruff cannot be clearly identified in any other American sources, except for the fact that when he enlisted, he was living in St. Louis in Ward 2. The cousin he mentions in the letter, the musician Severin Robert Sauter, also lived in this ward. In 1870 the census documents mention a thirty-four-year-old saloonkeeper named Charles Ruff who lived in the same ward as Sauter; if this is our letter-writer, he had cut eight years off his true age—something perhaps not unusual for a man married to a twenty-two-year-old. It is also possible, however, that shortly after his discharge, Ruff succumbed to an illness that had caused him to be hospitalized on April 11, 1865. This seems more likely, since he never applied for a war pension, and it would have been extraordinary indeed if he had survived after the war for a number of years without submitting an application.[4]

4. Muster Rolls, 41 Mo. Inf, Comp G, NatA. Information about Sauter in MC 1860: St. Louis/Mo., W. 2, #612; MC 1870: St. Louis/Mo., W. 10, Subd. 9, #1303. CD St. Louis, 1859–60; perhaps about Ruff in MC 1870: St. Louis/Mo., W. 10, Subd. 18, #2270.

49. Private Johann Christoph Penzler

Not much is known about Johann C. Penzler's earlier life, but it seems safe to assume that he emigrated for economic reasons. When he was born on August 27, 1829, his father, who had been a smallhold farmer, was already dead; and before Johann had turned three, his mother passed away. He grew up in Elxleben, a village with 1,200 inhabitants four miles north of Erfurt, in the Prussian part of Thuringia. We do not know who raised him, but his only close relative was his brother, Heinrich Jakob, a cabinetmaker who was twelve years older. Johann may well have learned this trade from his brother, since he earned his living as a carpenter until the end of the Civil War. Sometime before 1860 he moved to St. Louis and married Elisabeth Benack, from Hesse. He then lived for a while on his father-in-law's farm in Carondelet, St. Louis County, returning to St. Louis shortly before he wrote the following letter. A later letter contains at least a small hint of his liberal political views: he sent his children to a Turner* school three times a week.[1] In the 1870s he ran a saloon, and he died in 1882 at the age of fifty-three.[2]

SOURCE NOTE: Short as the available text may be, it is long enough to show serious deficiencies in spelling, grammar, and the construction of sentences. Not included here is one letter in the series from the time after 1865.

1. Information provided by the donor; KB (ev.) Elxleben; Neumann (1883), 266; MC 1860: St. Louis Co./Mo., Carondelet Twp., #838; MC 1870: St. Louis Co./Mo., Carondelet Twp., #23–24 lists Penzler with $1,400 in real estate. On the date of his emigration, see the letter of February 27, 1878, NABS.

2. CD St. Louis, 1875–82. His widow also appears the following year, CD St. Louis, 1883.

St. Louis, May 27th, 1865

Dear brother,

[20 ll.: correspondence; birth of a son; death of his three-year-old daughter; move to St. Louis] Last year times were very bad. The commanding general of the rebels, together with 3 other generals and 30 thousand men attacked Misouri, because most of our soldiers had gone with the main army to the eastern and southern states, so there weren't many soldiers in our state. That's why the rebels could go through the whole state without being held up very much. Wherever they went they took all the livestock, food, and all the men who could carry guns away with them, and they burned everything in their path. Then a militia or *Landsturm* was called up and outfitted with guns, and then the rebels were beaten back. The regiment I was assigned to served for 40 days, but I only went along for 30 days. We were posted 75 to 80 miles from St. Louis, but we had no enemy contact.[3] The rebels were just a few hours away from my father-in-law's farm, but then they went off in a different direction, since as much as they would have liked to plunder it, they didn't trust St. Louis.[4] On New Year's Day they held the first draft. I believe there's never been a war, at least in the civilized world [1 page missing][. . . .] to murder all the high officials of our government. Thus, on the 13th of April in the evening, our president of the United States Abraham Linkeln was shot to death at the theater, the secretary of war was stabbed in bed, but he is still alive and hopes he will recover soon. But they have captured the murderers and everyone involved in the plot—more than 100 of them—and the head of it, Jefferson Davis, the president of the rebel states, and we're expecting the end of their trial any day now.[5] The new president is a good man, he'll do his best to restore order.

Yesterday I read in a newspaper that in New York more than 5,000 immigrants had arrived within two days. Now that the war is over, they are hoping there will be a lot of immigration this year. [4 ll.: harvest is looking good] otherwise produce is still as expensive as before, and also clothing, but our paper money is now almost back to full face value.

[16 ll.: family; correspondence; greetings; signature; address]

3. Private John "Penzlar" appears in the muster rolls, Missouri StateA, of Comp B, 10 Provisional Regt., Enrolled Missouri Militia, organized in St. Louis on September 9, 1863; there is no mention of any duty in 1864, when Sterling Price launched his raid through Missouri.

4. For more details about the 1864 Confederate raids in Missouri, see Frick (no. 45).

5. In fact it was Secretary of State William Seward who was stabbed. Only eight of the suspected Lincoln conspirators were put on trial, and Jefferson Davis was not among them. On July 6, four were sentenced to death and the other four to prison terms. Smith (1982), 569–71, 578–80.

On January 11 the legislature of the State of Missouri abolished slavery and proclaimed the freedom of the slaves. I am enclosing this proclamation by our honorable Govenir Fletscher.

50. Private Anton Herman Bullenhaar

Herman Bullenhaar left Ostbevern, near Münster in Westphalia, in the summer of 1858 and went to Cincinnati to join a large network of acquaintances. He was the son of a farmer but was not entitled to inherit the farm, and this no doubt played a role in his decision to emigrate. Avoiding military service, the main reason his brother Joann Bernard had emigrated earlier, was not an issue, since he was already twenty-five years old. Bullenhaar's strict Catholicism was typical for the area he came from, the conservative Münsterland, but otherwise the family gives the impression of being quite engaged in the modern world. When his brother Joann died, after having lived in the United States for less than four years, he was a road contractor on projects worth thousands of dollars, with at least a dozen men working for him. What is remarkable about Herman is the fact that he learned English so quickly—after only ten months his written English was passable, despite his ignorance of spelling conventions. Although he worked south of the Ohio River in the slave state of Kentucky, he spent considerable time in Cincinnati, which no doubt exposed him to Republican newspapers written in German.[1]

[letterhead:] Cincinnati, December 27th, 1861
Dearest brothers and sister,
[. . .] I am still working in the country [. . .] and at the moment for an English* farmer named Johnsen Schmidt near Cinthiana in the State Kentücki, 75 *Meils* from Cincinnati on the Kentucky railroad, and I like it a lot [. . . .] A half an hour away there is a small town named Cinthiana. There are not a lot of Germans in this area, and most of the population is black.[2] Last year I worked for a German on the [*Tornpeik?*]. Here in America, war has

SOURCE NOTE: Bullenhaar is not a master of German spelling and grammar, and his Westphalian dialect shows through occasionally, but he writes more correctly than most German immigrants with a comparable level of education. Not included here is one letter from before 1860.

1. Complete transcriptions and copies of the letters of both of the brothers, as well as background information on the family, are in Schubert (1995). According to the local files, Herman emigrated without permission on July 26, 1858.

2. Slaves made up 30 percent of the population of Cynthiana; in fact, even in 1870 only eighty-nine Germans were living in Harrison County. USC 1860.1, 180–84; USC 1870.1, 356.

now broken out between the South and the North, and now all that anybody talks about is getting ready for the war. Everywhere you hear the unaccustomed, murderous hue and cry of war. The object of the war is the abolition of slavery. When on November 6th last year the Republican Abraham Linkoln was elected president, the southern slave states seceded from the North, and both sides are now fighting each other with unrelenting hatred. The Union, or the United States of America, has 33 states, and 15 of these are slave states and 18 are free states, and because the Republican Party is now aiming to free the slaves from their yoke, the slave states decided they would rather fight to the last drop of blood than give up their slaves. It's hard to say what the result of this war will be. The northern army already has more than 500,000 men, all volunteers, and many of them are Germans. Some of them who left Germany to get out of serving in the military are now helping to defend the flag of their new fatherland[. . . .] More than 100,000 northern troops have marched into Kentücki, too, and it will probably soon be the scene of a bloody war. There are several hundred men camped [. . .] about a quarter of an hour from us. If England doesn't get involved, the rebel South will hopefully soon be suppressed. Business is bad here and especially in the big cities, but most of the workers are now in *Cämp*, that means *im lager*.

[16 ll.: farming and weather] Next year a new Catholic church is supposed to be built here. At the moment, services are being held in a schoolhouse. Most of the Catholics are Irish, and the priests preach in English. I've been in the city of Cincinati now for a few days to celebrate Christmas. The soldiers have set up cannon all around Cincinnati to protect the city from enemy attacks. God willing, the rebel southerners will bow their proud heads and return to the stars and stripes, for it would be a shame if this wonderful land of freedom were to be torn apart. They pay good money in the army, from 13 to 27 a month, and a hundred dollars at the end of the term of service[. . . .] The North can still put another 500,000 men in the field, although the South can hardly raise another 500, and England leans toward supporting the southern *Conferazion.*

Hura for the Union en the Sisechen gohn tor Helle.

[30 ll.: his late brother's bequest for a church seems to have been embezzled and spent by his partner in the construction company] So I wish you a happy and joyous New Year, and a life that is cheerful and content. May the Lord keep and preserve the United States *of the* America in the indivisible bond of unity / Herman Bullenhar

Bullenhaar probably found it hard to resist his enthusiasm for his new fatherland and the temptation of the nearby army camp: on January 10, 1862, he went to Cynthiana and enlisted in the 18th Kentucky Infantry. After one and a half years of service, interrupted by two bouts of illness, he was killed in the battle of Chickamauga, Georgia, on September 20, 1863. The family in Germany was apparently never informed of these events. In 1874 Herman's brother Philipp Anton, who inherited the family farm, submitted an affidavit to the county court in Warendorf to the effect that he had had no news of his brother for more than ten years. He applied for a death certificate, which was issued on June 27, 1875.[3]

3. Muster Rolls, NatA; Schubert (1995), 94–100.

51. Heinrich Stähler

Heinrich Stähler was certainly a German living in America during the Civil War. The only question is whether he should be considered an immigrant or if his time in the country should be seen as the travels of a journeyman. An assessment of whether migration was temporary or permanent, however, is often only possible in retrospect. In Stähler's case, his son reported that after his father returned to Germany, he "suffered for decades from an intense longing to return to the States." At any rate, Stähler was in an excellent position to observe and assess the economic situation of the Confederacy during the war.[1]

He was born in 1835 as the son of a pastor in Müsen, near Siegen in southern Westphalia, and grew up in comfortable circumstances. He attended grammar school in Siegen and then the local mining college, not an unusual choice since the local economy was dominated by mining and ore production. He finished off his technical training with a course in metallurgy (1856–58) at the mining academy in Berlin. During the course of his studies, he also learned some English.[2]

In January 1860 Stähler left for the United States, where his technical skills were far more unusual and valuable than at home. He went straight from New York to Ducktown, a small town located in a copper mining area in southeastern Tennessee. The landscape in this part of the Appalachians was very similar to what he had

SOURCE NOTE: Stähler handles his German, untinged by regional dialect or English interference (though interspersed with phrases in passable English) with such skill, imagination, and subtlety that occasional lapses in spelling hardly count. His handwriting is unusual, however, in that it varies from very tiny and precise to normal size and sloppy. Not included here are additional letters in the series from 1860 (three), 1861 (one), and 1862 (two). Only transcripts are available for the letter of November 7, 1862, and the beginning of the letter of May 10, 1863.

1. See the biographical sketch in von Kindelsberg (1927).

2. Information provided by the donor; letter of April 2–7, 1860, to "my dear Elise," NABS. She was an additional reason for his return to Germany. Stähler was concerned that his deferment from his Prussian military obligations would expire (letter of October 15, 1860, NABS), and that April he wrote that he intended to be away for two years.

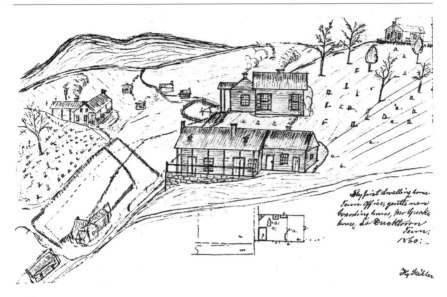

Sketch by Heinrich Stähler, "*My first dwelling house Firm Office, gentle men boarding house, Mr Specks house as Ducktown Tenn. 1860.*" (Otto Stähler)

left at home—although the population was much more sparse—but it seems very unlikely that he would have gone there by chance. The production manager of the copper works was a German, and most of the technical staff consisted of Europeans. Stähler, who was only twenty-five at the time, advanced within a year from being a laboratory assistant to become the director of the refinery.[3]

In terms of his ideological beliefs, Stähler tended toward European liberalism; for example, he seems to have sympathized with the Garibaldi movement in Italy. The influence of his southern environment, however, is also apparent. In a letter of October 15–16, 1860, he completely misjudged the prospects of the coming election: "Douglas, the Democratic senator, will become president." He also was quick to pick up white southern attitudes—or at least terminology—when it came to the race question: "I am in friendly correspondence with the plantation owner Mr. Traun in Alabama[. . . .] I hope to make the acquaintance of Mr. Traun in the future. His considerable experience in this country, and with his mind and spirit involved in everything new etc. (he's been here for 35 years, his *Nigger*[s] are said to love him like a father) it could be very interesting and profitable for me[.]"[4]

3. Information provided by the donor; HPL Indirect (i.e., usually via England), steamer *Leopard*, January 31, 1860. On the entire trip, he was accompanied by a miner from Müsen, who was perhaps going back to work after a trip home to Germany, and he met at least three acquaintances when he arrived in Ducktown.

4. Letter of October 16, 1860, NABS. Stähler uses the American epithet but treats it as a German word, forming the plural by pluralizing the possessive adjective instead of adding an "s" to

When Stähler arrived in the United States, he knew nothing about an impending war. Then, when Tennessee seceded to join the Confederacy in May 1861, both the situation in Ducktown and Stähler's life changed completely. Now suddenly cut off from northern markets, the copper works no longer had to compete with northern producers. Due to the Union blockade, moreover, Ducktown was also cut off from foreign imports, and demand for copper rose sharply because of the war. In terms of national copper production, Ducktown and Polk County were not terribly significant in 1860, with only 7 percent of the men employed in copper mining and only 5 percent of total output. For the Confederate states, however, Ducktown represented 85 percent of invested capital, half the workforce, and two-thirds of production. The autarky imposed on the Confederacy not only resulted in an increase in demand but also caused other challenges: material and food shortages, increasing transportation problems, and runaway inflation. Although he sympathized with the Union, Stähler did not miss out on this unique opportunity to apply his theoretical knowledge to these practical problems. He was also a firsthand, day-to-day witness of the industrial and economic shortcomings of the South.[5]

Refining works at Polk County *Smelter*
Ducktown, *Copper Mines* November / the 10th, 1861

Dearly beloved father, beloved mother and brothers and sisters,

Now it is no longer the ocean, over 3,000 miles wide with its waves and its tides, that separates and keeps us apart, making it both necessary and possible to keep in contact by letter—now it is the great torrent and flood tide of a fanatically inflamed tangle of peoples, which in a motley mixture of morning and evening, midday and midnight, South against North, has wriggled free of its quiet home and hiding place and rushes on with an inexorable roar, tearing to shreds and devouring the "great, young giant" that once imagined it could even dislodge old Europe from its fortress. The battle torch of war of this mixture of peoples has become inflamed across an expanse of land—their former glorious Union—that could almost accommodate all of Europe! And thus I am sitting here in my *Office*, stranded and kept apart from those who

the noun; italics indicate that the word (except in its plural form) was taken over from the German original. Traun is mentioned frequently; he was probably the brother-in-law of Stähler's favorite aunt in Berlin, with whom Stähler lived when he was studying there. According to Stähler, Traun owned twelve slaves; according to the 1850 census, he owned twenty-one. MC 1850: Dallas Co./Ala., Pine Flat Beat, #67, as well as the slave schedule of the same; MC 1860: Dallas Co./Ala., Old Town Beat, #160. Interestingly, several of Traun's ex-slaves did adopt his family name; the 1870 census shows ten black Trauns. MC 1870: Dallas Co./Ala., Pine Flat Beat, p. 540, 542; MC 1870: Dallas Co./Ala., Selma, W. 4, p. 691; MC 1870: Lowndes Co./Ala., Beat 4, p. 336.

5. USC M 1860.1, 571, 715, 735; Barclay (1947), 87–101. On the parallel case of the southern iron industry see Knowles (2001).

are most dear to my heart, in order to make an attempt to break, or at least circumvent, the *Cordons* & the *Blocade* of this great "South" with a letter to my dear homeland, now so far removed [20 ll.: friends caught between the lines].

I do not believe I am mistaken when I assume that you at home are better informed about the North by northern newspapers and other reports than by what I would be able to supply, since the North is now a distant, foreign country, and one can only correspond from here to there via Europe. But the northern reports will spread much that is false and untrue about the South. Although my sympathies are more for the Union, I cannot conceal from myself the fact that the ways and means used by the northern government in conducting the war & their success thus far have increasingly caused my interest in their fate to wane. And thousands & thousands of friends of the Union in the South have now become their open enemies, since the days at "Manassas" and other places in Virginia, where the northern troops behaved with such ignominy, and up until now the southern troops have been victorious almost everywhere. But still the South is suffering dreadfully from the *Blocade* and encirclement by the northern *Lincolniten* from whom significant progress is now being eagerly awaited any day (in the colder seasons it is easier to push forward). "All are freely giving their children, their money and other possessions to defend their rights (?) and I only hear this one opinion here, that our rights should be defended down to the last drop of blood," according to Mr. Traun's last letter to me from Alabama. It now becomes gradually more and more apparent just how dependent the South was on the North, as the effects of the *Blocade* are felt: "no money in circulation and we are feeling the effects of this civil war, in that nothing from abroad is available; there's a shortage of salt, we've had to give up drinking tea and chocolate completely, and most people don't drink coffee any more—we make the clothing and shoes for our *Nigger*[s] ourselves and will soon have to make our own as well etc.," as the knowledgeable Mr. Traun continues, who longs for peace but does not expect it for 4–5 years. The slave states will never reunite with the North under one government—but I don't want to go into the pros & cons of the [slavery question?]: it is now up to the god of battle, but we certainly would like peace soon or a change in the way this slow, ruinous war is going. According to Mr. Traun, "the whole thing is the result of a long-standing plan of the English government, who have had agents in the North & the South for fifteen years to bring this situation about, because the English were afraid of being bested, what with the American spirit of enterprise and the fact that they have caught up with them so quickly—and so, to bring about the ruin of America, they have ruined their own West Indian islands." At any rate, there is much truth in this gentleman's opinion [5 ll.: details].

With regards to our special situation in the *"Copper Mines,"* the smelting works and in particular our *Concentrations-Werk* here, *"the refining Works,"* have experienced a real boom under the *"Conforderacy of North America,"* and in October last month, the only copper works here in the South produced more than 182,000 [pounds] *of refined Ingotcopper*, a product that can match any copper in the world—and even this amount was not enough to meet the demands of the southern war secretary in Richmond, who wanted to make a *Contract* with the companies for 10,000 [lbs.] of refined copper per day. Mr. Trippel, my *Superior* under our *General* director, Mr. Rath [Raht], has been down in Cleveland for 3 weeks, where he is supervising the construction of a copper rolling mill, while I have started building a new 2nd refinery here, but now in the winter we can't get hold of enough wood and coal to keep up our current production levels[. . . .][6] Our refinery had frequent visitors this summer, *Gentlemen* & noble guests, and a few days ago a young Dr. & Professor by the name of Tuttle (*of the University of Virginia at Charlottesville*) was here again. He was sent by the government to work on the *Fabrication* of sulfuric acid, soda, sodium sulfate etc. in the *Copper Mines*, but all these plans are very vague, due to the circumstances at the moment. The young professor was sent up from Cleveland to see me, on the advice of Messrs. Raht & Trippel, and I assisted him in my laboratory. Soon our nice new laboratory here will be finished, but now we can't get any chemical reagents from the North & Europe. Mr. Tuttle studied with Wöhler in Göttingen and spoke German very well.[7]

Our copper is utilized immediately for casting cannon, percussion caps, saber hilts, etc. made in Richmond, Memphis, [and] New Orleans, among other places. Recently a southern artillery officer who was here (from Memphis) said that the loss of the *"Copper Mines"* would be a greater loss for the *"Conforderacy Government"* than losing Richmond. Mr. Trippel, who was

6. Dr. Alexander Trippel was born in Switzerland in 1826, emigrated in 1848, and moved to Ducktown in 1855. He appears as a mineralogist in MC 1860: Polk Co./Tenn., #950, which hardly does justice to the range of his activities; see Barclay (1946), 56, 66–69. Cleveland does not refer to the city in Ohio but to Ducktown's nearest railroad station, about forty miles away. Julius Raht was born in 1826 in Dillenburg, Nassau, only about twenty miles from Stähler's place of birth. He studied chemistry and mineralogy in Bonn and Berlin. He was probably a Forty-eighter; the family emigrated in 1850, after Raht's father, a judge, was banished from the town because of his democratic views. He moved to Ducktown in 1854 and in 1860 became head of all the mining operations and smelting plants in the area. Barclay (1946), 186–89.

7. David Tuttle (1835–1915), graduated summa cum laude from Harvard in 1855 and earned his doctorate at Göttingen in 1857. He served as a chemistry professor at the University of Virginia through 1861 and thereafter worked in industry as a technical chemist, until in 1886 he obtained a position at the Philadelphia Mint. *Who's Who in America* (1908–9).

called to Richmond last month with Capt. Raht, found an incredible activity in the factories there, where they were making war materiel day and night, and all other business except what is related to the war has completely slackened off. Fearsome iron plates for the prows of large ships are being made, so that even warships can be split apart by means of such a prow, large caliber cannon, shells, case shot etc.—but despite all of this there is a tremendous shortage of everything needed to equip the *Volonteers* here in the South, and if the South hadn't captured the arsenals belonging to the "*Union*" and been provided with weapons by Floyd, the secretary of war under Buchanan, the situation would be even worse.[8] Two companies of *Volonteers* have now been transferred from the "*Copper Mines*"; the first one is active in Kentuky, while the 2nd one will soon be meeting the enemy face to face in Knoxville. A friend of mine (an Englishman,* a bookkeeper last year at Raht's) is in the latter one, but earlier, he secretly organized a "*Union Company*" in East Tennessee, and now he is a second lieutenant on the other side (!)—The soldiers in Virginia are dropping like flies in the hospitals from fever and the cold, they have hardly any clothing, hardly any shoes and hardly a *Plänket* [blanket] with which to bivouac at night in the railroad stations, streets and *Camps* [28 ll.: prices; rumors of a northern invasion of eastern Tennessee]. If the northerners carry out their intended plan, then the *Copper Mines* & their works will fall into their hands -?- whatever happens, it is certain that the war is not over yet, and it will become even more fanatical rather than make the South give in. And should the North ever deal them a few blows, and up to now this has only been possible by the blockade—which is still incomplete—they haven't done so in the open field. In the battle at Manasas [Manassas] some of the German regiments parried & covered as well as they could for the *Yankey* mama's boys who were fleeing wildly and running in retreat. Hecker* & Siegel [Sigel*], the former heroes of Baden, are active in the northern ranks. According to Mr. Trippel, Siegel, a much-feared enemy and a northern general in Missouri, Rossenkrantz [Rosecrans*], a general in the mountains of West Virginia and also a German, and McCleland [McClellan] are the three northern generals for whom the southerners in Richmond have the most *Respect*—incidentally, the Confederates have much the better officers than the North—Mr. Lang saw "Hecker" with his "uniformed" regiment from Ohio marching through

8. Similar charges against Secretary of War John Floyd were often made in the northern press, even after a congressional investigation committee dismissed them. Shortly before he resigned from office in order to join the secessionists, Floyd had ordered 125 cannon transferred from Pittsburgh to arsenals in the South. Whether this was attributable to carelessness or conspiracy, the order was subsequently countermanded. McPherson (1988), 226; Smith (1975), 170–80, 187.

the streets of Louisville and Kentucky with music playing and the citizens of Louisville cheering them on their way as they marched to join General Anderson (the well-known hero of "Fort Sumter") in Cumberland.

Our payment has been quite regular up to now, every 2 months [. . .] but what value does this good & valid "paper money" have under the present circumstances?? A man like Mr. Raht, who already has his bundle safe in English banks, is carefully speculating on advice that is probably quite easy for him to come by, as one of the most important business leaders in the *Confôrderacy*, and buying beautiful farms, houses, carriages etc. on valuable land along the railroad [26 ll.: economic situation; friends; money matters; signature].

N.B.: the next mail boat from New Orleans to Matamorros & Tambico Mexico doesn't leave until December 10th, in other words one month from today, and if all goes well, this letter will reach you in early February '62.

<u>Ducktown</u>, November 7, 1862

Dearest parents and brothers and sisters,

[42 ll.: start similar to letter of November 10, 1861; mail service] As for me, I've been quite hale and hearty, aside from a few colds; I have a good position as manager or director of the new Polk County refining works here [7 ll.: details]. Since Trippel left I have been the sole head of the largest copper works—perhaps not in all America, but at least the largest in the Confederate States—we've produced hundreds of thousands of pounds for southern cannon, percussion caps, sword hilts, etc., since the beginning of this wretched war, and last year we were often able to produce more than 180,000 pounds every month, i.e. pure refined copper. Since the northerners were frequently close to the border of East or eastern Tennessee, but never actually in eastern Tennessee, the southerners are still in possession of the main railroad line between eastern Tennessee and Virginia and can put it to awful use, and with it our works, which has given us a tremendous advantage and continues to do so. Our foundry is situated very nicely [4 ll.: details].

But for some time now, things have been slowing down more and more; the workers off at war, the mines without powder, less and less equipment, everything prohibitively expensive, etc.—these are the reasons. But our *Bluestone* business and in the last 2 weeks our copper fabrication has been very brisk. At Christmas I started making *Bluestones*, or copper sulfate, at the refining works. 75 cents a pound—and a *production* of 300 pounds a day. Our *Product* is really quite wonderful, almost better than I ever saw in Germany in the Harz or at Freiberg.[9] I've also recently started to make *copperas*, or ferrous

9. Clausthal/Harz and Freiberg/Saxony were the two oldest mining colleges in Germany. Neumann (1883), 585, 313.

sulfate, and we're using our new 2nd refinery for this, which has now become quite a sulfate boiler (the old refinery produces copper). In Charleston, one pound of ferrous sulfate sells for $1.50 to $1.75[. . . .] There is an unbelievable demand for such materials in this country, and some of it is used to dye *homemadestoffe* or homespun cloth, and they also use it to feed the animals. But what good does my excellent position do me? What advantage do I have from the fact that Mr. Raht is so pleased with me, from being appreciated by the other notables? Clothing, food and everything else has become prohibitively expensive and unavailable. The *Blocade* is felt very much in this country, and the harvest was bad. The situation is dire—but there's no peace—*no peace no peace but independance from our deathely, hated Yankees—rather death, than subjugation.* (*Kein Friede, einzig nur Unabhängigkeit von den tödlich gehaßten Yakees— lieber tod-als Unterjochung.*) is their motto—and one can only have respect for these hordes in terms of their courage and bravery. I was quite mistaken about these people; they are anything but cowards; this they have proven a hundred times. Every day they prove how brave they are—what a pity that such bravery, such an ability to suffer deprivation, such achievements are based on such false principles. If the North had such energy and enterprise, the mighty colossus would have crushed this rebellion long ago—but as it is, never. And I fear that hundreds and hundreds of thousands on both sides are being slaughtered in vain for the great cause. The old man of 70 and the boy of 14 both speak with the same voice, show the same energy; there are men who would give 2 arms, legs and several lives if they could kill some *Yankees*—and men who've been beaten down and wounded 3 and 4 times voluntarily return to the fray after a brief recovery at home with their loved ones. And if an end to this fratricidal war does not come soon, where filled with hatred, fathers stand face to face against their own sons, brothers against their very own brothers— there will be a dearth of men in the population that will be absolutely enormous [10 ll.: pious wishes for peace]. My new annual contract expires in the middle of March next year; God only knows if I can come home then or not. If things continue like they are now, it could be very difficult [36 ll.: prices; Mr. Traun; postal and consular matters; signature missing].

Refining works, Ducktown Polk County, Tenn. November / 1862
Dear parents and brothers and sisters,
    These lines, like so many others, are addressed to you, without my knowing or finding out if they ever reach you; this letter will attempt to circumvent the *Blocade* with the help of our consul, via Charleston, S.C., and then it will leave for Europe from Bermuda [41 ll.: postal matters; no end of the war in sight]. Food and clothing have risen to prohibitive prices; there's no real money in sight, instead heaps of *confederacy currency* in paper, which is so poorly made

that the *Yankees* have easily *counterfeited* it and sent it into the country, and this doubly false money can only be distinguished from the original by the fact that it is better made. [50] dollars is about the smallest piece of paper in circulation, the prices of many articles have gone up 100-fold. We haven't had any coffee for more than ½ a year, nor any tea with *Supper*, and it sells for $15.00 per [pound] in Charleston. Rye is our substitute for coffee, corn— which used to be used only for *Nigger*[s] and livestock—is used in place of wheat [. . .] and everything and anything that is indispensable for daily life is enormously expensive—*home made jeans* (material spun at home) is usually the only kind of cloth to be had for clothing, and despite all the cotton and "*cotton is King*!!" ("*Baumwolle ist König*"—the motto of the southern aristocracy and leaders), more than half of the 4-500,000 *Soldiers of the confederacy* are dressed in rags, and more than ⅓ are barefoot and ¼ bareheaded. When one considers the achievements of this motley folk under these circumstances, one cannot help but grant that they are courageous, and perhaps even more so than the French—but it is still painful to have to pay sympathetic tribute to them, when one does not want to, and to feel antipathy toward those who are fighting for the only cause that one considers worthy of such tenacity, privation, and courage [21 ll.: details, similar to letter of November 7, 1862]. The war has been a beneficial shock to the laziness of the American *Ladies*, one which hopefully will be a blessing to future generations, so that even "women who used to be ashamed to be seen in their kitchens are sewing, spinning, and weaving and working all day doing all manner of household chores that their blacks used to do, etc." as Mr. Traun writes from Alabama, and as I have also seen myself. The *Ladies* are almost the *Yankees*' worst enemy, and the significance of this should not be underestimated, given the influence and the [role] of the so-called fairer sex in the United States. The *Ladies* make clothing for the soldiers, since the *Government* is unable to do much of this—the *Ladies* in the cities on the railroad lines have founded charity & humanitarian associations, set up hospitals, and the proud daughters of the Palmetto State (South Carolina) are even building cannon boats to defend Charleston, and the daughters of Georgia are working on batteries for the coast in Savanah.— What could such a people accomplish in peacetime, given such beneficial conditions! I must close now; may God Almighty grant that sooner or later I will be able to tell you in person what I cannot write here.—May this folk, so rigid when it comes to the Bible and their own imaginary virtues and piety, have their eyes opened and realize what will lead to peace.—My own personal situation is quite satisfactory—although I don't know how this kind of money will ever get me back to you, since the local *Currency*, naturally, is not worth much and is completely worthless outside the borders of the so-called Confederacy [28 ll.: conditions at the refinery; reports from friends]. It is also not much of a pleasure to travel by train. They used to be so luxurious, but now accidents happen all the time, since nearly everything that can be transported is shipped by rail, and they are now completely worn out and nothing is coming in from the North, except when the southern general "Stonewall Jackson" captures 20–30 fine locomotives à la Manassas in Virginia and ships them south [20 ll.: travel possibilities]. It is only now becoming clear how dependent the South was on the North because of its *Cotton* or *Baumwolle*: even the most basic necessities are lacking, instead of matches I make my own sulfur sticks, steel, flint and tinder, etc. But since all the men who work in manufacturing have been freed from *Conscription*, the South is starting to do better: salt mines are being discovered, there are saltpeter pits everywhere, sulfur makers etc. [27 ll.: November 14: military action in Tennessee]. Fare well, and think often of your faithful loving Heinrich

Ducktown, Polk County, Tenn., May 3rd, 1863
Dear parents and brothers and sisters,

[45 ll.: longs to be home] Under normal conditions, my personal position would leave almost nothing to be desired [. . .] and under different circumstances, being the head of our considerable business as well as running the chemical laboratory would be a pleasure & a joy. I can certainly say that Mr. Raht, the general director of all the mines and refineries, is pleased with me and would very much like to keep me on. Aside from our business relationship, he is very nice and obliging, and his family, who is doing very well, likes me very much. Last spring our *Central* administration started extending our mining operations in various directions, and even though there were delays and "breakdowns in one branch of the works," the other branch was very busy—I would really like to run a refinery like this at home in Germany someday, but unfortunately there's no chance, given the crowds of young people in mining and refining, and even less chance now, as I have heard, since all of the Prussian mining boards have been shut down, meaning that many state employees have to find jobs with the private companies.[10]—I have often regretted not having saved enough of the money left over from my passage to guarantee my return trip [27 ll.: money matters; went to visit Traun].

This letter is being sent to you via the goodness and kind interest of Consul de Voss in Richmond. The last lines that I received from Germany were letters from father and Aunt Traun that arrived in the spring of 1861 [27 ll.: they

10. Up until this point, mines in Prussia had been run as state enterprises, and mining personnel were civil servants.

Sketch by Heinrich Stähler, "*Refining works at Ducktown 1863.*" (Otto Stähler)

should intercede on his behalf with the Prussian military authorities; greetings; signature].

                                    Ducktown Polk-County Tenn., May 10, 1863
Dear brother and sister-in-law,
    [25 ll.: communication difficulties] On the surface, things have been wonderful for me, and for about 1½ years I have been in a position that in times of peace would leave almost nothing to be desired [50 ll.: career; war economy; as in letter of May 3, 1863]. Eastern Tennessee, between the western slopes of the Alleghanies and the eastern slopes of the Cumberland Mountains, has many sources of abundant and essential natural products, and now they seem to be digging them out, because of the high prices, for one thing, and to avoid *Conscription*, for another. This area is one of largest sources of support for the South, what with its underground riches and its agricultural production, and this is why it is so remarkable that the *Yankees* didn't make a major effort to take East Tennessee years ago and occupy it [7 ll.: details]. And what are the reasons and causes that have kept the great South thus far from exploiting nature's riches, from promoting industrial life and activity in its great dead fields, where there's nothing but "*cotton is King!*", *Baumwolle ist König*. This war is making the people here more agile and more *Yankee*-like in business and trade, but who knows if all these efforts do not come too late [10 ll.: two routes to get back to Germany, equally dangerous; one is via Richmond, through the front lines]. The other way is by *Oxen* or *mule trac* through East Tennes-

see over the Cumberland *montains* into Kentucky, the roads and passes (*gap's*) full of *Buswhakers and robbers* (*Buschklepper u. Wegelagerer*) and then there's yet another large army of *Yankees* marching from Kentucky toward Cumberland gap, the mountain pass where the 3 states Virginia, Tenn., and Kentucky meet. Aside from all these practical difficulties, which can get much worse depending on what is happening in the area, you still aren't safe and secure, despite a certificate proving one's *Citizenship of Prussia*, provided by the Prussian consul in Charleston. Recently, a young man from Lippstadt named Krossenberg left here and was captured in Kentucky and taken to a *camp of Instruction*, kept there, and forced to practice drilling etc. despite his Prussian certificate of protection. — And aside from that, you need a lot of money now to return home — and where can you get it? The local paper money here will get you as far as the border, and you can spend piles of the stuff every day (8.00 a day in a hotel), but no further [15 ll.: savings; copper prices]. In May 63 I took a *Tour* through several southern states to Alabama in order to visit Mr. Henry Traun, and on my way I passed through Selma and Montgomery, the capital of Ala[.] and previous *capital of the provisory government of the confederate States of America*[11] [6 ll.: itinerary]. Mr. Traun was quite well and lives a few miles from the river, 12 miles east of Selma, where he used to have his business. Surrounded by his slaves and their wretched huts, his house is located on the highest point of his little plantation of 230 acres. We spent a few enjoyable days together, although we did not harmonize in our views on what caused the war, the nature of southern institutions etc. It was often difficult for the old fellow to keep up a conversation in fluent German, and *he always turned into the english conversation, while I tried to Keep him in our beloved native language*.

On the trip I went to see many factories where they are busy, day and night, to achieve southern *Independence*. Factories where they cast cannon, make wagons, harnesses, leather, saltpeter, cannonballs etc. In Selma they had launched a gunboat a few days earlier, and hundreds of hammers and chisels were at work (I went on board).[12] The actual traveling, usually so *comfordable* in America, was quite unpleasant, the railroad cars full of ragged, wounded, stinking soldiers, everything in disarray and full of dirt, and you often had to stand for hours without getting a seat, in a crushing crowd & stench; one pleasant exception was the trip by steamboat on the Alabama River, and I

11. A detailed account of Stähler's visit is in von Kindelsberg (1927), 480–88.

12. Probably the CSS *Huntsville*, launched on February 7, 1863, or its sister ship, the *Tuscaloosa*, both four-gun floating batteries. *Dictionary of American Naval Fighting Ships* (1963), 2:490, 536, 577.

can imagine that in peacetime this is elegant and very *comfordable*, with fine *Saloons*, all illuminated, and southern *Ladies* playing the *Piano* and singing passionate songs about the fatherland and its sons, the *sunny, sunny South, glorious country, the brave boyes & man etc. dead and hell to the Yankees.* But what good does all the bravery do, the country is becoming more and more exhausted, and I believe that if they hadn't started off with better officers than the northern side, they would never have had a chance of keeping things together and in order. There's no question about it, the spirit and the energy of the southern government seems more lively than that of the North (all along, most of the officers in the United States Army were southerners, and a large number of the sons of the wealthy always went to the military academy at Westpoint, even a number of students who never intended to graduate as officers but to return to their estates or take up other studies. This is why some of the best southern generals, like Polk, who is a bishop in the *methodist episcopalian church*, or *old* "stonewall Jackson", who is a professor at the University of Virgin. Charlottesville, and other generals and excellent officers are preachers, doctors and the like, who went through the program at Westpoint and then traded in their swords for the pulpit, lectern, or an *Office*) [21 ll.: high prices]. God alone knows what will happen. I hope, God willing, to see you all as soon as possible. This letter is being taken by a German through the mountains into the North, and I hope it will reach you [20 ll.: postal matters; friends; greetings; signature].

Stähler continued his work in the copper refineries of eastern Tennessee until the fall of 1863. Then he traveled west, together with Raht and his brother, their two wives and four children, as well as several black servants. They crossed the Union lines two days after the battle of Chattanooga in late November. They were initially treated as enemies and held prisoner for two weeks, but finally they were issued new passports. Stähler then continued overland to Nashville, by steamboat to St. Louis, and then by train to New York. Despite numerous job offers, he returned to Germany in 1864. The following year he went to Sweden to run a copper refinery for an English company. Now rich in experience, he finally returned home to Müsen in 1866, got married, and began a long and successful career as the manager of a smelting plant, the founder of a steel mill, and a strong advocate of railroad construction, until he died in Müsen in 1909.[13]

13. Von Kindelsberg (1927), 494–95; information provided by the donor.

52. Kessel and Rückels Families

The Kessel and Rückels families were spread out across the United States, but they remained closely connected, as they had been in Europe. The two cousins Fritz Kessel and Johann Rückels were double brothers-in-law: Fritz was married to Johann's sister Regina, and Johann was married to Fritz's sister Johanne. Another brother/brother-in-law, Gottfried Rückels, was married to Amalie Schnutenhaus, who was also a cousin of the other four. All three couples immigrated to the United States from Rheda-Wiedenbrück in Westphalia, and during the course of the 1850s, all the other members of the Kessel family—the parents and seven other siblings— eventually came over. Left behind were the recipients of the letters: Mina Grimm, née Rückels, her husband, and Mina's parents who were living with them.[1]

The core settlement of the family in the United States was in Illinois, sixty miles south of St. Louis, where Gottfried and Amalie Rückels, Fritz and Regina Kessel, and another Kessel brother established farms in the fertile Mississippi Valley. The rest of the Kessel family lived about 200 miles upriver in northern Illinois. Johann and Johanne Rückels, however, settled in the border area of north Texas, not far from the newly established town of Fort Worth.[2]

The two extended families were not merely simple farmers; they were more like farm managers. Their Calvinistic creed was suffused with a strong faith in the pursuit of profit, and once in America, their entrepreneurial attitudes were unmistakable. In 1859 Johann Rückels wrote from Texas, "My idea is buy and sell, win or lose." Gottfried Rückels, who described himself in a letter written in 1877 as an "agriculturist with ambition and energy," had a similar attitude. If he had had the same good opportunities in Germany as one of his friends, he wrote, he would now be "a gentleman, riding proudly across my estates."[3]

Their opinion of the Civil War was predominantly colored by the economic

SOURCE NOTE: Even the short passage printed here shows that Johann Rückels's spelling and grammar are fairly weak, such that the message he tries to get across is not always clear. Amalie Rückels spells much better, though not really well, but she can express herself in a way that is easily understandable, despite the influence of her Westphalian dialect. Regina Kessel's writing is very similar to Amalie's. Not included here are the letters in the series from the time before 1860 (two) and after 1865 (ten), and additional letters from 1860 (two) and 1861 (two).

1. Information provided by the donor. According to the 1900 census, August Kessel was the first to arrive in America (1850), followed by his brothers Fritz (1851), Hermann (1853), Julius (1856), and Albert (1856). In 1856 Gottfried Rückels also arrived with his sister Regina, who then married Fritz in 1858. The Kessel parents and younger siblings also arrived before 1858. Johanne Rückels arrived in 1851, but her son, who came to America in 1854, was apparently born in Germany in 1852, indicating that she may have temporarily returned to Germany. MC 1900: Hancock Co./Ill., e.d. 36, #238; MC 1900: Jackson Co./Ill., e.d. 24, #64, #4; MC 1900: Stephens Co./Tex., e.d. 141, #246–47; Pension File, Albert and Julius Kessel, NatA.

2. MC 1860: Jackson Co./Ill., #650–51; MC 1860: Hancock Co./Ill., Wythe Twp., #1117.

3. Letters of November 27, 1859, and March 9, 1877, NABS.

effects of the conflict; they also showed little interest in German politics.[4] At the outbreak of the war, Fritz Kessel, Gottfried Rückels, and Johann Rückels were roughly the same age (twenty-nine, thirty-one, and thirty-six, respectively) and living in similar situations—all were involved in setting up their farms. Conscription policies in the North and the South, however, were very different.

JOHANN RÜCKELS

1860. / Fort Worth, October 28

Dearest parents and brothers and sisters,

[58 ll.: family; farming; farm prices] Otherwise, the country is very quiet, everyone is waiting for war, and our slaves are thinking they'll be set free, and business has gone down, on the 5th of November is the day we elect a new president, and as I see in the newspapers, things look bad in Germany, too. Grandfather always told me, though, that we'd see hard times in 1860, that Babel would fall, and I believe it. This is a new area here, and already a number of our towns have been devoured by flames—Dallas, for example, was burned down this summer—it was a pretty town, and many people were left poor. The plan was to destroy the town so there'd be no more shooting supplies, and then to free the slaves (or Negroes). The agitators were hung for their bad behavior, they don't fool around with things like that here, the next best tree is high enough[5] [29 ll.: farming; family; greetings; signature; address].

AMALIE RÜCKELS AND REGINA KESSEL

Jones Creek, January 27, 1862

Dearest parents, brother-in-law, and sister-in-law,

[8 ll.: correspondence; parents' health] Happy New Year, or in other words, we wish you all the best for the coming year! Yes, dear sister-in-law, you wrote about the unrest or war, and we must say things are looking very bad. Across the river from us over in Missouri, they have chased away many a *Farmer*, and destroyed a lot of things, set houses on fire, etc.[6] But over here where we live we haven't been affected. We are still happily living together

4. See letter of Regina Kessel, October 2, 1859, NABS.

5. The business district of nearby Dallas was destroyed by a fire on July 8, 1860, but it was probably caused by the extreme heat, not arson. In the hysteria that resulted, a white man suspected of being an abolitionist was lynched on July 17, a hundred slaves in Dallas were arrested, and three of them were hanged on July 24. A preacher who was opposed to slavery and had fled to Missouri was brought back and immediately lynched on September 13. McCaslin (1994), 22–27.

6. See Müller (no. 47), who lived not far away on the Missouri side and fled to join an Illinois artillery unit.

and still have enough to eat and more than enough of everything. This is because you can't sell anything and make money on it—you might as well give it
away. This is just the strangest thing, a war and yet prices so low. Oh, you dear
ones, don't you cry for us, times will change and things will improve. We can
only thank the Lord our husbands aren't involved, because every bullet hits
something, whatever it is. This year we would have paid off our debts, if we'd
been able to sell our 500 cords of wood, but no, not even for the cost of the
hewing. That is sad when you work so terribly hard and then can't get rid of
it. Yes, dear Mina, you're right, you can't escape.

No matter where you go, your fate will still find you, be it in the east or
the west.

Thousands have already been shot to death, and millions are still at it.
There are very many German volunteers, too—Julius and Albert Kessel went
as volunteers. They have a very good life in the army and get 18 dollars a
month and their uniform, but when they have to meet the enemy, it won't do
them any good[7] [7 ll.: prices of agricultural products are very low]. But in
the stores material and everything is so expensive—coffee 3 [lb.] for a dollar,
a *Berl* [barrel] of salt 6 dollars, it's unbearable, you always need more money.
We and the Kessels drink barley coffee in times like these [9 ll.: butchering
hogs; livestock]. We haven't had a letter from Johann for a long time, and we
think it's because Teksas is a southern state. That means letters won't get here
anymore. We hope he is still doing well. And that you will soon have received
a letter [27 ll.: news about friends; greetings; signature].

[REGINA KESSEL continues:]
Most dearly beloved parents, sister, brother-in-law, and child,

[53 ll.: religious consolation; pregnancy; her mother-in-law has moved to
live with the Kessel children in northern Illinois; harvest and prices; greetings; signature]

REGINA KESSEL
                                    Misisippi valley, April 7, 1862
Most dearly beloved parents, sister and brother-in-law,

[35 ll.: correspondence; birth of a child] Julius and Albert, my two youngest brothers-in-law who are in the army, write to us often. They wrote in
their last letter that they'd sent mother 75 dollars, and they'd get paid again in
March. They get 13 dollars a month and all their food, 160 acres of land and

7. Julius (born in 1840) and Albert (born in 1842) signed up in Warsaw, Illinois, in August
1861. They joined the Black Hawk Cav Comp, which later became Comp A, 7 Mo. Cav. Muster
Rolls and Pension File, NatA.

100 dollars when the war is over. Up to now they have always been in good spirits. The entire American army consists of volunteers, and even the Holssteiner fellow who used to chop wood for my brother is now a captain, getting 130 dollars a month. Everyone believes the North, where we live, will win, because the southerners have lost almost all the battles up to now. Let's hope the war will be over soon, and that we will get a better price for our grain next summer.

[61 ll.: farming] So, dear father and mother, I hope you stay hale and hearty, and don't scrimp your talers*—you should have things easier and more comfortable in your old age, for your children have enough to eat, even if they're not rich, and there's no want. We haven't heard anything from Texas, because no letters go there from here since it belongs to the South [6 ll.: greetings]. My Fritz and brother-in-law Johann send all their best, and be embraced in spirit by your daughter, sister, sister-in-law Regina Kessel [. . .]

AMALIE RÜCKELS

Jones Creek Randolph Caunty, Ills
Sept. 6, 1862

Dearly beloved parents and brothers and sisters,

[20 ll.: birth of a child; family] But we lack for nothing here, and we also have far too much work to do, so much that the two of us sometimes can't manage it all, but if you want to keep a farmhand for the whole year, it costs too much, because the crop prices are too low. Then it's better to leave some of the land fallow when you can't work it. The weeds grow 6 to 8 feet high here, and it's almost impossible to kill them. What with prices so low, clothing, sugar, coffee and other things are too expensive. But oh, dear parents, this is nothing compared to if my Fritz[8] had to fight in that great Seven-Years War, where so many thousand men are being slaughtered just for the sake of a few bigwigs. I certainly hope we won't be hit by the misfortune that my Fritz and Regina's Fritz will be taken from us. Oh, what would we poor women do then, as strangers in this country? For who cares about an American, *Jänky*? You probably know from the newspapers what the situation is like here. In the state of Illionois almost everyone went as volunteers, but they keep saying they're still going to draw lots.

I don't know what will happen then, because around here there are hardly any men left. They keep battling away against the South, but which of the two sides is the strongest? The North just got another 300,000 volunteers, but I

8. This does not refer to Fritz Kessel but to Gottfried Rückels, who was also called "Fritz" by his wife Amalie and his sister Regina.

don't know how big the army is in all. Can the higher-ups justify before God such a sacrifice of men, they're squabbling over things nobody understands. — But they say after these times will come a better one. Oh dear father, it's no good no matter where you are — out of the frying pan and into the fire! [63 ll.: hog cholera; harvest; livestock; children]. Albert and Julius Kessel are in the army. Albert got 1 bullet shot through his hat that took some hair with it, it was so close, so close.[9]

I don't know how my brothers are doing, we haven't had a letter in a long time. Our fruit did quite well this year, and my Fritz got me 10 bushels of apples to dry, for 10 to 15 cents a bushel, and we have a lot of our own peaches. In closing, all the best / Fritz and Amalia Rückels

REGINA KESSEL AND AMALIE RÜCKELS
Missisippi Valley, November 14 / 1863
Dear parents, sister and brother-in-law,

[81 ll.: family; crop prices; have bought another farm; livestock] Mother so wants to hear from Texas, but no letters from here get sent there, and we haven't heard anything from them since the war started. Many people think the war will be over soon. Julius and Albert are still alive, and two weeks ago they wrote they were about to fight a big battle, and may the Good Lord preserve their lives [8 ll.: family; greetings] My dearest ones, a thousand hugs and kisses from your loving daughter and son, sister and brother-in-law Fritz and Regina Kessel [. . .]
[AMALIE RÜCKELS continues?:][10]
Dearest parents, sister, brother-in-law and children,

[4 ll.: her mother's illness] But the Good Lord will keep an eye on her and make her well again, like He did with my dear Fritz. Last Wednesday he was able to get up again a bit for the first time, and he's slowly recovering his strength. He was seriously sick, but thank the Lord, he has recovered; and even if he won't be able to work for half a year, at least we can take comfort that he will never be fit for military duty. For they are still fighting away, they've killed 15,000 men already, and no one knows how many more they'll kill.[11] Many wives and children mourn their men. Oh how sad it is for such poor people.

---

9. On August 16, 1862, in action at Lone Jack, Missouri, Albert Kessel received a minor head wound, but he was back on active duty in September; Muster Rolls, NatA. The regiment in which both Kessels served spent the entire war in Missouri and Arkansas. Dyer (1959 [1908]), 1307-8.

10. It is unclear if the two letters belong together or not.

11. Ten times this number would be more correct.

[22 ll.: they don't want to repay their debts in Germany as long as wartime inflation continues; best wishes for a long life; health; greetings; signature]

REGINA KESSEL

Liberty, January 11, 1867

Dear father, sister, and sister-in-law,

[14 ll.: birth of a child] Now my dear ones, I must let you know that a few weeks ago we received a letter from Texas with the sad news that the Good Lord took His pleasure in calling our beloved brother to the Hereafter, and how? By means of the war. He also had to go to the war and was discharged because of illness in September 1865, and he died at home 1 month later, on October 3, 1865, of a liver inflammation. So you can well imagine what a sad situation poor Hane is in now, with 6 children, 5 girls and 1 boy, named Ernst, who is 14 years old. She writes that he is too young and too weak to run their farm, and they have 45 acres under the plow. Times were very dangerous and difficult for them during the war, and we always read about it in the newspapers, how Texas suffered so much. If our brother had believed us and moved up here, maybe he would still be alive now, but then man proposes, but God disposes. Now Hanne would like one of her brothers to come and live with her, but none of them want to because they are all married[12] [6 ll.: details]. So we wrote to Hanne that we think it's better if she comes up here, if she can sell everything there, and that someone will come to get her if she cannot travel on her own. All the brothers and sisters here will get the money together to pay for this. We're expecting an answer from her any day now. I think I wrote you last time that my Fritz got drafted, too, and that it cost us 350 dollars to pay for a substitute. These were hard times for us, too.

Otherwise we are doing quite well. The harvest was quite good, we harvested 400 bushels of wheat, and the highest price we got for it was 2½ dollars per bushel [13 ll.: harvest and prices]. Fritz and my brother Fritz got together last summer to buy a *Nigger* or (reaper) that cost 216 dollars.[13] My brother Fritz and another neighbor also bought a threshing machine in partnership last summer, it cost 375 dollars [37 ll.: family visit; livestock; encourages the

12. Albert Kessel married Mina Niekamp from Bielefeld, Westphalia, on November 3, 1866, in the Lutheran church in Quincy, Illinois. Pension File, NatA. Julius was the only member of the family with an Anglo American spouse, Ellen Woodrick. After she died in 1868, he married another American. Pension File, NatA.

13. This joking remark is one of the very few references to racial issues, but on March 7, 1875, Gottfried Kessel wrote, "I only have black farmhands, but they are faithful. I don't have anything locked up, everything's open." His sister-in-law is also listed in 1870 with a black farmhand in her household. MC 1870: Jackson Co./Ill., Kincaid Pct., #116.

family to emigrate; asks about relatives]. Now, dear sister, tell the other sisters of the death of our dear brother. Oh, the soldier's life was so hard for him in Germany, and here it cost him his life. But we trust and believe the Good Lord has granted him eternal joy [6 ll.: friends]. Thousands of greetings to you all, and all the best from your son and daughter Fritz Regina Kessel [. . .]

The widow Johanne Rückels ran her farm on her own until 1870. Then she married a widower with a roving spirit: originally from Georgia, he had worked before the war on a farm some 300 miles east of Fort Worth, and before 1880 the family moved another 200 miles west of the city.[14] In 1880 Johanne's eldest daughter died, leaving five orphaned children behind. But it is interesting that the children did not go to live with their grandmother or their aunts and uncles in Texas; instead, they were raised by their relatives in Illinois.[15]

And the Illinois branch of the family was in an excellent position to provide for these children. According to the 1880 census, Gottfried Rückels and his brother-in-law Fritz Kessel each owned farms worth $10,000. All but one of the Kessel siblings had settled nearby. Julius and August Kessel also ran well-established farms, and their army pay and bounties had no doubt been put to good use: their two farms, each 160 acres, were worth $4,000 and $2,500, respectively.[16] After the war, the letters from Gottfried Rückels and his sister Regina to their German relatives are full of praise of the advantages of the United States "for young, diligent people" and of exhortations directed at the next generation, urging them to immigrate.[17] Some of the letters are quite critical of opportunities lost—for example, Regina's letter of January 1, 1875:

> Dear sister, we would so much like to know [. . .] if all your children are still living with you or what they are doing, and wouldn't they like to come to America [. . .] and if they work hard and are thrifty, then they can buy some land in a couple of years and set up their homes, and then they'd get ahead, year by year. But you, dear sister, believe that what your son-in-law tells you is the truth[. . . .] But his opinions are very different from ours. He is a longtime servant of the king, who seeks his fortune and honor in faithfully serving the king. We German Americans think very differently. We think it is only fair and right when a young boy or girl living in Germany without any means, working hard for poor food, with no chance to get ahead, has the desire and

14. No official record of Johanne's marriage to James Jay exists, but their marriage is clear from the names, ages, and places of birth. MC 1860; Upshur Co./Tex., #1114; MC 1870: Tarrant Co./Tex., Pct. 1, #752; MC 1880: Stephens Co./Tex., e.d. 171, #15–16; MC 1900: Stephens Co./Tex., e.d. 141, #246–47.

15. Letter of Gottfried Rückels, July 17, 1881, NABS.

16. MCA 1880: Jackson Co./Ill., Degonia Twp., p. 31, Kincaid Twp., p. 5, 15; MCA 1880: Randolph Co., Ill., Vine Hill Twp., p. 9.

17. Letter of Gottfried Rückels, July 17, 1881, NABS.

the courage to found a new homeland in America, where they have the chance to make a new home, where they can provide a good living for a wife and children, free of problems and worries, and even be able to leave something to their descendants.

Regina's brother Gottfried Rückels most certainly did so, when he died in October 1891. "I'd never seen such a large and lovely funeral," she wrote.[18]

18. Letter of Regina Kessel, early 1892, NABS.

53. Dr. Hermann Nagel

Even though he left Germany a year before the Revolution of 1848, Hermann Nagel had much in common with the typical Forty-eighter. Born in 1820 in Pritzwalk, in Brandenburg, he was raised in an upper-middle-class family. His father, the town miller and drainage expert, died early, but this did not keep Hermann from attending boarding school and studying medicine in Halle, Würzburg, and Berlin, where he became active in a radical student association. He married the daughter of a pastor but remained a freethinking liberal both in religion and politics. As he later told his son, he was seldom interested in any book "unless the Government had denounced it." Nagel's immigration to Texas seems to have been motivated by equal amounts of political conviction and romanticism. Like many Forty-eighters, he tried to make a living as a "Latin farmer,"* and he settled on the prairie some sixty miles west of Houston, first in Bernardo, where his eldest son Carl was born in 1849, and then in Millheim, near Cat Spring, one of the oldest German settlements in Texas. In the 1860 census Nagel is listed only as a farmer, with an impressive $4,500 of property; in reality, the income from his work as a physician was indispensable, despite his original plans.[1]

Before the outbreak of the Civil War, the Nagels lived in a largely German-speaking world. Millheim had a German school, and about 1855 a *Gesangverein* (men's choral society) was established, along with a German-style bowling alley. In

SOURCE NOTE: For this series only transcripts of the original letters are available. Lacking the originals or facsimiles, we cannot be sure about Nagel's spelling and punctuation, but it is almost certain that a man with his education had no deficiencies here. What we can be sure of is that his German is colorful, imaginative, and impressively rich in vocabulary. Not included here are the fifty-one letters in the series from the time after 1865.

1. In the 1850 census, however, Nagel appears as a physician: MC 1850: Colorado Co./Tex., #226. The autobiography of his son Carl is an important source: Nagel (1935), 67 (quotation), 11–13, 20, 36, 47, 57–69, 96–97, 101, 122; see also Biesele (1987), 48–55; MC 1860: Austin Co./Tex., #802. Nagel left Germany with 2,000–3,000 talers*; his mother's property was assessed at 16,000 talers, according to Br. LHA P, Prov. Br. Rep. 2A I St Nr. 87, Bl 407–8, 424–25.

1856 an agricultural society was founded in Austin County, where Nagel and other "Latin farmers" from Millheim (including six graduates of German universities) could exchange ideas with the dirt farmers of peasant stock in Cat Spring. Despite their class differences, they almost all agreed when it came to secession: in the Cat Spring–Millheim election precinct, only eight voted in favor, and ninety-nine were opposed. Not surprisingly, Hermann Nagel belonged to this majority, but when the war broke out, this did not make his life any easier.[2]

Milheim, April 28, 61.

You must take this letter as it is written, scribbled in the greatest haste[. . . .] My dear brother,

[20 ll.: mail and money matters] It looks like we are in for hard times. I have expressed my opinions on our situation in the letter to Wolff; I still hold these opinions, with the significant change that I no longer believe in a restoration of the Union. From the point of view of the administration, sending northern troops into the southern states, although I find this acceptable, forces the Union loyalists here into resistance as well. It is hard to believe, but it's true, and what is even stranger, I even have these feelings myself. I strongly criticize this entire business (namely secession), I regard it as neither justified nor advantageous, but merely as the most unprompted rebellion there ever was, and yet it may come down to it that I myself go off to fight against the so-called invasion of the so-called abolitionists. You can well imagine how badly I feel about all of this. But it's strange how changing circumstances can be bewildering. Every day groups of 2, or 5, or 10, or 30 or more volunteers come here through [O.] and Milheim, cool-headed men, each with his own good *Rifle*, mounted and equipped at his own expense. They are all going to Indianola, where the United States troops are expected to land, and where about 1,000 of these troops have gathered. There they join the ranks to serve in the field. Seeing this, feelings of shame can overcome any man who is inclined to stay home quietly, just because he doesn't want to fight for something that is against his principles. I haven't read any proclamation yet from our governor calling all men to arms. But nevertheless, there is activity everywhere. Militias are drilling and everyone is getting prepared. I would give a lot to be able to put my heart into this; but it is impossible, and so my position here, along with that of many of my friends, is very distressing, most unsatisfactory, and there's no end in sight [8 ll.: correspondence]. When the current confusion is over, I intend to settle farther north with my family, but only if I am still

2. Biesele (1987), 50–55, 206, 209; Nagel (1935), 104, 117, 148–50, 193, 232; letter of October 3, 1862, abridged, NABS; Regenbrecht (1917), 30–33.

capable of making decisions and acting upon them, that is. I will be sad to leave Texas, a beautiful country that has offered me such happiness and satisfaction for so long, but I will have to. I will never be able to reconcile myself with the belief that slavery is the actual foundation of the state, that the continued existence of slavery is not merely a temporary necessity but the true essence and basic principle of the state, without which civilized society cannot exist [21 ll.: denies he was always unhappy in Texas]. Every day I say that I don't like it here at the moment, and I also express my wish to move to a freer country; but that will take a while in times like these, when things are not even worth their nominal value. And I am also kept back by a certain sense of shame, for leaving a country just at the moment it is overcome by misfortune, after having shared my lot with it so happily and willingly in better times [7 ll.: about the person delivering the letter].
Your brother H.

Milheim, October 3, 62.

Dear mother,

[6 ll.: about the person delivering this letter] As far as my family and I are concerned, we are doing well enough. We are not happy; that would only be possible for someone with no heart and sympathy for the sufferings of others, a true egotist. Our country is torn apart by this most terrible civil war, where fury and passion rage, often having to take the place of patriotism. The newspapers will have told you about the general situation. Slavery is the bone of contention. Here where we are, although things are probably better than in any other southern state, things look very bad. We only produce raw materials, so there's a shortage of everything beyond what we need to stay alive and to defend ourselves. There is already a lack of clothing and shoes everywhere. Coffee, rice, drugs, nails, tools are only to be had for their weight in gold; it's almost the same with salt. The well-to-do are becoming poor, but the rich are getting filthy rich; the farming class is ruined, but the merchants are earning dozens and dozens of thousands within a few months. Every man between the ages of 18 and 45 will be an active soldier in the field within the next 8 weeks. The only exceptions are the blind, the deaf, cripples, consumptives and the chronic, incurably ill, along with the officeholders, the overseers for the Negroes, shoemakers, tanners, millers and doctors. If I weren't already a doctor, I'd want to be a shoemaker. Just imagine, all the other men are gone, leaving their wives and children all alone, with no help, in a country where the men are needed more by their families than anywhere else, since most of the farm work can only be done by the men. I don't know how this can work out, and no one else does either. And then on top of this there's the black population in the country, who—even though they are generally quite easy to please—are suffering very much under the current circumstances and who have no doubt already taken over some of the strange ideas and wishes of the whites. They seem to be quite familiar with the name "Lincoln," and they probably associate ideas with this name that will cause a terrible blood-bath as a result. But in general I am not particularly afraid of Negro uprisings; small bands may try to run away, and they may be insolent and disobedient; but it will hardly come to a full-scale revolt, because in general, the blacks have had it too good. I do hope, at least, that I am right about this, although I must admit that I cannot form an opinion based on my own experience, since I live far away from the plantations and don't really know much myself about the blacks and their condition.[3] But even without slave uprisings, things look bad enough here [11 ll.: details]. Oh, you have no idea what a large-scale war means here, where several hundred thousand are working on half-tilled land, and only the basic necessities of life are being produced. The death rate in the army is horrifying; the reports are sometimes hard to believe. I know that if I had to go into the army, I wouldn't survive 4 weeks under these conditions. And so many are even weaker than I am, and yet they still have to go, with no exceptions. Only those men who are seriously ill are declared unfit for service, and the examination is so very strict and tough—it is dreadful. It isn't actually a medical examination at all, but a military one [33 ll.: family; about friends who are in danger of being conscripted]. I will do what I can; I am hoping for the best, but I am prepared for any eventuality, since the examination will probably be extremely hard. Still, I am a physician, and I know that both of the men are unfit for duty, and will try my best to convince the medical ex-aminer. But the medical examiners are outsiders, often ignorant persons, and they understand so little of what they are doing that they are unable to tell the difference between men who are truly unfit and those who are simulating. But enough [4 ll.: greetings; signature].

St. Louis, May 13, 1864

My dear brother,

[. . .] My son Paul has died, according to letters I received from my wife yesterday. I don't know how and when he died, because the letters refer back to earlier ones that I did not receive. He seems to have died before I left St. Antonio, and his passing was apparently peaceful and without pain.[4] My

3. Nagel's son could only remember three slaves in the settlement. Nagel (1935), 217.

4. Fearing for their lives, Nagel and his son Carl fled to Mexico via San Antonio, sailed from Matamoros to New York, and then went west to St. Louis. His wife remained behind with the younger children. Nagel (1935), 227–320, describes their flight in greater detail.

wife's words are vague, and this tends to confirm my suspicions, and Carl is convinced they are correct, that the boy became ill with sorrow when we fled, or that he even died of grief. That was his nature. And that closes his short chapter of life, one that was cheerful and harmonious, and I will never forget the innocent look in his deep, dark eyes. And what will my wife do now, that poor, self-sacrificing, woman, now so sorely afflicted? She is calm and collected in her letters (of December 22, 1863, to February 7, 1864), there are no complaints, she is only concerned about me and asks me to take good care of myself; she chats pleasantly with Carl and consoles him. But I know all too well what she has lost. So here I sit all alone and cannot go to her, I probably cannot even write a letter, and I writhe with fear, crying aloud like a child, all for naught. Patience, we must have patience. How, in Heaven's name, can I help my poor wife! [7 ll.: fighting his despair]. My wife still doesn't know where I am, but she has received a letter from Matamoros, in which I wrote I was thinking of going to St. Louis. If I had only stayed in Texas, I think our Paul would not have died. Oh! and how calm and reasonable were our thoughts about what we should do, and it seemed to us that I had no choice but to leave. I don't know what to think and am thrown from one idea to the next by the anxiety that tortures me [17 ll.: asks for pictures of his children; Carl's frame of mind and his own; greetings; signature].

St. Louis, August 5, 1864.

My dear brother,

   [. . .] I haven't heard anything from my wife or had any other kind of sign from my family. I know little more about Texas in general, just that my friend Schmidt told me that in a letter of April 11, his brother, who lives with his family in Houston (Texas), had talked about their great apprehension in the face of imminent anarchy and h[----]. Schmidt himself didn't believe there was much truth in this, nor do I, but he assured me that when he gets to Mexico, if he becomes convinced that the situation in Texas is really as serious as was claimed, he will do everything he can to get the rest of my family out of the country [45 ll.: no news since then; concern for his family; Carl's health; is thinking of sending him to Germany]. As for me, I am quite hale and hearty and can tolerate the climate better than all the rest of the Texas people who have sought refuge here, and I've even met up with some of my old neighbors and acquaintances who left their families behind like I did. Some of them have been here for years and haven't heard one word about their families. Most of them are from the southern Ona[-----] Distrikt, but they all long for beautiful Texas, just like I do, and probably none of them will stay here as soon as they have a chance to return to the South. I am the only exception; I don't want to go back, and only my wife's wish to remain there could induce me to make my home there again. What good is the beauty of the countryside and the climate, when the people who live there are like they are? I certainly didn't need to leave Germany just to watch my fellow human beings in Texas becoming increasingly depraved and stupid. As long as I thought Texas was part of the United States and wrongly assumed that the South would slowly but surely yield to the intelligence coming down from the North, I was perfectly satisfied, since I always feel quite at home as long as I have the freedom to fight, but ever since I witnessed this outbreak of brute force, viciousness, fanaticism, and the unbelievable perversion of notions of justice that I have seen in the South in the past 3 years, I've become apprehensive of living there any longer. The systematic demoralization of the Americans without slaves is so deeply rooted that it would be impossible to eradicate it without eliminating all the disciples of this worst of the worst medieval ideas [41 ll.: his medical practice is doing better and his social contacts have increased; money worries; greetings]. May you all be spared the suffering that weighs us down here and will continue to do so for a long time. Our nation, with all its faults and weaknesses, its arrogance and aversion to foreigners, as well as the vices and crimes found in certain groups of the society, is basically patriotic and good. Despite all the suffering that the wickedness and stupidity of its leaders have heaped upon us, I hope it is patriotic enough to persevere in the work of punishing the traitors and eradicating, root and branch, the cause of all our current woes—slavery. But heaven only knows how long we will still have to keep fighting. Our current government is blind, deaf, and awful, and there's no prospect of an end to our fighting as long as it is in power. With the best wishes to you all

Your brother H.

St. Louis, September 13, 1864.

My dear sister-in-law,

[7 ll.: apologizes for the delay] There has been little change in our situation, as far as I know. I have received some letters from my wife, and the most recent one, dated March 10, was 5 months old when it arrived. According to this letter, my wife was fine, as was Clara. Her words were calm and collected, she admitted she had had times when she was close to despair (which I certainly find hardly surprising), but she assured me that she had gotten over this now and was facing the future with composure [7 ll.: details]. The general situation hasn't gotten any worse, but my wife indicated that my absence was a good thing. She still has enough clothing and had collected enough money to pay the taxes, which were raised from the 10 dollars I usually paid to 300 dollars. She still did not know where I was[. . . .] That is a brief summary of the contents of my wife's letter. Later I had indirect news of her up to April 14, the day a young man fled from the vicinity of Milheim [Texas]. He arrived here a while ago and told me that my wife and daughter were well. They all thought I had gone back to Germany. According to this young man, the situation is getting worse every day, and a law was passed in the state legislature in order to confiscate all the property of those who have left Texas. I had anticipated this and put everything in my wife's name before I left, but this will hardly prevent those rogues from taking it. No law there can protect you from lawless bandits, only force. Many refugees have been arriving here from Texas lately, young men and men who like me have left their families behind [16 ll.: relatives and friends in Texas are suffering].

As for my personal situation, I make my living much the same as before. I have some patients, more than I could expect given the short time I've been here, and it's enough to support Carl and me, if the healthier season that is now beginning doesn't cause a sharp decrease in the number of illnesses in the small circle of my patients [13 ll.: otherwise, his life is simple and monotonous]. Carl has recovered quite well, especially in the last 3 weeks when he was staying out in the country with a rich American family[. . . .] I also make an exception and go out to see these people, who are always most anxious to show me their appreciation for the services I rendered to their eldest son in Mexico. When I met him there he was sick, in rags, and penniless, and I lent him 300 dollars, although he was completely unknown to me. He was the former adjutant of a well-known rebel general who had been welcomed and then left unaided by his fellow associates whose pockets were full of money [6 ll.: weather and health]. I follow our public affairs with great interest and hope that the rebels who are beyond all law, rights, and humanity, will received their just reward. We are, however, close to or even already in a crisis, and there are certainly enough shortsighted and wicked men among us who want to stop the course of history, but I think this will be in vain. Our best candidate for the presidency, Fremont,* the candidate of the Germans, has little chance of being elected, as things now stand, but he is the man for a radical cure. Lincoln's and McClellan's chances are unclear and haven't taken shape yet; much will depend on the success of our weapons, which have been scoring decisive successes of late.[5] Many things no one has even thought of may still happen quickly and unexpectedly. But one thing is beyond doubt, that the South will be crushed, if the North wants to, despite all the sympa-

5. On the election of 1864 campaign, see Nagler (1984).

thy in the English and French press for Jefferson Davis and his comrades. The only question is whether the North has underestimated the significance of the struggle and tires of making such great sacrifice. I certainly hope not, and see only one goal that must be reached for our true well-being and that of our children and our children's children, and the means to this end is war without reprieve [. . .] before I agree that we should make any peace other than a full-fledged one, based solely on the law and the demands of our progressive times, I would rather we fight and suffer, and suffer and fight, instead of making a rotten compromise and sowing the seeds of new action and bloodshed. My own personal life, as I am leading it at the moment, is hardly worth carrying on; it is only my hopes for the future that give meaning to the present [5 ll.: is bearing his fate with composure]. You advise me, dear sister-in-law, to read the Bible and go to church, or at least try if for once. I am so sure of the fact that this advice comes from the heart, sincerely sympathetic and well meaning, that I interpret it entirely and solely in this manner [9 ll.: was quite downcast at the beginning]. Nevertheless, dear sister-in-law, I must confess to you openly and honestly that a man like myself is a lost cause for the Bible and the Church, because of the fact that he knows both institutions[. . . .] I certainly appreciate the supreme teachings that are written down in it for us to follow, but are so seldom practiced in the world, either inside the church or outside it [. . .] and that's the extent of my appreciation of the merits of the Bible as the word of God [10 ll.: much of it is too cruel and contradictory]. My view of the merits of the Bible (when seen as God's word and revelation) leads directly to my attitude toward the Church, as a purely human institution imbued with all its shapes and shades by the various founders of the individual sects [8 ll.: has not set foot in a church since his wedding]. Still, I would be willing to assert that I do possess strong religious feelings, but they do not find any satisfaction in the practices of our church rituals and ceremonies [55 ll.: further freethinking reflections]. With that let me end this topic, a topic that for many years has occupied me much more than most people who know me only superficially could ever realize [6 ll.: no offense intended]. Give my best to Carl, Wilhelm and the other relatives, and in particular our good mother. I will leave it up to you whether you want to tell her all the details of our situation or not, since only you can judge the consequences. It seems to me to be a good idea, since you never know what still can happen, worse than now. Mother will know that we accept our fate as it comes, like rational people should, and that we are still relatively happy compared with thousands upon thousands of others in this otherwise so blessed land. We have had enough strength to endure the over-arching misfortune, and it would be small-minded and petty to despair over our personal one [10 ll.: greetings from Carl, who may be coming to Germany for a visit]. Your brother-in-law Hermann.

Even before the war came to an end, Mrs. Nagel followed her husband and son to St. Louis, where what was left of the family settled permanently—daughter Clara had also died in Texas. Although he arrived in St. Louis with only fourteen dollars and lost all his property in Texas, Dr. Nagel soon established a successful practice. In 1870 he listed $10,000 in assets, enabling his son to study law at Washington University in St. Louis. In 1872 the family returned to Germany for a year: both father and son attended lectures (in medicine and law, respectively) at the University of Berlin.[6]

Like many Forty-eighters, Nagel found it difficult to accept the imperfections of American democracy. In a letter of December 22, 1874, he wrote, "All in all, our political and administrative system, as it is managed by those in office, is completely incompetent, depraved, corrupt, and not in the least compatible with the basic principles that should infuse a republic. It is, instead, despotic and unbelievably capricious." Despite what he had suffered during the Civil War, he later turned his back on the Republicans, first supporting the Liberal Republicans and then, before his death in 1889, voting for two Democratic presidential candidates.[7]

Despite his earlier hatred of Bismarck, Nagel—like many other Forty-eighters— was caught up in the exhilaration of German unification: "[Bismarck] is the right man for our times and your position in it; at any rate he is a man after my own heart[. . . .] Yes, I am always happy now about Germany [. . .] that it is in such a good position and leading the other nations in its promises of greatness." As a free-thinker, he also heartily approved of the *Kulturkampf*, Bismarck's bitter struggle to subject the Roman Catholic Church to state controls, and praised the work of Charles Darwin.[8]

The liberalism espoused by two generations of the Nagel family also found expression in their openness toward Jews. Carl Nagel's schoolmate and "dearest friend for life" was a man named Washington E. Fischel, who later joined the elder Nagel's medical practice.[9] Carl married the daughter of a distinguished Jewish Forty-eighter from Louisville; her brother was Louis D. Brandeis, a prominent lawyer who later became a member of the U.S. Supreme Court.[10]

Carl (or Charles) Nagel also had a brilliant career in law and politics. He taught

6. Regenbrecht (1917), 33–34; Nagel (1935), 286–87, 300, 316, 377–81; MC 1870: St. Louis/ Mo., W. 8, #790. Starting in 1879, the Nagels had an elegant address at Lafayette Park. CD St. Louis, 1879–89.

7. Letter of December 22, 1874, NABS; Nagel (1935), 320–21; Regenbrecht (1917), 34.

8. Nagel (1935), 68, 377; letters of February 14, 1874, and December 22, 1874, NABS.

9. Nagel (1935), 339 (quotation), 342; letters of August 15, 1875, and April 8, 1876, NABS.

10. Brandeis (1971), 3–5, 17–18, 37–41; Wittke (1952), 86–89.

law at Washington University, was a member of the Missouri legislature and president of the St. Louis City Council, and was elected to the Missouri State Supreme Court. Unlike his father, he remained true to the Republicans, and his career reached its peak in 1909-13, when he served in President William H. Taft's cabinet as secretary of commerce and labor.[11]

11. Nagel (1935), 410, 412-19; Sobel (1990), 277.

54. Captain Robert Voigt, CSA

When the future Confederate captain Robert Voigt left Germany in 1850, he did not take much money with him, but he had other assets he could put to good use. He was born in 1832, the son of a senior foreman in the royal mines in Zschornau and Schneeberg in Saxony. When his father died in 1842, the family—including his six sisters—lived on his pension. Robert probably attended technical school, and he was certainly a gifted draftsman. Voigt immigrated to Houston, Texas, in the fall of 1850, and three years later his mother and younger sisters followed.[1]

Voigt assimilated rapidly into both German and American society in Houston, then a small but booming commercial town. In 1854 he was one of the founders of the Houston *Turnverein* [Turner*] and started out working as an architect. In February 1855 he married Anna Schweikart, the daughter of German immigrants, born in New York. Voigt's first son, also named Robert, was born in October 1856, daughter Selma followed in 1859, and second son Adolph was born around 1861. By 1859, the family must have left Houston. The 1860 census lists Voigt as a merchant with $5,000 of assets living in San Felipe, a village about thirty-five miles west of Houston. A short time later, he became the owner of a store and the postmaster in Industry, one of the oldest German settlements in Texas, about fifty miles west of Houston. Between 1859 and 1862, when he enlisted in the army, the value of his taxable property soared from $315 to $5,744. As his letters indicate, Voigt continued

SOURCE NOTE: Like most letter-writers with commercial or technical training, Voigt writes fluently and with a generally good command of the language, though there are occasional lapses in his spelling. His frequent use of English terms shows that both he and his wife were familiar with this language as well, but even after a dozen years in the country, English does not interfere much with his idiomatic High German—that is, he uses few German Americanisms. Not included here are a number of letters in the series written in 1862 (twenty), 1863 (three), 1864 (seven), and 1865 (one).

1. Justman (1974), 73, 83, 281-83, 295-97, 305-8, 315-16, 322, 328. Voigt's Saxon passport was issued on August 25, 1850. Brother-in-law Friedrich Sachs apparently preceded him, becoming a U.S. citizen with five years' minimum residency in June 1855, Voigt six months later in December. Index to Harris County Naturalizations, Houston Public Library, Houston, Tex.

to maintain good connections with the German and Anglo American business communities in Houston.[2]

The fact that the soldiers in his company elected Voigt to be their captain is certainly a sign of their respect and confidence. The question arises, however, just what it was that he and his company were actually fighting for. He writes himself about doing his "duty" for "our cause," without any further elaboration—slavery or slaves are hardly ever mentioned. Unlike his fellow Turners, who set up the first company of volunteers in Houston, Voigt enlisted only when it became clear that he would soon be conscripted, and then he tried to set up the conditions of his military service to suit himself. This was all the more true of the men in his company, who were primarily concerned with doing their onerous duty under someone they knew and trusted.

In ethnic terms, Voigt's company was highly homogeneous: apart from one Dutchman, five German Texans, and three Russian Germans, all 133 men were born in Germany. Over 100 of these men lived, like Voigt, in Austin County; but the fact that five more counties, stretching all the way to Houston, were represented in the company indicates that he was well known and had a good reputation. The other companies frequently mentioned in the letters, commanded by captains Henry Wickland and Otto Nathusius, a Houston merchant, were just as homogeneous— they included a handful of Bohemian and Swiss immigrants but only one clearly identifiable Anglo American. All together, these three companies were composed of Germans who lived in nine different counties, clear evidence that they felt it was important to serve in German units.[3] The rest of the legion was Anglo American. It was commanded by Colonel Thomas N. Waul, a wealthy plantation and slave owner from Gonzales, ninety miles west of Industry. All the units were mustered in for three years in Houston in April 1862 and then sent to a camp near Brenham for training.[4]

---

2. Justman (1974), 41, 73, 305-7, 315; Tiling (1913), 164; MC 1860: Austin Co./Tex., San Felipe Pct., #615; Property Tax Rolls, Harris Co., 1855-58, Austin Co., 1859-62, Texas StateA, Austin, Tex. In the first issue of the *Bellville Countryman* published on July 28, 1860, Voigt is listed as the subscription agent in Industry.

3. There were hardly any Germans in Captain J. W. McDade's company from Austin Co., mustered in on October 20, 1861; muster roll printed in the *Bellville Countryman*, March 8, 1862. See also Company Muster Rolls, Waul's Legion, Texas StateA. Nathusius, Wickland, and many of their officers were members of the Houston *Turnverein*. Tiling (1913), 166-67; MC 1860: Harris Co./Tex., Houston, W. 3, #996. August Süs explained his reasons for joining the army in his application for release from prison camp as follows: "Not seeing any possibility to avoid being forced into the Rebel Army I became a member of Company C" (Voigt's unit). Letter dated January 12, 1865, Notes from Foreign Consuls to the Department of State, RG 59, M664, Roll 5, NatA.

4. MC 1860: Gonzales Co./Tex., #610; Boatner (1959), 896-97. Waul ran for U.S. Con-

Camp Waul, May 28, 1862.

Dear Anna,

Today we set up the organization of our legion, and after the elections many of the men are going on furlough & I hasten to take this opportunity to write to you. Things here are quite fine, and if we stay here much longer, we'll get fat. Our Robert is very chipper and is not coming home unless you come to get him, he likes the *Camp* very much [20 ll.: instructions; food; regrets not having seen his mother; greetings]. With loving kisses from your / RobV.

Camp, Penoak Creek, Robertson County / August 24, 1862.

My dear wife,

[8 ll.: sixteen-mile march from Brazos; description of their location] Up to now, our march has gone quite well, since we left Camp Waul I haven't ridden my *pony* more than 4 miles myself, because I always let sick or weak soldiers from my *Company* ride, so they don't get left behind. Every morning at 2½ we have *Reveille* and at 5 o'clock on the dot all the wagons and knapsacks have to be packed and every *Company* has to be ready to march. We usually arrive at our new *Camp* between 10 and 11 o'clock, which depends primarily on the water supply[. . . .] Our entire *Commando* consists of circa 500 men and 28 *Mule* wagons. The band plays us a *Concert* every evening, and it is really interesting to see the *Camps* and take part in *Camp* life in general. At every meal I can eat twice as much as at home, although all we have to eat is *Bacon, Beef, Beans & Corn meal* and coffee, but it always tastes good. — Yesterday Ernst, Louis Kosse and I did a big wash in Brazos, we took off our clothes, sat down on a *Log*, next to our clothes and the soap, and had our fun with these chores [28 ll.: laundry; description of the river; are being sent to Vicksburg; correspondence]. Louis Kosse is sitting across from me and mending his trousers, and Ernst and the other lieutenants[5] are lying on *Blankets* and smoking their pipes, and the rest of the men are sitting and standing around their *Camp* fires and roasting barley for coffee, pounding *Beefsteak*, sifting cornmeal, mending clothes, etc.

[20 ll.: family photographs; greetings] With a thousand hugs and kisses
Yours / Robert

---

gress in 1859, but he was defeated by the Union-Democrat candidate Jack Hamilton. Buenger (1979b), 267.

5. Private Kosse, presumably Voigt's orderly, was the son of a Prussian engineer from Houston; both he and Lieutenant Ernst Scheurer were members of Voigt's *Turnverein*.

[letterhead:] Vicksburg,* Miss., October 5, 1862.

My dear Anna,

[6 ll.: has a lot of work paying the soldiers] We get paid ten cents per soldier for every mile that we did on foot from Camp Waul to here, which of course pleases everyone. Up to now we've done a total of 517 miles, with only one stretch (from Monroe to Tolula La.) of 60 miles via railroad, that makes a [Balance?] of 457 miles we've measured with our boots and shoes. I & the entire Company are in very good shape, healthy and in good spirits [17 ll.: description of the camp; march route]. I think the people living here must be plagued by fever, but the patriotism of the ladies is truly remarkable, in every house we passed by, the ladies came out on the balconies and greeted us with cheerful faces and waved their handkerchiefs in the air, and the closer we got to Monroe, the more belligerent the mood of the people, which gives every soldier a pleasant feeling [18 ll.: encounters with returning soldiers, wounded; signs of war; train trip from Monroe to Tolula]. Once we got to Tolula I spoke to Bob Jarmon from Houston, who was on his way home on furlough from Virginia; here we saw several bridges and houses that had been burned or destroyed by the northerners, on Tuesday morning we moved on, we had to do a Force March in order to get our equipment across the Mississippi that same day. On this route I saw the most beautiful Plantation I have ever seen or could have ever envisaged or imagined, gorgeous and beautifully furnished, it reminded me of a large noble estate in Germany [11 ll.: description of the route; destruction of the cotton harvest by the Confederates]. When we had marched to within about 8 miles away from Vicksburg, with the Mississippi on our left and no more than ½ a mile from where the Yanke Gunboats had been a few days earlier, we found the remains of a Yanke camp and close to 1,100 graves of northern soldiers who died of disease in the month of July, which is why the enemy withdrew and went to Memphis. This low-lying area must be a terrible place to live, at least for white people it is impossible, the air was so hot and oppressive that I was unable to march any further, it was the first time on the entire march that I gave out. I found some shade in a hut the Yankees had built out of Rails & Brush, and rested for about an hour, and then I followed my Comando and caught up with them before they got to the Mississippi at Vicksburg [39 ll.: strains and dangers of the march; successful river crossing; description of Vicksburg; explanation of the illustration on the letterhead; battery positions on the river bank]. I also had the pleasure of seeing 115 Yankee prisoners who recently arrived via R.R. This section of the city, near the river, was severely shot up by the Gunboats in the last bombardment. You hardly see any houses that didn't suffer, the Yankees wanted in particular to shoot up the *Courthouse*, but they couldn't hit it because the *Elevation* from the river was too high, but the houses below have been shot through and through, the *Bricks* don't seem to offer any resistance to *Cannons*, for the cannonballs rip holes in the walls half as big as windows [11 ll.: bomb damage]. Our batteries must have done good work as well, however, since they set one *Gunboat* on fire and sank two others, and the *Yankees* had to withdraw without having achieved anything [5 ll.: city fortifications].

It is certainly true that Texas hasn't seen anything of this war and hasn't felt any of its effects. The prices here are outrageous, civilians have to pay horrendous amounts, but as a soldier in the *Camp* I live much better from the rations we are supplied with than if I were to go to the best *Hotel*[. . . .]

The military has much better and more plentiful provisions than the civilians. We have lots of rice now, and tobacco keeps getting cheaper, because in the evening you have to smoke to keep away the 1½ inch-*Musquitos* that are quite a problem here on the river, that's the only real nuisance we have [11 ll.: pay; is sending money].

Everywhere we go we are respected as Texans, but it seems the people here have a different idea about Texans than they should. They seem to think we are half-wild savages as long as they don't know us, but when we get to know them better, they sometimes even admire the fact that we can read and write[. . . .]

You can tell everyone that all the men in my *Company* are well, and that I have also seen all the men from our area who are in Wickeland's *Company* & they're hale & hearty & no one should worry that we'll starve to death, we have enough on hand for quite a long time.

Give my best to the Schöders, Opincenskys, Neumann, Gollmer, Harde, Mr. Bartels, Fordtran[6] etc. / Yours / <u>Rob V.</u>

Holly Springs, Miss., October 18th, 1862.

My dear Anna,

You will no doubt be pleased to receive these lines via Louis Kosse; I would have written a week ago if I hadn't been so sure that I could arrange it with the *Colonel* that Louis could make the trip to Texas. I did this primarily so the people back home could get money from the men serving here, since soldiers have no need for money because they are supplied with everything they

6. Charles Fortran, an early emigrant from Prussia who had become very wealthy, owned twenty-one slaves and lived near Voigt in San Felipe; W. Bartels came from a wealthy farm family in Oldenburg, owned eight slaves and lived near Industry; see Schwarting (no. 56, letter of January 28, 1866). MC 1860: Austin Co./Tex., San Felipe Pct., #611; MC 1860: Austin Co./Tex., Industry Pct., #851; MC 1860: Austin Co./Tex., Slave Schedule.

need by the government, and the people at home can certainly use the money [28 ll.: correspondence; troop deployments; visits from friends from other regiments]. There are about 35,000 soldiers stationed here, all you can see are soldiers, muskets, cannon, etc. Our legion has made a good impression & is highly regarded; and I also want to mention to you that I could easily have been elected major in our legion for the second *Battallion*, had I wanted to do this. Most of the Americans wanted me to run, and the situation was such that I certainly would have been elected, but after careful consideration I turned it down. First of all, I didn't want to leave my *Company* as I had promised them I wouldn't, and if I had left they would have had to move to the last rank in the legion, whereas at the moment they have the third. Secondly, in the second battalion I would have had to command companies I wouldn't want to be together with yet [60 ll.: troop arrangements; new rifles; drilling; health; good rations; family; optimism; money and business matters; greetings; signature].

Camp Holly Springs, October 21, 1862

My dear Anna,

[36 ll.: correspondence; business matters; Anna's health] According to the new *Conscript Act*, I see that all the postmasters who earn less than $300 have to be mustered in & I am glad that I didn't wait but made my move in time. This new law will not please the men who claimed to be over 35 when they weren't. Please write to me how it affects our neighborhood [14 ll.: money matters; family; greetings; signature].

[letterhead:] Vicksburg,* Miss. / Camp Cold Water, *six miles north of*
Holly Springs, / Miss., November 3rd, 1862

My dear Anna,

[6 ll.: is in haste; in good health; nice new camp] A few days ago the entire legion got *Confederate Uniforms, grey Jackets with blue collars & cuffs, blue [pockets?], grey Caps* etc. Now the troops look magnificent, just as good as a German army & there's no lack of anything, and in a few days' time, we'll get paid again.[7] The only things we still need in the *Company* are woolen socks and gloves, these are hard to get here. If you could tell everyone at home about this, then when they get enough of them together, Louis Kosse can perhaps make *arrengements* to bring along the socks & gloves in a *Box*. Otherwise the men don't need anything, and it wouldn't be a good idea to send anything else

7. On October 30, 1862, Voigt distributed 119 caps, jackets, and pairs of trousers; receipt in Voigt's Military File, NatA.

along, because even now we can't take everything along with us, especially since we're getting new *Blankets* & shoes [22 ll.: visits from generals; health of the company; mail; greetings; signature].

> *Camp on* Hatchie River / 18 *Miles South of* Holly Springs
> November 12th, 1862

My dear Anna,

[13 ll.: has received three letters from Anna; troops have received new uniforms; major troop movements] We are making a major retreat, because the enemy advanced on us, which I don't like the sound of at all. Here in this camp, night before last I got sick with a *chill* & fever & I am very glad you sent along the fever *medicine* to Camp Waul, and it will certainly be very good for me. Tomorrow I will move on to rejoin the army, but if I don't feel well enough I will be taken care of in some private home until I am fit again, and you needn't worry in the least. I come first, and then the *Confederation*, I won't be a fool and ruin myself by destroying my health in the army. Otherwise I am fine, and from now on I will take more time for myself.

[8 ll.: whereabouts of his picture; false rumors about deaths] But there is some news; on our way back from Cold Water Camp, when we were marching through Holly Springs on the evening of the 6th of this month, Lieutenant Tränkemann fell sick, together with Otto Meissner from Kuykendall's *place*, and the two of them were taken to a German home not far from the hospital. Otto Bödecker was *detailed* to take care of the sick, and J. H. Jürgens went along without permission. At the same time there was a rumor that the *Yankees* were right behind us, but this was not the case. The next day (or that same night, I believe), Otto Meissner shot himself with Tränkmann's pistol, in the same room with the other four men,[8] supposedly out of melancholy and because of his illness [4 ll.: retreat on Sunday from Bullick Mills]. On Monday Otto Bödecker returned from Holly Springs to this *Camp* to his *Company* (Wickland's). He had left Holly Springs to avoid being captured by the *Yankees*, but Jürgen refused to go with him. I don't know if the *Yankees* are now in Holly Springs and if Jürgens has been captured[. . . .] Most people think that Jürgens wanted to be taken prisoner on purpose, but I doubt this.—We have several *Yankee Deserters* here as prisoners, they are tired of the war and say their entire army is demoralized and that Lincoln's [Emancipation] *Proclamation* caused commotion in Gen Rosencranze's [Rosecrans*] army. According to them, the southern army is in better condition and has much better pro-

---

8. According to the muster rolls, all four were from Austin County. Muster Rolls, Waul's Legion, Texas StateA.

visions than the northerners [6 ll.: business matters]. As long as you can pay off C. Ennis & [Co] with *Confederate Money*, you can accept money from the people who want to pay, but if you can't use it to pay any more, then don't accept it anymore, because if Ennis or Jordan can't be forced to accept it, then I can't be either, so make sure you watch out for *Shinplasters*.[9] Tell all the people who want to pay you and get their promissory notes back that you are not in a position to do *Collection* in my absence, and if you can get rid of *Confederate Money* and some, then go ahead and take it, but only on your signature, but if people don't want to do this, then just leave it be. And if they want to get nasty with you, then just be tough in return & tell them they should be more reasonable, what with my having left home, risking everything to keep the enemy away from the door, leaving you all alone at home, and now they come and want to trouble you [6 ll.: business matters]. If a fellow like Afflerbach comes in again, then throw him out & tell him he should take up a musket instead, because things won't get any better if he just stays home praying [25 ll.: details; business matters]. With regard to the battles here etc. I have realized it's not as dangerous as you think. I believe that more soldiers, especially the Americans, die of sickness than of wounds or gunpowder. We have two American companies in the legion from Houston County, [−] that have lost more than half their men to sickness, while in my *Company* and in Nathusius's, not one man has died[. . . .] Kiss the children from your Robert.

Camp Tippah Ford, 8 miles South
of Abbeville, Miss., November 14, 1862.

Dear Anna,

[5 ll.: exhausted from long march] The countryside here is very hilly and steep, all wooded, the Texas prairies are much more beautiful, and if someone were to give me some land here as a present, I wouldn't accept it. Also the people here are good for nothing, most of the settlers have northern *Sentiments* and don't like having anything to do with southern soldiers. They tried to charge me $2 for a chicken, and so I told them for that much money, they should go ahead and eat it themselves [18 ll.: strategic advantages of the camp location; retreat to a position eighteen miles north of Oxford; greetings; signature].

---

9. The South was already suffering from inflation, and Voigt did not want any of his debtors to pay off in devaluated currency unless he could also pay off his own debts with it. "Shinplaster" was a joking term for bills so devaluated they might as well be used as bandages. Cornelius Ennis was a businessman in Houston worth $400,000; MC 1860: Harris Co./Tex., Houston, W. 2, #901.

Camp Tippah *mouth*, November 18, 1862.

My dear Anna,

[9 ll.: correspondence] Dear Anna, I completely sympathize with your wish that I come home again soon, but I doubt that our wish will be fulfilled anytime soon. The North seems to be making every possible effort to outdo us with their *Forces* & if this is the case, the whole business will last for a long time. This year you will have to celebrate Christmas one time without me & butcher hogs and make sausage.

[15 ll.: winter quarters probably on the Tippah River; does not like Mississippi; is sending money] The *Officers* have no lack of food, but it is sparse for the soldiers, since we started our retreat the *Provisions* have dwindled. The soldiers ought to be treated better than this, and I hope that in a few days the situation will improve. We all have enough clothing, we only need *socks & gloves* as well as some *Blankets* & shoes, but the last two items should be arriving in the next few days [17 ll.: baggage transportation; provisions]. Gottfried (Emler) carries my *Knapsack*, so that all I have to carry is my coat, my saber, pistol and cartridge box, and my *Haversack*, in which I have the picture of you & Robert, my *Memorandum Book*, pipe, tobacco, matches, comb, soap and other light things. At camp, Christoph Baumann from New Ulm is my cook and Emler, or the commendable Gottfried, chops my wood, fetches water, packs and unpacks my things, polishes my boots, beats the dust out of my trousers, polishes my buttons, makes my bed and all the other furniture that it's absolutely essential to have in the tents. He is a great old fellow, keeps an eye on everything and takes care of everything for me, without my having to tell him what to do [21 ll.: details; laundry; is looking forward to seeing his family again; is concerned about them].

Ernst S. & Warnecke are sitting next to me and reading, it is 8 o'clock in the evening & the nights are too long to sleep through completely, so we pass the time telling stories & smoking tobacco, without having a drink because we can't get hold of anything [15 ll.: health of the men in his company; greetings; signature].

Camp Rocka Ford, Miss., November 30, 1862.

My dearest Anna,

[47 ll.: correspondence; is very busy; soldiers in good health; business matters] Don't forget to light the candles on a Christmas tree for the children, no matter what people say; just tell them it was my wish that the children shouldn't have to forgo their pleasure and joy because of the war. —

[13 ll.: Grenada, December 12: is very busy because of the retreat] but this evening when the train arrived I received the letters from you and Louis Kosse of November 24 with the tragic news that saddened me so sorely that my little Adolph has died. I cannot express my pain about this. Far away from home, all the hardships and difficulties I have had to bear were always lightened by my hopes of <u>seeing</u> my family <u>again</u>, of finding my dear family, upon my eventual return, well and as hale as they were when I left. And now fate wants to thwart my golden hopes. — Dear wife, all I want now, even more than before, is to be at home with you. — But I cannot, it is not permissible, and so, my dear Anna, I will willingly resign myself to the inevitable, and I only hope that you are able to do the same [10 ll.: correspondence; gravestone for Adolph; health]. On our retreat here, all our tents were burned and many things were thrown away so the wagons would be lighter and not get stuck. Some of the wagons that couldn't move fast enough were chopped to pieces or burned, so they wouldn't fall into the hands of the enemy that was on our heels and only one or two miles behind us. We were the *Rear-guard*, together with another *Infantry* regiment, our *Cavalry* & one *Battery* [18 ll.: war events]. On our *Retreat*, a number of men from my *Company* were so weak and exhausted they fell behind on the road and must have been taken prisoner by the *Yankees*. From my company, it was the following men: A. Doverg, F. Tegge, F. Raube, F. Gombel, C. Nattech, B. Retzlaff, F. Schlüns, J. Sydow, F. Treude, J. Treder, D. Willrodt, along with many of the men in Wickland's *Company*, including both of the Bödeckers, Ferdinand Schröder, etc. and 31 men from Nathusius's *Company* [19 ll.: war events; thinks they will retreat to Vicksburg*; correspondence; greetings; signature].

                                              Grenada, December 18, 1862.
My dear Anna,

   [27 ll.: correspondence; advises Anna to stay in Houston; family photographs] If there is any way for you to do this, I would greatly appreciate it if you could throw old Seeliger out of the *Store* as soon as you can. I am sorry to hear that he belongs to the Union party, and you can't be sure your *property's* safe when someone like that is living there. If Koch doesn't want to throw him out, then you could write to Ernst Knolle and let him know that it is my wish, and that he should do me a favor and make the fellow leave.[10] When you write to Knolle, write to him only in *English*[. . . .] If C. Koch also joins the *Unions-party*, the best thing to do is to get in touch with Knolle, because he at least has more sympathy for the men who went off to war than those who are op-

---

   10. The German merchant Ernst Seeliger was arrested in October 1863, together with four other men, and accused of treason to the Confederacy. After a lengthy trial, they were deported to Mexico in August 1864. Christian Koch was a farmer and cabinetmaker from Hamburg.

posed to our cause[11] [18 ll.: business matters; wants to send a sketch of the camp]. Duty is hard here, especially for me & Nathusius in the first *Battallion*, because the other *Captains* (all Americans) in our *Battallion* are sick. Almost every third day we are the *Provost Officers* in Grenada, we've cleaned up the town now and gotten rid of all the vermin, especially now that the people see our patrols won't stand for any nonsense, because a couple of days ago, when Louis Harde was *officer of the guard*, a drunk was resisting arrest and tried to ride away on his horse, but one of the soldiers shot him off his horse. Since then, all the tramps, gamblers, horse thieves etc. obey our orders [51 ll.: camp life; war events; correspondence; greetings; signature].

Grenada, December 29, 1862.

My dearest Anna,

[9 ll.: correspondence] On Christmas Eve (Dec 24) President Jeff. Davis & Genl. Joe Johnston arrived, and they were received by a 20-gun salute. That same day we had a large *Review* in front of President Davis, Genl. Johnston, Genl. Loring, Price, Tillghmann etc.[12] The weather was very fine, and there were 41,000 men in 4 divisions lined up on the Parade grounds, along with 116 pieces [6 ll.: the "Review"]. To give you an idea of the size of this army, let me tell you that it took 5½ hours for the troops to march by the President in close ranks[. . . .] Genl. Van Dorn was not present at the *Review*, because he had circumvented the enemy with 7,000 cavalrymen and was in Holly Springs. There he burned 1½ million worth of *Provisions* and *Quarter masters Stores*, took all the 1,500 *Yankees* who Genl. Grant had left to occupy Holly Springs prisoner, spiked all the cannon, and in general dealt a devilish blow to the *Yankees* who had chased us all the way to Coffeeville. He arrived so unexpectedly that Grant, who was in Holly Springs with his wife at the time, had trouble saving his own *Yankee* hide, and he had to leave his wife behind, who was taken prisoner by Van Dorn but then released[. . . .][13] The entire

11. Ernst Knolle was a German merchant with $34,000 in property, including nine slaves; according to the *Bellville Countryman* of February 27, 1861, he was one of the main people responsible for the fact that the Industry precinct voted eighty-six to two in favor of secession. MC 1860: Austin Co./Tex., Industry Pct., #1085; MC 1860: Austin Co./Tex., Slave Schedule; Muster Rolls, NatA. Two of Knolle's sons were in Voigt's company; E. H. Knolle's diary (in English) is printed in Hasskarl (1976).

12. General Joseph Johnston (1807–91), overall commander in Mississippi; Major General Sterling Price (1809–67); Brigadier General William W. Loring (1818–86); Brigadier General Lloyd Tilghman (1816–63). Boatner (1959), 699, 492, 839–40.

13. Major General Earl Van Dorn (1820–63) commanded a cavalry corps in Mississippi. Mrs. Grant was not taken prisoner; the day before she had left the town to join her husband in Oxford,

Cavalry burned their old double-barreled guns & were fitted out with beautiful *Revolving Rifles*. Everyone got new uniforms and excellent *Yankee* boots, the fellows were as pleased as punch, and everywhere they go they are met with cheers. Van Dorn also burned 6,000 stands of arms, all the *Amunition* and everything else the *Yankees* had in Holly Springs. He couldn't take anything with him, because he couldn't get any wagons there fast enough [12 ll.: has forced Grant's army to retreat]. In my opinion, things are looking good for our cause, especially after the battle at Fredericksburg* in Va., even though the *Yankees* are doing all they can to take the Mississippi away from us and want to take Vicksburg, which they can't do. But I still don't think we'll be coming home before 6 or 8 months, unless there's a rapid change in Lincoln's *Government*, although there may be a chance of this [39 ll.: Christmas in the camp; health; correspondence; greetings; signature].

Grenada, January 7, 1863.

My dear Anna,

[18 ll.: correspondence] Our armies have done very well recently, and finally there are some rays of hope for peace in the near future, at least you can read much about this in the reports in the northern newspapers, everyone is insisting that Lincoln should change his hardheaded opinion [77 ll.: optimistic about the situation in Vicksburg after the unsuccessful northern attack; New Year's celebrations; laundry; correspondence; greetings; signature].

Grenada, January 11, 1863.

My dearest Anna,

[11 ll.: correspondence; provisions] Charles Warnecke frequently provides me with various delicacies from the *Commissary Department*, like liver, tongue, brains, white sugar etc. And if a stray chicken lays an egg in the yard where his *Quarters* are, I can be sure he'll send it to me via Gottfried, when the latter goes to get *Beef* in the morning. And even when there's no *Bacon* or *Pork* for the others, I always get a piece, so you can see that I'm not about to perish [22 ll.: tent furnishings; Galveston, Texas, has apparently been recaptured; correspondence; greetings; signature].

Grenada, January 18, 1863.

My dearest Anna,

[20 ll.: weather; correspondence; is waiting for news about the birth of Anna's child] From other letters I often hear that Louis Harde and Gustav

---

Mississippi. Her horses, however, were seized, and her coach was burned. Boatner (1959), 867; Ross (1959), 134–37.

Loeffler write plaintive letters to their wives, and so of course they only receive answers in a similar vein. I think it is very foolish to make life more difficult for each other than it already is, because it certainly doesn't make things any better, and therefore it is best just to accept the situation as it is. As much as I would like to be with you, as much as I long to be at home again, and as much as I am convinced that this is also your dearest wish, I must admit that I would be ashamed to return home without having finished what we started here. So just be patient and remember, good work takes time. — In the northwestern states of Lincoln-land the wish for peace seems to be growing stronger and stronger [22 ll.: hopes for peace; instructions about son Robert's education]. He will now have the chance to speak English, and you should support this, but not to the extent that he forgets his German. — He shouldn't go to school yet, he would learn too quickly, and his physical *Constitution* is still too weak to keep pace with his mental abilities. If possible, he should do some gymnastics or at least some kind of similar exercises, daily and regularly. Have him get up in the morning before sunrise every day and wash his face, hands, and chest <u>thoroughly</u> with cold water, even when the weather is very cold [12 ll.: details; high food prices].

We do all sorts of things to pass the time on long evenings. I took along a guitar from the town, or rather borrowed it, or walked off with it from an old *Music Store* that is now being used as the *Commissary Department*, and it is used to rekindle the old times in our memories and practice the old songs. Last night we pulled *Molasses Candy* until about 11 o'clock, etc. [10 ll.: money matters; correspondence; greetings; signature].

Camp Snyder's Bluff, Yazoo River / January 30th, 1863.

My dear Anna,

[32 ll.: strenuous march to Yazoo City] The citizens of Yazoo City gave us a warm welcome and gave our soldiers everything they wanted, they took them into their homes and fed them in the friendliest manner. On the same day we boarded the *Steam Boat "35th Parallel"* [32 ll.: refreshments provided by the citizens; seventy-mile trip down the river; comfortable conditions; difficult march route to new camp]. We are only 9 miles as the crow flies away from Vicksburg* and every hour we hear the cannon of the boats that are trying to land. It will be impossible for the enemy to gain any ground here, no matter how many troops they send, they can just stay in their *Gunboats*, look at the hills, and shoot their *shells* that can't hit anyone up into the hills, and that is all [26 ll.: correspondence; greetings; signature].

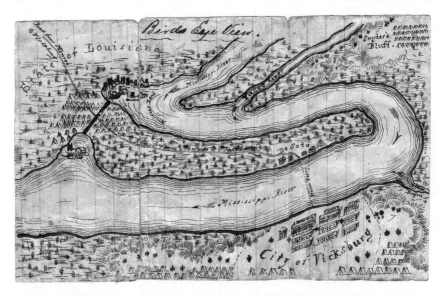

Map of Vicksburg drawn by Robert Voigt in letter of February 10, 1863.
(Center for American History, University of Texas at Austin)

Vicksburg, Miss., February 10th, 1863.

My beloved wife,

The weather this morning is very pleasant, today on my birthday, and I am pleased to choose this day to send a letter to you, although I don't know if and when it will reach you since it is possible that only one route, the only postal connection via Port Hudson, is still open [6 ll.: correspondence]. In our *Camp* on Snyders Bluff, we had no tents and we had some very cold weather, and three days of heavy rain, and we couldn't keep a single thread dry, even with the largest fire. I came down with a very bad cold, and I got so-called soldier's *Diarrhea* that I couldn't get rid of [4 ll.: went to Vicksburg to recover]. On the 5th I had myself driven here by *Ambulance*, and Henry Behrmann, who is also sick, came with me. We took up quarters with a German named Lipka. Besides the very friendly treatment we have received from him and his wife, we also get very good *Board*, and a nice room with beds and a stove. I am now living again as befits a white man, and the few days I have been here have restored my health completely [29 ll.: recovery; visiting other Germans; description of Vicksburg]. There will be a lot in the newspapers these days about the preparations being made by our side as well as by the *Yankees*, particularly about the *Canal* through which the enemy is trying to bring its troops into position below Vicksburg. This is hard to understand if you don't know the lay of the land, and to give you a fairly clear description of it, I am enclosing a small sketch that will give you a picture of the whole situation [65 ll.: has seen a company of Yankees on the river; daily life in Vicksburg; correspondence; is thinking of the family; greetings; signature].

Vicksburg, February 11, 1863.

My dearest Anna,

[20 ll.: correspondence; birthday celebration; health] I am very glad to hear that Seeliger is out of our *Store*. I was quite astonished about the women in Industry, they must have been drunk, or the devil must have gotten into them, because the fact that they wanted to kill poor old James with fire tongs shows they must have been out of their minds. That old Jew Seeliger is mostly to blame for this, since he's nothing but an old woman himself.[14] How happy I am that you are not at home, and if you think it is in any way possible, I would like it very much if you didn't go back to Industry until I come back home. This story is being told everywhere & exaggerated, and it will always remain a blot on the reputation of the entire settlement, and it may even have serious consequences for the future for everyone who lives there. And in fact the Germans in general, and especially the ones here in Wickland's *Company*, most of whom are our neighbors, behave at various times in a manner that makes one ashamed.[15] All of this often inclines me to the decision not to live with them in the future [31 ll.: correspondence; hopes for peace; correspondence; greetings; signature].

Vicksburg, February 18th, 1863.

My dear Anna,

[11 ll.: correspondence; health] I think it's getting to be time to try to get back to the *Camp*, because the *Yankees* started bombarding our *lower Battery* at midday [9 ll.: details]. I picked up my watch and have made the following observations: after you see the fire and powder smoke of the enemy battery, it takes 9 seconds before you hear the boom of the cannon. It takes 35 seconds

14. The attempt made in January 1863 to force the local militia into the regular army led to an uprising by the women, who chased off the enrollment officer. His deputy had to be defended with a pistol. Boethel (1965), 15. For information about Seeliger, see n. 10.

15. Sergeant C. W. Hander from Voigt's company noted in his diary on December 27, 1862, the rumor that "40 men from our legion have sworn an oath against us, and most of them are said to be Germans." Hander himself seemed to have reservations about the southern cause, observing on February 7, "several plantations were as large as small towns[. . . .] This is a lovely sight, but certainly not an inviting one, when you think of the Negro whips that are used so often." Hander Papers, Center for American History, University of Texas at Austin.

before the bomb hits, and sometimes they explode only 25 seconds after being fired. As long as the gunboats don't come closer and fire on the town, we will stay here, but if the enemy starts getting ready tonight to seriously bombard the town tomorrow morning, then I'll take off with Behrmann early in the morning, because the things might end up flying too close to our heads. The family we are staying with won't be leaving any earlier, either. On the night of the 13th to the 14th instant we were woken up by the loud thunder of cannon, I looked out of the window (our house is only 2 blocks from the *River*) and heard a *Gun Boat* passing by on the other side, but it was so dark you couldn't see a thing, and I don't think our batteries inflicted any damage on it [18 ll.: war events; greetings; signature].

Fort Pemberton, March 17, 1863.

My dearest Anna,

Yesterday I received the happy news, through a letter Loeffler received from his wife, that you gave birth to a healthy baby girl at the beginning of last month & that you and the baby were both hale and hearty. Dear Anna, my most heartfelt congratulations, I have been waiting for a long time for the happy news, and finally it has arrived. It cheers me up no end and makes me very happy, especially since I know that you and the baby are well. This letter brings you a thousand kisses from me [39 ll.: details; war action; his company has not suffered any losses; correspondence; shipping accident; confidence; greetings; signature].

Fort Pemberton, *near* Greenwood *on the* Yazoo River, March 30th, 1863.

My dear Anna,

[29 ll.: correspondence; description of the fortifications] I have already had to read enough about the situation in Austin, "Colorado," & Fayette County. The Germans there have put the entire *Nation* to shame & instead of being the protectors of the families whose men are now serving in the army, they are their worst enemies at home in their own country.[16] From what I have heard, they also have quite a lot against me & my name is supposed to be on their blacklist, but they should feel lucky they are still alive. These fellows will be in for a hard time [6 ll.: high prices; Anna should take good care of herself; soldiers killed in the war; greetings; signature].

16. In January 1863 German resistance to conscription led to the imposition of martial law in the three counties. Kerby (1972), 93.

Fort Point Laflore, April 26th, 1863.

My dearest Anna,

[11 ll.: correspondence] On the 13th of this month I received the *order* to take over the *Commando* in this place, a small town similar to Lynchburg and with almost the same geographical situation.[17] I brought my *Company* here, relieving a regiment from Mississippi, & took over the *Commando* on the morning of the 14th. I can assure you that I like it very much here, I am, so to speak, the <u>supreme ruler</u> & since the post is important and requires considerable responsibility, I find it even more interesting[. . . .] Here in the fort I have two rifled *Parrot Guns*, 20-pounders, & 2 Howitzers with 225 *rounds* of *Ammunition*. I am now training my company in *Artillery* & I am keeping them busy at this job, but the men like it so much that they all wish they could stay here until the war is completely over. This fort is on the extreme right of our entire line of fortifications & perhaps 4 miles as the crow flies from Fort Pemberton [21 ll.: description of the area; comfortable life in the fort]. Many of my colleagues (officers) in the legion would like to be in my position, they envy me my post & do not know why Col. Waul didn't order them here instead of me. My men have not been having a lazy time of it, but everything goes like clockwork. I don't hesitate to punish anyone if it is necessary, but I also make sure everyone gets something extra when they deserve it [12 ll.: details; health; greetings; signature].

Headquarters, Fort Pemberten, May 11th, 1863.

My dearest Anna,

[6 ll.: ordered to report to headquarters on May 5] When I arrived there, Col. Waul told me that he had been ordered to Snyders Bluff with his troops, but he was leaving behind one *Officer* in whom he placed great trust and 300 men, and he appointed me the commander of Fort Pemberton & *Post*. He gave me my instructions & the necessary papers. That same afternoon I went back to Laflore, had my pieces and *Amunition* brought on *Board*, and the next morning I left Point Laflore with my company and arrived here about 8 o'clock A.M. [7 ll.: details]. Aside from my company, I have enough *Artillery* to man 11 pieces, it is hard work for my company to fill all the posts, they can only sleep every second day. I don't even have ten minutes of free time a day myself, because I am always in the *Office* filling out passes and sending & receiving dispatches, and at the same time I also have to serve as the *Engineer* at the fort,

17. Lynchburg, Texas, was situated on a narrow promontory at the mouth of the San Jacinto River, near the present site of Baytown, east of Houston.

because I have 120 Negroes working there [59 ll.: details; accommodations; good provisions; correspondence; business matters].

Every day now we are expecting news from Vicksburg* and the area, the enemy is trying his best to take the town, but they will be forced to retreat in humility. At any rate, in the next few days (if it hasn't already happened) there will be a large battle there, and I wouldn't be surprised if our legion gets ordered to move from Snyders Bluff to below Vicksburg, since the *Yankee Gunboats* have already left Snyders Bluff. We sank another three of them, there are fewer and fewer enemy *Gunboats* & it won't be long before the *Yankees* don't have any more, they can't build them as fast as we destroy them. The entire army is full of confidence [12 ll.: correspondence; greetings; signature].

YazooCity, June 5th, 1863.

My dear Anna,

[13 ll.: correspondence] On the 20th of May I received an *Order* from Genl. Joseph E Johnsten [Johnston] to move all the pieces & *Amunition* to Yazoo City. I got started immediately & in two days loaded everything onto two steamboats, the company had to work very hard. On the 22nd I traveled down the Yazoo, and when I'd gone about 62 miles, we met up with all the *Steamers* that had been in Yazoo and got the news that yesterday the *Yankees* had landed in Yazoo City with two *Gunboats*, and so I had to go back to Fort Pemberton. When I arrived there I telegraphed Genl. Johnston in Canton to find out what I should do, and I received the answer that I should requisition wagons & get all the *Guns* & *Amunition* to the nearest *R.R. Station* and then move them on to Vaughn Station. On the 28th I arrived at the *Rail Road* in Verona, with 49 wagons & the large & small *Canons*, got everything loaded onto the train & on the 30th I arrived with the whole business in Vaughns Station[....] From Vaughns Station the cannon were ordered to move here to Yazoo City, since the *Yankees* had left the town again & our troops had reoccupied it. —I can't get back to the legion, which is now in Vicksburg, because the *Yankees* have completely surrounded it and no one can get in or out, unless he steals through at night, risking his life [8 ll.: details]. At any rate we are very fortunate not to be in Vicksburg, since three days ago a man from our legion arrived here [...] and he told me that that some 20 days ago, the legion had been involved heavy fighting that lasted 4 or 5 days. When he left camp, Major Cameron, Lieut. L. Papendieck, Williams, Upton, & several other *Officers* had been killed & almost every other *Officer* seriously wounded. Our legion has apparently suffered terrible losses & since then many more have no doubt fallen who we haven't heard about yet. I am really sorry about Papendieck. Löffler, Harde & Wickland are still unscathed. The legion apparently fought very well & was the best corps in Vicksburg[18] [17 ll.: his company is in good health; greetings; signature].

Near Vicksburg, July 17, 1863

Dear Anna,

I am a prisoner and am on my way to Vicksburg where I will probably be *paroled*.* Am quite well, hopefully we'll see each other again soon / Yours / Robert

Vicksburg, July 21st, 1863.

My dear Anna,

[5 ll.: correspondence] I was in Yazoo City in command of three batteries of *rifled 20 pounders*. Besides me, the 29th N. Carolina Rgmt. *Infantry* was there to cover my batteries, they were on my left flank in *trenches* and were supposed to hold off the attack we were expecting from enemy ground troops. In the afternoon of July 13th, the enemy came up the YazooRiver and the *Gunboat* [*DeKalb*?] first came into view, I opened fire & after we had exchanged shots for about half an hour, the enemy was forced to retreat. We had three hours of quiet, but about 6 o'clock in the evening I noticed that the enemy was trying to make another attack & I made preparations to receive them again, but at the same time a *Courier* arrived to inform me that the 29th N.C. Rgmt had left the trenches 3 hours earlier & was withdrawing & was several miles away on its retreat to Benton, so then I was all alone with my *Company* & it would have been foolhardy to defend ourselves. I prepared to retreat & had gone about 2 miles from the town by nightfall, when I suddenly heard enemy *Cavalry* behind me. I turned left off the *Road* & gave the *order* that all the men should lie down on the ground. The darkness concealed us & the *Cavalry* went on by, but right behind them were two regiments of enemy *Infantry*, the 20th Wisconsin & one from Illinois, who also marched by very close to us without discovering us, and so I was put in the position of being right in the middle of enemy troops. I stayed quiet the whole night, but there was no way I could sneak through & I had no choice but to surrender [6 ll.: details]. The *Yankees* treated me <u>very</u> well & were most polite, also to my officers and men, and all the other enemy officers & soldiers behaved most properly. Together with my *Lieutenants*, I was assigned to a room in a *Hotel* in Yazoo City as my *prisson*. Our *Boarding* is excellent, real coffee & everything else very fine. On July 16th

---

18. Papendieck, Löffler, Harde, and Wickland were fellow Turners* from Houston and officers in the two other German companies. Out of a total of 731 men, there were 245 casualties in Waul's Legion, including 47 fatalities. Tiling (1913), 167; Muster Rolls, NatA; Johnson and Buel (1987), 3:549; Hasskarl (1976), 25–27.

we were taken to Vicksburg. Here we were put with our *Company* in the *Jail yard*, but the next day, we *Officers* were released on *parole* of honor* & had to report every morning at 8 o'clock. Today we had to board a *SteamBoat* & will be taken as *prissoners* to a *Camp* in the North. I had hoped to be *parolled* here until we could be *exchanged* & was looking forward to coming home, but this *Cardell* [cartel] [19] only applies to the *prissoners* who were taken when Vicksburg surrendered. God only knows when I will be released, because on Lincoln's *order* from now on, no *prissoners* will be *parolled & exchanged*, instead they are to be held until the war is over. If we are as well treated up in the North as we have been since we were taken prisoner, I will be quite satisfied [6 ll.: details]. Fare well, dear Anna, don't despair & fret about me, stay well and don't let sorrow & worry weigh on your mind. Think of the children, kiss them a thousand times for me, and give my best to all.—I am well & am keeping my hopes up, all will turn out for the best. / *Adieu* / Yours / Robert [. . .]

Johnson's Island, Ohio, January 12th, 1864.

Beloved Anna,

[14 ll.: correspondence; mail is censored by several authorities] Today I am trying to get a longer letter through, although it is still uncertain, with the help of the *Corporal of the Post* for this prison, who is a German & will forward my letter after he has read through it. [21 ll.: repetition of the events in Yazoo City up until July 23] [. . .] on which day we left the town by *Steamer* & were brought up the Mississippi to St. Louis. Along the way, downstream from Helena, Kubitz & then Louis Kosse & F. Lillis escaped across the river during the night, I hope they have arrived home safely. On the 3rd of August we reached St. Louis, where we were kept in the Gratiot Street Prison until the 17th of the month [6 ll.: details]. The northern military that was guarding our prison in St. Louis was the 9th Wisconsin Regiment, made up entirely of Germans, who treated us very well, without exception. The officers did everything they could to make our situation as pleasant as possible [11 ll.: details]. These Union officers provided me with all the clothes I needed, tobacco, cigars, etc. and every now and again a few gallons of good St. Louis beer.—If I or any of my friends ever have the opportunity of meeting these hospitable men again, no matter where or under what circumstances, I will never forget to recall their friendship, and their names are: Capt. Hesse, Capt. Miller, Lt. Veit, Lt. Herman etc.[20]—On the 17th of August we left St. Louis

19. Agreement regulating the exchange of prisoners.

20. This Milwaukee regiment was named the "Salomon Guards" after the German lieutenant governor and was commanded by his brother, a Forty-eighter. Burton (1988), 109.

Program of a play put on by Robert Voigt and other Confederate officers in
prison. Note the unreconstructed subject matter and the stereotypical German
Union soldier. (Center for American History, University of Texas at Austin)

and arrived here in the afternoon of the 18th, just one year since we left Camp
Waul. Our prison grounds are 16 acres in size, surrounded by a high plank
fence. We are quartered in thirteen large, long buildings, and circa 2,600 prisoners, all officers, are here at the moment. The island is in Lake Erie in the
Sandusky Bay, about three miles from the town of Sandusky, on the northern border of the state of Ohio. The lake separates the United States from
Canada [21 ll.: the cold; lack of money].

About fifty men from my company were taken prisoner at the same time I
was, and they are now in prison in Camp Morton, near Indianapolis in Indiana. Brandt and I correspond every week. Adolf Steck and Jacob Bastian died
there last month, the latter on December 30th. Louis Baring was very sick but
is getting better now & Rudolph Sternenberg is still very sick (according to
Brandt's last letter). Emler, Marburger, and Grote have taken the oath and
are now in the Union army, and the others are all well. [37 ll.: visit from an
acquaintance; wants his family to move to Houston, for safety's sake; wishes

for a letter:] and in this case you must write in English, and leave the letter open for *Examination*[. . . .] [21 ll.: correspondence; greetings; signature].

Johnsons Island, December 22nd, 1864.

My dearly beloved Anna,

How great was my joy, how happy I was to receive your letter of July 25th on November the 1st. They were the first lines from you since I became a prisoner, and I carry them with me like a jewel, and I cannot deny that I even kissed the paper that your hand wrote upon, containing a thousand kisses from you and my beloved children [38 ll.: correspondence; health; hopes of being released; longing for his family; greetings; signature].

New York, April 11th, 1865.

My dearest Anna,

Finally, finally I breathe the air of freedom. On the 7th of the month I was released on Johnsons Island, left Sandusky the following day & arrived at Gustav Schmidt's in Brooklyn on Sunday the 9th [6 ll.: details]. I am in very good health & the good life here in connection with the comforts of my friend Gustav's house will have beneficial effects after such a long incarceration.

[22 ll.: correspondence; are Anna and the children on their way to New York?] Now that Richmond has fallen & Genl. Lee has surrendered the main army of the South to Genl. Grant, there might now be hope of peace in the near future, but I fear that Jeff. Davis may cross the Mississippi & try to defend his position with the troops in Texas, but I somehow doubt this & it seems almost safe to assume that in a short time peace will be declared in the South. If this happens, you could come here via Galveston & of course avoid great stress and strain. As I wrote to you earlier & explained, I do not want to return to Texas, nor can I, the children's education alone requires moving away from such a crude country, and after the war it will be full of even rougher people for the next few years. Don't be afraid for the future, dear Anna, I can put my experience & knowledge to even better use in a place like this than down there with such crude people [19 ll.: uncertainty about travel route and arrival of the family in New York; is thinking of her with love]. I cannot find the words to express what my heart feels, only fervent kisses would be able to relieve my overflowing heart. It is already night, and I still must write to Ignatz, mother & Selma & Conrad, so sleep well Anna, everything we have hoped and longed for will soon come true. / With a thousand kisses from your / Robert.

"A Prisoner's Melancholy," calligraphic poem by Robert Voigt, inspired by "a moonlit night in July 1864." (Center for American History, University of Texas at Austin)

When all is still in the midst of night,
  No noise my thoughts distract,
The call of a guard is the only light
  In the deadness of the black.
When Erie's waves do flirt and foam,
  And kiss by the light of the moon,
The west wind cools me as I roam,
  My thoughts enclosed in gloom.
And then my eye in the distance casts,
  To find my love ones, but alas,
Where I was loved, I now have left—.
  I weep and sigh—I am bereft—.
Oh wife! oh children! my precious life!
  Some thousand miles divide us,
No path permitted to my wife,
  No means to reunite us.
With hope trapped in a labyrinth,
  No prospect but a blackened wall,
My broken heart can find no splint,
  Wherever it may call,
In a thousand pieces, whispers a sigh
Asks fate: reunion, is it nigh?
But fate replies, crisp like a shot:
Maybe soon—or maybe not.

On February 11, 1865, Voigt had expressed his wish to swear the oath of loyalty to the United States and requested not to be put on the list of prisoners to be exchanged. It was April 7 before he could take the oath of amnesty, swearing to "support and defend the U.S. Constitution and abide by and support all acts of Congress and presidential proclamations having reference to slaves."[21]

Voigt's life after the war can only be sketched in rough outlines, but he never carried through on his decision to leave Texas. His numerous business connections in Houston were certainly helpful when, together with his friend Schmidt from New York, he started up an import business in the nearby port of Galveston. Robert Voigt died only one year later, at the age of thirty-five, probably of appendicitis. His wife lived only two more years at the most, but their two surviving children were well taken care of by the close family network in the area.[22]

21. Federal Military File on Captain [Voigt], Comp C, Waul's Texas Legion, Texas StateA. Hyman (1959), 199–218, provides a detailed description of amnesty proceedings but gives no estimates of how many Confederate officers applied for amnesty.

22. Justman (1974), 304–7, 315, 322. Voigt died before November 1867; guardianship proceedings for his two children began that month (Harris Co., Probate Minutes, Book F., p. 221), microfilm, Texas StateA. In 1870 the children were living with their grandfather Schweikart and their aunts in Houston, where Mrs. Anna Voigt was also listed in CD Houston 1867–68. MC 1870: Harris Co./Tex., Houston, W. 3, #70.

55. Captain Ernst Cramer and Ferdinand Simon

Ernst Cramer and Ferdinand Simon became brothers-in-law and were quite similar in terms of their social position both before and after they emigrated. Cramer came from a well-to-do family of millers and merchants in Schweinfurt, and when he emigrated in 1854 at the age of eighteen, he listed himself as a merchant.[1] Even if this reflected his hopes for the future more than the actual facts at the time, in his new home in Texas, these hopes became reality. Cramer was one of the first settlers of Comfort, a colony dominated by freethinking intellectuals and Forty-eighters some forty-five miles northwest of San Antonio. He traded various goods and did

SOURCE NOTE: In the case of Cramer, no valid statement on the original language can be made on the basis of the English translation (see note 5), though their similar background makes it seem likely that what can be said of Simon's German applies to Cramer's as well. Simon is not only able to write free of errors and with great fluency, but he also appears to enjoy displaying his mastery of the language. Even apart from the content, he is fun to read.

1. Information provided by the donor; HPL *Donau*, April 1, 1854. According to MC 1900: Blaine Co./Idaho, e.d. 26, #311, and MC 1910: Blaine Co./Idaho, Hailey Pct., p. 215, Cramer had immigrated in 1853; if this is correct, this reference could be to his second crossing.

Ernst Cramer.
(Charlotte Cramer
Lafrenz)

some farming and cattle grazing on the side. At least once, in 1859, he went back to Germany on business.[2]

Not much is known about Simon's background in Germany except the fact that he was born about 1826 in or around Darmstadt and arrived in Texas in 1854 at the latest, but perhaps as early as 1846. He apparently lived for a while in San Antonio, where in 1855 he married Carolina Bauer, who had recently arrived in the United States with her parents, sister, and brother. In the 1860 census Simon appears as a merchant in the small settlement of Leon Springs, fifteen miles from San Antonio on the stage road to Comfort. His household included his wife, two children, and a business partner who is frequently mentioned in his letters, Friedrich Kraut. The following year, Cramer, Simon, and brother-in-law Bauer each bought 500 acres of land not far from Comfort, farms that were either adjacent or at least close together.[3]

In Texas, Germans with a middle-class background were among the most vehement opponents of slavery. A group of freethinkers in Sisterdale, a nearby

2. Geue (1970), 61. On August 31, 1859, Cramer was elected first lieutenant in the Kerr County militia, evidence of his social standing. Bennett (1956), 187–88.

3. Marriage Records of Bexar Co., Book C, p. 287, microfilm, Texas StateA; Kerr Co. Tax Rolls, 1861, microfilm, Texas StateA; MC 1860: Bexar Co./Tex., #2000. Simon was naturalized in March 1859, so he must have immigrated by 1854 at the latest. Index to Bexar Co. Naturalization Records, p. 250, microfilm, Texas StateA. In the census "Darmstadt" could mean the Hessian state as well as its capital city, but in Simon's case the latter seems more probable. In 1859 Simon and Cramer already had connections to Comfort; see Biesele (1987), 176–77.

settlement of Forty-eighters well known to Cramer and Simon, played a major role in the creation of the antislavery "San Antonio Platform." Even in times of peace, however, free speech on this issue was quite limited: a former resident of Sisterdale, Dr. Adolf Douai, was fired from the editorial staff of the *San Antonio Zeitung* and chased out of the state because of his political agitation against slavery.[4] When Texas joined the Confederacy, the situation for people like Cramer and Simon became even more precarious, as the first letter indicates.

ERNST CRAMER

Monterey, Mexico, Oct. 30, 1862[5]

My Beloved Parents:

At last I have found the opportunity to write to you. I must take advantage of it even though I know of nothing pleasant to relate to you. Fate has dealt very harshly with me. It is beyond belief to think that any human being could come under such conditions of sorrow and great misery.

I had to leave Texas very hurriedly without the time to properly provide for my family. Also I live in a state of constant fear for their lives. My poor wife and small daughter are still in Comfort with my sister-in-law Mrs. Simon. My wife's parents are on my farm. Mr. Simon is in prison in San Antonio—in constant danger of being hanged. He may already have lost his life, for it is two months since I have heard anything of him. Leopold, my wife's brother, is dead—killed in a battle we had during our flight to Mexico. I live in such a state of anxiety that I can hardly collect my thought sufficiently to picture to you the life that I have been forced to lead the last few years.

I never thought that this disastrous war could last so long, and bring us all into such grievous circumstances.

I was married on the 17th of September in 1861 to Charlotte Bauer.[6] I have

4. Biesele (1987), 171–74, 196–203.

5. Cramer's original German letter has been lost, but his daughter Ottilie (born 1874) translated it into English, and it is her original translation that is included here (copy in NABS). Apart from a few misreadings of place-names in Texas that have been silently corrected, there is considerable evidence that the letter is reliable and authentic: the events are corroborated by other eyewitness accounts in Ransleben (1974), 86–120, and elsewhere.

6. They were married by a justice of the peace in Comfort; Simon and father-in-law Bauer were the witnesses. Kerr Co. Marriage Records, Book A, p. 44, microfilm, Texas StateA. The Bauers had arrived in Texas in 1854 or 1855; the fact that Charlotte was born in Prussia, her father in Sachsen-Altenburg, and her mother in Frankfurt suggests that she came from a mobile, middle-class background, even though her father was listed as a farmer and stock raiser in MC 1860: Kerr Co./Tex., #19; MC 1870: Kendall Co./Tex., Pct. 5, #69; see also Ransleben (1974), 23, 127–29.

already told you about her. I had a prosperous business—lived happily and contentedly—until towards the end of the year. Then military laws were enacted and every man between the ages of 18 to 45 was subject to conscription in the Confederacy. All of our friends in San Antonio as well as in our small town of Comfort—in fact—we felt that all of the West was in sympathy with the North.[7] And then came the first apprehension when we were threatened to be forced into the service of the South.

In February a Frontier regiment was organized of men who lived in our county and in the surrounding counties. It was for the purpose of protection against the Indians and only to be used in the service of the state of Texas. The young men of the counties joined and an intimate friend of mine by the name of Kohler [Küchler] (of Darmstadt) was elected Captain. He soon had a company together—all Germans[. . . .] Our Company had been formed of men gathered together with the understanding that as soon as the northern troops would come within reaching distance, we would join them. But it followed that our plans were overthrown in a most lamentable manner. Most of those in our Company, rather than be forced into the service of the South, swore that they would never enter into any service again.

Threats continued to become more violent and finally reached the stage where the men of the counties of Kerr-Kendall & Gillespie assembled to form a defensive organization. Up to this time Simon and I had taken no active part. We had been appointed to collect the property and war taxes for the counties of Kerr & Kendall and in consequence had not been interfered with or molested.[8] But as the agitation became stronger and stronger, we had to definitely take a stand for one side or the other. We resigned our positions and naturally joined our friends in support of the North.

The forbearance of the people seemed at an end. The Union flag was hoisted and the outbreak of a revolution was momentarily expected. On the 24th of March a meeting was called at a well [spring] named the "Barenquelle" between Freidrichsburg and Comfort.[9] Unfortunately at just this time the northern troops attacked at Galveston. That raised our hopes and gave us the

7. The German section of the county, around Comfort, voted fifty-three to thirty-four against secession; the Anglo American communities near Kerrville, however, voted in favor, forty-two to four. Bennett (1956), 136. The figures for Kerr County in Biesele (1987), 206, appear to be incorrect.

8. Part of Kerr County, including the village of Comfort, was split off and became the newly formed Kendall County, which explains the varying place-names in the sources. Gillespie County, with Fredericksburg as its county seat, voted overwhelmingly (400 to 17) against secession. Biesele (1987), 206.

9. Probably a spring on Bear Creek; a meeting was held there on July 4, 1862, and some of the participants lived nearby. Ransleben (1974), 205-6, 199, 202.

surety and confidence that the North would bring us help. The "Hurrah" for the Union echoed from all corners. Companies were organized and Officers for the different districts were elected. My Company, composed of 80 men, elected me Captain for the Comfort district.

The next day I was ordered to go to San Antonio for the purpose of joining our forces with the others from the different districts. I found everything well prepared there. But the spirit and enthusiasm that we had in our original organization was not there. I was told to await further orders. In my heart I knew that without help from the northern forces we were helpless [7 ll.: became increasingly disheartened]. And so we all came to the decision to maintain peace and quietness. It was no small thing to do. Every evening we met but delayed action from one day to another.

At last on the 15th day of April we were informed that the Union party in Austin had been forced to disband. Our hope had been built on the strength of the party there[. . . .] Our only hope was to be able to reach Mexico[. . . .] Now San Antonio and 8 days later our whole district was put under the laws of the Confederacy. Everyone must appear before the Provost within ten days and take the oath to support and be true to the Comfort division of the Confederacy on penalty of losing all properties. Then it was that I began to really know people. Excepting a very few, all took the oath, and also betrayed their officers. All Officers had to immediately flee for their lives. If anyone had told me 8 days before that such a thing could be possible, I could conscientiously have shot him.

Simon then also took the oath so that he could remain with his family. I took my wife to him. I had prudently sold my property to my father-in-law sometime before. And now, with a number of my friends, I departed into the mountains. There was Kuchler [Küchler]—two brothers by the name of Tegener [Degener] about my own age. They were sons of a very cultured and well-educated man who had to leave Germany in '48.[10] Franz & Moritz Weiss —Ernst Beseler—Wilhelm Telgman—Emil Schreiner—all educated young men of fine families. We formed a hunting party, hunted in the mountains, and were hunted and chased by soldiers. But we knew the country and every secret path and hiding nook too well to allow ourselves to be caught.

10. At the meeting on July 4, 1862, Cramer was elected captain of the Kendall County Company, and Hugo Degener was elected lieutenant. A man named Fritz Tegener was put in command, adding to the confusion caused by the names. Ransleben (1974), 195–96. The "cultured" man was Edward Degener (1809–90). Born in Braunschweig, he had been a member of the Frankfurt Parliament of 1848 and immigrated in 1850 to Sisterdale, Texas. After the war he was elected to two state constitutional conventions, the U.S. Congress (1870–71), and the San Antonio City Council (1872–78). Barr (1969), 146.

Early in July I had to go home. We were expecting a child. I arrived on the morning of the 10th and on the following day we were blessed with the birth of a small daughter. It was then that I felt my circumstances bitterly. I could not sit quietly for one instant. I had to conceal myself as though I were a thief. Because I knew that had I been caught I would surely have been hanged. I stayed at home for 8 days and then went 8 miles from Comfort to a well [spring] where I met my companions again.

Simon was under constant suspicion and his life at home was very unsafe—exposed to continuous risk—so he decided to come with me. Immediately thereafter all men up to the age of 35 were called. A death penalty if they did not appear. That made it more lively in our mountains. One by one we were joined by acquaintances until we numbered 20.

We decided then that as there were 600 men in the Confederate troops surrounding us, and as we wanted to uphold the law, we would go to Mexico where there might be a chance for us to join the northern troops. On the 2nd of August we started out. Leopold, my brother-in-law, provided our family with means for their livelihood for one year and went with us. At the well [source] of Guadeloupe we met 40 more men. 5 Americans also joined us and that brought our number to 68.

Our journey went very well as long as we were in the mountains. We had no suspicion of being betrayed or that we were being followed. On the 9th of August, late in the evening, we came to a narrow "draw" heavily covered with cedar growth. We stayed there, though without food for our horses. The next morning after riding barely two miles, we came to an open space—a meadow with fine grass and plenty of water[. . . .] It was an outer arm of the Nueces. We figured that Fort Clark was about 50 miles to the Southwest and that we were about 45 miles from where the San Felice joins the Rio Grande.[11] Our horses being hungry & tired we decided to rest there for the day and the next morning to continue on our way to the Rio Grande.

We proceeded to make our camp under the first group of cedars nearest the water. On this evening we were all quite cheerful, not having any omen that this place would be the grave for most of us. We sang and declaimed until late in the night.

About an hour before sunrise we heard one shot that awakened us. Immediately after came another & another. We leaped to our feet and were met with

11. Possible misreading; Fort Clark is actually about twenty miles away, located near what is now the town of Brackettville. "San Felice" probably refers to the San Felipe near Del Rio, which was about forty-five miles distant. On the location of the battle and routes of unionists and Confederates see Underwood (2000), 6–7.

a volley of about 100 shots. Leopold fell dead and four others were wounded. Then all became quiet. We held a consultation and decided to fortify ourselves as well as we could. That was quickly done and then followed a deadly stillness that was almost unbearable. I had given my word to Hugo Tegener [Degener], the older of the two brothers, to cover the right wing and was fully determined to stay and die at my post if need be. The chances to make escape seemed impossible. The soldiers greatly outnumbered us, had just as good position as we had and had at least 100 to 200 men available from Ft. Clark. And to add to our despair, the men who had joined us at the Guadeloupe deserted their posts one by one. At the end of the day, of the 68 men we had only 32 were with us. And now the soldiers charged. Three times they assailed us and each time we drove them back. Hugo and Heilmar, his brother, fell. Hugo's back was shattered by two bullets. He came to me, crawling, to bid me farewell. W. Telgman had been shot through the body sometime before, but kept his place bravely and continued to fight.

We rested about one hour and a half. But after another attack we realized that we could not continue to hold our position. Kuhler [Küchler], Moritz Weiss and I were the only ones that were not wounded. We decided to withdraw through the thick timber to the other side of the water. We took with us all of those not too badly wounded. Of my close friends Simon had a shot through the ribs. Franz had a shot through the heel and one through the lower part of the leg.[12] I had a shot through my pants and a shot had torn away all of the front of my shirt, but did not touch my skin. Of the others 6 were severely wounded.

Now we went forward up the valley very cautiously so as to leave no trace that could be followed. We had not traveled 2 miles when we met 6 or 8 of those men who had deserted us[. . . .] They begged us to be allowed to join us and as bitterly as we felt towards them we still could not refuse them & leave them there. We journeyed on until noon and still not the first trace of water. The wounded were exhausted so we made a camp for them in a sheltered place. Kuhler [Küchler] and Moritz remained with them. I started out again with a companion to search for water. About 4 o'clock we returned having found no water. As we came to the spot where we had left our companions we found no one there. We were too tired and weak to hunt for them. After resting for a while we proceeded to walk back to the battlefield. About two hours after dark we came to the water. As soon as we had satisfied our thirst we felt ourselves strong again. We emptied our powder horns and filled them with water. We meant then to continue our search for the wounded. Just then

12. Probably Franz Weiss; see Underwood (2000), 79, 90.

ten men appeared. They had been to the water but had hidden themselves on our approach. As the soldiers were still not more than 150 steps away—I suggested that we empty and clean every article that could be used to hold water and asked several of the men to hunt for the wounded and take the water to them. I wanted to go 4 or 5 miles further to try to get a deer at dawn. Everyone seemed satisfied with that plan because all were hungry. I left them without feeling any anxiety. Weber, who had been my companion all through the day, joined me. We were not fortunate in finding any game and came to the place where we had planned to meet about 10 o'clock. All of the wounded were there excepting Simon. He had become too weak to continue with them. I was almost frantic—was too anxious about him to be able to take any rest. It was a bright moonlight night and I hunted for him throughout the whole night. I had no success—he was nowhere to be found. I felt convinced that he was dead. I came back to our camp completely exhausted. I had had nothing to eat for three days and the anxiety and worry and strain was enough to exhaust the strongest man.

On the 4th day the soldiers withdrew. Then I went back to the battlefield to search for my friends and perhaps to see them once again. The sight was horrible beyond description. They had been stripped of their clothing and the bodies had been piled up one over the other in a large heap. Those who were still living when we were forced to leave them had been lined up and used as targets. Their faces and bodies completely riddled with bullets. It was heartrending and I could not linger there.

The next day with four others, I started back to my home to get provisions. On the 7th day we reached the first habitation and on the 8th we arrived in the outskirts of Comfort. It was a terrible day for me. I stayed in the thicket about a half a mile from my home and dared not go to my Lottchen. I could not face her with the news I had to tell of Leopold's death and Simon's.

The next day I went 18 miles further to the home of a friend to beg him to break the sad news to my sister-in-law and to the others. By the time that I reached my friend's home in Boerne I had a high fever.[13] For four days I was delirious. Had hardly recovered from my illness when I heard that Simon had been captured and taken to San Antonio. How it all happened I do not know to this day.

It was too dangerous for me to attempt to go home. Everyone was under suspicion. If anyone had even been suspected of giving aid to one of us they

13. Boerne, eighteen miles from Comfort on the road to San Antonio, grew out of a communistic settlement of Forty-eighters and was named after the radical author Ludwig Boerne. Biesele (1987), 172–73.

would have been taken and hanged. One hundred people had been hanged in less than that many days. Relatives of those who had been with us were especially watched. And so how it happened that Simon was still living, I do not know. In 6 days after I had arrived at Boerne, I went to Leon Springs. There I found the opportunity to speak with my sister-in-law. She had visited Simon in San Antonio and was very anxious about him.[14] She begged me to be careful and for me to try to get to Mexico as I was the only one left for them to depend upon[. . . .]

Through an earlier companion, Richard Brotze, I managed to secure a horse with the understanding that I leave immediately for the Rio Grande. He insisted on that and I could not blame him for had I been seen with his horse he would immediately have been hanged. I still had many dangers to face before I could get to the Mexican border and heard the whistle of many a bullet.

Küchler left again shortly after I did, together with Moritz and Franz and ten other good friends of mine. They had no trouble until they reached the Rio Grande. Just at the river they were attacked and under heavy fire had to leave their horses and ammunition behind. They had to swim the Rio Grande. Franz was shot and Moritz went to his aid and both were drowned. Four others were killed while swimming. Küchler is now the only one of my intimate friends that is left. He is safe here.[15]

Since speaking to my sister-in-law I have heard nothing of my family. I think, however, that no harm has come to them. If Texas is still in the hands of the Confederacy in the spring I feel that I must bring my family here. Our families are defenseless against attacks of Indians as well as at the mercy of all marauders. Because now all between the ages of 16 and 45 are called. Death and confiscation of their property, the penalty.

I am in great need of money and wish to draw on you for $100, hoping that the unfortunate and unhappy position in which I find myself will excuse it. I need the money to equip myself and straighten out my affairs so that I can return to Texas. I must return within 4 or 6 weeks so that I can make some effort to rescue my property[. . . .]

I think that I will be in no danger on the expedition because I know the way so well now. Am sure that I can find safe ways of traveling. Should, however, I

14. How or when Simon was captured remains unclear; on October 2, 1862, he came before a military commission on charges of "levying war" against the Confederacy and "secretly & covertly & in violation of the laws" attempting to leave the country. He pleaded innocent, but on October 10, 1862, he was found guilty of all charges and sentenced to death by hanging. This was apparently later commuted to a prison sentence. Barr (1969), 246, 270–72.

15. Eight men died at the Rio Grande on October 18, 1862. Ransleben (1974), 94.

be unfortunate and be killed, then, of course, the money would be lost to you [4 ll.: is sorely needed].

The outlook seems very favorable that the Confederacy in Texas will soon be played out. We are told that the northern troops are on the coast. If that is true we do not know positively, but the Proclamation of Lincoln not to divide the Union suggests that the North is in earnest. And we think that Texas would be the first state to be taken over. As long as Texas is not in the hands of the northern troops, it places the Confederacy in easy communication with the whole outside world.

A great deal of cotton is sold here. Exchanged for powder, clothing and other necessities. I have no idea how conditions are in the Union states. In fact I know nothing of the whole political situation. Since the blockade I have seen no newspaper. Here all the news of the States is withheld. I will write once again before returning to Texas.

Meanwhile I hope that you all are well. Please write to me. For you cannot know how much that would mean to me. To hear from you—how things are with you—the dear grandparents—brothers and sisters and the Franckes. No day passes that my thoughts are not with you.

Ernst Cramer / Monterey, Mexico / Adr. Sigm Dresely / Schwemian

FERDINAND SIMON

[postmark: San Antonio, Dec. 21 (1863)]
[address:] Mrs. Caroline Simon
Comfort / Kendall Co. / Texas

[start of letter missing. 13 ll.: urges his wife to look after her health] I am hale and hearty as usual, and with the greatest confidence and peace of mind, I am waiting to see what the near future will bring. I always have a deep feeling that I have survived the longest stretch of my misfortune and that I will soon be returning to freedom and happiness. I don't worry at all about how or when this will happen, and I don't waste any thoughts or concern on my current situation. Instead, I try to kill time as fast as possible, calmly leaving the decision up to fate in the future, but my inner feelings tell me that this decision can only be a positive one. So good night, sleep well, and dream sweet dreams of your faithful Ferdinand

Saturday morning, December 19, 1863

Good morning, my dear love, after I slept well until 8 o'clock, dreaming happily of you and the children, I didn't wake up until they brought breakfast [10 ll.: would like a pipe bowl for his birthday; is sending newspapers; greetings; signature].

My dearest Minna,

I was most happy to receive your last two letters[. . . .] I thank you, my dear child, and I ask you to keep on as you have been, loving your parents and cheerfully obeying them. This will make you loved by all and happy. When I am with you again, I will show you how much I love you. For now [. . .] hugs and kisses from your faithful loving father

Ferdinand Simon

[postmark:] San Antonio
Thursday, January 14, 1864.

Good morning, my dear Lina,

You don't write me anything about your health and your spirits! Make sure you don't forget to mention this every time, since you know how much I long for precise information about it. The best thing would be for Lottchen or mother[16] to write about it, because I don't really trust you to write me the whole truth.—As for me, I have always told you the unvarnished truth, and I can call on Kraut, Pascal, Degener,[17] Wille, Karsfeld etc. as my witnesses, all of whom were surprised that I looked so well and was in such good spirits.

I've been having pretty bad luck with my candle making [8 ll.: details].

Kraut was just here and brought me the heavy trousers and writing paper [12 ll.: details]. He also gave me a couple of large sausages, which were very well made and taste delicious. He said he had heard from Pfeiffer that Ernst had joined the army, but I cannot believe this, since then he would be committed until the end of the war, and that can still take 5–6 years. Please let me know exactly what happened[. . . .] My playing cards have gotten so worn out in the last 6 months that despite all caution and pasting, they're of no use any more. If Mrs. Fulton still has any, please send me a pack along with your next letter [21 ll.: correspondence; asks about the livestock; instructions; payment to Kraut].

16. Presumably Charlotte Cramer and Simon's mother-in-law Bauer. In March 1864 Charlotte Cramer, Carolina Simon, and their parents felt threatened by Confederate sympathizers and moved to San Antonio. Schuetze (1995), 136–37.

17. George W. Pascal, a judge from Austin, was arrested in 1862 for his support of the Union. Elliott (1947), 467–69. Edward Degener came before the same military tribunal as Simon, but one week earlier, having been accused of helping his sons to flee the state. He was sentenced to guarantee his loyalty to the Confederacy by posting $5,000 in bond. Barr (1969), 246–68. The court records make Degener's role in the entire affair appear much smaller than Cramer and other eyewitnesses reported; see Ransleben (1974), 105–6, 113. According to Nagel (1935), Degener had been released and, as of December 1863, was living in San Antonio.

Saturday morning.

My dear Lina,

[11 ll.: correspondence; visit from German friends unlikely] Yesterday I got the news that our case won't be investigated yet, and so we will be staying here for the time being. I am quite content with his, since the trip to Austin would not have been of any use. —One thing is certain, that we don't need to even think about an investigation or being released before the war is over. Instead, we must get used to the idea of putting up with several more years in prison. Because the same reason our witnesses could not be called up this time will remain in effect as long as the war continues.[18]

[14 ll.: purchases from the money he made on his candles; wishes for letters] I am hale and hearty and have nothing to complain about, except that our appetite is so large that aside from our daily rations we polish off a lot of bread and sausage with our coffee. With all the best to all from your Ferdinand.

The bleached bones of Simon and Cramer's nineteen comrades were gathered in 1865 and brought back to Comfort, where they were laid to rest with honor: the main speech was delivered by Edward Degener. The residents of Comfort erected a commemorative obelisk inscribed with "*Treue der Union*" ("Loyalty to the Union"), the only monument of its kind in the South.[19] The dedication ceremony was held on August 10, 1866, exactly four years after the battle of the Nueces, but Cramer and Simon were apparently unable to attend—at least they were not members of the group that traveled to the battlefield. Their private commemoration of the event, however, is revealed by the fact that both families named a son after their fallen brother-in-law Leopold.

There are only a few traces of Ferdinand Simon after the war. He seems to have stayed in San Antonio, where from 1866 to 1868 he only paid poll tax (a sign of limited assets). A couple of years later, he was assessed with trading goods worth

18. On July 3, 1863, the *Neu Braunfelser Zeitung* reported that charges of treason had been brought against Simon in the District Court in Austin, but that upon petition of the defendant, the trial had been postponed. It appears that Simon may have been released in late 1864; a Nueces survivor in Piedras Negras reported that "L. Simon and August Dücker had just arrived there. They had sat in jail in San Antonio for that long." The letter "L" is easily confused with"F" in German script, and later in the same paragraph he mentions a Ferdinand (no surname) who rode with him to Fredericksburg. Hoffman (1999), 502.

19. Of the sixty-eight names on the monument, all were German except Pablo Diaz, a Mexican orphan taken in by Germans. Ransleben (1974), 93–95, 124–25. The translation of *Treue der Union* on the historical marker as "Loyalty to the Union" is plausible enough and certainly not wrong. There is an alternative translation, however, which in view of the list of names on the monument might be preferable: "Those who were loyal to the Union." We cannot know which idea was paramount for the originators, and it may even be the case that the ambiguity was intentional.

Obelisk erected at Comfort, Texas, in 1866 to commemorate thirty-six comrades of Ernst Cramer and Ferdinand Simon: nineteen who fell at the Nueces, nine who were taken prisoner and murdered, and eight who died on October 18, 1862, crossing the Rio Grande. (Greg Krauter)

$2,500 (1870) or $2,000 (1871). In 1872 he moved to a farm of 200 acres near Boerne, and in 1878 both he and his wife died within less than a month of each other.[20]

Ernst Cramer fell back on his family's expertise and established himself as a miller in the Mexican border town of Piedras Negras. As of 1868 he also assumed the post of U.S. customs collector in Eagle Pass, Texas, across the river. In the mid-1870s he returned at least briefly to Comfort. Later he went back into business in Santa Clara, California. Finally, he moved to the future state of Idaho. In 1881 he built the first house in the town of Hailey, and then he ran a mill, built a store, and remained there until his death in 1916, surviving his wife Charlotte by two years.[21]

20. Bexar Co. Tax Rolls, 1865–71; Kendall Co. Tax Rolls, 1872–1878; Kendall Co. Probate Records, vol. D-2, pp. 1–14; all microfilm, Texas StateA. No one in the family appears in MC 1870. In 1880 daughter Minna had married a doctor from Prussia, and her brother Leopold (age fourteen) and sister Bertha (age eleven) were living with her; MC 1880: Kendall Co./Tex., e.d. 88, #174.

21. Telephone interview with Cramer's descendants Charlotte and Leo Brown, January 9, 1989; letter of appointment as collector of customs, April 14, 1868, copy in NABS; according to MC 1870: Maverick Co./Tex., #189, Cramer still had $1,800 of property, despite his losses during the war; MC 1900: Blaine Co./Idaho, e.d. 26, #311; MC 1910: Blaine Co./Idaho, Hailey Pct., p. 215. According to the census, his daughter Ottilie (MC 1900: Blaine Co./Idaho, Hailey Pct., e.d. 26, #110) was born in Mexico in 1874 and came to the United States the same year. Cramer appeared in the Comfort area in 1874 posting bond in an orphan guardianship and from 1875 to 1877 as the owner of approximately 2,625 acres; see Kendall Co. Probate Records, vol. D-1, pp. 285–86; Kendall Co. Tax Rolls, 1875–77; both microfilm, Texas StateA. Transcripts and copies of documents from Lee Brown; transcript of obituary in [Boise] *Idaho Statesman*, July 11, 1916.

56. Private Georg Wilhelm Schwarting

In 1855, at the age of twenty-three, Georg Wilhelm Schwarting made his way to Texas on his own, but he certainly knew what to expect when he got there. A compatriot from Oldenburg, Friedrich Ernst, had founded the town of Industry, the first German settlement in what would soon become the Republic of Texas. Prior to 1836, at least two people from Schwarting's immediate neighborhood near the mouth of the Jade River, followed Ernst. Schwarting's brother Gerhard also came over in the mid-1840s, but he moved on to California during the gold rush a few

SOURCE NOTE: Schwarting's "good education" may not have included economics, since he keeps writing "creditor" when he means "debtor," but it shows in his penchant for technical terms rarely found in private correspondence. His use of language is terse and unembellished, but his spelling and syntax, apart from a few lapses, are correct. Not included here are the letters in the series from the time before 1860 (three) and after 1865 (thirty-seven) and two additional letters from 1860 and 1864. For this series, only transcripts of the original letters are available.

years later. Georg lived in the small settlement of Round Top, twelve miles west
of Industry, and in 1860 no fewer than fifty-five Germans from Oldenburg were
living there.

Georg Schwarting had received a "good education" in Germany and probably
did not arrive with empty hands; his brother had taken 500 talers* with him when
he emigrated. By 1859 Georg had bought some farmland and cattle, and he did some
import trading on the side via his brother in Germany. His entrepreneurial spirit is
evident even in his first letter.[1]

Schwarting returned to Germany in the spring of 1860, but this had nothing
to do with the threat of civil war. Instead, he took over the "administration" of his
father's large farm and apparently tried to find a wife. He had sold his land in Texas
for $900 before he left, but he kept the money invested in Texas. When his father
dismissed him in the spring of 1864, he borrowed some money and returned to
America—this time via Canada and the North.[2]

[Chicago, May 1864]

[salutation missing]

[67 ll.: last part of a letter or travel journal; ocean voyage and arrival on
May 3] As you probably know from my first letter, when I was in Quebeck
I was still undecided, one hour before the departure of the train, whether I
should go west, north, or south [5 ll.: not happy in Chicago]. I had always
planned to move out to the country. But since I haven't received any answer to
my letters, I am planning to join an expedition of carpenters who are leaving
for Nasville Tenesse next week, to go and work for the government. The pay
is supposed to be 2½ to 3 dollars a day plus board, paid out every month in
good *Greenbacks*. The trip won't cost me anything. I have always longed to
return to a rebel state, since I actually belong to the rebels myself, and even
now I have more respect and esteem for a real Confederate, or rebel as they
are also called here, than for those who always sing the Union *for ever*, while
at the same time they are secretly undermining the country [21 ll.: greetings;
signature; address].

1. Emigration permit of Gerhard Schwarting, Ns. StA Oldenburg, Best. 70, Nr. 6013; Biesele
(1987), 43–45, 49, 51, 193 n. 8; letters of Georg Schwarting, February 13, 1856, January 25, 1859,
June 10, 1877 (quoted), NABS; Fayette Co. Tax Rolls, 1857–59, Reel #1075-01, Texas StateA,
Austin, Tex.; hand tallies from MC 1860: Fayette Co./Tex. (Round Top P.O.).

2. Letters of Georg Schwarting, September 26, [1859], February 29, 1860; letter by Anton
Bernard Schwarting to Georg Schwarting, April 7, 1860, which he did not receive, according to
a letter by W. Bartels from Texas, May 13, 1860; letter of Georg Schwarting, May 1864, and bill
of exchange of October 8, 1864; all in NABS.

Nasville, July 10 [1864]

<u>Dear brother,</u>

As you know from my last letter of last month, I didn't much like Chicago. And when I went out to the country to visit a traveling companion, we were treated with great disdain[. . . .] During the night, my traveling companion decided to become a soldier and enlist as one of the hundred-day volunteers. And so, after I had translated this plan to his boss, we left, and before the day was out, he had sworn his oath to the flag and joined a regiment that was bivouacked not far from Chicago and to be sent to the South the next day. He had fled Germany to avoid military service, not knowing he would enlist as a volunteer over here only a few weeks later.

If I hadn't signed up for the Nasville expedition, I would have gone along with Wilhelm, too. The pay is a good 32 dollars a month, but I hope to earn twice that much here, and I think I won't be mistaken. We are still in the city, but they say our company will soon be sent to Virginia to build bridges. Many of the men in our company have left the city again and gone home, they couldn't tolerate the climate anymore. Several more are still in the hospital, some are unfit for work and are still in the boarding house and waiting to be discharged.

But a few days ago an order came that no more discharges would be issued. Not more than about half the men are fit to work.

The heat has been unbearable lately. The work must be extremely urgent, whoever works on Sundays gets double pay. Day before yesterday, another 215 carpenters arrived in the evening to build housing for soldiers. They've signed on for six months like we did.

As for me, I probably won't be leaving this place until I go to Texas. I am certainly not in an enviable position here, since I am so lonesome and alone, but it is at least somewhat more enjoyable here than in Chicago. Here you can sometimes have a decent conversation with someone, even if they aren't compatriots. The Germans here are truly unbearable, at least the ones I've run into up to now. When they've earned a little money they think they own the world, and they can't decide how best to get rowdy, until some smart *Yanky* cheats them out of their earnings and tames them again.

[10 ll.: got Wilhelm a job as a farmhand] As far as other things go, I can't tell you much about it. We just live along or simply vegetate. You eat, drink, sleep at Uncle Sam's expense, and if you feel strong enough in the morning, you go work at the construction site. The unaccustomed heat makes your body so weak you try to avoid all exertion, mental as well as physical.

[18 ll.: business opportunities in the South] But to get back to earnings.

They aren't as much as you may think. Gold has gone up so much recently that you need to exchange 2½ dollars for one in gold.

To give you a clear picture of their real value, I am sending you a one dollar *Bill*. The smallest of these bills is worth five cents, and I don't know how large they get, probably up to a thousand dollars. These are the so-called *Greenbacks* (*grünrücken*) and they're the most acceptable because they are the safest. How may millions or how many thousands of millions of them are in circulation I can't tell you, but Uncle Sam guarantees them, and he still has the largest amount of *Credit*, should he go broke, everything will crash. Of course he could still put several more thousand million of his *Greenbacks* in circulation and still stay solvent, but what good does all the money in the world do you, when no one can vouch for its honesty? Poor people sometimes pay their debts better than the rich (U.S. Uncle Sam or United-States).
[21 ll.: about financial markets; address; greetings; signature]

Chicago, Aug. 15, 1864.

Dear brother,

Before I leave the land of the loudmouthed Germans and false *Yankys*, I want to entreat you one more time to please send me a receipt, and quickly. The reason I had to leave the land of the rebels again so quickly is the following: because like others, I couldn't tolerate the climate, and then with the new draft of another 500,000 soldiers, able-bodied men from all the towns of the eastern *Contingent* fled here to avoid being drafted, by working for the United States as government employees, and the town became so flooded with carpenters that a large number had to be dismissed. Only the most smooth-tongued sycophants kept their jobs, and the rest could go home again or hike on over to the *Front* (*Kriegsschauplatz*).

Most of them, of course, were forced to do the latter, some because they'd used up the money for the trip home, and some because they couldn't get a pass for the trip back. It is easy to cross the line into the war zone, but difficult to get out again. And they made every attempt to get hold of soldiers. From personal experience, I know just how hard it is to get a *Pass*, because even though my papers were in best order, it took me 2 whole days to accomplish what should have taken half an hour. And before they gave us even one cent of our pay, we had to swear our loyalty to the Union, saying that the oath had been sworn voluntarily and not out of fear of any financial disadvantage, etc. Everything is a swindle over here, both little things and big ones. The people who are the most stupid get the best positions. Certainly the new General Blair* got his position because he has absolutely no knowledge of military matters. But what difference do a few thousand human lives make? The only thing that counts here is personal advantage. As long as the leaders and commanders of the war haven't filled up their pockets with *Greenbacks* and satisfied their greed, there can be no thought of peace. *Herr* General Grant, who thought he and his 250,000 brave soldiers could crush the entire rebellion within a few weeks, hasn't taken any town like Petersburg, Mobile, or Richmont [Richmond], and instead of laying siege to these places, his brave army finds itself under siege, and they don't know how to get out of this situation. The rebels are laying waste to Pennsylvania.

But enough of this wretched war. Painful consequences will be inevitable.

I am glad that I am now on the road to recovery. Being sick here is worse than death.

Should the Union have the misfortune to reelect the current president, meaning that peace will be postponed for another 4 years, then I'll be going to Texas in the fall or the spring, and probably from there back to Germany. I just don't feel comfortable here in *Yanky*-land [11 ll.: correspondence].

Your brother / G. W. Schwarting

Oct. 14 [1864]

Dear brother,

After having survived our term of service, which only lasted four days, we are once again in freedom and staying with G. Brum. and Thdr. Hobby, where we're comfortable and holed up safe and sound. No one will come looking for us here, of course, but whenever we go out, it's scary as hell, particularly when we meet up with a guard. But it's not only our fault that we ran off, it was also because our superiors didn't keep their word and the negligence and stupidity of the guards was just too tempting. We had *entlisted* in the cavalry and were to be sent to New/orleans, but then we were equipped as infantrymen, to fill up the ranks of old regiments that had been shot to pieces, probably near Atlanta in Georgia. On top of this, as substitutes, we were separated from the regular volunteers and kept under lock and key, and we were only allowed to leave our prison when accompanied by a double file of guards with loaded weapons, while the volunteers could walk around the camp as they pleased. The next day we were sent to Springfield, and a few days later, on Oct. 9th, we were to be sent to the South. That afternoon a double file of guards had already brought us to the volunteer *Camp*, and from there an extra train was supposed to take us to the South. But the train was delayed. Evening came, and as soon as we were under cover of darkness, we disappeared into the volunteer *Camp*, then slipped through a poorly guarded spot in the shoddy fence and out into the open. We had to abandon all our baggage, of course, but we were richly compensated for this, since we'd had our bounties paid out in advance. Within half an hour of our departure, we reached the railroad to Springfield, got hold of some civilian clothing, and left on the next train to St/Louis. The next evening we arrived at Brumont and Hobby's without any trouble, and now we're in good hands and quite comfortable here, staying in a log cabin in the shadows of the woods[3] [8 ll.: description]. I think that as soon as the presidential election is over, we will try to go to Texas. The terrible rumors we hear from there, though no doubt exaggerated, have kept us back, otherwise we would have already tried to get there.

But now I am glad that we've thumbed our noses at those false *Yankys* and are out of boring old Chicago. Here we're among fellow human beings, where you can talk with someone and feel comfortable[. . . .] I think that soon, as soon as things have calmed down a bit, we'll be off to Arkansas. The times are too exciting to stay in any one spot for very long [22 ll.: about mutual friends]. All the best from your / G. Wilhelm. / Summerfield St-Clair County Illinois.

Little Rock, Ark., May 31, 1865.

Dear brother,

[23 ll.: correspondence] As far as politics goes, I can't tell you anything at all because I haven't read any newspapers for the last six weeks. What we hear is mostly *humbug* and lies so blatant you can see through them immediately, but you can't say what you think about things here. Since the president was murdered, anger at the rebels has risen to an all-time high, and some have had to pay with their lives for a careless remark. For about 2 months now I've been back in the service of the United States, and we've been sworn in as carpenters for a six-month term, with monthly pay of 7[?]5 dollars. Since nothing new is being built now that the war is over, and some things that had been started are even being torn down, we'll be out of work very soon. Every day for quite a while now, because of this, they've been letting a lot of workmen go. We, too, are expecting to be discharged any day now [6 ll.: travel notes to follow]. On the 10th of last month we were mustered in at St-Louis for a 6-month term of service, and the next day, under guard, we were brought to the shipyard and onto the steamer that was to take us to the South. Our expedition was 95 strong, made up of men from every nation, headed for an unknown and unidentified destination [154 ll.: travel notes]. The bends in the river were so narrow and tight that the boat was hardly able to navigate them. I've heard it's now been exactly one year since a large band of guerrillas fired on a *Packet-*

---

3. Schwarting and W. Porten sent a bill of exchange of $400 in gold to Schwarting's brother, with "Gerh. Brumont" and "Thedr. Hobby" in Summerfield, Illinois, listed as the return address. Letter of October 8, 1864, NABS.

steamer and forced it to surrender, and since then every boat on the Arkansas and on the White river has been getting shot at, but without much success. At the moment we don't need to fear any such attacks, because the bands of *Guilleras* have been significantly reduced, and it would be quite a hard task anyway to roam the woods at the moment, what with all the flooding.

[24 ll.: travel notes up to April 17] At ten o'clock we finally arrived in Duvals-Bluff, where we got off the boat, and a few hours later we arrived in Little Rock on the train. The town was silent and dead, all the doors were closed, and many of the windows were hung with black crepe. All the many flags that were flying were also hung with black. Civilians were wearing black on their sleeves, as were the soldiers, and they wrapped black bands around the barrels of their guns. Everyone was mourning the death of the President.

In the evening we were assigned to our quarters.

As far as the work goes, it is easy but not very interesting, except when pay-day comes, but that's something we can only enjoy once a month.

The war now seems to be over, much to the annoyance of many of the people working for it. Many men will now be dismissed from their profit-able offices and will have to look after themselves again. Those who still have their positions are doing everything they can to exploit this source of money as much as possible. This has taken its toll on us, too, since our rations, which used to be quite generous, have now become quite skimpy, and the pay of many workers has been cut by 15 dollars a month, with the rest disappearing in the bottomless pockets of the quartermaster.

Nothing new is happening here except for the occasional rebel or rebel sympathizer who gets shot, or a few *Guelleras* who get hanged.

Every day now we are expecting the arrival of an army of 60 thousand men who are bound for Texas in order to plague this state, which thus far has been spared the robbing and plundering of the soldiers [14 ll.: correspondence; greetings; signature].

Jan. 28, 1866

Dear brother,

[44 ll.: correspondence; advice about emigration officials] I am now back at my own place, at Zander's, and I have rented his farm along with 25 acres in a nearby field, in exchange for part of the harvest. Wilhelm got a job at Wilhelm Bartels's as vice-farmer, and he'll get one third of the harvest for this. This is a very good *Contract* for Wilhelm, because with an average har-vest he will be able to make as much as 250 to 300 dollars, and it is a good arrangement for Barthels, too, since all his Negroes have left him, and white farmhands are scarce. Bartels lost a lot during the *Conforderation*, not only his Negroes who are now free but also a considerable amount of *Capital* in cash, since his two creditors [debtors] lost everything in the war[4] [5 ll.: details]. Things are also looking bad for Kleinert, because his partner died during the war, and Kleinert married his widow. I don't know if he is completely bankrupt, time will tell. But Kleinert is presently insolvent.[5] As Kleinert himself told me, he and Rohde invested 37,000 dollars in Confederate *Bonds* [. . . .] I think my claim is secure, because Kleinert has given me promissory notes from other parties. My primary creditors [debtors] Robison and Gaither haven't done so badly.[6] Of course they didn't earn anything during the war, and have lost all their Negroes, too, but they are still solvent, they would still be solvent even if my claim was as much in thousands as it is in hundreds [31 ll.: details; land purchase].

The war is over now, or rather the front has been moved from the field into the halls of legislation. But the blood has not been shed for naught, slavery has ceased. Only time will tell, however, how the Negro will fare as a free worker. Whether they can become citizens or own their own land also remains to be seen, but they are free, and to my great joy I have lost my bet of 10 bottles of wine that I had with Lönneker. And when you get a chance, you're welcome to drink the same, to raise a toast to the blessings of freedom and the health of the United States [18 ll.: correspondence; advice about emigration; greetings; signature].

Schwarting's later correspondence with his brother is mostly concerned with business matters, but he does comment on social and political change in his part of Texas. What little he had to say about slavery before the end of the war was fairly neutral, and he did not shrink from doing business with slaveholders. Even the two

4. In 1860 Wilhelm Bartels owned eight slaves, including three adults; in 1870 only $4,000 worth of property was listed. MC 1860: Austin Co./Tex., Industry Pct., Slave Schedule; MC 1870: Austin Co./Tex., Pct. 5, #86. The Bartels, who were childless, were cared for in their old age by a former slave whom they had brought up and taught the German language; they willed him all their property at their death. Schmidt (1930), 88.

5. Henry Rhode, a merchant from Lauenburg, had assets of $80,000 in 1860, and his partner August Kleinert from Oldenburg had almost $12,000; each owned one slave. Ten years later, Kleinert was listed as retired, with $7,000 in property. His marriage to Mrs. Rhode is corroborated by the seven-year-old Louisa Rhode listed as living in his household. MC 1860: Fayette Co./Tex., La Grange Town, #1004, and Slave Schedule; MC 1870: Fayette Co./Tex., Le Grange, #92.

6. In 1860 James Gaither was a merchant with $17,000 in assets and eight slaves. Joel Robison owned a plantation and was Gaither's neighbor. He owned seventeen slaves and was listed with property worth $50,000, the value of which had shrunk to $10,000 by 1870. Fayette Co. Tax Rolls, 1860, microfilm, Texas StateA; MC 1860: Fayette Co./Tex., #419, #467, #469; MC 1870: Fayette Co./Tex., Pct. 3, #518, #527.

Germans with whom he had the most contact were slave owners. It is clear, however, that Schwarting did not mourn the passing of slavery, even though he had his doubts about the capabilities of freedpeople. In addition, Germans and blacks often shared a common enemy. In a letter written in the summer of 1866, Schwarting complained, "On July 25th there was an important election here, namely all the officials in the entire state were elected that day. We don't know yet which party won. It is high time we had an energetic government for a change, to put an end to all the rowdies. But the Germans suffer the most from this, and they are patient—otherwise, Judge Lynch would have long since put an end to these gangs."[7]

In the next letter of August 28, he mentions the problem again, but this time the victims are different: "The situation with the *Rowdy* gangs is increasingly alarming. The Negroes are the main targets—some have even been murdered, but the suspects always go free." In the next letter of May 1867, he distances himself from the Anglo Americans and their opinions: "We are still under martial law, which is no small irritation to the Americans, but the 40 soldiers who are stationed here in Roundtop can hardly keep the peace."[8]

In a Christmas letter written in 1867, Schwarting wrote to his brother-in-law for a change and included a more detailed description of the social and political situation:

> The former slaveholders, who have already been humiliated by the loss of their black property, have so far, as long as cotton prices were high, done all they could to keep their living and maintain their authority, but now their means to do so have been totally cut off[. . . .]
>
> It seems to me that politics are looking very bad. The Negroes have the same rights as the whites in every respect. They can hold office, from constable to president. A black subject can put himself forward as a candidate, and if he gets enough votes, he can hold the office of president for the next four years just like any white man.[9]

In Fayette County, however, it was German more than black candidates who benefited from the enfranchisement of freedmen. In the new state legislature the county was represented by a German from Schwarting's neighborhood in Round Top.[10] This had quite an impact, as a letter of November 1870 shows:

> Most of the rowdy gangs have moved on, as a consequence of some of their members being arrested, but horses still get stolen every now and then. The thieving Negroes are still trying to get by with being lazy. The slaveholders, whose power is completely broken, seem to have resigned themselves to their fate and are working their plantations again, although sometimes their ava-

7. The letter is dated May 10, 1866, but it must have been written over several months.
8. Letters of August 28, 1866, May 12, 1867, NABS.
9. Letter of "First Christmas Day" [December 25], 1867, NABS.
10. Boehm (2000) traces the career of this legislator, Robert Zapp.

rice and lack of character comes to light in legal disputes with their workers, whereas in the past all their disputes with free workers were put down by bribing the judges, and those with the slaves by the whip.[11]

Despite Schwarting's reservations about freed slaves, he obviously had more sympathy for them than for southern aristocrats.

In 1867 Schwarting married a German widow and acquired, so to speak, a complete farm and family. He supplemented his income by importing goods from Germany. In a letter of April 1867, for example, he ordered a variety of things from his brother: "I would also like a couple of cases of good rum and cognac, but since these drinks are subject to high taxes, they should go by the name of Bremen beer, i.e. filled into Bremen beer bottles, with the case well marked for safety's sake, and at the end where the case can be opened most easily, they should pack a row of real beer. You can't get along without humbug."[12]

At the end of the 1870s, Schwarting suffered increasingly from paralysis, and he returned to Germany twice in an unsuccessful attempt to find a cure. He also fell out with his wife and family and moved to California in search of a better climate. When his wife died in the mid-1880s, he got into a legal dispute with the children over her estate and then failed to provide for them, so that neighbors in Texas from Oldenburg had to help out. Schwarting himself probably lived off money he had inherited from his family in Germany. He survived well into his eighties, dying in 1916 in a German old people's home in San Francisco.[13]

11. Letter of November 16, 1870, NABS.

12. Letter of April 1, 1867, NABS.

13. Letters of June 10, 1877, February 27 [187?], April 4 [187?], May 2 [187?], May 25 [187?], December 9 [187?], March 13, 1880, June 4, [1880], January 4, 1882, June 3, [1882], July 4, [1882], July 14, [1882], August 12, [1882], September 6, [1882], November 2, [1882], November 17, [1882], NABS. See also letters of Wm. Bartels, Kreuzmoor, February 7, 1877, and May 6, 1882, NABS; Fayette Co. District Court Minutes, Book P: 699–701, Book R: 85–86, Reel #1468698, Texas StateA; Fayette Co. Probate Records, Book P: 333–37, Book Q: 35–37, 121–23 (guardianship hearings), Reel #964423, Texas StateA.

57. Private Ludwig (Louis) Lehmann, CSA, and Friederike Lehmann

Karl Ludwig Lehmann, born on Christmas Day 1824, was the son of a man who was a baker, farmer, and former town councillor of Havelberg in Brandenburg.

SOURCE NOTE: It is rare that the written language of a man and his wife differ as much as is the case here. Friederike Lehmann's spelling and grammar are distinctly nonstandard, her vocabulary is limited, and in several cases it is difficult to figure out what she means. Louis Lehmann's writing reflects his educated middle-class background; he handles the language easily and effec-

Karl Ludwig grew up in comfortable circumstances and graduated from a prestigious local grammar school. In 1849, together with his parents and three younger brothers, Lehmann left Germany and settled on a farm near Brenham, Texas. They were among the first Germans to locate in Washington County, but the following decade saw the growth of a substantial settlement, called Berlin, around the Lutheran Ebenezer Church that the Lehmanns had helped establish. In 1860, with a population of 600 whites and 320 slaves, the county seat of Brenham was no longer backwoods—it even had a railroad connection.[1]

Louis Lehmann, as he soon called himself, got married in 1854 to the daughter of a farmer from Westphalia, Friederike Clausmeier, and took over the family farm. By 1860 he had paid out his three brothers and built up a flourishing operation worth $3,400. With only one farmhand to help him, he brought in twenty bales of cotton—more than the average American with one to five slaves. A free labor system, therefore, could certainly compete with slavery.[2]

Washington County was a major cotton center. Located on the fertile plains of the Brazos River, the county ranked second-highest statewide in cotton production. Slavery played a key role there, and blacks outnumbered whites: the average plantation counted thirteen slaves, and eighteen had more than fifty. The only thing that made the county different from the classic image of the Deep South was the German presence in the area. A mere 4 percent of the county electorate dared to vote against secession, but even if these had all been Germans, they would have amounted to only one-third of the German population in the county. Lehmann's letters clearly show, however, that these voting patterns hardly reflect enthusiasm for the Confederacy or slavery as an institution.[3]

---

tively, with only a few slips in spelling. The two also differ in their use of English words. Friederike uses relatively few, but Louis's letters are full of them. Many of these terms, like *Biskits* or *Lehdies* (ladies), are spelled according to German rules (which are more closely phonetic). The influence of English, however, goes beyond mere borrowing: many English nouns and verbs have become so much a part of his language that they are declined or conjugated like normal German words: soldiers receive *Provisionen* (provisions), hogs are *aufgepennt* (penned up), soldiers are *gedrillt* (drilled), and fields are *gerentet* (rented). There are even a few cases where the structure of a phrase is English, but all the words he uses are German. This type of interference was fairly common among immigrants who had spent a considerable amount of time in America and interacted with Anglo Americans, particularly when a letter-writer knew that the recipient was also familiar with the language. Here, this was clearly the case, since Lehmann wrote all but one of these letters to his wife; and the last letter, written to his brother-in-law back in Germany, contains very little English interference. Not included here are the letters in the series from the time before 1860 (six) and after 1865 (five), and one letter from 1863.

1. Lehmann (1983), 1-16, 46-47; Biesele (1987), 56-57; Breitenkamp and Dabbs (1985), 145-60; Pennington (1915), 36; USC 1860.1, 486. The family took some 2,000 talers* with them, according to the emigration files in Br. LHA P, Prov. Br. Rep. 2A I St Nr. 90, Bl. 14-15.

2. Lehmann (1983), 46, 52, 79; MCA 1860: Washington Co./Tex., #392; MC 1860: Washington Co./Tex., #881; Jordan (1966), 67-68.

3. USC 1860.1, 285, 489; USC A 1860.1, 140-49, 282; Elliott (1947) 470.

Louis Lehmann.
(Edmund L.
Burnett, M.D.)

No matter what one thought of the war, it was almost impossible to avoid military service. Two of the Lehmann brothers, Julius and Hermann, joined a German Confederate unit in April 1862.[4] The need for soldiers in the South was so great, however, that even a thirty-eight-year-old man with five children aged nine and younger was not exempt. After serving in the militia in early 1863, Louis Lehmann was drafted and assigned to regular service in the cavalry that July. But difficult as his time in the army was, Lehmann felt the burden was even greater for his wife Friederike—"for you now bear the responsibility for everything." With only one servant girl and the occasional help from neighbors, she had to cope with five children and all the work on the farm.[5] Since he and his wife could use German as a "secret code," their letters are quite candid.

4. They served under Captain Otto Nathusius in Comp A of Waul's Legion; muster rolls, Waul's Legion, Texas StateA, Austin, Tex. See also Voigt (no. 54), who commanded a company in the same legion.

5. On January 1, 1863, Lehmann was sworn in for three months as first sergeant in a militia brigade. Texas Confederate Records, Reel 3, Texas StateA; Lehmann (1983); letter of November 22, 1863, NABS.

Friederike Lehmann
née Clausmeier.
(Edmund L. Burnett, M.D.)

LOUIS LEHMANN

March 8th, 1863

Beloved Friederieke,

[. . .] It is good that you got the $20 in gold from Petsch, for money is now very tight—and it was also a good idea to plant a lot of sweet *Potatoe*[s]—for by the fall, food will certainly be scarce and very expensive. In fact, the way you have taken on the farm so conscientiously is remarkable, and more than one could expect from a woman [4 ll.: instructions]. I only wish we would get our money so I could send it to you before it becomes completely worthless.— A. Müller can brag about his *smart*ness as much as he wants, but when he gets here he'll have to stroll right into the guardhouse.[6] There are several from our company who went off without permission and are in the guardhouse now,

6. August Müller from Brandenburg belonged to the same congregation as Lehmann. Breitenkamp and Dabbs (1985), 99; MC 1860: Washington Co./Tex., #1080.

and one man was only gone for 10 days. — We have roll call 2 times a day, and if someone's missing it gets *reportet*. —

Don't worry about the *Yankees*, they certainly don't intend to march into the country because they don't have enough wagons — although they could get them easily enough if they were serious about it. — The 7 men we thought had been taken prisoner have all returned [6 ll.: description of the camp; instructions]. I will try my best to come home in the middle or at the end of April. — Today is my turn to cook, and I can't write any longer[. . . .] Fare well, beloved Friederieke! Kiss the children and commend them to the Lord's care. I remain / your/ faithful husband / Louis Lehmann

A quick note   Dear W,

Give my best to Ehlerts, I will certainly be most grateful if he helps us with the plowing; also Hermann, Wehmaier and Schulte[7] [8 ll.: state of health; instructions].

                                        Camp near Richmond. Fort Bend Co. Texas
                                                                August 19, 1863

Beloved Friederieke,

[7 ll.: description of the march] In the last *Camp* before we reached Richmond, the *Colonel* had the regiment fall in, and then he explained to the men that he had received a message from Galveston saying that our troops on the island (3 regiments) had revolted and that the *Yankees* could easily take the island if they knew this. He (the *Colonel*) called on every Texan who was true to his country to step forward and volunteer to hurry with him to Galveston. About 200 men stepped forward — we Germans just stood still, along with about 80 Americans[8] — of the men who chose to stay, some were taken along to Richmond to look after the horses of the ones who went down to Galv.[9] — The *Colonel* took the volunteers right away on Saturday evening and headed off from our last *Camp*, 18 miles this side of Richmond, and on Sunday morning they left for Galveston via railroad on an extra train[. . . .] We are com-

---

7. Schulte was Lehmann's closest neighbor; all the others were related to Lehmann, either directly or by marriage, and all were founding members of the Ebenezer Church. Lehmann (1983), 56–57, 68, 80; Breitenkamp and Dabbs (1985), 69, 145–46, 150, 179; MC 1860: Washington Co./Tex., #288, #886, #882.

8. Lehmann and about a dozen of his neighbors and friends were almost the only Germans in the regiment, Terrell's Texas Cavalry. Judging by the names of its officers, Liken's Cavalry (35 Tex. Cav), to which Lehmann's Comp D was later transferred, was also predominantly Anglo American. Spencer (1982), v–vii, 101–65.

9. For more details see Spencer (1982), 3–5; some of the cavalrymen were disgruntled because they were afraid they would be permanently transferred to the infantry.

pletely in the dark. We heard civilians in the town saying that the troops on the island at Galveston had revolted because of paper money and their provisions, they're demanding as much paper money (for every dollar they are owed) as it is worth in gold, so 10 to one [9 ll.: details; description of his location]. Three days later [. . .] They say the business in Galveston has been settled, one of the rebellious regiments has apparently been sent to Louisiana, and the men from our regiment who went are still down there helping out with guard duty. —

Saturday, Aug. 23

Sternberg went back home yesterday morning, and F. Hodde left last night;[10] there is a lot of discontent in the *Company*, the captain is still in Galveston and our rations have become irregular, one day we have meat and the next day we don't, and it's the same with the fodder for the horses. — The *Ticks* are a real plague along the river. — An American in one of the other companies went mad a week ago, the poor man lost his wife and children, and he's been bound to a tree with his hands tied together — he is under guard day and night, and he screams the whole time. — Things are in disarray here, the doctor is almost out of medicine, and the sick are lying around under the trees. We haven't done any drilling since we left Wudderskreek, and the men don't know how to hold the rifles that we don't have anyway [19 ll.: encouragement; greetings; signature; "P.S. business"].

Camp near Eagle Lake / Coloredo County[11]
September 7, 1863

Beloved Friederike,

We stayed longer in the vicinity of Richmond than we had expected. On the morning of Sept. 2nd we left the *Camp* and crossed the Brazos with our wagons and horses at a shallow place above the narrows and followed the road to Columbus on the Coloredo about 50 miles away. For me, this *Trip* was the hardest I've had up to now. As a result of the bad water, many of our men were suffering from diarrhea, and I also had my share, so I was feeling very weak [22 ll.: details of the march; sickness; rations]. The captain came back, but the next day he rode back home to get the men who deserted at Richmond (about 8). Three have been caught already, including poor Sternberg with his

10. Both were Germans in Lehmann's company: Heinrich Sternberg (born 1833), farmer, father, and member of the Ebenezer Church; Hodde, an unmarried farmhand from Prussia, born about 1842. Breitenkamp and Dabbs (1985), 65, 103; MC 1860: Washington Co./Tex., #1145, #866.

11. Railroad station about thirty-five miles south of Brenham on the line to Houston.

crippled arm[. . . .] The 3rd lieutenant has also been sent to catch deserters, it is easy to run away here and very tempting, but the consequences! — ? The men who have thought it through are staying here — because the time is not yet ripe. — I think I will get a furlough shortly, and I think this is the best way to get to see my loved ones [6 ll.: rations]. We'll be leaving this *Camp* this morning and going up the Berhard (a *Creek*) or the Cummingscreek, I would prefer the latter because it is closer to Brenham, and there are Germans nearby[. . . .] No one knows what they have in store for us. We Germans have started up a little reading club and have been reading the newspaper regularly. Don't worry about my health, I am on the road to recovery and am better off than others who don't have anything, since now I've got coffee, sugar and vinegar and also some *Biskits*. I don't lack for money and buy things wherever I can. — But what are you and the children up to, are you all still content? — I often think of you when I lie under my tree in the quiet evening, and the moon lights up our nightly camp. So fare well and kiss the little ones. I hope that soon I can tell you myself how much I remain:

Your faithful husband / Louis Lehmann [. . .]

FRIEDERIKE LEHMANN

Brenham, Sept. 7th, 1863

Beloved Loui,

[8 ll.: correspondence; worries; rumors about where he might be] I wanted to write you much more, but for a week now I've had an eye infection so I couldn't put up with it, the main reason for my letter is that 2 companies of the militia have already been ordered to be prepared to march to Bohnham[12] on the 14th of September, and I am very much afraid that you will have to go there too. If you can get a furlough, try and get some good provisions to take along, and if that's not possible, we would be so happy if you could get some leave to come and see us. Maybe if you say that I am sick, you can get a furlough for an unlimited time, but if the Colonel won't give in and won't give you a furlough, then don't be afraid, it's not a deathly illness, and when it's over I'll be able to see as well as before. The children are much better now, Betti and Loui haven't had the eye infection, and they are busy picking *Katten*. Mile keeps picking too, and they will soon be through once. The children speak of you often, especially little Matthilde.[13] When the dog barks,

12. Bohnham was about 250 miles north of Brenham. The cause of the rumor was probably a group of mostly Anglo American opponents of the war who had assembled near the town; see Tatum (1934), 50–51.

13. The two eldest Lehmann children, Betti (Carolina Elisabeth), born October 29, 1854, and Louis, born December 1, 1856, already had to help pick cotton. Daughter Mathilde was born on

she jumps to the window, Papa's coming, bring me cake? Pretty dress, too? I go church. But dear Loui, don't lose heart, I have often prayed to the dear Lord to keep your health and that we might see each other again, and He will answer our prayers, so fare well and do not forget your / devoted / Friederike Lehmann / Schulte has gotten out of the militia [. . .]

[Nov. 18, 1863]

Beloved Loui,

[12 ll.: correspondence; is worried about all the rumors as to where he might be] You are so uneasy and worried about us, but we are all hale and hearty. My eyes got better after the first 3–4 days [7 ll.: has sewn all sorts of clothing] and the only thing missing from our circle is you, the head of the house, and the house is now so big and empty. It's been 4 weeks now since you left, and I often think, wouldn't it possible for you to visit us for another 4 weeks? [21 ll.: children; rumors about the war; the draft; a neighbor has left for the Mexican border]. That must be hard for the wife and parents-in-law, first the shame and then the trouble, and then everything they've worked so hard for is taken away from them and the children[. . . .] They say that Kron has lost all his sheep, his horses and Negroes up country, because of the Indians, and they say he wants to come back here again [14] [end of letter missing].

LOUIS LEHMANN

No. 2 [no. 1 missing] 5 days later / Sunday, November 8, 1863
Camp 25 miles west of Houston on the *road*
from Columbus to Houston.

Beloved Friederieke,

[18 ll.: correspondence; marching orders] All of our men who had gone to Galveston earlier, also our German friends Slotmann, Sternberg and Neinast, Cramer, were waiting for us at the *Camp*.[15]

March 1, 1861; the other children were named Gustav (born April 26, 1858) and Alwine (born February 5, 1863). Lehmann (1983), 47–50. "Mile" was the family maid, Emilie Weiss.

14. Georg H. Kron emigrated before 1848 from Hesse. He was one of the founders of the Ebenezer Church and was taxed for four slaves in 1862–63. The two other slaveholding Germans in the county each owned one slave. MC 1860: Washington Co./Tex., #1144, and 1860 Slave Schedule; Washington Co. Tax Rolls, 1862–63, microfilm, Texas StateA; Breitenkamp and Dabbs (1985), 145, 150, 156, 169.

15. William S[ch]lottman, farmer and father of a family, born around 1825 in Prussia, lived about thirty houses away from Lehmanns. Christoph Neinast was a member of the Ebenezer Church. For information about Sternberg, see n. 10. Friedrich Cramer from Hanover owned one slave. MC 1860: Washington Co./Tex., #851, #1043, as well as Slave Schedule; Breitenkamp and Dabbs (1985), 156, 182.

That evening, we each only got 5 cars of *Corn*, and the next morning only 6 ears, which has made everyone very unhappy. No new *Order* for us has arrived, and we don't know where we'll be going [21 ll.: rumors; consolation; signature; P.S.: instructions; correspondence].

                                   Houston, [------] November 22nd, 1863
Beloved Friederieke,
    [6 ll.: received a letter:] and I felt as happy as a child! I must have read it 2–3 times [21 ll.: was worried about her; has sufficient winter clothing and money]. You can't buy much here, since everything is too expensive. More than ⅔ of the *Store*[s] are closed, all you see on the streets are soldiers, but otherwise things look the same.—Today on a Sunday, when we went to church, we saw finery just like it used to be, the *Lehdies* [ladies] were sweeping the streets in their silk dresses and the little girls were dressed up like dolls [6 ll.: admired the gardens]. This Sunday morning I had to drive with the wagons to the railroad station and help load *Korn*—but that only took ½ an hour and then we visited the churches.—The *small pox* has shown up in town, so even though there are only a few cases, no soldier is allowed to stay in the town in the evening or at night. There haven't been any cases yet in the *Camp*, but don't worry about me, I have the medicine I got from Graul if it gets bad, and in that case they would move the military away from here.—Our German *Meß* [mess] is now 15 men strong, and every day 2 men take turns cooking, so it isn't too much work, but when we get some *Flauer* [flour] every now and then, they always say: Lehmann, you have to make *Biskits*. Because no one else knows how to do it.—The other evening we were singing some chorales, and it didn't take 10 minutes before we were completely surrounded by Americans who came to listen to our singing[. . . .] Since we have been here, we've done less than 2 hours of drilling, and I've only done picket duty once, that's why I have enough time left over to write you long letters. But even though we are lying around here with nothing to do, no one gets any leave, and without a pass or *Furloh* you can't leave. The other day I went with A. Müller down to the Hempstead railroad *Depot* shortly before the train left, hoping to see some acquaintances, and we saw that there were guards in front of each railroad car, not letting anyone on who didn't have papers—I watched the train leave with sadness, since it would have brought me home to you by evening, just like when little Mathilde watched us leave in the wagon for church, without taking her along.—Our *Company* has increased in size considerably this week, they're rounding up people from everywhere and sending them to Houston— they've been very tough in Austin County. There are several men from there who had been hiding in the *Bottoms*, and some who took part in the meet-

ings[16] a year and a half ago, and they brought them in locked up with a ball and chain, and they are stuck in prison. They say that one of them will be shot.—Thursday, Nov. 26, this morning we left old Terrell's regiment[. . . .] The regiment we have joined is called Liken's regiment (pronounced Leikens). This regiment has just been formed, and the men know even less about drilling than we do, and it is also still weak in number—this is an advantage for us, since we can gain some more time before they send us off to the enemy, who are now only down on the coast [29 ll.: troop dispositions; mail; instructions; address; greetings; signature].

[December 2, 1863]

[Beloved] Friederieke,

[12 ll.: has received new marching orders; equipment] We also received guns, old United States muskets, but still usable [—] and cartridge boxes. We don't care much for these guns and would have liked to have thrown them away—but we can't do anything about it.—Shortly before our departure, Houston was a colorful sight, the road from the *Camp* into the city was filled with soldiers from early morning until late at night, as well as with wagons with *Korn* and provisions for the soldiers. The presence of so many soldiers also led to an accumulation of loose women, since the houses on the outskirts of the town along the road to *Camp* are full of this low-down trash, and it is not unusual to see horses tethered outside in broad daylight; but in defense of the honor of the Germans I must say that they do not frequent such places.—Fritz Whitty[17] [. . .] knew no shame (despite a wife and children at home) and went to one of these odious places—and he got what he deserved immediately, a disgusting disease that was so bad that the *Captain* had to send him home—he had only been away from home and in the *Comp* for two weeks. [17 ll.: parade delayed their departure:] and we still had 25 miles to go to our new *Camp* (Sandy Point).—Despite riding at a trot, which meant we had a lot of *Trubel* [trouble] keeping our long muskets on the horses, we didn't get there until 8 o'clock in the evening.—From a distance we could see the watch fires of the troops camped there, and when we rode into the *Camp*, the *Boys* greeted us with a tremendous *Yell*, and then our men joined in too, and the yelling was so loud that if the *Yankees* had heard it, they all would have run

16. This refers to gatherings of war resisters, who were mostly Germans. For more details see "Introduction: German Immigrants and Politics in the Civil War Era," in this volume; Elliott (1947), 449–77; Tatum (1934), 46–49.

17. Probably a German named Witte from Lehmann's neighborhood. On prostitution in general during the war see Lowry (1994); and Clinton (1999).

away[. . . .] We were all very tired and swearing about our *Colonel* who had made us fool around with his dress parade for ½ a day [14 ll.: orders received and rescinded; conditions in the camp].

We went to see the *Captain* about Sternberg, about not making him come along with his broken arm, and he had the doctor write a certificate and sent him to the hospital in Chappel-Hill—if he were smart, he would have gone home [35 ll.: sending home unnecessary things; regiment rushed off in the middle of the night toward the coast, but it was a false alarm, no Yankees in sight; pointless and contradictory orders]. Now that we've had the chance to get to know our commanding officers better, [I] must say we are out of the frying pan and into the fire, for when we had that night march from Sandy Point, and the *Rehrgarde* [rear guard] (which has to chase after stragglers) came along at the back, they saw a human figure (next to a horse that was standing still) lying in a *Mudhole*. They pulled the man out of the mud, and *o weh!* They saw it was our *Colonel*, who was dead drunk and out cold—they left him lying there.—And when the *Colonel* arrived in Columbia, he was arrested[. . . .] The second *Colonel* (lieutenant *Colonel*) barely managed to escape the noose, because years ago he had rented out his field to someone, and then he wanted to run him off because he wanted to rent it out to another man who offered more money—and so he shot the first renter 6 times with his *Sechs schuter* [six-shooter] and then stabbed him over and over again with a knife—filthy lucre got him off[18] [8 ll.: descriptions of the route and the camp].

Camp 10 miles von Velasco, December 9th[19]
[CONTINUATION OF PRECEDING LETTER]
Beloved Friederike,

[11 ll.: warnings about false rumors of an invasion] And if the northerners really come, we won't be able to do anything about it, because the men don't want to fight, and they'd all just run away [26 ll.: farming matters; instructions; greetings; signature; address].

[ONGOING NOTES ATTACHED TO LETTER OF December 19, 1863]
Camp 8 miles N.W. of Velasco, December 9

Toward evening, 4 men deserted from our regiment with their [weapons] about 40–50 men were sent after them to catch them, the men stayed away

18. Colonel James B. Likens was accused of being drunk and unfit for duty for twenty-four hours. The lieutenant colonel was probably J. R. Burns. Spencer (1982), 159, 162.

19. Situated at the mouth of the Brazos River, about 100 miles downstream from Brenham.

until the 14th and didn't find anyone; some of them didn't even return and
went home. The troops are very disgruntled, and if this business isn't over in
a few months, they will hopefully all run off. —

Dec. 15. Most of the men in Terrell's regiment have received their *Bounti*
[bounty] (50 $) and also the men in our *Comp.* who went along to Galves-
ton have gotten their (50 $) *Bounti*, we have often fought with the *Captain*
about getting ours, but he doesn't do anything about it, or doesn't want to. —
Things are getting very lively here, that is between the mouth of the Colorado and the Brazos, there are 10–12 regiments, mostly cavalry, within 8–10
miles of here — Every morning several music corps (all of which are made up
of Germans) play when they change the guard — we don't care much for music
under these circumstances. The *Korn* for the troops comes down the Brazos
on *Steambote*[s]; the men in the regiment have supplied themselves with sugar
and *Molasses* from nearby sugar planters. They got it for free in the beginning, but then too many came, and they had to start paying for it. The *Order*
now is that no one can leave the *Camp* without a pass from the *Captain*, and
he is only allowed to issue two a day. — All around the *Camp* they've cut a path
through the woods, with sentries posted along it so they can see each other —
and when the horses need to be watered, they all go together under the supervision of a lieutenant — so that no one can sneak off [49 ll.: camp; provisions.
December 19: dress parade; troop dispositions; end of the war is coming].

<u>Happy New Year</u>! Camp near Velasco, Dec. 19th, 1863.
<u>Happy New Year</u>!!!

Beloved Friederieke,

[19 ll.: horse is heavily laden with the presents he received] As for the *Korn*
for the *Goverment* (the tithe), don't have it delivered! If the *Goverment* wants
to steal *Korn* from soldiers' wives, then let them come and get it themselves.
You can't just take it to them!! Why, I've been serving since the 1st of July,
haven't gotten my *Bounty* or any pay, and we'll never get anything! Plus having
to supply my own clothing — let the gentlemen Negro-holders who are sitting
around at home do something, too[20] [30 ll.: farming matters; instructions;
greetings; signature].

---

20. Because of inflation, the Confederate government tried to impose taxes paid in kind,
which were greatly resented. One cause for bitterness against the slaveholders was the fact that
for every twenty slaves, one southern white overseer was exempt from military duty. Tatum
(1934), 13–20.

Camp Horton *near* Velasco, Dec. 19, 1863

The orders to go to Texana were revoked today, and instead they announced a *Parade* and review *for* Gen. Magruder[21] [23 ll.: details]. During that maneuver, there wasn't one single *Hurrah* to be heard, unlike what usually happens.—On Dec. 20 the regiment received the new flag from the *Connel*, on which occasion he made a speech that no one paid much attention to and didn't receive even one single *Hurrah*—a sign that the men are fed up with this business.—In the night from Dec 21–22 I was on duty [. . .] when suddenly there was a horn signal that all the buglers on the line began to pick up, although it took one of them 10 minutes before he could get a note out because he was so scared, then in the distance gunfire could be heard and the call to "*saddle up*" was heard from all the officers.—*the "yankee's are coming"* Then there was great *Confusion* [. . .] and after ½ an hour of much flurry, the regiment fell in—a lieutenant had to search our company's *Camp* to see that everyone had left, and in each of the others (American messes) they found 3–4 men who had suddenly developed cannon fever, or had suddenly been so overtaken with sleep that they hadn't heard all the commotion—in short, it turned out that all the men who sound off like the greatest fire-eaters and always know everything better are the biggest cowards and had hidden themselves.—During all of this I stayed quietly at my post (but not without being somewhat nervous)[. . . .] I wasn't allowed to leave my post until I had been relieved—the lieutenant (who didn't know this rule) wanted me to leave my post, but I just laughed at him and told him he couldn't tell me what to do tonight.—After the regiment had ridden for an hour, the gunfire died down, and the *Order* came: *return to camp*. Then the "*boys*" let loose a *yell* that echoed through the entire woods and everybody was making jokes—the whole commotion was a false alarm (only the *Colonel* knew about it ahead of time). The shooting came from a *Comp*. that General Bee had sent out secretly for this purpose the night before.—All the men from our *Meß* [mess] had fallen in at the alarm, except for me, and this time they couldn't say anything bad about the Germans [4 ll.: moved camp].

Friday, Dec. 25[. . . .] Last night we sang various Christmas carols, it was already after 9 o'clock, and after we had been singing for about ¼ of an hour, the *Captain* sent word that we had to stop, since it was after 9 o'clock. We were embittered, but we had to obey—for the day before they had stopped a vesper service at another camp. They are quite strict with us here—but you

21. General John B. Magruder (1816–71) was a West Point graduate and the commander of all the troops in Texas; Boatner (1959), 501.

can only tighten a bow until it snaps—and it will, for there are now more and more signs of this—We had also baked a sweet cake (with cornmeal) since we have sugar and molasses, and I still had some cloves. And the little bit of spirits that I still had made a small punch for us [. . .] but all this was only a sad substitute, because our loved ones were missing! [6 ll.: little free time] Monday, Dec. 28, we had arms inspection with Gen. Bee, and after it was over he gave a wonderful speech and said that even if hundreds of thousands of *Yankees* were to come down, not one would leave Texas alive—we, of course, thought otherwise—and at the end he called for the *Boys* to give 3 *Hurras*, which drew a weak response from about 50 greenhorns [6 ll.: militias also disgruntled]. The planters nearby have demanded guards for their plantations, because the *boy's* stole everything from them in the beginning, and they're worse than the *Yankee's*—the hogs have all been penned up by the farmers, because otherwise they wouldn't have been able to keep any of them.—The weather has been very fine up to now, and nobody in our *Meß* (13 men) has been sick—the Americans get sick more often and try to shirk whenever they get a chance [13 ll.: fighting on the coast].

Camp Horton *near* Velasco / Dec. 31st, 1863

Beloved Friederieke,

[. . .] Rumors of the wildest sort are circulating in the *Camp* about the northerners, but they often prove to be unfounded—the real truth (unless we were there ourselves) is hard to come by, since our *Camp* is located so far away from any communication and cut off from the outside world like a monastery, there are no post offices in the area [. . .] newspapers don't get delivered, either (even to the people who have paid for them), so all we hear is what the gentlemen at headquarters think is good for us to know. It's even rumored that outgoing mail is opened and read (there's a German at headquarters). From now on, I'll adjust my style accordingly [12 ll.: Yankees are treating the civilian population well; weather; quarters]. I've heard that a law was passed in Austin that the last quarter of the militia that's still at home will be drafted, and in their place, ¼ of those in service will be sent home. The new law can't affect Schulte, because he is totally exempted and is not on any list. Send Horton about 20 bushels of *Corn*, and [if] they unlawfully try to draft Schulte, rely on Horton[22] [41 ll.: January 4, 1864: weather; conditions in the camp; instructions; greetings; signature]

22. This probably refers to George W. Horton, a wealthy lawyer in Brenham; MC 1860: Washington Co./Tex., #1.

[ONGOING NOTES, ATTACHED TO LETTER OF January 16, 1864]

<u>Camp between Caneycreek and Cedar lake</u>

[16 ll.: change of plans; moved into a new camp] There were still about 10 huts and [log] cabins there and our *Meß* was so fortunate as to get one of the best ones, much to the annoyance of some of the Americans—then we tried to make the house as watertight as possible by stuffing moss into all the cracks, and we made soft places to sleep for ourselves out of moss. Since there were several large *Farmer*[s] nearby, almost everyone (except our *Meß*) went hog hunting, the men had driven their hogs into the fields, but the *boy's* were so sassy that dozens of hogs were shot dead in the fields—the *Oberseher* [overseer] of the *Farm* complained to the Colonel, and a strong guard with an officer at the head was able to stop the foolishness [25 ll.: rushed to the coast at night, for naught]. January 10th [. . .] in the morning the *Yankees* started shooting again, we ran out onto the *Prairie*, and could see the battleship very clearly, along with the smoke every time they shot off a cannon, even though they were still 7–8 miles away. A fort is being built there, and the *Yankees* have their fun driving off the Negroes who are working on it with their *Bombschells* [24 ll.: land attack unlikely; thirty-two men died in a boating accident; only one death from a shell]

Saturday, Jan. 16, 1864—

Thursday noon 5 companies from our regiment, including our *Comp*, rode to the coast to *recognoscieren* (*skauten*) [scout] [12 ll.: details] and we (three) received the *Order* to ride 14–15 miles up the coast, and in case we saw anything suspicious on land or water, we were to turn around immediately and report [10 ll.: description of the terrain]. We got the order to load our guns, but we didn't want to kill anybody, and so we rode with empty muskets.—It was dark and quite chilly [5 ll.: details]. Strange feelings flew through my mind during this ride. If there were some soldiers who had landed ahead of us, easy to do from the boats, and then during the night had hidden themselves in the sand dunes along the coast, and if they were to catch us, then nobody would know where we had met our end, or later, if we had ridden another 15–20 miles, might [we] have reached good quarters??? —

If one could only know these things ahead of time, then one might be able to do something!?? [13 ll.: collected seashells; saw a northern ship]. The fort is anything but a fort!! A square surrounded by a trench and a wall of sand, about 80 Negroes are working on it day and night, but there is still not a single cannon.—The *Yankees* are keeping quiet on the peninsula, none of our men have ever seen any when they've gone scouting [7 ll.: antiwar rumors]. Desertions are more and more common here, and in 4 weeks' time things will get even livelier.—Many of the *boys* seem to like the coarse, rough soldier's life, but most of the older men are thoroughly sick of it, there have been several mission preachers here in the *Camp* who have held services (in English), one of them is still here, and I have never heard anyone preach any better in English. They have set up a place with seats for church services, but the rough boys don't come to these meetings [8 ll.: received marching orders, but for naught].

Letter no. 2, Saturday evening, January 16, 1864 [CONTINUATION]
Beloved Friederieke,
[9 ll.: correspondence] *Korn* is getting low around here as well—the area down on the coast will soon be eaten up by the soldiers, and if the *Yankees* should·come, the Negroes will be brought up from the coast to our region, so yours will be eaten up as well, and *Korn* will run low where you are, too, before there's another *Krop*; hopefully something will turn up before mid-February and March—I am heartily tired of this forced soldier's life (slave life) [25 ll.: longing for peace; greetings; signature; address; correspondence; business matters].

Business [attached to previous letter?]
I am repeating here in case you didn't get my last letters!—Petty can work the following land! [4 ll.: details]. I don't really want Petty's Negroes to come this side of the *Brench* [branch: creek] so that you have *Trubel* close to the house—if this is possible.—Schulte should plow the land that we need, then take what he can manage for himself, the rest is for Wehmeier, and if he doesn't need it all, give the rest to Petty[23] [4 ll.: details]. They can't take Schulte, because he is not on the lists and is *exempted*, go and talk to Horton yourself, if they try to take him by force—and send him 20–25 bushels of *Korn.*—For every 4 families, 1 man has to stay at home [14 ll.: farming instructions; provisions]. According to the reports of deserters, the *Yankees* have 20–25,000 men on the peninsula and their commander, General Banks,* is still in New-Orleans and will be bringing along another division, so they can eat us for *Brekfäst*[24]—the military governor appointed by Lincoln is in Indi-

23. G. M. Petty, born around 1811 in Tennessee, owned a farm worth $15,000 and at least four slaves. He lived three families away from the Lehmanns; see MC 1860: Washington Co./Tex., #878; Washington County Tax Rolls, 1861, microfilm, Texas StateA.
24. Lehmann overestimates the size and the seriousness of the invasion, which was primarily designed as a warning to the French in Mexico. *DAB*, 1:577–80; Kerby (1972), 186–88.

anola, his name is Jack Hamilton. — We still haven't gotten either our *Baunty* [bounty] (50$) or any of our other pay — but don't send me any money, because I still haven't touched the 10 $ you sent me. We also have very few opportunities to buy anything. — And this money is so bad it isn't worth anything — don't pay your war-*täx* yet! —

[. . .] If we are actually sent west, the distance from home won't be much more than from here. — On our map (that we bought in Houston) we always calculate the shortest route home, but unfortunately, we've never been able to realize our plan — / all the best to Müller's wife, he is in good health!

Tuesday, February 2nd, 1864 / Camp Hardemann

Beloved Friederieke,

[22 ll.: correspondence; farming matters] Yesterday we got 48 $ for 2 months — I am sending you 40 $ of this in this letter that is enclosed in A. Müller's letter, since I can't get much of anything for it here, and this money isn't worth anything anymore, 30 for one dollar silver in Houston. — Last night 190–200 men rode off from 2 regiments near us because they were going to have their horses taken away and be made into infantry. — *Korn* is so scarce here that they want to turn most of the cavalry regiments into infantry, our regiment is supposed to keep its horses because we belong to the brigade that will go west. — We are still here where we were when I wrote my letter of the 28th, 30 miles from the coast. — Some of the planters here have moved further inland, because they are afraid of the *Yankees*. — Since we left the coast, the *Yankees* have taken 9 of our men prisoner. — Our regiment is supposed to march to Victoria soon — the *Yankees* are 9,000 strong in Indianola[25] but are treating the citizens very well, one woman had 2 turkeys stolen by the soldiers, the next morning she went to the *Yankee Colonel* and he gave her 10 times as much coffee and sugar as the turkeys were worth. — I am still quite healthy, thank the Lord, and the Germans who are sick are also recovering. — May God keep us all in his fatherly protection and give us peace soon. Kiss the children and keep me in your thoughts / your faithful husband / Louis Lehmann [6 ll.: wants mail; address].

---

25. Indianola is on the coast on the southwest side of Matagorda Bay; Victoria about thirty-five miles inland.

In the piney woods, 60 miles from Alexandria
(Midday) Wednesday, April 27th[26]
Notes along our march / in Louisiana.

On Monday the 25th, we crossed the Sabine rivver below Loganport and
were then on Louisiana soil[. . . .] In the evening we arrived in Mansfield
[. . .] 3-4 miles from the town there was a battle with the *Yankees* recently,
the first one this spring—here we saw the first horrors of war, all the houses
were filled with wounded men, and I saw various groups of *Ladies* bringing refreshment to the wounded; in the various battles we have lost more than 3,000
men, killed, wounded, and taken prisoner (including more than a thousand
dead).—We have taken no more than 3,000 *Yankees* prisoner—the *Order* that
the *Captain* received here was to march as quickly as possible, day and night, to
the regiment, and the men were supposed to take nothing more than a *Blanket*
with them [8 ll.: details]. My sausage stands me in good stead, but the weight?
In the evening we rode out of the town until midnight.—3-4 miles out of
town, we came upon part of the battlefield, which we recognized from the
stench of the dead horses.—From here to Plesant Hill (22 miles) our troops
had followed on the heels of the *Yankees* and attacked them, as was clearly
shown in the bullets that were stuck in the pine trees, the dead horses, and
the graves on the roadside. The entire area is a dense forest of pine trees, and
where there was an old field, the *Yankees* had regrouped and stood up to our
men.—But one must say in their defense, the *Yankees* didn't burn down any
houses. Of course, they did take the bacon and *Korn* away from the farmers.—
Although folks claim that they lay waste to everything, that's a lie! [6 ll.:
Yankee gunboats threatened to run aground] Since we've been in Louisiana,
we've confiscated (stolen?) *Korn* 2 times already, one time from another *Gou-
vermentswagen*, and 1 time from a large wagon train (a Louisiana *planter*, who
had fled from the *Yankees* to Texas and was on his way back with more than 100
Negroes and 30 wagons)[. . . .] Our regiment is supposed to be another 25 to
30 miles off, and by the time we get there they may still be that far ahead of us,
but we don't mind, and if the *Capt.* weren't with us, we might get lost [24 ll.:
April 28: description of the battlefield at Mansfield and the destruction caused
by the war along the road]. In Mansfield we had gotten guns, cartridge boxes
and cartridges, I would have much preferred to take along my bacon.—<u>Friday,
April 29th</u> / All along the way we rode down the Cane rivver valley yesterday, about 30 miles, the fields were planted with *Corn*, but most of the fences

26. After four weeks at home on furlough, ca. March 19 until April 16, 1864, Lehmann attempted to catch up with his regiment, which had been sent to fight the Union invasion of Louisiana.

were down and lying around in heaps, our *Train's* had come through and the troops had marched through. — The houses, *Gin's*, Negro-houses, and *Kornkribs* lay in smoking ruins, we didn't see any people living there, and not an ear of *Corn* will be planted here this year. — Finally, after 13 days of hard riding, we met up with our regiment [9 ll.: commanded to a new position]. They don't know yet if the *Yankees* will leave this part of Louisiana or risk another battle; it is clear that they've been beaten — they didn't know that all the Texas troops were here and didn't think our men would attack them. They've lost more than 200 mule wagons, because they were surprised.[27] — But down here they didn't burn all the houses. If the owners were there and swore an oath of loyalty, they didn't destroy anything. — But they do take the *Korn* and bacon, if they need it, wherever they find it — that's why Texas can consider itself lucky that they haven't come down there.

Friday, April 29, 12 o'clock noon, 8 miles from / Alexandria

Beloved Friederieke,

The 4 weeks I spent so happily in your midst now only seem like a pleasant dream from the past. Who would have thought that 13 days would bring us into the interior of Louisiana, very close to the *Feds*, only 6 miles away? I have seen 3 battlefields — but no enemy!! The 4 weeks at home were good for me, not only at home but also here — otherwise I would have been with the regiment in a skirmish — because our regiment launched an attack on the gunboats, quite suddenly when all the men were working on the decks. Our men had crept up close to the high riverbank on their knees like Indians and fired several salvos on the ships, and they say that more than 100 were killed and wounded — none of our men were hurt — because they were protected by the high riverbank [38 ll.: encouragement; greetings; signature; route description; business; notes].

In the field below Alexandria, La. <u>Friday noon, May 6</u>, 1864

<u>Sunday</u>, May 8th

Beloved Friederieke,

It's only since we've been here in Louisiana that we've seen what it means to be a soldier in the field — we used to think things were hard in the *Camps*, but in the field it is different [7 ll.: details]. The landscape here is very pretty, the Red rivver valley, crisscrossed with lovely wide streams, on which [only] large sugar plantations are located, looking like nice towns with all their Negro-

---

27. Northern losses were even higher than this, 250 loaded wagons; see Kerby (1972), 306.

houses, which admittedly are almost all empty, because the young, strong Negroes were taken away last spring by the *Feds*. The same is true of the draft animals (mules and wagons) so that the few crippled old Negroes and women and children are left to plant a little eating *Korn* with a hoe—and on top of this, the poor creatures are in constant danger of having their houses shot to pieces or burned by their friends or their enemies, so that whenever we are camped near plantations like this, or when we pass by, the Negroes start taking their belongings to safety. Up to now I have been in 2 skirmishes, but I haven't been injured, thank the Lord. In the first one, I didn't even get a chance to fire my gun, and in the second one, just 1 time—but I am sure I didn't hurt anyone. But it is certainly a strange feeling when it's the first time, and you see all the preparations being made—once you're in the midst of it, it's easier.—Our *Comp.* only has muskets, and when there's a skirmish then the other *Comp.* that have Enfield rifles go in front, because they can shoot farther.[28]—There's no point in worrying about me, for the Lord who can protect me is everywhere, and I certainly try to be very careful [23 ll.: reassurances; greetings; signature].

> *No 1—in the field 12 miles below* Alexandria, La

Notes [56 ll.: details of the skirmishes of May 3 to May 7]

Sunday, May 8: When our troops have to retreat, they burn down all the corncribs, it is a painful sight to see this destruction glowing in the sky in the evenings. First the *Feds* take away the best Negroes and mules, and now the remaining grain is set on fire, our troops break open the sugarhouses and destroy more than they eat. This area is being completely devastated. Our men have destroyed several *Transport* steamers and gunboats on the Red rivver.—Sunday, [actually Monday] the 9th of May—the *Feds* are not to be seen today, much useless riding back and forth on our part [16 ll.: details].

Tuesday, May the 10th We are camped today near Marksville, we don't know what we are supposed to be doing here, they say more troops will be arriving—the *Feds* are still 3 miles from here [16 ll.: mail service; reassurances; greetings; signature; address].

---

28. The Enfields imported from England were rifled muskets with four to five times the range of their smooth-bored predecessors, another sign of how poorly equipped many of the Confederates were; see McPherson (1982), 193–97.

FRIEDERIKE LEHMANN

Brenham, May 17th, 1864.

Beloved Loui,

On Thursday, May 5, I received your dear letter of April 24. I was at church, and Müller's wife, mother, and mother-in-law were there, too.[29] They asked me to come with them and to open the letter about Louiziana. You can well imagine that we were not a little shaken up that you all were so close to the enemy. I went home immediately, I didn't want to be with the others, I preferred to be alone and to have my thoughts with you. I received the other letter of April 30 on Pentecost, May 15 [6 ll.: regrets his hardships]. I don't even want to think what would happen if the *Jenkees* came here, I wouldn't know where to go with the children. Mrs. Petten says that a northern general is coming to Texas with 7,000 men, that old Magruder is also coming back, and if this is true, then maybe you will come back again too, which I would like very much [65 ll.: Petty, the Ehlerts, Müllers and Schlottmans came by to hear the news; words of comfort; signature; hymn verse; business matters] Recently in Brenham 170 bales of cotton, 2 *Waarhauser* [warehouses] and *Korn*, and now Hoffman's *Stoor* [store][30] have been burned, two southerners with northern sympathies, traitors, are said to have set fire to them, they'd already put them in *Jeel* [jail] and they were supposed to be shot, but the next morning they were gone [10 ll.: they have enough clothing]. The *Korn* for the *Guwerment* [government] hasn't been picked up yet, and Petti says they may not pick it up at all, because all the men are gone. What do you think, can I sell some more of it? I borrowed 24 dollars from Schulte for wool, but there's no rush to pay it back, *Korn* now costs 12–15 dollars.

Ehlerts, Schulte, Wehmeier, and Hermann send their best.[31] Herman has to be in Columbus on May 25, otherwise he'll be treated as a deserter, but he thinks he can get out of it again.[32] On May 6 all the sick were back in Brenham, almost all of them had been declared fit for duty, they thought maybe they could just make cartridges or take care of the wounded. Holt and Meier are still at home[. . . .] The night before Pentecost they found [Thormann] and Böcke and two others, they say that Schmit betrayed them [10 ll.: Schlottman's wife asked about him]. I asked Emilie about staying on, she said if the

---

29. Presumably they were attending Ascension Day services.

30. Probably R. Hoffmann, born around 1835, merchant from Hesse with assets valued at $6,200, according to MC 1860: Washington Co./Tex., #1111.

31. For information see n. 7.

32. Lehmann's brother Hermann, discharged in August 1862 on grounds of illness, was conscripted again toward the end of the war; see Lehmann (1983), 56–57.

war is over by Christmas she would marry Hackburg, otherwise she'll stay on.[33] [...]

LOUIS LEHMANN

New Orleans—La—June 15, 1864

Beloved Friederieke,

You are no doubt very worried about me, but for no reason, thank the Lord! I wrote 2 letters from our regiment in Louisiana, and an open one in the English language since I was taken prisoner.—I had been sent off from our *Comp*, together with another German, on detached duty that lasted 3–4 days—during my absence our regiment received marching orders and crossed the Red rivver, but we who'd been detached, we couldn't get across anymore because of the *Fed* gunboats. On Sunday May 15, the *Feds* attacked us near Marksville and chased us back some 3 miles, on Monday they took up the fight again early in the morning, our men answered with a fearsome cannonade, but they had to retreat by midday, and I was taken prisoner along with others.[34]— My horse had hardly had anything to eat for 2 days, and I hadn't eaten anything the day before, either.—The man who captured me, a *Sergeant* from a Missuri cavalry regiment, treated me just like I might have expected from a *Gentleman*. He let me keep all my private belongings (of course I had to give up my horse and saddle, but he let me ride the whole day to Gen Emory's headquarters)—then all the prisoners had to march on foot, which was not very amusing in the dust and the heat. We got the same food as the soldiers, that is *Kräckers*, some sugar, and good coffee (my coffee mug was my old companion), we marched for several more days, and when we heard cannon thundering in the distance, because our troops were harassing the *Feds*, during this time we kept marching with the vanguard of the *Fed*. army, with columns of infantry and cavalry that stretched for miles, and a lot of artillery, all marching in the utmost calm and order, certainly not to be compared with an army in defeat, and then there were the enormous wagon trains, all moving forward in an orderly fashion.—In Simsport we arrived at the Atchavalaya, where there was an entire fleet of steamboats[....] After we had waited there for one day, the 170–180 of us prisoners, Texans and Louisianans, were brought on

33. Apparently Emilie Weiss, their maid, stayed on another year; on January 1, 1866, a Henry Hackburg and "Amelie Vice" applied for a marriage license. Washington Co. Marriage Records, p. 324, microfilm, Texas StateA.

34. According the Roll of Prisoners of War in NatA, Lehmann was taken prisoner on April 18, 1864, near De Glaise; in fact it was May 16 or 18, 1864. For more information on the battle near Marksville, see Spencer (1982), 49-50.

Ludwig Lehmann's entry in the Roll of Prisoners of War of the Union army gives the wrong date of his capture but the correct date of his exchange (July 22, 1864). (National Archives, Washington, D.C.)

board a steamboat, and about 24 hours later we arrived in New Orleans, where we were put in a large, massive *Cotton* press that consists of massive buildings surrounded by a 16-foot wall[. . . .] We get 1 loaf of bread a day (made by a baker, we can't even finish it)—and ¼ [lb.] of salt beef, ½ a tin can of beans, or rice, or *Potates*, and coffee 2 times a day (bad, with chicory)—everything is cooked for us and served in the mess—there are more than 1,100 prisoners here—I was very happy to meet up with Marold's *Comp* and with Remmert, several men are sick and in the hospital, where they get better food and care and things are clean.—The officers, including A. Klaeden,[35] are in a special

35. The predominantly German Comp E, 16 Tex. Inf, in which Wm. Remmert served, was commanded by G. T. Marold, a silversmith who emigrated from Altenburg in 1851. In 1860 Adolph (A. W.) Klaeden, born in Havelberg, was working as a clerk and became first lieutenant in the company. His sister was married to Lehmann's brother Adolph. Muster Rolls, 16 Tex. Inf, Texas StateA; Geue (1970), 104; Lehmann (1983), 12, 55, 56; MC 1860: Washington Co./Tex., #11, #31.

house in the town. We sleep in bunks, 3 on top of each other like on ships, and although we have a place to wash, there's a lot of vermin.—The citizens sometimes send food and clothes for the sick. Our situation is fairly bearable, there is talk of exchange, but if disease should break out here, we would probably be sent to St. Louis, or most of the men would probably take the oath, to avoid the danger of becoming infected[36] [4 ll.: religious consolation]. *St Louis Hospital in New-Orleans*—June 30 [13 ll.: had diarrhea and swamp fever; was put into the hospital; treated very well] I thank the Lord! that I was put in the hospital and am rid of my fever—a few times the women of New-Orleans have also brought some good soup or some cake—There are good people every-where!—I've been here for a week now, and they say we will be exchanged—I would have liked to stay here for another week to regain my strength—if it doesn't affect my exchange, then I will stay here for a while, since I can't do any marching yet.

[. . .] I will do my best to find some way to come home again—Evening of July 26, 1864. Alexandria (Louisiana).

After having heard about being exchanged so many times, at midday on July 21, they suddenly said "get ready to leave" [13 ll.: exchanged for Yankee prisoners and sent by steamboat to Alexandria, Louisiana]. I had hardly set foot on land and was lying half-asleep under a tree, when A. Müller came riding up, I was very happy to see him—he is well and sends regards to his wife.—

There's a rumor that we (the prisoners) will get 60 days' leave—if I can't get any leave from headquarters, then I hope to get it from the regiment, since I don't have a horse [letter breaks off].

Near Brenham Washington Co, Texas, Jan. 1866
Mr. Friedrich Clausmeier, Warden at the Lüneburg prison.
We request that this letter please be forwarded to all our brothers and sisters / L.L.
Dearest brother-in-law,

Years have passed by without our knowing anything at all about our loved ones in the old homeland! The years of this unhappy civil war have weighed heavily upon us, but thanks be to God, His protective hand has led us all safely through it, we are all well, and our property has remained intact. We would so much have liked to send you some news, if we hadn't been cut off by the *Blokade* from the entire world, and the route via Mexico was too insecure to be used.—The news that reached Europe in the newspapers during the war,

---

36. Prisoners had the option of joining the Union army and hence coming free.

about our situation in the South, was largely exaggerated and did not reflect the truth, since all the news came from northern sources and was therefore biased.—The two big parties before the outbreak of the war in the United States were the Democrats and the Republicans, the latter were also called "Black-Republicans" because of their sympathy for the Negroes in the South and were mostly to be found in the northern states of the Union, while the Democrats were mainly in the South, but also some in the North.

In the presidential election of Nov. 1860, when the Democrats were split, the Black Republicans got their presidential candidate Abraham Lincoln elected to the presidency. The majority of the Democrats in the South did not expect good things for their slaves from the Republican majority in *Congress*, they thought they would change the *Constitution* of the United States (which protected slavery in the South and its continued existence) and set the slaves free.[37] The leaders of the Democrats, therefore, tried to stir up the people in the South against the Union (the North), and the press was of great assistance here—except for the German press.—

Speakers deluded the great masses into thinking we only needed to leave the Union (through a referendum)—everything would be peaceful, England and France would recognize us as a separate confederacy (with slavery—how absurd!), and protect us from the United States, if necessary—enough said! The people were deluded—and voted, although only by a small majority, for secession from the Union.—And now began a dark period in the history of the South, freedom had to yield to military despotism, the honorable *Patriot* Sam Houston,[38] who was governor of the state of Texas, tried in vain to prevent the people from making this ill-considered move, but all for naught, the flood could not be stemmed, he resigned from his post voluntarily, the most influential friends of the Union like Jac Hamilton and thousands of others, including many Germans, had to flee the country to save their lives [16 ll.: Confederate war measures]. In the beginning, the South raised its army from volunteers, but when the war reached such gigantic dimensions, and *Präsident* Lincoln threw his armies against almost every state in the South, the South sought refuge in *Consription*, the like of which has never been carried out in any civilized country. The first draft was for 18 to 35-year-olds, without

37. In fact, Republicans did not have a majority in Congress until southern Democrats walked out after secession, and the Lincoln administration posed no immediate threat to slavery where it existed.

38. Sam Houston (1793–1863), hero of the Texas Revolution, two-time president of the Republic of Texas, and U.S. senator from Texas for fourteen years, was elected governor in 1860, but he was removed from office (not voluntarily but without resistance) in March 1861 for refusing to swear an oath of loyalty to the Confederacy. *DAB*, 9:263–67.

making any allowances—the widow had to send her only son, the mother with 7–8 helpless children had to give up her husband. If the poor were hit by this fate, they received support from the county [40 ll.: economic disaster in the South]. This *Conscription*, which was hard enough when it started, became the crudest despotism toward the end—special search companies scoured every farm, and no men under 50 were spared—and the men over 50 were put in the militias.

Many of the men who were subject to conscription (mostly Germans) hid themselves in the woods or went to Mexico. At the start of the war, there was a severe shortage of weapons—old rusty double-barreled shotguns were used, even in the coastal batteries on Galveston Island they had logs painted to look like cannon, intended to deceive the enemy and keep them from landing.— All the imports and exports from Texas during the war went via Mexico (on wagons) and cost 30 cents per pound [8 ll.: details; end of the war]. No segment of the population rejoiced more at the coming of peace than the Germans, who hadn't had any stake in the matter anyway—the war gripped the country with an iron hand, in almost every house a husband or brother had been torn away, or even worse, was mourned after[. . . .] When the news of the surrender of the army in the eastern states arrived, our Texas army just dispersed on its own, every soldier took his gun and went home, and in the city of Houston, where there were government workshops, arsenals, ammunition depots, etc., everything was plundered by the soldiers as they were leaving. Entire wagonloads of powder were thrown in the river, and in short, the end of the southern *Confederation* gave a true picture of the entire rebellion. The main result of the war is the *Emanzipation* of the Negro—4 million blacks have received their freedom this way, and this will cause great upheaval in our agriculture.—The majority of the Negroes have signed on as farmhands, but almost all have left their former masters.—Most of the Negroes, of course, don't yet know what to do with their freedom, since without any schooling, their emancipation came too suddenly; they think that now they only have to work as much as they want to, and because of the fact that we depend solely on the blacks here, the farmers are very apprehensive—especially since immigration to Texas completely stopped at the beginning of the war. We all hope that immigration from Germany will increase tremendously, because there is a great need for workers here[. . . .] Dear brother-in-law, much as I hated to, I had to join the army and fight for a cause I never approved of. I was attached to a cavalry regiment, and I had to take part in the campaign against General Banks* in Louisiana in the spring of 1864, I witnessed a series of important battles, and in one of the last ones I was taken prisoner and transported to New-Orleans, where I was kept with about 800 other Texans until the end of

July, then exchanged and sent home (to our southern headquarters). — With
no money and sick to boot, I had to make my way with other fellow sufferers
on foot from Louisiana to the first Texas railroad station (about 150 English
miles). When I got home, so completely broken down that I couldn't walk for
a week, my wife hardly recognized me. She hadn't heard a word about my capture, because I was not in a position to send any news, and rumor had it that
I was dead. These were sorrowful times, both for me and for my wife [. . .]
but thanks be to God, it was His mercy that preserved our lives and property,
and we give thanks to Him. I received 60 days of leave when I returned, and
was not back in service through the end of the war (May 1865) — premeditated
illness — knowing the doctors — was of great assistance here. — A civil war in a
republic is the greatest misfortune that can befall a country! I expected it here
for a long time, but circumstances forced me to stay. But the existence of the
United States is now more firmly grounded than ever before, the stumbling
block of "slavery" has been cleared out of the way, and the southern states,
and in particular Texas, will soon recover from the effects of the war, since
the latter saw no enemy within its borders. — The new Präsident Johnson, who
follows a conciliatory policy toward the South, is very popular here. — There
are only a few United States troops here, just enough to keep order[. . . .] Our
Farm became quite dilapidated during the war, since nothing could be looked
after properly, and now white farmhands are not to be found anywhere! [8 ll.:
offers to finance immigrants in advance]. The Ehlerts's are still well, but the
war left an irreplaceable breach in their family, for Friedrich, who served as a
sergeant in a German company, met his death in a battle in the state of Arcansas — his parents were only able to find relief in religious consolation [17 ll.:
news; greetings; signature; address].
[FRIEDERIKE LEHMANN continues:]
Dear sister Christine
[19 ll.: family; business matters; greetings; signature].

As Lehmann's last letter suggested, the Confederate defeat caused many political
and social changes in Texas. In the first postbellum session of the state legislature,
Washington County was represented in the upper house by a former slave, Matt
Gaines, and in the lower house by a German, Lehmann's comrade-in-arms Wilhelm
Schlottman, both of whom were Republicans or "radicals." During deliberations on
a new school law, Schlottman and the half dozen other German representatives all
voted against the clause prescribing segregation.[39] But most of the idealistic plans

39. Dietrich (1973), 171–74; *House Journals of the 12th Legislature* (1870), 803. Letters by
Schlottman and other relatives were published in Kammeier (1994), 45–67; an 1869 letter (p. 57)
indicated that he had rented land to three black tenant families.

of "radical Reconstruction" foundered due to lack of funds, the enormity of the tasks, and the impatience of many citizens, including Louis Lehmann.[40] It seems that his earlier animosity toward the slaveholders was now directed more toward the freedpeople, and this change in his political sympathies is corroborated in the letter of March 15, 1875: "We are now pleased to have a good government, since the Democrats have taken the rudder; the newspapers in Germany have no doubt reported about the corrupt governments in the other southern states where the Negro party is in control of the government.—The *Civil*-Rights-*Bill* that recently passed Congress is an insult to whites and even harms the Negro, because it will cause many disputes—and be of no benefit to anyone."[41]

Lehmann's support for the Democrats was welcomed by the English-language newspaper in Brenham; it railed against the alliance of "the German vote of the county with negro-radico swindlers." Apparently, Lehmann had only recently changed party affiliations, and clearly not all Germans followed his example. Washington County remained under Republican control until 1884, with the support of most of the blacks, about half of the Germans, and a handful of courageous Anglo Americans. As long the Republican Party remained in power, blacks served as deputy sheriffs and jurors, and the local courts treated them relatively fairly. The Democrats were only able to take over in 1884 by the use of violence and threats against blacks. In the extremely close election of 1886, a Republican revival was only prevented by stealing the ballot boxes in three Republican precincts, lynching three black Republicans, and chasing three leading white Republicans out of the area. At least one of these men was German: the lawyer and editor Carl Schutze.[42]

As for Louis Lehmann, he seems to have increasingly identified himself with white southern society, far more than had been the case during the war. When he

40. On March 15, 1875, Lehmann wrote, "The state *Constitution* requires the establishment of free schools throughout the state[. . . .] The thousands of Negro children, whose parents (former slaves) own no taxable property, must therefore be educated at the expense of the whites (the property-owning classes)[. . . .] The blacks here are an expensive legacy for us!" In 1878 240 white and 256 black children were enrolled in the Brenham schools. Pennington (1915), 49. For more information on race relations in the area, see Kelley (2000).

41. The "radical" Republicans were only in power in Texas from 1870 to 1873. The Republicans in the South were neither as dominated by blacks nor as corrupt as has often been claimed. The Civil Rights Bill of 1875 prohibited racial discrimination in public transportation, inns, and restaurants, as well as on juries, but not in schools. McPherson (1982), 560–63, 576–77.

42. *Brenham Banner*, January 14, 1876; Niemann (1989), 391–420. Two years after his departure, Schutze wrote to Lehmann's brother Julius, who had helped finance his newspaper: "[I] am afraid the *Mob* will put on the same show in this election that we went through 2 years ago. Violence and intimidation will once again be the main weapons used to intimidate the Negroes and if need be control the *Ballotboxes*. What consequences does the *Mob* need to fear? The officials are the main instigators and leaders of this murderous gang[. . . .] I can imagine that these are just the rascals who are doing their best to play themselves up as friends of the Germans and stir them up against the Negroes, just as they stir up the Negroes against the Germans." Letter of Carl Schutze, August 22, 1888, NABS.

died in 1904, the obituary in the local English-language paper emphasized his status as a veteran: "He seen [*sic*] service in the Confederate army, was true to his colors and made an enviable reputation as a soldier by the promptness and fearlessly [*sic*] with which he discharged every duty assigned to him." His funeral was attended by "old comrades" from the local chapter of the Confederate veterans' association, of which he had been a "warm and fraternal" member.[43]

43. Newspaper clipping in NABS, probably from the *Brenham Banner*, published shortly after Lehmann died on April 23, 1904.

EPILOGUE: RECONSTRUCTION

Although the Civil War permanently settled the issue of slavery, much still remained to be determined in the aftermath of the war about two interrelated issues: the position of ex-slaves in the political, economic, and social system of the South and the political re-formation of the ex-Confederate states. However, it is striking how little attention was devoted to these issues in the letters written home by Germans, especially if they lived outside the areas immediately impacted by slavery.

There were exceptions, of course. John Bauer (brother of letter-writer Georg, no. 46), lived just a few miles south of the Iowa border in a Missouri county with fewer than 100 slaves in 1860, a negligible 1 percent of the population. But he proved to be well informed about national politics and fully in tune with the view of radical Republicans, when he wrote on February 2, 1867:

> Our hypocritical president, who during the time of war wrapped himself in the resplendent robes of a true friend of the Fatherland, has finally taken them off, revealing in his true light what he really is, a friend of those who tried to destroy the government with sword in hand. This baneful man has sown much evil[. . . .] He has dealt with the rebel states as if no one had any say in the matter. *Congress* disputes this right[. . . .] It is hard for them to give up their rights as American citizens, but this must happen, everything must be made anew, otherwise all the blood was shed for naught and the fruits of victory lost and it would not be long before they started selling people like cattle again.
>
> Much better a second war.[1]

Bauer continued to offer a running commentary on national politics, noting the incongruity of the Liberal Republican coalition in a letter written on Election Day 1872: "The Democratic Party has lost every election since the one in 1856; this time they resorted to a major trick & united with a certain small party which has given itself the name / liberal Republicans, / many of these people used to be the worst enemies of the Democratic Party, but since they don't see all their wishes being fulfilled by the current president,

1. Letter of John Bauer, February 2, 1867, NABS; for more on John Bauer and a wider selection of his letters see Kamphoefner, Helbich, and Sommer (1991), 149–81.

they thought that this way they could prevent his reelection, acting out of revenge & envy."[2]

Although Bauer does not mention it, among the Republican defectors were many querulous German radicals who had opposed Lincoln from the left in 1864; for all their differences with autocratic Prussia, they still missed the incorruptibility of its bureaucrats. The Liberal Republican candidate Horace Greeley presented the spectacle of a lifelong abolitionist crusader preaching reconciliation with the South—an eccentric, teetotaling fanatic trying to attract beer-drinking Germans. Carl Schurz* captured their mood on the evening of Greeley's nomination when he sat down at the piano and played Chopin's Funeral March. Mercilessly pilloried by German American caricaturist Thomas Nast, Greeley carried only six former slave states and died just a month after his humiliating defeat.[3]

John Bauer maintained his keen interest in national politics down to the end of radical Reconstruction; his analysis of the situation on February 1, 1877, penetrates to the core of the matter:

> Our presidential election is still not decided to this day & God only knows how it will be decided. The fight is now in *Congress*[. . . .] The campaign was so heated that one candidate only had one more [electoral] vote than the other. Both sides accuse the other of fraud. In the slave states, the blacks were forced under threat of their lives to vote like the ones who have the upper hand wanted them to & many were shot & hanged. It is shameful, even heart-rending, the atrocities committed during this election.[4]

Although it may have escaped Bauer's notice, southern society was not entirely polarized along racial lines during Reconstruction. About one-fifth of all southern whites voted Republican in 1872, and they, in turn, made up about one-fifth of all Republican voters in the region. Like the wartime unionists from whose ranks they often came, they were concentrated in several heterogeneous positions outside the southern mainstream: conservative former Whig planters who were often reluctant secessionists; white yeomen from the poorer hill-country areas of the South outside the plantation districts, who often had little use for planters or their slaves; and in the few areas where they were present, Germans and perhaps other immigrants as

2. Letter of John Bauer, November 3, 1872, NABS.

3. Nagler (1989b), 415–38, esp. 416 n. 4, 428; Foner (1988), 488–511.

4. Kamphoefner, Helbich, and Sommer (1991), 178. Bauer's view of the election is confirmed by Foner (1988), 564–82, and McPherson (1982), 598–604.

well. This was especially true in Missouri, which elected Republican Carl Schurz to the U.S. Senate in 1868. Likewise, in Texas, another Forty-eighter, Edward Degener—whose two sons died trying to flee the Confederacy (see the Cramer-Simon letters, no. 55)—served as a Republican congressman from the San Antonio area. Similarly, in New Orleans, German-born Michael Hahn was one of the leading Republicans.[5]

As has been seen in this volume, Germans who lived in former slave states did comment occasionally on various aspects of Reconstruction politics and race relations. But the most striking impression from this collection of letters is how rarely other writers' mental horizons extended below the Mason-Dixon Line once the actual war was over. In this edition, any substantive comments by letter-writers on issues of race or sectional politics in the Reconstruction era have either been reproduced in the infrequent letters dated after 1865, or they have been excerpted in the editors' note following a given letter series. In most instances, the silence is deafening. True, post-1865 letters have survived for only about half of all the writers included in this volume, in some instances because the writer himself was deceased, or in a few cases because a writer had been reunited with the wife to whom he had been writing. There are three instances where a soldier who was writing back to Germany survived through the war and many years thereafter (Horstmann [no. 13], Martens [no. 38], Schorse [no. 42]), but only the war letters have been preserved—an indirect indicator of the relative importance that some recipients, though perhaps not the writers themselves, placed on the war in comparison to its aftermath. But the surviving post-1865 letters of approximately half of the writers in this volume give unambiguous if mute testimony to the low level of interest in events and developments in the postwar South on the part of all but a handful of writers in the North. This is all the more striking in contrast to the high level of interest found at all levels of immigrant society in the wars of German unification under Bismarck in 1866 and 1870–71, and the numerous comments these events elicited in letters home.[6] If German immigrants were at all similar to their Anglo neighbors in the North, these letters add to the mounting evidence that the failure of Reconstruction resulted not only from white southern hostility but also from northern indifference.

5. Foner (1988), 46–50, 182, 297–305; Campbell (1997), 45, 207.

6. Kamphoefner (1997), 105–6; Kamphoefner, Helbich, and Sommer (1991), 141–42, 169, 430, 485–86.

GLOSSARY

BANKS, NATHANIEL P. (1816–94): Without any military training when appointed a major general of volunteers by President Lincoln in January 1861, Banks had little success as a commander, but as an influential politician at the state and national levels he contributed considerably in terms of money, recruiting, and beating the drum for the Union cause.

BLAIR, FRANCIS P., JR. (1821–75): A lawyer and politician in St. Louis, Blair was elected to the U.S. Congress in 1856 as a Free Soil candidate with strong German support. Although a slave owner, he opposed the expansion of slavery and played an important role, with the cooperation of local Germans, in keeping Missouri in the Union. He became one of the more competent "political generals."

BLENKER, LUDWIG (LOUIS) (1812–63): Born in Worms, Hesse, Blenker fled Germany due to his involvement in the 1848 revolution and settled in New York as a farmer. His reputation as a revolutionary helped him raise a German American regiment under his command (8th New York Infantry). In August 1861 he was appointed a brigadier general of volunteers, and he commanded a brigade and then a division at the first battle of Manassas. His headquarters was best known for its pomp and luxury. After the battle of Cross Keys, he received his honorable discharge and died six months later.

BUTLER, BENJAMIN F. (1818–93): A successful Boston lawyer, Butler served as a Democrat in the Massachusetts state legislature. As a delegate to the Democratic national convention in 1860 he voted for Jefferson Davis and John C. Breckinridge, but in the course of the war he became a Republican. Five days after the fall of Fort Sumter, his 8th Massachusetts Infantry relieved the almost defenseless capital city of Washington, and shortly thereafter, he was the first to receive the rank of major general of volunteers. From May to December 1862 he was military governor of New Orleans. As an administrator he was quite effective, if highly controversial: he and his family and friends made large amounts of money. Despite a series of failures as a commander, he continued to serve in the east until January 1865.

CHANCELLORSVILLE, VIRGINIA, BATTLE OF (MAY 1–6, 1863): General Joseph Hooker, commander of the Army of the Potomac (some 134,000 strong), halted his advance at Chancellorsville to wait and see whether the

Confederate Army of Northern Virginia (a force of 61,000 led by General Robert E. Lee) would advance or withdraw. In a daring maneuver, Lee left only 15,000 men to confront Hooker's main force and sent 30,000 men under "Stonewall" Jackson on a twelve-mile march through a seemingly impenetrable wilderness of woods and underbrush. These troops surrounded Hooker's right flank and attacked O. O. Howard's XI Corps from the west. Most of these regiments were facing south at the time, unprepared, and as evening approached, many of the men were relaxing or cooking supper. They were so thoroughly routed that it was impossible to bring up reinforcements for several hours. The fact that this corps consisted primarily of German regiments, already regarded as mediocre, dealt a crushing blow to their reputation. After two days of continued fighting, Hooker finally retreated. He had lost 17,000 men, and the Confederates suffered 13,000 casualties. This clear defeat was a shock to the northerners, and their morale plunged. And southerners mourned the loss of Jackson, who had been fatally wounded.

COPPERHEADS: This pejorative term was first used in July 1861 by the *New York Tribune* to refer to members of the "Peace" faction of the Democratic Party who advocated the immediate negotiation of a settlement with the South. The term was created by their political opponents; referring to a poisonous snake that hides and strikes without warning, it was used to accuse the "peace Democrats" of disloyalty.

CRIMINALZEITUNG: This German-language weekly newspaper appeared from 1852 to 1911 under titles that changed frequently and were often variations on "*New Yorker Criminal-Zeitung*" or "*Belletristisches Journal*" or some combination of the two. The publication was widely read by Germans throughout the country, had a wartime circulation of approximately 4,000, and was known for its quality journalism. Letter-writer Albert Krause (no. 22) wrote some war reports for the paper.

DRAFT RIOTS, NEW YORK (JULY 13–16, 1863): Four days of escalating mob violence in New York City, set off by protests against conscription, amounted to the worst riot in American history. Irish immigrants, in particular, caused considerable property damage, burning Protestant churches, missions, and most notoriously, an orphanage where 237 black children barely escaped with their lives. Eleven African Americans were killed (far fewer than reported at the time), and about the same number of policemen and soldiers died in the fight to quell the uprising, along with more than eighty rioters.

ENGLISH: Many German immigrants and German Americans, even some educated ones, used "English," "Englishman", and "the English" when they meant "American" or "Anglo American." The reason is simple: they designated neighbors and strangers by the language they spoke. Still, occasionally they did mean what they said, using the term to refer to persons from Britain (or Canada, a British possession), and sometimes it is impossible to decide exactly which is meant.

FORREST, NATHAN B. (1821–77): A self-made man from Tennessee, Forrest grew rich as a slave trader and cotton planter, and he raised and equipped a Confederate cavalry unit at his own expense. A long string of successes, some of them quite spectacular, led to continuous advancement, and in February 1865 he became lieutenant general. Forrest had a legendary reputation as a cavalry officer, and many specialists still consider him the best cavalryman who ever lived. He was also responsible, however, for the massacre of Fort Pillow (April 12, 1864), in which his troops slaughtered more than 300 black soldiers after they had surrendered. This—and the fact that he later founded the Ku Klux Klan—has earned him the deserved reputation as an extreme advocate of white supremacy.

FORT FISHER: In late 1864 there was only one gap left on the Atlantic coast that could be used by blockade runners: the Cape Fear River, gateway to Wilmington, North Carolina, some twenty miles upstream. Fort Fisher stood guard on the coast at the entrance to the river, massive and heavily armed.

FORT(RESS) MONROE: The fort built at the tip of the Virginia peninsula formed by the James and York Rivers remained in Union hands. It was used to land the troops sent down the Chesapeake Bay to mount General George B. McClellan's Peninsula campaign (April–June 1862) to take Richmond from the southeast.

FREDERICKSBURG, BATTLE OF (DECEMBER 13, 1862): The Union Army of the Potomac, commanded by General A. E. Burnside, tried in vain to storm the Confederate positions that were located behind the town, on high ground and behind good cover. The Union army suffered one of its worst defeats of the war—some 12,700 casualties (out of 105,000)—while the Confederates under Lee and Jackson lost 5,300 out of 72,500 men.

FRÉMONT, JOHN C. (1813–90): After attending college in Charleston, South Carolina (1829–31), Frémont became a mathematics teacher in the navy and then a mapmaker in the army (1838). Before his resignation from the army in 1848, he was part of several important expeditions to explore and survey the West. He ran unsuccessfully as the first Republican presidential candidate in the 1856 elections, and in 1861 he was appointed major general and commander of the Department of the West by Lincoln. On August 30, 1861, he issued his own startling emancipation edict, freeing the slaves of all Confederate activists in Missouri. This won Frémont praise from Germans and abolitionists but led Lincoln to remove him from command—one of the factors precipitating his abortive candidacy for president as a radical emancipationist in 1864.

GETTYSBURG, BATTLE OF (JULY 1–3, 1863): Hoping to score a political victory in the North and abroad, General Robert E. Lee had invaded Pennsylvania. On the first day the predominantly German XI Corps of the Union army was routed, as they had been at Chancellorsville,* but Union forces withdrew to a strong defensive position resembling a fishhook. The last major Confederate offensive on the third day, Pickett's charge against the Union center, collapsed with a loss of nearly half those engaged. The casualties sustained in these three days of fighting were immense: the Federals lost 23,000 out of 85,000 men, and the Confederates 28,000 out of 75,000.

GRIERSON, BENJAMIN H. (1826–1911): Before the war, Grierson was a music teacher and a merchant. As commander of the 6th Illinois Cavalry during the Vicksburg* campaign in April 1863, he was ordered by General Ulysses S. Grant on a diversionary expedition into the heart of Mississippi with a 1,700-man brigade. He covered some 600 miles in sixteen days, fighting and winning many skirmishes, tearing up telegraph and railroad lines, and burning a large number of freight cars and depots, before rejoining the Union forces near Baton Rouge. This spectacular raid, which confused the enemy and allowed Grant to cross the Mississippi unopposed, drew great acclaim in the North, and Grierson was promoted to brigadier general of volunteers.

GUILDER: A unit of currency (abbreviated fl.) worth forty-one cents, used in many German states and the Netherlands in the nineteenth century.

HECKER, FRIEDRICH (1811–81): A lawyer who was actively involved in the 1848 revolution in Baden, Hecker immigrated and settled on a farm near Belleville, Illinois. He was active in the Republican campaigns of 1856 and 1860 and joined the Union army as a private. He was promoted to colonel but then had a falling out with his superior officer and resigned. He later commanded the (German) 82nd Illinois Infantry.

KRYZANOWSKI, VLADIMIR (1827–87): Born in Prussian-Poland, Kryzanowski immigrated to the United States in 1846. He raised and commanded a German-Polish regiment (58th New York Infantry, the "Polish Legion") and was appointed brigadier general in November 1862.

LATIN FARMERS: This term was used to designate well-educated, politically idealistic German immigrants who bought farms in the United States, even though they often knew more about Latin than about farming. After all the money they had brought with them from Germany was used up, many had a very hard time of it, and some came to a tragic end.

MAXIMILIAN VON HABSBURG (1832–67): The cultivated and sophisticated archduke of Austria was the younger brother of the Austrian emperor, Francis Joseph I. In a scheme devised in part by the French emperor, Napoleon III, a deputation of conservative Mexicans offered Maximilian the imperial throne. He accepted and sailed to Mexico in the spring of 1864, accompanied by French and Austrian troops. Once on the throne, he tried hard to implement a range of liberal reforms. Even before his arrival, however, the U.S. Congress had declared that the United States would not tolerate the establishment of a monarchy in Mexico. Internal political strife and the departure of the French troops (in March 1867), sealed his fate: he was tried by a Mexican military tribunal and executed on June 19, 1867. In the United States many regarded him as an autocratic invader of democratic North America, in blatant violation of the Monroe Doctrine.

NEW MARKET, BATTLE OF (MAY 15, 1864): This battle ended General Franz Sigel's* attempt to march his Union troops through the Shenandoah Valley. Having sustained heavy casualties, he was forced to retreat to Strasburg, Virginia, and shortly thereafter, he was relieved of his command.

OSTERHAUS, PETER JOSEPH (1823–1917): Born in Koblenz, Osterhaus was a Prussian officer who supported the 1848 revolution and was forced to flee the following year. After several stops along the way, he settled in St. Louis. In 1861 he served as a major and then a colonel in Missouri, and in 1862, having been promoted to brigadier general (volunteers) he fought in various battles in the western theater—Vicksburg,* Chattanooga (Missionary Ridge), and, by this time major general, in the Atlanta campaign, as well as on Sherman's march to Savannah and through South Carolina. After the war Osterhaus worked in the U.S. consulate in France and then in Germany, where he died. The most successful foreign-born commander in the Union army was not the politically influential Carl Schurz* or the hapless Franz Sigel,* so well loved by German Americans, but Osterhaus.

PAROLE: During the Civil War this term referred to the release of prisoners on word of honor. Under normal conditions, this meant that parolees could only return to fight in their units when they had been exchanged for soldiers from the other side.

PORT HUDSON, LOUISIANA (MAY 27–JULY 9, 1863): A fortified town about twenty-five miles north of Baton Rouge, Port Hudson was the last Confederate stronghold on the Mississippi River. On May 27, 1863, Union troops launched an unsuccessful attack and then began a siege of the town. On July 9, 1863, as a consequence of the fall of Vicksburg,* Port Hudson and its garrison of 15,000 troops formally surrendered to Major General Nathaniel P. Banks.*

ROSECRANS, WILLIAM S. (1819–98): A descendant of eighteenth-century Dutch immigrants, the West Point graduate (class of 1842) from Ohio served in the engineering corps until 1854, when he resigned to become an architect and civil engineer. In early 1861 he was appointed brigadier general in the regular army and gained renown in western Virginia. In the summer of 1862, now a major general (volunteers), he began his celebrated campaign in Tennessee that forced the Confederates under General Braxton Bragg into Chattanooga and then back out of the city. He was blamed, however, for the disastrous defeat at Chickamauga (September 19–20, 1862) and was replaced by Ulysses S. Grant. This effectively ended Rosecrans's role in the war; in 1867 he resigned his commission.

SCHURZ, CARL (1829–1906): Schurz, a university student and participant in the 1848 revolution, escaped from the besieged fortress at Rastatt and fled to England, and finally immigrated to the United States, arriving in 1852. He joined the Republican Party at an early date, was a delegate to the 1860 Republican national convention, and campaigned for Lincoln as an orator. He was then appointed minister to Spain, but in early 1862 he returned to join the Union army as a brigadier general of volunteers. In recognition of his services, he advanced to major general in March 1863. A lifelong reformer and journalist, he represented Missouri in the U.S. Senate from 1869 to 1875, and from 1877 to 1881 he served as secretary of the interior under President Rutherford B. Hayes.

SHILOH, BATTLE OF (APRIL 6–7, 1862): After capturing Fort Donelson, General Ulysses Grant marched south to Pittsburg Landing on the Tennessee River, where he encamped his troops. Here he was surprised by a massive assault that almost pushed his troops into the river. The next day, the Union forces regained the ground they had lost, and the Confederates withdrew to Corinth, Mississippi. Although both sides suffered casualties that were roughly equal (10,000 men) and both sides claimed victory, the Confederates gave up the field and most of Tennessee, and a route to dividing the South via the Mississippi River had been opened.

SIGEL, FRANZ (1824–1902): Sigel graduated first in his class at the military academy in Karlsruhe and served in the Baden army until 1847. He became minister of war of the 1848 revolutionaries and, after their defeat, escaped to the United States. At the outbreak of the Civil War he was a teacher in St. Louis, where in August 1861 he was appointed brigadier general in the Union army. He took part in campaigns in Missouri and Arkansas, and then in March 1862 he was promoted to major general and ordered east. There he served as corps and division commander, but with so little success that he was relieved of his command in May 1864. Despite this, most German Americans idolized him.

SUTLER: An officially appointed civilian vendor was attached to each regiment of the Union and Confederate army and allowed to sell the soldiers approved items such as tobacco, foodstuffs, reading material, and other provisions, often supplying credit and unauthorized alcohol as well. Enjoying a monopoly, they had a reputation for cheating and price gouging.

TALER: A unit of German currency worth 71.4 cents, but the term was often used to mean a U.S. dollar.

TURNER: The Turner movement came to the United States with the Forty-eighters, and before the beginning of the Civil War, there were more than 100 organizations (*Turnvereine*) of Turners in the United States. Following the teachings of the original founder of the movement, Friedrich Ludwig Jahn (1778–1852), activities focused on gymnastics and physical fitness, but members also tended to be freethinkers and political activists who were deeply committed to republican ideals. In 1860 the national organization supported Lincoln in the 1860 election, and when his first call for volunteers was issued, many Turners living in the cities—usually healthy young men just the right age for recruitment—joined the Union army en masse. They made up sixteen German regiments and played an important role, especially at the beginning of the war.

VICKSBURG CAMPAIGN (JUNE 1862–JULY 4, 1863): No other Independence Day was celebrated with such relief and jubilation in the North as July 4, 1863. The previous day had brought news of the decisive victory at Gettysburg* and of the pending capitulation of heavily fortified Vicksburg on the Mississippi River. Set on 200-foot bluffs impervious to gunboats, this fortress had withstood attacks from several quarters during the winter of 1862–63. But in the spring Grant mounted a brilliant amphibious campaign that ended in a successful siege. With the enemy confused by Grierson's* raid, Grant marched his troops down the west bank of the river, then ferried them across unopposed on April 30 with transports that had run the batteries at Vicksburg. Abandoning his supply lines and living off the land, Grant struck inland toward Jackson, marched 180 miles in two weeks, and defeated several divided Confederate forces nearly as large as his own, then swung back and enveloped Vicksburg on May 17. When direct assaults failed, the Union settled down for a six-week siege. It ended with the surrender of 30,000 troops, opening the Mississippi for its entire length and cutting the Confederacy in two.

BIBLIOGRAPHY

Archival Sources

Germany
  Address Books
    Braunschweig, 1846
    Schwerin, 1859–61
  Archives
    Brandenburgisches Landeshauptarchiv Potsdam
    Gemeindearchiv Heumaden
    Generallandesarchiv Karlsruhe
    Hessisches Staatsarchiv Darmstadt
    Landesarchiv Schleswig
    Landeskirchliches Archiv Stuttgart
    Mecklenburgisches Landeshauptarchiv Schwerin
    Niedersächsisches Staatsarchiv Oldenburg
    Niedersächsisches Staatsarchiv Wolfenbüttel
    Stadtarchiv Braunschweig
    Stadtarchiv Eberbach/Neckar
    Stadtarchiv Ehingen
    Staatsarchiv Hamburg
    Stadtarchiv Korntal-Münchingen
  Newspapers and Periodicals
    Der Gemeinnützige (Varel), 1863
    Lahrer Hinkender Bote, 1863
    Warnemünder Zeitung, 1895
  Parish Registers (Kirchenbücher)
    Evangelical
      Abbenrode
      Alten Buseck
      Bietigheim
      Dresden, Dreikönigsgemeinde
      Eberbach
      Elxleben
      Engelrod
      Lombach
      Mahlum
      Ritzebüttel
      Rodenkirchen

        Röhrenfurth
        Stade, St. Wilhelmi
        Unterschefflenz
    Roman Catholic
        Haslach
        Schiffweiler
  Passenger Lists
    Hamburg Passenger Lists, 1857, 1860, 1861, Staatsarchiv Hamburg
United States
  State and Local Archives
    Center for American History, University of Texas at Austin, Austin, Tex.
      Barthels Papers
      Hander Papers
      Lehmann Papers
      Voigt Family Papers
    Houston Public Library, Houston, Tex.
    Indiana Historical Society, Indianapolis, Ind.
      Brucker Papers
    Maryland State Archives, Baltimore, Md.
    Minnesota State Archives, St. Paul, Minn.
      Rochester State Hospital Case Books
    Missouri State Archives, Jefferson City, Mo.
      Muster Rolls and Pension Files
        10 Provisional Regiment Enrolled Missouri Militia
        27 Enrolled Missouri Militia
        54 Enrolled Missouri Militia
        75 Mounted Infantry Enrolled Missouri Militia
        Franklin County Home Guards
        St. Charles County Home Guards
    Nodaway County Courthouse Maryville, Mo.
      Deed Books
    St. Louis City Hall, St. Louis, Mo.
      Marriages
    Texas State Archives, Austin, Tex.
      A. J. Hamilton Papers
      Muster Rolls and Pension Files
        16 Texas Infantry
        Waul's Legion
      Texas County Records, microfilm
    University of North Carolina Library, Southern Historical Collection, Chapel
      Hill, N.C.
      Kock Papers
    Washington Historical Society, Washington, Mo.

Western Historical Manuscript Collection, Columbia, Mo.

U.S. National Archives, Washington, D.C.

Muster Rolls and Pension Files

Regimental Books

29 Michigan Infantry (Descriptive Books)

45 New York Infantry (Order Book)

116 New York Infantry (Morning Reports)

35/74 Pennsylvania Infantry (Order Books)

Record Group 59—Records of the Department of State

Notes from Foreign Consuls, M664

Record Group 92—Records of the Office of the Quartermaster General

8w2A, Box 3, 1403

Record Group 94—Records of the Adjutant General's Office

Adjutant General, New York, Box 3073

Adjutant General's Office, Enlistment Papers: U.S. Army

Adjutant General's Office, 1862, W620, Box 154

Krauseneck Trial, February 1–3, 1864, Courts-Martial, Box 588 No P-2935 VS 1864

War Department, Special Orders Nos. 31, 49

Enlisted Branch Letters Received, 130-100-1865, 9w3, R23, c. 31, Series 13,409, Box 290 (Steamer North America)

Record Group 153—Records of the Office of the Judge Advocate General

Betge Trial, Court-Martial Case File, KK 407

F. Brunner Trial, Judge Advocate General, Courts-Martial, NN 131, Files 1809–1994

Turner-Baker Papers, M797, Roll 129, Baker

City Directories

Chicago, 1858, 1865–90

Houston, 1867–68

Milwaukee, 1858/59–1860/61

New York (Manhattan), 1853/54, 1861, 1946

Peoria, Illinois, 1882/83–1901/2

Philadelphia, 1862–82

St. Louis, 1879–1910

Washington, D.C., 1862–66, 1870

Will County, Illinois, 1859/60

Manuscript Census

The U.S. Manuscript Census is available in National Archives microfilm publications. Footnote citations include sufficient information to locate an individual state; county; township, ward, or enumeration district; and family or page number.

Minnesota State Census Manuscripts, 1885, Minnesota Historical Society, St. Paul, Minn.

Newspapers
    Anzeiger des Westens (St. Louis), 1866
    Baltimore Morning Star, 1885
    Bellville (Tex.) Countryman, 1860–62
    Brenham (Tex.) Banner, 1876, 1904
    Buffalo (N.Y.) Courier, 1913
    Cape Girardeau (Mo.) Democrat, 1892
    Jackson (Mo.) Deutscher Volksfreund, 1892
    La Grange (Tex.) State Rights Democrat, 1861
    Neu Braunfelser (Tex.) Zeitung, 1863, 1865
    New York Times, 1858, 1860–65, 1882, 1887, 1896, 1898, 1913, 1916
    New Yorker Criminal-Zeitung und Belletristisches Journal, 1863–64
    St. Charles (Mo.) Demokrat, 1861–70
Parish Registers (Kirchenbücher)
    St. Paul's Lutheran, New Melle, Mo.
Passenger Lists
    New York, 1849, 1851–54, 1857, 1860–62
    New Orleans, 1854
Published U.S. Census Returns
    Cited according to the numbering in *Bibliography and Reel Index: A Guide to the Microfilm Edition of United States Decennial Census Publications, 1790–1970*. Woodbridge, Conn.: Research Publications Inc., 1975.
    USC 1850.1
    USC 1860.1
    USC 1870.1
    USC A 1860.1
    USC M 1860.1

Published Sources

Andreas, Alfred Theodore. 1885. *History of Chicago*. Vol. 2. Chicago.
———. 1886. *History of Chicago*. Vol. 3. Chicago.
Arndt, Karl J. R., and May E. Olson. 1965. *German-American Newspapers and Periodicals, 1732–1955: History and Bibliography*. London, U.K.
Auspurg-Hackert, Dagmar. 1984. "Deutsche Auswanderung nach Texas im 19. Jahrhundert." Ph.D. diss., Ruhr-Universität Bochum.
Bacarella, Michael. 1996. *Lincoln's Foreign Legion: The 39th New York Infantry, the Garibaldi Guard*. Shippensburg, Pa.
Bailey, Anne J. 2001. "Defiant Unionists: Militant Germans in Confederate Texas." In *Enemies of the Country: New Perspectives on Unionists in the Civil War South*, edited by John C. Inscoe and Robert C. Kenzer, 208–28. Athens, Ga.
Barclay, R. E. 1946. *Ducktown Back in Raht's Time*. Chapel Hill, N.C.
Barr, Alwyn. 1969. "Records of the Confederate Military Commission in San Antonio, July 2–October 10, 1862." *Southwestern Historical Quarterly* 73:143–74.

Basler, Roy P., ed. 1953. *The Collected Works of Abraham Lincoln*. Vol. 5. New Brunswick, N.J.

Beiträge zur Statistik der inneren Verwaltung des Großherzogtums Baden. 1855. Vol. 1. Karlsruhe.

Beiträge zur Statistik der inneren Verwaltung des Großherzogtums Baden. 1857. Vol. 5. Karlsruhe.

Bennett, Bob. 1956. *Kerr County, Texas: 1856–1956*. San Antonio, Tex.

Bergeron, Arthur, Jr. 1989. *Guide to Louisiana Confederate Military Units, 1861–1865*. Baton Rouge, La.

Bergquist, James M. 1971. "People and Politics in Transition: Illinois Germans, 1850–1860." In *Ethnic Voters and the Election of Lincoln*, edited by Frederick C. Luebke, 196–226. Lincoln, Neb.

———. 1989. "The Forty-Eighters and the Republican Convention of 1860." In *The German Forty-Eighters in the United States*, edited by Charlotte L. Brancaforte, 141–56. New York.

Bernstein, Iver. 1990. *The New York City Draft Riots: Their Significance for American Society and Politics in the Age of the Civil War*. New York.

Bibliography and Reel Index: A Guide to the Microfilm Edition of United States Decennial Census Publications, 1790–1970. 1975. Woodbridge, Conn.

Biesele, Rudolph. 1987. *The History of the German Settlements in Texas, 1831–1861*. San Marcos, Tex.

Biographical Directory of the Indiana General Assembly, I. 1980. Indianapolis, Ind.

Biographical Sketches of the Members of the 42nd General Assembly of the State of Indiana. 1861. Indianapolis, Ind.

Biographisches Lexikon der herausragenden Ärzte aller Zeiten und Völker. 1962 [1929]. Vol. 5. Munich and Berlin.

Blum, Virgil C. 1948. "The Political and Military Activities of the German Element in St. Louis, 1859–61." *Missouri Historical Review* 42:103–29.

Boatner, Mark W. 1959. *Civil War Dictionary*. New York.

Boehm, Theodora Vanderwerth. 2001. "Robert Zapp, German Texan Politician." M.A. thesis, Texas A&M University.

Boethel, Paul C. 1965. *The Big Guns of Fayette*. Austin, Tex.

Brancaforte, Charlotte L., ed. 1989. *The German Forty-Eighters in the United States*. New York.

Brandeis, Louis D. 1971. *Letters of Louis D. Brandeis, Vol. I: 1870–1907*. Albany, N.Y.

Brandel, Friedrich. 1901. "Geschichtliche Mitteilungen aus Peoria." *Deutsch-Amerikanische Geschichtsblätter* 1:22–24.

Breitenkamp, Edward C., and Jack Autrey Dabbs, eds. 1985. *Church Records of the Pioneer German Families of Berlin, Texas*. Bryan, Tex.

Briegleb, Klaus, ed. 1968. *Heinrich Heine. Sämtliche Schriften*. Vol. 1. Munich.

———. 1975. *Heinrich Heine. Sämtliche Schriften*. Vol. 6. Munich.

Bright, Eric W. 1999. "'Nothing to Fear from the Influence of Foreigners': The Patriotism of Richmond's German-Americans during the Civil War." M.A. thesis, Virginia Tech University.

Brinkmann, Tobias. 2004. "The Dialectics of Ethnic Identity: German Jews in Chicago, 1850–1870." In *German-American Immigration and Ethnicity in Comparative Perspective*, edited by Wolfgang Helbich and Walter D. Kamphoefner, 44–68. Madison, Wis.

Brown, Thaddeus C. S., Samuel J. Murphy, and William G. Putney. 2000 [1965]. *Behind the Guns: The History of Battery I, 2nd Regiment, Illinois Light Artillery.* Edited by Clyde C. Walton. Carbondale, Ill.

Buenger, Walter L. 1979a. "Secession and the Texas German Community: Editor Lindheimer vs. Editor Flake." *Southwestern Historical Quarterly* 82:379–402.

———. 1979b. "Stilling the Voice of Reason: Texas and the Union, 1854–1861." Ph.D. diss., Rice University.

———. 1984. *Secession and the Union in Texas.* Austin, Tex.

Burnham, Walter D. 1955. *Presidential Ballots, 1836–1892.* Baltimore, Md.

Burton, William L. 1988. *Melting Pot Soldiers: The Union's Ethnic Regiments.* Ames, Iowa.

Byrne, Frank L., and Jean Powers Soman, eds. 1985. *Your True Marcus: The Civil War Letters of a Jewish Colonel.* Kent, Ohio.

Campbell, Randolph B. 1997. *Grass-Roots Reconstruction in Texas, 1865–1880.* Baton Rouge, La.

Capers, H. D. 1893. *The Life and Times of C. G. Memminger.* Richmond, Va.

Catalfamo, Catherine. 1989. "The Thorny Rose: The Americanization of an Urban, Immigrant, Working-Class Regiment in the Civil War: A Social History of the Garibaldi Guard, 1861–1864." Ph.D. diss., University of Texas at Austin.

Cheeseman, Bruce S., ed. 2002. *Maria von Blücher's Corpus Christi: Letters from the South Texas Frontier, 1849–1879.* College Station, Tex.

Clark, John E. 2001. *Railroads in the Civil War: The Impact of Management on Victory and Defeat.* Baton Rouge, La.

Clark, Robert T., Jr. 1980 [1937]. "The New Orleans German Colony in the Civil War." In *Die deutschsprachige Presse der Amerikas*, edited by Karl J. R. Arndt and May E. Olson, 3:661–88. Munich. [Reprinted from *Louisiana Historical Quarterly* 20:990–1015.]

Clinton, Catherine. 1999. *Public Women and the Confederacy.* Milwaukee, Wis.

Cole, Garold L. 1988. *Civil War Eyewitnesses: An Annotated Bibliography of Books and Articles, 1955–1986.* Columbia, S.C.

———. 2000. *Civil War Eyewitnesses: An Annotated Bibliography of Books and Articles, 1986–1996.* Columbia, S.C.

Cook, Adrian. 1974. *The Armies of the Streets: The New York City Draft Riots of 1863.* Lexington, Ky.

Cunz, Dieter. 1948. *The Maryland Germans: A History.* Port Washington, N.Y.

Current, Richard N. 1976. *The History of Wisconsin: The Civil War Era.* Madison, Wis.

Dean, Eric T. 1997. *Shook over Hell: Post-Traumatic Stress, Vietnam, and the Civil War.* Cambridge, Mass.

Deiler, Hanno J. 1980 [1901]. "Geschichte der New Orleanser Deutschen Presse." In

Die deutschsprachige Presse der Amerikas, edited by Karl J. R. Arndt and May E. Olson, 3:617–60. Munich.

Dennett, Tyler, ed. 1939. *Lincoln and the Civil War in the Diaries and Letters of John Hay*. New York.

Dictionary of American Biography. 1927–36. Edited by Allen Johnson and Dumas Malone. 20 vols. New York.

Dictionary of American Naval Fighting Ships. 1963. Vol. 2. Washington, D.C.

Dietrich, Wilfred O. 1973. *The Blazing Story of Washington County*. Rev. ed. Wichita Falls, Tex.

Domschcke, Bernhard. 1987. *Twenty Months in Captivity: Memoirs of a Union Officer in Confederate Prisons*. Edited and translated by Frederic Trautmann. Rutherford, N.J.

Draper, Hal, trans. 1982. *The Complete Poems of Heinrich Heine*. Cambridge, Mass.

Dünnebacke, Anton. 1938. *Geschichte der Familie Dünnebacke*. Bigge.

Dyer, Frederick A., ed. 1959 [1908]. *A Compendium of the War of the Rebellion*. Washington, D.C.

Eaton, Clement. 1964. *The Freedom-of-Thought Struggle in the Old South*. New York.

Ehlmann, Steve. 2004. *Crossroads: A History of St. Charles County, Missouri*. St. Charles, Mo.

Elliott, Claude. 1947. "Union Sentiment in Texas, 1861–1865." *Southwestern Historical Quarterly* 50:449–77.

Engle, Stephen D. 1993. *Yankee Dutchman: The Life of Franz Sigel*. Fayetteville, Ark.

Ernst, Robert. 1949. *Immigrant Life in New York City*. New York.

Faust, Patricia L., ed. 1986. *Historical Times Illustrated Encyclopedia of the Civil War*. New York.

Fehrenbacher, Don E. 1981. *Slavery, Law, and Politics: The Dred Scott Case in Historical Perspective*. Oxford, U.K.

Foner, Eric. 1988. *Reconstruction: America's Unfinished Revolution, 1863–1877*. New York.

Formisano, Ronald P. 1971. "Ethnicity and Party in Michigan, 1854–1860." In *Ethnic Voters and the Election of Lincoln*, edited by Frederick C. Luebke, 175–95. Lincoln, Neb.

Förster, Stig, and Jörg Nagler, eds. 1997. *On the Road to Total War: The American Civil War and the German Wars of Unification, 1861–1871*. Cambridge, U.K.

Fredrickson, George M. 1971. *The Black Image in the White Mind: The Debate on Afro-American Character and Destiny, 1817–1914*. New York.

Friedrich, Carl J. 1950. "The European Background." In *The Forty-Eighters: Political Refugees of the German Revolution of 1848*, edited by Adolph E. Zucker, 3–25. New York.

Geary, James W. 1991. *We Need Men: The Union Draft in the Civil War*. DeKalb, Ill.

Genealogical Abstracts from Kendall County, Texas Probate Records. 1986. Boerne, Tex.

Gerstein, Ludwig. 1934. *Geschichte der Familie Gerstein*. N.p.

Geue, Ethel Hander. 1966. *A New Land Beckoned: German Immigration to Texas, 1844–1847*. Waco, Tex.

——. 1970. *New Homes in a New Land: German Immigration to Texas, 1847–1861.* Waco, Tex.

Gienapp, William E. 1986. "Who Voted for Lincoln?" In *Abraham Lincoln and the American Political Tradition*, edited by John L. Thomas, 50–97. Amherst, Mass.

Glazier, Ira A., and P. William Filby, eds. 1988–. *Germans to America: Lists of Passengers Arriving at U.S. Ports.* 67 vols. to date. Wilmington, Del.

Gonner, Nicholas. 1985–86 [1889]. *Die Luxemburger in der Neuen Welt: Illustrierte Neuausgabe in 2 Bänden.* Edited by Jean Ensch, Carlo Hury, and Jean-Claude Muller. Esch-sur-Alzette, Luxembourg.

——. 1987. *Luxembourgers in the New World.* Edited by Jean Ensch, Jean-Claude Muller, and Robert E. Owen; translated by Gerald L. Liebenau and Jean-Claude Muller. Vol. 1. Esch-sur-Alzette, Luxembourg.

Goode, James. 1979. *Capital Losses: A Cultural History of Washington's Destroyed Buildings.* Washington, D.C.

Gould, David, and James B. Kennedy, eds. 2004. *Memoirs of a Dutch Mudsill: The "War Memories" of John Henry Otto, Captain, Company D, 21st Regiment Wisconsin, Volunteer Infantry.* Kent, Ohio.

Goyne, Minetta Altgelt, ed. and trans. 1982. *Lone Star and Double Eagle: Civil War Letters of a German-Texas Family.* Fort Worth, Tex.

Grebner, Constantine. 1987. *We Were the Ninth: A History of the Ninth Regiment, Ohio Volunteer Infantry.* Edited and translated by Frederic Trautmann. Kent, Ohio.

Haas, Oscar. 1968. *History of New Braunfels and Comal County, Texas, 1844–1946.* Austin, Tex.

Hackemer, Kurt. 1999. "Response to War: Civil War Enlistment Patterns in Kenosha County, Wisconsin." *Military History of the West* 29:31–62.

Hargest, George E. 1971. *History of Letter Communication between the United States and Europe, 1845–1875.* Washington, D.C.

Harris, James F. 1989. "The Arrival of the *Europamüde*: Germans in America after 1848." In *The German Forty-Eighters in the United States*, edited by Charlotte L. Brancaforte, 1–15. New York.

Hasskarl, Robert A. 1976. *Waul's Texas Legion, 1862–1865.* Ada, Okla.

Hattaway, Herman. 1997. "The Civil War Armies: Creation, Mobilization, and Development." In *On the Road to Total War: The American Civil War and the German Wars of Unification, 1861–1871*, edited by Stig Förster and Jörg Nagler, 173–97. Cambridge, U.K.

Heil, Walter. 1979. "Auswanderung nach Amerika im vorigen Jahrhundert dargestellt am Beispiel Ludwig Wilhelm Müller aus Bad Vilbel-Massenheim." *Bad Vilbeler Heimatblätter* 19:3–13.

Helbich, Wolfgang, ed. 1985. *"Amerika ist ein freies Land . . ." Auswanderer schreiben nach Deutschland.* Darmstadt.

——, ed. 1988. *"Alle Menschen sind dort gleich . . ." Die deutsche Amerika-Auswanderung im 19. und 20. Jahrhundert.* Düsseldorf.

——. 1996. "American Reconstruction and German Reunification: The Limits of

Comparative History." In *Different Restorations: Reconstruction and "Wiederaufbau" in the United States and Germany: 1865, 1945, 1989*. Edited by Norbert Finzsch and Jürgen Martschukat, 352–72. Providence, R.I.

———. 1997. "Immigrant Adaptation at the Individual Level: The Evidence of Nineteenth-Century German-American Letters." *Amerikastudien* 42:407–18.

———. 2002. "Dietrich Gerstein: Ein Achtundverziger, wie er selten im Geschichtsbuch steht." In *200 Jahre Vereinigte Hoffmann- und Ludwig-Stiftung: 1802–2002, ein Familienverband im Strom der Zeit*. Edited by Hoffmann- und Ludwig-Stiftung, 81–86. Detmold.

———. 2004. "German-Born Union Soldiers: Motivation, Ethnicity, and 'Americanization.'" In *German-American Immigration and Ethnicity in Comparative Perspective*, edited by Wolfgang Helbich and Walter D. Kamphoefner, 295–325. Madison, Wis.

Helbich, Wolfgang, and Walter D. Kamphoefner, eds. 2002. *Deutsche im Amerikanischen Bürgerkrieg: Briefe von Front und Farm 1861–1865*. Paderborn.

———, eds. 2004. *German-American Immigration and Ethnicity in Comparative Perspective*. Madison, Wis.

Helbich, Wolfgang, Walter D. Kamphoefner, and Ulrike Sommer, eds. 1988. *Briefe aus Amerika: Deutsche Auswanderer schreiben aus der Neuen Welt, 1830–1930*. Munich.

Hess, Earl. 1983. *A German in the Yankee Fatherland: The Civil War Letters of Henry A. Kircher*. Kent, Ohio.

———. 1997a. "Tactics, Trenches, and Men in the Civil War." In *On the Road to Total War: The American Civil War and the German Wars of Unification, 1861–1871*, edited by Stig Förster and Jörg Nagler, 481–97. Cambridge, U.K.

———. 1997b. *The Union Soldier in Battle*. Lawrence, Kan.

Hicken, Victor. 1991. *Illinois in the Civil War*. 2d ed. Urbana, Ill.

Higham, John. 1981 [1963]. *Strangers in the Land: Patterns of American Nativism, 1860–1925*. New York.

Hippel, Wolfgang von. 1984. *Auswanderung aus Südwestdeutschland. Studien zur württem-bergischen Auswanderung und Auswanderungspolitik im 18. und 19. Jahrhundert*. Stuttgart.

Historical Statistics of the United States: Colonial Times to 1970. 1975. 2 vols. Washington, D.C.

History of Franklin, Jefferson, Washington, Crawford, and Gasconade Counties, Missouri. 1888. Chicago.

The History of Nodaway County, Missouri. 1882. Vol. 1. St. Joseph, Mo.

History of Pennsylvania Volunteers, 1861–1865. 1872. Vol. 2. Harrisburg, Pa.

History of St. Charles, Montgomery, and Warren Counties. 1885. St. Louis, Mo.

History of Warrick, Spencer, and Perry Counties, Indiana. 1885. Evansville, Ind.

Hoffman, David R. 1999. "A German-American Pioneer Remembers: August Hoffmann's Memoirs." *Southwestern Historical Quarterly* 102:487–509.

Holtmann, Antonius, ed. 1999. *"Für Gans America Gehe ich nicht Wieder Bei die*

Solldaten . . ." Briefe des Ochtruper Auswanderers Theodor Heinrich Brandes aus dem amerikanischen Bürgerkrieg 1862/63. Bremen.

———. 2005. A Lost American Dream: Civil War Letters (1862/63) of Immigrant Theodor Heinrich Brandes in Historical Context. Translated by Eberhard Reichmann. Nashville, Ind.

House Journals of the 12th Legislature of the State of Texas. 1870. First Session. Austin, Tex.

Hyman, Harold M. 1959. To Try Men's Souls: Loyalty Tests in American History. Berkeley, Calif.

Johnson, R. U., and C. C. Buel, eds. 1987. Battles and Leaders of the Civil War, Being for the Most Part Contributions by Union and Confederate Officers. 4 vols. New York.

Jordan, Terry G. 1966. German Seed in Texas Soil: Immigrant Farmers in Nineteenth-Century Texas. Austin, Tex.

———. 1989. "Germans and Blacks in Texas." In States of Progress: Germans and Blacks in America over 300 Years, edited by Randall Miller, 89–97. Philadelphia, Pa.

Journal of the House, Missouri 25th General Assembly, Adjourned Session. 1870. Jefferson City, Mo.

Justman, Dorothy E. 1974. German Colonists and Their Descendants in Houston: Including Usener and Allied Families. Quanah, Tex.

Kammeier, Heinz-Ulrich. 1994. "Halleluja, jetzt sehen wir Amerika": Auswandererbriefe aus dem Kreis Lübbecke und Umgebung, 1836–1889. Espelkamp.

Kamphoefner, Walter D. 1975. "St. Louis Germans and the Republican Party, 1848–1860." Mid America 57:69–88.

———. 1980. "Dreissiger and Forty-Eighter: The Political Influence of Two Generations of German Political Exiles." In Germany and America, edited by Hans L. Trefousse, 89–102. New York.

———. 1987. The Westfalians: From Germany to Missouri. Princeton, N.J.

———. 1991. "German Americans and Civil War Politics: A Reconsideration of the Ethnocultural Thesis." Civil War History 37:226–40.

———. 1997. "'Auch unser Deutschland muß einmal frei werden': The Immigrant Civil War Experience as a Mirror on Political Conditions in Germany." In Transatlantic Images and Perceptions: Germany and America since 1776, edited by David E. Barclay and Elisabeth Glaser-Schmidt, 87–107. Cambridge, U.K.

———. 1999. "New Perspectives on Texas Germans and the Confederacy." Southwestern Historical Quarterly 102:441–55.

Kamphoefner, Walter D., Wolfgang Helbich, and Ulrike Sommer, eds. 1991. News from the Land of Freedom: German Immigrants Write Home. Ithaca, N.Y.

Kaufmann, Wilhelm. 1911. Die Deutschen im amerikanischen Bürgerkrieg. Munich and Berlin.

———. 1999. The Germans in the American Civil War. Edited by Don Heinrich Tolzmann. Translated by Steven Rowan. Carlisle, Pa.

Kawaguchi, Lesley Ann. 1994. "Diverging Political Affiliations and Ethnic Perspectives: Philadelphia Germans and Antebellum Politics." Journal of American Ethnic History 13:3–29.

Keil, Hartmut, and John B. Jentz, eds. 1988. *German Workers in Industrial Chicago: A Documentary History of Working-Class Culture from 1850 to World War I.* Urbana, Ill.

Keller, Christian B. 2001. "Pennsylvania and Virginia Germans during the Civil War: A Brief History and Comparative Analysis." *Virginia Magazine of History and Biography* 109:37–86.

Kelley, Sean Michael. 2000. "Plantation Frontiers: Race, Ethnicity, and Family along the Brazos River of Texas, 1821–1886." Ph.D. diss., University of Texas at Austin.

Kerby, Robert L. 1972. *Kirby-Smith's Confederacy: The Trans-Mississippi South, 1863–1865.* New York.

von Kindelsberg und Martinshardt. 1927. *Heimat- und Familiengeschichten zur Dreihundertjahr-Feier der Evangelischen Gemeinde Müsen.* Edited by Evangelisches Pfarramt Müsen. Müsen.

Kleinau, Hermann. 1968. *Geschichtliches Ortsverzeichnis des Landes Braunschweig.* Hildesheim.

Kleppner, Paul. 1979. *The Third Electoral System, 1853–1892: Parties, Voters, and Political Cultures.* Chapel Hill, N.C.

Knowles, Anne Kelly. 2001. "Labor, Race, and Technology in the Confederate Iron Industry." *Technology and Culture* 42:1–26.

Küffner, Cornelia. 1994. "Texas-Germans' Attitudes toward Slavery: Biedermeier Sentiments and Class-Consciousness in Austin, Colorado, and Fayette Counties." M.A. thesis, University of Houston.

Lehmann, Elizabeth. 1983. *Roots and Branches of Ludwig Lehmann, 1700s–1983.* Brenham, Tex.

Levine, Bruce. 1992. *The Spirit of 1848: German Immigrants, Labor Conflict, and the Coming of the Civil War.* Urbana, Ill.

Logue, Larry M. 1993. "Who Joined the Confederate Army? Soldiers, Civilians, and Communities in Mississippi." *Journal of Social History* 26:611–23.

———. 1996. *To Appomattox and Beyond: The Civil War Soldier in War and Peace.* Chicago.

Long, Everett Beach, and Barbara Long. 1971. *The Civil War Day by Day: An Almanac, 1861–1865.* Garden City, N.Y.

Lonn, Ella. 1951. *Foreigners in the Union Army and Navy.* Baton Rouge, La.

———. 2002 [1940]. *Foreigners in the Confederacy.* Chapel Hill, N.C.

Lorenz-Meyer, Martin. 2000. "United in Difference: The German Community in Nativist Baltimore and the Presidential Elections of 1860." *Yearbook of German-American Studies* 35:1–26.

Lowry, Thomas P. 1994. *The Story the Soldiers Wouldn't Tell: Sex in the Civil War.* Mechanicsburg, Pa.

Luebke, Frederick C., ed. 1971. *Ethnic Voters and the Election of Lincoln.* Lincoln, Neb.

Macha, Jürgen, and Andrea Wolf, eds. 2001. *Michael Zimmers Diary: Ein deutsches Tagebuch aus dem Amerikanischen Bürgerkrieg.* Frankfurt.

Marschalck, Peter. 1973. *Deutsche Überseewanderung im 19. Jahrhundert. Ein Beitrag zur soziologischen Theorie der Bevölkerung.* Stuttgart.

Marten, James. 1990. *Texas Divided: Loyalty and Dissent in the Lone Star State, 1856–1874*. Lexington, Ky.

———. 2001. "Exempt from the Ordinary Rules of Life: Researching Postwar Adjustment Problems of Union Veterans." *Civil War History* 47:57–70.

Martin, David G. 1987. *Carl Bornemann's Regiment: The Forty-First New York Infantry (DeKalb Regt.) in the Civil War*. Hightstown, N.J.

Die Matrikel des Collegium Carolinum und der Technischen Hochschule Carolo-Wilhelmina zu Braunschweig. 1983. Hildesheim.

May, Robert E. 1985. *John A. Quitman: Old South Crusader*. Baton Rouge, La.

McCaslin, Richard B. 1994. *Tainted Breeze: The Great Hanging at Gainesville, Texas, 1862*. Baton Rouge, La.

McDevitt, Theresa. 2003. *Women and the American Civil War: An Annotated Bibliography*. Westport, Conn.

McPherson, James M. 1982. *Ordeal by Fire: The Civil War and Reconstruction*. New York.

———. 1988. *Battle Cry of Freedom*. New York.

———. 1990. *Abraham Lincoln and the Second American Revolution*. Oxford, U.K.

———. 1994. *What They Fought For, 1861–1865*. Baton Rouge, La.

———. 1997a. *For Cause and Comrades: Why Men Fought in the Civil War*. New York.

———. 1997b. "From Limited War to Total War in America." In *On the Road to Total War: The American Civil War and the German Wars of Unification, 1861–1871*, edited by Stig Förster and Jörg Nagler, 295–309. Cambridge, U.K.

Mehrländer, Andrea. 1998. "'Gott gebe uns bald bessere Zeiten . . .': Die Deutschen von Charleston, Richmond und New Orleans im Amerikanischen Bürgerkrieg, 1861–1865." Ph.D. diss., Ruhr-Universität Bochum.

Metzenthin-Raunick, Selma. 1953. "One Hundred Years Neu Braunfelser Zeitung." *American-German Review* 19:6, 15–16.

Miller, Randall M., ed. 1989. *States of Progress: Germans and Blacks in America over 300 Years*. Philadelphia, Pa.

Moore, Bill. 1977. *Bastrop County, 1691–1900*. Wichita Falls, Tex.

Mosman, Chesley A. 1987. *The Rough Side of War*. Garden City, N.Y.

Nagel, Charles. 1935. *A Boy's Civil War Story*. St. Louis, Mo.

Nagler, Jörg. 1984. *Frémont contra Lincoln: Die deutsch-amerikanische Opposition in der Republikanischen Partei während des amerikanischen Bürgerkriegs*. Frankfurt.

———. 1989a. "The Lincoln-Frémont Debate and the Forty-Eighters." In *The German Forty-Eighters in the United States*, edited by Charlotte L. Brancaforte, 157–78. New York.

———. 1989b. "Deutschamerikaner und das Liberal Republican Movement 1872." *Amerikastudien* 33:415–38.

Neumann, Gustav. 1883. *Geographisches Lexikon des Deutschen Reichs*. Leipzig.

Nieman, Donald G. 1989. "Black Political Power and Criminal Justice: Washington County, Texas, 1868–1884." *Journal of Southern History* 55:391–420.

Nodaway County, Missouri, Past and Present. 1910. Vol. 1. Indianapolis, Ind.

Öfele, Martin W. 2004. *German-Speaking Officers in the U.S. Colored Troops, 1863–1867*. Gainesville, Fla.

Official Army Register of the Volunteer Force of the United States Army for the Years: 1861, '62, '63, '64, '65. 1987 [1865]. Edited by United States Adjutant General's Office. 9 vols. Gaithersburg, Md.

Official Roster of the Soldiers of the State of Ohio in the War of the Rebellion, 1861–1866. 1886–95. 12 vols. Akron, Ohio.

Parish, Peter. 1975. *The American Civil War*. London.

Patrick, Charles, ed. and trans. 1999. *Giesecke's Civil War Diary: The Story of Company G of the Fourth Regiment of the First Texas Cavalry Brigade of the Confederate States of America (1861–1865)*. Manor, Tex.

Patterson, Gerard A. 1997. *Debris of Battle: The Wounded at Gettysburg*. Mechanicsburg, Pa.

Pennington, Mrs. R. E. 1915. *The History of Brenham and Washington County*. Houston, Tex.

Pflanze, Otto. 1990. *Bismarck and the Development of Germany. Vol. 1: The Period of Unification, 1815–1871*. 2d ed. Princeton, N.J.

Pierce, Bessie Louise. 1957. *A History of Chicago*. Vol. 3. Chicago.

Portrait and Biographical Record of St. Charles, Lincoln, and Warren Counties, Missouri. 1895. Chicago.

Potter, David M. 1976. *The Impending Crisis, 1848–1861*. New York.

Priesner, Paul. 1981. *Die Auswanderungen aus Ehrenstetten und Kirchhoffen nach Nordamerika in der zweiten Hälfte des 19. Jahrhunderts*. Die Geschichte der Gemeinde Kirchhoffen und Ehrenstetten, Vol. 3. N.p.

Pula, James S. 1976. *The History of a German-Polish Civil War Brigade*. San Francisco, Calif.

Ransleben, Guido E. 1974. *A Hundred Years of Comfort in Texas: A Centennial History*. Rev. ed. San Antonio, Tex.

Record of Service of Michigan Volunteers in the Civil War, 1861–1865. 1905. 46 vols. Kalamazoo, Mich.

Regenbrecht, Adalbert. 1917. "The German Settlers of Millheim before the Civil War." *Southwestern Historical Quarterly* 20:28–34.

Reinhart, Joseph R., ed. and trans. 2004. *Two Germans in the Civil War: The Diary of John Daeuble and the Letters of Gottfried Rentschler, 6th Kentucky Volunteer Infantry*. Knoxville, Tenn.

Report of the Adjutant General of Illinois for the Years 1861–1866. 1901. Vol. 4. Springfield, Ill.

Report of the Adjutant General of Indiana. 1865. Vol. 2. Indianapolis, Ind.

Robertson, James I., Jr. 1988. *Soldiers Blue and Gray*. Columbia, S.C.

Rorabaugh, W. J. 1986. "Who Fought for the North in the Civil War? Concord, Massachusetts, Enlistments." *Journal of American History* 73:695–701.

Rosenblatt, Emil, and Ruth Rosenblatt, eds. 1992 [1983]. *Hard Marching Every Day: The Civil War Letters of Private Wilbur Fisk, 1861–65*. Lawrence, Kan.

Ross, Ishabel. 1959. *The General's Wife: The Life of Mrs. Ulysses S. Grant*. New York.

Rousey, Dennis C. 1992. "Aliens in a WASP Nest: Ethnocultural Diversity in the Antebellum Urban South." *Journal of American History* 79:152–64.

Rowan, Steven, and James Neal Primm, eds. and trans. 1983. *Germans for a Free Missouri: Translations from the St. Louis Radical Press, 1857–1862*. Columbia, Mo.

Ruggles, Steven, Matthew Sobek, Trent Alexander, Catherine A. Fitch, Ronald Goeken, Patricia Hall, Miriam King, and Chad Ronnander, eds. 2004. *Integrated Public Use Microdata Series: Version 3.0* [Machine-readable database]. Minnesota Population Center [producer and distributor]. Minneapolis, Minn.

Schafer, Joseph. 1971. "Who Elected Lincoln?" In *Ethnic Voters and the Election of Lincoln*, edited by Frederick C. Luebke, 46–61. Lincoln, Neb.

Schem, A. J., ed. 1869–74. *Deutsch-Amerikanisches Conversations-Lexicon. Mit specieller Rücksicht auf das Bedürfnis der in Amerika lebenden Deutschen*. 10 vols. New York.

Schick, Susanne M. 1994. "For God, Mac and Country: The Political World of Midwestern Germans during the Civil War Era." Ph.D. diss., University of Illinois at Urbana-Champaign.

Schmidt, C. W. 1930. *Footprints of Five Generations*. New Ulm, Tex.

Schöberl, Ingrid. 1990. *Amerikanische Einwanderungswerbung in Deutschland, 1845–1914*. Stuttgart.

Schroeder, Adolf E., ed. and trans., and Carla Schulz-Geisberg, ed. 1988. *Hold Dear, as Always: Jetta, a German Immigrant Life in Letters*. Columbia, Mo.

Schubert, Werner. 1995. *Auswanderung aus Ostbevern. Dokumentation XII*. Ostbevern.

Schuetze, Julius. 1995. "My Experience in Texas, 1886." Translated from "Texas Vorwärts." *German-Texan Heritage Society Journal* 17:120–37.

Scott, Robert Garth, ed. 1991. *Fallen Leaves: The Civil War Letters of Major Henry Livermore Abbott*. Kent, Ohio.

Smith, Elbert B. 1975. *The Presidency of James Buchanan*. Lawrence, Kan.

Smith, Page. 1982. *Trial by Fire: A People's History of the Civil War and Reconstruction*. New York.

Sobel, Robert, ed. 1990. *Bibliographical Directory of the United States Executive Branch, 1774–1989*. Westport, Conn.

Spencer, John W. 1982. *Terrell's Texas Cavalry*. Burnet, Tex.

Spurlin, Charles D., ed. 1992. *The Civil War Diary of Charles A. Leuschner*. Austin, Tex.

The Story of the 55th Regiment Illinois Volunteers Infantry in the Civil War, 1861–1865. 1887. Clinton, Mass.

Tatum, Georgia Lee. 1934. *Disloyalty in the Confederacy*. Chapel Hill, N.C.

Tiling, Moritz. 1913. *History of the German Element in Texas from 1820–1950 and Historical Sketches of the German Texas Singers' League and Houston Turnverein*. Houston, Tex.

Trefousse, Hans L. 1982. *Carl Schurz: A Biography*. Knoxville, Tenn.

Ueberhorst, Horst. 1978. *Turner unterm Sternenbanner*. Munich.

Underwood, Rodman L. 2000. *Death on the Nueces: German Texans "Treue der Union."* Austin, Tex.

Utley, Robert G. 1988. *Cavalier in Buckskin: George Armstrong Custer and the Western Military Frontier*. Norman, Okla.

Vinovskis, Maris A., ed. 1990a. *Toward a Social History of the American Civil War: Exploratory Essays*. New York.

———. 1990b. "Have Social Historians Lost the Civil War? Some Preliminary Demographic Speculations." In *Toward a Social History of the American Civil War: Exploratory Essays*, edited by Maris A. Vinovskis, 1–30. New York.

von Wiese, Benno, ed. N.d. *Schillers Werke in 5 Bänden*. Vol. 4: *Gedichte. Prosa*. Cologne and Berlin.

The War of the Rebellion: A Compilation of the Official Records of the Union and Confederate Armies. 1880–1901. 128 vols. Washington, D.C.

Warner, Ezra J. 1959. *Generals in Grey: Lives of the Confederate Commanders*. Baton Rouge, La.

———. 1964. *Generals in Blue: Lives of the Union Commanders*. Baton Rouge, La.

Weyand, Leonie Rummel, and Houston Wade. 1936. *An Early History of Fayette County*. LaGrange, Tex.

Who's Who in America. 1908–9. Chicago.

Wiley, Bell. 1943. *The Life of Johnny Reb*. Indianapolis, Ind.

———. 1952. *The Life of Billy Yank*. Indianapolis, Ind.

Williams, T. Harry. 1952. *Lincoln and His Generals*. New York.

Wilson, Joseph. 1981. "The Earliest Anglicisms in Texas German." *Yearbook of German-American Studies* 16:103–13.

Wittke, Carl. 1945. *Against the Current: The Life of Carl Heinzen*. Chicago.

———. 1952. *Refugees of Revolution: The German Forty-Eighters in America*. Philadelphia, Pa.

———. 1957. *The German-Language Press in America*. Lexington, Ky.

Woodruff, Mrs. Howard W. 1969. *Marriage Records of Franklin County, Missouri, 1819–1858*. Kansas City, Mo.

Work, David. 2004. "Lincoln's Political Generals." Ph.D. diss., Texas A&M University.

Yox, Andrew P. 1985. "Bonds of Community. Buffalo's German Element, 1853–1871." *New York History* 66:142–63.

Zucker, Adolph E. 1950. *The Forty-Eighters: Political Refugees of the German Revolution of 1848*. New York.

DONORS OF LETTERS AND MATERIALS

Albrecht, Otto: Balch Institute for Ethnic Studies, Historical Society of Pennsylvania, Philadelphia, Pa.

Albrecht, Wilhelm: F. F. Brockmüller, 74078 Heilbronn.

Augustin: Dr. Gert Durchschlag, 22609 Hamburg.

Barthel-Odensaß: Antonie and Herbert Fischer, 34223 Fuldatal-Knickhagen; Margarete Knauf, 34376 Immenhausen.

Bauer: Helga Bauer-Reinhardt, 79104 Freiburg; Catherine Nulliner, Phoenix, Ariz.

Boffinger: Maria Drettmann, South Venice, Fla.

Bönsel: Karin Tavenrath, 47443 Moers.

Böpple: Emma Klein, 70619 Stuttgart; Karl-Georg Schahl, 70619 Stuttgart.

Brucker: Indiana Historical Society, Indianapolis, Ind.

Bullenhaar: Werner Schubert, 48346 Ostbevern.

Buschmann: Werner Schubert, 48346 Ostbevern.

Cramer: Prof. Dr. Jürgen Reulecke, 45279 Essen; Charlotte Cramer Lafrenz, Portland, Ore.; Leo D. Brown, La Jolla, Calif.

Dieden: William S. Bailey, Seattle, Wash.

Dünnebacke: Dr. Maria Thiemann, 46567 Recklinghausen.

Dupré: Brigitte Leiß, 91056 Erlangen.

Eversmeier: Dr. Roland Vetter, 69412 Eberbach (Stadtarchiv Eberbach).

Francksen: Hans H. Francksen, 26969 Butjadingen; Franke Francksen, 26180 Rastede; Prof. Dr. Antonius Holtmann, Universität Oldenburg.

Frick: Stadtarchiv Lahr (Nachlaß Karl Fleig), 77933 Lahr; Dr. Joachim Sturm, Stadtarchiv Lahr.

Gerstein: Klaus Gerstein, 57072 Siegen; Barbara Gerstein, 44357 Dortmund.

Härring: Harald Schuhkraft, 70197 Stuttgart.

Heinzelmann: Paul Elwert, 72160 Horb.

Herbst: Jochen Krebber, 51109 Köln; Anton Efinger, 78554 Aldingen.

Hermanns: Ellen Hausmann, 40721 Hilden.

Heubach: Dipl.-Ing. Robert Eichhorn, 30880 Laatzen; Kurt Hayn, 96523 Steinach.

Hoffmann: Peter Schwinn, Philips-Universität Marburg, 35032 Marburg.

Horstmann: Hartmut Reinecke, 26129 Oldenburg.

Keppler: Paul Elwert, 72160 Horb.

Kessel: Heinrich Grimm, 33378 Rheda-Wiedenbrück.

Kessler: Dr. Roland Vetter, 69412 Eberbach (Stadtarchiv Eberbach).

Klausmeyer: Maryland Historical Society, Baltimore; Hedwig Reismayer, Millbrook, N.Y.

Knoebel: Paul Priesner, 79102 Freiburg; Giesela Zens, 70117 Freiburg.

Krause: Gerhard and Ingborg Krause, 69522 Heidelberg.

Krieger: Gustav Adolf Kaper and Hanna Kaper, 26316 Varel.

Kühner: Annemarie Gätschenberger, 74842 Billigheim-Katzental; Lisbeth Keller, 74850 Schefflenz.

Leclerc: Herbert Leclerc, Bundespostmuseum, 60596 Frankfurt.

Lehmann: Werner Gronarz, 47199 Duisburg; Ludger von Husen, 45770 Marl; Elizabeth Lehmann, Brenham, Tex.

Martens: Ingo Wichmann, 24768 Rendsburg.

Miller: Walter Heil, 61118 Vilbel.

Monn: Gerhard Schwarz, 89143 Blaubeuren.

Müller: Martha Ohle, 27721 Ritterhude.

Nagel: Erwin Horstmann, 53474 Bad Neuenahr-Ahrweiler; Anne A. Watson, Marion, Mass.

Pack: Institut für Historische Landeskunde des Rheinlands, Bonn (Nachlaß Scheben); Friedrich Denne, 66578 Schiffweiler.

Penzler: Karl Penzler, 45279 Essen.

Petasch: Gerlind Voermanek, 37139 Adelebsen.

Richter: Dr. Andrea Mehrländer, 12161 Berlin; Willy Rönsch, Dresden; John F. Kennedy Institute, Free University of Berlin.

Rossi: Dr. Friedhelm Zwickler, 65232 Taunusstein.

Ruff: Lisa Winkelmann, 72406 Bisingen.

Schmalzried: Michigan Historical Collection, University of Michigan, Ann Arbor.

Schorse: Georg Wittich, Braunschweig; State Historical Society of Missouri, Columbia, Mo.

Schwarting: Daisy Neidhöfer, 22119 Hamburg; Wulf Neidhöfer, 26316 Varel.

Simon: Karl Gebert, Houston, Tex.

Stähler: Otto Stähler, 44135 Dortmund.

Strohsahl: Hermann and Margarete Jelten, 27574 Bremerhaven.

Treutlein: Prof. Dr. Gerhard Treutlein, 69121 Heidelberg.

Uterhard: Klaus Ohlerich, 38302 Wolfenbüttel.

Voigt: Center for American History, University of Texas at Austin.

Weinrich: Raymond Weinrich, Puyallup, Wash.

Wesslau: Heinz Wesslau, 32756 Detmold.

INDEX

Note: Letter-writers and their families have not been included in the index because they can be located through the table of contents.